You're in *high school* now

You're in High School Now: **Julian's Sophomore Year, Part 1** Eldot
Q Press/One Spirit Press, 625 pages, (paperback) $25.00
978-1-893075-77-1 (*Reviewed: June 2015*)

This charming novel continues the story of Julian, from author Eldot's series Julian's Private Scrapbook. Set in the early 1960s, it follows Julian's coming age as a gay man through the first half of his first year in high school, as he makes new friends, learns about girls, and navigates this strange but exciting new world.

The title refers to the refrain his mother and her friend continually use when explaining to Julian why he must pay attention to his clothes now and other new "rules." Julian's only real concern is his mother's interest that he take out a girl. Since he is only romantically interested in his scoutmaster Mark, that presents an obstacle. Fortunately, he attracts the attention of Rita, one of the school's prettiest girls, who invites him to the Sadie Hawkins dance. Julian's complete ignorance about Rita's intentions during the dance and the car ride afterwards (as well as his description to his mother later) provides some of the novel's funniest scenes.

Julian is certainly experienced when it comes to sex, however. He continues the explorations he discovered at scout camp the previous summer, both as an initiate in a secret society of like-minded boys, as well as with Randall, recently moved from Washington. Randall, a victim of bullying at his previous school, is instantly drawn to Julian when he sees him, and they form an immediate, deep friendship. Julian introduces Randall to his scouting troop and takes an interest in his photography, and Randall is deeply impressed by Julian's drawing skills. The two bring out the best in each other.

While not every reader will appreciate the sex scenes, they are sensitively drawn and important to the story. The only complaint this reader has is waiting for Part 2, where it seems the situation will become complicated. Well-written, with engaging, likable characters, this book skillfully presents the challenges and pleasures boys who love men face in growing up.

Also available in hardcover and ebook

You're in *high school* now

Summer and Fall, 1962

a romantic comedy

by

Eldot

Julian's Sophomore Year, Part 1

Q Press
Portland, Oregon

In grateful memory to James B. Hall,
my first writing teacher

Publisher's Note:

This book is intended for a mature audience. It is not written to serve or encourage prurient interest; it contains no pornography or graphic language, but there are several intimate male/male passages. Readers who are offended by that should not read this book. All the characters in the story were 64 years of age or older at the time the story was written in 2014. Any similarities or references to actual persons have been systematically modified to eliminate any basis for recognition.

By the same author:

The Julian's Private Scrapbook novels:

Barr's Meadow
The Poker Club
The Shooting Gallery
Thunder and Lightning
The Champions

eBook only:
Inside the World of Eldot
The Little J and Roger series

Author's Note:

Set in the 1960s, this novel presumes some background knowledge that many contemporary readers do not have. A glossary provides explanatory information to offset that. An Index of Characters is provided to assist in understanding who everyone is and which are more important.

Additional back-of-the-book extras are provided to enhance the reading experience. A brief note on style elements comes first. A special appendix amplifies a major episode, freeing it from burdensome explanations.

This novel is unconventional; the subject of sexual orientation and activity is central to the story and is dealt with honestly. Readers who are uncomfortable with the subject should be prepared to skip over a few passages.

Julian's Sophomore Year is a work of fiction, though elements of it originate in true life experience. Any similarity to real persons is coincidental and unintended; some of the places exist, but are used fictitiously.

LCCN: 2015943460

ISBN: 978-1-893075-77-1

Library of Congress Cataloging-in-Publication Data

2015.

1. GLBT—Men 2. Fiction—Romantic Comedy

I. Title.
A44. 2015
813.306

Q-Press
Portland, Oregon
www.onespiritpress.com

Table of Contents

Visual and Editorial Materials

Key to symbols

Segment End, Non Text

Jump Forward in Time

Chapter End

Jump to Concurrent Event or Viewpoint

Flashback Segment

Preface to
Julian's Sophomore Year

After a few months of nagging, I began to pay attention and the Muse got her way at last. That, and a few very nice prods from readers of the *Julian's Private Scrapbook* series, convinced me that there was more to write about Julian. I'm not sure how long this "phase" of his story will run, since I'm not in charge, really. I have come to understand that it isn't over until the Muse decides it's over. I have to accept that Julian's life, like most, has many chapters—even chapters within chapters. This book is one such—the first year of high school is special for most of us; it certainly was for Julian.

The grand social purpose that motivated the *Julian's Private Scrapbook* series lurks in the background, unsolved as always: social change is never as rapid as one would like. There are still bullies, there are still boys who don't know what to do about their life. Laws and institutions remain inadequate and clumsy, sometimes indifferent or cruel. So it's worth the effort to add a positive chapter or two.

About all I can do is insist that it remain fun and interesting. I hope that you are able to enjoy the ride as well. It's not supposed to be more work.

Eldot

1 Registration day

Wait a minute… something's not right.

Julian looked straight ahead: the top part of his head wasn't there… it was out of sight above the mirror. He stepped off the stool… whoa. Now I can see my entire head. What's going on here? The last time I did the whisker check I stood on the stool; well, duh! I *always* stand on the stool—I always do this the same way. What did I look like last time I did this? It was only a couple of months ago, just before summer camp. Thanks to Geraldine, I let my check-ups go this summer; I was busy all the time working on her crew.

Could I grow that much? This can't be right…

He raced to his bedroom, snagged a pencil from the drawing table, and stood tight against the closet doorjamb—he had been keeping track of this since the third grade. Careful to hold the pencil level, he rested it on the top of his head and drew a mark on the frame. He turned around to check.

"Wow!! Must be *three inches!*"

He bent close: the inscription under the previous mark read June 1, 1962: 5' 3 ½". He raced back to the table for a ruler. I need an *exact* measurement. Put the ruler tip on the *zero* mark, Julian… yep… two and five eighths. He stood back and calculated…

"Five feet six and *one eighth*!" he hopped up and down with glee. "I did it!" Winning a bet with Sid is *so* sweet. He bet I'd never be 5'6" by the start of the 10th grade. Guess what, Sidney!

> Beep-beep-beep! <

A car horn! Yow! They're here already. Blast… no time. I'll do the whisker check after I get back. Julian didn't have a bet going about that—but whiskers had always fascinated him. He wanted to be the first one to see—to know that he too would be able to *shave*. Since he was a little kid sitting on his grandpa's lap, that had been an important goal. Rubbing his grandfather's stubbly chin was a favorite memory. "Gotta scoot!" He grabbed the envelope of school papers and his sketchbook.

"When Sid finds out I made 5 feet 6 he'll be *so* mad…" chances to impress Sid are hard to come by; he won't be expecting this. With a chortle he headed for the front door.

"Oh, wait!" he slid to a stop. "I forgot to put on my shoes!" The hardwood floor was well polished in several places—Julian rarely wore shoes in the house; sliding to and fro was standard practice when Mom was away at work—hard on the sox maybe, but… he hurried back to his room.

> *E contare, oh oh oh...* < Dean Martin crooned from the kitchen.

Oh, yeah—I hafta turn the radio back up. Mom always wants the radio blasting away when she's gone. She has this screwy idea that it will frighten away burglars. Lately, he'd been turning it down when he was home alone; some songs got really boring—the words are so stupid. Some of the older songs are okay; the best ones don't have any words at all.

"Good morning, Julian," Marjorie Thomas grinned.

Such a lovely boy—always smiling. A good influence, too—keeps Sid out of mischief. Goodness, how *dark* he is; he must have been at the pool all summer. Her boy burned too easily; he was allowed to go twice a week, in the morning.

"Oh—hi, Mrs. Thomas." He hopped in so fast that he didn't notice that Sid was behind the wheel. His eyes opened wide. Sid is *driving!*

"I got my Learner's Permit last week," Sid said casually, as if it were an everyday event. The expression on Julian's face had just made his day.

Julian cursed silently... I'm *never* ready at times like this. Look at him, wearing dark glasses like a race car driver! He deserves a really good wisecrack. Dang! with his mom sitting right there... better cool it. Maybe I can get him later.

The trouble was, Julian never thought about that kind of thing; wisecracks didn't come to him naturally like they did to Sid. I'm just like Charlie Brown—too stupid to figure things out until later. A *Learner's Permit!* How am I gonna get one of those? He forgot all about bragging about how tall he was and scooted forward to watch. How good is he at this? Huh... looks easy enough... musta been practicing. Driving a car! That's one thing Julian hadn't thought about, actually.

They were on the way to the Jackson High School Registration and Orientation. Classes start first thing Monday—four days away. All new students were required to attend, preferably with their parents. Mom has to work, so I'm tagging along with Sid. The forms are all signed; a check for the fees is there, so I'm set. This will be just like camp—they always have to organize and orient you when you're new. The assembly at the end of last year told all about it.

According to Mom, this is one of the most important days in my life. I'm not worried. I probably should have thought about it more; other than making sure to sign up for an art class, I don't have a special plan. Most things are required, so there isn't much point in worrying about it. The main thing is taking it seriously, which is no problem. What I didn't expect was for it to come so soon; it seems like summer just started, and now it's over. Summers used to last a long time—I was always glad it was over so I could do school and scout stuff. Having a job must cause that; I had so much fun I didn't think about much else. I hafta think about other things, now.

Julian had mixed feelings. At Wallace Junior High, the ninth graders were king of the mountain; at Jackson High, the sophomores will be back at the bottom, just like the seventh grade was at Wallace.

Stories about hazing and initiations were sort of scary—the idea of pants being run up the flagpole sounded funny—as long as it was someone else's pants. But I have friends in high places—the Flaming Arrow patrol will come to the rescue.

At the start of the summer he was promoted to the elite Flaming Arrow patrol by Mark, the scoutmaster; now he was in training to become the next Troop Scribe. Scouting was the most important thing in his life, and being given responsibility like that meant everything. And, now that summer is over, not only is school starting, so is *scouts*.

Wow… the high school appeared at the left. It's gigantic! How many *floors* are there!? Squinting enhanced his focus… *three*! Think of that! I've seen it before; Mom drove by it one time. I didn't pay much attention because I was just a little kid then. *Three* sets of double doors are propped wide open—must be airing it out or something. It's *dark* inside. Boy… at first you could be afraid of a big building like that—the huge front doors look like a gigantic open mouth just waiting to swallow up hundreds of kids.

One kid is gonna be pretty small in a place like this… so *many* kids, more than any school I've ever been in. He pictured himself in a vast sea of students all in a rush to get to class on time. I'm not worried… I'll figure out how to do things—just because it's big isn't a reason to be scared.

Several architectural features caught his eye as they drew closer to the corner. What a great place to draw… man, there must be half a dozen views just in the front. Look at that! A gigantic pedestal with a bronze plaque stood in the middle of a large circle—atop it, the flagpole. He ducked slightly so he could see the entire pole… the flag looks just as high up as the *building*. Whoa… what would you do if your pants *did* get up there?

Soon they were around back; finding a parking space was easy—so far, twenty or so cars were in the lot. Looks like we're early. It was an average summer day—heat waves shimmered above the blacktop already. A big sign over a door said Registration. Must be a gymnasium or something.

Julian joined the A-H line while Sid and his mom went over to the P-Z line. Three lines… smart… the wait won't be that long, then. They should do it that way at camp. I remember *that* line… it took forever before I could do the swim test; they only had one line. He looked around to see if there was anyone he knew—Jeremy should be here somewhere. Nope.

Well, here I am at last. Registering for high school is like anything else: you get to stand in line. Truth is, he missed being out in the bright sun, missed working with the guys… standing in line is boring, even if it isn't very long. He shifted his weight to the right leg, consciously assuming a position that had a special meaning. Mark always stood this way, and Julian made it a point to assume the same stance. He spent a lot of time studying this position—every night before going to bed. Hidden safely behind the clothes in his closet were the drawings he had made of Mark at Camp Walker. These were secret drawings that only Mark knew about; one of them, maybe his favorite, showed Mark standing in this position with his back turned.

Most days it was the only time he got to be with Mark. One day Zack and the yard crew helped him rescue some panels of cardboard from the dumpster behind the hardware store—perfect for a backing. Now I don't have to fight the curl caused by being rolled up in that tube. The drawings are large—as big as his drawing board; that made it easy to pretend that it was the real Mark; after a few seconds his imagination made the drawings come alive—fantasy did the rest.

Man alive, it's stuffy in here—even if it is still morning.

Julian was used to being outdoors; he had spent the summer working on Geraldine's yard maintenance crew. They made sure all the houses up for sale looked perfect. She also managed several apartment complexes, and they did the grounds for those. He figured the main reason he got the job was because his mom and Geraldine were close friends; his mom worked in Geraldine's real estate office.

Working outdoors all day was fun. The crew was a happy bunch of guys joking around, singing, telling stories during the breaks. It was his first work experience—his first exposure to the world outside home and scouting; I was the only teen on the crew. Sometimes they poked fun—especially when I didn't get their jokes—but they weren't mean about it or anything. Three of the crew guys were black—brown is more accurate. But they liked to be called black for some reason. No big deal. Some folks called them colored, which doesn't make any sense at all. They're fun to work with.

Especially Zack—he had an endless supply of stories and loved to pull my leg—I never knew whether he was funning me or not; that's what he called it. "I'se jes funnin' ya," he would say.

Julian was easy to "fun," because he never expected it. That's one reason Sid usually got the best of him. But for Julian, being "funned" was fun. He didn't take himself very seriously, so he wasn't offended. It was part of getting to know these guys—especially the Blacks. Never got the chance before—they all live so far away. Mom says that they're just people like anybody else. I'm gonna miss those guys. Yesterday was my last day. Geraldine said I could work Saturdays if I wanted, but with scouts and everything, I won't have time.

Manual labor was new to Julian. As with everything, he dove in and gave his all. They let him work in his cutoffs, too—it was casual, natural, and invigorating to work in the sun. Geraldine was pleased with his work. She said that if it weren't for my hair, she'd think I was half Cherokee—I always took my shirt off, so I got a pretty good tan. Thanks to the sun, my hair got even more blond than before.

The reason I took the job was to earn enough to buy my school clothes. I've never done that before—never even thought about it until that night at camp—after that talk with Mark. That talk in the cabin was really important… afterward, I looked at myself in the mirror… I saw myself waving goodbye to that little kid… the little kid that used to be *me*. I wasn't sad about it… it was something that had to be; just like Lucy's kitten had to grow into a cat. I hafta start doing my share.

So when I got home I had a long talk with Mom about things. That's when we asked Geraldine to add me to the crew. I think

I earned enough money to get what I need—which is just about everything, except hiking boots. I grew over two and a half inches! No wonder nothing fits me anymore. Shopping with Mom tomorrow will be fun; she promised to get the shoes—that will help a lot. I didn't spend anything all summer, 'cept the times we stopped for milkshakes on the way home. Otherwise, it all went into the savings account, first thing.

The best thing about the job was it helped to keep his mind occupied—he missed being with Mark at night and in the morning. During camp it was easy to imagine that they were a couple since they actually lived under the same roof. Taking Mark his coffee in the morning, watching him get ready for bed at night… wow, that was hard to give up. Now all he could do was pretend… he had not seen the real Mark all summer.

Pretending came easily enough. Julian was introspective by nature; an only child, his creative ability prohibited loneliness: since no one else was around during the day, he talked with himself. It didn't matter whether he was happy, sad, puzzled or just in the mood to be silly. Curiosity about everything drove him; it gave him a sense of purpose. His self-analytic process became a habit of mind; he was likely to converse with himself silently or aloud. Paying attention to what was happening in his head gave him stability. His ongoing task was learning patience. Things never happened fast enough. That's where his "inside guy" came in handy; thanks to his warnings, Julian had been saved from disaster more than once.

Out of habit he opened his sketchbook and looked around. He always had an eye out for interesting things. There hadn't been a chance to draw since camp, and he missed that. I expect to do at least one new one today; something is bound to pop up—everything here is new. Now that school is starting, I'll be able to draw a lot more—no more yard crew. I never took the sketchbook to a crew job: no time to draw. Besides, what if it got hit by one of the sprinklers?

One of the biggest things that happened at camp was discovering that drawing was so *important*. He'd always enjoyed it and took pleasure in it, but now it was special. It made him feel different to do it—especially the portraits. It was like nothing else. He had no words to describe it, but he knew it was something he was meant to do—something he was *supposed* to do. But you don't go around talking like that, or they'll think you're a nut case. I still haven't talked to Mom about it, but I think she understands. She amazes me sometimes by what she knows.

There are other things like that—things you don't talk about. Some you don't want to talk about, some have to stay a secret. He was good at keeping secrets. No one, certainly not Mom, knew about his Big Plan, either. Boy, if the yard crew knew that! Don't even think about it.

—m—

Rita Mitchell had always been partial to blonds; the one in the line to her left was more than interesting—way, *way* more. I wish he would turn around. If his face looks half as good as his rear end… she might have spotted her first challenge of the year. She nudged her friend. "Who is that boy?" She spoke softly so her mother couldn't overhear.

"*Which* boy?" Barbara whispered back. "There's only about a hundred in here." She glanced back quickly… her mother and Rita's were preoccupied with the upcoming bridge tournament—too busy to pay attention; just as well.

"The blond with the fabulous suntan… in the striped T-shirt." Rita nodded to the left; she didn't mention the *very* tight short pants.

"Oh, *that* boy." Barbara recognized the fluffy blond head at once; she looked at him critically—someone needs to get that kid a high school outfit. "Julian Forrest." She blew a small bubble and with a rapid snakelike movement, sucked it back into her mouth. "I was in fifth grade with him." We weren't friends, especially. "He was a cub scout, I think." She blew another mini-bubble. > *snap* < "Looks taller now. He's a friend of Lucy's, I think."

"*Lucy?!*" Rita looked back in amazement. Lucy, the painted doll? Since when has she had that kind of luck? Rita couldn't *stand* Lucy Graham. If she has her hooks into this one, the challenge had just transformed into a Top Priority Rescue: it would become her mission in life to—"Oh!" Rita held her breath: she couldn't believe her eyes.

Julian looked upward to the right and turned… he gazed at various things with his camera eye, his pre-sketch composition eye. Unaware that he was displaying his considerable physical attributes, he began a slow, 360 degree turn. He paused … the geometric intricacies of the folded up basketball hoop is a possible subject… he tilted his head left, then right. Hmm… he continued his slow pan… the cages around the overhead lights are interesting, but…

Rita was spellbound—the profile—*perfect.* Look at that *tan!* Blonds *never* tan like that; look at his *arms!* What's he looking for? She leaned close and muttered, "I would *kill* to have hair like that."

Barbara glanced over. "Yeh… don't you just *hate* that? I bet he doesn't even need to comb it in the morning." All her life she had to slave away at putting up her hair. "There's no justice in this world." She focused on forming another bubble—her goal today was to make them smaller—make a quieter snap… sort of a click.

When Barbara didn't comment further, Rita wasn't surprised… Barb's not that far along socially… obviously, she had not used the summer very well… still has her Junior High brain—expects the boy to be in charge, do the calling, the deciding. I need to bring her up to speed. Rita was way ahead there—she had landed her steady almost a year ago while she was still in Sheldon Junior High. Going out with Tracy was a scandal for some: he was a year ahead of her in school. So what if she was ahead of the game? She had proven to herself that she was ready, and that's what mattered. So she knew how the high school operated. She was a part of the upper class social scene already. Registering for high school seemed like a formality more than anything.

Rita had just spent another summer up north with cousin Val. Thanks to Val, she had learned many essentials; first of all, if you expect that call or decision to go the way you want, some planning has to be done, steps have to be taken. Boys are so *clueless*; they can't think ahead more than a day or two—they can be properly steered as long as you plan it right.

She nodded, thinking to herself: Barbara would be perfect. Using confederates at various stages was the new strategy this year. Not only did that contribute to success, it provided protection; reputation safeguards were essential. Barbara didn't know it yet, but she had just been taken on as an apprentice, or lieutenant. She needs some training before anything. First thing will be to wean her from that bubble gum.

Julian continued to search, but nothing really appealed to his eye. Standing in this line is the problem: the angle is all wrong. If I could go over there by the end of the bleachers and look back this way…

Rita's eyes did a *careful* survey, not a casual check; Val had first trained her in this skill in the seventh grade. Every summer she spent a month with Val and her friends up at the family "cottage" on Greenwich Bay; every summer got more sophisticated—it wasn't as overstocked with boys as Newport, which worked to their advantage. Of course, the boys down here aren't as experienced or as rich, but they have the same equipment; it's more of a challenge sometimes—it takes a little longer, but that adds to the fun.

At times she considered herself "relegated to the provinces," to use her cousin's terminology. Instead of allowing her to attend the *best* schools, her father had overruled her mother. He was bound and determined that she attend public schools and learn to function in the real world, not the world of upper class New England that had produced her mother. He wanted his daughter to grow up at home, not in a boarding school.

Rita had come to the conclusion that it was smarter to go along with her father's wishes about school, so she didn't protest. This made it possible for her to spend the summer at cousin Val's with his blessing; aunt Lillian was eager always to make up for the presumed hardships of having to live "down south." For her, anything below New Jersey was down south, including North Carolina. Rita, like most people she knew, didn't think of herself as a southerner. That applied to South Carolina and Georgia—places like Alabama and Mississippi. North Carolina was not at all like those. It wasn't a northern state either—it was in the middle. She agreed with her father: all that Rebel vs. Yankee business was nonsense. But she allowed Aunt Lillian to take pity anyway—why not? It was nice to be pampered a little.

Cousin Val wasted no time: the previous year's experience was compressed into a concentrated summer of fun and frolic. Rita had returned home fully trained and more than ready. She was the flip side of the fox protecting the henhouse: she was a minx patrolling the rooster pen.

Rita focused on the legs—just as tan as the rest… if this is how they grow them over at Wallace Junior High, wow. She doubted if any could top this blond, but you never know… there might be more surprises. Val says it always pays to keep an open eye. She narrowed her eyes slightly and sighted in: like a lioness peering through the tall grass, taking careful measure before pouncing. Her fingers flexed, performing slow, catlike contractions.

It might be smart to look around anyway. Tracy is just too… what's the word? How about *boring*: all he can talk about is football. I won't discard him yet, though… he might end up being a big star. If so, she was already in place where it counted. No point in throwing that away, is there? But it's a new school year, a new school—an upgrade is worth considering. This one has the looks, no doubts there. Her survey had reached the feet; she checked out the shoes and socks… *very* end of summer; he's saving his good clothes for next week… obviously not a jock; what did he use to get that tan? Maybe he's a swimmer! *Ooo*, yes. There were swarms of those at the bay this summer. Reggie comes to mind—yes, yes—supine on the beach, enjoying another application of sun cream from her expert hands.

Where do you suppose this one's tan line is? She pictured him on a boat dock with the shirt gone and a Speedo in place of the short pants. Rita was fond of Speedos; they worked wonders when Tracy wore them. The assets are gathered together so nicely… maybe I won't be in a hurry—he's a lot of fun to play with when he's in his Speedo. She checked out the tight shorts again… what color Speedos would this one wear? Turquoise would be perfect with that hair.

She glanced at the clock… ten minutes? Feels like I've been here an hour. She pulled a fan from her purse and put it to use. A stuffy gymnasium was not what she was accustomed to. The building isn't air conditioned. Too bad they can't postpone school for a month or so. Being forced to wear a closed collar blouse doesn't help. Halter tops and summer casual wear aren't allowed. She returned her gaze to the blond masterpiece.

Rita could find no flaws, aside from the clothes. Although… the tight shorts simplified assessing what they were covering… very promising. The T-shirt looks very sixth grade—but form fitting, which makes it fabulous. The eyes…I haven't seen his eyes. If only I was closer—will this line *ever* get moving?! He's going to be finished and on his way before we even get close to the table. She ran through some names in her memory bank… who do I know that knows Lucy? That's a tough one… *nobody* knows Lucy. Wait: I know, I know… Sharon. It's been a while, but I can talk to Sharon. She nodded. The plan had begun to take shape.

—ʋʋ—

Woop—the line had moved forward again. Julian took a few steps and closed the gap. He was behind a kid he didn't know. The back of his head, and the neck were inches away. You don't get a chance to study the back of a head all that often… not this close, anyway. The hairline in the back, for instance… it isn't a solid line at all. There's some of that real fine hair, too, the white peachfuzzy kind like I have—or… do I still have that? I didn't get to check on that before Sid showed up. Julian felt his right temple and cheek… not sure. Attention to detail was one reason people liked his drawings—and part of the fun was showing details… like that small mole just above the neck of the T-shirt… I don't have any of those. The curlicue thingys in the ear—why do ears have those, any way? They're all different… must be like fingerprints or something.

Sure is stuffy… I miss being on the crew right now… when I got too hot and sweaty, I could count on Marty to hose me down good if there wasn't a sprinkler running. The guys got a kick out of doing that.

Without thinking, he bowed his legs and dipped slightly to free himself from a bind on the left side. It was easier if you were wearing your cutoffs; all you had to do was reach up your leg and tug the side of the skivvies loose—and scratch a little, maybe. On the crew, nobody thought twice about freeing up things down below when they got in a bind. You had to do that pretty often sometimes—especially if your skivvies are too tight and you're sweating a lot. You can't do much of anything if your sack is pinched, so you take care of it—no big deal.

Not today: I'm wearing my scout shorts, so I can't do it that way. I have to reach down from the top to pull myself free when I'm in these. Mom bought me these for camp three months ago, and even *they* are too tight. I hafta get new scout stuff too, I guess. I know: I can get that tomorrow when we go shopping for school clothes—Julian smiled wide. I'll get to see Mark! That's where he works.

Man alive! He tugged again from the outside. I sure wish I had on my cutoffs.

Rita smiled: even though she was back several feet, she understood what the blond had just done so ungracefully. Tracy did that all the time. She thought it was crude until he explained the why and what. It was unconscious, almost a reflex like any old itch. But, thanks to Tracy, she knew how it loosened things up… oftentimes visibly. She waited for the blond to turn around again; another look would be nice. Could be very nice. She focused her attention on the backside. Mee-yow! One day, her hands would hold those—on the dance floor first, of course. Her right hand worked the small fan with determination while the empty fingers of her left hand flexed in anticipation.

2 Special sale day at Oglivy's

Mark crossed the sales floor in great haste. Is it a universal rule that some emergency has to come along at the last minute? Don't the Powers That Be realize that I have to make a pit stop just like anyone else? He had just spent the last five minutes changing the tape in the shoe department cash register. Why that was so urgent, no one could say. But Ardith was about to have a fit if it didn't get done *now*. He wondered if he was in charge around here or not.

At last! I can take care of this—not a minute too soon. He hurried into the men's room and unzipped. Wow. Any longer and I would have wet my pants!

The relief was immediate and intense; he closed his eyes.

> *whoof!* <

Disaster averted. It took a while, the tank was very full. I shouldn't have had that third cup of coffee. The Musak background is a little loud. I may need to adjust that. He did another mental run through of the key departments—teen and young adult clothing in particular. The advertising blitz had been heavy. We're ready—every line is in stock; the loss leader tables should hold all day. There'll be plenty when Julian and his mother arrive.

When Francine called last night to ask about school clothes, I advised her to wait at least an hour after the doors open. The crazies take over for that long at least. Oglivy's Back In School Weekend Sale always draws a huge crowd on the first day. The first hour is very hectic, nothing like Penny's or Sears have to face, but bad enough.

It will be good to see Julian… I haven't seen him since the Fourth of July parade. Mark didn't want to admit it, but he missed having Julian around. After our two weeks at camp, I got accustomed to having freshly brewed coffee delivered first thing in the morning. But it was more than that: the companionship had meant a good deal.

What Mark didn't anticipate was the after-effect of having been close to Julian so much of the time—a bond of sorts, a friendship, if that's the right term, was formed. Not seeing him for the last two months has been—what's the right word? Disappointing, certainly… almost uncomfortable. Not that I can't make my own coffee, of course—but I miss the end of the day conversations. It was a thrill to see him develop intellectually, and to be a part of it. With talent like that, he has excellent prospects.

Mark had never been truly close to any of his scouts, but Julian was special. Even so, thinking about him or any of the boys was generally avoided. It was just as well that camp came to an end. Julian had a great experience, but needed to move on. He took a summer job and now he's about to enter high school. It will be a busy year. He'll do well—he doesn't need me to hold his hand.

Just as well for me: today is my own first day: I'm in charge of the sale this year. Being promoted from purchasing to Assistant Manager came as a surprise. Remarkable for a man my age: twenty-eight in three weeks. He had mixed feelings about it. A career in retail sales had never been his goal, but having a degree in business was ideal. Now it's assumed by everyone that I've found my place in the world. Maybe so. The job here at Oglivy's was exactly what I needed when I took it—without Erik I needed a place to hide; the little office upstairs was perfect. It felt like a trap once in a while, but they have always been good to me. They deserve my best effort today, that's certain.

As Mark neared the end of his task, a different sensation began—it felt like Roger was enjoying this. He glanced down. Hmm…

Roger was indeed enjoying himself; a slightly puffy state had replaced his On Standby state—this sometimes happened after being employed to keep the bladder valve closed tight; tension relieved in the one muscle was transferred to the other automatically; a simple, basic principle—nature's version of dissipating excess energy by routing it from one area to another. Roger was happy to oblige.

Roger had been given his name late one afternoon when Mark was a boy scout; as a lark, his circle of friends had adopted special names for their below the belt boy toys. It had facilitated some of their extracurricular activities greatly, and it added an element of fun. He continued to use the nickname after scouts—it's convenient. Now that he was a scoutmaster himself, Roger's appellation wasn't something he could share with his boys.

"No time, big fella." Mark gave Roger the customary drip flips, lest a droplet make a late exit. Telltale spots appearing near one's fly were not acceptable. "I have to open the doors in a minute." His watch said three minutes, to be exact. Puffy or not, Roger had to be tucked away and zipped in. As he washed his hands he gave his hair a check—no problem there. By chance he made eye contact in the mirror.

You shouldn't have done that, stupid—especially at work. Every time he looked directly at the eye, the face looking back accused him. The promise he had made to that face had not been kept. For weeks it had been asking a question that he didn't want to deal with. I can't stop to think about this now—I only have seconds—it's my job to unlock the doors and greet the public with a welcoming grin.

Tonight—after I get home… a silent oath would have to do. *I double promise.* Mark had been putting off dealing with his inner demon for weeks. He had run out of excuses. Roger was not returning to sleep as ordered, either; a Roger revolt at work would be disastrous. I have to pay full attention to the job, or else. He pressed Roger down flat and hastened out the door.

Roger, was delighted with the rough and tumble of the hurried transit across the store. It helped postpone the daylong nap he was about to take.

—∾—

Phyllis Simpson was skilled at appearing busy when she had nothing to do. She'd been ready for the doors to open for half an hour, but she knew better than to be seen standing around idly—especially when the new floor manager would be making his rounds. Her station behind the cosmetic counter was ideal; centrally located, most women had to pass by whether on the way to clothing or housewares. Another advantage was proximity to the changing rooms and restroom facilities. Knowing full well where the new manager had gone in such a hurry a few minutes ago, she waited eagerly. His reappearance fulfilled her expectations perfectly.

As an executive for the town's most popular men's clothier, his attire was always impeccable—all the employees at Oglivy's Emporium were expected to wear and exemplify what was being offered for sale—*especially* the new manager—the *dapper and sexy* new manager. His well-fit slacks, as they should, demonstrated the new men's line perfectly—its flat front was more than attractive on a man in such excellent physical condition. With those eyes, the medium blue tone is particularly flattering.

Moreover, as Phyllis knew well, walking vigorously toward the front of the store placed demands on any pair of trousers; in motion, the occupant between the left front pocket and the fly was often discernible—in this instance, tantalizingly so.

Recently, she had made a decision to explore certain "possibilities." A little off duty playtime with this wow of a specimen would suit her just fine. What she had just beheld confirmed her resolve. The wedding ring was not a deterrent; as a matter of fact, married men were preferable, provided they're not newlywed. They tend to know their way around in a bed; saves time. All she was after was a little fun. All work and no play, as the saying goes, make Mark a dull boy… she gave his backside a considered look as well.

Being older and more experienced gave her an edge. Eight years, maybe nine? She was approaching forty, but it didn't show… she always paid attention to what counted, and she didn't look a day over thirty. Mark must be *almost* thirty… even if he doesn't look quite 25. He's ready for a little extra-curricular romp—the famous seven-year itch must need to be scratched about now.

She nudged a space open in the center of her mental trophy case. How long will it take to bed this one? By the holiday rush he should be needy—before then would be nicer, but it's never wise to hurry these things—especially when there is a company policy standing squarely in the way. Three to four months? Probably not that long. I'll want another one in the meantime... I can always play with Ray; he's been flirting with me for weeks. One of these times I'll drop in on a slow day... see where his wordplay goes when no one is around. A late lunch on Tuesday would work... he enjoys bringing me refills.

She glanced at her reflection—the new rose tint looked good—it's subtle enough. Mark would be drawn to that over anything bold or dark. Lashes look good... she was ready for him to drop by. What he would respond to was unclear at this point, but she was good at this. It won't take long to figure that out. In the meantime, I'll rack up some sales. That *always* opens executive doors.

3 Julian's new clothes

When it came to putting on school clothes, Julian had never paid much attention to style and that kind of thing. Whatever was handy—as long as it wasn't too dirty and fit all right—that's all he cared about.

Now all of a sudden he was supposed to pay attention to that other stuff—or try to. The trip today to buy new school clothes did not go the way I expected at all. Always before, I just tagged along and let mom decide what to get. All I ever had to do was try things on; that way she could tell if they would last long enough. She always buys the next size up, which is smart. That way I don't grow out of them before the year is over—a good thing the last two years, for sure.

It looks like those were the good old days. Today, Geraldine took over. Julian had not expected that, but it wasn't a surprise. She was his mom's best friend as well as her boss—and for the last two months, his boss too. All the money he earned this summer was from working on her landscape crew, so he was grateful. But she always does things in a big way; she has to run things all the time, no matter what it is. "Don't mind me," she says, "I'm just along for the ride." Then she says, "Not that one, dear," and picks out what she wants you to wear.

He had learned a long time ago that sometimes she meant the exact opposite of what she said. You could get into big trouble if you didn't take that into account. Geraldine was *never* along for the ride, *especially* if she kept saying she was. It looked like she and his mom were in cahoots on this school clothes thing. That wasn't a surprise either.

"You're in high school now," she says for the hundredth time. Trouble is, they never tell what that means. I'm supposed to know that automatically. It must be a whole bunch of things because they say it all the time about all kinds of stuff. What I wear and how to wear it is only the latest. When I get up in the morning until I go to bed, no matter what in between: I'm supposed to remember that I'm in high school now. As if I could forget! If it's all that important, they should put out a handbook. Man. All he could do is shake his head and put up with it.

The ladies had gone back to the office at last, leaving Julian to sort out all the clothes. So, with the radio blaring away in the kitchen keeping the burglars away, he stood staring at his bed, trying to organize the task. The radio is so annoying… if I was trying to draw I'd go turn it down first thing. I'll do that in a minute. I can put up with Dean Martin. They play him a lot on that station.

When it came to clothes, Julian didn't care one way or the other. *Clothing-smothing* was his attitude. He was quite content to turn over all the style questions to Geraldine and his mother. After all, they're the ones who had to look at him—might as well keep them happy. The only reason to look in the mirror was to comb his hair—or do his weekly check on what was happening with his ever-changing anatomy. Lately that had been of special interest, especially what was going on "down below." Yesterday I discovered that I don't need the stool any more to get a close look at my face. One day the first whisker will appear—that's supposed to happen in high school. The ladies don't talk about that for some reason.

Something else is going on with them, though, besides scheming about what I'm supposed to wear. All summer long Geraldine made smart-alecky remarks about how the girls were gonna be hard to fend off when school starts, and stuff like that. The guys razzed me a little too. All during the shopping trip she raved at how they were going to love me in this or that.

No point in arguing about it—they'll get their way in the end anyway. Besides, it's to my advantage to play along. Why make them suspicious? I like girls well enough, considering—but not the way I'm supposed to. When it came to "looks," it was boys and men that caught his eye. But even there, he was biding his time. After what he learned at camp from Danny and Nick and Tom—and don't forget Geoff! Julian knew where he was going and pretty much what to do when he got there. That was his Big Plan. Staying in the cabin had made it possible to understand the dimension of that. The timeline had to be adjusted, but the goal is the same as always: I will be ready when Mark wants me. I decided that a long time ago—the night Mark came to the house and invited me to join Troop Nine.

Hands on his hips, he looked in wonder at the small mountain before him. I've never had this many clothes in my life… piled on the bed like this, looks like I bought out half the store. Where to start? First I'll sort by type into smaller piles… The goal was to put them away by the days of the week. Organizing them in the right combinations before hanging them up in the closet made the most sense. That way I won't wear the wrong socks with the right shirt… Geraldine filled me in on that. It's easy to see what goes with what—any dummy can tell that. It had never occurred to him to pay attention to that while putting on clothes.

"Never wear the same outfit two days in a row," Geraldine said. That's another thing that's going to be different. Before now I had two kinds of shirt and one kind of pant. I always had different colors of socks, but I never fussed over which ones to put on. Now they have to match my shirt because "I'm in high school now."

Do they have people checking on what you wear? Is there a committee that awards points and keeps track, like in scouts? What do they do if you wear the wrong color of socks? Spank you and send you home to change?

Let's make Monday blue day. He put the blue shirt at the left end, on his pillow. Ah: two different pair of blue argyle socks. That's easy—one has diamonds with the same sky blue color as the shirt. The other one will start a leftover pile at the right end. Pants… Levi's, suntans, or the Bermuda shorts? Hmm… depends on how warm it is outside. He put all three pair to the side. Pants don't have to change every day. A white T-shirt went onto the Monday pile; every day gets one of these. I'm supposed to wear a fresh T-shirt every day, no arguments. Honestly; it isn't as if I was like Pigpen. Last year I wore the same T-shirt for two or three days sometimes—if mom wasn't watching. Of course, they weren't white like these… it took a while to look used. I'm gonna miss my striped T-shirts. Secretly, he sympathized with poor little Pigpen—always surrounded with dust and dirt no matter what; if nothing else, you had to admire him for being different.

Before now, only one decision to make: clean or dirty. Of course, I never had clothes that were *very* dirty. Mom always sweeps through without warning, picking up whatever isn't put away; she washes it whether it's dirty or not. Sometimes, I tried to hide things but it never worked; she'd rummage around and find it anyway. Annoying. They weren't dirty: why waste the soap and water? Mothers have funny ideas sometimes, that's all there is to it.

Tuesday: how about making that coral day. This is the first orange shirt I ever had—or is it pink? It's sort of both; another Geraldine inspiration. Wait: she said that was a Friday color. He moved the coral shirt to the right. Let's make Tuesday yellow.

"You hafta hang things up from now on," he warned himself. Otherwise these would wear out too fast because of his mother's laundry sweeps. One thing about clothes—if they've been washed a lot they have an oldish look. Having bought most of these with his own hard earned money, he had a new respect for what shirts and pants had to put up with. The laundry is a lot harder on clothes than I am. One day I need to ask about that: how many washes can a shirt take? Maybe *Consumer Reports* says something. I'm gonna make Mom hold off washing them until I've worn them at least twice.

Two kinds of shirt were new: turtleneck T-shirts and a Rugby shirt; both had long sleeves. I had to talk them into the Rugby shirt; only kind that had stripes. I like stripes. That was the other surprise—all this stuff was from the *men's* department. I'm too big now for boy's sizes—they have all kinds of stripes in the boy's department. Oh well. *You're in high school now…* No more striped T-shirts.

They don't let you try on turtlenecks in the store. What do they look like? Might as well see… Mom and Geraldine are back at the office for the rest of the day, so I can put one on without all the yak-yak and oohs and ahs. He took off all his clothes; might as well do this right. Besides, I'm due for another progress check.

Why do they call these turtlenecks, anyway? They don't look like turtles. Which one should I try… light blue, light brown, and canary yellow. The canary is supposed to go with my hair. Why does it made a funny crinkle sound? Oh… a layer of tissue paper inside; some pins keep it folded up. Why do all these shirts have pins? These will come in handy on the bulletin board… he started a pin pile over on the drawing table.

He unfolded it and pulled it on. It's kind of like the sweater Mom got me a few years back… super warm. It smells new… which means practically no smell at all. After she washes them, that's when they smell *clean.* Wow, it's *long!* The thing goes halfway to my knees! The cloth feels like a T-shirt but softer. He went to the bathroom for a look-see.

The neck is too long… he rolled it down a little, like a sleeve. Feels different, having my neck all covered up… he looked closer, trying to remember what a turtle looked like. Do they have a bunch of extra skin around their neck? Hmm… I thought they had real skinny necks. I'm gonna check the encyclopedia. The only critter I know of that has extra stuff around the neck is a buzzard.

Close up, the yellow of the shirt was a little darker than his hair; he backed away… Huh. From a distance, they're pretty close, at that. Chalk up another one for Geraldine. His eyes looked down to the shirttail… not quite halfway to my knees, but it's below the skivvy line. There's Little J… pokes out farther when he isn't tucked away in a pair of skivvies. Julian swung his hips back and forth… mmm… Little J likes being wagged like that… ooo!

Thanks to Danny, Julian had a name for him. On the second day of camp, Danny took him into the supply tent after KP to relax. That was a super important thing: that's when Julian found out that he wasn't the only one who liked boys. After Danny gave me my first ever massage, he introduced me to "Little D." That's the name Danny had for his stiffy. It was so *funny!* Anyway, it made sense, so I copied the idea: it's a lot easier to say Little J than the usual words. The usual words sound kind of uggy anyway.

Little J is eager to harden up as usual; most of the time he does that on his own. Sometimes that's okay because it feels so good. The trouble is, I can't hide him like I used to; I have to figure out different ways to sit and stand when people are around. Once in a while I see other kids with stiffies… it looks kind of silly and awkward. I don't dare look too long, or Little J will wake up and give me the same problem.

He wagged again… *ooo…* Little J is up all the way! With the shirttail pulled down tight his outline is *impressive.* I never thought that before… he lifted the shirt to see the difference.

From the kitchen, the radio blared, *"I've got a one track mind… Maybe I'm a stubborn fool…"*

Julian laughed at the coincidence. "One track mind sure fits… just look at you!" He wasn't a Bobby Lewis fan, but his song was right about Little J, for sure. Huh… uncovered he doesn't look as big. Ooo! I just had an idea. He raced back to the bedroom. "Let's see how Little J likes the new skivvies."

Rummaging in the pile reminded him of the best part of the day: when Mark came over to say hello. Being close to Mark was a challenge, but thanks to summer camp, he had learned how to keep Little J under control—most of the time.

The minute we entered the store I looked—it wasn't hard to spot him, since he's so tall; he's a bigwig around there, always on the move checking things and helping out. One reason this trip was special was getting to see Mark. When I saw him heading our way, I pretended to pay attention to Geraldine. I had to work all summer, so it would have been hard to come in here—besides, coming to the store without planning to buy something would look kind of suspicious.

Today he wasn't in his scoutmaster uniform. Wow, was he ever cool looking. Mark's dress slacks weren't very good at hiding things—the new style is smooth and tight across the front. Julian forced himself to turn away—if I'm not careful, Little J will wake up… don't need that! Mark's presence never failed to give Julian a buzz. Woo… he's here! Julian didn't need to turn around: that aroma always caused a tickle behind the balls.

"Howdy, neighbors," Mark tapped the cart cheerfully. "I see you're selecting the best quality; I approve, naturally." He gave Julian a friendly nudge on the shoulder.

"Oh, Mark!" Francine was delighted to see him; she touched his arm. "You've met Geraldine, haven't you?"

Mark smiled, "Yes, indeed." He had bought his house from Geraldine. Everyone in town knows Geraldine.

Geraldine winked flirtatiously. Mark always gave her fantasy life a boost. "You're just in time. This young man needs an expert opinion that only you can provide."

Mark's eyes opened wide.

"Underwear," she winked again. "First hand experience is always more reliable, I'm told."

"No argument," Mark grinned. One area he never handled was ladies undergarments. He gave Julian a nod. "If you'll come along with me, *young man*, I'll show you what we have." He gestured to the right, then paused a second: "have you stopped by the handbag department? We have several new fall items."

"Ooo, what an idea!" I need something new. "Why don't you meet us there?" She'd spotted a hat in the window on the way in… might take a look at that too. She waved a ta-ta and looked at Francine happily. Perfect timing. She liked it when that happened. It reinforced her belief that much of life was meant to be—today was proving her right once again.

"Thanks," Julian said quietly so the ladies wouldn't hear. He was ready for a break. Shopping with Mom was bad enough, but two ladies? Besides, now he could do what had been his real goal: look at Mark's bright blue eyes for a minute—that's always special.

"Don't mention it," Mark laughed. "It looked like you needed a breather." It was great to see Julian, as a matter of fact. The summer tan has transformed him. Working in the sun all day will do that… I did that when I was in school. "So, you took the day off?"

"Nope. Wednesday was my last day. Gotta get ready for school; it starts on Monday." He pulled the cart forward.

"Stupid me; I knew that."

"Went to registration with Sid yesterday; I signed up for Art class."

"Excellent. I want to know how that goes." He turned to the left. "I promised Sarge you'd get lessons, you know."

"Really?" Wow. "I miss him." Sarge is this neat old guy at the camp; I call him Uncle Max. I hafta write him a letter about school. Man. I'm glad I remembered that. He gave me the drawing board and those large sheets of paper.

"That reminds me—I need to come over and do a Scrapbook review. The first troop meeting isn't far off, you know."

"Mmm, yeah!" *Perfect!* Sitting next to Mark going over the scrapbook is my *favorite* thing. "It's ready—even the parade is in there. But I didn't have time to draw much new stuff, what with all the yard jobs." Oo, this will be great! There are some he hasn't seen! Besides, the drawings look different when they're put into the scrapbook. "When?"

"Well, tonight's out—I'm on duty here until nine o'clock. But I'm off all weekend… since you're not working, we can do it any time tomorrow or Sunday. Let's ask your mother." Francine usually keeps us supplied with cookies and lemonade. "I'd like to get it done before you have schoolwork to worry about."

Darn—just *one* of these times, he wanted to do the Scrapbook without Mom fussing in the background. One of the special treats at camp was looking at the scrapbook and talking about stuff just before lights out. We'd sit there, next to each other, looking at each drawing, just the two of us.

"Here we are!" They approached the underwear department. "What kind of underpants do you like?"

Gosh. "Kind?" Underpants are underpants… usually they're annoying. "I didn't know there was different *kinds.* Mom always gets them." Julian's eyes strayed momentarily—he wanted to see how things looked when Mark walked. What he saw refreshed his memory nicely.

"You'll be glad you took care of this in person. There's no such thing as perfect underwear, but some kinds are better than others." He stepped over to a low countertop and pulled a small stand out from underneath; it had a curious adjustable mechanism on top; two arms swiveled apart; each had a vertical shaft with a prong hanging down on the inside. It was specially designed to help demonstrate the features of men's underwear.

The salesman stood at the ready, expecting to assist or to take over, but Mark dismissed him with a nod. "I'll take care of this one, Carl." He grabbed the tailor's tape that Carl always kept around his neck.

"Stand still a minute." He measured around the waist and hips. Julian had grown considerably since camp; still a small, but medium isn't far off. "You're in luck. We have lots of choices in your size." With a wink he tossed the tape back to the salesman and stepped over to a nearby rack. "What kind do you have now?"

Julian didn't expect to see such a variety—wow. "Last summer Mom got me some of those." He pointed to a package of Hanes briefs.

"Do you like them?"

What a question. Hmm. "No, come to think about it."

"Can you tell me why?"

"Too tight around the leg… and the opening in front is hard to work." I always pull the front down rather than fuss with that stupid opening.

"Okay. Here's what we'll do." Mark took several packages of skivvies off the rack. He opened one and fitted a pair onto the prongs—the tension kept the briefs in place. He put a hand inside and pushed outward to simulate their being on a person.

That's when Julian lost the struggle with Little J. Seeing Mark's hand creating that fake bulge was just too wonderful to describe… especially when he demonstrated how secure the opening was by poking his middle finger out from inside. Wow. Memories from the cabin popped into view… it was no trouble at all to pretend what he was looking at.

"As you can see, this pair is pretty secure." He removed his hand from inside and showed how it worked being accessed from the outside. "These are kind of tough to get into."

"I hate that." It always takes both hands to do the job.

"Now you try it."

Julian was glad the other guy had moved off to wait on another customer; he repeated the test… pretty much what he expected.

Mark fitted another pair—very different. They tested four different brands. Only one was easy to get in and out of. A pair of boxer shorts was next.

"Ever tried these?"

Julian shook his head.

"One nice thing about boxers is they aren't tight around your leg. Some guys like being loose down below." He poked his finger out the front slit. "The larger sizes sometimes have a button in the middle. Guys who are big need that, or you-know-what happens." He poked three fingers out of the opening.

That caused a giggle; Julian pictured Tom in a pair of these... he'd need a button for sure. Right off, one advantage of boxers was obvious: if a stiffy needed attention, they'd be real handy.

"Another advantage is it's easier to free yourself."

Free myself? He tilted his head.

"You know, when your balls get stuck down low, between your legs."

Julian blushed. He did know; he never expected Mark to say that, though. Wow.

"Last and *least*, is the bikini brief." Mark handed him the package. "It doesn't have an opening at all, of course."

Huh... the drawing looked kind of like a pair of Speedos. "Why..." how do I phrase this without using the word sexy? Where are you, inside guy...

"Some guys like everything to be tight, in a bunch. Some pants aren't good at covering things; these can help make up for that."

Julian kept a straight face... if Mark was wearing these, the nice bulge hanging to the right wouldn't show nearly as well.

"One drawback is that you can usually see the line going across your buns." Mark winked. "Top secret: that's one reason some guys wear these." With a knowing smile he turned sideways and pushed his right hip outward to highlight the line under his blue slacks.

Julian's expression was wonderful. Mark chose not to explain further.

Little J just went full... no way to stop him. That particular contour, line or no line, was one of Julian's favorites.

"Some athletes like the secure feeling these can give—sort of like a jock strap."

"OH! Those are on the list. I need one of those for P.E.!" I've never had a jock strap before. I saw a few last year: the sports guys had them.

The athletic supporters were on the next rack. Mark did not demonstrate those either—he just tossed a couple of pair in the basket. "Best to have a clean one on hand when the first one has to go to the laundry."

Julian nodded his approval. Mom would have bought two automatically. He picked up a package and looked at the illustration.

"First pair?"

Julian nodded. Odd… I always wondered why these things didn't have a back other than the straps. They'll probl'y tell about it in class.

Inadvertently, Julian had stepped away from the cart; his "problem" had become visible: the scout shorts couldn't hide what had developed. Indeed, Mark doubted if they could hide an erection half as big as Julian sported nowadays. I had the same problem when I was a teen. His new Levi's will hide things well enough. Mark knew better than to suggest putting them on now; he had to pretend, as usual, that he didn't notice.

"You're taller. You grew quite a bit this summer."

Julian grinned. "Yep. Two and five eights inches!" It meant a lot that Mark noticed. I never did get to brag to Sid.

"Wow—no wonder you need to get new clothes; that's over an inch a month!" Julian bulged just about everywhere. "You're going to need a new scout shirt too."

"We got one already." That was the first stop.

"Excellent. So—" he gestured to the pile of underwear: "any questions?"

In fact, Julian was dying to know what brand Mark wore.

Well, since he asked… Inside guy prompted.

About time you showed up… Julian cleared his throat. "Um ... what kind do you like?"

"Hard to tell… like you, I can't say I *like* any of them. Truth is, I try all of them out." He shrugged; "part of the job, y'know. I try to know as much as I can so that I can help customers like you," he grinned. "The most important thing is to get them big enough." Mark looked at the stack of open packages. He debated with himself a minute. "You know, at the rate you're growing, I think maybe you should get some mediums."

Julian nodded. Tight skivvies are a real pain.

Mark stepped over to the rack, plucked a medium sized set and added them to the pile. "Tell you what: you can be my assistant tester. You can report on which ones you like and why. That way you get them for half price!" He plopped everything into the shopping basket.

One nice management perk was the ability to discount on the spot. He gave Julian his signature pinch, high up on the shoulder. "Let's go find your mother."

Julian snapped out of his reverie and returned to the present. Man alive, what a difference being with Mark made, even for a little while. "The whole world looks better, that's all." He pulled off the turtleneck and tossed it onto the bed. I wonder what he'd think of me in *that?!* Pretty silly… although… I wonder. Did I get anything today that Mark would like?

You mean something that would make you look good to him, don't you? Inside guy was on the job, as usual.

Well, yeah. Geraldine is out make me look good to the girls. What if Mark doesn't like me in this stuff? How could I tell, anyway? Maybe these things make me look… I don't know…

You mean like a teenage kid?

Well, yeah. That's one thing I learned in the cabin. He made it pretty clear that he wasn't allowed to have anything "special" to do with anyone under eighteen. Do these look like teen clothes?

We got them in the men's department.

Yeah, that's true. Except for a necktie, these are pretty much what guys like Mark wear… maybe I'm okay. The thing is, I never pay attention to what people wear. I always look at their face and think of what they're like as people, on the *inside*.

That's not true… when you look at Mark you pretty much look at everything.

That's just Mark. Although… I do pay attention to what he wears. He looks sexy in just about anything. 'Course, I spend most of the time imagining what's under the cloth.

Don't I know! One track mind, that's for sure.

Boy, I must have looked really awful today… all my old clothes are so small.

Mark doesn't care about stuff like that. He treated you the same as always—he gave you his special pinch.

Ooo, yeah. Remembering it was almost as good. Little J thinks so too: he's tingling again. Julian looked down at the pile of underwear… I want to see what those bikinis are like. I know! Now that Little J's going strong, this is the perfect time. He tore open a package, pulled on a pair and dashed to the bathroom.

Wow. These make me feel horny. He turned around to look at the line across his buns… just like a Speedo all right; it's about halfway up the bun. Mark said some guys want that to show on purpose. Why? I was afraid to ask. Maybe Nick knows. It's always safe to ask him about that kind of thing.

The tan line sure looks strange… I didn't pay any attention to that before. A border of white skin above and below the bikinis showed where his cutoffs had blocked off the sun… showed how dark the tan really was. Zack always made sure I greased up. I think

Geraldine told him to do that. That's why I didn't get sunburned like Danny did at camp. Huh… the bikini sure doesn't cover very much.

He faced front again. "How am I gonna test all these skivvies with you showing off like that?" Little J pulsed happily as if to say, 'test them all this way; I can stay up.' Julian pulsed him a few times to see how they handled the stretch. Little J wanted to point sideways. There isn't any other place for him to go in these things.

Not much point in those that I can see… Inside guy offered. When it came to matters below the waist, he tended to comment whether it was asked for or not.

For some time now, Julian's habit of talking to himself when no one else was around had become a standard device for thinking things through. Last summer that process had refined itself, fortunately. Now, in addition to the dum-dum who looked back at him from the mirror, the Inside guy had appeared, as if by magic—a good thing, too. The inside voice had stopped him from doing some really stupid things as far as his plan for Mark was concerned. He had gone to camp with a super hot idea: lure Mark off to a remote place in the forest, and somehow, trick him into making a play of some kind. It hadn't been thought out in any detail, but with two weeks to work things out, it was easy to assume a way to achieve his goal would come along.

Boy was I ever wrong about that! And it was the Inside guy that helped me figure out things. I came close to doing the exact wrong thing more than once. The last time was in the middle of the night—I discovered by accident that Mark was out of bed—he had wandered off somewhere. In spite of the protests of the Inside guy, Julian went searching, and found him sitting alone on a stump. I didn't go close, but I could see that he was really sad about something. The Inside guy stopped me from getting too close—Mark didn't know I was there.

After he came back to the cabin was when I found out two important things: first, that he was remembering someone that had died… someone he loved—and that he wasn't ready to think about someone to replace him. Second, I learned that the person was a *guy*. That was *so* important. It told me that there *was* a chance… but that I had to wait.

For how long didn't matter; *as long as it takes* was his new motto. Meantime, my job is to learn and prepare so that when the time comes, I'll be ready—Mark will know, and will want me. Of that Julian had not one doubt—especially now that Inside guy is here to stop me from screwing everything up.

Of course, the Big Plan was Top Secret; Inside guy was the only one that knew. None of his scout buddies knew.

Better keep it that way, too, said Inside guy; he was still in on the discussion.

Julian had learned very early it was smart to pretend about some things. Especially about liking boys instead of girls. Years of having mommies pester him about who his girlfriend was had trained him well; what to say and do… all he had to do was help them think he was just like all little boys were supposed to be. Half the time a smile and blush did the job. They *loved* it when he did that. So he didn't have to think about girls at all. The ladies filled in the blanks the way they wanted.

He hadn't spent one minute thinking about what girl to be after or trying to impress. When I see guys hung up doing that I am so glad I don't have to bother; if I don't have some scouting thing to do, I improve my drawing—a better way to use my time; more *fun*, too.

However: as Geraldine had said a jillion times, "You're in high school now." The summertime prodding about having to fight off swarms of girls had developed into kind of a scold: now I have to impress them with all these fancy clothes. I'm not worried; as usual, they told me what to buy, and what to wear—so, that solved that. I'll do like always: just smile.

His eyes returned to the bikini. "Do you think anybody on the crew wears these?" he asked the boy in the mirror. The face shook its head. "Nah." Julian agreed. Still, he was a little curious about who would like them. I don't expect to like them much. I have enough trouble with Little J as it is. He pulled them off and watched

Little J bounce up and down happily. The inside guy didn't need to make a wisecrack.

One by one Julian tested the advantages and disadvantages of each style with a stiffy going. The Jockey pair was best at hiding Little J; the boxers did that too—they also made it easiest to make adjustments or do "whatever."

Time out: Little J insisted on being satisfied. Julian was happy to let him have his way. But first, do something about that blasted radio!

Does your chewing gum lose its flavor
On the bedpost overnight
If your mother says don't chew it
Do you swallow it in spite...

The volume knob got a fast left twist. "Take that!" He didn't dare turn it off, but it was low enough so it couldn't reach his room. Chewing gum on the bedpost! What a screwy thing to sing about. Julian didn't chew gum, but putting it on a bedpost seemed like a stupid thing to do—besides, his bed didn't have bedposts like his mom had. Anyway, Little J had a better idea of how to spend the next five or ten minutes... they rushed back to the bedroom.

He pulled his pillow out from under the blue shirt and plopped it near the edge of the bed, then reached over to grab the Kleenex box... it's a little early for this; might as well get it out of the way. Working around a pile of clothes didn't pose a problem. He hopped up, stretched out, took Little J into his right hand, and closed his eyes.

An imaginary picture of Mark trying on a pair of bikini briefs appeared. Julian had a considerable bank of images in his memory, most from the cabin at Camp Walker—without Mark's knowledge, of course. The bikini style would be full the minute he put it on; Mark is pretty big down there. If he got a stiffy, it would have to poke up over the top. Picturing that helped him have a really great time-out session with Little J.

Afterward all the skivvies were re-tested in reverse order—this time with Little J asleep. Before long his first report was ready: he didn't really like any of the briefs, but the BVD pair had the best front door. All the S sized ones will be too small around the leg by Christmas.

He distributed the skivvies—I'm supposed to change those every day too, along with the T-shirt. I'll start with… he shrugged. The day of the week doesn't matter with these… might as well start with the bikinis. The boxers were put at the end.

4 TV dinner

"Thanks a bunch, Ben. See you on Monday," Mark tapped the top of the car and waved a grateful farewell. On days when Pat was out of town, he had to depend on others to give him a lift when it was this late; five miles is a little far to walk. The bus made its last run at 8 o'clock. One of these days, I have to get a second car… this happens too often.

Mark checked his watch—almost *ten*. No wonder I'm tired. His legs did not want to go up the front steps. Not surprising after being on his feet for almost sixteen hours. The daily totals were gratifying, but he was less enthusiastic about closing at nine on Fridays. "The downside of being management," he observed, unlocking the door.

The air that met him inside was unpleasant, as expected; being sealed in the house all day in late summer guaranteed that. He began the usual route to turn on the air conditioning: living room first. I'll hit the bedroom after I get supper started. He opened the downstairs bathroom and kitchen windows; natural air circulation always helps. It's cooling nicely outside; it won't take long for this place to be livable again.

Too late to do any serious cooking, but I'm starving. He opened the freezer compartment—let's see… there's fried chicken, turkey, more fried chicken, and… Salisbury steak. Which one cooks the fastest? What says the back of the box… same time on all of them: 25 minutes at 425 degrees. You'd think I'd remember—I do this often enough. Fried chicken won the toss. He turned on the oven and set the timer. Onto the rack you go! The TV dinner slipped out of the box eagerly. No point in waiting for the oven to preheat… I'll just add five minutes.

"Shower time," he announced, and headed for the stairway.

Mmm… the next best thing to a massage is a long hot shower. Mark took his time… Pat isn't here to scold me about wasting water. He enjoyed relaxing under the spray.

The day began to play back in his mind as it usually did, in bits and pieces. Odds and ends about inventory passed by… Marie had an unexpected run on towel sets… need to put in an order first thing Monday… hosiery had problems too. Household items… sales were slow there. But that was to be expected this time of the year. Clothing met their goal and then some. Phyllis had a great day. She sure knows how to move inventory.

His mind didn't linger on the workday any longer. He emptied his head of worldly concerns and focused on the physical pleasure of hot water spraying relentlessly on his weary muscles.

It was good to see Julian again. Has he ever changed! He's grown over two inches since camp! Must have put on ten pounds—and the suntan! That summer job made a giant difference. I noticed at the end of camp that he was growing fast—he got a good start there. One of the most fascinating things about scouts was seeing boys jump in size so rapidly. Every year a new set of clothes—in some cases, two. They're certainly good for clothing sales.

There were several boys like that today—some of them, like Julian, look fantastic in the new line of clothing. The older boys looked especially attractive. Of course, boys had never been of any interest sexually; men his own age or older—that's all he had ever known. One man, in fact. Aside from playing around at scout camp, he was without experience. He had just one love in his life and had never strayed—or been tempted to, even six years later… no: seven! Wow—next month it will be seven years since Erik died.

But something was going on someplace inside his head, and it wasn't possible pretend otherwise any longer. It was time to find out why he wasn't always in charge these days.

Ever since the "close call" at camp, Mark had been unsure of himself. The experience with the "California Kid" had shaken him; something had changed inside his control center or whatever it's called. Geoff was his name; a very mature lad from Atlanta. Evidently I have to be on guard once they're full grown. Once they're that mature, they can be appealing—simple as that. That's new. Never before had even the most mature scout been of interest sexually. None of his own boys had ever drawn his eye.

Mark wasn't *terribly* worried—when it was a matter of self-discipline and control, he was sure of himself. Take a risk just because a sexually precocious kid like Geoff is flaunting himself? No way—even if Roger is itching for some exercise.

Still, Roger is a problem more and more… Mark glanced down to verify what had been trying to get his attention: being washed and rinsed had awoken Roger; the extended stay under a warm shower had stimulated him even more. Not a surprise; it didn't take much to do that lately.

He turned off the water and reached around the shower door for the towel. A loud buzz was sounding downstairs.

Was I in there that long?! He dried his hair hurriedly and set out for the kitchen; racing down the hallway is awkward if you're trying to towel dry yourself at the same time—nothing can be done to prevent a trail of wet footprints.

"Sorry, Roger; not now—supper's ready." It was sort of fun skipping down the stairs with him waving back and forth. But Mark wasn't about to give in whenever Roger wanted. He wanted to be in charge of that—he *needed* to be in charge of that.

The blast of hot air from the oven punished him for being unprotected. He grabbed the towel from his shoulder and wrapped around his waist; it would have to serve as a bathrobe. *Wow*, is this hot! Onto the counter with you! The foil cover resisted, but came off, releasing a puff of steam... *mmm*, smells like a million. He fetched a plate and some flatware. A glass of wine was required... there we are. Feast in one hand, wine in the other, he headed for the den. Sitting alone at the kitchen table didn't appeal: he wanted to be comfy and distracted.

Mark didn't watch a lot of television, but something besides the sound of his own chewing would be nice. The Friday Night Movie on channel 7 had started already... looks like Bogart tonight. Perfect company for a late supper; the Strato-Lounger wasn't ideal for dining, but it would serve; eating here meant not having to get up and move afterward. He planned to stay in one spot, off his feet, until bedtime. The T.V. table was wide enough to accommodate his Swanson's deluxe chicken supper, the glass of wine, and today's small stack of mail. I'll sort that while I feed my face.

Yep... the extra cooking time helps. The meat practically falls off the bone. This is tasty.

His eye focused on the T.V. screen. Volume is too low... phooey. I don't want to go over there, I just sat down! Why don't they come up with a way to turn up the volume from a distance? You can fly a model airplane with a remote control, why not a T.V. set? I haven't seen this one... looks like they're in the tropics... an old guy and a pretty girl... must be his daughter. Maybe I can get the gist of it anyway. He took a long sip of wine. MMmm... After that shower, twice as powerful. The label said California, 1961... must have been a good year.

Mark took his time... enough hurrying today. By the time he was finished eating, who was what in the movie had been sorted out; always did like Leo G. Carroll. He extended the footrest and settled in to watch. Bogart and a couple of others are pretending to repair a roof. No idea why...

Mark rarely fell asleep watching television. But after a double shift at the store, a long hot shower, a full stomach, and an 8 ounce glass of Zinfandel, he dozed off—a relaxed, contented man. The air conditioner in the living room provided an ambient sound that complemented the low volume of the TV, and may have contributed to the series of dreams that began to parade through his mind.

It was a sound sleep—physical exhaustion combined with the stress of being responsible for the fiscal well being of the store made sure of that. The dreams weren't strong enough to surface to his conscious mind. After a good two hours of sleep, a sharp sound made him flinch. "Huh—?" What caused that?! Oh… the fork slipped of the edge of the TV tray.

The last image in his memory was a snake in the picnic basket… was that in the movie? Must have been. White snow and a soft hiss had replaced the movie; the television station had gone off the air. > *yawn* < He stretched… wow. There's a snake in my lap too: Roger was on duty helping to control his bladder: *that's* what woke me up. "We need to visit the boys' room." Groggy, he returned the recliner to its vertical position and stood… Man! I was out for the count…

"You need to go to bed, stupid."

Why is my left arm half numb? Doesn't like to sleep in a chair I guess. That *sound!* turn that infernal thing off! Groggy still, he made his way across the room.

> *klik* < Much better: the annoying hiss was gone. Mark wasn't wide awake, but that's okay—didn't want to be… might not be able to fall asleep again. An autopilot somewhere in his head was in control. Wine glass and empty TV tray in hand, he systematically shut off the lights and the air conditioner on the way to the kitchen. At the foot of the stairs a wagging Roger alerted him: the towel… where? … it fell off somewhere along the way, I don't usually parade around in nature's own—

"Get it tomorrow," he continued up the stairs. A glimpse of himself in the full length mirror at the end of the hallway did not faze: "tomorrow." He pushed away the image with a wave of his left arm: Roger was standing in full salute again, unapologetic.

The image of Roger was put out with the hall light, but emptying a full tank meant doing battle with him, *then* I can get back to sleep.

Again he had put off dealing with what was happening in his subconscious… another broken promise. "Some day you'll pay if you don't take care of this."

Tomorrow: I have all day tomorrow. Roger relented, and Mark finished his last errand of the day.

He crawled into bed and slipped into a deep sleep almost at once—the long workday and the wine were his ally in the struggle with his conscience.

Roger, however, didn't feel sleepy at all—he'd been a good boy all day. He had an "inside connection" with the control center in Mark's subconscious—another series of dreams was put into the production line. The protective shield Mark had built up the last six years was crumbling—his libido had been sidelined long enough.

Mark had always avoided thinking about personal matters; all his life he had tried to hide who he was from the world. He thought of himself as being a fraud, essentially. Counseling to deal with his sexual orientation would only lead to disaster. He wasn't wrong or mistaken to feel as he did: he was born this way. Becoming a martyr to defend his identity made no sense either. It was possible to lead a "normal" happy life and excel without personal secrets interfering. The brief time with Erik had proven that he was a healthy worthwhile person; he didn't need to explain or justify himself to anyone.

The mistake was presuming they would always have one another to share whatever problems or challenges came along. Alas, what fate had in store for them came suddenly, without warning—and Mark was not prepared. That late night flight to Boston eliminated their future. They had done nothing to plan for such a possibility. For three years they had simply enjoyed being together—thrived on being together. Mark used those memories to build a protective shield. Since there would never be anyone like Erik, it was futile if not sacrilege to seek a replacement. It was a self-imposed standard—Erik had nothing to do with it—he would have counseled Mark to move on; sadly, the subject never came up.

But after six years of fantasy and denial, loneliness gradually replaced consolation. Sleeping alone was not fun. Biological imperatives and requirements began to percolate through layers of self-discipline, and reinforced his growing psychological need for companionship. Increasingly, the real world provided sights and experiences that pierced his armor. Once again, inner needs began to respond to external stimuli.

That's what Roger was all about. Mark was confused and annoyed by his unruliness and demands; he did not understand that Roger's behavior was a symptom of inner change. His period of mourning was over, whether he wanted it to be or not. The guilty conscience every time he looked in the mirror was due to his disinclination to be introspective. He didn't want to face this… even though deep down he knew that he'd have to, eventually.

Seeing Julian today was particularly significant—images in his unconscious that had been floating randomly for months were set in motion. Summer camp was full of self-denial. Mark thought that it was Geoff's bizarre attempt to seduce him that must have started all this. It was a big part of it, but it had begun earlier in subtle unsuspected ways. One reason he had built a wall between himself and Julian was the subconscious awareness that one day Julian would be mature—he would be like Geoff, only much more attractive—maybe irresistible. That could be his downfall—or, just maybe, his salvation. In the meantime, in his conscious mind, Julian was strictly off limits, by definition.

Roger made it a point to chip away at that wall whenever he got the chance.

5 Scrapbook Sunday

Another droplet of sweat ran down Julian's cheek—he grabbed a tissue from the Kleenex box just in time. The action was automatic, almost unconscious; he'd had to do that a lot this afternoon to protect his work. A drop of sweat—or any kind of liquid—meant stopping at once. You can't draw on wet paper, simple as that. That would wreck everything…these had to be done before Mark arrived. That's why, on a hot Sunday afternoon, ever since they had had come home from church, Julian had been at his drawing table doing finishing touches. He'll go over the new scrapbook pages right after supper—they have to be as good as possible.

The weatherman must be out to set a new record for high temperature today—typical for the last day of summer vacation; oh well. Usually, the last day was reserved for splashing around at the pool; not this year—not with Mark coming over. Man, I hope it isn't this hot at school tomorrow!

Alleviating the atmospheric conditions in his bedroom wasn't easy on a day like this: the window was wide open and the electric fan was on the high setting. It was doing its best—but it had to be aimed away from the table slightly because it kept flipping the pages. Wearing cutoffs helped a lot—they made it easy to run through the sprinkler in the back yard. But stopping every five minutes to go outside doesn't make sense if you expect to get much done. He wiped off his forehead and scooted his chair back a few inches; sitting in front of the fan while checking the drawing helped some—"Mmmm…" evaporation! He closed his eyes and enjoyed the breeze. The sound was his friend too—it helped mask the radio in the kitchen. Mom is a radio addict, unfortunately—her only known shortcoming.

This was the last drawing about summer camp. An experiment—kind of tricky, too: the first time he'd ever tried to depict what something looked like after dark. There are lots of interesting things to see when it's dark, but figuring out how to draw them is *hard.* This one was supposed to show what you saw if you looked up the aisle of the bus at night.

After stopping for supper at that drive-in and watching the sunset, the last part of the long bus ride home was at night. Lots of guys had their pillows along and took a nap. Might as well; not much to do in the dark… home was over an hour away. In the drawing, all you can see is the outline of the seats and some of their heads. The hardest thing to get right is the row of little lights going up the aisle—the moonlight coming in the windows on the left side is *very* tricky halfway down the bus, Jeremy has his pocket flashlight on, showing something to Justin. They're so small you can't tell who they are. That's the main problem with the scrapbook—the pictures have to be small enough to fit on the page; then you have to leave room to write a description and tell about what's going on—it doesn't do much good if the description is on the next page.

"What I need is black paper and a white pencil." Boy, I bet that would be even harder. Do they make white pencils? Maybe that art class will teach me what to do. He narrowed his eyes and scanned the drawing. Nope… he shook his head; this "experiment" is falling short, that's all. I'll take it out if Mark wants.

I need a magnifying glass...drawing the small heads that were supposed to be Justin and Jeremy is super hard... They made Julian smile proudly—thanks to me, they became friends on the last day of merit badge class. Justin was Julian's buddy in Forestry, and Jeremy had been his pal all the way through grade school. I asked Jeremy to show Justin how to row a canoe, and that's all it took. It was terrific to see Justin come out of his shell. He's super shy and serious about everything. Jeremy is the perfect buddy—he isn't shy at all; they like the same kind of things.

Julian spent a lot of time at camp learning about friendship. It was different at camp—you could take time to think about things… watching others helped him understand himself and his own goals. I have a lot to learn about friendship and romance before I can expect Mark to take me seriously; watching Nick and Tom helps a lot… They had what he was going to have, someday, with Mark.

I'm about the luckiest kid around, if you think about it. Being the youngest ever to be put in Flaming Arrow, for instance. How lucky is that?! I ought to make a list sometime of all the lucky things in my life. Living down the street from Mark… being asked to join the troop by Mark… being promoted to Flaming Arrow by Mark—living in the same town as Mark…

It's not only Mark that's lucky, you know, reminded Inside guy.

Yeah, yeah, I know. I just have him on my mind today, is all. I had to do without him all summer.

Maybe Mark was glad to have some time to himself…

Julian was a little worried that he might have become a pest. Mark did wander off a couple of times after lights out…he had to be by himself. At first I felt bad because maybe I was in the way. But after Mark told me about losing his friend… his love, I knew that it wasn't my fault. I felt so sad for him, it's *awful* when you can't help.

Rested and freshly showered, Mark stood at the bathroom mirror, shaving. Unusual thing to do on a Sunday afternoon, but this was a special occasion—supper with Julian and his mother. He had high expectations: last year Francine invited him to supper a few times; her cooking is outstanding. A fresh shave was a basic requirement whenever he visited a scout at home. Of course, Julian and Francine had become close as friends and neighbors; but Mark was a bit of a stickler for traditions and appearances—it would never occur to him to relax his standard. Especially with Julian: Mark was mindful of the progress he had made during summer camp—neutralizing Julian's adolescent "fervor," for want of a better term.

Mark didn't want to call it a crush, but that's what it was. The idea that he could be the object of desire for someone as young as Julian was a little disconcerting. From his own boyhood experience, he knew better than to ignore or dismiss it. But as an adult, he knew better than to allow it any room to develop. He had taken a page from his own scoutmaster's book there: face it head on and face it early. Establishing precise protocols and rules made it impossible for Julian to continue his fantasies, whatever they were. Having been a scout himself, he had a fair idea of what they might be. It wasn't that long ago… what, twelve or thirteen years?

As a boy, Mark had never allowed himself to have a crush on anyone—too scary. It didn't matter if they were his own age or not. Admittedly, Erik was four years older, and I worshipped the ground he stood on. So I understood Julian and was able to empathize. My solution was to place him so close that he couldn't maintain the constant staring; that worked instantly. Julian didn't realize it, but I placed him in the cabin for protection, primarily—from the older boys as well as from himself. Promoting him to the Flaming Arrow patrol connected him with boys who could take care of his sexual curiosity and urges without taking advantage. The strategy worked perfectly. Julian's infatuation faded and I became more like a mentor—a roommate. Roommate rules, it turned out, established the appropriate boundaries quite effectively. Mark was quite pleased with himself for coming up with the stratagem. It was fun to have him as a "roommate."

He rinsed off the remaining shaving cream, dried his face and did a final inspection: job well done. Stupidly, instead of cheerfully bragging aloud, he made eye contact in the mirror again. *Blast it!* His cheerful mood vanished—the face in the mirror had just made the usual demand.

"All right! What do you *want* from me?!" Mark didn't have a good reason to put him off this time—at least half an hour remained before he was expected for supper. Arriving early wouldn't be fair to Francine; the walk might take all of two or three minutes.

The answer to his question was just becoming visible in his peripheral vision: Roger. Again.

"What do *you* want?" Why would I be getting an erection now? It's late Sunday afternoon, I'm about to leave for a very nice supper, and I have not been doing or thinking about anything that would stimulate Roger. But there he is anyway, demanding attention. Annoyed, he looked accusingly at the face in the mirror. It didn't help a bit.

One problem was his fundamental disinclination, if not aversion, to being introspective. Basic macho male pride had determined it was virtuous and manly to ignore these things. Mark was intelligent enough; he had sufficient formal education to provide a basic approach to analyzing his problem. But years of inactivity in the realm of soul searching, if not outright avoidance, had left him ill prepared to sort out what was happening. He had always preferred to leave well enough alone—being unprepared was the perfect excuse. It was more convenient to rationalize: things would sort themselves out eventually, so why bother?

The truth is, a hunch about what was going on lurked just under the surface, there wasn't any way to forget what happened at camp: blasted Californian. Somehow, he found a weak spot that I didn't know was there. Under the clever guise of wanting to know basics of close order drill, he set out to tempt me into, well, to have a sexual adventure of some kind. He even showed up after midnight, fully expecting to hop into my bed.

The fact is, I was tempted. That's what nags at me. How could that be? Such a thing had never happened before. If Julian hadn't been in the cabin, I could have given in. I *might* have. I didn't know I was vulnerable—even slightly. After Erik died, I relied on his memory—I didn't want anyone else, I didn't *need* anyone else. Then suddenly, out of nowhere, this exotic creature appears—waltzes, more like—and blindsides me in the HQ where I'm busy planning my winning play for the water polo team. The oldest ploy in the book worked like a charm: simple flattery. I bought his act without suspecting a thing. He sure knew what to do; I figured that out later. When he showed up in the middle of the night, I realized I'd been in his sights all along.

Fortunately, I had come to my senses by then—not only that, I had protection: Julian. What a surprise—it was living up to Julian's expectations and image of me that provided the strength I needed. Best of all, Julian slept soundly through the entire thing—to this day he has no idea of the service he provided in my hour of need. That will remain my secret.

He looked down at Roger again, with a frown. "So *why* are you up, anyway? Geoff is hundreds of miles away in Atlanta. He has lots of opportunities close by—he doesn't need me, thank goodness—or you. Until this minute, I didn't give him a thought all summer."

Roger remained at his maximum—mute, as always. Infuriatingly mute.

It was true: Mark had not given so much as a passing thought to Geoff since camp—yet for the past few weeks, Roger behaved as if he was receiving long distance calls from him or someone on a hidden line. Something was at work here—whoever or whatever it was, it had *nothing* to do with Erik, and that was very troubling. Being unfaithful to Erik's memory was unthinkable—yet that's what Roger seemed to be demanding: it wasn't memories of Erik that caused this. That's what Mark did not want to accept.

He scowled at the reflection: "The answer is *no*!" I'm not about to cave in and "satisfy" Roger now. I wonder if I could talk to Pat about this. She's *almost* a doctor… maybe I should see a specialist—she probably knows who I should see. They have a pill for everything these days, don't they?

With determination, he turned his back on the mirror. "So, what should I wear?" scout uniform? Technically that was appropriate; going as a scoutmaster to review Julian's work on the Troop Nine Scrapbook sort of decides the question—although, she did say something about being neighborly. Well, we'll see. He walked toward the bedroom, determined to prevail in this power struggle with Roger… I have to show him who's boss around here.

—ɯ—

Francine hummed happily as she assembled another kebob; this song was so *cheerful*. She was partial to Dean Martin anyway, and *Volare* made her feel ten years younger. No matter that she didn't know any Italian—it was a happy song, and she was in a happy mood. She didn't mind the heat... well, that wasn't true, but the opportunity to prepare a special Sunday supper reduced it to an inconvenience. The opportunity to do this didn't come very often. She enjoyed it for several reasons—fifteen years ago, her mother had spent weeks and months training her to make the perfect Sunday supper, among other things. She had hopes that Francine would find a good man to take the place of the husband that had betrayed her; toward that end, she believed that being trained as a superb cook was the first order of business.

Other than successfully teaching her how to cook, events hadn't worked out quite as mother envisioned. But preparing meals was enjoyable and challenging. She might have made it a career if Geraldine's offer hadn't come along. The real estate business was probably the better alternative. The pay wasn't very high, but it was secure, and it allowed her to spend more time with her child. Why be in a hurry to marry again? In any case, being just a mother gave her purpose enough. In truth, she was proudly selfish—why share Julian with a strange man? Why take a risk like that? The next one might be just as unfaithful as the first. Her duty was to her little boy... her perfect, beautiful little boy. What a treasure. It's hard to believe he's in high school already; if only he didn't have to grow up. He's growing so *fast* now—he's taller than I am.

She paused to check her preparations... Mark could arrive at any time. Salads are ready, iced tea is ready... table is set, kebobs are started... what have I forgotten? Oh: the watermelon. Julian can bring that in after we've cleared the dishes—

> ***Ding-ding!*** < The doorbell sounded.

Francine looked at the clock: perfect! Mark is always so punctual. That made it possible to do a main dish that relied on precise timing.

"Julian!" she called out. "Mark is at the door. Will you take care of letting him in, please? I need to keep an eye on things in here."

She peeked into the oven—these need to be turned in about thirty seconds… scorched kebobs will not do.

"Yow!" Julian leapt out of his chair and raced from his room.

—~—

The apparition that opened the door caught Mark by surprise: it's the fifteen year old Alexander, reincarnated. Gleaming with perspiration, he's left the Macedonian sports arena to greet a visitor to his father's court. The unclad torso glistened as if it had been vigorously engaged in a wrestling match; the pale blond hair, a mix of gentle tufts and curls, framed the handsome youth's classic, eager face.

But the grin, absolutely disarming, was completely Julian. The illusion dissolved instantly: this is a young artist, not a warrior. This was a face Mark knew well; it had greeted him every evening when he entered the cabin at Camp Walker. Seeing Julian barefoot and in his skivvies was routine at camp—in the late evening, it was his custom to work at the table while Mark made his final round of camp visits. The cabin was always warm at day's end—it held on to the heat it had absorbed during the daylong bake in the sun. Quite sensibly, Julian shed his uniform at the first opportunity; he was ready to hop onto his cot the minute the lights out command was given.

Tonight it's cutoffs instead of skivvies—and a deep tan. A couple of months of manual labor out in the open had done a nice job. At the store, Mark had only seen his head; much more had changed. Julian was considerably taller and more developed, the boy he had grown accustomed to in the cabin was becoming a young man.

Mark shouldn't have been surprised—but he was. Like Francine, he wasn't ready for Julian to grow up.

"Hi, Mark!" Julian was so glad to see him—wow, *look* at his clothes! looks like a golfer! Instead of the summer scout uniform, a nifty blue polo shirt and cream colored Bermuda shorts. The combination made his blue eyes stand out even more.

"Howdy—I hope I'm on time." He didn't let on he'd been surprised.

"Yep—come on in. Mom's in the kitchen." He led the way with a skip. Wowee… his brain busily calculated… those *sexy* clothes! how am I going to check him out without getting caught? "Hey, Mom—guess who's here," he giggled happily.

Amused, Mark shook his head; Julian's spontaneous behavior was as fresh and innocent as ever—his physical development hasn't spoiled that. He followed behind, unable to avoid passing through an invisible cloud of freshly shed pheromones—a surprise that, fortunately, his self-discipline enabled him to ignore.

Francine wiped her hands hastily on the apron as they stepped into the kitchen. "Your timing is perfect! It's almost ready to put on the table!" She was pleased and flattered that he had taken the trouble to dress so fashionably. She turned to Julian, about to suggest he show Mark to his chair when she noticed. "Lord have mercy! Julian! Where are your manners?!" She pointed to his room. "At least put on a shirt—we have company tonight!"

Julian was startled by her brusque rebuke—company? It's *Mark*! Mark isn't *company*. He sees me like this all the time. "But Mom, it's so hot!"

"You have lots of nice new clothes—please, Julian."

She's right, Inside guy interjected.

"Okay, okay." He looked at Mark. "Sorry… be right back!"

She watched him turn and skip out of the kitchen. "Boys!" She shrugged with a smile, and gestured to the table.

Mark laughed heartily. "On a day like this, who can blame him? Besides, I don't think of myself as company, really." He sat in the chair he always occupied when visiting the Forrest family. Sensing the growing sweat rings under his arms, he envied the freedom of boyhood.

"I know… and you're right—I didn't mean it that way… please don't take offense. You're not company at all—you're a part of our family. It's just that all this week we've had such a time with him, Geraldine and I. He has no idea what he'll be facing when high school starts tomorrow. Sometimes you wonder if *anything* is getting through..."

—m—

Julian didn't try to listen to what his mom and Mark were saying. The sound of the fan made that impossible anyway. Scratching his head, he stood in front of his closet where the new shirts were lined up all nice and fresh for starting school. What's the big deal about putting on a shirt, anyway? Sometimes she is hard to figure out.

Why wear a bunch of stupid cloth when you're working in your bedroom at the drawing table, and even with the window open and the fan on, it's still almost 90 degrees? Like always when it was very hot and humid, all he had on was his cutoffs. I even took off my skivvies—not that it helped much. At least there's a little air circulation down there... besides, Mark saw me like this in the cabin all the time—no big deal.

Julian was oblivious to social niceties like dressing properly for a dinner guest. Impressing people by what he put on never entered his head. It had never mattered, really, what they thought. There wasn't much he could do about how he looked: he was born this way, so why worry? Tuning out the hyperbolic adulation his mom and Geraldine dished out had become automatic; without thinking, that policy extended to what he wore—made things a lot easier. It didn't register in his mind that he might actually want to be worth looking at. He had begun to see others as attractive—Mark, especially. But he was slow to connect dots, generally; it hadn't dawned on him that to another boy—or to a grown man, even—looking attractive might be important. In his mind, clothing was worn to keep a person warm; on a super hot day, what's the point in wearing a lot of surplus cloth?

You know, maybe you should think about this some. Inside guy was on the job.

Think? what about? what shirt to put on?

Think about why, not what.

I don't get your meaning.

Why would it matter if you wore a shirt?

Beats me.

Figure it out: what would you think if Mark arrived barefoot wearing only cutoffs?

Wow. That would be *something.* He pictured that in his head briefly, drawing on his memory file of Mark in the cabin. That would be *hot!* Oh-oh… what about Little J? A minor tingle reminded him that a shirtless Mark always made Little J restless, or worse.

What else would you think?

Julian pondered… even though it was yummy, I'd think it was kinda weird, actually.

Exactly. So what do you think Mark thought when he saw you open the door?

Yow… I doubt if he thought I was yummy. Weird? I don't know. What's so weird about a kid opening the door in his cutoffs?

Nothing.

What's the big deal, then?

You want Mark to think you're just a kid?

Whoa… Julian could hear Geraldine clucking in the background. 'You're in high school now…' now I get it. "Sometimes I'm so stupid!"

No argument there.

So… what shirt then? He stepped forward to view the row of new shirts—they were arranged in order, starting tomorrow: blue, yellow, green, purple and coral. "I wore the green one to church this morning… Mom thought that one would look nice."

This isn't church.

Oh… yeah.

Which one do you like best?

Gosh… truth is, I don't care that much, one way or the other. I'm sorta new at wearing fancy shirts. The blue one stood out… maybe he'll like this—

Because he's wearing a blue shirt?

I didn't think about that. Maybe I should wear the coral one?

That's Geraldine's favorite.

Hmm. She's an expert. "Coral it is!" He pulled it out, hanger and all, and stretched it out on the bed. The matching socks were hung on the bottom wire. Do I hafta to put on the socks?

No reply from Inside guy. Hmm… she said put on a shirt. What would he think if I put on the whole outfit?

*Now **that** would be weird.*

At least we agree about something! He slipped on the shirt. "Ha!" he grinned: she didn't say I had to button it.

Remember, now: no staring.

I know, I know…

I mean it: you know what happens down there when—

I promise. With a giggle he skipped out of the room.

Francine was delighted; both Mark and Julian were busily consuming their third kebob, and both salads were almost gone. Seeing your work appreciated is always rewarding—but this evening she took special pleasure in watching the dynamic between Julian and Mark. Gracious—Julian ate just as much food! She had not realized until now how much his appetite had changed… last time Mark was here for supper, Julian ate much smaller portions and took *no* seconds.

We are so fortunate to have Mark… the *perfect* role model. How different from Julian's father. If he were single and about ten years older, he would be exactly what my mother had in mind… I wouldn't have put up a fight.

"I have more makings in the refrigerator, if you're still hungry."

"If only I had the room!" Mark was completely satisfied. "A perfect meal for such a hot day."

"Mm!" Julian agreed, his mouth too full to form words.

"Thank you; a few minutes under the broiler and it's done—the room temperature is hardly effected. I made the potato salad yesterday, so there was no need to slave over a hot stove."

"If you ever decide to give cooking lessons, I want to sign up." Mark wasn't kidding. He'd already decided to do these kebobs himself. They'd be faster to cook than a TV dinner, and a lot tastier.

"Me too," Julian chimed. Come to think about it, I should ask if I could help out in here. I need to know how to do these things anyway, eventually; cooking for Mark one day was part of his Big Plan.

"I considered writing a cookbook a few years ago, but…" she paused—Geraldine used to nag me about it. "The world doesn't need another cookbook."

"Maybe not, but *I'd* buy one." Mark drained his glass of iced tea. "Maybe I could talk you into jotting down how to do this one. I don't see how it could be better; if it's half as simple as it looks, we could do it on the next campout."

Francine was flattered. "Well, except for the potato salad it would be easy enough—I've always wanted to do something like this in the back yard," she shrugged. "A table out there on a day like this, with a breeze during the meal—that would make it *much* nicer."

Mark's eyes lit up; he looked at Julian. "I'll bet they make a kit for picnic tables and benches," he winked. "Be a good weekend project."

"Wow, yeah!" he looked his mom—the only concern was whether she could afford it. "Umm, how much would something like that cost?"

"I don't know for sure, but the biggest part of the cost for anything like that is labor. I'll bet Sears has something, or Wards… maybe Murphy's Lumber, even. There's probably a newspaper ad. They might even be on sale—it's the end of the season."

Darn! If only I was still working for Geraldine. Julian looked at his mom for a hint—she had to make every penny count. This month she already bought my shoes; and there were the school fees… he didn't know anything about managing money other than to make sure there was enough before setting out to spend it.

"It sounds like a fine idea… why don't you find out what it costs, Julian." Francine wanted to say yes, but she did have to look first before leaping. She looked at Mark. "We have watermelon for dessert—would you like that now, or after you do the Scrapbook?"

"Afterward." He patted his stomach. "By then there'll be room." He stood and gestured to Julian. "Time to do the dishes."

Julian jumped up and went into action. This was a favorite thing—instead of his mom, it was Mark at his side. Last year Mark had made a point of forcing mom to sit and watch while we did the dishes. Best of all, now I don't need the stool to put the dishes away!

Francine was grateful that Mark wanted to look at the Camp Walker drawings in sequence. She had seen most of them right after Julian came home—he leafed through his sketchbook the next day, excitedly telling about his camp adventures. But he went so fast—I'd barely started to look at one when he moved to the next.

That was special, just the two of us—it was like old times. We used to do a lot together—sharing the day's events after I came home from work… playing hide and seek, romping on mother's oval rug. She grinned… I still have to tell him to put on a shirt; he's mostly boy, in spite of his size. Unlike her friend Geraldine, she wasn't especially eager about what was coming in the next months. Before long she would have to teach him to drive the car—then he'll begin to develop a social life. Scouting will have to allow room for other things: in other words, girls. I'm not ready for that—why can't he just stay the way he is?

Reluctantly, she had to agree with Geraldine; it was time to pay attention to those things; but she also knew Julian—he was unlikely to abandon scouts overnight. He's devoted to scouting and to Mark—it's hard to imagine that a girl could ever eclipse them completely. That's not hard to understand—just watching Mark examine each drawing carefully and read every word was enough; she could see the respect and care he gave to his boys—and they thrive on that. Julian spent the entire day doing last minute touches on this when he could have been at the pool escaping the heat.

Removed from the sketchbook, these drawings are very different… being nestled in a narrative makes them more like illustrations. She had never gone to a summer camp herself, so this was very helpful. Along with the letter he sent from camp, this helped her feel a part of the experience—it filled a troublesome gap. It was the only time in their lives they had been separated. It was certainly worth the money—but seeing him off on the bus that day was one of the most difficult things she had ever had to face.

She read the hand printed caption under the drawing Mark was examining:

Johnny hails the rescue team as he climbs out of the well. "I found him! He's down here, you guys!" Johnny had found the lost dog, all by himself!

Johnny? I don't remember anyone in the troop named Johnny…

"I didn't know you did this one over again," Mark was very impressed. "This used to be a cartoon."

“Yeah… Justin liked it a lot, I thought it deserved a better job.” It was one of the first drawings I did at camp...I learned how to draw better. “I gave Justin the first one.” That was fun...he turned so *red*.

Mark bent down to look more closely—remarkable. Uncanny how Julian portrays the likeness of a person—some of their character shows too. He turned to Francine. “Do you know Justin?”

“I don’t think so… I may have met him once, you know, after a meeting.”

“This is a good snapshot. You couldn’t do better if you had a camera.” There was no doubt in his mind that he was, in fact, looking at Justin. “Julian used his face to illustrate a story written by another scout.”

Julian felt a special glow when Mark complimented him. It meant everything—Mark liked what he had done. It didn’t exactly hurt to be sitting right next to him, either. The reverberation of his voice always gave him a fuzzy glowy feeling, something like he felt when Mark pinched his shoulder in that special place. That and his aroma were combining to challenge Inside guy’s control over the situation: Little J was beginning to tingle.

Francine experienced a sudden onset of goose bumps—Julian’s instant blush just now made him look so *precious*… Mark’s praise hit her as well; it was always nice to have someone reinforce the high opinion she had of her boy. Mothers are rarely objective about that—certainly she never claimed to be.

Julian was a little worried— controlling Little J with Mark this close wasn’t easy. I got fairly good at it during camp, but now…

Better not let him do that, Inside guy warned.

I know… I’m out of practice. It’s been almost two months since I sat next to him like this. Julian could feel Little J awakening on the right side of his crotch. Not having any skivvies on was a mixed blessing—if Little J grows very much, he might peek out far enough to be noticed! These cutoffs are pretty short. The possibility was *scary*—that thought helped Julian arrest Little J's progress… puffy was as far as he was allowed to go.

Glancing back and forth at Francine and Julian just now, Mark was struck by how alike their faces were: the deep brown eyes, especially. The smile was the same, too… Julian didn't look at all like a girl, and Francine didn't look masculine in the least—yet they look so *alike*. Maybe that explained why he felt so welcome here. Last year when we sat at this table Julian was noticeably shorter—now their faces are at the same level. Another indicator of how he has grown. With that tan, he looks like he just came in from a day in the surf. The coral color of his new shirt certainly sets off his eyes—proof that stocking the new Daytona Beach collection was a good idea.

Mark wasn't an artist in any way shape or form—but he was skilled and informed when it came to selecting wardrobe items—that was an important aspect of his job at the store—he was the one who placed the orders. What Oglivy offered was largely his decision. His professional eye measured how well this shirt suited Julian—it was gratifying to see how right he had been to stock this item. Julian's appearance didn't need improving, of course—but a shirt's job is to enhance and support even the best looking; this combination is outstanding.

Mark's subconscious mind was also busily registering information. More than direct visual data was being collected about the person sitting so close at his left: the pheromones that had jolted him earlier were part of the mix. The coral shirt did not detract one bit from their potency, either. Fortunately, his ability to focus had joined forces with his remarkable will power: he was able to avoid thinking about what his peripheral vision and his nostrils were recording. This kept Roger in line for the time being… a slight puffy state was all he was able to attain.

Francine remembered the next drawing."You didn't finish telling me about archery. How did you do? Did you earn a merit badge?"

"Just barely. I could hardly pull the bowstring. I finally got a bull's-eye on the last day." He held out his right arm. "I didn't have this yet." The bicep he had developed working for Geraldine was clearly visible when flexed. "I should have waited until next summer." He pulled back the sleeve with his left hand and flexed again. "I did my share of lifting on the crew, Zack saw to that." He grinned at Mark.

Mark reached over and gave the bicep a manly squeeze. "You're right! It's the genuine item." He winked at Francine. "I remember what it was like to have spaghetti arm. That's a big problem when you're a boy."

"For sure!" Julian laughed.

Mark sat back "Let your mother feel that!"

Julian blushed and leaned across Mark's lap, grinning wide.

"My word!" Francine squeezed her boy's arm as instructed, with a nervous giggle. She didn't recall ever seeing him flex a muscle before; it shouldn't surprise, yet it seemed out of character somehow. Julian never boasted or bragged… but this wasn't that, exactly. *He's embracing his manhood—as he should. I have to get used to that.*

Mark raised his left arm and flexed. "So let's compare."

Julian held his arm next to Mark's, and they flexed together.

"Man!" Julian exclaimed. He squeezed Mark's arm, then his own.

"Don't sweat it," Mark laughed. "I have a few more years into mine—you'll catch up soon enough."

For the better part of an hour, Mark continued his meticulous examination of Julian's work—it was leaps ahead of last year's pages in both quality and output. The quality reminded him of the full size drawings Julian had made at camp—the one of Sarge, the Camp Quartermaster was a revelation; perched on the stool in front of the work table, the old ogre was transformed. He was like a mellow grandfather… Julian had seen the real man and preserved him on paper.

The drawing of the medic tending to Geoff's wounded foot is framed and mounted on the Camp Director's office wall. It looks like a Norman Rockwell Saturday Evening Post cover—without the comic exaggeration. I can't forget the ones he drew of me—wow. One day I'd like to see those again. Those cinched it for me—they're why I gave Sarge my word that Julian would get art lessons. I meant it too—if the high school doesn't have a good art teacher, I'll find one. Like Sarge, I know what it means to see myself portrayed by Julian's keen and perceptive eye. Hmm… I wonder how I can see those again… I'm certain Francine doesn't know about them. Julian promised to keep them confidential—and safe.

Last summer, seeing those drawings was a profound experience—they connected me with Erik like nothing else ever had. The impact was powerful—it frightened me a little—I needed them to be put away. I have to be ready before I look at them again. He had no idea what that required; but the next viewing needed to be private—Julian should not be there. One day I'll ask to borrow the tube he keeps them in.

It did not occur to Mark that those drawings might assist in the growing struggle he was having with his inner demon. Had he known, he might have arranged to borrow them sooner. Meanwhile, they remained safely hidden in Julian's closet—but they were not stored in that tube.

Only a few pages remained—Francine was amazed at what her boy had produced. What an achievement! The range of activities depicted was far more comprehensive than she had imagined—the brochure Mark had shown her last spring showed some of this, but it didn't begin to convey what it would be like—certainly not the way the scrapbook has. To think that all this was packed into *two weeks*—I would have guessed it was twice that. Scout camp is not just swimming in the lake every day, is it?

Julian's rapid artistic growth was not a surprise—she knew what his father could do. It pleased her greatly that Julian had trained himself without Adrian's help. It verified his innate ability—his skill is all his own. There's no denying that his talent was inherited, but his father's presence wasn't required. As far as Francine was concerned, it would have been disastrous to have him in the picture. And now, just when he needs a father figure, he has Mark. What good fortune. He's a far better man for that job. She didn't share Geraldine's belief that things happened because they were meant to, but it certainly seemed to apply in this case.

From the living room, a faint, familiar sound:

> *ding- ding ding ding... ding ding ding ding...* <

Grandpa's mantle clock had begun its eight o'clock toll. The familiar Westminster melody was a comfort as well as a reminder that they had been at the table a long time; before too long, it would be bedtime—tomorrow is the first day of school.

"Goodness!" Francine was amazed at how much time had gone by.

"Time flies by when you're having fun," Mark smiled, ready to turn the page.

Julian ignored the clock; he wasn't usually given to biting his nails, but Mark was about to look at the last drawing.

"Another new one!" Mark bent close. After squinting briefly, he grinned. "Has Jeremy seen this yet?"

Julian about wet his pants. "How could you tell it's Jeremy?!"

The puzzled look on Julian's face was wonderful. Mark looked at the drawing again. "I don't know—you tell me, you drew it."

Julian was speechless. He looked at it again, up close.

Francine bent forward to look... she knew Jeremy well. Hmm...

"It *is* Jeremy, right? and that's Justin." Mark enjoyed this. He remembered seeing them use the pocket flashlight on the bus. The image on the paper evoked that memory perfectly—they didn't need to be depicted with accuracy.

"Gosh." Julian was going to apologize for how crudely he had done this one, but now...

It still isn't a very good drawing... Inside guy was on guard; no point in allowing you to get a swelled head.

Yeah, but how can he tell it's them? I can't tell, myself!

"Watermelon time," Francine pushed away from the table. "You have room now, I presume?"

"Do I ever!" Mark closed the scrapbook with a big grin.

"It's been chilling for hours in the back yard." She stood and went for the dessert plates. "Be sure to turn the hose off, Julian."

Julian leapt out of his chair and trotted toward the back door—he'd forgotten to check on the watermelon. What if the hose slipped off somehow?

Mark watched Julian disappear through the back porch door with a touch of nostalgic envy—it was fun to be a boy. Odd how obvious that is now... yet at the time it didn't mean much to me either. Eagerness reigns at that age; there's no need to hurry, but you do—that's part of being a boy: hurrying, never stopping to enjoy. This had been so wonderful, going over the scrapbook with Julian—that was such a reward at camp. I have missed that as much as anything. He looked at Francine. The evening had been such a pleasure, he didn't want it to end. "He's come a long way."

Francine set the plates on the table and returned her chair to its regular place. "Yes, he has. To be honest with you, I wish it wasn't going so fast."

"I know what you mean," he nodded. "Unfortunately, we don't get to make the rules."

After a long pause, Francine spoke. "There's no way I can thank you for all you've done for Julian. I..."

"No need. No need at all. It has been a privilege. I mean that sincerely. I'm fond of all my scouts, but Julian is special—I can't deny it."

> ***Bam!*** <

Julian’s elbow clipped the open door as he came in, forcing it to slam shut. It’s hard to be graceful when you’re carrying a huge dripping wet watermelon.

“Can I cut it open?” he asked eagerly. I’ve never done that. With care he put it on the empty plate his mother had put in place… there. “It’s nice and cold!” he grinned. He didn’t mention that he had almost dropped it on the way. Wow… that would have wrecked everything.

The spectacle of Julian bearing the huge melon was both comical and exotic. The unbuttoned coral shirt flapped happily, framing the tensed muscles of his torso. The expression on his face was a delight to his mother, who saw her boy working to prove himself.

It wasn’t just the midsection that struck Mark’s eye—the cutoffs, and what they were covering, were impossible to ignore. He got a good look before he forced himself to avert his eyes.

6 Lunch on blue shirt day

The bell rang; 4th period was over at last. Julian was *famished.* He stood up and stretched. From what Mr. Frankel had just said, Biology was likely to be his least favorite class. The prospect of peeking at the insides of a frog—or inside anything, for that matter, did not appeal. Especially just before lunch. This class meant business, though: instead of desks, they sat at these long black tables. These spell trouble for the frogs, for sure. A faint chemical smell in the room hinted that mysterious things happened here.

Tomorrow we get assigned a lab partner; I wonder who I'll get. I recognize a few of these kids, but I don't know any of them. I'll cross my fingers and hope for the best. He gathered up his stuff—man alive, *look* at these *books!* Every class so far except P.E. had supplied a big thick textbook. It's all I can do to get this pile under my arm. *Ugh…* are these *heavy.* For having stuff to tote around, this is a *lot* worse than junior high. If I didn't have a locker down the hall, I'd have to borrow mom's suitcase.

The first day of school had always been a favorite, and it still was—but high school was very different: for one thing, he didn't have Sid or Jeremy in any of his classes—or anyone else he knew. Having a buddy along had always been a part of things. I hope it's not this way the whole day. The problem was that registration… if I'd been in the same line as Sid, we could have made sure we had at least *one* class together. Except for Art, we're taking the same things. At least Jason and Tom are in my P.E. class—but there's no homework to do there. One thing I liked about P.E.—everyone is mixed in together like in scouts; it's not just one grade.

Wow: the hallway is packed! I'm not the only one in a hurry to feed myself. Trouble is, the locker is at the other end of the hall; at least it's up here—all the sophomore lockers are on the third floor. They were assigned during first period class. The only thing inside mine is a sack lunch—which I am eager to eat. Amazing how hungry you can get sitting behind desks all morning.

This is ridiculous… tomorrow I'm gonna wait a few minutes. It's so crowded! all I can do is scoot in little duck steps. I don't see anybody I know, either. Oh well… I'll just scoot, then. He looked up at the ceiling—might as well, since I'm not getting anywhere. The super high ceilings made the hallway seem open; large globes hung down on metal rods like space ships lining up to be assigned a mission somewhere. Changing the light bulb in those must be a pain.

At last! here it is… locker number 1145. Let's see... the combination, oh, yeah, now I remember. Right three turns: > *whsss... klik.* < Left, two turns: > *sss... klik.* < Right, one turn: > *sss... klik.* < This works better than the one I had at Wallace—that took both hands and a swift kick.

> ***klank!*** < Mission accomplished: there it is on the shelf, right where I put it this morning. Don't need these until tomorrow… the textbooks went onto the locker floor. The three-ring notebook is different—I hafta take that along… it has everything I need this afternoon… most important, my sketchbook is inside. He tucked it under his left arm—this way I won't hafta come back for it. He grabbed the lunch.

He closed the door firmly and spun the combination wheel a few turns. Miss St. John told the class about doing that… she said sometimes people had things stolen just because they hadn't made sure it was locked. Spinning the knob after it was shut was supposed to do that. Mr. Snead said the same thing about the P.E. lockers. The idea that someone would go around stealing from lockers was awful; nobody ever did that at Wallace. Geraldine giving her "you're in high school now" speech came to mind.

I'm tempted to sit down right here, I'm so hungry… I don't have a plan. Sid and Jeremy had first lunch; they're on the way to their fourth period class. The cafeteria is too small to take everyone at the same time, so they split the building into halves. If your 4th period class is in the north part of school where the math and science classes are, you have to take second lunch.

It isn't as crowded now. Maybe I can find *someone* I know in the cafeteria. Practically everyone I've seen is a stranger. They're expecting a record number of kids this year—over 1500, they said. He glanced here and there … so far nobody familiar.

I just thought of something—like me, most kids have new clothes. Maybe everyone puts on new stuff. That figures, come to think about it. Maybe kids I know are there, but I don't recognize them. A variety of vivid colors moved in front of him—no one will ever recognize me in this fancy blue shirt. I like it, but when I looked in the mirror this morning I felt weird—sort of like I was in disguise. Mom said I'd get used to it. So far, I haven't seen anyone else wearing one this color. Like me, most of the boys have brand new jeans; never washed denim looks dark and feels so stiff—I forgot about that.

Before all I wore was a T-shirt. Now I have to wear a fancy shirt *over* the T-shirt, even if it isn't cold. What Geraldine said is true: nobody is wearing just a T-shirt. Hmm… small comfort; it annoyed him to be a conformist unless there was a good reason. "You're in high school now" isn't good enough… that's just like the old "because I said so" reason. Being reminded that he was still a little kid, not old enough to understand things was a major pain. Oh, well; no point in arguing.

He was enthusiastic about everything so far—except for the frogs. This place is about three times as big as Wallace. At least I haven't gotten lost—that orientation tour on registration day helped a lot.

There's the north stairway—excellent. It's down to the cafeteria at last. This part is nifty—I hafta draw this up, for sure. Two eight foot wide staircases flanked a gigantic atrium. It's impressive. If you use the inside railing, you can see the whole area while you go down. The atrium is two floors high—it stands right on top of the cafeteria; those skylights must be over 30 feet up! Everything here is tall; the classroom ceilings are ten feet.

Halfway down he stopped to look … the space below is used for different things; lots of trophy cases and exhibits; I have to check those out—hey, benches! *There's* an idea… some kids are eating their lunch down there! I don't have to go to the cafeteria after all. There's an open one. Great! From that corner I can make a drawing of the stairway. I have to snag that before someone else gets it… he picked up his speed. The smells coming from the cafeteria were *yummy*—another reason to get a move on: his tummy was complaining again.

—∞—

Randall Hallstrom was just as glad to be in this school as not, even if it was thousands of miles from everything he had known all his life. Having to move here was a blessing in disguise. It saved him from having to deal with Nels and his band of toughs every day. At Pullman High where he would have had gone, surviving them would have been a full time job.

This school is huge—twice as big as PHS—which is scary in a way; on the other hand, it's a lot easier to disappear when there's a crowd. One positive factor: I'm starting on an even playing ground; every kid in my classes is just as new at this school as I am. So far, he had no strong feelings about the place; the occasional southern accent was interesting. Odd how that works—not everyone has an accent. Everyone seems friendly. I haven't seen any obvious Nels types… but I'm not stupid enough to think they won't show up eventually. The first day is supposed to make everyone look good. So far, that's worked out.

I like the classes so far, and the teachers—I hope Woodshop is interesting. It's a consolation choice—they don't have a Photography class. I was sort of hoping they would, being a school this large. I need a class in the basics of color photography. I always have to send that out for processing—very annoying. Randall's hobby was his favorite thing: secretly, he hoped to make photography his profession.

The cafeteria is well run; less than five minutes in line. A spot over to the side near the stairway looked good… two guys were at one end, friends obviously. Randall sat at the other end. Surveying the area and its occupants as he ate made good sense. Curious by nature, familiarizing himself with the environment was a basic. The entire student body could never fit down here, but there's plenty of room for half.

He focused on the lunch—not what I would have expected back home. I might not be able to eat it all: an unfamiliar vegetable—deep fried… it's a slice of something with large gummy seeds inside. Corn bread, a butter patty, and a casserole with noodles and chunks of chicken. Tastes as good as it smells, too. A carton of milk and two Oreos.

The kids here are a happy lot, joking and having a good time with friends. That's encouraging, actually. Of course, these are early days. Everyone is busy impressing or being impressed. Randall was inclined to be cynical at times, having been an unsuspecting victim more than once. Not all these cheerful bubbly people are as nice as they look on the outside.

He was not a good looking person himself, and that was just fine; the best thing about that was obvious: no one ever gave him a second glance. If they did, it could mean trouble. That's why he always wore something generic and boring—dull tan, dull green, dull blue, dull grey—suntan pants usually. They help you fade into the background.

He wasn't anti social, but experience had made him cautious. One or two friends would be nice. Eventually I'll find a kindred spirit. Even though Randall didn't wear glasses, he was always tagged as a bookworm or a nerd, and that was okay—it was a safe place to be, all things being equal.

It was wise not to be the center of attention for several reasons. Not only was it uncomfortable, it was dangerous: he was not like most. He did not have the usual goals and tastes. His likes were, to be honest, abnormal. He liked books, he liked the outdoors, and he liked boys.

That had to be kept secret or another Nels and crew would be on his case. So, as he scanned the area, it was important to offset his tendency to spend a tad more time on boys when his eye landed on them. He wasn't looking for anyone or any type in particular—that's just where his eyes always landed, unconsciously. That had been true for a long time now. At times it seemed like a handicap—especially when some of the loudmouth macho types like Nels were about. If his opinion were to be sought—which, thank the stars, it never was—he wouldn't have been able to offer one. He did not look at or care one whit about what obsessed them… always raving and blathering about tits and snatches. Disgusting. Evidently it was all their tiny minds had room for. None of that girl stuff interested Randall.

He was still a virgin, if that was the right word to use. In the third grade one time, he had an experience—fondly remembered—with Davey Reynolds… if only that could have happened again. But ever since, all he had was his imagination. If only Nels and his bunch were right! Somehow, they had pegged him as a queer, and they made as if he was out there having all kinds of fun sucking on guys. If only. How they figured out that's what I wanted is a mystery.

A sip of milk and two Oreos remained. I'll save these for seventh period: into the shirt pocket you go. The sound of the last sip of milk entering the straw notified anyone near that his lunch was finished. Now what? I have a huge amount of time on my hands. Lunch is a full period long. Just gawking at people isn't very smart. According to the student guide, the halls are open, as well as the immediate campus… so let's explore. That's a good way to spend the rest of the period. He checked his watch: 12:15. Almost half an hour left. First, get rid of this tray and dirty dishes; the line isn't far away.

The student guide has a set of floor plans in the back; he pulled it out of his rear pocket. Might as well explore the ground floor; most of my afternoon classes are down here. With his trusty clarinet case in hand, he set out to find the band room. If nothing else, it helped him look legit.

—∞—

Julian had just made an executive decision: from now on, his lunch sack would need two sandwiches. Even with carrot sticks and an apple, his tummy was not even close to being full. He had been wrong there; he told his mom this morning that one was enough, since he wasn't going to be working with the crew all day. Maybe I'm used to big lunches now. Maybe those extra sandwiches were why I grew so much this summer. Hmm…if you look at it that way, another sandwich is a good idea: I still need to grow another six inches. Reaching six feet was a goal I set the first time I saw Mark. That was a long time ago—three years! Lots of guys around here are that tall or taller; maybe I should go for six foot one.

The aroma from the cafeteria was tempting, but he wasn't that desperate. Besides, I don't want to lose this spot. He wadded up the lunch sack; what are you supposed to do with trash around here? There—across from the stairwell. I can toss this on my way to 5th period class. He parked it on the bench.

So… > *Klack!* < He opened his 3 ring binder.

Time to remove the sketchbook—this ring thing made it easy to keep everything handy. From the zipper pouch came a brand new No. 2 pencil. Now then… he turned his attention to the north staircase. This view is almost perfect. Let's see… squinting may look odd, but it helps you locate the most important elements when you're forming a composition. Vertical… this one has to be vertical; he put a dot where he wanted the forward corner of the lowest step—that will determine where everything else goes.

Ooo! most everything is a straight line… the ruler!… might as well use it for this one. He removed it happily; the ruler had holes in just the right place. I never thought about why those were there until I got this binder. These binders are *terrific*. I'm gonna get one to use at scouts.

Now then… his eyes looked upward… I want that skylight in… another dot set its location. A clear idea of composition formed in his mind… a new drawing at last! I've been waiting all *day* for this.

—~—

Randall stopped to look at the pictures on the wall. Next to the door labeled Student Government, the student body officer pictures were enclosed in a large frame; the 8 x 10 portraits made them look like movie stars; pretty fancy. Too bad they used glossy paper—portraits should always be on matte paper. The main office was directly across the hall.

This building continued to impress. It's in excellent shape for being this old. That's the way they built these in 1926. I noticed the date on the cornerstone when mom and I registered last week. This second tour is a good idea—the orientation tour was hurried; to be honest, I didn't pay attention very well. The orbs hanging from the hallway ceiling are elegant. One would have expected long fluorescent tubes. Must be too expensive to convert… reminds me of Dad's building on the campus. Same architect probably.

Well here we are, back at the cafeteria entrance. The ground level was interesting and easy to cover—the gymnasiums, P.E., auditorium, band and music occupy the major part… offices, a few classrooms, and the senior class lockers—nothing unexpected or out of the ordinary. Still, it pays to know where things are. Shop class is in the out building. He checked his watch: ten minutes until the first bell; plenty of time left. Let's go up to the atrium. I can wander around there before going out to the Woodshop.

During the orientation tour he had taken a cursory glance at these trophy islands; might as well see what they have on exhibit. Ah: the first one is a collection of drama and stagecraft awards. Interesting, but not my thing, especially. Maybe the technical side would be worth checking into… say, maybe they could use a photographer. He stepped around the corner of the exhibit case… !!!!!

It's *him!*

The bright sky blue shirt and wavy blond hair he beheld twenty feet away were unmistakable.

Randall was locked in place. I saw this kid in history class, second period! For the first time I was sorry I'd sat in the back; this guy was in the front row. I couldn't take my eyes off him. When he walked by on the way out I almost fainted.

What should I do?!

Compelled to stare, he was afraid—it must be wrong to do that. But I *have* to. It's both scary and thrilling. His stomach was behaving oddly and his groin was doing something he didn't recognize—it was something very nice, though. He wanted to hide and peek out from some secret spy hole and snap on the telephoto lens… nothing like that around here. Besides, I don't have my camera anyway. I don't dare get caught staring… he glanced both ways… no one is paying attention to me yet. I'll look at him a minute… I *have* to look at him. What is he doing… he's *drawing!*

Randall watched, fascinated and awestruck. The last guy I expected to see, sitting right there, all alone. He swallowed and took a deep breath, still unable to move. It's a good thing he's a fair distance away, doesn't know I'm looking at him. I wish I wasn't such a coward. How can I get a closer look at his face. He's so *tan!* Randall backed part way behind the exhibit case—I can duck out of sight quick if he looks this way.

—ꟺ—

Julian had the major stairwell elements roughed in. Time to place some other things—trophy cases and benches. These will help a lot, they're interesting. Rapidly he placed a few locator dots… now then… people. Might as well put in a few of those. This drawing rates a serious effort. It felt *terrific* to be doing this.

During camp he had figured out that he would do two types of drawings. The usual kind for the Troop Nine Scrapbook was simple for the most part—cartoony or simple sketches to show what was going on in a patrol or a badge study, or something. But others were worth spending time on. Those needed more detail, more *spirit*. He experimented with conveying what he felt as a person when he looked at a scene. It helped him select what to emphasize or skip over. That made a huge difference when I started to do portraits. I could tell I was on the right track, too—it was like I was in the picture touching things—I could almost feel them appear on the paper.

That's why the two he did of Mark were so powerful. I didn't appreciate how powerful until the night Mark saw them. His reaction was so thrilling and so scary. I had to promise to keep them hidden in my closet. That was a bonus—from the first I planned to give them to him. Now I have to keep them safe for him instead—which means I get to look at them when I want to—when it's safe, that is. Julian's secret wish was to do another one someday… but next time, Mark will be like those museum statues: no clothes.

Julian did not know how or why he had this talent. It was odd; as long as he could remember, he liked to draw. I asked Mom about it once but she didn't know. I could tell it made her happy, because she always told me how good it was and gave me paper and crayons and stuff. Then she got me a real drawing table—I was in the seventh grade. Until last year, I used it for building models, mostly—now I'm going to use it for drawing more of those big pictures. It's perfect for that. Somehow I hafta get more of those large sheets… I wonder what they cost.

Before now he had no goal like most kids—some wanted to be a fireman, or a policeman, or whatever their father was. But Julian didn't have a father to imitate, so he never formed a goal about what he wanted to do when he grew up. When the time comes I'll figure it out; besides, Mom is always there—she always knows what to advise. She's not like some moms, who decide everything for you, whether you want them to or not. Between Cubs and Boy Scouts, all kinds of possibilities had come along—of course, the main goal is Mark. Whatever I end up doing, it has to be something he'll approve. After what I learned last summer, it's obvious that it will be something to do with art—everyone said that, even the camp director and good old Uncle Max—and Mark said so too. So it's decided.

He paused a minute to look at his sketch: should I plan to do a big one? Hmm. Too early to decide. Besides, my first art class is coming up right after typing. A real art teacher! Exactly what I need.

> ***Baaaaaaaaaz!*** < The piercing buzz of the passing bell overrode the background noise of the atrium and the cafeteria below.

Lunch is over, Julian: you can plug in the people tomorrow. He held the tablet out for a final check… needs lots of work, but not too bad for something this complicated. I have all week. He put the ruler and sketchbook back into the binder and snapped it shut. The pencil went into his shirt pocket—that way I won't forget to sharpen it the first chance I get. Dull pencils are useless. Typing class, here I come. Nick will be glad I'm taking that. He grabbed the wadded up lunch sack and set off with a satisfied grin. It felt so good to have done something today besides sit and listen.

On the way to the stairs he passed this guy who was looking at him; he smiled back… looks kind of familiar. Is he from Wallace? Hmm… I can't place him.

—~—

Randall's day had just been made as special as any in his memory: he *smiled* at me! Heartbeat going off the chart, his mouth was dry, and his knees weren't feeling at all reliable. He leaned against the case to steady himself. Wow. I've never felt a reaction like this before. A double take now and then, no denying that… this is something else entirely. I have to get a handle on this. He felt elated and frightened at the same time.

He shook his head in an attempt to regain control. I'm so lucky I didn't duck out of sight—I couldn't move… I was frozen by fear and fascination at the same time. Is that what a deer feels like when he watches the approaching car that is about to end everything? I lost track of time… he checked his watch. It seems like ten minutes has gone by but it's only been a few seconds. Odd… He looked up the stairway… there—about halfway up the first section. Randall swung around and hurried to the stairs—I have to see where he's going. The fact that he had class in the opposite direction didn't matter—being late on the first day wasn't a good way to start, but it was worth the cost.

Skipping every other step, he reviewed those unbelievable seconds by the exhibit case. I got a very good look… he must have spent the summer on a beach somewhere. His *eyes*! I didn't see them in history class this morning. They're *brown!* Tomorrow, I'll sit a lot closer to the front of the room—or to wherever he sits.

Randall was intelligent enough to realize he was in a precarious state of mind, unsure if he could stay in control of himself. A sense of dread grew… he was being drawn by a force that couldn't be resisted—like a moth circling the 250 watt bulb in the living room torchiere. His is a dance to the death; Randall didn't sense that kind of danger, but he felt that kind of pull. It was an exhilarating state of being; he had not been here before.

7 Birch Street: Monday, 9 p.m.
one week later

at 1082 NE Birch Street, Mark and Pat

The deep bass undertone was a vibration as much as a sound; coming from the west side of the house, it told him that Pat was home. Sound waves from the engine penetrated and passed through everything between itself and his Strato-Lounger. Mark had not taken any college courses in physics, so he didn't know how to explain the phenomenon; as far as he knew, sound radiated in every direction—no idea how far. Presumably it's Pat… he glanced at the clock… who else would be pulling into the driveway at this hour? Ah… she turned off the engine at last. Good… the vibrations felt altogether too pleasant down below. Awakening Roger was certainly not needed. But it was good to know it was a car motor that was running out there.

She's early tonight. Good. That means we can talk about the transportation situation. Double good; it will help keep me awake until bedtime. Indulging in a second glass of wine had not helped sort out his nagging unsolved problem. But that doesn't mean I'll stay awake worrying: wine is wine, and a second glass always makes me drowsy. Going to sleep early means waking up early. The day always starts wrong when that happens.

—∾—

Pat let herself in the front door this time. Rather than go in through the kitchen, she had taken the time to walk back down the driveway to wave a friendly salutation. She would have gone over for a brief chat, but Francine was about to drive away with Geraldine. They're likely off to meet a client—the real estate business often made inconvenient demands. As a professional woman, I understand completely; being sociable with the neighbors regularly is almost impossible. Pat didn't have anything in particular to say, but she was socially "aware" enough to know that in a suburban neighborhood it behooved one to be friendly, at least.

Her mother had made the need for that clear a hundred times if she had done so once. "That Smith woman," she would cluck. "Who knows *what* she's up to…"

It was safe to assume her mother's busybody mentality was still the norm. To many of the housewives around here I'm thought of much the same way Natalie Smith was by mother years ago. But to be fair, when I was a child most women were at home all day; minding other people's business was part of the program. That and keeping up with the soap operas; professional women were suspect, generally… still are.

As she put her handbag and keys on the credenza she realized that it was quiet—no TV on? Strange. She stepped down the hall and peeked into the den. One glance told all—it was one of those nights: the photo album was at Mark's side, not in the bookcase. He was in his recliner staring at a silent picture on the television set… behind the scrolling screen credits a determined tall man marched up a dusty street pumping his rifle—mowing down unseen villains.

She moved forward and put her right hand on his shoulder. "One of those days?"

"Yes and no." The question didn't offend; he didn't have any secrets from Pat—the photo album usually meant that he was reliving the past.

She massaged his shoulders gently. He's wearing his lightweight lounge pants and a T-shirt—nothing seems amiss.

"Mmm… thanks." He rotated his head.

She waited for him to explain.

"I'm glad you're here," he leaned forward, indicating that a massage was not required just now. He stood and grabbed the empty glass: time for some iced tea. "I need to talk about getting another car."

"Ah, I wondered when that would come along." She followed him into the kitchen, but she wasn't satisfied; the photo album had not been out for some time… there must be a reason.

—~—

at 1012 NE Birch Street: Francine and Geraldine

Francine returned the friendly wave that came from three houses down the street.

"What do you think of her?" Geraldine hadn't seen or heard about Pat Schaefer for over a year.

"Hard to say. I almost never see her." Mark's wife seemed gone more than anything. "She's always friendly."

Geraldine wasn't inclined to gossip. Still, it was odd: Mark was highly visible about town, but rarely seen with his wife. Sometimes that foretold unhappy days. The plus side of that was easy to see: it could mean that their house would be back on the market. If so, Francine could have the listing.

"She's studying to become a licensed M.D. On top of her job at the hospital, that must make for an awful schedule." She's still young enough… Mark's age, or thereabouts. Certainly not thirty.

"I see." Geraldine understood. When they bought the house I sensed that Pat wasn't the family type… too bright and efficient. She related to that, of course. Raising children had never appealed to her, either. Playing aunt to Julian took care of her motherly needs—*and* sisterly needs— conveniently and sufficiently.

"Amanda's?" Geraldine tended to frame her intent as a question—it gave the illusion of being flexible.

"Perfect." Any other suggestion would have been out of character—and they needed the relative privacy of an Amanda's booth. Geraldine's "girl talks" often got down to cases; being overheard was not a good idea, generally. Francine was grateful to Geraldine for lots of reasons; she always set aside a time and place for personal matters—it was never a subject at work. Likewise, shoptalk wouldn't be a problem tonight.

When Geraldine called, she didn't announce her agenda; it would be about either Edwin or Julian—unless something else was brewing… one never knew. In any case, she insisted on going out. Presumably, she didn't want Julian to overhear anything. He doesn't need a baby sitter, so a girl's night out isn't a problem. Supper tonight was wonderful as usual: his enthusiasm and reports about his day were the highlight of her own day. Staying connected to him was always her top priority. As long as Geraldine didn't interfere with that, she could ask almost anything. She's a wonderful friend, idiosyncrasies and all.

Francine turned to wave again at Pat, but she had disappeared into the house. One day I'd like to have her over. She is a bit of a mystery.

—∞—

"It isn't a matter of economics—we can afford another car easily—it's a matter of principle." Mark didn't believe in the so-called two-car ideal of the American middle class family. He was not trying to "keep up" with anyone. But then, that was one of his and Pat's secrets—it might be time to re-think that… appearances do matter. The truth of the matter was simple: the philosophical satisfaction of making do with one car no longer served his needs.

Pat listened patiently to Mark's concerns about buying a second car. He didn't need to go to all this trouble, but she listened and pretended to be fully engaged; that's what he needed her to do.

She and Mark went way back—they had been friends in high school. She used to have a crush on him. They dated once, and it had fed a wonderful fantasy: one day they would come back from their separate colleges and get in touch like always—they had been good study buddies; intellectually, they had always clicked. Alas, for one reason or another, it didn't happen; she dated others but none of them compared to Mark. Some time in the future, maybe a way would be found. Meanwhile, their friendship was powerfully important. So when Mark called that awful night, she jumped to his side at once. She had not known about Erik. But as Mark went on she grew to understand—and rather than take offense and feel hurt, she felt his pain as a friend; it meant the world that it was she he had come to for help.

It forced her to take stock—in spite of her mother's constant nagging about still being single, her own goals had been unaddressed—she still held a residual hope about Mark. Her mother tried everything; she didn't want her daughter to become an *old maid*—translation: a lesbian. Mark's family had been nagging behind the scenes in a similar way—of course they didn't know about Erik, but they had met him.

After a few weeks Pat came up with a plan—a plan that seemed nonsensical at first glance: get married. She didn't do so with any illusions or expectations. It wasn't subterfuge; it was enough to be his friend; he was like a little brother that needed her protection. In some ways that was a good description of their emotional relationship.

Her focus had then turned to professional goals; personal issues like love, children, and all that could wait. Those might come along, but she was in no hurry—her job was clear. Be a good "sister" and become a physician.

Ironic to be sure, yet it proved to be the perfect solution: they had made two sets of parents enormously happy. Other than occasional grumbles now and then about not being grandparents, they remained happy and supportive. Mark was free to escape into scouting and bury himself in office work at Oglivy's, and she was free to pursue her professional goals. Their activities complemented each other; a few appearances in public and they were set: free to be themselves, double income to boot.

That's why the matter of purchasing a second car was so simple. Mark could have just gone ahead and done it unilaterally—but that's not the way he does anything. It was his nature to think of others first; the financial impact didn't concern him—rather, the effect it would have on her routine, her convenience. Aside from the absence of a sexual element, Mark was the ideal conjugal partner. When he had finished his unnecessarily complex proposal, she joined the discussion.

"Thanks, Mark. I'll be honest—my conscience has bothered me for months." Her schedule was about to make matters worse. "In January I'll be gone overnight a lot because of the intern requirements… so the time for a second car has come."

"You sure you're happy with what you're driving?" He was prepared to go all the way and use their car as a trade-in for two new ones.

"Oh yes… I know it and like it, and there's nothing wrong with it. You should get what you need." Pat chose not to make any suggestions; cars were one thing she knew nothing about. Something small would be nice… commuting to Oglivy's doesn't require much. Maybe he'll get something sporty—one of those MGs would be perfect. A colleague at the hospital had given her a ride in one. A sports car might be a good way to have an outlet other than scouts.

They worked out a plan for parking. Generally, Mark was the first to leave in the morning, which meant he would need to park his on the outside. When she got home every night, they would have to shuffle, unless he was off at a scout meeting when she got home.

"That was easy," she said cheerfully and stepped over to the refrigerator. Mark had not moved, which suggested that he wasn't in a hurry to get back to the television set. They had discovered instant iced tea recently—the perfect evening companion. She added a few ice cubes and returned to the table.

"You said yes and no." She refilled his glass. Time to talk. Sometimes he needed a gentle nudge.

Mark frowned, searching for a way to explain; he did not understand what was going on. “It’s not the same, now…” he looked up, frustrated. The blank look on Pat’s face showed that she needed to know more—he assumed that she had noticed the photo album. “The pictures, I mean. Looking at the pictures… it’s different.” He paused… “Really different.” He rotated the glass slowly between his hands; a small condensation ring had appeared on the Formica tabletop, providing a focus point.

Not only was Pat his best friend, but she had some psychotherapy courses in her kit bag now; she had a much better knowledge of how to listen.

Always before, the photo album had helped him relive the wonderful times with Erik. A good cry usually followed—painful, but cleansing somehow, too; he always felt better afterward. All told, it helped. Tonight there were no tears, no feeling better afterward. “They don’t give me the old ‘fix,’ know what I mean?”

She tilted her head to indicate she needed more.

Mark puzzled about this a second time. I tried to figure this out a few minutes ago. “It’s as if they were in my *parent’s* album or something—they’re the same photos, but… they seem old… as if they were tinted in that sepia brown. Only they aren’t…” he shook his head, confused.

Pat understood at once. “Sounds to me like you have moved on.” This is *major*.

“Yeah.” Mark shrugged. “Maybe. A lot of *good* it does me.”

“So there isn’t a new face appearing in the crowd?”

“Ha! Where am I likely to find *that?!”*

“Mark, this is nineteen *sixty two.* There are lots of opportunities now.” Nowadays, any medium sized town has a way to find ‘company.’

“Right.” He nodded sarcastically.

"I'm *serious.* There *are.*" She had talked to a few colleagues about this very thing. Unknown to him, she paid attention to that. In theory, their relationship was sort of "live and let live," no strings. That was the theory; in practice, the caring sister was always on silent duty.

"I might have some ideas. Tell me some more—are there other signs? I want to know if you're ready—really ready." The worst thing would be for him to go on a date and be wiped out by his aging and obsolete conscience. His fidelity tended to be absolute; it had crippled him for six years now.

Mark pointed downward: "For months I've had trouble with you-know-who, you-know-where." Again, he was reluctant to mention what had happened last summer. Too much about that midnight episode continued to intrigue and taunt him. Escaping the snare so cleverly set by the California Kid was laudable—but he had also denied himself something he wanted: admitting it was something he needed wasn't a consideration yet. That was a ways off, still trapped in his subconscious.

Pat laughed; Mark was such a prude at times. "I am almost a doctor, you know; you don't have to be so *polite.*" She pointed to the hospital ID badge on her lapel.

"Yeah, I know… tell me, then, doctor: why am I subject to arousal so often? It's almost like I was fifteen again." Roger used to behave; more and more he's a constant threat.

Pat smiled. "Is it caused by anyone I know?"

"No! It's not any one person—any *person* at all." This wasn't exactly true, though he didn't harbor an attraction for Geoff. No one else knew about the "midnight ride," and he planned to keep it that way. In fact, that's when this seems to have started.

"Just an increased libido, demanding attention?" There were clinical signs here…

"I don't know… I suppose that's it. In high school—say from age 15 to 19, Roger was always a problem."

Pat laughed. "I'd forgotten you had a name for him." That had always tickled her.

"So how do I *control* him?!" Word was, monks took something to fix that. Some kid said that at camp years ago…

"My knowledge is theoretical, of course: my guess is you need to have a more active sex life." She waited for a reaction; none came. "You have denied yourself for a long time, you know. Maybe Roger wants to play catch-up." The urge to giggle wasn't easy to suppress.

Mark was reluctant to relate details about his way of dealing with that—lately, the same choice had to be made every night: left hand or right hand. The problem was, Roger wanted more; he was ready during the day as well—morning, afternoon, Mark never knew what to expect these days.

"The problem, or part of the problem, is at the store. I never know when it will happen—or come up, to be more precise." He looked at Pat directly. "I haven't told you about Phyllis."

Pat was taken aback: Mark, attracted to a *woman*?

"She's been making a move on me—it's happened before. Usually all I need to do is cite company policy, chapter and verse." How to describe this difficulty politely was a challenge. "The new trouser style lends to the problem. It's hard to hide anything. A couple of times I'm sure that she noticed that Roger was… 'awake.' She can't help seeing what's there, can she?"

Pat nodded. She had seen his problem herself from time to time, even before the new style. Mark was a full sized man, no doubts there. "So she assumes she's the cause of your condition?"

"You tell me." Trying to interpret a woman's thoughts was way beyond his ability.

"I haven't met her, but it wouldn't surprise me. She could be looking for a way to justify believing she has prospects. I take it that the wedding ring is not much help."

Mark shook is head. "She's a good employee, otherwise. Letting her go would be a big problem. I'd have to have other grounds. I wish I knew how to shift her attention onto someone who needs it—or wants it."

Pat took a sip of tea and planned her next comment. An idea had just come to the surface…

—~—

Geraldine slid into the booth at Amanda and June's with a frown. What she wanted, she realized too late, was a martini. Supper had been a hurried affair—not even a glass of wine. No time to change clothes, either. Hmm. They don't have a liquor license here, or I'd order *something*. That Fredericks woman talked for *hours*—would have gone on all night if I hadn't cut her off; strangest client I've had in years. If I hadn't planned to spend the evening with Francine, I'd have headed straight for Harold's Leading Edge. They make a superb martini. Geraldine rarely went to a lounge in the evening—unless, of course, it was with someone *special*. "Thanks, Arlene," she did a quick survey. "Slow night."

The waitress nodded, placing the water glasses before the ladies. Mondays were always slow after eight o'clock. Worst night of the week for tips; Geraldine was a delightful surprise. She's always good to me. "The blueberry pie is especially good today."

"Drop back in five minutes. I'm not ready to make important decisions just yet." The background music… it might be up a little too high. Masking restaurant noise is desirable as long as you don't have to shout over it to be heard. As it was, there wasn't anyone who could overhear. That suited just fine: she was on a mission tonight. All week I've been waiting for some sign, some indication that my effort and expertise made a difference. So far there hasn't been a word… not one word—*nothing*. Hard to believe. Waiting in the wings, so to speak, was not Geraldine's style. She had seen to it that Julian's wardrobe was perfect. He *had* to make a splash. Francine hasn't volunteered any news; I intend to find out what's going on.

Francine liked Arlene… always so thoughtful. “Thanks.” She took a sip of ice water. The accent candle on the inside of the table had been lit. They must be… of course: it’s after nine. This late they cater to clients seeking a more romantic atmosphere. The overhead lighting is reduced. Ever since last summer, she took notice of these things. Romance—or the possibility of it—had nearly upset the applecart last summer. She was over it for the time being, but… the low light and candles did remind her of a very nice evening last summer.

Geraldine hadn’t decided whether to have anything more than tea… coffee at this hour would be stupid. A big dessert would be double stupid. If Francine is interested in ordering, I’ll let her decide.

“Hmm… do you suppose they can warm the blueberry pie?” Warm blueberry cobbler was a specialty of her mother’s.

“They will tonight. Perfect. With a scoop of vanilla ice cream?”

Francine nodded eagerly.

Geraldine was struck by that—in a flash she saw where Julian had acquired his extraordinary cheerful countenance: from his mother. It was one of Francine’s most endearing, winning qualities. She didn’t show it very often.

“So.” Time to get on with it. “Any reports about the first week?”

“He’s excited about his classes. You know Julian: sits right in front and grins wide. He’s in love with his three ring binder. You’d think it was a miracle invention or something. I never thought about him not having one in junior high…”

“What about the wardrobe?” Most of all, what did the girls have to say?

“He’s meticulous about that… a fresh outfit every day. He makes sure to get my approval before we leave.”

“You still take him to *school*?”

“Of course. But he walks home afterward.” That was a major concession.

Hmm. "That's a start." Francine's overprotectiveness is Julian's biggest problem.

"No mention of girls falling all over themselves to catch his eye, I don't suppose."

Francine shook her head. "It's only the second week. Once he's in a routine with his classes, he'll begin to deal with that." His socializing skills were an open question. He made it through junior high without a girlfriend. To be fair, there wasn't much time, what with scouts. "Not a word about scouting all week. That's a first."

Geraldine was disappointed; evidently the clothing didn't have the effect she was after. Unfortunately there's no way I could supervise… hmm. Too bad I had to let him resign from the yard crew… at least there I was in a position to make a few suggestions… a prod here and there maybe… and being exposed to a bunch of men whose first and last thought of every day was a woman didn't hurt.

Arlene returned, order pad poised. They ordered the pie and ice cream. Once she was out of hearing, Geraldine was back on task.

"I want to know what you plan to do about…" how do I say this?! "his getting a girlfriend. Or two, or *three*." Julian had not had so much as *one* date in his life. "He's in *high school* now!"

Francine had mixed feelings. "He's not like his father, that's for sure." In fact, he seems to be just the opposite.

Geraldine sat back; maybe that's part of the problem. "How much does he know?"

Francine stared at her hard: "Nothing. *Not one thing*." Her tone was as cold as steel. That was an absolute she would not violate.

The intensity of the response surprised; Francine's contempt for Julian's father had not diminished one bit. You'd think that in fifteen years she would mellow a *little*. Nope. That line was permanent; pointless to argue about it. That's one area that defined a basic difference in temperament between herself and Francine.

Francine had married young, two years out of high school. A modeling job at the art school made a huge difference—her stipend was a little slim. The sculptor was an incredibly sexy man, a veritable Apollo. He was an accomplished lover as well—and for a time, he was besotted by his pretty young model. However, once they were wedded and bedded, and she had been in the family way for several months, his insatiable nature reasserted itself.

Geraldine didn't know the details, but one day Francine came in on her husband when he was "breaking in" his latest model. The marriage was finished in an instant. The divorce was swift and its terms harsh: the father would never see his child again. He had no rights. The downside for Francine was no support requirement either—but that was just fine with her. She dropped out and returned home, her college career on hold.

Geraldine had been the one to help her get through all this. They had been good friends, and she stayed in touch. After five years of pleading, Francine agreed to move here and settle down. Her aging parents had passed on; enough was left in the estate to get a good solid start here.

One thing that Geraldine had never shared—and never would—was what happened after Francine returned home. As an "intermediary," Geraldine had met with Adrian more than once. It didn't take long for Adrian to appreciate her "efforts." The brief fling was *very* nice. For a few weeks it was difficult to do much else. That's one reason it was so fascinating to watch his son grow up. Aside from his eyes, Julian was a carbon copy of his father—the hair especially. Sneaking a hint or two to Julian about his father crossed her mind once in a while, but her regard for Francine was too high. She would never betray that trust. Still, it's uniquely thrilling to watch Julian grow up.

Maybe she's afraid he'll turn out like Adrian. I don't see any danger of that, not at this stage. He won't behave like his father. Francine has done well in that regard. Maybe too well. Geraldine cleared her throat and assumed her big sister tone of voice. "Have you talked to him about girls?"

Francine tensed… Geraldine means well, but…

"That's what I thought." No need to press the point. "I don't mean to tell you your job, Francine, but you need to pay attention to this. What if he doesn't learn what to do, how to date and relate to women? You have to learn that in high school."

Francine didn't disagree with that, but…

"He's becoming a handsome young man. His cute-little-boy days are almost over." In another year, *gorgeous* will be the only word. As it is, everything we bought came from the *men's* department.

"What if…" she had not expressed this concern aloud before… "What if he doesn't like girls?"

That notion stopped Geraldine cold. "Not like girls?" I watched him closely all summer: he was right at home with the working men. "Why would you think that?" There's nothing effeminate about Julian.

"Look at his room—model planes, forest scenes, drawings—no sign of a girl *anywhere*."

Geraldine debated whether to ask this or not… "How carefully do you look?"

"Carefully? What do you mean?"

Patience, Geraldine, patience… Francine is as naïve as her boy. "What if he's hiding something?" Several weeks ago she had put it into Zack's head to give Julian a copy of Playboy after work. He must have it stashed somewhere.

What an annoying thing to suggest. "I am not about to peek under his mattress or paw through his things." That would destroy her relationship with him in an instant. "If I have a good reason, I'll ask. Julian would never lie to me." She gave Geraldine a sharp expression. "You know that as well as I do."

"All right, all right… I apologize." Unfortunately, she's probably right about that. Julian did not have an ounce of talent when it came to deception… a serious weakness. In the morning I'll ask Zack about that Playboy… maybe he has some idea if it had any effect. She had chosen Zack because he and Julian had become buddies of a sort. It was cute the way Julian mimicked Zack's swagger and light hearted "no big deal" approach to life.

She pursued the subject from a different direction. "Didn't he used to have a girlfriend? Wasn't there something a few years ago…

"You mean *Lucy*?" Francine smiled a second then paused. She debated with herself for a moment then decided to go ahead; it was a long time ago.

"Probably; I didn't remember a name. Why?"

"I didn't tell you about this because he swore me to secrecy at the time. He was *so* mortified, poor child." Francine chuckled. It seems humorous now.

Geraldine sat up, all ears.

"You have to swear you'll never let on you heard about this."

Geraldine raised her right hand as if she was in a courtroom. This has to be good.

"One day after school…"

The pie and ice cream arrived just then. The aroma of freshly heated berry pie commanded their attention immediately.

What a *brilliant* idea, this. All of a sudden, Geraldine was *ravenous*.

—∾—

Pat looked across the table. Mark appeared so helpless… her heart went out to him. She went to the point. "Why not go on a date?"

Mark could hardly believe his ears. "A *date?!*"

"Sure. Why not? You're of age." She smirked.

"Be serious."

"I am being serious. All you need is a way to arrange it." She winked. "It so happens, I can do that easily."

This chat had taken an unexpected direction. He was at a loss to find any way to express what was going on in his head.

Pat reached across and patted his hand. "Really, Mark. It's not such a big thing. I know several guys who would *die* to get a chance to meet you. You have no idea." She knew three who would *leap* at the chance.

Mark's memory flashed back to what it was like in high school… afraid to answer the door almost. Fearful that someone would find out that he was "that way," the notion of meeting someone of a like mind was never considered. He had never gone looking. All he could dare was hope that on a campout one of his scout buddies would get horny. When he was a freshman in college, he and Erik had discovered each other by accident—they couldn't stop themselves. His purpose in life had been discovered. Then, seemingly just as fast, Erik was gone. Helpless now as well as then, he looked up with a sheepish grin. "Umm… I've never been on a date."

Pat was stopped cold by that claim… she frowned. "Mark, this is *me*. We went to high school together, remember?" Of course he went on dates. "You went on a date with me, in case you have forgotten."

Mark shrugged. "Yeah, but that wasn't the same thing." He could see that she didn't understand. "Tell me: what is a date?"

Pat paused… "Well, it's when you go out with someone… you know, just you and her… or whoever…"

"Uh huh. And why do you go on the date?"

"To have a good time."

"And?"

"Well, you know, to see how well you get along, to see if they're someone you want to know better… maybe someone you'll really like and…" this is all so obvious.

"Right." He paused for effect. "I've never done that." With eyes steady, he looked at her directly: "I went on four so-called "dates" in high school. I remember every one of them. None were for the reason you just gave. I went for one reason: to *fool* everyone. I didn't want *anyone* to know that I was… that I…" even saying the dread word was as distasteful as ever.

"You knew *then*?" This is news.

"I didn't *know*, maybe, but I was afraid I was. The only thing that turned me on was messing around at Scout camp. That's where I discovered what I liked and wanted. That was my only experience when I met Erik." He shrugged. "Short history. To this day, you are just about the only person who knows about him." As a couple, he and Erik had made no friends—too risky, too daring. They took pleasure in living a secret life.

Pat was genuinely surprised. She knew that Erik had become Mark's life, for all practical purposes, but she did not know *how* important. This is a little tougher than I thought. Still, that doesn't change the prescription, does it?

"Here's what you do: get used to the *idea*, at least. In a week or so, let's talk again. By then you might be ready to help me make a plan. You need to join the world, Mark."

Mark felt an odd mix: grateful and ashamed. "You are so good for me… how did I get so lucky?" It was true. She was his lifeline.

Pat blushed. It was mutual. Mark did not know what he meant to her; she intended to keep it that way, lest he grow self conscious or defensive. She had as much of his heart as she could ever hope for, and was content to be his "sister." Second best is better than nothing. She stood. "Time to retire, boys and girls." She patted his shoulder on the way to her room. Getting out of uniform and taking a nice long shower was next on the agenda.

Mark nodded. Wow. The last twenty minutes had drained him. Go to sleep? Not likely, now. He swiveled out of the chair and stood. Uh-oh… I don't *believe* this… Roger had just made himself known again. Damn. "Why didn't I ask about the monks?"

A squat loosened Roger up somewhat. Time to turn everything off and go to bed. Maybe ignoring him will work. He turned off the kitchen light and headed for the den.

—ʍ—

Geraldine shouldn't have been surprised to find that blueberry pie was indeed superior when warm. More years than it was comfortable to admit had passed since her tongue had been subjected to this exquisite experience. Warm pie is dangerous—especially blueberry; it could be habit forming. That could be disastrous… maintaining a presentable waistline requires vigilance. There's no point in becoming a dieting fanatic, but one needs to be sensible… an extra five pounds perhaps, but not an ounce more. It's altogether too hard to lose weight. One excess a week—two on *rare* occasions. From this day, warm berry pie will be held in reserve… limited to an annual indulgence.

Francine stopped to sip her tea; a glance to the left told her all was clear. She looked up at her friend's expectant face. "He was in the second grade. Once in a while I dropped him off at Maxine Graham's to spend the after school hours. The office had problems keeping him entertained from time to time."

"Mmm," Geraldine nodded. I remember well. The boy went through every coloring book and used up all the crayons. She rolled her eyes.

"She was a very imaginative little girl. Inventing new fantasy games was her specialty. Julian had complained about having to play "house." This time, Lucy persuaded him to play a special revision—she called it "Dress Up." You know Julian—he always agrees to do whatever anyone asks without thinking. He is incapable of suspecting an ulterior motive."

"Ulterior? In the *second* grade?"

"I doubt that it was *planned*... But I'm getting ahead of myself; it was Lucy's idea to *trade places* as well as dress up. She planned to dress as the father, and Julian was assigned to dress as the mother."

"Wooo!" Geraldine tried to picture Lucy in her mind... Graham, Graham. Hmmm. Nothing appeared... not one of my clients.

"Lucy was thorough. Everything was prepared in advance, including the script in her head. They were to play out a full day, beginning by getting up, fixing breakfast, dressing for work, and so forth. Father would come home after a hard day, mother would complain about having too many chores as she served supper; then they would watch TV and go to bed." Julian had described this in detail.

"Sounds like fun," Geraldine chuckled.

"I think it was, for a while. But it went very bad." Francine paused to take a bite... the ice cream is melting.

Geraldine happily followed suit; the pie was cooling fast. She proceeded to clean her plate as thoroughly as possible with the tools provided. This *is* dangerous... a strong urge to order a second slice tugged at her resolution—it was all she could do to refrain from licking the plate. Resisting the urge made her feel strong and virtuous; regretfully, the plate was still in view... unfortunately, all she could do was slide it close to the edge where Arlene would see it—the sooner it's swept out of sight the better.

After a sip to rinse her mouth and a dainty pat with her napkin, Francine continued. "Lucy led him into her bedroom; everything was set up. They had to pretend lots of things, naturally. First they prepared by putting on pajamas. They needed to start the day by getting out of bed, you see." Francine wasn't sure about some of this, so she plugged in what must have happened. "They turned their backs to each other, undressed, and put on the pajamas. Two pair had been set aside; she had to pretend that the pair she put on was her father's. Once they were ready for bed, they placed their clothes neatly side by side so that they could be put back on when they got up."

Geraldine enjoyed this immensely. I wish I had been that clever… a boy came to mind that would have been perfect.

"So, they climbed into bed, pulled up the covers and closed their eyes. Lucy issued directions along the way as needed. After a minute of closed eyes, she imitated the alarm clock going off."

"That's right!" Geraldine laughed. "You said they had to *start* the day. Spending the night before was not in the script!"

"Exactly. Well, the surprises came soon enough. Nothing was said about how to remove pajamas and put on underwear." Geraldine's facial expressions made telling this fun. "He didn't think twice about it and undressed at once. He didn't realize that he was being watched. When he pulled off his pajama bottoms, he was surprised to hear a squeal. Lucy pointed at his little willy: 'what is *that?'* she asked."

Geraldine covered her mouth.

"Julian looked down at himself to see what she was talking about and then across to her. He discovered that she did not have one. He did not know that basic fact."

"Oh, my g— *Francine!*"

"I assume they paused the game while they made a closer study. Julian allowed as much later on, but didn't go into detail. He couldn't believe Lucy was missing such an important piece of equipment. Back to the game: he proceeded to put on Lucy's clothes, and she put on his. He had to pretend to fix breakfast while she pretended to read the morning paper. After breakfast it turned sour.

"She pretended to be a good husband by kissing her pretend wife on the cheek before going off to work…" Francine paused a minute. "I just thought of something. He didn't seem to mind that. At least he didn't say anything that suggested he was bothered."

Geraldine was pleased to hear that. "Yes, that is interesting; little boys are usually annoyed by that aren't they?"

"I always thought so, but… anyway, this is where the story gets interesting: after closing the pretend front door, she went around the back and reappeared behind him as a secret invisible helper; she had to show him how to get made up—he had to pretend to go shopping."

"No!"

"Yes. She sat him down at her toy dressing table and showed him how to put on lipstick, rouge, eyeliner, perfume and face powder. She had raided her mother's dresser and went all out. After a while, she just took over. Evidently, her little vanity mirror was covered, because he didn't see what she had done until after she was finished.

"What did he think?!?

"I'll get to that in a second. Lucy was so pleased with herself that she had to show him off. I don't think she had any idea what his reaction was going to be. She took him by the hand and led him downstairs. I'm not sure what Maxine was doing—something in the kitchen. I gather she screamed with delight. Her words, however were the wrong thing to say. She told Julian he was prettier than almost any little girl she had ever seen. I guess Lucy was a little put off by that. Anyway—Maxine took him by the hand and led him to the mirror in the hallway, where she kneeled down and compared her makeup to his."

"Good grief."

"I know. He didn't recognize himself, of course. When he compared the two faces he was horrified. He said he put an end to the game then and there." Francine paused. "Actually, he didn't, according to Maxine; she said he went back upstairs without a word to finish the game. He didn't go into detail about what they did before I dropped by to pick him up. By then he was cleaned up and back in his own clothes.

"Julian held his feelings close; it took him three days to tell me about it. Maxine was appallingly insensitive. After that day he never agreed to spend an afternoon at Lucy's." Needless to say, he didn't see the humor.

A long pause. "Well." Geraldine's brain was humming over this information. "It seems we have some repair work to do."

Francine doubted that. "It was a long time ago… *second* grade, remember."

Geraldine had reservations… childhood traumas can be long lasting in their effect. She had a demon of her own in that category. I need to think about this. Her Julian plan was now on temporary hold. This was most unexpected. I wish I had known about this before. Suddenly she was adrift, and that was uncomfortable. Geraldine liked to be in control.

Francine indulged herself for a moment… remembering Julian telling about this was special. It was the one and only time he'd had trouble telling her anything. It was probably the first time he had been embarrassed. It meant the world that he had been able to open up about it finally. It was one of the best "mother" moments ever; being there when your boy needs you is not only important to him, but it's important to you: nothing is more satisfying than knowing you have fulfilled your purpose.

Geraldine emptied her glass of iced tea. Glancing across the way, she caught Arlene's attention: a nod and raised glass gave notice that her services were required. Julian is on hold: so be it. There is a second issue—this one rather touchy. As if it was simply time to change the subject, she adopted an off-hand attitude and tone of voice. "So… what's the news from Edwin?"

Francine took a deep breath. "With school starting and everything, you know… I haven't given that any time." That was on a back burner now.

Geraldine was pleasantly surprised. "No letters?"

"I haven't answered his last one… that was what… three weeks ago."

So… he's not putting on pressure, then. Good. The prospect of Francine pulling up stakes and moving to Florida had haunted her for months. The vacation we took while Julian was away at camp introduced a real, viable romantic candidate into Francine's life. That was not the plan, but it had happened. It's wise to keep my mouth shut for the time being. With luck, this will cool off completely. Without thinking, Geraldine checked her watch—an unconscious but sure signal that she was ready to leave.

Francine was grateful that Geraldine didn't push her about Edwin. Doing that could cause her to lose her objectivity. If I decide to go with Edwin, it has to be clean, on its own merits—not in reaction to pressure from Geraldine.

The waitress appeared with the refill pitcher.

"No more, Arlene; I've changed my mind." Geraldine pointed at the empty pie plates, still perched on the edge of the table. "I'm trying to think of a way to punish Francine for leading me astray." She scooted out. "I shall return," she announced, and headed toward the ladies room.

Arlene gathered the dishes and gave Francine a friendly wink; obviously, suggesting the blueberry pie had pleased Geraldine; that meant a good tip tonight, if experience was any guide.

Francine knew better than to try picking up the bill—Geraldine always insists on paying; her planning to depart signal was clear, as usual. She'll find me in the waiting area up front.

All in all, the talk had gone well; maybe Geraldine will back off a little now… She means well, but her plans for Julian, whatever they are, have to be held at bay: he has to have growing space; Geraldine's plan is not his plan.

Francine frowned… Geraldine's suggestion that he might have secret girlie pictures tucked away rankled. Of course he doesn't have anything under his mattress: I change his sheets… I'd have seen them. The very thought made her feel guilty.

Avoiding the issue of Julian's sexual development had been her conscious policy; she rationalized that it wasn't important to know particulars. What useful purpose is there in evoking memories of his father? Julian's uncanny physical likeness tended to make it hard to avoid at times. She wasn't about to tar her boy's image with the sins of his father. He has shown no sign of his father's promiscuity—she planned to keep it that way. When Julian marries, it will be for keeps; he will be a faithful husband.

On the other hand, what if he doesn't like girls? What then? That would require the attention of someone other than Geraldine. Julian is not a sissy—he will be a man, one hundred per cent. Maybe he's one that has to wait until his thirties before finding a mate. I've heard about that. In any case, it's a good thing I'm not counting on having grandchildren right away.

She stared out of the entry window, eyes unfocused… Geraldine is right about one thing: it is time to deal with this. I haven't been avoiding it, exactly… but I haven't been paying very close attention, either. Julian is growing up far faster than I expected; adjusting to that reality isn't easy. I haven't talked with him about a career path either. I need to get busy.

8 Meatloaf for lunch

Art Frankel patrolled his classroom silently, observing the hard working test takers with care. Doing this helped fill in what couldn't be discerned from reading their paperwork. He had a good eye for spotting a student in need of attention. Often the ones who need help are the ones who are afraid to ask for it. So far so good: everyone seems to be engaged… no one seems to be in trouble. The sound—or lack of it—during an exam is a good yardstick; everyone on task meant lots to read over the next few nights.

Two weeks into the term, first unit done; the team assignments seem to be working out well… years of experience taught that if a student team wasn't properly matched at the start, one or both would do poorly—or worse, fail. Friends were generally bad lab partners—so were "couples." Next worse were the social elite types; *preventing* combinations was key in their case—mostly guesswork, since all were new at the school. Worst of all was hormones in full bloom; those were the most difficult to fit. The symptoms didn't always show—girls were especially adept at keeping their cool.

It's too bad the course calendar can't be rearranged: we don't deal with hormones until the end of the year. By then, it's too late for some, of course… post something… the opposite of *post mortem*; is there a Latin euphemism for that? *post oops-couldn't-stop-in-time*. The Snyder boy in the back row is a perfect example: he needs to know that material now. Not a day has gone by this term that his rebellious "lap partner" hasn't been a distraction. He tries to hide the problem, but good luck… how could anyone hide that? What he needs is a size ten codpiece; wrong century. Some hungry lass will help him find relief before long; odds are he'll sire before the end of the semester. At least his lab partner is able to ignore it; Jenkins is a late bloomer.

He paused to look at the Forrest/Johnson team. They're doing better than expected. Perhaps I was too hasty to judge in his case. I pegged Julian as a classic social type—splashy wardrobe, good looks, Palm Beach suntan… doesn't behave according to type: doesn't crave attention or seek special favors. He looks like a leading candidate for class president or yell king but acts like a plain ordinary boy. It's early in the year… events may catch up with him. But putting Beth with him has worked well—she's starting to come alive. I've never had a girl as frail and frightened of the world. To give full credit, Julian is a gentleman—treats her like a next door neighbor. Visually, they are opposites. Funny how that works sometimes.

He glanced at the clock: thought so.

"Time's up. Hand me your papers on the way out. Thanks, everyone." The bell rang as he headed for the door. He enjoyed making the small gesture of accepting their papers in person—a smile helped remove some of the terror that lurked in their minds; this was their first major test in his class.

That bell was the best sound Julian had heard all day: time for lunch. He sat back and exhaled… Boy. That was something. That's about the toughest test I've ever taken. He looked at his lab partner with a grin. "I think I passed it!"

Beth nodded. "It wasn't so hard after all." He'll be fine; we reviewed everything twice.

"Easy for you to say," Julian laughed. "You're naturally good at this stuff."

> *klack!* < He opened the three ring binder at the Biology tab; man, if it wasn't for this, I'd be lost in this class. Three new worksheets today…

"There's one more." She handed him a sheet he had overlooked.

"Thanks, Beth," he glanced at it. "Wow." A list of assignments for next week. How did I miss this? "I don't know what I'd do if you weren't paying attention. You hafta promise to never be absent, okay?" He put it at the front of the Biology section. Mr. Frankel's handouts were always pre-punched.

Beth nodded silently, and turned red. Miss this class? *never*.

"No, really, I mean it." He grinned wide. "I'm lucky to have you instead of some of the kids in here. You understand this stuff a lot better than I ever will. I bet you get an A on this."

If only I didn't freeze up when he talked to me. "I'm sure you did fine. You're not stupid." Beth was often in danger of wetting herself when Julian talked to her directly. His deep brown eyes and dark eyelashes were always so *happy*… they were *intense*. With that smile, it was hard not to faint. The pattern on his shirt made it worse—it seemed to be in constant motion, like a mobile in a gentle breeze.

"I was never any good in science. Now that I've got you, I'm not worried."

> *klack!* < He snapped the binder shut.

As usual, Beth watched him pack up—a favorite moment every day. I am *so* lucky… to think of all the people I could have been assigned, but no. Mr. Frankel was her secret hero for this.

He stood and tucked everything under his left arm. "See you tomorrow."

His mind is always somewhere else when he's headed toward the door; that's when she could watch him unnoticed. > *sigh* < I don't know what I'd do if he ever waited for me… would he ever walk to the cafeteria with me? I'd wet my pants for real. It's stupid to fantasize about it, but…

Today, Julian had earned his lunch. He had to satisfy himself about one thing, though. He handed Mr. Frankel his test paper. "Number three was a trick question, wasn't it?"

Frankel kept a straight face. "Trick?" He looked back in earnest. "Depends on how you look at it, Julian. In a way, Life is a trick question, isn't it? Still, we have to come up with an answer, don't we?" The expression on his face was a bonus. One kid in a hundred had the guts to ask about that question—I always put it on the first test of the year. Amazing, sometimes, what I get back. He was eager to read what Julian had put down.

Julian frowned as he left the room. It *had* to be a trick question:

3. What are the best kind of shoes to wear in the lab? Explain.

(a) enclosed toe shoes (b) sandals
(c) flip flops (d) none of these

Tests never have a question that stupid. He shook his head, frustrated. I bet Mr. Frankel is just like Sid—always trying to pull one on you when you least expect it. Oh, well. Enough of that! He set out for his locker, walking double time… I have a new drawing to start!

—m—

Randall was in a *big* hurry—geometry let out a little late today… I have to get into position! Studying his blond demigod's movements and habits closely for the past week had paid off: knowing exactly what Julian would be doing during lunch made life easier, for sure. The problem now is getting to my locker in time. I have to fetch my clarinet and most of all, my *lunch*—it's needed for cover as much as anything. If only my locker wasn't at the wrong end of the hallway. I feel like a salmon fighting my way upstream—but I'm navigating through a river of *people*. I should have taken care of this during the last break. I didn't think of that until this minute. I can't believe how stupid I am at times.

Lunch had become his favorite period—admittedly, he was feasting his eyes more than his stomach. Every day the first task was locating himself properly: being seen would be a disaster. Watching him is such a pleasure—I've never done anything like this before. Someday I'll get to meet him… Randall had fantasized any number of approaches, but still couldn't figure a way. The *worst* thing would be to foul it up. That fear kept him at a distance… I need a foolproof plan, that's all there is to it.

I lucked out in second period; I was able to sit closer on the second day—it didn't make any difference because Mr. Quimby proceeded to assign seats. He prefers his classes to be seated in alphabetical order. That put Julian in the second row—that's how I learned his name. I ended up in the next row back, three seats to the left. It isn't right next to him, but maybe it's better that way; the view is perfect.

What a *wonderful* name, what a *perfect* name. Julian Forest… just *saying* it gives me goose bumps. I do that when no one is around—or at home after everybody is asleep. Yes… a perfect name for a perfect face, a perfect *everything*.

Now in second period I can see him all the time—he doesn't have to turn around—I can watch him for as long as I want. What a profile… it's a good thing they have desk chairs in that class. They hide The Problem well enough. The Problem—Randall's euphemism for the inevitable swelling in his lap that followed when he stared too long at various parts of Julian's anatomy. Not the usual reason to be fond of World History, of course. Luckily, there has been no need to get up and move around during class.

Randall had done a great deal of detective work and research in the last two weeks. He knew quite a lot now—such as what classes Julian had and when. I even followed him home one afternoon—that was scary. Almost got caught. I was late getting home, but Mom came home even later. Marietta didn't tell on me, so I owe her one. One of these days I'll follow him again with my telephoto lens along. The only problem with that is what to do with the camera during school. Rule one: don't attract attention; a lone sophomore boy carrying a fancy camera case could be the best way to alert the Nels types.

My Blond Prince is a puzzle in many ways, though. He talks to some friends once in a while, but there's no way to tell what they talk about—they're always too far away. I'm paranoid about being seen—I make sure to keep at a safe distance. Most amazing is the fact that there isn't a girl glued to his side. How could someone that handsome and that well-dressed not have a flock of them hanging all over him? Because of that, a cautious optimism underpinned his thinking—it wasn't smart to make any assumptions.

Blast it! I could swear the hallway is more crowded than usual... if only there was a way to go over or around them. Getting in position early today is important: yesterday it looked like the drawing was finished. I couldn't see it, but from the way he checked it over, it must be done. That could mean he'll be moving to a new location; where that might be is the question. One of these days he'll find somewhere to draw besides the atrium—that could be *today*. That's why having to wade through all these people is so exasperating. If only I could run... there's no way through... I *have* to see where he's headed.

Those blasted girls! A bunch of them are clogging the hallway. One of them is grabbing at something.

"...give that *back!"* a girl dressed in dark red shouted angrily as she grabbed at a small book.

"In a *minute!"* the one dressed in green insisted, pulling it free.

Man alive! Suddenly they were directly in his path...

Julian had to swerve to the left all of a sudden to avoid running smack into a couple of girls that had just backed out in front of him. Why don't they look where they're going?

"Whoa—*yow!*" someone in a dark blue shirt is going around them on the other side!

> ***Krumpp!*** <

Head on collision—stars, flashes... forced off balance, he spun around—

> ***Bam!*** <

Julian's shoulder struck a locker door… he slid to the floor, stunned. It took a couple of seconds to recover… ooo… my forehead… wowee, that hurts. His left shoulder was sore—it had taken the brunt of the fall.

Instead of slowing down, Randall deftly dodged to his right, confident that a small burst of speed would get him around the arguing girls in plenty of time. Unfortunate; unable to stop or change direction, there was one choice—close his eyes or watch the inevitable. It happened very fast—three seconds. To Randall it seemed like several minutes… every detail was crystal clear, magnified as if filmed in slow motion.

I'm headed right at someone—*oh no!* it *can't* be… beautiful brown eyes and flowing blond hair are zooming in… yellow shirt… red lines… green squares… I studied that this morning—

> ***Krumpp!*** <

A billion stars flashed and everything went dark.

Randall did not hear the screams and ruckus that followed. He was out cold, having struck his head a second time on the shiny asphalt tile floor.

Julian heard squeals somewhere, but they were vague. I better rest for a minute… I'm a little woozy. What happened? I remember sliding down on my knees… *My books!* …scattered every which way. The boy in the dark blue shirt is laying face down a couple of feet in front of me. Gosh… he sat up and reached out…

"Clear away, please… everyone stand clear!" Frankel was there in seconds—only a few feet away when it happened, he was locking his classroom, about to go to lunch. There's no mistaking the sound human skulls make when whacked together. Not a good sound.

First aid training in college years ago had provided a basic working knowledge; he checked for a pulse—no problem there. He braced the boy's head with care and lifted the left shoulder… slowly, gently he turned the boy onto his back. It's *Randall!*

Randall's eyes opened as he was being lifted—a vision, a wonderful magic vision appeared—he's right here! Brown eyes, blond hair… I'm looking straight up at him—he's kneeling right in front of me. How can that be? How can he be lifting me up like this? I can see both his hands…

"Easy, son, easy…" Frankel was relieved… the boy's eyes are opening. A good sign… hasn't been out long. Randall was one of his better students in 7th period.

"What happened?" It's my Biology teacher holding my head. He blinked several times… things didn't look right… is this a dream? A pain, a major pain in his head told him that he was awake.

"You took a nasty fall and banged your head. We'll get you down to the Nurse pronto." He looked over at Julian. "How about you?"

"Wow… umm…" Julian felt his forehead. A small bump was forming. "I think I'm okay…" he touched the tender spot cautiously. "I felt woozy for a minute, but I'm all right now." He looked down at Randall with concern. I know this kid from somewhere… don't know his name though.

How long is the nurse going to leave the thermometer in my mouth? She's busy with the other kid—Randall, I think they said. He was knocked out cold, so they're all fussed about him. She said we both had a Class Two whatchacallit, so they aren't taking any chances.

Julian looked over at the desk—the nameplate said Esther Rosenthall, RN. Seems to know what's she's doing. Boy, if only I could get this thing out of my mouth… he cleared his throat and swallowed the extra saliva that had pooled.

"OH, I'm sorry, dear," Nurse Rosenthall turned toward him. "I'll bet you thought I had forgotten all about you." She removed the thermometer and looked at it closely.

He smiled gratefully and watched her face… she's an expert, for sure. You can tell they're an expert when they don't let you see what they're thinking. I'm not worried; except for the pulsing lump at the top of my forehead, I feel fine. Still, I'd feel better if she said *something…*

"How's the pain now? Any change since you came in?"

He thought for a second. "Pretty much the same, 'cept I can feel it throbbing a little more now." The trouble is, I'm getting hungry… it wouldn't be very cool to complain about that…

She nodded. "Yes, that will last a while—but if it doesn't stop pulsing in the next 30 minutes, please tell me." She touched it carefully. "The skin isn't broken," she said to herself. No need to put on a dressing… an ice pack if it doesn't stop growing.

Thirty *minutes?!* I'm *hungry…* what about lunch?

"Have either of you had a concussion before?" She looked at Randall, then Julian.

Julian had no idea—didn't recognize the word.

"I thinks so, but it was a long time ago," Randall had heard the term more than once, and knew it was kind of serious.

"How long ago?"

"I was in the third or fourth grade—I got bonked good by a foul ball one day. I didn't think it was as bad as they made out… hurt like blazes, but it didn't knock me unconscious."

The nurse was relieved, but… "Do you remember if there were any aftereffects?"

"I had a bump on top my head. It didn't last long, a few days or so." The best after effect was providing a good reason to avoid participating in the activity ever again.

"And what about you?"

"OH! I remember, yeah..." Julian nodded. "I knocked my head pretty good last summer. At camp we had this lightning storm in the middle of the night. I whacked my head against the wall when I woke up."

Obviously the nurse wants to know more... "I don't think I was knocked out or anything... I woke up because of the thunder. I was kinda woozy for a while. Mark made me sit still and wrapped me in the quilt real tight—it was pretty cold all of a sudden."

"Where did you hit your head?"

"On the wall."

"I mean where on your head... can you remember that?"

"Oh, yeah, sure. I had a bump right here." Julian put his finger on the spot. "Kinda neat... it was sort of like a little walnut trying to pop out of my head," he chuckled. He was proud of it for some reason. "It went down by the end of the week. After a day or two it didn't even hurt." It stayed tender 'til after I came home. Once I started working on the crew, I didn't notice it at all.

The Nurse took that report very seriously—today's bump was only an inch away... better treat him as Class 2 just to be safe. She stepped over to her desk and turned on the lamp. Then she went to the door and flipped off the overhead light.

"Boys, I'm afraid you will have to stay here for the time being. Both of you have had a concussion—that's always a serious thing; how your head is treated afterwards is very important. Most of the injury is inside your skull where you can't feel very much if anything. It has to heal—if you do too much too soon, you could have bigger problems as time goes on. Eventually, you will need to see your family doctor—I'll be sending a note home advising your parents to be sure you do."

Julian was not happy—the idea that Mom will have a doctor bill to pay is not welcome. I'll try to talk her out of it.

The nurse stepped over to the far side of the room and pointed at a window: "For now, I want you to rest." Two narrow beds separated by a small table filled a tiny side room. “If you feel cold, there is a blanket folded at the foot. I’m going to leave you for a few minutes, but I won’t be away long.”

Julian and Randall looked at each other. Neither had expected this. They looked at the wall clock—

“Umm…” Julian wondered about going after his sack lunch.

“Don’t worry about lunch. That’s where I’m going—the cafeteria will put together a tray for each of you.” With a wink, she whispered, “You don’t have to pay for it, either: that’s because I get to decide what goes on the tray.” She flipped over a sign that hung in the door window as she left the room.

“Are we supposed to take a nap, or something?” I don’t feel sleepy.

“Sounds like it. Maybe after we finish eating.” Randall was amazed that he had been able to talk—and to sound halfway sensible. The conflicting forces within him were without precedent; confusion of this kind was new. Not being in control of the situation or of himself was bizarre. Am I in a crazy dream? I’ve just been spoken to by *him*… by Julian Forest himself! I don’t want to alert anyone, but my heart rate right now must be about to set a record. It’s not due to the lump on my forehead; the nurse didn’t say anything about my blood pressure—I wouldn’t know what it meant if she had. But she’d freak out if she took it now—it must have doubled.

The meeting he had prayed for but feared more than anything had started. Unable to think, let alone *do* anything was like floating in outer space. I have to get a grip somehow… I’m not used to being unprepared. To begin with, there’s the bothersome fact that I might have a serious injury… but that’s nothing compared to what I’ve done: *it was my fault*. If I hadn’t been running up the hall—

“I’m sorry I ran into you like that.” Julian figured he’d caused the collision because he hadn’t been paying attention. “I was in too big a hurry to get my lunch.”

Randall couldn't believe his ears. "No, no, it was all *my* fault." I feel so *awful*. "I was going too fast. When those girls started to pull at that book… they were doing a tug of war over someone's diary, I think." I saw that in plenty of time to stop. Gosh… look at the bump on his forehead… I caused that. He reached up to feel his own bump… ooo.

"So *that's* what they were doing." Julian touched his bump too… still the same. "I tripped over something and couldn't stop." Keeping a diary is too risky. That's why I never do that. If anyone found out about that kind of stuff, it would be a disaster. I'm the only one who knows about my Big Plan, and that's the way it's going to stay. Otherwise, Mom—or worse yet, Mark—would find out. That would only ruin my whole life, that's all; diaries are a stupid idea.

Same problem with drawings… I had to remove the secret drawings from my sketchbook—those were trouble waiting to happen; if the wrong person saw those… man, oh man. Who draws nude pictures of anybody? Boy, if Sid had seen those… close call, that's what.

Unconsciously touching his bump again, Randall watched Julian… I wonder how bad his is. Was he knocked out too? I'm afraid to ask.

A dead spot in the conversation revealed that neither boy knew what to say. Julian broke the silence. "You know, I've seen you someplace but I don't remember where. You didn't go to Wallace, did you?"

Randall blushed. "No… I'm new. We just moved here." He must have seen me looking at him after all…

"Oh." Where have I seen him, then?

"Is Wallace the Junior High?"

"Yeah, Wallace is where I went. There are three Junior Highs. Wallace is the best, naturally." He performed an exaggerated nod, showing that he regarded school pride with a degree of disdain.

This peek into Julian's mind had raised the pedestal even higher: he has a brain too.

"What's your last name, anyway? Mine is Forrest." They had been using their first names in here, no point in saying those.

"Hallstrom." He tilted his head and shrugged: "My dad is second generation Swede."

"Wow! I've never met a Swede before!" Automatically he reached out. "Put 'er there!" Randall Hallstrom… neato name.

Holding Julian's hand! Randall was in heaven. Such an event had not been imagined in any fantasies. The smile… no word could describe what happened when Julian Forest smiled—he seems to *radiate* or something. It causes a glow… it takes over your brain… an electric charge zoomed down his spine and landed behind his balls—it didn't fade. He folded his hands at once to cover himself.

"I don't know what my dad is…" Julian puzzled a second. "I never asked about that. I just know it has two r's. Dunno why." Mom doesn't want to talk about my dad. I don't usually talk about that stuff.

*Two r's… Forrest…*that made the name even better…

The door opened and they both turned—Mr. Frankel carried in a small stack of books. "Hi boys; how're your heads?"

"Okay," they said in unison. They looked at each other, grinning at the coincidence.

Frankel put the books on a table beside the door. "You're in luck. Someone thought to gather these up." He stepped closer. "Dark in here." He looked at Randall first, then Julian—the bumps were clearly visible; not a surprise. "Where's Mrs. Rosenthall?"

"Getting us some lunch, I guess;" other than using the beverage line, Julian didn't know what that involved.

"Ah, yes; she would. You are in luck there, boys. She is a highly qualified nurse. Be sure to do whatever she says." He gestured at the ceiling. "She knows enough to have the room dim like this. Bright light can be bad for you after a head injury."

The door opened again; the nurse entered, followed by two kitchen assistants.

"Hello, Mr. Frankel," she said, unsurprised… he's the kind of teacher that always follows up on a student. "Thanks for getting these boys squared away and down here so quickly." She frowned. "Why are you two still sitting out here?" With a shooing gesture, she herded them into the small room. She turned to the lunch bearers: "Put those on a table and push them in." Two bedside tables were standing by the interior window.

Julian went first—it seemed that Randall wanted it that way. The bed by the window drew him at once; being the curious type, keeping an eye on what was happening made sense. I doubt if I'll be falling asleep; all this is overdoing things. Randall is the one who needs this. My job is to keep him company, mostly. Being a new kid and all, it figures they'd want me to help out.

That's a load off my mind… Randall did not want to decide which bed to take. In fact, whatever is left over is all I have coming, if that. It's amazing how friendly and nice he is… I never thought about what he would actually *sound* like. Still fearful of making matters worse somehow, Randall remained silent unless spoken to… at least I'm not panicking. It feels safe to talk to him… best be careful anyway. At least he isn't upset or angry with me. To think that he tried to take the *blame!* I did not expect that at all.

With great interest, Julian watched the small bedside tray moving toward him: hungry was not a strong enough word to describe his condition. Starving was more accurate. Meatloaf, creamed peas 'n onions, a slice of bread and a carton of milk. Looks more like a start than a full lunch. He smiled to himself: no sweat… eventually I'll figure a way to retrieve two sandwiches, cookies and an apple from my locker.

Randall regarded the tray; am I hungry? Maybe, a little. The sack lunch in my locker wouldn't be any better—maybe not as good.

The cafeteria lunches are excellent, generally—I started bringing my own when I realized how much longer I could watch Julian drawing in the atrium—they help disguise what I'm doing; it's relatively easy to use a sandwich or an apple like a duck blind—they help me disappear. Besides, if he ever decides to go somewhere else to draw…

Nurse Rosenthall took note of Randall's hesitation to eat. "You don't have to eat any more than you want, but you should have something. Then you need to rest." His injury is the one to worry about.

"Umm…" This is awkward. "What if you hafta… you know…" Julian sometimes had to visit the boys' room after he finished his lunch.

"Oh, yes. If you need to use the restroom, please tell me—I'll take you to the faculty lounge. It's right next door. I'll leave this door open until after you have eaten." She looked to see if there was another question. "I'll be at my desk if you need anything."

Julian started at once. Excavating the thick slice of meatloaf came first. "Mmm," he nodded. "Not bad." Is there a ketchup packet… nope. Oh well.

Randall stared, fascinated. I've never sat this close. Food was the last thing on his mind… he watched as long as he dared, then looked down at the tray. What am I going to do? Any minute he'll finish eating—then he'll be looking at me. A terrifying thought… what will he think? The yahoo that caused his concussion is sitting right there… I must look as stupid as I feel…

"Not hungry?" Julian dipped his spoon into the peas 'n onions. "Yummy stuff," he advised. I wonder if they let you go for seconds.

Randall snapped out of it. He smiled sheepishly and scooped a spoonful of peas… they had served these before. I like them a lot.

After they'd chewed a while, soft music came through the doorway. The nurse had turned on the radio by her desk. Julian liked whatever it was. Then he figured it out: that's supposed to help us get sleepy. She knows what she's doing, all right. Whenever Mom turns on that kind of music I get sleepy.

About halfway finished, the silence had begun to bother Julian: time to get acquainted. Mark says it's good to meet new people and find out where they come from. That's what we always do in scouts.

"So, where did you move from?" he asked offhandedly.

"Hm?" Randall was taken off guard; he hadn't expected to be asked anything. "Oh… Pullman. Pullman, Washington."

Julian's eyes opened wide. "Gosh. I've never… *Washington?*"

"Washington the *state*. It's way over on the west coast."

"Whoa! I've never known anyone from out west." Oh, wait: Geoff was from out west too. "Is that by California?" Let's see now… we studied that in the sixth grade… He tried to remember the map—

"Sort of—Oregon is in between."

Julian was thrilled. I always wondered what it was like out there… "Are there lots of Indians?" His imagination kicked in. Maybe it's like on TV. All of a sudden, Randall had become very interesting.

Randall chuckled. Dad mentioned being asked a question like this. People around here think there's still a wild west. "You must watch Wagon Train, right?"

"Not every time, but yeah. It's pretty good." Mom likes the wagon master. She says he's like Grandpa Mattson. 'Cept he doesn't have a pot belly.

"I hate to disappoint you, but I've only seen Indians from a distance. Mostly, they live on reservations, as far as I know." Pretty lame answer… what else can I say? "The biggest difference is we have lots of mountains… and the climate is different. Otherwise, it's pretty much the same as here… y'know, roads, cars, airplanes."

Julian nodded. It was good to get this information from a person that knows. I figured they didn't use covered wagons any more, but…

Randall had been put at ease by Julian's open and friendly manner. A huge weight had lifted from somewhere. The unexpected relief unfroze him, enabling his nose to report in: attention returned to the lunch tray. With enthusiasm he addressed the meatloaf: I'm hungry after all.

Julian finished his tray first—more filling than expected, it had triggered the call from Mother Nature he had expected. The usual wise sayings popped into his head, the ones the crew guys used when they had to go—somehow it didn't seem right to use any of those; he'll probably think they're crude or stupid. Well, they are crude and stupid. So, he simply stood and pushed the bedside tray out into the main room.

The Nurse looked up. "Thank you. How do you feel?"

"Full, actually. Thanks."

She pointed to his head.

"Oh…" He reached up and touched his bump. "Yeah. Still hurts some, but…" he held his finger there… "the throbbing has eased up some."

"Do you want an aspirin for the pain?"

Julian frowned, suspicious: "What does that do, exactly?"

"It speeds the circulation and reduces the swelling. With a full stomach, it should work faster."

Hmm… he tried to read her thoughts: she's good at keeping a straight face. "The thing is, is it a good idea, or just something to make me feel good?" I hate being babied.

Boys are so predictable—they have to prove their manhood. "Both. But if you would prefer to feel the pain…"

"Okay." Julian nodded. "But just one, okay?" That should be enough to tell if it works. Mom gave me one of those when I was in Cubs; I don't remember if it did anything. He watched her fill a small glass with water and take a pill out of a bottle on the counter. So… it doesn't have to be kept in a special medicine drawer.

She handed Julian the water and the aspirin. "Pop it in the back of your mouth and swallow quickly, or…" too late.

"Gaaa!" Unfortunately, he had not been paying attention. The taste is *awful*

> ***Bleah!*** < Shaking his head didn't help at all; goose bumps ran up his arms and his eyes watered; he stuck out his tongue… that doesn't help either

"Rinse it down with some more water."

The cold water renewed his pressing problem. "Umm, I need to…"

She had been expecting this. "Follow me. I need to escort you."

He shook his head in a futile attempt to shed the acrid taste from the back of his tongue—aspirin had just been put at the top of his *don't-take-any* list.

—◦—

Wow… wait 'til I tell Sid about this! The Faculty Men's Room! That's something he hasn't done, come in here! It's a lot different from the Boys' Room. It's *teeny*… a small sink for washing hands, one urinal mounted on the wall with a shield on the left side to protect the sink—and a toilet. That's in a regular steel rest room booth, to the right. Not a whole lot of room in here—a line would have to wait outside. Lucky all I have to do is number one… he stepped over to the urinal.

The trouble with new Levi's is they're so hard to unbutton. Everyone told me to get the button kind instead of the zipper. Even Mark said they were the best. They never said why. Julian undid his belt and began: you hafta undo the belt first or the buttons are worse to get into than the stupid skivvies. A break-in period is required.

They hafta be washed a bunch of times so they're not so stiff. Then they're easier to use; some of the guys in P.E. just tug on both sides at the top and *p-p-p-p!* the buttons come undone all by themselves. I tried that once—not a chance. How many times do they have to be washed? Problem is, you can't ask anybody or they'll think you're weird.

Unbuttoned at last, he stepped forward and pulled the skivvies down from the top as usual; skivvy front door openings are a pain. That's another reason you have to undo the belt; you can't pull down the top of your skivvies if the belt isn't unbuckled. That's true with a zipper fly too, actually, unless you use the stupid opening. He frowned: why do they call them *flies*, anyway? Words like that really annoyed—they don't make any sense. Fly? How? Where are the wings?

About halfway done, the door opened: a big heavy man came in—Julian had never seen him before. Must be a teacher though—he took a glance at Julian, nodded, and worked his way into the toilet booth. Reminds me of the French cook at Camp Walker; sideways or straight in, either way's a squeeze.

Small bathrooms have certain acoustic qualities; every minute sound is reflected and seems magnified. Julian had never had occasion to be this close to a fat middle aged man relieving himself; picturing in his mind what was making the noise coming around, under and over the partition less than a foot away upstaged everything. Entertaining, certainly, if a little scary—students weren't supposed to be in here. The stream that noisily pierced the bowl of water was impressive… not a tinkle. It brought to mind what he had witnessed on the landscape crew—this guy could match Zack, easy. Big guys whizzing is an amazing thing to see—and to *hear*.

Julian buttoned up and stepped over to the sink—he always washed up when anyone else was around; otherwise, why bother. He made a quick job of it, hoping to leave before the teacher came out—there wasn't room for two at the sink. Didn't *quite* make it… before he could turn to leave, the mountainous man emerged from the booth. Julian smiled sheepishly, and acknowledged the man's nod. Funny mustache… Julian opened to door to the lunch area and took a step…but before the door closed behind him, a bizarre sound—

"*Huhm-h-hrwabnobble…*" the man made a fake throat clearing sound in a futile attempt to mask a rather huge fart.

Julian's eyes went wide and he did a beeline for the lounge door. He didn't look to see if anyone else had heard that—but they had to, didn't they? There must be a dozen teachers in here… I hope no one thinks it was me.

He made it to the door with a straight face, but it was work. As the faculty door closed he took a deep breath and sighed in relief; the aroma in the cafeteria was complex, but it smelled like lunch; the exit from the Faculty Men's Room had been made in the nick of time.

The problem now is controlling myself: if I break out laughing, everyone will wonder why. They'll think I'm pretty weird, laughing all by myself. It figures that someone will recognize me; even if I don't eat lunch in here, people I have class with do. Lucky the nurse's door isn't far away—maybe I can scoot back in before anyone sees me.

Why do I think farts are so *funny*? The thing about farts is that you have to be there—farts are one of those things that aren't funny to hear *about*. Besides, people don't go around talking about farts—that would be kind of weird. I won't be able to laugh until I'm home and no one else is around.

Always, for as long as he could remember, farts made him laugh. Especially when I was little—Grandpa got into trouble doing that and had to go out onto the porch for punishment. He used those made up words too… that was one of Julian's earliest and fondest memories. Maybe I am weird.

I'm pleased with this one—drawing Randall is more fun than I expected. Julian had gotten permission to get his sketchbook after

Randall fell asleep. I fibbed a little and told the nurse I wanted to jot a few things down before I forgot. She said that would be okay—I'm not supposed to do any reading, though. He glanced over his shoulder... maybe I can do one of her after I finish this one. I'm supposed to be in Art class right now anyway... I hate missing that most of all. Doing this will help.

He focused on the ear and how the hairline ran along behind... wait a minute... I *know* that ear! The small mole, the uneven line... I *studied* that. His mind raced through a series of mental images he had filed away... Registration! I *knew* it! I stood right behind him in line. What a relief! That's been bugging me all afternoon. No wonder it was so easy—I already know this ear. Interesting nose—a little larger than average, but straight. It's different to draw eyes closed—that's a first. He leaned closer and squinted... eyebrows and eyelashes—you don't get to look at those up close every day... they're dark brown, like mine; too bad the light is so dim in here...

Randall was having a familiar dream...

...he was hiding behind a huge oak tree. Nels and his bunch are on the prowl as usual... they haven't spotted me yet. that's the way I want to keep it. especially since I don't have anything on again. every once in a while that happens and I don't know why... I'll be someplace and discover that I forgot to put on my pants. why would that be? how to get somewhere without being seen is always the problem.

I can hear them yakking and laughing it up, bragging about something. that's what they always do... it means they're on the lookout for someone to pick on... someone like me... peek around the tree and see if they're heading this way... oh no! Petey spotted me. he's the short one... what can I do... can I climb up? no way. I have to make a run for it...

why are my legs so... they feel like lead... are they following? yes they are... I'll duck around that corner... rest a minute... maybe my legs will get back their strength. peek and see how far away they—

wow! it's *Him!*

He *stopped* them: He's standing there, hands held out wide, blond hair shaking away. where did He come from? I don't believe my eyes… I need to look again. Nels is running away… so are Petey and Fred. it's a miracle. suddenly the golden haired Boygod turned… He's coming straight at me with a huge smile… what am I gonna do? He'll see me—the brown eyes, the black eyelashes zoomed close … oh no! He'll see my huge hard on…

Randall jerked awake and sat up—

Julian sat back and grinned. "Good morning in the afternoon!"

"Wha—what's going on?!" Randall was disoriented… the face in my dream was so *real*… and when I woke up, it was right *there*—the *same* face… Julian Forrest's face. "Mmm…" he felt kind of stupid. "I guess I went to sleep after all."

"Yep… 'bout an hour ago."

"Wow…" I didn't expect to do that… he rotated his head to clear the minor crick in his neck. "What time is it, anyway?"

Julian looked at the clock above the nurse's desk. "3:15 School's almost over."

Randall touched his bump… still there.

The door opened; the nurse had heard them talking. She focused on Randall. "How do you feel?"

"Fine, I guess."

"You can come out into the main room. Your mothers will be here soon to take you home. I'd like to check a few things again before they arrive." She led them out.

Woo… the lights are brighter than I expected. Julian had to squint for a second to adjust. The nurse poked a thermometer into his mouth again; Randall got one too. Nurses and mothers and their thermometers! He rolled his eyes and looked at Randall with a shrug.

Randall suppressed a giggle… don't want to bite the thermometer in two. He watched the nurse wrap the blood pressure cuff around his arm. What does that show? I never thought about that before. Luckily he'd been able to sit down and hide his problem before it was noticed. With any luck, it would recede quickly.

Julian spotted a small mirror on the wall. An idea popped up.

"I can't find a thing that needs fixing, boys." She pretended to be disappointed. "I have no choice but to let you go home." She paused for a courteous laugh, but it wasn't forthcoming. "But you need to be careful for a few days. No P.E. the rest of the week. No running, no jumping, no wrestling around. Don't read any more than you have to, don't watch too much TV. Your brain needs to make its own repairs. If you give it too much work, it can't do a good job. Understand?" Her stern I-mean-business look underlined the instruction. She held it until they nodded. "Good. Your mothers will be here any minute." She returned to her desk.

Julian waited for Randall to look his way. "C'mere. Let's compare bumps!" He stepped over to the mirror with a big grin.

Without hesitation Randall leapt up. Standing next to Julian didn't freak him out like he expected. The bumps were not in the same exact place, but it was possible to stand so both could be seen at the same time. They studied the reflection briefly.

Julian touched his lightly and then reached over to touch Randall's. "Hmm." I'm not sure. "You try it."

What can I say? "Feel pretty much the same, really." Actually, Julian's felt warm… *very* warm. It would have been nice to touch it longer, but…

"Wait. Stay right there." My three-ring binder has a ruler.

> Klack! < Julian preferred precision when it pertained to body parts—whatever they might be. He returned to the mirror and measured the reflection of Randall's bump. Then he tried to measure his… "My arm is in the way." He passed the ruler. "You do it."

He measured the reflection. "Seven eighths. What did you get?"

"One inch. You win."

Randall had his doubts. The distance from the mirror could distort the true answer. He turned to Julian and measured the real thing. "Ah, I thought so. Yours is an inch too."

"Really?" Julian took the ruler and measured Randall's… very close. "I think you have a little more… maybe a sixteenth…"

"Call it a tie."

Julian grinned wide. "Put 'er there!" He reached out and gave Randall a vigorous handshake.

The exact same sensation as before… maybe even more powerful. It caused Randall to swell automatically; his face felt flushed… I must be blushing like crazy. Fortunately, Julian had stepped over to put his ruler away. I don't think he saw anything… he glanced at the nurse. She was writing stuff down and didn't see either. He returned to the chair quickly and sat. Lucked out that time, for sure. Crossing my legs will take care of hiding things; I'll be okay by the time Mom gets here.

Eloise Hallstrom was mildly impressed by what she had seen at the school, and by the other boy's mother. Pleasant enough, certainly, but not a bridge player. Her boy is polite and well mannered. She glanced over at Randall. He still seems dazed. The nurse said he'd be fine as long as he didn't overdo and reinjure himself. He can watch television for a few days instead of practicing his music. She said that would be fine. All is well…

Her train of thought returned to that last hand… something about Roberta… she's usually better at bidding. Contract Bridge requires concentration. I wonder if anything's wrong at home…

A state of absolute euphoria had swallowed Randall whole. This was the best day of his life, hands down. He had been unbelievably wrong about Julian—he is so much more, so much better than I ever guessed. And he likes me! Well, not the way I want, not yet… but…

the handshakes and… *feeling his bump.* Oh boy oh boy. Maybe he'll let me do that again… The fantasy machine was gearing up for a huge night.

His excitement, fortunately, was hidden under the books on his lap. He did a test… ooo. Little did his mother know that he was able to lift three books *and* his notebook with a single pulse. Lap calisthenics is a fun diversion when it isn't possible to "take things in hand."

—∞—

"I was impressed by the nurse," Francine Forrest had not thought to find out what the school offered in the way of first aid.

Julian nodded his agreement. "She even gave us a free lunch." Ohmygosh! My lunch! It's still in my locker—two of Hazel's homemade cookies are in that sack.

"That's nice…" they must have a way to cover that. Cafeterias always make extra, don't they? She looked over at his forehead. "How long did she say you'll have that knot?"

"A week, prob'ly." Too bad it's so visible. The one at camp was partly covered by my hair. He frowned; how are you supposed to tell people that you got a concussion by running head on into somebody? Without looking like an idiot, that is—way to go, dum-dum. "I'm sorry, Mom." The nurse practically ordered her to take me to the doctor. "How much does it cost to see Doctor Overstreet?"

"Don't worry about that."

"What about work? Did it cause any trouble to leave early?"

"No. Thanks for asking." Geraldine wanted to come along, but I wouldn't hear of it. "I can go back to the office once you're all tucked in."

Tucked in? I don't want to go to *bed,* of all things: tonight is the Flaming Arrow meeting!

"I can still go to scouts, though, right?"

She turned to face him. "I thought the first meeting was next week."

"I'm in Flaming Arrow now. We hafta meet ahead of time and plan stuff." Now I understand why the meetings go so well all the time. Mark is super smart about things like that.

"As long as you're not running and jumping." Being under Mark's supervision made all the difference.

"Mark is ordering pizza—we get to meet at his house." That was something he had been waiting to do for a long time: go inside Mark's house. He had spent a lot of time thinking about that. I figure that since I'm the new guy, I won't have much to do but listen… and look around. I have a plan figured out already.

He touched the bump. Hmm… maybe this will come in handy… what if I hafta lay down or something? Maybe he'll let me lay down on his bed…

Now, now… don't go getting any wild ideas… Inside guy was on duty again. There were times when that was lucky; but there were times when he was a major pain.

Francine kept silent while Julian sorted out his experience… he didn't need a scolding—he's kicking himself plenty hard already. He always punishes himself more than I would. It was an accident, after all. Unusual—he's not a clumsy boy by nature, like some of his friends.

She had recognized the other boy's mother at once. Geraldine took great pains with her last summer. We found a very nice property near the Country Club. Her husband didn't much care, as long as it was within walking distance of the University; typical professor. It didn't come as a surprise that the woman didn't remember me—it was three months ago. Geraldine showed the property—all I did was background research.

"The Hallstrom boy is nice… seemed rather quiet."

"Yeah, nice kid; kinda shy… well, being new and all, that's what you'd expect: they just moved here…" He turned to her with the interesting news: "they're from *Washington* the *state!"* Julian considered that—when you think about it, that made being in an accident even harder for him. "He tried to take the blame." That was impressive. "He took a long nap, so I didn't get to talk with him very much—but we both have Mr. Frankel for Biology."

"Oh, that's interesting. I think his father teaches that at the university." A special kind—I overheard him telling Geraldine.

He turned to his mother, amazed. "How do you know that?" Every once in a while she pulls one like that—surprises my pants off sometimes, what she knows.

Francine enjoyed teasing Julian—it was harder to do all the time; being informed was one of the benefits of being a parent.

"Mothers know lots of things," she grinned.

Stupid question deserves a stupid answer… Mom usually outfoxes me. He liked that, actually. It was a game they had played all his life… it reminded him that he was a very lucky kid; he had just about the best mom around. He looked out the window, happy about life in general. Except for missing those classes, things turned out great today… I probably missed something important in Geometry. Otherwise I'll be okay. And I have a new friend. That's always a good thing.

Julian shifted his thoughts back to Randall. Say, maybe I can invite him to scouts sometime. Is he too old to join? Hum… do they ever let kids visit? I'll ask Mark. I think he would fit right in… maybe he was a scout out west, like Geoff…

9 The Flaming Arrows meet

Julian was early for the Flaming Arrow meeting on purpose. This way I'll have a minute with Mark before everyone gets here—as the low man on the totem pole, I won't get much attention once the meeting gets going. Besides, since I live a few houses up the street, it figures I'd get here first. For once he had won an argument with his Inside guy—he's *always* chicken… afraid I'll slip into my old ways. I compromised on what to wear—I wanted to put on my Bermuda shorts. Instead, I'm wearing what I had on today at school. Inside guy won there. Before pushing the doorbell button he studied the door, the handle, the address numbers… every detail is important. The porch light is so cool. Okay: here goes… three deep breaths… he pressed the button.

> *Bling-bling, bling-bling; bling-bling, bling-bling* <

Neato… his doorbell plays that tune. Grandpa's mantle clock plays that.

The door opened wide— "Hey, there he is!" Mark was delighted to see Julian—I haven't seen him since the last Scrapbook session. "Come in, come in. You're the first to arrive.

Julian felt vindicated; the big grin on Mark's face had proven his point. He took another deep breath… I've been waiting to do this for a long time. Going inside this house was like entering a shrine. Be cool, Julian.

Mark noticed the bump at once. "Hey, what happened to you?"

"Hm?" Julian had forgotten about his forehead.

"Your head!" The storm incident at camp came to mind at once.

"Oh, that." Julian smiled sheepishly. "I ran into this kid between classes by mistake." He shrugged. "No big deal."

Mark frowned. "A bump like that *is* a big deal, Julian. Don't go playing the tough guy with something like that." His boys often did this—play tough because they didn't want to look like a wimp. "What did they tell you at school?"

"The nurse said we had a Class 2 something or other. She made us both lie down for the rest of the day." Overdoing it in my opinion; now I'm probably behind in Geometry.

"Good for her. Did you tell her about hitting your head at camp?"

"That's why she made me stay."

"Good." He held Julian by the shoulders and stared him straight in the face. "You are signing up for the First Aid badge, first chance you get: hear me?" He waited for a nod. "You'll find out about concussions. You don't want to take any chances with those, Julian." Mark experienced a strange, unexpected sensation… this is not the little boy I held by the shoulders at camp. I noticed that at the store, too—he isn't so little any more.

Julian knew what Mark was doing and why; it didn't stop him from being thrilled. Having Mark hold him was a rare exotic pleasure any time, for any reason. Never mind the risk… he waited for as long as he dared before agreeing. "Okay," he nodded. The tingle down below had started.

"Right. Now let's go into the kitchen and get you something to drink." He closed the door and led the way.

What a nice surprise: Mark is in some kind of leisure pants, almost like a jogger's outfit. The fabric clings tight; around the back, it makes his butt look so darn *sexy*… I didn't get a look at the front.

Just don't get caught staring, okay? Inside guy warned.

Don't worry: I have lots of things to look at. Julian had made a list in his head of what he'd want to remember. Everything about Mark was important, not just his pants.

Julian appeared calm, polite and interested on the outside—inside he was jumping with joy and doing somersaults. Because I came so early, Mark is giving me a tour of the whole house—he didn't want to just sit and talk. Julian's photo eye recorded everything—especially the bedroom and the bathroom… those details will come in handy when fantasy hour comes along. Asking personal questions is off limits naturally, but twin beds? And the bathroom—it looks like the one at camp: only shaving gear. Where does his wife put her stuff? I thought I'd see lots of female things like Mom has… our bathroom is crammed *full* of her stuff.

The hallway is lined with photos—sort of a scrapbook substitute. Lots of scout and school photos, including some from when Mark was in Troop Nine.

"This is my scoutmaster," Mark put his finger below the tall figure at the end of the last row. "I wish I had more photos from back then. This was taken when I was a First Class." He put his finger below a small face in the front row.

Julian bent close to get a good look… this is what he looked like at my age. Everyone is so small… but I can tell it's Mark… something about the shape of his face… he was hot back then too… Julian felt a sudden buzz run down his spine. Standing close like this is so wonderful… his voice is so mellow… it causes a faint tickle under my left ear.

Careful, now, Inside guy warned.

I know! It's a good thing I wore my new Levi's tonight. Between the voice and the aroma of his dream man less than six inches away, Julian was going a little crazy inside. Little J was about two thirds up already.

"This is Tip O'Malley, my Patrol Leader…" Mark ran his fingertip along the front row; the Panthers were in front, since they were the high pointers that year. He laughed: "and this is Terry; Terry Nelson."

The kid in the center was overweight. Reminds me of Bruce.

"You remember him; Terry's the one who came up with that campfire jingle I told you guys about." The blank look on Julian's face revealed that he didn't remember. "You know, 'The Fizz, the Fuzz, the Fizzy Fuzz?'"

"The Farting Post song!"

"Right. Terry was quite a character. Great sense of humor, full of jokes—and full of farts." Some of the sounds that kid could make! He moved on. "This is my Eagle picture… and this is my Graduation picture."

Wow… these are special. Julian concentrated hard: these had to be in his memory, ready for quick reference. The Eagle photo especially—a full length snapshot in his summer uniform: short pants. Julian leaned in for a close look while Mark continued going down the hall… wow… *wow*—

Oop! Mark had opened a door and started down a set of stairs; Julian hurried to catch up. What's down here? Washer, dryer… workbench… a few boxes… everything's in its place. Just like the upstairs: nothing loose… no piles of magazines or books. Mark and his wife are super tidy types. No way to tell what the last project was. What do they do at home?

"I don't do a lot down here, but I like to fix things when I can—saves money so I can throw parties, y'see." He pointed to the bottle in Julian's hand. "You ready for another Nesbitt's?"

Julian looked down… plenty left. "I'm okay for now." I don't want to fill up on pop. Throw parties? That had to be an exaggeration; Mark never throws parties. I'd have been able to tell, since I live so close. Maybe he means scout stuff like tonight.

"Let's head back upstairs. The gang will be here any time." He stood back so Julian could go first.

"Okay." So, the tour is over… except for one room…must be hers. Maybe she has her own bathroom and bedroom? On the way up the stairs, Julian's imagination set to work while he took the liberty of making a minor adjustment; his eyes had remained on Mark's front side too long. The lounge pants are more like pajamas than sweat pants... not wearing any skivvies.

It's good manners for a host to go up the stairs last—it prevents the guest being left behind in the dark when the light is turned off. Even so, walking up a set of stairs behind Julian would have to affect anyone who paid any attention at all to what was in front of him. Even if one's mind is on something else, as Mark's was, when such a sight is that close, it makes an impression. He was not thinking along those lines at all, and was not prepared for a sudden unexpected urge—one he had not had for a long time. He forced his attention to shift to the handrail.

Unknown to Mark, something *subconscious* was going on; following behind Julian had another element—a secret pleasure. Certain sights and sensations get filed away deep inside the brain. Mark had a file—several files—that he knew nothing about; they were tucked away for future reference and use, unknown and undetected by his conscious mind. One such file had Julian data exclusively. Mark did not know that the file existed; nor did he know it was open wide, hungrily gulping fresh new information. The input received a week ago at Francine's supper table was joined by a fresh image of Julian's remarkably well formed derrière.

Frankie was having trouble paying attention. He hadn't gone to summer camp, so he didn't have much to contribute to the proceedings. Thanks to the fates, I had to work all summer—otherwise I'd have lost my job. I needed the money, pure and simple.

So, as the official Bugler, he had not been there to provide the wake-up call mornings, nor Taps, the lights out command. *Lucky for me they're a forgiving lot.*

"You want a car, you get to pay for it," his father said, a thousand times at least. His father was a generous man, but meant what he said. *Insurance, gas, repairs… always something. That reminds me: I need a new distributor cap. I should have enough…*

On the other hand, having wheels meant being able to do lots of things—when he wanted, with whom he wanted. That thought led his eye back to Danny. *Hmm… too busy being a big shot. We haven't found time to see who won our bet. Better do that pretty soon before we fade back to winter white. I didn't get as many tanning sessions in as I expected—sort of tricky in town. If Danny's face is any guide, he might have won. But I want to see the proof; the bet was specific: the one with the best tanned butt wins. What was the prize… probably who gets to go first.*

'Going first' meant shooting first, of course. Frankie didn't care much about the order—he enjoyed the doing as well as the being done. *But we had to have some kind of prize.*

This line of thought had caused his favorite discomfort… he crossed his legs again. That obscured the bulge effectively on a sofa or in an armchair. Checking out Danny had awoken his pride and joy, surprise, surprise. Another factor contributed to his condition: the new kid in the patrol. Julian was appointed to help Nick out with all the reports and minutes. *He's the one with a tan—too bad I don't have a bet with him.*

Danny used to talk about him… I'll bet he got to fill in for me at camp… Danny can't control himself when he's seriously horny. That wavy blond hair and what's hiding below would tempt anyone. So far I haven't been able to tell much about what he's got down there…

"… Speaking of that," Mark looked over at Frankie. "Have you anyone in mind for yours?"

A long pause… the silence caused Frankie to look up—oh-oh. Everyone is looking at me. "Oh… uh, what?"

"Welcome back to the meeting." Mark cleared his throat. "We're talking about the change in command, remember? Are you going to train your replacement, or do we have to put an ad in the paper?"

Frankie blushed. "Sorry. I haven't done anything about that." Well, it is months away…

"Do you know if anyone already in the troop would work?" He held up his copy of the Troop Roster.

Frankie flipped to that sheet in his packet. "Lessee, Don is in Marching Band." He scanned the list.

"Can he play a bugle?"

"Dunno." He had no excuse for this. Mark told me at the Parade to figure this out and I clean forgot.

"You will have a name before the troop meets next week?" Mark's question was an order.

Frankie nodded.

> ***Bling-bling, bling-bling; bling-bling, bling-bling…*** < The Westminster chime melody burst from the wall.

Julian flinched; wow… the doorbell fixture was just above his head.

"Pizza time!" Mark gestured for someone to follow him to the door. "I need a hand." While I pay the delivery boy, the patrol can take everything into the kitchen.

Everyone followed, eager to be of assistance.

Julian had been looking forward to this… he always had an appetite nowadays. One slice from each box: Pepperoni, Hawaiian Delight, and Gino's Special Combination—that's one I've never tried before. I don't get pizza very often. Mom always gets the

Hawaiian or Chicken Triple Cheese; I don't much care for that one, myself. Boy, does this smell great!

As he took the first bite he looked around the table… it's so good to be here with the guys, sort of like being back at camp—I'm sitting right by Mark, just like I did at camp, with Nick on my other side. Only we're not in uniform tonight—fine with me, especially considering what Mark is wearing.

Tom, the Junior Assistant Scoutmaster, oldest in the group, is directly across. His best friend—and steady boyfriend now, is Nick, the Troop Scribe. I got to know them real well at camp, especially since I'm Nick's assistant. I get to take over the Scribe job when he graduates. I'm so lucky! youngest ever to join the Flaming Arrow patrol.

Sitting next to Tom is Danny—he's in training to take over Tom's job. Now he's the Senior Patrol Leader… he lives in the house right behind mine. The difference tonight is that other guy—the Troop Bugler. He's next to Danny, at the other end of the table. I don't know him at all—he's a senior, like Tom.

"So, how did you get the bump?" Nick had missed hearing about it.

Julian finished chewing his mouthful before answering. "I ran into this guy in the hall today; had to spend the afternoon in the Nurse's room."

"Huh." Nick looked closer. "Must have been some collision."

"Yeah—he was knocked out." Julian didn't really want to talk about it. The bump wasn't exactly a sign of nimble footwork. What was I gonna ask him? Oh, yeah… the bikinis. Can't do that now… Nick's about as smart as they come, and Julian could talk to him about almost anything. But not with Mark right here; that would be pretty stupid.

His attention shifted across the table—look at Tom's pizza! Piled high with extra tomato and onions… Mark's is loaded up too. Man: how can they open their mouth wide enough? Mark just gave Tom a wink. What's that about? Maybe I should add some on mine... Julian selected a few rings of raw onion from the plate in the center of the table. That's another thing Mom never has around. Kind of nifty the way they crunch.

Frankie gave Danny's knee a double nudge under the table—their old signal. Had to be cool about it—everyone's so close it's impossible to say anything out loud.

Danny feigned ignorance at first—the signal wasn't expected, but it should have been. How could I forget? We haven't talked about our bet! Thanks to Tony, I clean forgot. Frankie doesn't know about Tony and me... no one does. Danny had a short tug of war with his conscience... he was stuck. If I don't honor it, Frankie will find out about Tony. That settled it: lucky we're sitting at the same corner. When no one was looking, he returned a triple nudge... that was the signal for "you bet!" After the meeting would be perfect. He was eager to show off his tan buns, actually. I suffered a lot to get those; tonight will be payday. Wait until I show him what I learned at camp! Frankie doesn't know about Geoff. He fanned his legs to loosen Little D up—his other appetite was vying for attention, now that Frankie had brought it up.

"After we finish eating," Mark announced, "we'll draw the campout assignments." The schedule of troop meetings was now firm; this particular team is probably the best one I'll ever have.

Tom delivered a deep loud belch. Terrific thing, carbonation.

"Well said," Mark nodded. "That reminds me—if anyone has a need, the Farting Post is down the hallway, second door."

Everyone laughed heartily except Frankie.

Danny leaned over... "tell ya later." Frankie didn't know about the Farting Post because he wasn't at camp.

Tom stiffened... then sat back. "False alarm." He popped the last enormous bite into his mouth and got up to get another slice of Gino's Combination.

Mark had a twinkle in his eye… a nice one was brewing. He had learned years ago how to direct everything to the lower exit. Odd what you learn in scouts… the fellowship at the table tonight is just like being back at Camp Walker. Last summer was one of his best camps if not *the* best. This bunch is like family.

KP went like clockwork; Mark concentrated the leftover slices into a single box and popped them into the fridge. Tom and Nick collected the dirty dishes and proceeded to the sink. Julian waited for Mark to hand him a dishtowel. It was just like camp; too bad we can't do this every night… the glimpses when Mark moves back and forth! Whoever bought him those leisure pants deserves an award.

Frankie pulled Danny to the side. "How about I give you a ride home?" He raised his eyebrows up and down a few times.

"I live right around the corner, ya know," being coy on purpose—Frankie is needy tonight.

"Gotta give you a ride in the car first—I souped it up some," he gave Danny a small punch on the shoulder.

"Well, that's different," he nodded. A glance over his shoulder told him no one was tuned in. "Need to go by your place on the way," he winked, sealing the deal; Frankie's room is a lot better than mine. More comforts and less parents.

"Here we go," Mark had a small half-gallon bucket in his hand. "This year we're drawing lots. Each piece of paper has a month and a patrol on it. You are drawing the campout you will go on as an official from the Flaming Arrow patrol. You'll report to the troop how they perform. You will be able to give individual points and demerits. But they have to be explained at the troop meeting after your campout." He looked around for questions. None came, so he went around the room; each person drew a slip.

Julian was sitting next to Nick as usual, with his notebook ready. His slip of paper read: *May: Tiger patrol…* woo. Who do I know in the Tigers? He showed the slip to Nick.

"May. Lucky draw—you'll probably have good weather." He checked his: *April.* He nodded. More than likely rain, but April is okay. March is the one you don't want.

"Read out your assignments so Nick can put them down." Mark felt one coming. "Be right back…" he hurried down the hall.

Frankie looked at Danny…what's going on? Why is everyone paying attention to Mark? After a few moments of silence,

> ***Baa-aa-ri-IP!*** <

Mark's backside exploded with considerable force—a push halfway through, causing it to grow louder at the finish.

Everyone in the living room roared with laughter. The bathroom acoustic amplified and added a slight echo. They applauded as he came back into the room. Julian looked at Mark in amazement. While it was funny—farts always are—it seemed so strange… Mark actually enjoyed them, took pride in them. But only with the Flaming Arrow Patrol. It was that way at camp, too. It was a side of him that the rest of the troop never saw. What an odd way to be special.

It made Julian feel privileged, in a way. But how to join in the "fun" himself was a problem: he didn't have much experience. At home, it wasn't allowed. His mom was just like grandma about farts. She always punished grandpa by making him go out on the porch. It was funny—I think maybe he did it on purpose. He always gave me a grin and a wink on his way out. Except for last summer at camp, Julian couldn't remember ever cutting one loose. What *causes* those, anyway? I don't feel a thing back there.

"Ten point bonus for being the first!" Tom cheered. His wasn't ready yet. As former members of the Panther Patrol, he and Mark did their best to honor the special Panther after dinner tradition.

Mark took a gracious bow and sat in his easy chair. After the laughter died down he spoke. "Now, for the good of the order, sort of: on Saturday I will be shopping for a car. If anyone is interested, I'd appreciate company."

There was a pause.

"Y'see, I don't know much about buying cars. I want to get one that will come in handy for scouts… y'know, for campouts and day hikes." The expertise he needed was right here—Tom and Frankie, certainly.

Tom leapt at the opportunity. "Man, yeah! *Cool!* I can borrow our car, I'm pretty sure." I helped Mark run errands once before when his wife had the car.

Darn it! Frankie couldn't join in. He had to work Saturdays now that school had started.

"Great. Lunch is on me afterwards." He looked around to show that everyone was invited. Half a dozen boys piling in and out of various cars is bound to be a lot of fun. Saturdays are supposed to be fun. I hope the salesmen can handle the challenge.

"Ten o'clock all right?" Tom wanted to sleep in. Nick is planning to "party" a little after the game.

"Perfect." Mark stood. "It's a school night, guys. Better call it a day." Too bad the party has to end; he was savvy enough to know when to send kids home. It was a good meeting—a great start to the year.

As the boys filed out he stopped Julian. "How's the bump?" He bent close to look.

"Okay… it doesn't hurt any." Mark can look and touch all night. He let his eyes fall downward—the temptation to pull those leisure pants down was hard to resist … they seem to invite it. One day…

Mark studied the bump closely… it's about the same. "Did you put any ice on it?"

Julian shook his head.

"Sometimes that helps the swelling. Ask your mom about doing that before you go to bed." He gave his signature shoulder pinch.

Julian had been hoping he'd do that…one of my favorite sensations—the special tickle behind my balls. Only Mark caused it, always with that pinch. Little J likes it a lot too. He continued to gaze at Mark's mid-section.

That's long enough... Inside guy had come to the rescue again: better not get caught staring.

"Okay," Julian looked up with his signature happy face grin.

"See you on Tuesday night,"Mark stepped onto the porch to wave good night. Julian's sunny smile always caused him to respond in kind.

"Can I come on Saturday?"

"You bet! I'm counting it." Mark did not mean to exclude Julian at all—everyone in the patrol needs to be there. Watching him skip down the steps is a delight. Boy oh boy, did he ever grow the last two months. Remarkable. Francine must be sprinkling Vigoro on his breakfast.

Returning to his living room had an unexpected effect. Closing the door brought silence... the sudden quiet was like a punch in the gut. He made a beeline for the den. After spending the last two and a half hours with his boys, silence was not welcome—not welcome at all. Stopping to think about why won't help. Filling the empty house with sound is essential. What's on TV tonight?

The lingering aroma of pizza was a mixed blessing...aha! A glass of red! That will help. Mark never indulged himself in front of the boys. That could lead to requests that he didn't dare grant. When I was in high school, we conned a teacher into letting us have a glass of beer at a picnic one time... the poor guy. We never let him alone after that. No one ever told, of course... why wreck a perfect thing? He must have been glad to see us graduate. That's one mistake I won't make. Cutting farts with them is risky enough. He did an about face and headed for the wineglass rack.

—∾—

Tonight felt different. Julian had pulled the drawings out from behind the clothes in his closet, his usual ritual. The meeting supplied fresh images—the first in a long time. Mark wearing lounge pants especially. They showed off more than the fancy clothes at the store—o' course, he looks sexy in anything he wears. These were baggy and loose around the legs, almost like pajamas. I wanted to cuddle up next to him and watch TV. The inside guy poked me good though, and I snapped out of it.

He savored the memory of the evening, replaying it from the minute Mark opened the door. How fabulous to be there—and have Mark all to myself. It brought back memories of the cabin. The best moments of his life were at the end of the day when just the two of them were there, alone in the cabin. Sometimes three, if I count Inside guy. To be fair, I have to do that.

Darn right. If it wasn't for me, you'd have been tossed out after the first night.

That's true; you saved me more than once from doing the wrong thing. One night I almost snuck into Mark's bed. Talk about *stupid!* That's the worst one. But a few times, like tonight, I was *right* to do something. If I hadn't gone looking for Mark that one time, I would never have found out about *him*, and what he meant. He was the person that Mark loved—and still loves, even though he's dead. If I hadn't…

Yeah, yeah, you're right. You don't need to brag about it.

His attention returned to the drawings. I remember the night that I showed these to Mark; it was the high point in my life. I was scared to death he wouldn't like them—at first I thought he hated them, but I was wrong. I still don't understand it—he got tears looking at them; I almost fainted—I forgot to breathe, I was so shocked.

"I just figured something out!" I *saw* him! Tonight, when Mark showed me his bedroom! The picture on the dresser!

Yeah, and you almost went over to look at it…

I wish I had, to tell the truth. If I ever get the chance again, I will, too.

He reached forward to touch the drawing—this was where Mark was looking when he started to cry… well, not *cry* exactly… Julian closed his eyes and remembered the moment—I was on my knees, right next to him—he reached out for me. We sat there a long time in silence, studying the drawings. That's when I looked up and saw his face. Julian had never seen such a profound and complex expression on anyone's face before. But emotionally he understood it somehow. Mark was sad and happy at the same time and a tear ran down his face.

Mark said it helped him remember stuff. Suddenly, these drawings had become more than Julian intended, more than he understood—even though he had drawn them… I felt special while drawing them, but this is more than that. One day I'll understand—I made a promise to myself about that. Meanwhile, I hafta keep these safe in my closet… That's what Mark asked me to do… he didn't want to take them home. He didn't want anyone else to see them. Only Mark and I have ever seen them; that's the way it would always be. Julian never felt a need to show off his drawings—he preferred to give them away. These are Mark's, not mine.

Julian looked down at his lap. Little J has gone to sleep. Huh. The usual reason for looking at these is gone now. I was gonna imagine how those lounge clothes would look, and… oh well. Maybe I'll do that tomorrow.

He got off the bed and returned the cardboard panels to the back of his closet. After turning off the light, a final thought: I should get some of those lounge clothes. They look comfy. Julian didn't want to admit the real reason—whenever it was possible, he tried to do whatever Mark did.

OOee! Julian's eyes popped open: pressure in his lower intestine had formed unexpectedly. I was almost asleep… oh-oh… I know what's going on! He stuffed a pillow back there to muffle the sound. He didn't know if it would be a noisy one or not… One thing he did not have at home—would *never* have—is a farting post…

Ooop!

He giggled guiltily. She couldn't have heard that one—it wasn't very big. Mom is as bad as grandma when it comes to farts. Hey, I just figured it out: that's the reason we never have Gino's Special Combination pizza… or onion slices.

10 Tuna fish and bologna

Friday already! The week had *zoomed* by. Julian was glad because of what was going to happen tomorrow: the Flaming Arrows get to help Mark pick out a *car*! Any chance to be around Mark automatically put everything else aside. I don't know anything about cars… I need to go along just to learn; someday I'll have to know about that stuff.

Lunch in one hand, 3-ring binder in the other, he had reached the big tree—his new noontime perch. Giant roots fanned out from the trunk, creating a cozy place to settle into. Old trees like this are special—like grandparents, sort of. Sitting outdoors in the shade is so much nicer… the fresh air, the light breeze… open space is great for drawing. You can see the sky; shadows make everything more interesting. As long as the weather holds out, I'm gonna draw outside. He sat cross legged and made his usual lunchtime arrangements: sketchpad and pencil at the ready, lunch sack open on the left, first sandwich in hand, wax paper peeled back.

This is more like it! Lots of room to spread out—I don't hafta squeeze everything onto a bench top. *mmm…* tuna fish today… *yum.* > *sniff-sniff* < The smell made him feel good—like everything is going the way it's supposed to. For as long as I can remember, Mom made these on Friday. He reviewed yesterday's progress while he tackled the sandwich.

Randall had watched Julian draw all week in secret, hiding out of sight as always. Completely frustrating… impossible to find a vantage point. He's so far away it's sort of futile. Binoculars and telephoto lenses made no sense—too impractical and risky. Monday's collision and the aftermath had complicated everything. Julian tried to take the blame, but I know better: it was all my fault. I feel so guilty; all week I just wanted to hide. I even went to history class late so he wouldn't see me—he doesn't realize I'm in the same class. I stayed as invisible as I could… I'm pretty good at that. But the more I thought about it, the more I remembered how friendly he was in the nurse's room. Today I'm going to take a *huge* risk: allow myself to be seen. I worked up enough courage, finally—but going over there uninvited is out of the question.

Jackson High's front entrance featured three sets of double doors; a set of eight divided glass windowpanes occupied the top half of each door. The effect was stately and palatial—it came as no surprise that Julian had chosen the entrance as a subject. Ironically, it had turned out to be the only practical vantage point from which to watch Julian draw. The optical effect of the sun hitting the surface of the glass negated its transparency; as long as Randall stayed inside, he was invisible.

He peeked through one of the panes in the southernmost door… yes: he's there. The coast is clear… a boy and his girlfriend are sitting on the bottom step over on the left side—their regular place for lunch—they've been there every day. This is it, Randall. Pretending to be calm and collected, he opened the door and stepped out. Three paces took him to the lip of the top step. So far, so good; he sat down and put the clarinet case across his knees to serve as a table; he opened his sack lunch and removed a sandwich.

He took a big bite and chewed slowly, looking to the right as if there was something over there worth seeing—obviously, I have to pretend I don't know he's out there. From his vantage point, I'm sitting right in front of one of the doors. How long will it take to recognize me? Not looking at him is so *hard*… what if he *doesn't* recognize me?

—∞—

The light at this time of day is bright, but not like a month ago; it's a lower angle… I'm glad I waited. The shadows look more dramatic. I've never drawn a set of doors before. Julian looked across the lawn… considering that I've only worked on it three days, it's looking pretty good. I was going to start it on Monday, but that's the day I bumped heads with Randall. Say, now… I haven't seen him since that day. I wonder if… whoa! Is that… I think it is!

"Hey, Randall…" Julian stood and shouted: *"Randall!"* he waved hard until Randall looked his way. "Come on over!" Neato! he's eating his lunch too! Think of that: right on the front steps…. What a relief—I thought maybe he was hurt worse than they thought, or something. I want to compare bumps again.

Randall was thrilled—his hunch had paid off! Oh boy—look at him wave! Is a teacher anywhere in sight—nope! He grabbed his case and cut straight across the lawn, walking as fast as he could, sandwich in hand. What the heck! He broke into a run.

"Hey, long time no see!" Julian felt an urge to give him a hug—but they both had their hands full.

Randall nodded happily; he had to catch his breath.

"I thought maybe you ate in the cafeteria." He sat back down. The music case is new…

"Used to… sometimes though it makes sense to eat outside—you know, as long as the weather stays nice." Wow… he's so *friendly*. It felt right to sit down without asking permission.

"Mmm," Julian agreed, his mouth full of tuna. He swallowed after a few seconds and focused on Randall's bump. "Still there, I see."

"It's a lot better now though." He reached up and touched it automatically. It's half as big.

Julian reached across and touched it lightly. "Does it hurt much?" He leaned forward so Randall could do a return touch. "Mine's not bad if I leave it be."

"Nah, not anymore." Randall's dream of the day had just come true: I touched Julian's bump. *Woo!* It was as if a bolt of electricity had run up his arm: it headed right for his crotch. He blushed and put his hand in his lap—just in case. It wouldn't be long before his Problem returned. Goose bumps formed on his arms.

Reassured, Julian's attention returned to his sandwich. I really like these. Mom is real good at lots of things, but tuna fish sandwiches are right at the top. I could eat these every day. It's a lot of fuss to make the insides just right—she uses hard boiled eggs and sweet pickles as well as tuna… sometimes she lets me help mix everything together. It's one of grandma's recipes, I think. He glanced at Randall's. Bologna. Not one of my faves.

Neither felt impelled to make conversation; Julian returned to assessing his drawing while he ate, and Randall returned to assessing the artist—while his heart rate slowly returned to normal.

Being this close was revolutionary—I don't dare stare like I usually do, he'll notice… He studied Julian's face in short glances—the lips, the eyes… the sheer *beauty*… wow. I can't believe I'm here, sitting right next to him; I've *never* had this kind of luck in my entire *life*. I could kick myself for being such a coward—I could have been out here all along. Gradually his eyes moved downward… the rest of this blond demigod's body was so wonderful. Finally, the drawing came into view: his eyes nearly popped out.

Julian wadded up the wax paper and tossed it into the bag. He withdrew the apple and took a healthy bite. The detail in the recessed doorway isn't right—needs some work. He was about to ask if it was okay to draw while they talked, but the look on Randall's face stopped him. "What's wrong?"

Randall stared at him. "Wrong?! Nothing's *wrong*," he nodded at the tablet. "How can you be so *good*?" Until he looked at it he'd no idea of Julian's ability. "It looks *professional*."

"It's not *that* good." Being complimented is okay, but that was a little overboard; surprisingly, it felt nice.

"Can I look at it? I mean, up close?"

"Sure." It would have been rude to say no; Julian wasn't looking for a bunch of praise though. I have an idea about how good it is—and how *not* really great it is too. Thanks to Mr. van Horn, I know what to look for when I draw stuff. He sat back and watched. Intriguing… what does he see? I never thought about that… what other people see. Huh.

"Can I… umm…" It just occurred to Randall to ask if he could look at the other drawings. He'd been so absorbed looking at the artist, it never occurred to him. I watched some of them being drawn, but I have no idea what they look like. They must be pretty amazing.

"Sure, go ahead." Randall's face and blue eyes are interesting. You don't get a chance to study someone's face up close like this every day—unless they're asleep of course. That was fun to do. Interesting… hum. I thought Swedes had blond hair. His is dark brown. Maybe his mom isn't a Swede. That must be it. That's why I have brown eyes: because of my mom. He nodded. I remember now, I saw her in the nurse's office. She has dark hair too… but her nose wasn't unusual. He must have his dad's nose. The instrument case caught his eye. Sort of like Frankie's… I wonder what he plays.

Randall turned the pages with care—as if it was a priceless ancient document like they talked about in World History. It wasn't just that Julian had drawn these…they were so incredibly *good*. Never having paid attention to drawings, he had no way of judging them… his only personal experience was back in elementary school. It took no time at all to determine that I had no talent whatsoever, so I never tried. But I saw Julian draw these—from a distance, admittedly—there's no way these could have been copied or traced. How does he *do* this?! They make me feel like I'm right there in the atrium! The next page delivered a huge surprise—he sat up and looked at Julian in shock.

Julian saw Randall's jaw drop and glanced down. "Oh, that." He chuckled. "I hope you don't mind… I drew that while you were sleeping in the nurse's room." That was a challenge; the light wasn't very good.

It took Randall a while to adjust. This makes me look a lot better than I ever did before. He knew that for a fact, having spent some time looking in the mirror. Boy, would I like to have a copy of *this*. He looked more closely… there it is: he even put in the bump!

Watching Randall study the drawing is fun… I'd like to have him do a pose, like Leonard did at camp. Maybe after he knows me better he'll give permission.

It's hard to believe these drawings; I've never seen anything like this. Reluctantly, Randall turned the page—the drawing in progress was next. He compared it with the building across the way… you'd think he had a camera built into his head or something—but that isn't it either. The drawing is more interesting than the real thing. How can *that* be? He handed the tablet back. "Thanks for letting me look."

"Sure, no big deal. Any time." The praise is nice… makes me feel good, sort of. Maybe we have a special connection because of the bumps. "Okay if I draw some?" I have an idea about the trim detail—working on a small sheet like this has its problems.

Randall gulped, afraid to ask: "Is it okay for me to stay?"

"Sure. I can talk about stuff when I draw. I do that all the time." Why do people ask that, anyway? I never did understand that. Why would I mind?

Awed, Randall watched. He felt so privileged, so lucky… and so horny. A few traces of a very special aroma had wafted his way when he returned the sketchbook. Julian was not just an artist, not just a beautiful demigod: he was a real *boy*, and he smelled like one. Randall inched a little closer to watch. His nostrils were hungry.

The tile segments above the arch have a problem—squinting doesn't help. I'll have to take a good look at those when I go back in… are they molded or painted? Molded I think. I need some binoculars.

Randall watched Julian's drawing hand—the fingers especially. The slightest move made the pencil do wonderful things. The mechanics involved… it had never occurred to me to notice such a thing… let alone the artistic results. The fingernails are so *delicate*…

"So," Julian tilted his head and reconsidered the angle of the shadow… always tricky this time of the day… "When did you move here?"

"When?" Not expecting to converse, Randall was startled. He had to think for a second. "In July… yeah, it was in the middle of July." How could I forget! It was so hot and muggy."

"Whereabouts is your house?" One of the vertical lines on the left side of the arch needs to be smoothed out a little.

Randall watched Julian's face, fascinated. The tongue poked out of the corner of his mouth—here is this kid, drawing a masterpiece and talking away as if he wasn't doing anything out of the ordinary… never mind that he's too beautiful to describe. "Oh… umm, we live off 48th, over by Griffin Park." Look at that *tongue!*

"Woo-ee, that's *nice*, over there!" Geraldine sold a house near there. I worked on the hedges. Everyone has huge yards over there. "That's close to the university, isn't it?"

"Yeah. My dad works there. He wanted to be in walking distance. He's into walking." That was an understatement.

"I live on Birch Street between 10th and 11th." No need to point out that it's not as classy a part of town.

"Oh." Randall didn't mention that he knew that already. "I don't know my way around town yet."

"I reckon it's a couple of miles from your place."

Randall nodded. Twice that—I know that well enough! I walked home from there once. Julian's shirt caught his attention—wears that every Friday—unusual color—makes me think of Disneyland and southern California. Coral orange or coral pink? It could be called either one. He should be on a surfboard instead of drawing under a big tree. A stray breeze fluffed the wavy blond hair and tugged at the page… it doesn't faze him a bit; he just draws away.

A sudden urge almost took over—he wanted to stand up and run around the tree and shout something, anything—it didn't matter what. His brain was a traffic jam of emotions. To relieve the pressure, he closed his eyes for a moment and took a deep breath. I have to get in control. He had never felt such intense feelings all at once—gratitude, joy, amazement, wonder…an unleashed yearning that he couldn't identify. Randall was used to having a quiet, peaceful, boring life. That was changed now.

"Ooop…" A puff of wind tried to turn the page. "Not finished yet, please…" Julian grinned. "Don't mind me," he glanced at Randall. "If I talk to the wind, don't think I'm nuts—I talk to myself too." Randall's blank look told him that an explanation would help. "See, if I bawled out the wind for messing with my page, all it would do is blow some more and make me mad. The wind won't stop for li'l ol' me. So instead of getting mad about it, I say something silly. That way I feel happy instead. I get more done when I'm happy."

Randall had never heard anything like this. He was being called upon to do a whole new kind of task: his hormones were screaming at full volume, he was being bombarded by the strangest mixture of homespun philosophy and artistic sophistication imaginable, and his deepest fears had been vaporized by this simple open friendly person. He had no idea what to say or what to do. So he *did* nothing. With any luck, I won't spoil anything.

Julian was concerned. "I just thought of something…" his on-board scout manual had opened: *you're supposed to be friendly and help new people*. "I've never moved to a new town." He paused a second. "Except that we moved here when I was five. I wasn't in school yet, so I don't remember too much." Grandma and Grandpa was about all, really… "It must be hard to do… I mean, you don't know anyone at all, do you?" I never thought about that before. What would I do?

It wasn't a question, and Randall didn't have an answer—all he could do was shrug in agreement with the sentiment.

"Tell you what: let me show you around a little. You can meet some of my friends—you'll like them, I know. I'm sure they'll like you."

"Really?" Randall's eyes opened wide. This was beyond anything he had imagined.

"Sure!" It just hit him: "What are you doing tomorrow?" What better than spending some time on Saturday with Randall? Showing off someone from Washington the state isn't something you can do every day. Yeah… how do I get Sid into this… he's never met anybody from out west…

It was the best day of his life, hands down: before the bell rang he had been invited to help Julian and his pals pick out a new car for their scout troop. Randall just happened to know about that—he and his dad went camping a lot. Some cars were hardy, others better not venture off paved roads. I'm supposed to show up at nine in the morning—he wants me there early so that he can show me all his models first. Incredibly, he likes me—I'm now his *friend.* Randall pinched himself on the way up the steps. Wow.

11 Summer into autumn

a: Mark 1 **b:** Francine **c:** Julian **d:** Randall **c:** Mark 2

a: Mark 1

The resumption of regular scout activity was precisely what Mark needed; it demanded enough attention and energy to offset the loneliness that had been growing slowly since the summer.

The outing to purchase his new car was a particularly happy time, resulting in an additional occupant for his driveway: a brand new Ford Country Squire nine passenger station wagon. The rusty maroon color and faux wood panels provided more elegance than he wanted, but the boys thought "Chestnut Metallic" was *cool.* It wasn't the most rugged vehicle available—but the extra bench seat in back and the luggage rack on top swung the deal; a trailer hitch was the only add on—every other "extra" was already included: custom wire wheels and one inch white sidewall tires. Before he'd had it a week, the entire troop had been given a ride. Since they all wanted to be "the one in front," that took a while.

Every boy wanted to know what the back seat was like too. It was more than curiosity—sometimes it was a long drive to a camping or hiking site. Being stuck in the middle in back automatically meant getting a major case of Tired Butt. Mark came up with a way to deal with seating: he created the position of Wagon Master—this individual assigned the seats. His job was to devise a rotation schedule that guaranteed fairness—trip distances were divided into segments equal to the number on board—as a distance segment was reached, he would call for a stop so everyone could shift one position to the right. A new Wagon Master would be named for each trip. Beforehand, Tom, the Junior Assistant Scoutmaster, appointed the Wagon Master from the list of scouts scheduled to go on the trip.

A Name The Car contest was announced at the first troop meeting. Each patrol was eligible to put forward a single nomination. The October meeting reserved time for the patrols to huddle and start their search for the winning name. They were expected to finish the task at their next patrol meeting. The vote was scheduled for November.

Pat, meanwhile, kept a discrete eye on Mark. Shortly after their conference about getting a second car, she set out to find what he needed. She had primed a colleague, a good friend as well, to take on the task of bringing Mark out of his scout hidey-hole into the world of big boys. Peter Gustafson was his name, an RN who, like Pat, had ambitions to become a fully licensed medical doctor. The difference was, of course, that he was a single male—one who also preferred the company of a man when it came to sex. He also happened to be unattached, and about Mark's age.

Pat did not know if he was the "solution," but she was right about him being an ideal person to take Mark by the hand and get him out of the house. Peter had his work cut out for him—Mark was not eager to venture out, in spite of the fact that he knew he should. Fortunately, Pat was there to push.

For one reason and another, they had spent nearly an hour just driving around. Peter was nice enough a guy, no problem there. But where to go? Mark was paranoid about being seen by the wrong person—or anyone, for that matter. I'm too well known by too many people in this town. I don't dare go into a tavern or a cocktail lounge—aside from an occasional beer or glass of wine with a meal, I don't drink. If I show up in one of those places and a parent sees me, what then?

Finally, a hotel restaurant and lounge near the university came to mind. Here they could order something light and sip a glass of wine without drawing attention.

"This is nice," a place to land at last! Peter took off his blazer and laid it flat on the bench—he expected to be here for a while, and didn't want to worry about creasing his best coat. What a relief; he gave the room and its occupants a quick assessment and sat: I am ready to get something to eat. The booth was surprisingly comfortable—Miles Davis playing in the background set a good tone.

Mark nodded. "I was here once a few years back." He checked around again to see if anyone he knew was in sight. "I should have thought of it sooner." The sound system in the adjacent lounge is a nice surprise—it will help keep the conversation private.

Peter held his tongue… he'd been filled in by Pat, so he understood why Mark was so fearful. Still, it is a little annoying… it isn't as if I look strange. I'm not wearing anything out of the ordinary. But time is getting on. "I enjoyed the tour. I would never have found out about this town's ins and outs, I'm sure."

Mark shrugged, oblivious to the implicit sarcasm.

"But I still don't know anything about *you*." There. Cornered him at last.

Mark nodded, sheepishly. "Sorry."

"No, don't be sorry. From what little I know, I can tell this must be hard for you. But until I know you better…" he shrugged, uncertain now if he was dealing with a patient or a prospect—could be either. A slow approach would be wise. He's exactly as Pat described: hot. *Very* hot… certainly knows how to dress; eyes as intense a blue as I've ever seen.

Mark took a deep breath and blew out a puff of air. "Okay. The thing is, I'm really new at this… or new at…" he stopped and looked Peter in the eye: "Is this a *date*?"

Peter laughed gently—the expression on Mark's face was disarming and revealing: I'm sitting across from a boy in a man's body. "Well, it *could* be, I suppose." Finding the correct phrasing here is essential—especially if it were to become a date. "Pat didn't tell me much, other than you were lonely, you were inexperienced, and you needed to be shown around so that you can see who and what is out there." He watched Mark closely to see if that was accurate—and if there was anything more he needed to know.

Mark nodded. "That's about the size of it."

They paused while the waiter placed water glasses and menus on the table.

The waiter made eye contact with Peter and each knew at once who he was looking at; he had already checked out Mark and dismissed him as a prospect—looks straight: wedding ring, no pinkie ring. "Do you need time? Or…"

"Something light that goes well with…" Peter pulled the wine list over for a glance. "Unless, you have something in mind?"

Mark shook his head. "I prefer red wine…"

Peter perused the list. "The Bordeaux, I think."

"We have a very nice brisket, unless you'd prefer a seafood plate." He returned Peter's look and held eye contact without blinking—this one doesn't need any help.

Peter looked at Mark to see if he had a preference. He is so uptight. "Beef?"

"Sounds good." Mark didn't know what a Brisket was, but whatever this restaurant served would be okay.

Peter nodded. "Make them both medium, please. Tossed green, and vinaigrette." He smiled back at the waiter, leaving things open. He handed him the menu, taking a rapid second glance at the trouser front. Regrettably, the slacks were black. From the perspective of a curious eye, those are worthless in low light.

The waiter bowed slightly, and collected Mark's menu.

Peter nodded a silent instruction to Mark: *watch him*. When the waiter was well away, he asked: "What do you think?"

"Think?" Mark frowned. "What do you mean? The order?"

"No, the *waiter*."

Mark shrugged. "Knows what he's doing… the wines, the food… what's to think?"

"His name is Albert and he's available tonight after his shift. If I'm interested, I can say so when he brings the wine. He prefers bottom, but could go either way. He is average in size, probably six inches."

Mark's jaw dropped. "How can you tell all *that*?!"

The expression of shock was a *treat!* Peter was delighted. If nothing else, this will be a lot of fun.

"First Rule: pay attention." Peter held up his left hand and pulled down a finger each time he identified a point: "One: the lapel badge gives you his name; Two: he looks you straight in the eye and forces you to blink first—that means he is available; Three: he suggests a specific menu item that goes with the wine you have mentioned—in this case, the brisket or seafood. Four: as he walks away he puts enough swing into his backside to indicate it is available, and Five: when he first arrived he stood with enough tilt to show a clear hint of what he was packing—he hangs to the right. Up full he would be around five and a half or six." Peter took a sip of water.

Mark's jaw had remained open—he dipped his head, stunned; he was unprepared for anything like this.

Peter smiled kindly; class was in session.

—ᨖ—

b: Francine

Geraldine gave a sideway glance, a sign of her displeasure. Hilda was on duty tonight. She didn't much like Hilda, sorry to say. Too frumpy by half. If it weren't for the little Amanda and June's bonnet, her hair would make a good fright wig come Halloween. I wish she would hurry up: how long can it take to slice a piece of carrot cake?

Be patient Francine, be patient. Geraldine had been testy all day; no telling why. Francine had learned long ago to bide her time when her friend—and employer—was in a mood. Geraldine had bad days now and then for no apparent reason. But this was my idea, this meeting. When the coast was clear, she began. "We had the talk," she said, keeping her voice even.

"The talk?" Geraldine looked at her closely. "*The* talk?"

"Last night, after his pal Randall went home."

Geraldine tilted her head "Randall?" That's a new name.

"A couple of weeks ago they met rather abruptly in the hallway—collided head on. After spending the afternoon in the nurse's office, they became bosom buddies." Boys do that.

Geraldine frowned. What's this got to do with Julian getting a girlfriend?

"Never mind Randall and all that. I can tell you later. What you want to know is what about Julian and the Female Race, right?"

That made Geraldine sit up straight.

"After we washed the dishes last night we had a sit down in the living room, at my request…"

"Sure, I like girls. What do you mean?" Julian wasn't expecting that question… I thought she wanted to talk about school; oh well, no reason to worry. He and his mother were used to talking openly about anything. But this wasn't a question he had heard in a long time. When I was little, that's all the moms could talk about. They gave up, finally. I never knew why.

"Well, isn't it time you had a girlfriend?"

He knew what she meant but chose to dodge. "I have lots of girl friends."

"Oh?"

"Yeah. I see them at school all the time."

Francine worked to keep this non-threatening. "I'm glad to hear that. Can you tell me about any of them?"

Julian wasn't ready for this… he grabbed at the first name that popped into his head. "Well, sure. There's Beth," he grinned wide. Perfect choice. "She's my lab partner in Biology." The interested expression on her face is clear: obviously I'm supposed to say more. "I like her a lot. Thanks to her I'm gonna pass that class—prob'ly get a B at least."

"What's she look like?"

What am I supposed to say to that? She looks like a girl.

Better not get wise here. Inside guy had just checked in.

"Well, she has blond hair—kind of straight though, and darker than mine…" lessee… "she wears one of those pin thingys to keep her hair off to the side, y'know, so it doesn't hang in front of her face. Blue eyes, I think… yeah, blue. She's a little short, maybe."

"What's her last name?"

"Johnson, I think… yeah, *Johnson*."

"Is she pretty?"

"I s'pose." Odd question… "I never think about that. It's what's inside that counts," he grinned. That's what she always used to say when I was little. Truth is, that's what he believed. Julian had never cared much what people *looked* like, boy or girl. He was so used to being told he was pretty, he discounted it. That kind of talk, no matter who it was about, was disregarded.

Francine could see she wasn't getting anywhere. She had never played mind games with him—they had a lifelong history of openness and honesty; she wouldn't ruin that for anything. This is my own fault—it's been a long time since we had a direct talk like this—not since he was in the seventh grade, not since he started boy scouts. But he's had no problems, nothing needed attention—he always comes to me if there is anything at all. Admittedly, I've been assuming Mark would be there to handle any "boy" problems that came along.

"Julian, I'll come to the point. I'm worried, a little. Now that you're growing into a man, there are things you need to know and learn. Being a man has…" she searched for a way to say this.

Oh-oh… I'm not ready for this… what should I do? I can't tell her the truth, can I?

No, you're right about that, Inside guy agreed.

"I'm sorry you don't have a father here to talk about this, but we've been able to get along up to now, haven't we?"

"Yeah, sure, Mom." He had never felt deprived; Mom is the greatest.

"High school is more than learning English and Typing and History. You need to learn what it is to be a man who can go out into the world and stand on his own. That means more than finding a job. It means finding a wife. You want to marry someone whom you love and whom you want to have your children."

Julian was dumbstruck by that statement. He had been expecting to dance around the subject. I should have known better. Having children of my own? Whoa. Such a thing had never entered his mind.

"High school is where you learn how to do that." She watched him closely—resisting the urge to hug him instead… she could see his discomfort.

"Gosh…" he grasped for something, anything to say. Inside guy was no help here at all. "Umm… I never think about that stuff." That much was the honest truth.

"I know. That's why we're having this talk. It's my job to pay attention to more than your food and clothing."

Julian knew that, of course… but hadn't given it any thought—never needed to.

"Let's go at it from a different angle." This is the hard part. She cleared her throat. "I assume that you have learned about the birds and the bees," she looked into his eyes.

Julian blushed and nodded.

"I'm not worried about you getting a girl into trouble, or anything like that, but…" Francine realized that she was in over her head… this subject needs a man. "I'll be honest, Julian—there are things I don't know and can't teach you." She fiddled with her fingers. "It's my fault, in a way, that you don't have a man here to lead you through these things." This wasn't the time to explain that, either. "I don't want you being led astray by rumors and locker room talk…" or by Geraldine's yard crew, for that matter. "I want you to promise that if you have questions or problems that need a man's attention, you'll ask Mark to help you."

Julian couldn't believe his ears.

"I plan to have a talk with him about this. I'm sure he'll be there to give you any advice you need." He's practically a member of the family; for several years she'd thought of Mark as being like her boy's older brother.

Panic alert: the *last* thing he wanted was for her to talk to Mark about this.

You better head that off, if you can.

Right… that would make Mark think like a *father.* Bad idea.

Francine held on to her proverbial hat: this part had to be mentioned.

"I know that you are mature enough to get into trouble. I also know that there are some girls who would be willing to let you try." There always are.

His eyes opened wide: did she just say what I thought she said?"

Yep.

"I would guess that you haven't been tempted yet…" asking indirectly seemed prudent, but she had no reason to think otherwise.

"I *never* think about that stuff!"

Francine doubted that; his laundry showed signs once in a while. He isn't as active as his father, thank goodness—but he inherited Adrian's good looks as well as his talent. The potential for the other "attribute" could be there too—Adrian's appetite for seducing women had no limit.

"What about your friends? Do any of them have girlfriends?"

He shook his head. "I think some of the guys in the troop, the older ones do, maybe." The truth is whenever any of the guys talk about girls, I tune out.

The trick question worked: he knows perfectly well what I mean by girlfriend… something else was clear: she had gotten as much information as she was likely to get. Becoming an inquisitor wouldn't help anything.

"Julian, I want you to start thinking about this. Maybe you and Sid, or you and Randall could team up and have a double date—go to a movie, or something. That wouldn't be so hard, would it?"

What do I do? He gulped. Where are you, Inside guy?! Nothing… I'm all alone here. He couldn't see a way out. But take a *girl?* To a *movie?! What* movie?

Francine dared not make it a demand, but she remained firm and waited for an answer.

Better go along with this… we can figure something out later. The Inside guy had come through just in the nick of time.

"Okay." He gave his mother his best innocent little boy look. "A movie." Sid or Randall? Maybe Jeremy…

"By the way—you should feel free to invite Beth over. I'd like to meet her."

"Something wrong with the cake?" Hilda had stopped by to do refills. Neither lady had taken a single bite.

"Oh!" Geraldine jumped, startled. She hadn't noticed that the carrot cake had been delivered. She lifted her fork, slightly embarrassed. "Mercy… I forgot all about the cake…" how long has it been here? With a small smile, she took a bite. The interruption enabled her to reflect a moment on what she had just heard. Francine's performance is an eye opener. I have not been giving my "little sister" enough credit… nowhere *close* to enough. She took another bite. Mmm… this is tasty.

Well timed, Hilda! Francine appreciated the break… her "report" was almost finished. The carrot cake looks wonderful… *mmm…* "Delicious!" I should have ordered it with a scoop of vanilla…

c: Julian

When Geraldine's car pulled away Julian leapt to his feet as if freed suddenly from invisible straps. He paced back and forth: he had a problem. Sometimes it's easier to think when you move around.

"She's gone off to talk about me and *girls*," he informed the room out loud. That seemed to help some, saying it aloud. It proved that he understood what was going on, at least.

They've been doing that a lot, going out to talk about stuff. They used to sit in the kitchen and yak away for hours; now they take off instead. Put two and two together: 'fraid I'll listen in, prob'ly.

It makes sense: they're in this together. Ever since I joined her crew, Geraldine went out of her way to make wisecracks about girls and stuff. I thought she was just having fun; for as long as I can remember, she always made jokes, even when I was a little kid. It used to be about my hair. At least she doesn't try to fluff it up anymore.

But you're not a little kid anymore.

I know that! So does she, I guess. Always talking about how the girls in the high school are gonna have to get in line, I'll be in such demand… I didn't think anything about it 'cause I thought she was doing it to help me fit in with the crew—well, they are a bunch of studs. They always talk about that kind of thing.

Then there was the school clothes … they were in *that* together, for sure… now it's *dates*. He stopped pacing… gotta go. He headed for the potty.

Leaving the door open so that he could hear if they came back unexpectedly, he performed the tedious unbuttoning procedure required by his new Levis. Brother! I'd be in trouble if I was in a hurry! He pulled himself out at last and aimed at the bowl.

"I don't suppose *you* have any ideas." Little J was busy draining the tank. He never answers anyway; might as well be deaf, he never listens to me… has a mind of his own. Julian finished, put Little J back inside and started to button up.

Grrr... it takes forever to unbutton and button these… I still don't see why they're better than zippers. Hmm. I need a pair of those lounge pants. Heck with it! Julian's patience had run out. He took his pants clear off and kicked them aside. I don't need those on anymore anyway. It's not that long until bedtime.

Out of habit he stepped over to the washbasin. Not to wash his hands—he didn't bother when no one was around. Why should I? I'm clean down there, I didn't get any splashes on myself, so why's it such a big deal? Rules for rules sake were a pet peeve. Self-respect required that they be ignored whenever possible. He checked his face, his hair. Everything looked okay. "So what are we going to *do*?!"

The dummy in the mirror never knows anything. "Where's that line of girls that Geraldine talked about all summer?" If I knew, I could grab the first one and go to a movie.

The face in the mirror looked back with an expression of terror: what do you do when you take a girl to the movies? Aren't you supposed to hold hands? *Eew.* His nose twisted in disgust. Oh… I just remembered… an un-flushed toilet is a major no-no around here. He stepped over and pushed the handle. Back to work, Julian: he took a short run and slid across the hallway into the living room… perfect: his toes touched the edge of the rug. It's been a while since I did that. Sometimes it was helpful to walk around grandma's oval rug while figuring things out. Toe to heel, careful to stay right on the edge as if it was a curb, he was back on task.

Whatever I do, I have to protect my secret. One day they'll figure out I like boys; I want to delay that for as long as I can. What he did *not* want them to figure out was his love for Mark. He had decided long ago who his life mate would be; that was beyond question. Ah! *That's* what I'll do! Talk to Mark!

He went to his room and headed for the closet. Maybe if look at him long enough, I'll figure this out. Those drawings do help—they come to life sometimes… sometimes I can hear Mark talking. That's another top secret.

Last summer Mark had posed for two drawings—the first was a seated position, the second standing. Julian's opinion alternated about which one was the best… it depended on his mood, or his need at the time. Usually one became stronger than the other when they were side by side.

Achieving his life goal was going to take longer than he first thought. That's what I learned at camp; but I also learned that I was *right*—not that there was ever a choice. When I looked into his eyes that first time, I knew. I wasn't even a scout yet, but I knew. And Mark *is* getting closer—I can feel it. When he gave me that tour the other day, and when he held me by the shoulders… Julian's eyes blurred and he faded into a glow of warm affection…

Yeah, yeah, just don't make too much of that…

"Well, you have to admit it was special—and he gave the shoulder pinch."

He wouldn't do that if he knew what it meant to you.

I bet he would… Actually, I'm afraid Inside guy could be right about that. That's one reason I keep it secret. I still think it shows how he feels deep inside. He wouldn't do it otherwise.

Julian stared at the drawing, waiting to hear Mark's voice—the voice he used when he talked seriously about things. What would Mark advise? What would he do? Julian looked into the eyes… the steady, strong blue eyes. Well, he'd stand back and be calm, for openers. He wouldn't be afraid, that's for sure. He'd be brave about it, and find a way to get on.

Now you're talking.

Mark wouldn't *show* it if he was afraid. He'd know that would just make it worse. Yeah… it's coming to me… I hafta talk to Tom or Nick. I bet they had to take a girl to a movie once. I bet they know what to do. Maybe they can help me figure out who to ask… hold on! Mom already told me what to do!

"A double date!" Perfect. Wait… would Sid want to do that? Hard to imagine. Jeremy? *Randall?* That's another problem.

I wondered when you'd get around to him.

I think he has a crush on me, y'know?

Brilliant. What gave him away? The staring or the stiffies?

Yeah… reminds me of myself. I useta be that way around Mark. Man, I must have looked real stupid. Now I know how Mark must have felt all last year. It's a miracle he put up with me.

Took you long enough to figure that out.

Well, I did, so take it easy. I just hope I didn't wreck things for good.

As long as you don't get in a big hurry, you'll be okay; Mark has to be ready, and you do too.

I guess you're right. Well, we can figure Randall out later. What about Mom and Geraldine? Do we have a plan yet?

Inside guy was silent.

Hmm. Okay: we say we'll go on a date. We don't have to say who with, or when yet. Nick will help there.

That won't be enough.

You're right. Besides, they'll want to know *who*, right off. Who… boy. Who *could* I ask on a date?! No idea. Let's see… who do I know? Other than Beth, I don't know any girls. I can picture a few, but I don't know their name… why would I? Do they have a girl list anywhere? If I saw a name or two maybe… boy, this is gonna be *hard.*

Muttering a silent thanks, Julian returned temporary Mark to his hiding place. He wasn't needed for anything else tonight—the talk with Mom and the movie thing had upstaged Little J's usual bedtime sport.

Don't forget: your pants are still in the bathroom. Inside guy was good at remembering details—especially ones that could lead to embarrassing questions.

"Yeah, yeah, okay." Not that it was a bad thing to do or anything, but Julian never left his pants behind. Stupid to invite questions. After I do that I'll head for the back porch and get this morning's paper; might as well see what movies are showing… at least I can pick a good one. Getting his head around the idea of sitting next to a girl all the way through a movie was… he didn't even have a word for it.

—∾—

d: Randall

It was a toss of the coin whether to walk or ride his bicycle. The bicycle made it possible to keep going if his spot was occupied, which it was, sometimes. Randall was used to meandering around a college campus—in Pullman it was the only area of town where

Nels and his toughs never lurked. A university has many who, like himself, need to get off by themselves to think. There are lots of good places here, and he had found several.

Solitude was essential from time to time—at home it was interruptions, interruptions. It never failed: the second he stopped practicing his clarinet to do a little thinking, either his sister, or mother popped into his room without warning. Another reminder to pick up his room he did *not* need. In the park he could concentrate on things. These days, of course, it was Julian that occupied his thoughts. One of these days I'll figure out a way to get a photo. One thing I've noticed about Jackson High School is the complete absence of cameras hanging around student necks. Taking mine to school could be an invitation to disaster.

My favorite place, at last! no one is there—I lucked out. He dismounted and walked the rest of the way. The bicycle had a ready made perch against the back of the giant sweet gum. Excellent: no one is coming up the path. Where it led didn't especially interest him; once in a while a jogger came along… maybe it's a loop or something. This spot would be ideal for taking promotional snapshots. From here one can see the west part of the campus and the dormitories. The view is pleasant—especially now that autumn has begun in earnest. A readymade cushion of deep red and orange leaves was waiting to accommodate his meditations. He pushed a few more in place. It's early in the season; the leaves are still soft and pliable. He picked one out and examined it closely as he sat.

Randall had never been particularly sensitive to artistic values, but watching Julian draw had caused a heightened awareness; some things that had always been right in front of him were visible suddenly, now that he bothered to look. For example, the intense colors in this leaf: an amazing phenomenon. The pigment transformation was a biological miracle that had always fascinated him, but now another dimension took precedence. The view across the campus had an impact, a new meaning, for lack of a better word. The beauty, the sheer pictorial beauty before him would have gone unnoticed before now. The variety of trees, the different stages in the annual cycle—some were still green, others were yellow, orange or red—some were a mix. What a privilege it is just to *see* this! Goose bumps ran up his spine.

Conditions are ideal today: the late afternoon light is perfect. He had brought along his 35mm camera to document this spot, this time in his life. Keeping a journal was not his thing, but maintaining a photographic record was. Thanks to his grandfather, it was second nature to keep that up. One day, when I'm in my rocking chair, I'll be able to relive the good times, times like now. My trusty tripod is strapped to the bicycle frame. After that's set up I'll get few exposures… this vista is outstanding. The late afternoon light is perfect.

Maybe I'll send one to Jimmy—tell him about life in the east. A snapshot might get his lazy writing hand busy for once. I'm glad I'm here, but it would be interesting to know what it's like to be a sophomore at Pullman High—it's half the size of Jackson. He mounted the camera and sighted in. Now… a few shots using the zoom lens… *amazing* what this thing can capture. He removed the camera from the tripod and changed lenses. I want a few close-ups—these leaves are incredible. Good thing I have color film loaded. Kodacolor negative film had become his favorite: truer color; *and*, you can see every photo without having to set up a projector.

It seemed a shame to put away the camera, but there wasn't anything else to capture—and the light is about to call it a day. I want to sit and watch it fade; the changes will be interesting.

Back on his makeshift cushion, he leaned against the trunk and took a deep breath—almost a sigh. It feels so *good* to be here, to be looking at this scene, to be appreciating its quiet and glorious beauty. Not the same old science nerd, am I? Studying the incredibly handsome and lovely Julian has done something to me. He makes the whole world look beautiful. A wonderful new feeling welled up within—slowly, a feeling of contentment with life, the world… Eyes closed, he rested his head against the trunk.

A review of the day's visual treats—the ones that couldn't be captured on film—began in earnest. The gentle autumn breeze offset the warmth of the setting sun… almost in a trance, it was easy to picture the breeze playing with Julian's wavy golden locks… a couple of weeks ago it did that under the giant oak in front of the school. The memory made him giggle—the breeze had flipped the sheet of paper… 'Ooop!' he says, then asks the wind to behave because he was still drawing. I mean, who asks the wind to behave?! Who would even *think* about doing that?! He's such an *original!*

Randall opened his eyes and looked up: the leaves were flapping away in the breeze as usual, unaware they were being gradually tugged loose. "Hang in there." Might as well take a page out of Julian's book.

A sudden blush of embarrassment struck: what would father think if he saw me indulging myself like this? What would he say about what's going on in my head? Randall loved his father dearly, but had no illusions about following in his footsteps. He's a giant of a man for openers—a Swedish Erik the Red. Not likely he'd ever notice my odd behavior, so the thought wasn't scary. What about the rest of the family? My sister could have a field day and make life miserable, but that wasn't likely either. Mother? She'd be mildly annoyed, but that's about it. No, I'm all alone in this, and that's just fine. All I need to do is keep my cool… what other people don't know won't hurt me—that's always been my working hypothesis. It was almost true—except for Nels, of course. But his kind hasn't appeared around here yet.

That's to Julian's credit too. He's included me in his circle of friends, and they accept me, no questions asked. No gang of redneck cowards is going to mess with Julian's bunch.

Time out. He paused to replay Julian's eyes.

Randall had evolved a reverie sequence: think about this or that, then stop the analytic wheels and focus on one of Julian's features. There are so many… hard to get through them all. First up today—eyes: long black eyelashes… dark brown eyebrows… How to describe the warm, deep brown of his iris? A *rich* brown that makes my heart rate increase. Is there a name for that shade? Hmm. Ahh, I know: I'll ask Dad. He's a regular walking encyclopedia of Biology. Randall opened his eyes and examined the leaf. …huh. It's so *intense*. He studied it for a moment, fascinated. Right: I'll take one of these along—after he expounds on the reds and oranges, I'll ask about eye colors.

A familiar sensation below drew his attention; a shift in position was required. As usual when thinking about Julian, a pleasant side effect had begun; when no one was present, whatever course it sought was allowed—within reason. Unzipping to take care of the demand wasn't allowed—holding off to do a proper job "after hours" at home was an invigorating task in itself. Tonight will be triple nice—having been super hard at least three times since school was out meant a lot of pressure had built up; releasing it is both required and pleasurable.

Another topic, please; always wise… helps divert attention from the crotch. One thing is highly curious: Julian's apparent indifference to girls. He didn't even turn his head when those girls walked by today—he never paid attention to them in the atrium either. Most guys would have—he seems to be girl proof. But he doesn't look at boys either—I'd have noticed that. It's really odd.

It's a miracle that the girls haven't found him yet. He has to be the best looking boy in the sophomore class! He has no idea how handsome and sexy he is. He must have had a bunch in Junior High—but all he talks about is what he did in scouts. Well, that's understandable, in a way.

Time out. Randall paused to replay the crotch. Sometimes movement or change in position gives a good idea of what's tucked away—especially when he wears the Bermudas. The 501s are too new to be of much use. After a few dozen trips though a washing machine, that's when you want to get a front row ticket for 501 Levi's.

He must have seen me—but *has* he? I get a stiff one every time I'm around him, but I don't think he ever notices. For a long time I tried to hide it, but I don't think it made any difference: he never looks down there… at *any*one. That is *weird.* We sit right next to each other sometimes doing homework—it's all I can do to keep my mind on what we're doing. He smells so *sexy* up close. My boner wants to pop out and start firing… once I thought I was going to explode right there! I did drip a lot. He didn't see a thing, as usual—all he did was go over the stuff about the Sphinx again, and the theories about what it was holding between its legs—a temple or an entrance to a secret passage? It's a good thing I'm a coward—my temple door was ready to open…

> *sigh* < Looking up into the branches helped get his mind off his own crotch. Amazing… there are so many leaves up there. How long does it take for all of them to fall off? Several flapped busily in the breeze. They're *tough*, aren't they? What makes them give up and float down here? Ah, there goes one… he followed its meandering course downward.

That car buying trip was a lot of fun. Hmmm. A couple of those guys looked pretty hot—

Randall laughed out loud: maybe they issue some kind of secret repellant spray or something, like they have for mosquitoes… makes them girl proof. Not that I'd need any myself. What I need is the opposite: a secret spray that attracts wavy blond haired boys.

e: Mark 2

"What do you think?" Jerry was very interested to hear Albert's report on the two walk-ins in the corner booth. He had been keeping watch the entire meal.

"The one on this side is definitely a 'member of the club'; the other one? hard to say… straight or in the closet." He put the dishes into the bus tray. "No dessert, but they want another glass of wine. They're not in a hurry."

"They're not a number, then?" He polished another glass.

"Not now." He was amused by Jerry's total lack of subtlety. "But they could be. It's obvious that they don't have room in their evening for the likes of you and me."

Secretly, Albert hoped that the shorter of the two, the "member of the club," might show up by himself later. He did ask about closing time. But nothing was definite. They're having an intense conversation about something… I wish I had a hidden mike in that booth.

"Poo," Jerry pouted. He had a nice fantasy going about the one with the fabulous build. He could wrestle me to the ground in seconds. I love to lose wrestling matches. With those thighs clamped tight I'd be powerless. I could pretend to resist, but... *look* at him talk. Closet? I don't think so. He's been talking up a storm for hours. They look about the same age... maybe they're getting caught back up... maybe he's been gone a while... maybe he's reporting in.

—∾—

Without realizing it, Peter had become jaded about prospective playmates—if that is what the remarkable man across from me is to become. Mark's unpolished candor forced a quick reassessment of approach... and purpose. Fascinating just how inexperienced and closeted he is. I've never met a man so clueless—especially one so hot! Peter was smart enough not to make any moves, but it takes a while to get used to being a listener—I'm not in a position—yet—to make any plans. A lot of background information is needed before I can think in those terms.

During the meal Mark had given a full report of his childhood and teen years. Once started, he opened up completely: he'd never had a crush on anyone in school—all he had done was play around a few times at scout camp. That's common enough... that's where many guys first explore, satisfy their sexual curiosity—mostly for fun. For Mark it was more meaningful.

"See, for a long time I was *afraid* I might be queer; I wasn't attracted to girls—I was almost repulsed." He grimaced. "Big breasts, especially..." he shook his head, still disgusted. "Gross—it seemed like that was all my friends could talk about."

Interesting... I wonder if Pat knows that. Peter didn't interrupt to ask.

"At scout camp I discovered what I liked very quickly. Sex was a game at night; feeling guilty about it was silly. Too many guys were doing it; it wasn't considered "queer" at all. A couple of them were a little too experienced, though, to think that it wasn't what they did at home."

Mark had never shared these things with anyone other than Erik. He had never known anyone he *could* talk to about it. Tonight's conversation gave him a sense of release, of unloading. Liberating—an unexpected but welcome aspect of the conversation. Peter's openness and interest was *enormously* helpful. The wine didn't hurt, either.

"Then you went to College, and everything changed?" Peter was delighted by Mark's charming naïveté. He had forgotten what it was like to be "new."

Mark looked at Peter with a sheepish grin. "It sure did." He was about to continue, but the fresh glasses of wine had arrived. Peter had ordered a chilled rosé to be the after dinner companion.

Mark just remembered what Peter said earlier, and looked up—sure enough, there's the nameplate; Alfred is looking at Peter… check below—the light is too dim to see anything. Maybe it takes practice… Amazing; I would never have guessed the things Peter said. When the waiter left, he looked at Peter apologetically. "Sorry."

"Sorry?"

"I didn't pay attention until it was too late. What did I miss this time?"

Peter laughed. "Nothing new, really. He knows that he and his friend will have to look elsewhere tonight."

"Friend?"

"Mmm. The one at the bar. He's had his eye on you all night. He's polished those glasses at least three times."

Mark turned his head slowly… the guy wasn't looking at him. "Are you *trained* in this stuff?!" Peter's skill is mind boggling.

"I never looked at it that way… *practiced* is a better word." He chuckled. I'm dealing with a man who has no idea what cruising is. I learned this in high school; it's like learning to *read*, it's so basic. Mark skipped that stage somehow. "You were just about to enter college, I think." He wanted Mark to finish his story—the *interesting* part is next.

"Right." Mark inhaled deeply, not altogether sure he could keep his cool telling about this. "I was nineteen years old when I first saw him. I was in Western Civ class sitting up front as usual; he came in the side door and went up to the professor. I got a real good look at him. It was one of those bolt of lightning things. We had never seen each other before that minute. He happened to glance over at me while he talked to the professor—our eyes met and I went all hot and fuzzy. He was only about twelve feet away. That first look was burned into my memory forever."

Peter understood the feeling, though his own experience wasn't as powerful.

"He was a Grad Assistant; helped the professor grade tests and papers for his freshman classes. One day he graded one of mine... He wrote me a note on the bottom."

Peter fought the urge to comment.

"There was a great big A circled in the corner. The note next to it congratulated me on doing such a fine job. It said that he would be waiting for me at The Gables—at ten o'clock the next morning." Mark could feel his heartbeat pick up as he remembered this. "I really freaked out."

Peter took a sip of rosé. Mmm...temperature is perfect. "Gables?"

"A small café just off campus; they have little private booths. The seatbacks reach clear up to the ceiling. I didn't know it, that was our first date. Freshmen *never* went there!" Mark chuckled. "I thought they wouldn't let me in the door, but no one batted an eye. I peered around the counter in front to see if I could spot him and sure enough, there he was waving at me to join him about six booths down the narrow passage."

Mark took a sip of wine and relaxed a minute. "Can you imagine for a minute what you were like right out of high school up here?" He pointed at his head. "And what you would feel like if your greatest idol, say someone like Marlon Brando, or whoever was sitting right there looking at you, smiling, paying one hundred percent of his attention to you?"

"Ooo," Peter cooed. It was fun to imagine.

"That's *exactly* what I felt like as I sat in that booth with Erik. I felt dumb and stupid and hot and fuzzy and silly and gloriously happy and the luckiest person in the world all at once, and I was afraid to say a word."

Peter chuckled.

"We spent two hours talking. *Two hours*, if you can believe it. Mind you, we had not said a word to each other *ever* before."

"What did you talk about?"

"I don't know, a little of everything… silly stuff about my home town, buddies, scouts, whatever came to mind. He drank in every word as if it was important." Mark paused. "Two hours was long enough; I bet you know what we did next."

"Let's see, now… you're sitting in a booth with this hot guy you have flipped out over, you've been talking for two hours… you haven't even got up to go to the john or anything, and you've been drinking soda pop or coffee all this time. Plus, he's making you crazy hard: you can't jump him right there, or you would."

"Can you read minds too?"

He giggled. Mark made it real easy; Peter felt like he was there in that booth.

"So, anyway: he said 'Come to my room. Now.' Simple as that." Mark tried to repeat the intonation Erik had used exactly. "It was a command… but it didn't sound like one. It sounded like a *solution*—like it was a math problem, or something. It was a sensible, logical thing to do. So, that's what I did."

Mark felt a rush just now—Peter's interest and support had made it possible to bring this memory to life—something he didn't anticipate.

"He lived a mile away… awkward at first—no way to hide our "condition." After a few blocks we were able to drop our hands—it's all we had to cover our fronts… I don't know if anybody noticed us or not—I was busy stealing glances at him the whole way, which didn't help. I couldn't keep my eyes off him… he was so *hot*… you know what I mean?"

"Indeed," Peter nodded, guessing at sizes… Erik must have been packing a nice one.

"He had a tiny one room studio apartment above a garage—with a small bathroom. We headed in there right away. I've never had to take a leak so bad. We had fun at once, dueling with our piss. We both had a gallon."

An image of this appeared in Peter's mind: crossed golden streams.

"It was almost like a small cabin, come to think about it—it had a kitchen over in one corner. The living room and bedroom were the same; his sofa pulled out to be the bed. From the john he led me over to the sofa and stared me in the eye for the longest time… then one piece at a time took off all my clothes—slowly and carefully, as if I was fragile. That was so special." Mark paused—he had just dropped a large tear—a happy tear, with just a trace of sad.

This was an important moment… Peter was perfectly still.

Mark recovered after a minute. "Then, we made love. For twelve and a half hours. He gave me lessons one, two and three, a mid-term and final exam."

"Wow." Peter was not ready for this news. Twelve hours!

"We had to take a lunch break. It was Saturday by then. After midnight; we ran six blocks to a pizza parlor, but it was closed. We found an all night grocery store and pigged out on day old deli sandwiches."

Peter sat back and exhaled. "Wow."

“I was nineteen and real needy, and all I had ever done was goof around with a few boy scouts. I had a whole lot of catching up to do. Erik got right to work on that. He got me all caught up… and for three years kept me caught up, too.”

Mark reminisced briefly in his mind… the variations, the repetitions, the frenzy, the soft poetic interludes of that first night. These were not details to be shared. “Mmm-hmm!” he hummed in agreement with himself. “I spent a lot of time in that little room—in my second year Erik let me move in.”

Peter looked at his glass… then at Mark. There was more to hear.

Mark looked at his watch. It was late, but not too late. He wanted to get it all out. “One more, I guess—unless you want to call it a night?”

“Not on your life. I have all night.” He did, too. Mark has yet to tell about the most important years of his life: knowledge about that is crucial to the task at hand. Moreover, it was an experience that Peter had always longed for and never been able to achieve. Who knows? Maybe I’ll gain as much from this as Mark. He waved at the bartender, and showed two fingers. Albert was busy elsewhere.

Mark took a deep breath and relaxed for a minute. Recalling that first day with Erik was always so wonderful—even more wonderful to recount it aloud to someone who could understand what it meant. What I still don’t understand is why I need to do this. Something inside seems to be pushing me… until now, I would never have considered sharing it with *anyone*—certainly not a stranger. And that’s what Peter is—a stranger. Well recommended, but a stranger all the same. I should feel guilty. Erik didn’t give his permission to reveal our secrets.

Well, for better or worse, I’ve started. Nothing is worse than a job half done. I just hope this guy is as good as Pat thinks.

12 The Hayden Park Campout

prelude

"Who's that down there with Julian?" Tony was looking out of Danny's bedroom window. They had just finished a very nice after school "snack."

Danny slipped on his skivvies and scooted over to look. "Oh, that's Randall. He's a new kid—from out west. Julian has taken him under his wing, I guess. He came along when we went to look at cars with Mark."

Tony just got an idea. "What do you think about him?"

Danny hadn't given any thought to Randall. "He's a nice kid, kind of a nerdy type—doesn't like to be called Randy."

Tony gave a nudge to the ribs. "For the *Initiation!*"

"Oh…" Danny paused. "I never thought about that… he's not a scout."

"That doesn't matter."

"Huh. Could be okay… he knows camping stuff. Talked about climbing mountains with his dad…"

Tony slid the window up and leaned out. "Hey, Julian!" Always act on a hunch Tony, that's me.

Julian looked up to see who had called. "Hey," he waved back. It's Danny and Tony! He grinned wide.

"What are you guys up to?" From this distance all he could see was their heads and shoulders.

"I'm showing off my clubhouse!" He had built this out of old fence boards when he was a Cub Scout.

Whoa… Randall couldn't believe his eyes. I recognize one of the guys up there—he was on the car buying trip last Saturday. The other one is even cuter… I've never seen him before. Most amazing was the fact that neither one had a shirt on… That's the kind of thing Randall noticed right off.

If he'd been standing behind them, he'd have been able to see that the lower half was equally unclad, save for Danny's just-slipped-on skivvies. Except for the skivvies, that's the very image that flashed into Randall's imagination. It was logical; why would *any* clothes be off? Considering the time of day and the relatively cool temperature this afternoon, there had to be *some* reason… he dared not think what he was thinking… but there they are. Meanwhile, he took in every detail… every wonderful detail possible without his telephoto lens… from a distance of thirty or forty feet at a sixty degree angle from below, that lens would have come in handy.

Tony cupped his hand and spoke louder: "Hold on a minute, okay?" He muttered to Danny: "have you been in there?"

Danny shook his head as he rubbed the goose bumps that had popped out on his arms… the air outside was a little chilly. "Never did go in, actually." I meant to, but…

Tony shouted, "We want to see. Be right down!" He zipped back to the bed.

Danny loved Tony's impromptu ideas—they always surprised and amused. "What are you…"

"Quick, put on your clothes. I just figured it out. We can invite both of them. It'll be *perfect*." He had been trying to find a way to play with Julian. This is *ideal*. "Do you have a gate, or do we hafta go around?"

Danny giggled. "Around." I'm not worried about Julian, but the new kid… ooo-ee.

"Wait 'til you meet Tony!" Julian laughed. He gestured at the shed-like clubhouse. "As you can tell, there's nothing for them to see. But Tony will have fun with it anyway."

"Is he another scout?"

"Yep. He's always clowning around. You'll like him. I think he holds the troop record for demerits; always needs to do extra stuff to get points."

"Demerits?" Randall frowned.

"Sure. How else would they be able to handle a guy like Tony?" Julian had never got any himself.

The very concept was unattractive—built-in abuse of power; I'm not a class clown, but I'd be in trouble for something—not making my bed in the morning, for openers. Mom has given up on that finally. He glanced up at the window… still open. No shirts… I doubt if they'll appear down here like that. Not in October.

Randall was frantic—Mother will be here any minute to inspect. I have to have this room shipshape or the deal is *off.* The opportunity is too promising to miss: a two-night campout with *Julian?!* Are you *kidding?!*

And his two scout friends—his *hot* scout friends, hot scout friends who take off their shirts upstairs after school! A couple of other guys too. He giggled to himself. Ever since he'd gotten home his imagination had been going *crazy.*

His dresser drawers were stuffed—didn't want to close them until the last minute, just in case a late discovery needed to be tucked in. He performed a methodical scan of the room starting with the northwest corner.

Think of it: TWO NIGHTS!

He felt a surge of gratitude toward his father—all those hiking and climbing overnights were like money in the bank. I don't know anything about scouting, but I can climb, hike, and hold my own at a camp stove. From what I've seen of the country around here, these guys don't have any idea what roughing it is.

Well… if that's what this trip is really about. Something was fishy about it—the supply list, for one thing. The gallon canteen and mess kit were no problem, but air mattresses, *required*? And what do you need a blanket for if you have a sleeping bag? They're supplying the tent, so I don't need to pack mine in. The way they talked about the other two guys was strange… they aren't part of Julian's troop. It's not an *official* scout campout. > *giggle* < That's one detail I didn't mention.

The desk! For Pete's sake, Randall! He opened the top drawer and scooped all the loose papers and pencils in. I can sort these out later…

Eloise Hallstrom sat in the living room listening with great pleasure to her favorite Chopin recording—Rubenstein, of course. It was a welcome alternative to the usual afternoon fare—Randall's clarinet practice down the hall. As she watched the minute hand on her wristwatch she noted that the music seemed especially zestful today… it suits the occasion—the deadline she had set was approaching. She was entirely pleased for the first time since they had settled here. Well, not *entirely* pleased. But she had gained the leverage needed to force Randall to deal with *his* room, at least. Randall had inherited a disdain for tidiness from his father. They both had an aversion to putting anything away. Random Order was their phrase for Utter Chaos. I'll never find a way to coerce Helgar into reforming himself, but Randall is within reach once in a while.

And, for once, he wants to go camping with someone *other* than his father. Perfect. Usually it's Helgar's trip, and I'm powerless. In two minutes I will appear in his doorway to see the magic. If I ever get the chance, I'll be sure to thank whoever made this invitation. Maybe they'll do it again. Monthly would be ideal.

I won't be too fussy, but he doesn't know that. Being in a position to grant such a large favor was a pleasure in itself. Seeing the happy face she was about to cause was a bonus. Ah! perfect... the last bar of the mazurka began as she stood; she let it finish as she stepped across the living room. How fitting: I was Randall's age when I learned that piece. I'll arrive seconds after the deadline.

Ungh! Blast! the bottom drawer won't close... > *skree...eep!* <

Wow. I just hope she doesn't want to inspect inside. He stood and put his hands on his hips, the closet is good, the bed is made—oo... he stooped to look underneath. A *sock!* He grabbed it—there! under the pillow just in time.

"Well, now..." Eloise approached the doorway and took a quick glance. Yes! Better than I expected. The music stand by the window caught her eye—that and the desk had been unearthed—both looked ready to be of service.

"I remember this room," she smiled as if seeing an old friend after a long absence. She faced her boy. "I am pleased." She made a point of walking in and doing a slow tour—she was not looking for a flaw, but wanted him to think otherwise. The look on his face was wonderful. She paused to run her forefinger across the top of the desk. I forgot what this looked like... still in good condition. She stepped over to the window, looked out briefly and turned around for an overall survey. How long will this last? She glanced at the score on the music stand—is that the Mozart? Probably. She pursed her lips. "One final thing..."

Randall's eyes opened wide in dread.

"I want you to photograph this. Keep a print on your bulletin board." She suppressed the urge to moralize, and looked at him kindly. "Thank you, Randall. Have a good camping trip." She opened her arms and accepted his hug. He didn't do that as often nowadays. She patted him on the shoulder wistfully.

"Thanks, Mom." He maintained his cool. Jumping and shouting had to wait until later—after she's out of hearing range. Then I'll take a couple of pictures—camera's ready to go.

Packing in...

October 19 had arrived at last: six boys had been champing at the bit all week to get out of the classroom and into the woods. This was not an ordinary campout. Three were "Masters," and three were "Initiates." The official name or organization was secret—known only to those who had reached the mysterious Fourth Level. That meant that they had been through three of these "ceremonies," and were regarded as Grand Masters.

The days were getting short, no time to waste—sunset came at 5:30. The hike was less than a mile, but they had to set up camp; they could cook supper in the dark if they had to. It was doable as long as they didn't dally. It was worth the strain—starting on Friday after school meant *two* nights. The weather forecast was clear and cool—meaning it would get down into the forties by midnight. Perfect cuddling weather! Of course, for Tony, any kind of weather was okay for that when Danny was the cuddl-ee.

Tony was sort of the center figure—it was his idea to recruit Danny and the other two. It would be a good one, no doubt about that. The look on Chuck's face a few minutes ago at the trailhead told him that his candidates were "acceptable." Louis never breaks a grin, so there's no way to be sure about him; best poker face I've ever seen.

Tony "discovered" Danny near the end of summer camp—it was a powerful experience; for the first time something he couldn't control had grabbed hold. Remarkable, since Tony was experienced and sophisticated in the area of sex play—frolicking with others was his favorite pastime—the more names on the list the better. The idea of committing himself to a single person had never entered his mind. Danny had changed that; Tony had not noticed anyone else for three months.

His reputation, however, caused him to come under scrutiny by Louis and Chuck. He did not know either of them; they were seniors and lived way across town. That was not a problem; Tony was outgoing and unafraid of just about anything, and his reputation for being easy to meet and fun to be around was well deserved.

Their invitation was intriguing; understandably, Tony was flattered. His devotion to Danny had not waned—the romance was still new and exiting. But long experience led him to believe that managing a frolic on the side was no problem. They talked him into joining in a little fun one afternoon, and afterward invited him to a four man one night version of the "Initiation" the next day. It was so *hot!*

Afterward, he had his first ever guilty conscience attack.

So he faced it like a man and told Danny what had happened. The need to do that demonstrated his commitment. Conveniently, that gave Danny the opening he needed to tell about Frankie. Danny was a one-at-a-time type, generally speaking, and even though it was settling a bet, he too felt bad about it later. After they had their talk, they enjoyed one of the best lovemaking sessions ever.

But Chuck came around again and again, urging Tony to play some more, to go to the next "Level." Tony wasn't interested—but when Chuck suggested that he could recruit another person, he thought of Danny—and how he would like to experience the "Initiation" with him. Then they pressured him to round up *three* guys—that way they could have a regular full-blown two night ceremony.

Doing that qualified him for Level Two and made him a "Junior Master." Titles were of no importance to Tony, but he had always liked to "play" a lot, and "improve his game." These guys had a new twist, for sure. So, what's the diff if Louis and Chuck want titles?

Here they were, hiking to a campsite in Hayden Park, of all places. In the summer, scouts didn't think much of the place—it was too close to home and overrun by Cub Scouts. He hadn't been here since those days. But this time of the year it ought to be just fine. The parking lot was empty—I've never seen *that* before; we might be the only ones here tonight. Chuck said they use it all the time. They liked one location in particular because it was seldom used by anybody, even in the summer.

Tony glanced above Chuck's head… the sun is going down fast. But we'll make it okay; Chuck sets a good pace. Tony just realized something—our place in this line must be on purpose: the three "Initiates" were next, followed by Louis, the other Master, at the end.

Danny had been assigned to carry the stoves. They weren't heavy, but the sloshing sound of the white gas annoyed. The two single burner Colemans looked like sawed off lanterns. These simplified cooking, and were a lot easier to tote than a pack full of firewood.

The guys in charge know what they're doing, though—when we got to the parking lot, they had already divided stuff into six piles; everyone had to carry about the same weight. Considering that everything has to be packed in as well as back out, that's important.

Loads averaged 30 to 35 pounds, gallon canteen included. The tent was the biggest item—over 40 pounds. Of course, Danny had considerable experience organizing hiking trips; that was one advantage of being in Troop Nine—more so now that he was Senior Patrol Leader. So far, these guys measure up. All I had to do was pony up three bucks for the grub; they had everything figured.

Danny's thoughts shifted to the "other" aspect of the trip—the after dark part. Leave it to Tony to find wild things to do! Tony and Danny had discovered each other at the end of summer camp, and had been inseparable ever since. Well, *mostly*. Frankie wanted to settle up on our bet, so I had to honor that. Doesn't change how I feel about Tony. When he told me about these guys I felt a lot better—and I told him about Frankie. It wasn't a matter of making us even—it was more a matter of sharing. So it made sense for us to join in this Initiation thing together; it will strengthen us even more.

I feel a little guilty—Julian and Randall don't know about the after dark stuff. I don't know too many details myself—Tony said he swore to keep everything secret. Being in suspense is kind of fun.

Julian had always enjoyed hiking, but today he'd been assigned to pack in two dozen eggs—that's something I never did before. They're well protected, but still—if I trip and fall… not good. The surprise was all those envelopes… they said we'd be doing some kind of Biology study; we have to collect lots of samples—kind of like what I did in the Forestry badge at camp. It might come in handy. Both Randall and I are taking Biology… maybe we can get extra credit or something. I'm gonna get plenty for Beth too, if I can. She deserves it.

My first campout this year; I've been so busy with school and stuff… I don't even know if the Wolves have gone on their campout yet. We had one last fall. Gosh. The bad part of high school is getting all split up. I almost never see my old friends anymore because of the schedule. Randall is okay, but I miss goofing around with Sid and Jeremy. Being in the Wolf patrol was a lot of fun.

It's so good to be back outdoors; camping is one of my favorite things. I wouldn't mind doing it every weekend. What a lucky thing, this trip. Because of this, I didn't have to do that movie date thing this weekend. Course, I haven't figured out what girl to take anyway… Maybe I can get Danny off to the side and ask about that. I bet he and Tony have done that. I was afraid Mom was gonna say no to this hike at first, but I lucked out.

Randall was used to two-man campouts, sometimes three, if Walt was along—he was one of Dad's grad students at Washington State. Six is a whole new adventure; this *particular* group of six is interesting, to say the least. At first, the prospect of camping overnight with Julian was all I could think about… that I might stand a chance, somehow, by accident or whatever to *actually…* but that's crazy. Besides, we won't be in a two-man tent. What are the chances of doing anything with Julian when four other guys are in the same tent? On the face of it, not so good. But from the beginning, something had nagged him about these guys. They're up to something. If my suspicions are right, maybe something will happen. Unfortunately, Randall had no experience of any kind when it came to sex play; he wasn't able to imagine anything very specific.

For him, fantasies and wishful thinking amounted to the same thing: in all probability, he assumed, nothing will happen. Nonetheless, he was ready and eager to do whatever these guys had in mind.

He stopped that train of thought. I don't need to develop The Problem on the trail, please.

I've studied Tony and Danny as much as I can, considering. Julian was right about Tony being fun. So far they behaved like buddies and nothing more. But the image of them looking down out of that window side by side was etched in his memory. They looked so *beautiful* up there… no other word for it. Not something you see every day.

The organizers are interesting… a little intimidating. He had never spent time with older kids—big usually meant bad; safer to avoid being around them. But Chuck and Louis, for being seniors, are amazingly friendly. They've gone out of the way to make me feel welcome and equal. I'm certainly carrying an equal load… must be over thirty pounds, plus all my camera gear. I've done that before. At least here it's all pretty much on flat land.

They don't know what mountains are around here. Back home we'd gain a thousand feet before setting up camp. I doubt if there's a hill around here over five or six hundred. I've spent time in the North Cascades and the Sawtooths. I guess if you go to the west end of the state by Tennessee and Kentucky there are some that get up there half way… still, calling the Appalachian Range mountains is stretching it.

Randall had a good supply of Tri-X; thanks to the geniuses at Eastman, I should be able to get plenty of good shots. I can always push it if I have to... I sure wish they'd hurry up and invent a high speed color film.

He had been well trained by his grandfather, a professional portrait photographer. It was a fun hobby, and documenting mountain trips with his father was valuable field experience. Secretly, photography was his top choice as a career. He had his camera gear along as usual—tripod, lenses, filters—close to ten pounds all told. Dad will be interested in seeing some plant close-ups… naturally, I'll take a few snapshots of the campers… as many of Julian as I can get away with. I got a good group shot at the trailhead. The light is just about gone for the day.

Mmmm… a very nice whiff—being right behind Julian was another piece of luck: my olfactories are starting to throw a party. If that continues, I might develop The Problem anyway.

Setting up camp…

Danny paused to catch his breath. Everyone was sitting around in front of the tent blowing up an air mattress. I've never seen this kind of tent before. It'll be cozy tonight, that's for sure. Six air mattresses will fit in there, but there won't be a whole lot of room left over. From what Tony said, that's the whole idea. Too bad these guys don't have a pump for this. You'd think they would, if this is a regular thing like Tony says…

Julian had never used an air mattress before; luckily, Randall's dad had an extra. Cool… I didn't need to bring my ground cloth. When we finish blowing these up, we're supposed to take them inside there—but I don't see how they can all fit. Is there some way a hexagon makes extra room? We haven't studied hexagons in Geometry yet. Maybe I'll learn something ahead of time…

Randall kept an eye out—for what he wasn't sure. The hexagon tent added to the mystery. These guys know their stuff; they told us where to stand and what to do. We had it up and ready in under ten minutes. The faded I.D. tag on the storage bag read: "U.S. Army type M-1950 Arctic 5-man shelter." Louis said it's good enough to use in the Arctic, too. It has a flap in the roof for a chimney, even. I guess not using a stove is why we can fit in six guys. Louis ran ropes from the top of the center pole to a couple of trees… wonder why. Huh, too high for hanging things on; must be for extra support or something… at least no one will bump into them. I wonder if Dad has ever used one of these.

Tony stopped blowing into the air mattress valve and broke up laughing. He couldn't help himself. The irony of the scene around him was too much for his funny bone.

"What's so funny?" asked Chuck, putting in his plug. He was finished.

Hayden Park

Hayden Park was a combination City/County operation. The vast plot of woodland, five miles long and two miles wide, was honeycombed with trails; daytime picnic and recreation areas could handle large groups; 60 overnight camping sites were accessible by trail. These were arranged and spaced to assure privacy, but not isolation. Campfires were allowed in season, but campers were expected to provide their own fuel and use the designated campfire rings. A few single lane safety roads made maintenance and fire control possible. These were not open to the public. No motorized vehicles were allowed. It was possible to spend a weekend remote from civilization virtually in the middle of town—the only missing ingredient was a mountain stream. Three parking areas provided running water and restroom facilities, as well trail end drop off points; these allowed people to use the camping areas without having to leave their cars overnight. Attempts to connect the camp areas to city water and sewer had failed twice at the ballot box. Campers had to pack in their water; portable chemical toilets were strategically located along the access roads. There was no staff, no reservations—it was first come first served, year around. No firearms were allowed and hunting was prohibited.

In 1886 Joshua Hayden deeded the land to the city and county with the stipulation that it be developed for recreation only; it was never to be sold or divided. It came with a private trust fund dedicated to assure its maintenance; even during the Depression the fund prospered. Thus, the park cost the taxpayers nothing, other than a Sheriff's safety patrol on major holiday weekends. The community took pride in keeping it safe and clean; it had always operated on the honor system. Originally located at the north edge of town, by 1950 it was surrounded by suburbs.

Hayden Park

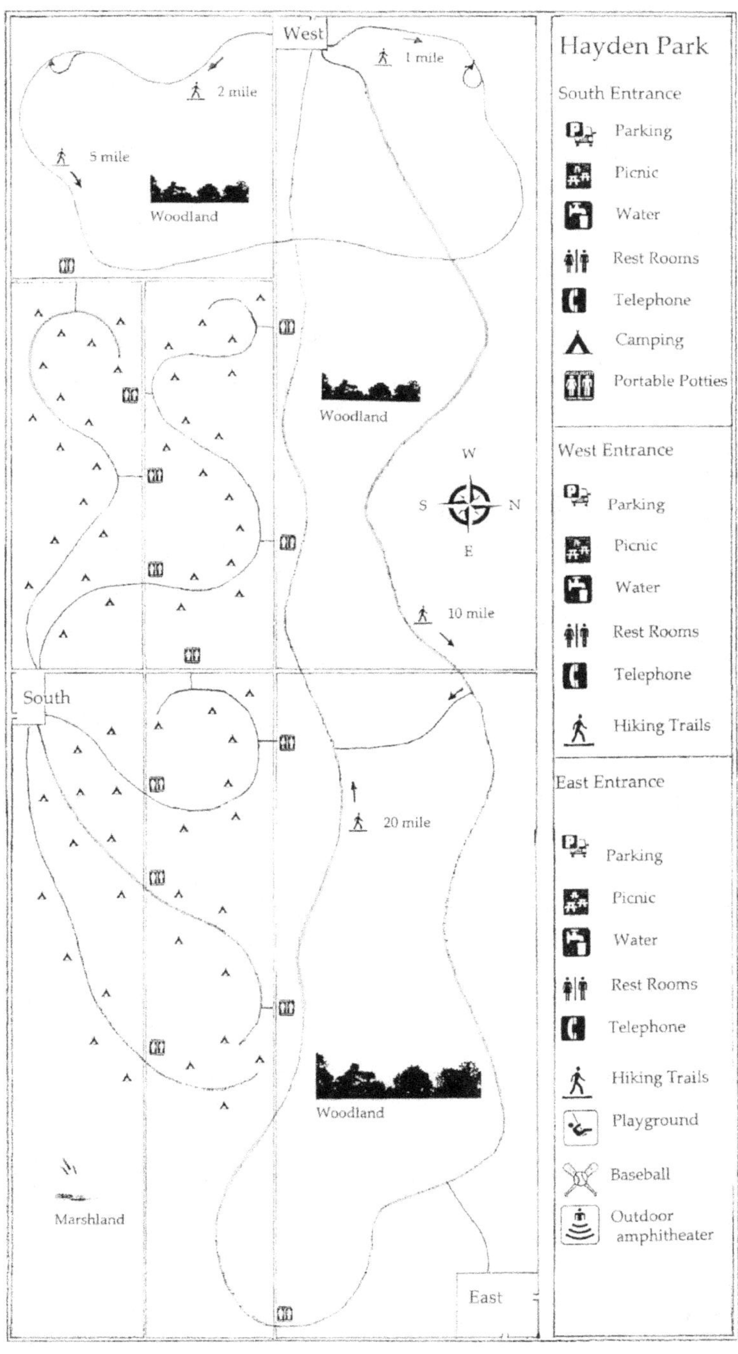
West
1 mile
2 mile
5 mile
Woodland
Woodland
W
S
N
E
10 mile
South
20 mile
Woodland
Marshland
East
Hayden Park
South Entrance
Parking
Picnic
Water
Rest Rooms
Telephone
Camping
Portable Potties
West Entrance
Parking
Picnic
Water
Rest Rooms
Telephone
Hiking Trails
East Entrance
Parking
Picnic
Water
Rest Rooms
Telephone
Hiking Trails
Playground
Baseball
Outdoor amphitheater

"Never mind. Just something I thought of…" he got control of himself and resumed filling his air mattress. He didn't dare answer Chuck's question. No way could he tell anyone what he was thinking. Knowing what Chuck and Louis are up to, that's my problem.

"Okay you guys," Chuck stood. "When you have them inflated bring them to the tent. Be sure they're sealed tight: no slow leaks allowed. While Tony and you guys fix supper, Louis and I will set everything up for the night. Bring over your sleeping bag, pillow and blanket too." Chuck disappeared into the tent. He rechecked the pole… it's secure. Its base had been moved outward toward the entrance, making the center area free and clear. The ropes were meant to keep it stable. He placed his mattress in its pre-assigned slot and waited by the opening. The plan required that the Initiates not know what arrangements were being made inside.

Tony boiled the hot dogs while Danny and Julian spread the tarp. That would have to do as a serving area. Other than the stone fire ring, the sole campsite amenity was eight log sections that served as seats. If there had ever been a table at this site, it had rotted away a long time ago and been used for firewood. That's one reason this site wasn't used much: no picnic table.

The setup disappointed Julian—I expected to have a big campfire going by now. No way to do that with the stoves in there… maybe we'll start one after supper; I wouldn't mind having one now. It's too cold to take coats off.

"No mosquitoes," Randall was pleased to observe; assembling the line of condiments was his assignment.

"Too cold now, prob'ly. The swamp is at the east end of the park. It's dried up now. The winter rains will get it going soon enough." Julian wasn't worried about mosquitoes anyway—they don't like me much.

Danny watched the remnants of the day disappear… no color. "I can't get used to the days being so short. We just got here."

Randall had looked at the horizon a while ago… "It's already dark where I come from. Pullman is ten degrees farther north." Up there, we'd have to take off from school right after lunch. A hike after school would start in the dark. He joined Danny and watched the water come to a boil. That takes a while here. I'm used to camping at a higher altitude.

Each stove had a gallon can on top, three quarters full of steaming water—that had emptied one and a half canteens. Four and a half gallons remained—plenty, but there was no water to waste. The Coleman stoves looked lonely and out of place in the circle of river rocks. Ordinarily, campers had a healthy campfire to cook on.

"How come you don't put in the hot dogs to start off?" Danny thought they might cook sooner if they could heat up with the water.

"My dad told me that this way they almost always split open; makes 'em taste better." Tony liked the way they looked when they did that—kind of gruesome. He plopped the first one in. "They cook up faster, too, when they split open."

The boys clustered around to watch. In seconds, one split; the aroma leapt out at them: mouths began to water at once. Hungry, hungry, hungry: it had been a full day at school, and the hike in wasn't exactly a vacation.

The meal consisted of hot dogs and potato chips; they had a choice of Tang, instant milk, or Quik. Simple, fast, and filling. There wasn't a lot of talking; they had just learned a better way to boil hot dogs: when split open, they hold lots more catsup and mustard.

Since he didn't know anyone else, Randall settled next to Julian automatically. The "seats" are too close to each other. Tree segments; practical, but it's impossible to talk privately—too bad. I wanted to get Julian's opinion. It's obvious that the two big guys have a plan of some kind. When I carried my sleeping bag to the tent, Louis took it inside for me—same with my pack. Why wasn't I allowed to go in there? They must be assigning us a slot or something… very strange. I'm too chicken to object… I was sort of hoping my bag would be next to Julian's.

Julian took a big bite: *mmm!* this is so *yummy*. I don't get these very often. Mom never cooks them at home. At the Fair or when we go to the beach is when I get a chance to eat these. Can I eat all four? Somebody else can have my last one. The tent caught his eye… I've never slept in a tent that had a pole in the middle. What were those guys up to in there? No point in trying to see anything—they kept the flaps closed. Whatever they were doing, it didn't require a lot of talk. I didn't hear a peep. When they came out to join the chow line, neither one said a thing. I wonder if Randall has any ideas…

Why don't you ask? Inside guy just checked in.

I don't want to rock the boat. Danny knows these guys, so does Tony. They must have a good reason. Some things are supposed to be a surprise—makes it more fun.

Also makes it hard to back out…

The cautionary note was unexpected. Why worry? Two of these guys are my *friends*. Whatever Chuck and Louis are up to, can't be that big a deal. Back in Cubs they used to do stuff to spook you before lights out—tell ghost stories and stuff. It's probably something along that line. Halloween is coming up, so…

Chuck had been keeping his eyes on the initiates, just in case. It looked good, really. They must have an idea of what's coming—they're scouts, and they're in high school, so they're ready. Tony sure was. Chuck had every reason to think that this would be one of the better romps he and Louis had had the pleasure to organize. "Okay, guys. As soon as we put everything away, we'll make a trip over to the portables. We'll do that as a group."

"How come?" Tony wanted Chuck to explain why; in his opinion, it was stupid to be so mysterious about everything. It takes away from the fun.

"We don't want to interrupt things later. Once the Initiation begins, it must continue until the end."

"Oh." Tony nodded. "Makes sense." The expression on Danny's face verified his concern. Now he's relaxed again. The other kids look easier about it too.

Chuck gave the initiates a reassuring nod. "Once we're into it, you'll understand."

The lids were put on the condiments, and everything was tucked behind the left flap of the tent—they didn't want anything to tempt the night critters; these woods had a healthy raccoon population. Another precaution was taking the used water well away from camp—dumping it at a distance would help draw away nocturnal camp robbers.

Chuck turned on his flashlight. "Lights on, everyone," he started out. The cluster of portable toilets was less than a quarter mile away, but it was possible to make a wrong turn. They went in the same order as the hike in—Louis bringing up the rear. The string of flashlights looked out of place: in case any animals had not noticed, Man was here.

The Initiation begins...

"Grand Master," said Chuck in a quasi-chant, addressing the dark opening of the tent as if it was a cave. "I have the pleasure to present three initiates." He crossed his forearms and held them level. His legs were spread apart in a formal ceremonial stance.

"Your news is welcome, Senior Master," came a deep even-toned reply from inside. "You may proceed." It was the voice of Louis, lowered to sound impressive.

Chuck did an about face and gestured to Tony. "Junior Master, you may present the Initiates." He turned and entered the tent.

It was Tony's job to lead them into the "temple" one at a time. He stepped over to Danny and tied on a blindfold. His movements were not particularly ceremonial—there had not been a rehearsal.

"*Junior Master*?" Danny chuckled.

"Yeah, yeah," he spoke softly so Chuck wouldn't hear. "Just play along, okay? Take off your coat and carry it with you."

Julian and Randall looked at each other, unsure how to react. They watched Tony lead Danny to the tent opening. Why the blindfold? The sun had set an hour ago, and there was no moon at all tonight. They took off their jackets and waited their turn. It was chilly already—below 60 for sure… no breeze, no crickets, nothing: absolute quiet.

"You shall be called **Delta**," said the deep voice. Tony pushed Danny's head down so that he wouldn't bump into the tent—the top of the split that created the entrance was under five feet; you had to duck down when you went in. Tony pulled open the left side of the tent split, and Danny was led inside.

Randall sensed that this was all a game. Apparently we aren't supposed to talk. He gave Julian a bemused grin; hard to tell what he thinks—in these trees, the starlight is minimal.

Julian's question had been answered—namely, what everyone was going to do after the potty run. The Initiation had started already—might as well; it's cold and we don't have a campfire. It should be warmer inside.

When Tony returned to put on the next blindfold, he gave Julian a smile and a wink. Danny told me all about breaking him in at summer camp; he should be able to figure out what's coming. I'll keep a straight face—no point in letting him know too much.

Julian had been high on his *personal list*—the special list of as yet untasted yumyums. The list had been put aside when he took up with Danny at the end of summer camp. Tony did not regret that; the ceremony this weekend would remove Julian's name from the list; he didn't regret that either.

Julian was called "**Epsilon**."

Randall's turn: Tony gave him a wink too—no point in letting him worry. I don't know Randall at all; but he's Julian's pal, maybe he has some idea about what's going on. If not, well… too late now.

Randall appreciated the wink, but wasn't sure what it meant… probably just something to reassure me. I wore one of these in grade school once; we whacked at that hanging Mexican thing… a goat—or a burro? First grade stuff. The blindfolded kid had three minutes to hit a dangling paper maché animal with a stick. If time ran out, the next kid tried. The idea was to break it open. Whoever succeeded won the toy inside—everyone helped themselves to the candy that spilled all over the place. I'll bet these guys are up to something a tad more advanced, it won't be raining candy kisses in there. Oop… we must be at the tent.

"You shall be called **Zeta**," said the deep voice. "You may enter."

Why Greek? Maybe that gets explained later.

Tony lifted the flap. "Hand me your coat and take off your shoes." He gave Randall's head a light push downward and followed behind.

It felt slightly warmer… these tents must hold in the heat… well, it did say Arctic. He unlaced and removed his shoes. This explained the short delays… someone, probably Tony, took the shoes away.

"Remove your pants and hold them out to the side," Chuck's voice instructed.

I knew it! I expected something like this. I've heard about fraternity initiations. These guys must have a connection with one of those… that explains the Greek letters. Just so they don't plan to do any paddling…

His pants were whisked away; someone took his left hand and guided him forward.

This is strange… a step up. It took a second to figure out why it felt so odd underfoot: I must be standing on one of the air mattresses. But it's smooth, no round top ridges… he was placed somewhere. From behind someone held him by the waist and shifted him slightly… I'm being positioned. It didn't feel threatening… just a little wobbly.

"Welcome Initiates," the deep voice of Louis began. "I am **Alpha**."

In spite of himself, Randall felt goose bumps run down his neck and arms. Being in total darkness sets you up for that…

Julian wondered if he was supposed to hold his hands behind his back or in front, or what. I hope we get to sit down pretty soon; it's hard to hold steady.

"During this ceremony, you will use your designated letter name; it is how you will be identified by the others. It is given for you to hold in trust until the rite is concluded. Should you succeed and advance to the next level, you will be given a new name for that ceremony."

Yow… what am I called again? Julian had never heard it before… a foreign word… eppy something…

"There will be no need to speak. During the first step, you will be allowed enough light to follow the instructions and learn the Letter Names of those present. You will use only those names during the ceremony."

Randall had no problem with that. *Zeta*. That's easy enough…

"The everyday world has been shut out. Soon all light will be extinguished. The ceremony will be conducted in total darkness. Your task is to learn a new level of understanding and communication—you must rely on your memory alone; you will learn to employ your other senses at a higher level than you have ever known. Welcome to the entrance of an ancient and sacred mystery. Its name is known only to those who have completed the Four Stages. Tonight you will begin; if good fortune is yours, tomorrow you will complete the First Stage."

Danny wanted to laugh, but controlled himself. Tony never said anything about all *this*.

"We will now form the Circle of Energy. You may lift your blindfolds temporarily—do not remove them completely. Please sit cross legged and be sure your knees touch the knee of the person next to you, on both sides."

Randall welcomed this instruction. He raised the blindfold—a faint reddish light, sort of like a darkroom safelight, but not as bright, made it possible to see shapes. He snuck a glance—I guessed right: Julian. Louis is on my left… he's the one doing all the talking.

Julian was disappointed; it's still dark in here. A flashlight must be on somewhere, but it isn't being allowed to let out much light. Who is where? I must be in the middle—I was the middle one brought in… Danny must be on my right.

Danny was happy to sit—stable at last. He looked down: the air mattresses had been joined together end to end and side by side under a large giant sized flannel sheet; I can make out where they meet. It's comfy—one large area… like one big padded wrestling mat. *Ooo.*

With a little scooting and shuffling, it didn't take long for the circle to form.

Having a bare knee come into direct contact with another person's is, for some, a pleasant surprise. When it happens on both sides at once, the effect is beyond surprise—it is more like a jolt.

At once a unique current began to surge—mysterious, pleasant, thrilling: the six point zig-zag "circle of energy" had been formed. Each point a pair of knees… each point essential to form the circuit—six crotches, now connected, hummed silently as they searched for a common frequency.

A pleasant glow was felt at the base of six spines—the result: six wakeup calls. There was no way to stop the thrilling sensation—not that anyone wanted to—erections began to form at once.

Louis placed the flashlight in front of himself, pointed toward the center; the thick red sock surrounding it dimmed the light significantly. He picked up a deck of cards; after shuffling them he placed them in the center of the lit area and spoke:

"Each person will draw a card and pass the deck to the left. The one who draws the highest value is chosen to begin…"

Randall paid close attention: Louis is reading this from a prepared script… it looks like 3 x 5 notecards… this is planned in detail…

Danny glanced around… why not just start? I'm ready *now*.

Grand Master Louis continued: "**Gamma** is appointed to draw the first card. The person to his left will be next, and so forth. As we go around the circle, you will speak your name; pay attention as you hear the name spoken at each place in the Circle of Energy. It is important to learn the names as soon as you can."

Julian's eyes had adjusted to the dark… I can see who is where; that's a relief. Now I can figure things out… remembering those odd names will be a lot easier…

Tony began the process; he reached forward, selected a card and placed it in front of him face down. He nudged the deck toward Danny. Danny selected a card and pushed the deck to his left. The four others followed in order until the deck was back in front of Tony; the circle was complete.

Tony flipped his card over. "Gamma has a six of Hearts."

Danny flipped his card. "Delta has a ten of Diamonds."

Oh boy… huge problem… Julian racked his brain… nothing… not even a remnant of his Letter Name was there. He flipped his card… "Um… Queen of Clubs." He grimaced.

"Epsilon has a Queen of Clubs." Louis came to the rescue.

I am *so* embarrassed. At least it's mostly dark… epsilon… epsilon… epsilon… if only I could write it down… epsilon. What kind of word is that, anyway?

Randall was sorry he hadn't helped somehow. He flipped over his card. "Zeta has the Ace of Spades." Oh-oh… that's the highest card!

Louis was next. "Alpha has the 3 of Hearts."

One card remained, one more Letter Name to hear: "Beta has a 4 of Spades." Chuck placed his card face up.

Randall gulped and reached for the cards. He slipped his Ace into the deck. "Zeta." He passed it to his left. Each person followed the example: they returned the card to the deck and spoke their Letter Name. Alpha… Beta… Gamma… Delta… Epsilon. When the deck was again in front of Zeta, he handed it to Louis.

The Grand Master gave the deck a shuffle and placed it behind, out of sight. He resumed his deep tone. "We will now begin the unveiling. Zeta drew the high card; he has the honor to be first. He will remove his shirt and speak his Letter Name. He will put the shirt behind his back and the person to his left will then remove his shirt and speak his letter name, and so it will go around the circle."

Without hesitation, Randall removed his shirt and tucked it behind. "Zeta," he nodded at Louis. What a relief: looks like no one is going to get paddled.

Louis removed his shirt and said, "Alpha." Chuck removed his shirt and said, "Beta."

The others followed in order; Tony was "Gamma," Danny removed his shirt and said, "Delta." Julian remembered and blurted out "Epsilon!" before he took off the shirt.

Randall started the second round by removing his T-shirt. "Zeta." Alpha had helped by giving him a light nudge. Focused on doing what he was supposed to—and learning the Letters—he didn't think about where this was going.

Alpha removed his T-shirt and gave his name. This process was repeated over and over, one article of clothing at a time. It might have seemed tedious, but it served the purpose well: soon everyone knew all of the Letter Names and where they were in the circle.

The methodical removal of clothing also guaranteed that the fifth and last item would be special and spectacular. Each person had to stand and face the center of the circle as he removed his skivvies.

Bravely, Randall stood: "Zeta." His circumcised six inches bounced cheerfully several times, waving hello to five pair of eyes that had been awaiting its appearance with great interest. Everyone's eyes had adjusted to the low light—seeing the essentials was no problem at all.

How did I do that so easily? Must be because I had to go first—didn’t have time to think about it. Before he could sit down, Alpha stood up.

“Alpha.” Louis flipped his skivvies behind his back.

Until this minute, the only erection Randall had ever seen was his own. Other than a few tantalizing trouser bulges, he had only fantasy and imagination to go on—he couldn’t believe his eyes. The largest cock in the world had just sprung free at his left.

Julian smiled—not at the size—Alpha wasn’t as big as Tom—not many are; but it will be easy to identify *Alpha* in the dark. Next to Zeta, it was super huge; you don’t see those differences when everybody’s sitting. So: Alpha equals Big One; Zeta is Little One… all I need to do is to figure out a way to remember these weird names. Why is that so important? He watched carefully… Beta has a big one too, but it curves to the left. Tony is next… I’ve wondered about him… Gamma. hmm. No easy hints there, just not as big … now Danny: that’s easy. I know Little D already. Danny is the guy that showed me how to do everything at camp.

Oop my turn… I’m last. He stood and removed his shorts. “Epsilon.” He tossed them behind and glanced down. Oh… I look like Zeta… Julian felt a little better because he’d remembered the name; as long as I can remember the word I’ll be okay. He glanced a second time… Zeta has more hair down there. Not surprising… mine got a late start…

Randall had been waiting for this moment… whoa… he’s circumcised, like me… are we the smallest ones? Huh. I thought he was bigger…

“You will now lower your blindfolds.” When Louis could see that they were in place, he provided more light and waved silent instructions: Tony stepped behind Julian, Chuck stepped behind Randall, and Louis stepped behind Danny. On cue, they held them by the waist and nudged them into place.

The Initiates were spaced evenly into a line at the center of the tent, at the end of their own air mattress. Later they would discover that their sleeping bag, pillow, and blanket were directly behind them. They would have no need to hunt for them after the ceremonies were suspended for the night.

Alpha spoke again: "Please spread your legs apart and put your hands behind your back." He waited for them to be in a comfortable position, and motioned to the other masters to move around in front; this was their first action position.

"The first sense you will learn to perfect is Touch. A Master will demonstrate this for you. When he is finished he will speak your Letter Name. You will then get on your knees and follow his example; when you have recognized who he is, speak his Letter name." He relocated the flashlight to the side. The dim light allowed the Masters to perform the introductory instructions with precision… they reached forward.

Someone's right hand gently took hold of Randall's cock—what a *feeling!* It was a revelation: it glowed with pleasure. Whoever it was began a routine. Wondrous… he forgot to pay attention to specific details at first… whoa. I'm being *explored...*

Julian hadn't realized what was going on until the last minute—he was still preoccupied remembering those Letter Names. But when someone took his cock in hand, everything changed. Someone is running his finger around my tip. My shape is being traced as if it was being drawn…whoa…wonderful—I *feel* what I look like… I can see what I am, only I'm *huge*… gigantic…Ooo! that's where I'm the most sensitive. His artistic skill had come into play: I'm looking at myself in some kind of fourth dimension mirror—I see myself from the inside out…like a galaxy, a gigantic pulsing neon outline filled his field of view.

Danny had not expected this, but he was delighted; whoever's fondling Little D knows what he's at, that's for sure. Ooo, yes… a favorite sensation: slowly pulling down the foreskin. Man, staying still while someone is tracing every inch of your cock, up and down, back and forth…feels very strange.

Randall had never imagined anything like this… a fingertip was following a line around his genitals—down one side, around behind his balls, and up the other side… he had not realized that his scrotum was capable of feeling *pleasure*…

Wow… I *like* this—Julian had never had his balls included before. Danny didn't do *this* at camp…

Danny recognized this part. Tony had done this to him after school one day… must have been just after he was initiated. But that isn't Tony's nose. Mmm…

Randall's heart rate had accelerated considerably. It's a good thing that this is so tender and slow. Otherwise… oh! Something slid up the side—a *nose!* I'm being *sniffed!*

Julian's nostrils awoke when he felt his sack being nosed; he hadn't been paying attention to anything besides what was being done—but the air in here smells *sexy*…

The tightly woven arctic fabric performed as designed: hold heat in and keep cold out. Pheromones and body heat emanating from six horny boys had begun to create an enriched atmosphere. No time limit was set for the first stage, but it took less than five minutes for two hands and a nose to trace, caress, and learn every millimeter of the other individual's manhood. How it felt, how it pulsed, how it smelled was entered into memory. To the person being examined it seemed infinitely longer—the requirement to stay still became a sweet agony.

At last, the time had come; Randall sensed it at once: he's gone… the "surveyor" had withdrawn.

"Zeta," said a voice. The first Initiate had been identified and announced.

It took a minute to adjust; now I'm supposed to get on my knees and find out who said that—who spoke my Letter name. He reached forward… nothing there… he moved his hand to the right—a leg. Aha! he's standing up. Carefully, slowly, he moved his hand upward… oh, boy—for the very first time he had someone else's hard cock in his right hand. Wow. It's huge, it's *enormous*… and… the skin is *loose*! Ah! Uncircumcised! whoa… I always wondered about this…

"Epsilon," said another voice.

Julian looked forward to this. Why did it take him so long to identify me? I guess you're supposed to be thorough. My turn! He reached out and oop! Someone's tummy! Oh, yeah… I'm supposed to get onto my knees. Sure enough… mmm. Nice. I know about this! He had played with four uncircumcised cocks at camp, so he knew pretty well how they worked. Let's see… he held it and squeezed lightly. Medium to large. It's either Tony or Danny—no: either Gamma or Delta. He started tracing the head first… ooo-ee, do we have a drip? He pulled the foreskin down all the way and spread the droplet out; it was enough to coat half of the underside. He continued the fingertip exploration around the top and down the side of the scrotum… lots of hair down here…

"Delta." The third identification had been announced.

Danny was super ready… he recognized Alpha's voice. Why did he take so long? He must have drawn it out on purpose… I can't be that hard to identify! He got onto his knees and reached forward… yow! It *is* Alpha, the big one. Hmm. Do I have to tell the minute I know, or do I get to pretend I don't know yet? Silly question: let's pretend it's a surprise… *Oo-ee*, it takes both hands…

Randall was fascinated by the way foreskin behaved—even though the shaft is as hard as a rock, the skin glides like a layer of soft silk. He tested its limits—up all the way it almost covered the crown; down all the way the shaft felt super tender. He twisted it right and left… interesting. I can't do this with mine… wow… He pulled the skin down with his left hand and held it in place while his right hand went through the tracing routine. The head is super sensitive… I wish I could look at it, actually see it…

Julian wasn't practiced at this; but the surprise encounter with Doug that morning in the Panther camp was kind of similar. He wanted to be examined close up, so I said sure: he had a bent down one, and I wanted a good look. This one is regular… very nice…

must be Tony… it's bigger than Little D. Going through these tests is fun… I'll make sure to do everything. Boy, this is making me super horny… they didn't say anything about sucking though… too bad. Should I call him Little T?

*No no no: it's **Gamma**, stupid!*

Inside guy is here! With him helping, I'll get those names straight.

Danny enjoyed exploring Alpha… it was like an enlarged version of himself, in a way. The blood vessels were more prominent, and the crown was broader. There's plenty of foreskin; I can pull it clear over the tip even though the shaft is hard. The balls hang down more than mine… Alpha must use a *sturdy* jock strap. It's too big for doing what Tony likes…

Randall had explored Chuck's huge curved instrument and, though he didn't really want to let it go, the time had arrived. He pulled his hands away— "Beta."

"Gamma," Epsilon announced a few moments later. Julian was pleased—he just realized that he would be playing with Gamma again: why else would they want me to know it so well? So I can find it in the dark!

"Alpha," said Delta. Danny was ready for whatever was next. Tony said this would be hot, and he was right.

The Grand Master spoke: "Congratulations, Initiates. You have all passed the first test. Sit back and listen carefully. You are about to be told what is required next, and what you will be doing for the rest of tonight."

Chuck gave Tony an elbow in the ribs and a wink to show his appreciation for providing such excellent candidates. All in a line, they looked marvelous. He was eager to play with all of them—and he would before they broke camp on Sunday.

Alpha continued: "Your next task is to reach out to your first Master—the Letter Name you learned; you will be taught how to employ your hands—and, later, your nose. No other sense is to be employed or explored. Others will be added in due course—first to be mastered is the sense of touch."

Julian frowned. Darn. I wanted a taste. Maybe that's tomorrow.

"When you have released the sacred fluid, you are to spread it across your partner's body. This honored lotion is a special gift. As you do this, speak your Letter Name. As the lotion evaporates and cools, prepare for the second exercise. When all three Initiate names have been spoken, instructions will be given."

Randall was tempted to pinch himself to be certain—is this really happening?

Alpha continued: "At my command, you will remove your blindfolds and hand them forward."

Alpha paused, as the instructions on the card indicated. "Last of all, let me repeat: the only word spoken aloud will be announcing your name after you have completed the exercise. Does anyone need the instructions repeated?"

There was no request. Alpha nodded to the other Masters to position themselves for the first exercise. He turned off the flashlight and tucked it behind. He reached forward with both hands. "Remove your blindfolds and hand them forward." When he had all three he tucked them behind and gave the order. "Initiates, find your first exercise partner."

Each Initiate reached forward, and found his partner right there, waiting; the program proceeded as planned.

Due to the prolonged preliminaries, many were too far along at the start; the Masters prevented early ejaculations by giving a clear stop signal. After a pause, action was resumed; it was essential to experience a range of techniques before the first climax.

Beta began by pulling Zeta's scrotum downward with his left hand; with his right he gave the shaft a delicate, slow upward stroke. Randall followed his lead…

Randall had never thought about trying different things—other than trying his left hand once, he'd always sought the fastest finish possible. Manipulating another person at the same time I'm being stroked is incredible.

Mildly surprised at Gamma's first move, Julian followed his lead. A slow, circular massage, somewhat like Danny's lesson that day in the cabin—only he kissed me at the same time… I wonder if Gamma will do that…

Danny was grateful he had been told to follow the lead… otherwise, he wouldn't have the faintest idea how to handle something this large…

The Masters instructed the Initiates in the art of mutual masturbation by example and suggestion; no pre-set pattern or sequence—each followed what felt right. Motions or patterns that drew no response were replaced and others tried. Gradually, each individual learned to communicate his own level of pleasure and to detect what pleased his partner. It was similar to learning to dance. The rhythm was generated from within; the activity was silent, yet sounds were present… general, vague, suggestive—an occasional intake of breath… and with the first ejaculation, soft groans of pleasure.

The second round was much like the first—after the Masters shifted positions, the Initiates were instructed to engage with their second Letter person. It took longer to reach completion; the activity differed because the individuals fit together differently, and spending more time allowed for more experimentation. The action was still restricted to the hands and nose.

By the end of the session, each had an intimate knowledge of two other boys' sexual equipment and how they were able to give pleasure in return. It was burned into their mind and memory; and, they knew themselves on a new level—what they had and how it worked, and how to give pleasure to another person. They had begun to master the skill.

It was fortunate that Julian didn't have to search for his sleeping bag because he was exhausted. It was right behind him, just as Alpha said it would be. Fortunate, because crawling in was about all he was able to do. At least the no-talking rule is still in effect. No late night yak-yakking on this campout. We're supposed to stay silent until we leave the tent in the morning to fix breakfast. It will take that long to sort out this odd, strange, wonderful thing—and to decide if I want to see it through a second night.

> *yawn* < Julian wasn't sure if he would be able to sleep. Little J isn't sure either—he's doing some odd things on his own… small pulses or something. That's a new thing too… I hope he didn't have to work too hard or anything… maybe he'll calm down in a minute.

Randall's brain was numb, and his balls felt strange—drained most likely. He was proud of himself, but unsure why. He had achieved something, but he wasn't clear about that either. Instinct kicked in and he crawled into his sleeping bag. Best of all was the rule about no talking. He wasn't ready to look anyone in the face, let alone say anything. Moving to this end of the country from Pullman was nothing compared to where he had travelled tonight… he didn't know where he was, and he wasn't really sure where he had come from… but he realized that it wasn't possible to go back, either. He wasn't worried about falling asleep—that never worried him. Sometimes he stayed awake all night, other times he dropped off the minute he was down. He had turned that over to whatever was in charge of that a long time ago.

Danny was pleased and a little surprised.Over the last few weeks he'd had a small preview of what happened tonight because Tony had done some of these wonderful things; but it was different because it was so much more detailed and extended. Being able to do these things with someone other than Tony was a surprise. Somehow that wasn't a problem… in the end, it will make Tony and me better together. Chuck and Louis have some kind of program here, though; it's too complicated for them to have invented it… I wonder if the other levels are like this… I wonder if anyone else is going to take part in it… When do they let us talk about it?

Danny yawned and snuggled into his bag. I was going to curl up with Tony tonight, but… he reached over his head to touch… by accident, he had learned that their bags were opposite each other, head to head, almost touching.

Tony's hand was there, waiting… he pulled Danny's hand to his lips and gave it a quiet prolonged kiss.

That was all Danny needed… that moment was the best part of the evening.

13 Initiates day in the park

a:Danny b:Julian c: Randall

a. Danny and Tony

Tony checked to make sure that both Louis and Chuck were well gone, not just out of sight… yeah, they're far enough. He moved quietly until he was right behind Danny. "Boo!" he whispered.

Danny turned around, startled. "I thought we weren't supposed to talk."

"I won't tell if you don't," Tony puckered his lips.

Danny kissed him, as requested—and as expected.

It became more than a love peck; it was crucial that Danny be okay with what had gone on last night. Tony didn't want anything to mess up what he had going with Danny. This ceremony thing is kind of kinky—that's okay if it doesn't foul anything up. The idea was to make what they have even better.

"So, you're okay?" He played with Danny's curly hair absentmindedly. The kiss was wonderful, and reassuring.

"Yeah, why wouldn't I be?" He ran his right hand around behind Tony's waist and gave a reassuring tug.

Tony shrugged. "I don't know, it's just that I'm not used letting anyone else play with you."

"I thought we had that figured out." They had a long talk about that before deciding to come on this trip.

"You're right. So what do you think?"

They sat down cross-legged and faced each other. They had a long-standing rule about not showing their affection in public; they weren't stupid. But when they were alone, the opposite was true.

Danny was glad Tony was being himself and stretching the rules. Tony had never met a rule he didn't want to "test" real good; that was one reason Danny was so in love with him. He does stuff I'd never dare to, even if I thought of it. He looked him in the eyes for a minute—he hadn't done that yet today. What I want to do right now is borrow Randall's camera and take a picture. He looks so fabulous this morning. Danny was still amazed at what happened inside when Tony stared into his eyes like this… too bad I hafta talk.

"It's different… kinda neat, in a way. I never expected to take so *long* though." He grinned slyly. "That part will be interesting when it's *your* turn."

Tony laughed. True enough: they had never been able to control themselves and extend. Instead, they just rested a little and went for a second helping.

"When is it our turn, anyway?"

Tony rechecked to see if they were still alone. Silence… no breeze this morning. The angle of the sun and the color of the remaining leaves certified that autumn was well along. Not cold enough yet to make their breath visible, but that would change before long. Nothing moved out there. "I'm not supposed to tell," he winked.

Danny gave him a skeptical look. "Why not?"

"Beats me." Tony hadn't been attentive when that part was discussed. His favorite bulge had begun to form in the lap opposite—he touched it gently. "You, down there: you have to wait until after dark."

Danny blushed; Tony always gave him a stiffy; he'd never timed how long it took.

"We're together *first* tonight. But you don't know that." He licked his lips.

"Mmm," Danny approved. Perfect; I don't want Tony to be last. By then I might be too pooped out… doing *three* is a big challenge. The last one is supposed to happen after we're asleep. Alpha said this morning that a Master would find them in the dark and perform the last part of the ceremony. Weird. So, I'll be awakened by Chuck. He's the only Master left, after Tony; Louis was the first one last night.

"What's all the secret stuff for, anyway?" His frustration began to show. "Why aren't we supposed to *talk*, even?!" If they said why, I missed it.

"Dunno. The one I was in was a one-nighter in Chuck's basement. There were four guys instead of six. One thing was different though. I could hear other things going on. I think the other guys did more advanced stuff." He thought a minute. "It figures if you think about it; I was the only new guy, so they just did the first level with me."

Danny's eyes went wide. "What were they doing?"

"Can't say for sure, but I could hear slurpy sounds… hard to tell what was going on… I was busy myself, y'know."

Ooo… maybe we could add a little tonight when it's our turn. No, better not—Tony gets carried away… we might bump into one of the other guys.

"So when we got up in the morning, we just had breakfast and went on our way. It wasn't a campout. Chuck's folks were out of town."

"Did you use the oddball names and everything?"

"Yep. Everything was pretty much the same. But I was the only new guy. What it came down to was each of those guys taking a turn with me. *Whoo!* I was so tired out…"

"So who was the other guy?"

"Called himself Alpha. But his real name was Phil. Phil Young, I think. They told me later. He's in college."

"Alpha… so did he run it then, like Louis?"

"Yeah." Tony reflected. "I think he might be the one that brought Louis and Chuck into whatever the club is. I guess it's a club."

"Funniest club I ever heard of. I bet they don't read the minutes of the last meeting."

Tony thought for a minute. "Y'know, Chuck has a cousin that goes to college—a football player. He's well known—famous, I guess."

"What's his name?"

"Don't ask me; I never pay attention to jocks." Tony had an active dislike of organized sports. Generally he regarded anyone on a team as a lower life form. "Ask Chuck… no, wait. Don't. I don't want them to know we're talking instead of picking wildflowers." He looked around. What wildflowers?

"So we're *not* supposed to be talking then?"

Tony grimaced. "I don't know, for sure. They didn't sit me down and go over the rules." He frowned. "I think maybe they're leaving something out, or…" he didn't want to admit that his attention had shifted and he didn't get it all. I didn't ask them to repeat anything.

"Why are we supposed to be collecting all the plant junk, anyway?" It's almost winter; not much around except dead grass and leaves.

"I think it's just so we have something to keep busy, so we won't talk."

A sound at the left made them freeze in place… something had moved in the brush. A fluffy grey tail wagged into view, swished a few times, then disappeared. A second later a squirrel appeared and hopped forward lightly—its mouth stretched open wide, holding an acorn. It paused momentarily then hopped another two feet and paused again. They watched silently; it stared right at them, but didn't seem to know humans were present. It moved forward again, always in two or three foot lengths, until it was across the clearing.

"Why do they hop?"

"Don't know… I took Biology last year, but I don't remember anything about squirrels." Tony wasn't a pet owner either; animals didn't much interest him.

"They seem to be all air." My dog likes to chase them—otherwise, I haven't thought about them much. "What's it going to do with the acorn?"

"Bury it. I remember that much. They store it for later when it's snowy or cold. The ones they forget turn into trees."

"Mmm." Danny just had a thought: "*Say:* is there a merit badge in biology?"

Tony grinned at him. "I never thought of that! I bet there is! They have a *million* merit badges." Tony always needed to earn points and credits for Troop Nine. The first meeting is Tuesday. "Let's check that out! This stuff might come in handy!"

Danny gave him another kiss and stood up. "Might as well fill these bags." He checked his watch. "Three hours 'til lunch." The idea of getting credit for this was attractive.

"By the way: don't forget to give me 25 points for going on this campout. Having a few bonus points ahead of time is a good idea. I was even up by the end of summer camp." This year won't be so bad… Andy is the new Patrol Leader—he's better than DumbCop Dale; Dale always had it in for me.

b. Julian and Louis

As far as Julian was concerned, the best part of the day so far was breakfast. Tony did a great job making scrambled eggs. Instead of bacon, he fried up cubes of spam. When they were all cooked and toasty, we broke open a dozen eggs right over the pan while he stirred; he flipped it over and over 'til it was done. Fast, easy, and tasty; explained why they brought along that huge frying pan. The donuts were okay, considering they were a couple of days old and mashed flat in places… whose pack were those in, anyway? A cup of hot cocoa, and we were good to go.

Julian had never cooked anything all by himself. It would be a good idea to pay attention; someday I'll need to know what to do. Danny is good at it; he cooked breakfast for the Arrows at summer camp. One of these times I'll ask Mom to teach me some things. Maybe I could surprise her someday and have supper ready when she gets home—or breakfast in bed, maybe. 'Cept I don't know if she would like Spam; it's another thing we never have.

I'm in a better mood now; ever since we got started, Louis has stuck to me like glue—he must be a guard or something. I guess he's gonna make sure I don't talk to myself. Oh well.

You probably would, too. Inside guy was there to help him stay in line.

If it wasn't for the fact that he had been assigned to Louis for the day, Julian might well have decided to sneak back to the tent, get his stuff, and hike home. Inside guy had talked him out of that:

What about Randall? You can't just leave him here.

Julian couldn't argue with that. The rule of silence is so *unreasonable*, that's all. That weird wake up call this morning: I was sound asleep when all of a sudden somebody shakes me by the shoulder and tells me to put that stupid blindfold back on.

They had all these instructions and I wasn't *awake* yet. One thing was clear: Once outside the tent, we're not allowed to talk about what went on inside. The trouble with that is, we're not allowed to talk inside either, other than to say those stupid names. What is *that*? Am I supposed to get some kind of secret message from the spirit world or something?

What really griped was being treated like a little kid: too young or too stupid to be told why things were set up this way or that; why can't they just be honest about it and say what's going on? All his life he'd resented that, deep down. He didn't complain about it usually, I'm smart enough to know it would only make me feel worse; besides, it wouldn't do any good.

All right: so what about last night? How is that going to do me any good? At camp I made a rule: having sex with someone else is allowed as long as it helps get me ready for Mark. Last night qualifies, but what about tonight?

Wait a minute… I just had a thought. A BIG thought. The image of Mark wearing those leisure pants… those pants that clung to his buns like a coat of paint; they showed off the front side real good too.

Julian was adept at the art of imagining things, a well organized library of images in his mental filing cabinet helped—one drawer was dedicated to Mark. He began to plug in some of these with the new kind of memory he was introduced to last night. Mark is about the same size as Beta. By accident I saw him completely hard once in the cabin—only for a second; too fast to tell if it curved like that… but…

Inside guy isn't objecting. He generally remains silent if he's okay with my line of thought. This will pass the time. That last memory of Mark had been gnawing at him to be put on paper. But it had to be in a separate tablet—a secret one so I don't have to tear out the pages. One of these days I'm gonna get a new sketchbook—one that's reserved for secret drawings.

Picturing the subject of a drawing in his mind prior to putting pencil to paper was his favorite method of starting anything important. It's the perfect activity to keep me occupied while I scrounge around for interesting plant samples. I know what to do there—I did a lot of this at camp with Justin. The Forestry merit badge class spent several days collecting things. I sort of know what to look for… he bent down and tugged at a small tuft of grass. Remember now, get two of everything.

While he collected samples, his imagination took over… A special Mark drawing, for sure, but I just might draw what I played with last night. I might as well have seen them—I can almost see them this very minute. He grinned at the idea: boy, where would I hide those?!

Louis was attentive, keeping an eye out for any signs that the blond kid was having trouble. That was important—tonight will be even tougher. So far, so good. Ah… that's better… he just adjusted himself; that means he's is going over things… good. That's a big relief.

—∞—

c. Randall and Chuck

"There's a bunch of acorns over here," Randall aimed his camera and took a good *in situ* close up shot. He wasn't sure if Chuck was looking for these. In fact, I'm not sure *what* Chuck is doing besides keeping me under surveillance. It's obvious that they designed this part of the event just as carefully as the part in the tent. Each Initiate is accompanied by a Master, and we've each been led to a different part of the forest. I don't believe in coincidences: they're making sure that Julian and I don't talk about what went on last night.

"Great!" Chuck answered. "Grab one or two extras. See if you can find ones that don't look exactly the same." He had been watching closely; so far, no signs of trouble. During breakfast I had some second thoughts—he is a little green… caught on fine last night though… learns fast.

When Chuck wasn't looking, Randall tried to match what he could see this morning with what he had felt last night. Chuck was Beta, the first one. His eyes wowed. I would never have thought that my first experience enjoying another boy's cock would be what happened last night! Maybe the rule about not talking is smart… The chance to just *think* about it is welcome; I need to sort it out in my head before anything else.

Randall had a highly organized and segmented mind. A part of it was fascinated and curious; another part was a little frightened. He had been dumped into a deep lake and no one was willing to toss him a lifesaver. He was being tested like he never imagined possible. Sink or swim? Something like that. I wish there was a way to sneak a look at what's printed on those 3 x 5 cards.

He scooped up a few acorns and tossed them into a bag. This is a good spot to shoot the wide area. He grabbed the tripod and set it up. Let's see… a few reference shots to please Dad… he mounted the Yashica medium format. Color prints are costly—one 12 exposure roll will have to do the job. He reset the film speed on his light meter and took a reading… the light this morning is *excellent*. The crisp air is bracing—autumn is one of my favorite times of the year. The humidity is within bounds at last. Adjusting to that was the biggest task after moving here last summer. Eastern Washington is usually in the thirties in the summer.

Here I am, collecting plants and leaves and lichen flakes as if I was on a biology class field trip. It made sense in an odd way—it gives me something else to focus on. I assume we get to keep this stuff… I can use it in Mr. Frankel's class. With the photos and samples, I could do a pretty good report on Piedmont flora in October. Somebody is into that stuff, not to mention any names. Father will love these snapshots.

I got some good candids of Julian at breakfast. Too bad I don't have an infrared flash… some snapshots inside the tent would be *very* nice. Thinking about five guy's cocks was beyond any fantasy I could have imagined. But now here I am, collecting bits of dead and dying plants, experiencing sudden flashbacks of two of them as if I had known them for years! I can still feel them—*smell* them, even.

Up to now, his big dream had been to find a way to play with Julian… he had no idea until now what that would be like… Wow:

tonight, this very night, I'm going to do *exactly* that! Will he be first or second? The third is supposed to be a Master—either Alpha or Gamma, since I had Beta last night. He glanced at Chuck again. Whoa. Amazing what you don't see in a guy's pants. More amazing to know what's in there, even when his back is turned.

They have it all figured; but telling us what's happening or going to happen isn't the way this club works. I guess it's a club… they won't say its name though. Pretty weird… the whole thing is weird, come to that.

Although, it is engineered with skill. Complex formulas are at work here. This wasn't invented by a couple of high school kids. How did Louis and Chuck get pulled in? One of them must have a connection on campus. This has to be from one of the fraternities; they're big on secret initiations. I'll bet they have a predetermined grid—all they have to do is plug in the names; Alpha said this morning that by the time we're done tonight, we will have "learned" all five. I couldn't figure that out how to set that up without a tablet of graph paper and a couple of hours free from interruption. What kind of formula would that require, anyway? Another thing I can't ask Dad… he snickered: I keep running into those.

The one thing that had begun to worry Randall was Julian—not so much *when* we'll be put together, but what he will think—will he like what I do? He'll be comparing me to four other guys. It's not fair! They're all *experienced.* What if he *hates* the way I do it?

It's stupid to worry about that, but I can't help it. It's my first time! If only I could talk with him beforehand and explain somehow, and ask him to understand… what if he never wants to do it with me again? This is sink or swim… I *have* to do well with Julian! *Everything* depends on that.

"I've got some nice sweet gum pods over here," Chuck announced.

Randall took a deep breath. The interruption to his thoughts was welcome. He had almost thought himself into a hole. Keeping his mind off it for a while was a good idea.

"I could use one of those; thanks." He stepped over to Chuck, ready to aim his close-up lens.

Chuck smiled back. Looks like the kid is gonna make it. He sure knows about cameras.

14 The Sadie Hawkins date

Oblivious to the sound her shoes made as they struck the floor tile, Rita Mitchell marched down the empty hallway with determination; she had found a way to deal with Tracy. She was still furious. For the second week in a row, Tracy had pulled this stupid trick. Once was bad enough, and she had tolerated it. Tracy didn't know that she had done some checking, and knew what was going on: the so-called "reception with important alums" was nothing of the sort. Under the banner of getting a football scholarship, he was sneaking off with Barry Webster and his cousin to a stag party. His fraternity was raided for showing triple X movies a year ago, and now they're doing it again.

Cousin Val told me about those movies—they're all the rage in the Ivy League frat houses. Val saw part of one. The fraternities pass them around from campus to campus.

Rita was smart enough to hold her temper in check—throwing a tantrum wouldn't do any good. No, that would make me look immature—he'd just go ahead anyway. I have to get his *attention*. This will do the job nicely—and if it doesn't, I might go ahead and dump him. She didn't want to, but she would if it came to that. Tracy was just being a stupid horny guy; getting him under control again was worth the effort. Besides, her ego was at stake—what if word gets out about what Tracy and Barry have been doing? Embarrassing doesn't begin to describe it. Her *reputation* was at stake.

Lynne and Barbara were on either side as she reached the second floor landing. Getting them excused a few minutes early "to work on Girl's League business" was easy enough; I'm in solid with Miss Fredericks—acquiring the hall passes was not a problem.

When I saw the blond cutie in the hallway on Friday it came to me in a flash: the boy during registration! I got so busy doing other things that I forgot all about him. Seeing him inspired me instantly: I'll take *him* to the Sadie Hawkins dance—Tracy will be out in the cold. That will do the trick. I'll wait until the *last* minute to tell him… she grinned with narrowed eyes. No one beside herself and her two friends would know until it was too late for Tracy to do anything about it.

She steered her "lieutenants" over to right side; a twenty foot strip of wall was free of lockers… the perfect place to lay in wait.

"He'll be coming from Miss Nielsen's room." She pointed to the left. "You can't miss him. He has wavy blond hair; as cute as can be. All you have to do is block both sides—so there's no way around when I step in front of him, okay?"

—~—

Julian left the typing class refreshed. An odd feeling to have after an hour of boring keyboard drill, but he was grateful: it felt terrific to *not* think about anything—especially *it*. He didn't have a name or a word for what happened at the campout, so he just called it "it." He had recuperated, but barely. His first full night of sleep was *packed* with dreams. Parts of that weird ritual popped into my head and gave me such a stiffy it kept waking me up. After a while that got really annoying; didn't matter to Little J though.

It's a little better at school, but Little J is always looking for an excuse to go puffy. He was a problem in English class, but not history. P.E. was so-so; all those guys in the shower were a challenge. He was just as frisky as ever in typing class—that's always one of Little J's favorite times; he doesn't show much when I wear the Levi's. He glanced down… hmm… shows when I walk. Anyway, it's packed with kids along here—no one can tell.

I shouldn't have done the second night… but I couldn't figure a way to back out. Besides, how could I? I'm glad that Randall was the first one… kinda nice, actually. Danny was second—old home week; like being back at Camp Walker. But the last one was Mister Big—Alpha… Big Al for short. I was too tired to get much out of it. Big ones are… hmm. I need to find a new word; it's stupid to call *everything* weird, even if it is.

How do I get those things out of my head? At least for a day or two… I wonder if Randall is having the same problem. He looked okay in History class. We still haven't talked about it. Didn't show up for lunch today either… just as well, I suppose… I'm kind of chicken to bring it up. I've never had that kind of problem before. Maybe after school we can talk… yeah… after school. The next class will help… Art is my favorite. The rest of the world disappeared when Julian was in Art class. He turned the corner and headed toward Mr. van Horn's room.

The traffic always thinned out along here, making it possible to walk a little faster. The sensation below drew his attention… darn. Little J is still up quite a ways. I can tell from the way he presses against my right leg. He glanced downward… It would be nice if he was asleep by the time I get there… walking doesn't help. I can't make any adjustments in the middle of the hallway, either—someone would see.

"Here he comes… everyone ready?" Rita fluffed her hair to give it a fresh from the outdoors look.

Her "crew" nodded in the affirmative.

Julian was especially eager to get to Art today—a demonstration of something *new*. Mr. van Horn didn't do those very often, so this is special. I've never used charcoal before; this is going to be fun.

All of a sudden his way was blocked—three girls had stepped into the center of the hallway. Since this was the Junior Class locker area, he figured these girls were juniors; he didn't think anything was out of the ordinary. He could just smile and go on around—no big deal.

"Hi," said Rita, in a cheerful friendly tone, stepping directly in his path.

Julian stopped in mid step. He didn't know too much about Junior Class girls—actually, he didn't know anything about Sophomore Class girls either—especially ones from the Rally Squad and Dance Team, like this one. I recognize the outfit: the sophomore outfits have a solid red skirt. Julian generally avoided all that school spirit and rally assembly stuff. Watching long rows of girls in short skirts jumping up and down in front of a screaming mob isn't my idea of entertainment. Besides, they're mostly from the rich part of town—have to be to pay for those uniforms. It looks like she wants to tell me something. Hope it doesn't take too long.

"You're a sophomore, aren't you?" she was surprised by what he looked like up close; fortunately, she had her script planned.

"Uh…yeah." What else can I say? He rubbed his nose unconsciously… her perfume is kind of strong.

"What's your name?" It took some effort to maintain her cool: he's *much* better looking than I thought!

"Er… Julian." He glanced at the other two girls… looks like they want something. Maybe they're working on a project… probably recruiting helpers. I know: I'm about to be drafted to work on a decoration committee.

"I've never met anyone named Julian before!" she exclaimed. "You're my very first!" Her "look-pure-and-innocent-smile" gave way to a "look-at-what-I-just-found" glow.

Her friends muffled a snicker.

She had not seen his eyes before: they aren't blue, but *brown*… puppy dog brown! With *perfect* black eyelashes and dark eyebrows. The summer tan is fading, but his skin tone is still very *very* nice—freckle free, too!

Julian blushed, unsure if he should say anything or not. What she said wasn't exactly a *compliment*, although it might have been meant as one. She seems nice enough, even though she stinks of perfume.

"I'd like to check something, do you mind?" Rita had been hiding the pale yellow Gerbera daisy behind her back. She brought it around and held it up in front of his face. Look at his *eyes!* She studied them closely while he focused on the flower.

If someone puts a flower an inch from your nose, you pretty well have to look at it. Sort of medium sized, it's kind of stout, for a flower. The light yellow color looks almost like poster paint… For a minute he thought it might be a fake, but when the girl ran her finger across the petals he could see that it was real. He nodded, assuming that she wanted to compare it to the color of his hair. He ran into that a lot. He couldn't figure out why they made such a big deal about his hair all the time. All his life they did that. Especially Geraldine.

Rita held the flower by the side of Julian's head. "What did I tell you?" she asked the girl at her left. The flower was a surprisingly good color match at that.

Lynne's eyes had been focused on a much lower area of his anatomy. She could see an indication of what might be Rita's real objective. Nibbling at her fruit twist, she nodded slowly. "You've got an eye, all right."

"My name is Rita." Tilting her head slightly, she delivered a coy smile. "Thank you for helping me win a bet." She held out the flower for him to take. She studied his lips. Yes… *very* yes.

Julian looked at it for a moment… she wants me to hold it for some reason. "Oh—okay… uh, Rita." He took it and examined it up close to be sure it wasn't painted. > *sniff-sniff* < Nothing.

"And thanks for accepting my Sadie-Daisy." She curtsied, and took a last measured look before turning around to lead her friends down the hallway. I have made a real discovery! "Be seeing you," she said, as they hurried off.

Julian watched them walk away, whispering and giggling between themselves. The bright red and white Cardinal Dance Team outfit emphasized her rather short girlish figure: narrow waist and wide bottom. No thanks. So they didn't want me on a committee. That's a relief. Just betting on my hair. He shook his head and looked at the flower again. What am I supposed to do with this? I don't really want it. Is there a wastebasket around here? Nope. Come to think about it, I saw another girl carrying one of these—a bright red one. Odd. Hey: maybe Mr. van Horn can use it; he's always arranging odds and ends for us to draw. Might as well poke this into one. He skipped ahead—don't want to be late!!

This was Ralph van Horn's tenth year at Jackson High. With Joe Stoddard, the ceramics and woodcraft teacher, the two person art department was in high demand. Ralph took the drawing and painting classes; one day he hoped to add sculpture if he could get the budget approved. He had been looking forward to this day for over a week. I can't wait to see what my star pupil will do with the new medium. Impatient, he fussed with the materials a little; everything was set up at the end of last period. He was always pleased when Julian entered the room; he's a little later than usual. Julian is special—the biggest talent I've ever had in class. I moved him to the center of the room so more students could watch him work and learn from him; it's almost as good as having a full time assistant.

Julian glanced at the clock as he headed for his seat. Wow, just in time. Those girls almost made me late. At least Little J is shrunk up completely now… probably the perfume.

A small commotion on the far side of the room meant class hadn't started; several girls were whispering and giggling something. Julian glanced over—they're looking at me. He tilted his head… are you talking to me? When he looked over they went silent. He shrugged and turned his attention to getting settled—books always go under the table to free up drawing space.

He did not notice that each of those girls had a bold colored Gerbera daisy on her table. He didn't find out the significance of that until after school, when he ran into Nick.

When Julian placed the flower on the desk, van Horn grinned. I'm not surprised. The flowers were distributed this morning. Some girl was bound to be on her toes and snap him up. As far as Van horn knew, Julian was up for grabs. He isn't driven by social pressure like so many boys his age—he's focused on developing his extraordinary talent. That's why he's such a delight in class.

The bell rang. Julian had his sketchpad open and ready, and his eye on the narrow black stick that had been placed dead center on his table.

"Good afternoon, ladies and gentlemen," Mr. van Horn began. The rapt attention from Julian was like a shot in the arm. He picked up a new charcoal stick and held it up. "You each have one of these. Before you do anything, however, you need to know some basic rules of the road..."

15 Sorting it out

Geometry was a good way to end the day. Julian liked Mr. Withers; his dry sense of humor and his ability to make mathematics visual made it interesting. Visual was where he thrived; the nifty thing was that he started seeing geometric relationships in his drawings. At first his awareness of angles and space had been instinctive... but now it became a conscious part of composing a scene—it was another tool. It's a lot more interesting than algebra was last year.

I was gonna ask about hexagons after class, but Inside guy advised against it. Just as well; Julian's opinion of the Initiation had begun to sour. He had begun to suspect that the hexagon last weekend had little to do with squeezing in a sixth air mattress—or connecting with a secret Mystery of the Universe. It had more to do with what tent Louis could borrow from his dad.

Here I am, thinking about it again... he shook his head to free it up. Instead of going to his locker, he turned left: I'm gonna find Randall and see if he's okay. I can grab him when he leaves Mr. Frankel's room. The longer I go without talking about it, the more uncomfortable I get; I bet it's the same for Randall. Mr. Frankel's room is only five doors away, so... I'm in time—good. He's just now coming out.

Randall glanced at Julian and looked down awkwardly. He didn't expect Julian to appear unexpected like this—usually, it was the opposite; I always hurry to meet Julian at his locker after school. I don't know what to say.

"What's the matter? Hey, *Randall*. It's me: *Julian*."

Randall looked up sheepishly. "I thought you were mad at me."

"Mad?!" Julian was shocked. "I'm not mad at you! Why would I be mad at you?" After what we've been through, how could I be?

"I don't know." He glanced up at Julian's face and realized at once how stupid he had been. He blushed, embarrassed. "I'm sorry… I… I'm all confused about things…"

I was afraid if this. "Campout, right?"

Randall nodded.

"Well I'm confused too, if you want to know the truth. So that makes two of us." He put his hand on Randall's shoulder. "Get your stuff and let's go talk about it, okay?" To heck with those guys' rule.

"'Kay." His locker was close by. He felt a whole bunch better, now. Julian's cheerfulness was exactly what he needed.

Julian watched carefully as Randall exchanged his Biology book for History; he seemed nervous and jittery, fumbling awkwardly for his clarinet case… did I do something to make him feel bad? He searched his memory. The problem was the rule those guys passed about not talking. At first I was glad; I didn't *want* to talk about it. I didn't know what to think, let alone say. I figured it was smart to do what they said. But now… now I need to talk about it. Looks like Randall has the same exact problem.

The end of the school day is marked by a sudden flurry of activity and bustle. The happy cacophony of lockers slamming, people yelling, laughing, hurrying to get to an activity or to go home: perfect cover for an awkward silence—just what the two friends needed to get their bearings. Going to their lockers, figuring out what books they needed to take home, putting on their jackets, winding their way through the hall to the stairs with someone they knew… by the time they were at the exit to the bike racks, they almost felt normal again; the queasy feeling was gone, replaced by growling stomachs. As they approached the bicycle rack, Julian had an inspiration.

"Wanna go to Sparky's?"

"Yeah!" Randall grinned wide. "I've been by it, but never gone in." The popular drive-in was a couple of blocks from the school; it's the kind of place you went to *with* someone.

"They have super milkshakes." Geraldine's crew stopped there sometimes after work.

"That's a great idea… they have a bike rack, don't they?" Julian's nod set him at ease. Randall had started riding his bicycle to school the second week. It put him into the nerd colony automatically, but he preferred that anyway. At Jackson High, you either drove your own car or rode with a friend who had one—or you walked. Otherwise, you were "nowhere." If you were a Nerd, you rode a bicycle; a music instrument case completed the image perfectly. If your mother brought you to school, like Julian's did… well, there wasn't a word for it. People just smiled sympathetically.

His parents said that he could have his own car next year provided that he maintained a four point GPA all year—in other words, forget about it. A four point means an A in every class. How am I supposed to get an A in P.E.? Everybody knows only jocks get an A in P.E.

No point in getting upset about it. In the first place, he had no need to parade his masculinity—the main motivation behind most guys getting a car. One or two might need a car for a job, but most of them just want to show off—pick up chicks and impress them with how much noise the muffler makes. Besides, driving a car would likely attract the attention of the Nels types, I sure don't need that.

Proximity to the high school made Sparky's Drive-in a logical destination during lunch and after school. Always busy, sometimes overflowing, Julian picked up the pace. Today luck was with them… they found an open booth right off. The simple menu was encased in a plastic stand on every table. The milkshake flavors were located at the bottom… Julian scanned the list; I had a chocolate and a strawberry last summer. Maybe today… *Lime*? Mmm…

What intriguing flavors... *Pumpkin*? *Peanut Butter*? Do they mix any of these? Randall had a yen to try a combination chocolate and peanut butter...

The waitress appeared with two glasses of water and an order pad at the ready. On the short side, her fully developed top appeared very large; the low cut of her blouse allowed more cleavage than was permitted at school. A recent graduate from Jackson, she was efficient, if slightly impatient—sophomores weren't her favorite. They never order more than a coke, and never tip. The older, bigger boys usually ordered a burger basket; they came in later. The daisy peeking out of the blond boy's pocket caught her eye; she gave him a wink.

Julian didn't know how to react, so he pretended not to have noticed. Her Betty Boop hairstyle and overdone makeup made her a bit of a cartoon. Neither boy knew who Betty Boop was, but it was clear that Georgia (the name on her badge) was on parade. When she left with their order, Julian smirked and rolled his eyes. Randall broke into laughter. It was a perfect tension release.

A stack of books and a large coke plopped down suddenly right next to Julian's water glass. "Now I've seen everything." Nick scooted in with a gentle nudge to Julian's ribs. He gave Randall a friendly wink; he was helpful when we went shopping for Mark's new station wagon.

"Wow, hi Nick!" What a surprise. He gave Randall a reassuring smile. This is great! Of all the people I know, Nick is the best one to ask about stuff—especially personal stuff. They had become close buddies at camp. Julian was instrumental in helping Nick and Tom set up their secret bedroom.

Randall remembered Nick; he wasn't particularly happy to see him, though; how am I gonna talk about those guys and their Greek letters with him here?

"I saw you guys come in; what do you think of Georgia?"

"Georgia?"

"Yeah, the waitress. She doesn't usually flirt with sophomores, you know." Nick spotted the flower poking out of Julian's shirt pocket. "Maybe she's jealous."

Julian had no idea what he was talking about; he stared back, his expression a complete blank.

"The flower!"

Oh... "This?" I forgot all about the stupid thing. He pulled it out—huh: not wilted yet. I didn't know I still had it.

"Yeah! Who's the lucky girl?"

A sinking feeling... "girl?"

"Sure. Who gave you that flower?"

He paused for a minute... what did she say her name was? It took a minute. "Rita, I think. Yeah, Rita."

"What's her last name?"

"Dunno. Why?"

Nick broke into a big laugh. "You better find out! She's taking you to the Sadie Hawkins Dance!"

"What?!"

"Every year, the girls get to ask the boys out. Only girls are allowed to do the asking. It's *required.* Whatever girl asks you first gets you. The girls can swap if they want, but not the boys."

"That's about the craziest thing I ever heard of. Is that in the Student Handbook?" I knew I should have read that...

Nick laughed. "I wouldn't doubt it." The look of panic on Julian's face was real. "Hey, it's not *that* bad. You don't have to pay anything. The girl has to do that—she picks you up, takes you to the dance, and buys your refreshments... the whole thing. All you have to do is go."

Julian looked across the table: Randall was equally shocked.

"When you took that flower, you were saying yes. Even if another girl wants to give you one of those, you still have to go with whoever snagged you first. ...*Rita*, did you say? I don't know any Ritas."

Now I see what Mr. van Horn was talking about; he said it would make my life simpler if I kept it poking out of my pocket... said I should do that for the rest of the week. So that's why they use such a sturdy flower...

Randall was grateful to learn this... just in case. I doubt if any girl would try, but if they did... "So if you refuse to take it, you're okay?"

Nick shook his head. "Better to take it. Otherwise, you get on a blacklist. Some guys have been messed with pretty bad. They gossip about you, call you names, generally try to make your life miserable."

"Whoa..." Dating girls—Randall had not faced the issue yet. I've been lucky so far; my parents don't care much about that stuff, fortunately. Maybe I should plan to be sick...

"I don't get it: why would a girl I've never even seen before want to take me to a dance?" Must be some mistake.

"Don't ask me," Nick shrugged. "Never had the problem; maybe she's a secret admirer." It's not hard to figure why—Julian is as good looking as they come.

Randall's eyes blurred suddenly—he'd just realized the implications of this: what he had feared from the first: a girl had discovered Julian. It was bound to happen. The question is, what will he do? Will he—perish the thought—like her? Rita... not a very common name. I have to find out who she is... competition was not something he knew much about—but he wasn't going to sit idly by, not when it came to his friendship with Julian.

Julian had an idea: "When is it, anyway? Friday after the game?" Maybe we could spend most of the time watching football or something...

"No, no, no…" Nick pulled out his student handbook. He always carried it along. He flipped to the calendar. "November 10. It's a Saturday. Julian, this is one of the biggest dances of the *year*. It's almost like the *Prom*, it's so big."

Prom… that word was vaguely familiar. I always ignore words like that. Should I ask what that is?

No, but you better do some homework about all this stuff. Inside guy had come awake; survival issues were being discussed here.

"What if you don't know how to dance?" Maybe there's a way out…

"I guess you have to find someone to teach you." Man… Nick scratched his head; this is one problem I never had to face. "Don't look at me. I don't know how to dance either. I'm one of the lucky ones who never get asked. Hey: maybe Tom could… he had to go last year." It helps to have a bunch of big brothers help you get over the hurdles. Plus, Tom's good at faking things. Nick looked at Julian closely. I get it: he doesn't have a girlfriend… all he does is scouts; I should have known that. He doesn't have an older sister like I do… No wonder he doesn't know anything.

"I know how to square dance… sort of." They taught us how in the fourth grade… that wasn't so bad. It was kinda fun… do-si-do and all that… I've forgotten most of it.

"I don't think that will help much. I'm pretty sure they do modern stuff… you know, like on American Bandstand."

"Oh." I saw that on TV. Geraldine said something about that when we were buying school clothes. *B o r* -ing…. I changed the channel.

Maybe this is lucky... Inside guy interrupted… *maybe you won't have to do the movie date after all!*

Say! That's right! Another hot idea just popped up: when I tell mom, she'll tell Geraldine, and *they'll* teach me how to dance. "November 10?"

"Yep. You have about two weeks to get a costume and learn how to dance." He winked at Randall. "No problem for a guy with your talent."

"Costume?"

"Sure. It's a theme dance. Everyone dresses up to look like one of the Dogpatch characters… you know, in *Li'l Abner*."

Li'l Abner… Julian never paid attention to the funnies, other than *Peanuts* and *Rip Kirby…* oh, and *Pogo*: I always liked the idea of a possum being best friends with an alligator.

"You don't read *Li'l Abner*?" Nick faked a shocked expression. "What's the matter with you… are you some kind of weirdo or something?"

"Darn right! Weird is my middle name. You can call me JW for short."

They broke up laughing; the milkshakes arrived. Georgia checked Nick's glass. "Refill?"

"Sure! Cherry Coke." He passed her the empty glass.

Julian and Randall addressed their milkshakes. Just the thing; their minds were taken off personal problems temporarily. First, they had to taste each other's shakes. Surprise: Julian liked the peanut butter chocolate better than the lime. Randall liked the lime best. They traded; tummy and tongue were delighted.

Nick watched this closely—it just occurred to him that maybe they were more than just friends. He thought about that while they played with the milkshakes. Maybe, but I don't think so. Julian doesn't seem to have a crush on Randall, at least. It usually shows, somehow. Julian is the same as always… Randall I don't know well enough yet. Could well be though… he sort of reminds me of myself: the wallflower.

Nick had no idea where Julian was when it came to romance. I keep thinking of him as too young, too pure… stupid of me. It's easy to see why he was asked to the dance: he's grown a bunch since camp… he's downright hot now. I'm so wrapped up with Tom I don't notice things like that right off.

After a while, Julian and Inside guy had it figured out: all I have to do is break the news to Mom, and everything will get fixed: she'll tell Geraldine, and Geraldine will take over. She won't be able not to. She'll teach me to dance *and* make my costume. It'll be just like the school clothes thing. She was in her element that day. Not only that, it will take care of the movie problem… for a while, at least. Inside guy had come through again!

Now then… Julian looked across the table: Randall. Why did he think I was mad at him? Looks okay, now… hmm. Seems to be hitting it off with Nick; that's good. Maybe Nick can help out… maybe he knows those guys. "Say, Nick,"

"Hm?"

"Do you know a couple of guys, their names are Chuck and Louis. I think they're seniors."

Nick nodded his head. "I don't know them, but I know who they are."

Randall's eyes went wide; he couldn't believe Julian would bring *them* up…

From the expression on Randall's face, Nick knew instantly that something was amiss.

"You know anything *about* them?" Maybe he's heard of the 'Initiation.'

"Not really. Why?"

"They're friends of Tony's."

Nick rolled his eyes. Tony. Anything is possible with Tony in the picture. From Julian's tone of voice, something needs attention. Tony is in the Troop, after all. "Friends?"

"Well, sort of…. He turned to Nick directly. "Tony and Danny took us on a campout with those guys over the weekend."

"Oh. I didn't know they were scouts. What troop?"

"I don't know… they never said. Maybe they aren't scouts." Julian looked over his shoulder to see if by chance anybody was listening. He spoke softly. "Maybe campout is the wrong word… they called it an 'Initiation.'"

Nick frowned. Something struck him as wrong about this. "Initiation? Into what? A club or something?"

Julian checked to see if Randall wanted to say anything. He was looking down, picking at his fingernails.

"That's the thing. It is, but it isn't." He fussed with his straw, searching for a way to tell about this. "See, we didn't know what was going to happen at first. We thought it was just a campout. I think Danny and Tony knew what was going to happen, but they didn't tell us anything. It seemed okay at first, you know, a little weird, but…"

Nick noticed that Randall was very uncomfortable.

"You remember last summer, when you and Tom gave me that surprise party?" He looked Nick in the eye. "It was kind of like that."

Nick's jaw dropped open wide.

"Only it wasn't like that at all." Julian looked around again. "It was all in the dark and we weren't allowed to talk." He glanced across the table. Oh-oh. "Randall?"

Randall looked up. His face was white—he was close to panic.

"Randall! Nick is our *friend*. He *knows* stuff. He can help." In fact, he may be the only one who can.

Nick stretched out his hand… he kept it there until Randall reached back. Nick grasped it and squeezed gently. He waited for eye contact.

"You can trust me, Randall. You really can." He waited while Randall sorted out his emotion.

Randall looked from Nick to Julian and back again… he'd never had a friend at this level—always he was left alone and unable to reach out. This was so new and so genuine it was a little overwhelming. He nodded mutely and smiled. A tear ran down his cheek.

Julian just had a flash insight. "Was that your *first* time?"

Randall nodded.

"Whoa…" now I see why he's so messed up.

"What did they do?!" Nick was alarmed. "Do we need Tom?" If those guys got out of line, Tom could handle them, no sweat. He looked around at the wall clock. "He'll be through with football practice in an hour or so…"

"No, no" Julian shook his head. "It wasn't anything that *bad*, really, it was just so *weird.* The thing is, they wouldn't let us *talk* about it."

"Yeah," Randall nodded his head fervently. He looked directly into Julian's eyes, pleading to be understood. He had talked himself into believing that Julian hated what they had done together, that he'd never want to do anything ever again.

"Wow." Nick looked around. "You know, maybe we should find another place to talk."

"Boy, yeah." Julian scratched his head. "We can go to my house…" It's not far, about a mile.

Nick bit his lip. He glanced at the clock. "You live close to Mark, right?"

Julian nodded.

"Let's do that. But we have to talk along the way… I have to be back here to meet Tom after football practice. What do you think?"

"Sure." Julian checked to see what Randall thought. Randall nodded his approval.

"Great." Nick slid out of the booth. "Be sure to leave a nickel for Georgia."

Julian tilted his head.

Nick his put his fingertip to his temple. "Good memory. She remembers if you leave a tip. Next time you come in, you'll be glad." He nodded emphatically, placing his nickel on the table.

A nickel made the milkshake cost 30 cents… no big deal.

Nick checked his watch as they walked into Julian's room… I need to leave in ten minutes. He looked around. "Cool." Model airplanes overhead, and a big table covered with drawings. The Troop Nine Scrapbook was there, along with his Assistant Scribe steno tablet. "How's typing class?"

"Okay. I've got the hang of it; I should practice more." He pointed—Mom's Royal typewriter was in its case under the end of the table. Taking it out was a bother, but leaving it on his desk all the time was silly. Drawing stuff is more important.

Randall assumed Nick would take the chair, so he sat at the foot of Julian's bed… it felt kind of bold to do that. But after that campout this room seemed to welcome him; anyway, there's no place else to sit.

Nick bent down to examine the typewriter. "I've never seen one in a travel case like this." He opened it up. "This is cool. You ought to see mine. It's pretty ancient compared to this." He squatted down and typed a few words. "Nice."

"Mom got that in college, I think." Or maybe it was a graduation present. Yeah, that's right… Grandpa gave her that.

Nick stood up. "So, to get back to Louis and his tent…" He pulled out the chair and turned it around. "My bet is he got pulled into that club or whatever it is by his brother or a cousin. It's a college thing, for sure."

"That's what I thought too," Randall nodded. The Greek letters pretty well gave that away. "At first I was afraid they were going to pull out a paddle."

"Paddle?!" Julian kicked off his shoes and hopped onto the bed; he adjusted his pillows to make leaning against the headboard more comfy.

"Yeah. In Pullman one of the frats got in hot water because they hurt one of their new guys pretty bad. That's a part of getting initiated as a member—fifty whacks or something like that." He shrugged. "I don't know if they all do that; their paddle was drilled with holes so that it hit harder."

"Ouch!" Nick laughed. "Maybe this one tests how good you are at doing special things in the dark!"

Randall and Julian looked at each other.

"They *said* it was a test!" Randall nodded; "they said if we passed we would be invited to do the second level."

"Yeah. I figure the second level must be taste… y'know, kissing and… well, *tasting*." Julian wowed his eyes and licked around his lips. I wanted to do some of that.

Randall turned red. He had thought the same thing.

"Makes sense." Nick gazed at the model planes swinging over Randall's head. "The third and fourth? Did they say anything about the other levels?"

"Nope."

"That's the trouble," Randall's frustration was boiling. "They didn't say anything about *anything*—outside the tent, especially."

"And we weren't supposed to talk about it, either. They said we had to use only our sense of touch and smell. No other sense—no tasting, no seeing or hearing." I really would have liked to include sucking. Especially with Gamma.

"Maybe that's level three." Nick found the whole thing very strange. Although, he was sort of wondering about Tom and himself trying some of it… could be nice. "But they didn't hurt you guys any…"

"No, nothing like that… just the opposite. The whole idea was to make everything feel perfect… the best possible." Tired me out, though. "I was sure glad when it was over, y'know?"

"Me too." Twice in one night was hard… a first for Randall. *Three* times on Saturday.

Nick was intrigued. I'm gonna talk to Tom about this. He might know those guys… "When do you know if you passed?"

"They didn't say."

Randall clarified. "They said if we passed we'd be invited to the second level. They didn't say how long that would be."

Hmm… Nick pondered that. Probably when they get good and horny again… better not say that aloud. "What did Danny and Tony say?"

"Nothing. Sunday after breakfast we packed everything up and hiked out as if nothing had happened. We were back home by lunchtime."

"It looked to me like they had a good time." Randall had paid attention to them. "They seemed to be thinking and remembering stuff from the tent." Well… pretty hard not to do *that*…

Nick checked his watch. "I have to get back to Sparky's. Tom always meets me there after practice. I'll do some checking around. There must be other guys that have done this…"

"Yeah," Julian agreed. "They ran it like it was a regular thing, all right."

"Louis read everything from 3 x 5 cards."

"So you don't think Tom needs to "take care" of these guys?"

“Nah.” Julian laughed. “They’d prob’ly invite him to join.” He grinned; “Tom could show Alpha what being big is really like.”

“For sure!” Nick laughed, and checked his watch. “Gotta shag or I’ll be late.” He stood up.

Julian followed him to the door; Randall tagged along. He didn’t want to go home yet, so he hung back.

“Thanks, Nick.” Julian waved gratefully as he skipped down the steps.

Nick gave a thumb up and jogged up the street.

He turned around to face Randall. “See what I mean? Nick is *so* smart. I knew he could help us figure it out.” Thanks to that little conference, Julian had come to a decision. “You aren’t in a hurry to go home are you?”

Randall shook his head.

“Good.” Mom won’t be home for an hour, at least. “Let’s go back to my room.” He closed the door and headed there at once. When he reached his bed he hopped back up to his perch. “Kick off your shoes and come on up.” He pointed to the space in front of him.

Randall’s eyes popped wide open. He complied at once. He sat at a respectable distance; this is new. Usually, Julian brings in an extra chair; we always sit at the table to do homework.

Nick ran the bizarre story through his mind as he jogged along. It was strangely attractive. Tom and I might be able to use a few new techniques; obviously there are things to learn. *Noses!* If Randall hadn’t been there, Julian might have gone into more detail. He laughed aloud, remembering that special thank you party at Camp Walker when the troop was off at the Sunday service. Amazing! Julian had proven that he wasn’t at all shy or afraid to play… showed Tom and me a thing or two! Danny had appointed himself the task of breaking Julian in, and he did a first class job! Julian's outstanding show and tell proved it. Hard to imagine it when you look at him… boy.

Still, this thing is annoying…they should steer clear of sophomores. They're too green to do such advanced stuff. Strip poker is about as much as they can handle… regular strip poker—not what Geoff's Poker Club does. So Tony got them into this… it figures. That's who I need to check with. He owes me for setting him up with Geoff. Yes… he's the one to spill the beans on those guys. I can quiz him after the troop meeting tomorrow night.

—∞—

"So…" Julian crossed his arms and looked for the right words. "It's okay with you if we talk about it some more, isn't it?"

Randall nodded.

"Good." He paused. "See, I didn't want to talk about this kind of stuff with you before."

Randall knew *that* well enough…

"But now… I mean, face it: you are Zeta and I am Epsilon, and we got to know each other pretty good!"

"Yeah," he chuckled, blushing.

Julian smiled warmly. He waited for Randall to look up—he wanted to look him in the eye. He reached out. "Put 'er there, Zeta."

Randall took his hand… it was different this time. Last time was in the nurse's office. Unexpectedly, Julian pulled him into an embrace. It was awkward, and incomplete, but it was wonderful. He felt tears begin to collect. When Julian let him go he was both sorry and grateful.

"Here's the thing…" Julian paused.

You should save that for later… Inside guy stopped him in mid sentence.

Julian paused, glad Inside guy was on the job—good timing, guy. You're right: I don't need to give him the bad news first. I have to let him know that we can't be boyfriends the way that he probably has in mind. But that has to be later; Inside guy is right about that. He changed course.

"I think it was really bad for them to invite us without checking us out. It was bad enough for me, but I didn't know that you had never done anything before. I mean, you must have been scared to death."

Randall shook his head. "No. I suspected something was up when they invited us." I had put two and two together about Danny and Tony. "It figured that it was going to be a sex party—I could tell that from the way they talked."

"Really?" Julian was amazed—and impressed.

"Yeah. I was really excited about it. I've wanted to try stuff for a long time, but I didn't know anybody… I'm kinda chicken to say much…"

"Makes me feel pretty stupid… I didn't suspect a thing!"

"Wow. What *did* you think?"

"I just thought it was gonna be a camping trip. Extra points. We get points for going on campouts. It helps in qualifying for stuff. You can't advance to the next rank if you just sit around, y'know."

"You didn't suspect *anything*?"

"No. When they wouldn't let us see into the tent I knew something was up. I expected scary stories, or something. Besides, I was expecting to get all those plant samples for biology. And I didn't know Tony—he's always funny, but I've never talked to him before, actually. I always like to meet guys in the troop I don't know." It helps when I work on the Scrapbook if I know these guys.

Now that he thought about it, Randall wasn't surprised. Julian never shows any interest in sex.

"I was just like you until last summer… I knew—or thought I knew—what I wanted, but I always figured I was an oddball, y'know? I didn't think anyone I knew felt the same way. Boy, was I wrong!" He laughed. Then he stopped short and looked at Randall with a straight face. "You have to promise you won't tell, okay?"

Randall nodded his head.

"No, really *promise*. There's nothing worse than talking about people behind their back."

He raised his right hand. "I really promise." No one had asked him to swear an oath like this before. He felt a rush.

"Excellent." He could tell that Randall meant it. He's not a scout, but…

He's okay… Inside guy was in on this, all the way.

I think he is too. Since Danny was in the Initiation, he figured it was okay to tell about what we did at camp—still, it was essential to keep his name secret. Julian felt strongly about this; especially since Danny was a friend, and he was in the troop.

"Where was I?" Julian thought back… "Oh… camp. On the first morning at camp, I was assigned to do KP with Danny. KP means 'kitchen police:' doing the dishes, basically. We got done early, that's when he took me into the supply tent and… it was weird: he wanted to give me a *massage* and…" he pointed downward, "play with Little J."

"Little J? Who's that?"

"Oh, wait… you don't know about that yet…"

Take your time, take your time…

"Sorry—see, it wasn't until later that he told me that he had named his stiffy Little D. So that's when I named mine Little J." He smirked. "It's kind of neat to have a name. Between you and me, I like Little J better than Epsilon."

"Little J!" Randall laughed. "That's perfect!" He looked down to his own crotch… the usual problem when he was with Julian had begun to take shape. He gave it a pulse and grinned. "Hello, Little R!"

They had a good laugh. It relieved one kind of tension and increased the other kind.

"Well anyway, that was *my* first time—in that supply tent with Danny."

An instant image of Danny—or Delta formed in both their minds. The memory was fresh, like it had just taken place. For Julian, he was the first one on the second night of the Initiation… one of the best of the five.

The advantage of—or the problem with—the campout memory was unique: the "picture" was not what a mental image usually is. The Initiation memory was tactile, not visual. It triggered a three dimensional "felt" memory, complete with remembered aromas… the memory of Danny was vivid and strong, as if he was handling it this very minute. Danny's wonderful manhood was uncut… but Randall had never actually *seen* it.

Julian hopped off the bed suddenly. "Be right back." He ran to the kitchen to turn down the radio: if Mom arrives unexpectedly, I won't be able to hear her with this thing blaring away. He looked out the back door to make sure Randall's bike was out of sight and secure. Just to be double safe, he ran to the front door and locked it as well; either way, I'll hear her using the key. I'm supposed to keep it locked anyway. Julian had decided to play—this time, *not* in the dark. I don't want her coming in on me and Randall.

Don't forget: you have to tell her about the dance, Inside guy reminded.

Right. He raced to the bedroom and left the door wide open. Inside guy is okay with playing with Randall a little—just so I don't forget to keep an ear open.

He stood with his hands on his hips and regarded Randall silently. Little R was at his maximum; Little J would be in a minute. "What do you say we forget about Alpha's rules? I want to show you a little of what I learned at camp."

It took a minute to process that. He looked at Julian in disbelief.

"You hafta get off the bed so's I can pull down the covers," Julian grinned. "It's easier to take off your clothes down here." He pulled off his shirt and draped it on the back of the desk chair.

Randall leapt into action.

"Put everything in a neat pile just in case we hafta get dressed quick." This is the first time he'd ever done anything in his bedroom. The thrill of that was a bonus.

Being told to take off all his clothes in Julian's bedroom was the last thing Randall ever expected to happen. Somehow his automatic switches were able to do that—a good thing, because his brain was frozen in a state of disbelief. Little R was certainly ready. As he took off his last sock, he noticed that his clothes were folded neatly in a pile just where Julian pointed… I don't remember doing that… He turned and faced Julian. Whoa… goose bumps zoomed down his back. Standing before him was the magnificent blond demigod in the *flesh*. What he was looking at surpassed all his fantasies. His heart was going a hundred miles an hour.

When Randall was standing there, ready, Julian took a careful look; his artistic eye kicked in at once. He imagined three drawings. But that would come later—

A new sensation upstaged his artistic response—looking at Little R had completed a new circuit; the visual image merged with the tactile memory image: the combined components seemed to swell, to glow—Randall's erection seemed to *radiate* energy. Little J is doing the same thing! Amazed, he looked up at Randall's face… he's experiencing it too…

"Whoa…" they said in unison. For a moment they stood transfixed, staring at one another and themselves. It seemed like a long time, but after twenty seconds or so the effect faded. A remnant of the blush that had roared across their foreheads made their temples glow… their erections pulsed at maximum, as if they were talking to each other.

"Was that supposed to happen?"

Randall shrugged. "Don't know…"

Julian liked what that felt like, but he didn't know what it meant. "Did we wreck things?"

"Wreck what?"

"What if we weren't supposed to look at each other until the next level? What if that was supposed to be part of the next Initiation?"

"Gosh… I never thought about that…" Randall frowned. "But they didn't say *not* to look at each other…" they didn't say *anything*.

"Right." Besides, I haven't made up my mind yet if I'll do the second one. I'm not sure at *all*. Nick didn't seem to think much of it.

So, then… back to my plan. "Let me show you what we did in that supply tent first; then we can hop onto the bed." Julian got onto his knees and examined Little R up close. Gently he pushed it to one side, then the other, examining and assessing the state of Randall's genital forest. He pushed downward in order to examine the hair follicles at the top, lifted the scrotum and peered underneath. He took close visual note of the details learned so well by touch during the Initiation. Engrossed, achieving a visual confirmation of what he knew was there wasn't particularly erotic, but it was fascinating.

The difference between this and Danny was enormous; Danny's stiffy was the first, other than his own, that he had ever seen. I already know this one really well—the Randall session in the hexagon was the first one Saturday night. The memory was vivid—positive. We're almost the same down there; Randall might be a teeny bit larger around. No need to test how it works—I know that by heart already. But *seeing* it was important. Now I know Little R a lot better. He stood.

"Now you get to take a close look at Little J."

Randall was in heaven for sure. Best of all, I was wrong about Julian not liking me. Now, incredibly, I'm looking at Little J close up… I never *dreamed* of doing this… it's so… there weren't any words in his vocabulary. The effect of the careful visual survey amazed him; it combined with the other memory seamlessly… it was as if someone was turning up the volume on the hi-fi set. The piano morphed into an orchestra. Now he could see the source of that incredible aroma… Julian's *spoor*… nothing else smells like that. When he was ready, he stood.

Julian continued. "That was the first thing I did: look at it carefully. I had never looked at one of these up close before. The second thing we did was a teeny version of what we did in the tent during the campout. We took turns beating each other off, one at a time." He paused. "It sounds silly now… but *then* it was… like an earthquake in my head, or something, y'know?"

Randall nodded. Earthquake in the head fit what he was going through right now.

Julian stepped to the head of his bed and peeled back the covers… "Bedspreads are too bumpely…" Besides, it had to be kept out of range. Unexpected squirts onto his fancy bedspread would be bad: mothers notice that kind of thing. In fact, they keep an eye out for it—Mom told me that herself by mistake.

He hopped onto the bed and beckoned. "You can lie down on the other side." He fluffed up the pillows and placed them side by side.

Randall jumped up and crawled over. He followed Julian's lead and lay on his side, his right arm forming a headrest. He stared at Julian, rapt.

"The second 'lesson' Danny gave me was an accident. He had a bad sunburn and needed to have sun cream put all over him." > *giggle* < "His butt was *very* pink. He had lain out in the sun both swim periods."

"Pink *butt*?"

"Oh—I forgot to mention that at the lake you had to swim naked. Only the lifeguards wear bathing suits...Speedos." He wowed his eyebrows.

Randall's jaw dropped.

"It surprised me at first," he grinned, "But it wasn't a big deal; no females are allowed in the camp."

Could I do that without getting a boner? P.E. is bad enough...

"Once you're there with a few hundred guys all splashing around, you don't even notice. The Speedos are what look sexy. I felt bad at first, 'cause I didn't have any hair down below yet." He chuckled. "I still don't have much. But you already found that out on Saturday night." It was sort of embarrassing—his crop of pubic hair was still pathetic: about four dozen at the last count. At least it's dark, like my eyebrows. I was afraid it would be blond like my head.

Randall glanced down at Little J. True, there isn't a lot... I don't mind.

"Anyway: I was telling about the second time. It was an accident; when I put sun cream on his buns, I didn't know it, but it gave him a big stiffy. So when I turned him around, there it was. At first I figured he had a sunburn there too—"

"Yow!" Randall grabbed himself without thinking,

"He didn't, but thought lotion would be a good idea anyway." Julian grinned. "Sneaky... he knew all along what it would feel like; he just wanted an excuse to play with Little J again; said it felt super good when I rubbed Little D with sun cream, so he talked me into undressing so he could show me."

The expression on Randall's face was a treat. Telling this to anyone had never entered his mind before today. It was fun to remember, too. I was so stupid back then.

It was only three months ago, silly... Inside guy didn't want him to think he was an old hand at this.

"To be honest, I didn't mind being tricked. I still didn't know anything other than what we had done the day before. Have you ever beat off using a cream, or your saliva?"

Randall shook his head… sounded kind of weird.

"It's different… feels great, but it's kind of messy. You hafta wash up when you're done, so you can't do it just anyplace." He thought a minute. "The sun cream didn't have much of a smell, but I hated the greasy feeling on my hand afterward. Saliva is better."

"Saliva?!"

"Sure… you just lick your palm and fingers real good; you have to keep doing that once in a while, 'cause it starts to dry on you." Julian licked his right palm until it was well coated and reached down and took Little R in hand for a small demonstration. After what they did Saturday night, why not?

"Whoo…*mmMmm*…" Randall was surprised and delighted and thrilled.

"If you want, we can do that in a little while…"

"Wow, yeah…" why wait? Randall was smart enough to not ask that, but he was very ready.

"See, I think it's best to tell you about more stuff first. I don't want you to think I'm some kind of sex fiend or anything." Julian remembered back to when it was all he could think about. That was the best thing about camp. Now he knew what he needed; didn't have to worry and think about it all the time.

Randall blushed, afraid that he might become one of those… I do think about it a lot…

"I wish there was some way for you to go to that camp next summer. You can learn *lots* of stuff." He grinned, "'course, you're not supposed to be doing that stuff at all. But lots and lots of guys do; there's so many chances; when you're not doing merit badge work or official stuff it's easy to sneak off and play around; if you're lucky, you can play after lights out. I didn't, but lots of guys did."

Giving specific examples would violate his own rule, so that was out. Tom and Nick were busy a lot, and Danny—he and Tony probably snuck off someplace after lights out. They weren't boyfriends before camp; now they're steadies.

"The third time, Danny showed me something new: how to suck."

Randall's eyes went wide… that was his own secret goal: always had been, thanks to Nels. I never thought about it until he started calling me those names.

Julian had skipped over the snorkel and how he and Sid had played in the cabin. Maybe some other time. Today his job was to help Randall out by showing him what he could—just the basics—and also to help him understand that they couldn't be boyfriends like Nick and Tom are. This is where Julian drew the line: the kissing part would have to be skipped. Kissing would be dishonest.

He cleared his throat. He wasn't sure how to get this started.

"I thought, if you want, I can show you that second lesson of Danny's, you know, the sun lotion one."

Randall held his breath… is this *really* happening?

"Then, afterwards, we can talk some more about stuff, y'know?" He looked Randall in the eye to see if he wanted to.

Randall's voice was trapped behind a locked door somewhere… he nodded.

"Okay." He sat up and faced Randall. "We did it on our knees because Danny's legs were sunburned so bad that's all he could do. We could do that, or sit." When Randall sat across from him he realized that he had never tried it sitting. Julian didn't want to do it lying down… that might make it too easy to kiss. They had been on their knees in the Initiation too; the problem was his knees always complained after a while.

They tried sitting across from each other…no good cross-legged; can't reach very well. They splayed their legs wide apart, Julian laid his left leg over Randall's right, and Randall laid his left leg over Julian's right. They scooted as close as they could… not bad!

Julian grinned wide, nodded; he licked the fingers of his right hand and filled his palm with saliva.

Randall grinned back and did the same… man oh man I have waited so long for this…

It was exquisite at once: the effect of lubrication on what they had learned to do during the Initiation was incredible. They closed their eyes automatically and focused on that for a long time. They had learned each other so well in the dark that they knew what and when and how already; it was just *better*. And they were able to prolong… they didn't need to talk.

As they reached the apex they opened their eyes and looked down and watched what was in their right hand—they wanted to see it happen. It was rapid and it was plentiful. And because of their sitting position, well aimed.

The first two ejections struck the torso opposite; the rest overflowed over their hands. When they were finished they sat still, hands in place. The experience had been better than either expected, and they wanted to hang on to it for as long as possible.

Randall was first to look up… Julian's face… wow. This image he would remember, forever… no camera could capture this.

Julian opened his eyes and grinned. He nodded. "Good one!" The bead of fluid running down his chest had turned cold and begun to tickle. He took his hand away from Little R. "Let's go clean up." He pulled his knees up and swung to the right to slide off the bed.

Randall watched him in awe… he had never imagined seeing a naked Julian walking away, casually, as if it was something he did every day. His backside is just as magnificent and beautiful as the rest of him. He slid off the bed and hurried to catch up.

Julian turned on the hot water tap and reached for a washcloth. He glanced up in the mirror. The dummy looking back at him, as always, didn't have a clue about what to say.

You can't tell him yet... Inside guy warned.

Yeah, I know. Why wreck a perfect afternoon? Why hurry? Besides, I still want him to pose.

Randall was tempted to lick his fingers as he had that night in the hexagon tent after he had massaged Julian's chest. That was not what I expected—no taste at all. This would be different… why didn't I think of that back in the bedroom? I can't do it without Julian seeing… next time. There will be a next time—I know that now. I'm not going to do anything to ruin that.

Julian saturated the washcloth, squeezed away the excess, and turned to wash off Randall's chest. "This is the opposite of the Initiation, but…"

The warm cloth felt very nice. He took it from Julian and returned the favor. If only I could wash the whole body, the whole magnificent body… maybe someday.

"C'mon, we can rinse off our hands together." A glance at the mirror reminded him of the last time he stood with Randall like this… comparing bumps. This is different… it looks nice… but only nice. He turned off the faucet and grabbed a hand towel. Randall can use it first.

Randall handed back the towel and watched Julian dry his hands. He was unable to think right now… this afternoon had exceeded his wildest dreams, and the dream was still running. Standing bare *naked* with him in his *bathroom?!* Are you *kidding?!*

"There. Let's go back to my room." He followed on purpose to see Randall's backside… buns are okay… not what I'd call "choice," exactly… but they're nice; certainly worth drawing.

Instead of riding, Randall walked his bicycle home. I don't want to arrive back home for a while. Sorting out what happened today was more important than spending another half hour practicing—the clarinet was one thing in his life that needed no attention; he'd learned all the music weeks ago, and the concert was another month away. This afternoon topped everything; together with the campout thing, *boy*. I'm not used to so much important stuff happening all at once. Like always, there was absolutely no one in the world he could talk to about this; he had to sort it out for himself. Luckily, it was wonderful and happy stuff. The trick is not to mess anything up…

> *Brrrr!* < It's getting *cold…* the headwind isn't too bad; my knit cap helps, but I don't have any gloves. I've faced worse… I hope it isn't going to rain.

What amazed him more than anything was being asked to pose while Julian drew him. Amazed didn't begin to describe it. Who wants to look at a drawing of me?! A photo would be bad enough, but a *drawing?!*

Instead of putting clothes back on, they had spent the next half hour buck naked in that bedroom. Julian ran into the kitchen and came back with a stool. He had me stand there with my right foot on the stool, my left hand on my hip, staring at the bulletin board while he started this drawing. He has a *huge* drawing board—the paper is just as big. This wasn't the sketchbook he uses at school. Once in a while I glanced over to look at him draw, like I always do… I couldn't see what it looked like, but watching him is so wonderful—especially when he doesn't have anything on! He giggled… Little R appreciated the view too.

Now *that's* a good idea, having a name for him. He reached down to make an adjustment; Little R appreciated that train of thought.

We had to stop after a while; didn't want his mom to know about this. Since she was due home any time, we had to get dressed and put everything back so it looked like we were doing homework. The incredible part is that he wants to work on it again tomorrow before we go to the scout meeting! I had forgotten all about that—the scoutmaster invited me when we were shopping for that car.

We didn't do any history. No TV tonight. Tonight it's hi-fi and homework.

One thing is puzzling, though. Once in a while, I get memory flashes of the other four guys in the Initiation. Why is that? All I want to remember, really, is Julian. But… I like remembering the other ones. In fact, I want to see them, too… I even want to do the saliva thing with them. Does that mean I'm going to be a sex fiend? Randall wasn't sure what being a sex fiend entailed. It sounded kind of bad…

—⁂—

The radio was back up the way his mom liked, the front door was locked, his bed was made, and the history book was open on his table. The afternoon had gone rather well after all. Julian's conscience was satisfied—he'd found a way to deal with Randall's crush without hurting his feelings. A lesson or two should be enough. After the Initiation, it made no sense to be standoffish… that would only hurt his feelings…

And make him suspicious, Inside guy observed.

Right. Keeping the Big Plan secret is always top priority. Randall is a smart kid—it wouldn't be hard for him to figure out about Mark and me. We'll call it The Private Lesson Strategy; keep him happy and unsuspicious.

Careful now... you don't want to give him false hopes.

Good point. I'll be careful; I'll just be the same guy as always… behave as if nothing special had happened. No special boyfriend looks, stuff like that… I'll concentrate on the new portrait. Working on that makes me feel so *good.*

He propped it up on the seat of the chair and stood back… knees. I need to work on knees. "Thank you, Mr. Withers!" He had achieved an interesting composition by making the angle of the left arm half the angle the knee made on the stool… looks more interesting.

Well… time to put it away. I can look at it later. He took it to the closet and tucked it behind, out of sight. How much time do I have? He checked the alarm clock on the nightstand; I could have anything from ten minutes to half an hour. She doesn’t always come in at the same time. The real estate business doesn’t close down at 5:30—it closes whenever the customers leave. If she went grocery shopping, it might be super late.

Doing that close-up examination of Randall reminded me: I haven’t checked down below for a while. Besides, after all this activity it might be a good idea to have a look. I’ve had more sex in the last three days than I’ve had in the last three months!

That’s an exaggeration... the inside guy chimed.

Yeah, yeah, I know. He went to fetch his mom’s hand mirror. “But you gotta admit, it’s been pretty busy lately,” he said aloud. Little J has certainly proven himself... I wonder if it shows. He grabbed the mirror off his mom’s dresser and hurried back to his room. He always used this for a close up look—the back of the mirror magnified things real well. Helps when you’re trying to count hairs.

16 Naming the Country Squire 1

"How did I ever get along without you?" Mark gave the dashboard a loving pat as he turned off the engine. Aside from the challenge posed by parallel parking, he had grown quite fond of the Country Squire. Inching into a parking spot felt like driving an aircraft carrier. But: thanks to this massive land schooner he was able to dash home to refresh and change clothes in plenty of time for the Troop Nine meeting. Before it was always an I-just-barely-made-it thing. The city bus was economical and philosophically correct, but it took a *long* time: now I'm home in fifteen minutes—I have over an hour! "What are we going to name you?" Tonight the nominations are due.

Scouts is the perfect antidote just now, too. Supervising fifty bundles of energy will take my mind off the weirdest weekend of my life. Peter had taken him for an overnight "adventure" in Raleigh. It was supposed to be fun and do all kinds of terrific things for his social life. That part of it backfired: I haven't one name to put into my address book, not one face I can remember. The "fun" part was still a matter of internal dispute. Peter was delighted with the outcome; Mark had mixed feelings about it; mixed at best.

Out of habit, he hurried into the house. Taking a shower was uppermost in his mind. He always showered at the end of the workday, but today he hoped it would help get his mind in shape for the scout meeting—a nice hot shower sometimes helped rinse away more than perspiration; anything to get my mind off Saturday night.

Years of performing the same sequence of actions can lead to a high level of automated behavior and efficiency. After six years of racing the clock on scout nights, Mark had honed down walking into the house, showering and dressing to seven minutes; he was as much a creature of habit as the next man, so today he was in the shower in under five.

It had been an average day at the store... no special frustrations to deal with, no self-debriefing needed. Things were stable, the week ahead promised to go smoothly. A nice hot shower is very relaxing, nonetheless—maybe too relaxing: it didn't take long for his mind to stray in the wrong direction. A shower can be so *conducive;* the mind tends to wander where it will. Maybe it wasn't the best way to get his mind off Raleigh after all...especially since, now that he had a car, there wasn't such a hurry...

After stopping for a bite to eat, we went to this place on the edge of downtown Raleigh called The Pompeii Health Club and Spa. It sounded grand—it looked quite grand on the outside. It could have been a hotel at one time, but there was no doorman—only a ticket window. The décor imitated a Roman emperor's villa—when you went past the lockers and up the stairs, it turned out to be a colossal steam bath with "extra features." Some of the Roman décor had faded or flaked away; what wasn't hidden by the steam had a more modern, *recently* decayed quality; they need to shut down for a week and do some repainting.

They had registered at a nice motel within walking distance and taken separate rooms—the idea was to have plenty of flexibility later on. Peter's plan was to have each of them "connect" with someone and bring him back to the motel for a follow-up to whatever they did or started to do at the spa. It seemed sound enough; Peter had done it a few times himself and vouched for its safety and discretion—not to mention its purpose: to relieve sexual tensions and frustrations. Mark had a lot of those to relieve; he reasoned it was worth a try, especially since Peter vouched for it. He was grateful—he would never have been able to venture into a place like this by himself. It was far enough from home to eliminate his fear of being recognized. This had been his main stumbling block from the beginning.

The Pompeii had begun as an exclusive private club just after the war, but they were forced to open it to the public. A larger customer base was required to keep the place open; the membership dues were high, and too many had dropped away. Members still determine the policies and procedures.

The entrance was sort of awkward; instead of presenting a member card, you bought a ticket as if you were going to a movie; a small booth jutted onto the sidewalk. A push button alerted the booth operator that there was a customer waiting. He slid a small panel to the side and, after satisfying himself that the customers were of age, cheerfully sold the tickets. Inside, you presented the ticket at the reception window. The waiting room wasn't designed to accommodate many people—it was a pass through to the dressing area.

What may have been a lobby had been walled off and converted to a book and variety store that featured special toys and paraphernalia. Its main entrance was outside on the corner, making it appear to be a separate business. The bookstore had its own clientele and was not operated by the spa staff. The spa had a discreet entrance to the bookstore from the small waiting room. Another door, marked "Private," was the entrance to the basement, where a small fifty seat movie theatre showed triple X movies. Entry to the basement was controlled by the bookstore cashier. When the fee was paid, the customer was buzzed in.

A new feature downstairs was a coin operated arcade: a dozen small private booths lined a wall outside the theatre; five minute film loops cost ten cents per view. Peter had investigated all of these features at one time or another, and told Mark about all the possible ways to spend an evening—or week, if you wanted to do it all properly.

Peter agreed with Mark that the spa would be enough, thanks.

When they gave the attendant their tickets, he passed them each a key and a bath towel. The key opened both the locker and the door to the locker room. No one could enter without a key; sensible: riff raff wasn't likely to make it past three levels of security. Everything was covered by the entrance fee. No food or beverages were allowed… drinking fountains were available.

You could leave and return without having to pay again—they stamped the back of your hand and held onto the key—some guys liked to visit the "bookstore," or have a time out in the bar and lounge next door. Owned and operated by the Pompeii, it had a disco area as well as a small restaurant; no cover charge if you showed your hand stamp. The stamp also qualified you for a discount if you needed to rent a room for the night in the small hotel above the restaurant and spa. That also had a separate entrance for the general public. Peter had a mixed feeling about that part of the complex. The motel was more expensive, but it provided more amenities and felt more secure.

You could pay an extra ten dollars for a massage if you were interested. They gave you a voucher chip to present at the massage room. Maybe next time—the price was reasonable, but Mark wasn't in the mood for a massage. I haven't had one since Erik died… it was one of Erik's specialties. Not remembering Erik is one of the main reasons I'm here.

No one supervised the locker area; two rules were posted: no smoking and no clothing of any kind permitted beyond the door to the "spa." So we undressed and stowed our clothing in the locker. The key ring was worn like a bracelet around the wrist or ankle; it had a small plastic tag with the locker number. Mark's was 77, Peter's was 78; there must have been over a hundred and fifty lockers. Evidently the place is popular—about a third of the lockers were in use. Did that mean it was a slow night? Mark rather hoped that was the case; the notion of being surrounded by fifty naked men was more appealing to a neophyte than a *hundred* and fifty. Bath towels wrapped around their waists, they went through another secure door. It opened to a landing at the base of a six foot wide stairway: deep maroon carpeting with gold detailing along the outside created a sense of opulence. Faux torches mounted on the wall every six feet lit the way; the spa occupied the bulk of the second floor.

Peter's plan was to give a mini tour first, to show what was where. The double doors at the top were not locked. We encountered a sign first thing: by direction of City Ordinance number 56 dash 123 or something, and dash 456 or something else, we were hereby ordered to shower before going anywhere; comforting to know that the health department was looking out for everyone's well-being. The shower area was to the right. No one was on duty, so the city relied on the honor system—that too was comforting.

They draped their towels on a hook and stepped in. Over twenty showerheads were available, spaced about three feet apart. Floor tile continued the Pompeii motif—a mosaic replica occupied the center: a couple of nude warriors were charging off to battle in a chariot. A decorative border lined the edge.

Showering in front of Peter wasn't a problem. Mark wasn't particularly attracted to him; he was fit and attractive enough, but… no magic there. It was a matter of courtesy to use adjacent showerheads; it didn't bother him that Peter was checking him out… he had expected that to be part of the program. One thing did annoy: I showered at home just a couple hours ago. Had I known, I would have saved the water.

A couple of men came in a few minutes later; one gave Mark a big smile and a wink. A good reminder of why he was here, it hit him a little strongly. He'd never had that happen: a blatant flirtation from someone he had never *seen* before? Mark did not know the codes or the signals—Peter had not given him any special preparation on that.

He didn't want to say yes or no inadvertently by doing the wrong thing. If I'm polite or courteous, does that mean I have said yes? I'll keep a straight face—stay absolutely blank—neutral. He turned his back to the guy. What if he comes up from behind? He gave Peter a what-do-I-do? look.

Peter stepped over and patted him on the left bun. He spoke softly: "I'm not being fresh. That pat just told him you are taken; finish rinsing and we'll leave." Peter glanced over and smiled at the man with a kind but regretful look. No point in alienating him… who knows, maybe later on… Peter had been with a wide range of men over time; he could find a way to play with most, including that one. For the present, it was a delight to pat Mark's backside at last; he'd been hankering to do that all evening. Mark didn't know the standard translation.

"Thanks… I wasn't ready to do anything yet." An understatement for sure; it's a good thing Peter was handy and had an eye out.

"Sure. Let me give you the tour now. Once you know your way around, there won't be any reason to be afraid. Remember: most of these guys are just like you and me. Every one of them likes men; each one is horny tonight—that's why he is here; somewhere in this place, just what he needs awaits. If he doesn't find it, it will find him. Same thing goes for you; so relax, take it easy… okay?"

Mark nodded. The pep talk helped… this is so new and unfamiliar. He didn't want to admit that he was afraid… but he was. I wonder if Erik knew about this place… I thought he knew about everything…

"Up ahead are the large group rooms." They walked forward into the gallery, about sixteen feet wide; fake marble columns every ten feet or so gave the effect of being the center or mall in a classical temple or forum. Several men moved about slowly or stood in a languorous pose; one studied a statue, trying to simulate its stance. The massage center appeared on the right.

Mark peered in the glass door; one table was in use, the other masseur was watching a small TV set. The décor matched the stairwell and gallery—faux torches and fluted columns every six feet. The glass doors were a modern intrusion.

The carpeting had changed to a more practical indoor/outdoor synthetic material—very tight nap with no padding. Understandable; showers and steam baths meant slippery floors otherwise. The area could have been an atrium had it not been under several stories of a downtown building; in its heyday it may have been a grand ballroom. Three life sized statues spaced about eight feet apart stood in the center—all replicas of famous sculptures—nude, of course. Mark didn't know much about the subject, but a handsome nude male standing on a pedestal here and there was impressive—and it helped set a mood; they were lit with special lights. Opaque plastic panels overhead dimmed and diffused the area lighting—the torches mounted on the wall were electric—primarily decorative, they lent a late afternoon quality to the light. The first statue was a life size replica of Michelangelo's David.

Opposite the David was the **Mark Antony** room—the source of the steam. In the center, a tubular grille, inserted between a statue and its four foot high pedestal, issued irregular puffs of steam. Different sized holes in the ingenious rotating sleeve created the illusion that you were wandering around in the clouds. Mark did not recognize the statue, but it too must have been a replica. At times it appeared to be floating in a cloud. The figure didn't have a full erection, but it wasn't sporting a sleepy mini dick like the David; he wanted to stay and look at it more closely, but Peter was headed somewhere. Low volume nondescript music provided a relaxing ambience—loud enough to mask most conversation.

We moved through the hot odorless fog slowly—you could see ahead about four or five feet, sometimes a little farther; the floor was warm and wet. Peter led us around the statue so I could get an idea of how the room was set up. A double tier of wooden benches ringed the room. More steam issued from wall vents under some of the upper benches… as far as I could tell, a couple dozen guys were scattered at random in the fog. A hundred or more could squeeze in if they had to. Some used their towels as a modesty shield, others not. The two guys that had an erection were not doing anything with them or each other; they appeared to be meditating.

Peter gave a dismissive shrug and a grin. They headed to an empty space on the lower bench and sat. The plan was to get an idea of what it felt like to sit in the dense hot humid air, then make a quick exit. It didn't take long to appreciate the "pleasure" of sitting on a bench engulfed in hot steam.

Mark gave the statue a closer look. An excellent view of the backside presented itself—the figure seemed in motion with all the steam roiling around its feet; buns clenched, pelvis pushed forward slightly…purposely ambiguous; a forward or upward motion was easy to infer. It verged on being erotic; the eye of the beholder was expected to provide the final ingredient from within himself.

It shouldn't have been, but the statue was a surprise. That, combined with a couple of men sporting erections are what this place is about. He wasn't shocked or offended—or aroused. But it was so casual, so matter of fact… the observation helped put him at ease.

"It's unusual for an overt show of affection to occur in here," Peter spoke just above a whisper… "but it's not against the rules. Some guys sit in here alone for a long time. Personally, five minutes is about my limit." He stood. "Shall we?" He gestured to the exit.

Mark did not object.

"I have a Scandinavian friend from Minnesota who loves that room—spends half an hour then hops into the pool." Peter shook his head at the thought and led the way.

Next, across from a massive statue of a nude Hercules leaning on a club, a spa room called the **Julius Caesar** occupied the center position of the complex. Two small spas accommodating up to six were on the right; a couple of middle aged men occupied the far one; they needed to go on a diet if they weren't already. The water bubbled vigorously, fed from below by jets of water and air. At the left, a large oval pool about thirty feet long looked inviting… like a very classy back yard swimming pool. A bronze statue in the center invited the eye—surrounded by a variety of blocks that served as seats or platforms for reclining, none were occupied. Again, Mark didn't recognize the statue; it was another perfect body—considerably younger than the other statues, the reclining figure was propped up on his right arm, his left raised to greet a companion.

The water was three feet deep; an underwater bench ringed the pool… Chrome handrails on either side showed where the steps were located. Mark stooped to dip his left hand… cool after the steam room.

"Come on in for a second," Peter left his towel by the ladder and descended; he squatted to submerge himself.

After the steam room, it seemed cold. The main purpose became clear. This was better than a shower, for sure.

"Hard to believe, but it's almost body temperature," Peter grinned. "Too warm, according to Sven. He wants to see snow and ice around the edge." He waded over a few feet from the underwater steps and sat on the bench. "Medically, it's a good idea to lower your body temperature after being in that steam room; it's wise to rest in here until your heart rate lowers back to normal. This bench is ideal."

Mark sat down next to him—ooop… everything but his neck and head was submerged. Man alive—what does a short guy do in here? Sit cross-legged? He glanced around—a dozen or so men were seated on the opposite side. Their heads appeared to be floating on the surface—what a strange phenomenon. The statue drew a second look; is it based on an under age model? Of course, in ancient times naked youth was admired openly. Nowadays they wear scout uniforms…

"On a busy night you'll see guys reclining on those blocks surrounding the statue. Again, there aren't any behavior rules; but I've never seen any intimacies in here." He grinned with an underwater nudge to the knee. "That's what we'll get a peek at next." He got up and waded over to the ladder. "There's no point in drying yourself off—you'll just get wet again." He left the pool and wrapped the towel around his waist. "Your towel will be saturated before long anyway—and you don't get another one."

Onward to the last large area, the **Tiberius**; the statue opposite was a satyr—viewed from the right side its enormous erection, poised in readiness, commanded attention—it had been sculpted lovingly in *great* detail. Tiberius also featured steam. The only visible difference from outside, other than a triple row of hooks with towels hanging on them, was the lighting—or lack thereof. It was not just dim: it was *dark*.

"We won't enter this one," Peter said with a knowing grin. "This is the 'groping room.' Anything can happen in the dark, and does. You have to be ready, willing and *very* adventuresome. You leave your towel outside. Notice the continued absence of any rules posted by the entry." He stood close and leaned into the six foot wide arch, like the other rooms, there was no door; he cupped his ear.

Mark stood close… sounds were there all right—soft moans… slippery sounds, a mild slap… *action.* His imagination flared: am I hearing an *orgy* of some kind? His eyes went wide.

Peter nodded. "Not for beginners." As an afterthought, "No wooden benches in there—wrestling mats and padded platforms." They moved across the hall past the satyr… the erection wasn't visible from the other side. The view back down toward the entrance was impressive—the backsides of the Hercules and David statues were as stunning as the front.

Peter stopped in front of a wide doorway—one of four along that side of the gallery. A corridor stretched ahead about forty feet, perpendicular to the gallery. "These doorways all enter the Honeycomb." He pointed to the name above the arch: **Welcome to the Honeycomb.** The classical frame matched the other named rooms. "Let me describe what you're going to see—talking in there is very bad manners.

"Originally, this was an exercise and weight room full of barbells, bench presses and a variety of body building machines. When the club turned into a public bath, those were replaced with what you see now." He drew a floor diagram in the air—a backwards and upside down capital E with an extra branch. "It's a network of corridors between rows of small private cubicles. Each has a single bed, a chair, and a side table. The area lighting above provides what light there is; there is no separate light control inside. The walls are seven-foot high partitions—they don't go all the way to the ceiling. If you need to play in the dark, you're out of luck—unless you're willing to go back there." Peter indicated the "groping room" with his thumb.

"What are these cubicles for?" Stupid question, but I'm new around here.

Peter tilted his head and considered. "Whatever you like. You can lock the door and take a nap if you want to. What you need to know is the function of the door." He pointed down the corridor to one that was standing ajar. "If it's open, that means it's available—

even if, *especially* if, someone is inside." He gestured with his arm. "If the door is closed, that means it's occupied: go away.

"Here's the way it works. When you walk through the network of corridors, you are on parade. You may wear your towel or not—I do; when I want to be invited in, I remove it or let them have a peek. You are showing who you are and what you have to everyone whose door is open. If they like what they see, they will invite you to enter with a gesture of some kind. Meanwhile, they are showing who they are and what they have to offer. If a guy is lying on his stomach, he is telling you he likes to be bottom. If he is holding his cock, that means he wants you to play with it, or be a bottom. If he's sitting in the chair with a towel covering his lap, he is saying go on by. If he flips the towel open, he wants you to enter."

> *gulp* < This is a lot to absorb… I'm not ready for this. Mark looked around… is there a place where I can just sit and think for a minute? He scratched his head. What should I do now?

"I'd offer to guide you through, but that would mean that we wanted to recruit someone to join in a three way." Peter shrugged. "Not my thing; sorry."

Mark's eyes opened wide: "Mine either."

"So, it's time to play. What do you want to do? There is no specific order to follow."

Where to start?! I'm lost in the wilderness here. "What did *you* do the first time?"

Peter thought back. It was a while ago…"To begin with, I walked around the gallery looking at the statues while I worked up enough courage to go into the Honeycomb." I remember now. "I was invited into a room and…" he paused; instead of describing what had taken place, he offered a smile. "After a while we went to the steam room." A good time, that night.

Mark nodded… that made sense; the simplicity appealed. I'll do a walk through just to see what's there… yeah. I don't have to stop. "Is this where you start?"

"Usually, yes. I've tried the steam room first, or the pool… I've never tried the Tiberius *first.* It's a last resort for me—others do a beeline for it right off. 'Different strokes, y' know." An afterthought: "if you don't see anything that arouses your interest," he smiled at his own pun, "just settle into an empty cubicle and strike a pose; eventually, what you want will pass by—just be sure to invite him in." With that, waving a merry ta-ta, he sauntered into the Honeycomb, ready to play.

What a strange sight… Mark watched him "parade" past the first set of cubicles. It hit him suddenly: now *I'm* supposed to do that. All by myself. Usually I like to be on my own, but this… yikes. Do I do it now, or… I'll let him go a ways first… I don't want to be right on his heels.

Fake vines crawling along the partition tops drew his attention. This is supposed to be outside in a Roman garden… a garden of pleasure. Togas have been replaced by bath towels. Oh-oh: Peter just turned the corner.

Mark took a deep breath and exhaled… *hoo-boy…* I do *not* want to do this. Here goes… he swallowed hard and started his parade, towel securely covering his essentials. I feel like I'm about to lose my virginity—that's stupid: I gave that to Erik years ago.

With a grimace, he walked down the center, preoccupied by his gait and what to do with his arms… it took some concentration—how fast am I supposed to walk? Peter forgot to tell me about that… Oh! I forgot to look into the rooms! Peeking into someone's private space was so counter to everything he had known, everything he *believed*; he'd passed by three before he realized his error. You're supposed to *look*, idiot! He slowed his pace. The next cubicle had a guy lying face down… that overweight scoutmaster at camp sprung to mind. Disgusting. Moving on… this guy is sitting in his chair—a beard, a big grin, and a massive hard on that curves downward. No thanks. Mark did not make eye contact with either of those. He approached the corner and slowed down, expecting to see Peter. I don't want to catch up with him too soon… he peeked around—what?! The passage is empty! Peter is nowhere to be *seen*!

Did he go into one of these cubicles? *Already?!* What do I do now? He continued onward. Each stretch has about eight of these little rooms, four on each side. The next group had two empties and three that were closed tight; Peter must be in one of those. I'll walk by slow… maybe I can hear something… no. Press on. All of a sudden a man turned the corner ahead and came straight at him. Gosh… I thought this was *one way*. What am I supposed to do… smile? Not unless I want him, right? Before he had figured out what to do, the guy had passed by. This isn't as easy as Peter said.

I see how this works: the rooms are meant to be looked into from one direction… that's why there's two way traffic; you go through one way, then turn around at the end and come back. He looked above the doors… one side had even numbers, the other odd. I'm headed in the odd direction… hah! tell me something I don't know…

About halfway through the network it became obvious to Mark that his endeavor was pointless… the level of frustration and tension intolerable. I need to take a break… he stepped into the next empty cubicle. A simple hook and eye locked the flimsy plywood door; a magnetic catch held it tight. He stepped over to the so-called bed and sat on the edge.

Why didn't I do this *sooner?!* His heart was going a mile a minute. He closed his eyes and took a few deep breaths. After a minute he looked around. It's a trifle Spartan… bed? slab is a better word… no springs. It's *narrow*; two's a crowd on this.

Calm down Mark, and take stock. I've looked into eight—no, nine of these. None of those guys were suitable—some were decidedly *not* of *any* interest, *whatever*; he grimaced at the thought. Well, given my present frame of mind, no one would be. The guy that walked straight at me *might* have worked… he'd gone by before I got a good look.

Mark closed his eyes and thought about his situation. He had made a promise to Pat, and he had an obligation to Peter. Peter is certainly holding up his end of things… If it were not for those factors, he might well have called a halt to all this and headed back to the motel. But Mark was not a quitter, and keeping his word was essential to maintaining his self-respect.

I have to change my approach to this; I have to leave this area for the time being. I'll return to the steam room and stay there for as long as I can stand it, then go to the pool. Maybe that will make it possible to relax… then I can come back here and start over. He stood and looked back at the bed… reminds me of Lumpy Louise—his name for the awful kapok filled mattress in the scoutmaster's cabin at Camp Walker. Impossible to sleep on; some featherbeds from the quartermaster made it tolerable. Well… this isn't for sleeping, is it? He surveyed the room again… I've never been in a jail cell, but…

The bare walls were a comfort of sorts—no mirror. Looking at myself right now would be more than I could take. I still have a long time to spend in this place… and I'm on my own. Other than the chair and this small side table, there's nothing here. He pulled out the drawer. *Aha:* a box of Kleenex, a jar of Vaseline and a tube of KY. Well. That clears *that* up. Peter was right: I can do whatever I want to… or not. He peeked under the chair. That's where they keep the wastebasket. He pulled it out far enough to see that it wasn't empty. Gingerly, he nudged it back out of sight.

So… now that I'm all calmed down I have to get back on task. It's just like real life, Mark: *deal* with it. He unhooked the door and headed for the Mark Antony room, almost directly across the gallery.

The fact that he didn't see anyone right away was a relief. Where should I sit? The only way to find out is explore… He wasn't planning to make a "discovery" right off; he wanted to sit and work up a sweat. The situation would be funny if it was someone else: my body is engulfed in steam and my brain is in a fog all its own—either way, I can't see where I'm going.

Is there a good place to sit when you'd just as soon no one would… he caught himself in mid thought: don't be so *stupid*, stupid: you're *here*. Just DO it. If someone makes a pass, for crying out loud, catch it. He headed toward the steam unit and veered right… the benches were obscured by steam, but visible. Instinct told him to climb to the upper level. I'm in luck: no one in sight. He sat and leaned back, resting his head against the wall. What if someone comes up here… he half hoped/half dreaded the prospect of a hand sneaking across his thigh.

The statue emerged teasingly from the fog from time to time… I sat on the opposite side before, with Peter. Now I'm looking at it head on. Appearing between swirls of steam, its face almost hypnotic—it seemed to move toward him—yet Mark knew it was fixed in place. The music and the swirling puffs of steam formed an optical illusion: the eyes seem to stare at me, beckon me to approach, to caress, to set it free. Hands on the hips, the pelvis thrust forward as if presenting a special gift… Mark shut his eyes. The image of the partially tumescent cock remained, still seeming to move forward—

Aside from browsing through a Playboy magazine once, he had never seen any pornography; otherwise, he had no experience with visual prompts. At first the statue fascinated—a good thing it's solid white. If it was flesh colored, wow… he shook his head to dislodge the image, *willing* it to disappear. I need to think about something else—better yet, come up with a *plan.*

He relaxed and paid attention to the background music, such as it was. I previewed a sound track like this for Oglivy's. The theory is to slow the shoppers so that they take longer. Supposedly they buy more if they move slowly.

Thinking about work here makes no sense Mark! You have a *job* to do… it's impossible focus on anything; it's simply too hot. It's like being on a long uphill hike with a sixty pound pack… all I can do is endure.

Either I'm lucky, or whatever I'm doing is code for don't-bother-me—no one has approached. Whew! This heat is awful… hot steam saunas are not my thing. I didn't know that until now. At least I have learned *something*… the weekend isn't a total loss. I have to get into that pool.

He stood and made an unexpected discovery: Roger had taken it upon himself to puff up—*considerably*. Mark didn't comprehend what had happened at first; but the friction of the damp terrycloth scratching Roger's tip got his attention. All the better reason to get into that cold water! Maybe that statue had had an effect after all—it threw a switch in my subconscious or someplace and sent Roger a secret signal; it's not the first time Roger has acted independently.

Mark did not leave unnoticed. Shortly after he passed out of the steam, another bather followed. The tented towel had been observed … could be what he had been waiting for.

Mark had not learned that everyone here was always looking at who else was here. If someone walked in a beeline from one point to another, it drew extra attention. If they avoided eye contact, it meant that they were busy—or revealed that they didn't know what they were doing. Persons who were looking for someone, or who wanted to attract, *sauntered.* Their destination was a person, not a place. Mark did not realize that at any one time at least six and as many as twelve had him in their sights—the ones loitering by the statues had followed his movements with great interest. He hadn't noticed any of them; they might as well have been part of the décor.

He didn't pay attention to who was or was not present in the spa either—his goal was to cool down. He pulled his towel off at the railing and stepped down into the pool. The water was perfect—the cooling effect will take care of Roger. Submerging for several seconds helped… his body temperature began to adjust. He waded along the bench a few feet and sat, presuming that no one would be along here either. He leaned back and rested his arms along the top of the underwater bench. His neck and head were above the water; again, he closed his eyes for a time. Again, he was unable to focus his mind on anything in particular.

When his eyes opened again they were aimed at the statue of the youth—this vantage point gave the boy's backside an idealized yet alluring quality; I wonder what it looks like on the other side. On the other hand, those ancient sculptures always have small dicks, so why bother? The delectable buns could have been modeled after a number of boys in Troop Nine. He had made it a policy to *not* study those backsides. The longer he looked at this sculpture, the more he realized how wise that policy was. The curly locks resembled several boys he knew well—Julian or Danny, certainly—maybe Tony. The face would be angelic, of course—statues had idealized faces too…

He looked away at last—dwelling on which scout could have posed for the object in front of him was a bad idea anyway. Eventually, he noticed that a dozen or so men were in the pool, also sitting quietly on the bench—funny; I didn't see them when I came in. A couple were only a few feet away. He did not look at them directly. And again, he was not approached. Evidently you have to give people some kind of eye contact… good to know. It increased his comfort level; he had begun to feel safe and secure… what am I worried about? No one is going to pounce on me.

Under most circumstances in the outside world, that would not be a wise assumption to make. But here, the rules were different. He had happened upon one of the better ways to avoid being approached: don't make eye contact. For most men here, eye contact of some kind was an essential part of making an approach. Only the most accomplished player proceeded without seeing a signal of some kind—usually via their eyes. For those who were daring and who didn't need to be polite, the Tiberius room was always at hand: to enter was to give permission.

Mark's body temperature returned to normal after a few minutes. How long have I been here? Hard to say… what time is it now? How do you tell time around here? I haven't seen a wall clock anywhere—wait: the massage room… above the TV set. Good. I can check that at some point. How long should I stay here? Am I ready to go back into the maze? What is Peter doing now… what if he's finished already… what if he needs to go back to the motel? That's silly; it hasn't been *that* long… Calm down, Mark, just calm down. Think positive: you can do this. It will take a little time, but you can do it.

His brain told him he should be doing this, but his heart was not in it. A frustrating tug of war, and he was pulling at both ends.

He reviewed the men he had seen once again. They weren't *all* trolls… to be honest, I haven't given them a truly serious look. Why was I so hasty, so eager to pass every one by, regardless? Peter's comment came back to him… "they're just like you and me…" They aren't dragons or monsters. They deserved a chance… more to the point, *I* deserve the chance. I have to face the fact that I've been halfway hoping for a disaster of some kind; part of me wants to prove that the idea to come here was bad in the first place. His rational mind continued to fight that off. His conscience and good sense wanted this to succeed. There's more to life than selling clothing and herding boy scouts on weekends. He also realized that this was like everything else in life: if it's important, I have to work for it.

Oh-oh… he looked down. The water feels lukewarm now… Roger finds it quite hospitable… conducive, in fact. He hasn't receded after all. On the contrary: the clear water enabled his eyes to confirm what he felt down there. Do these physical conditions bring that on? Mark had asked this same question several times in the last month. It doesn't take a spa to wake Roger up. Roger has a mind of his own.

Admittedly the physical sensation is enjoyable. The fact that Roger was acting up again reinforced the point: Roger doesn't depend on what's going on in my head at all. That's what had convinced Mark that he was free of the past, for all practical purposes. He didn't feel guilty about being here. He felt silly and stupid, and a bit frightened, but not guilty. He glanced down… Roger is trying to make me feel horny.

What should I do? I'm not about to stroke the pork here and now… returning to the Honeycomb is a possibility… on the other hand, I don't look forward to walking by any of those open doors wagging an erection. And it will be up by the time I cross over to one of those entrances. Like it or not, Roger is running his program, whatever it is, this very minute. And when Roger is up, there's no hiding him.

I know: I can duck into that dark fog, find a corner and take care of this! Then, after Roger goes down a little, I can duck back out and find an empty cubicle. At last, a *plan*. He opened his eyes, stood and made his way back to the chrome handrail. He wrapped his towel around hurriedly and scurried out—Roger is winning the race.

Again, he was noticed, and again he did not notice. He was followed, of course. Mark did not realize that he was one of the more outstanding and now upstanding specimens in attendance this evening. He was the sort that was noticed at once. It did not require a rumor mill; word did not need to spread. Regulars at the spa had antennae somewhere… their heads and eyes turned almost before he appeared. He remained oblivious to this—as befits a novice; that status was also observed. Greenhorns and new faces were always a treat because they haven't learned better. By the time he entered the Tiberius room, he had a following. Anyone with an erection had that. Mark was followed in seconds by two from the spa. The steam room hopeful was close behind, and the one across the hall by the Honeycomb entrance was in such a hurry to catch up, his towel missed the hook and fell to the floor.

Mark hung his towel on one of the hooks and ducked in rapidly. He thought, incorrectly, that he'd been clever and surreptitious about it. In fact, only he would not have noticed. When he entered Tiberius he was not expected, but he was hoped for. Several had placed him at the top of their want list; they would know if he showed—his silhouette would give him away the minute he crossed through the steam.

Not having entered before, he did not know how the area was laid out and what was done where. He assumed that it would be like the other steam room, basically. Ah, he was *so* mistaken. The steam issued upward from a grate that stretched across the entrance—it functioned as a semi-transparent curtain. If there was a column or statue in the center it wasn't visible… nothing was. The aroma was not bland like the other steam room—in here a distinct male odor prevailed, like a workout room or a locker bay during half time. Sweat and body fluids from many men mixed and, intensified by the steam, permeated. Sexy, dense air flooded his nostrils, it *stimulated.* He didn't have time to analyze that, but Roger knew at once that he had arrived. It was several degrees cooler than the other steam room—somewhere between 80 and 90 degrees; more like daytime on a Florida beach, without the sun or the fresh air.

Mark had forgotten one important detail: Peter mentioned that the floor was padded.

Wha—! *no traction!*

> *Sw-i-pp*— whump! < *Ouch!* His left shoulder took the brunt of the impact; flat on his face he zoomed headlong into total darkness… into the unknown.

… nothing to grab onto… can't stop… it's slippery, like grease…

In a steamy room, smooth vinyl wrestling mats accumulate moisture. Soon it becomes slippery—one does not simply walk across. If one tries, as Mark did, he slips instantly.

If no one else is around, no problem—even if you're off balance and your efforts to correct add to the problem by increasing your velocity. On the other hand, if you slide face down directly into a cluster of horny men in the Tiberius Room, you are a greeted as a long awaited delivery: you are welcomed with open arms—with groping hands, open mouths; erections seek your mouth, your butt, your hands. It is *party time*! No introductions, no warm ups: zero to a hundred in seconds.

The "lubricated" floor offset the friction that would have caused mat burn—but it enhanced the velocity. The welcoming committee was sure footed enough to absorb the impact and to spring into action without pause—collision with the jumble of feet and legs had been expected. What seemed chaotic at first was anything but—he had joined a complex ballet of writhing bodies caressing one another. Smooth hands explored his thighs, his calves, his buns, shoulders, arms—too many hands to count. As he lifted himself up onto his knees, his torso became part of the sensual, rhythmic choreography. The muted background music provided a pulse, a calming, a sense of belonging. Instead of claustrophobia, he felt celebrated. Resistance was pointless.

Only after he had escaped did Mark begin to appreciate that a method, a protocol, prevailed, even there. No one fought over what they had discovered; first come first served. Someone helped him get up partway—but kneeling was as far as he got.

He had no idea who had sucked him, but whoever it was knew what he was doing. The one behind had not tried to enter him, but instead did a hump and slide between Mark's buns until he unloaded. He was replaced by a second guy who aimed underneath; the one servicing Roger around front grabbed with his free hand and finished him off at the same time. The guy trying to kiss his lips gave up when he didn't get a response; he shifted to the earlobes and neck. On both sides someone used his hand as a channel for their throbbing staff; they even demonstrated how they should be held to provide maximum pleasure—they surrounded his hand with theirs and pressed tight: feeling their emissions move upward and escape as they pumped was unexpected and thrilling and impossible to forget.

Why didn't I escape? Why didn't I roll away from them somehow and crawl out of that place? Why did it not enter my mind to lash out with a solid punch at any of those men? Why did I *enjoy* it?!

Mark sat behind the locked door of his second cubicle of the evening and tried to make sense out of the past ten or fifteen minutes. He had never done so much in so little time. He had no idea who had been in there with him. He had a strong sense that given the chance he would recognize at least two of the erections, the ones that had used his hands. What the rest of the person looked like was a complete mystery. Other details sprung into his mind; hands and fingers had massaged and explored every inch of his body—tenderly, lovingly, as if a committee of blind people was memorizing him, massaging him, worshipping him from stem to stern.

No statuary or structure was in the center of that room: *I* was the statue. A *live* statue.

He looked down at Roger. What *is* it with you? Roger was still up two thirds! He wants *seconds*!

Roger was that way *again.* Reviewing the Pompeii episode in the shower wasn't very smart; Mark didn't want to take the time to indulge him the way he had in the Pompeii cubicle—Danny and Julian will be here before long. Now that I have a car, I'm returning the favor. Up to now, one or the other gave me a ride when Pat wasn't home; we all live on the same block.

"Maybe *after* the meeting, if you're good." Roger wagged naughtily as Mark dried himself off. "Quit that now, or I'll go get some ice." Roger did not like anything cold. Ice was the ultimate weapon. Mark combed his hair and checked his shave… everything was in order.

After I'm dressed I'll recheck the materials I assembled this morning; it always pays to take a last look. He headed into the bedroom.

He pulled the new pair of slacks out of the closet and laid them flat on the bed: a late addition to his scout costume. Since the scouts have changed from olive green to tan, I can take advantage of the opportunity: the new Haggar line uses a synthetic fabric, lighter and more comfortable than the standard scout gabardine—their British Khaki is a perfect color match. The meeting will be a lot easier in these—ninety minutes isn't terribly long, but why put up with those heavy gabardines? Wearing these made the day go a lot easier at the store. After a while, you forget they're there—they never pinch or bind in the crotch. That alone made them worth the extra ten dollars. That and the fact that unlike suntans, they're wrinkle free permanent press. Ironing pants is a bore; now it's a thing of the past. They should make shirts out of this. Who would I write to about that?

I need a single edge razor blade… the stitches around the label have to be removed. While foraging in a drawer for the blade, his mind wandered back to Saturday night…

I took advantage of a pause in the frenzy to duck down and scoot backward on my hands and knees. Over my shoulder I could see light spilling in from the gallery. I turned around and went as fast as I could. No one tried to stop me—at the time I chalked that up to sheer luck. Now I think I was being allowed to leave. It's obvious: those guys *knew* I was leaving; my silhouette must have shown that. A clear outline of whoever is between you and that opening is automatic. I have no idea how many guys were in there, or how many "worked" on me. I wasn't harmed in any way. They were out to give as much pleasure as they expected to receive. They could have held onto me and kept going—I was outnumbered, what: ten to one? Twelve? No way to tell.

The fact that I was trapped is scary now. Why wasn't I scared at the time? Maybe because of what Peter said… "these guys are just like you and me…" I wasn't forced to do anything. Without realizing it I had agreed to what was going on by not struggling. I didn't fight back at all. I resisted being kissed, and that was respected. Someone poked tentatively between my cheeks… he didn't force his way in; he could have—I was held in place by activity on every side… but after a couple of probes he chose to press my cheeks together tightly and do the outside hump. Was he waiting for permission? How would I have given it? I'm glad it didn't happen. After six years of abstinence, I'll have to go there *carefully*. Only with someone I know and care about. That was Erik's preference—granting that privilege will never be accidental. Say… he looked up and thought a second: someone in there *was* doing that! I could *hear* them.

Why didn't I fight it? How did they know I wanted and liked what they were doing? I didn't know it myself! Is there a button somewhere, a secret permission button that they knew how to activate? If there is, it must poke way out: that's the first sex I've had with another person in six years, going on seven. The irony is I didn't see any of them—I wouldn't know one even if I ran across him. So much for making a "connection."

When I grabbed my towel outside I couldn't tell if I was getting the right one—thirty or forty must have been hanging there. I sat in that cubicle *forever*, with the door *closed*. What a blessing, that refuge! Maybe that's one reason those rooms are there. That place is *engineered*, isn't it?

He glanced down again; Roger had not backed down one millimeter—if I don't deal with him, he'll keep this up. "I'm going for the ice!" He stepped to the dresser and grabbed a pair of briefs. Generally, he let his crotch air dry for a while after showering… cuts down the itching that develops down there later on. "Maybe if I put these on now, you'll get the idea!" He slipped them on and headed out of the room. There’s a cube of ice in the kitchen with Roger’s name on it. I’ll grab a root beer while I’m at it.

“What I want is a glass of wine.” He usually had one around this time of day—not on a scout night; after the meeting, maybe. I grabbed a burger on the way home, so I’m squared away. Another benefit of having that car: I can use drive thru windows!

The kitchen clock told him he had twenty minutes: plenty of time. He fetched a bottle from the fridge and popped off the cap. He took a swig and opened the freezer to grab an ice cube; Roger had receded half way, but Mark didn’t trust him. “Just to be sure, I’ll do you when I get upstairs—”

> *Bling-bling, bling-bling…* < The Westminster chimes sounded in the living room.

What?? He looked at the clock again. It’s Julian and Danny—they’re *early*! Awkward, but… they’re in Flaming Arrow—they’ve seen me in skivvies before. I’ll let them in then dash upstairs. He hurried to the door, root beer and ice cube in hand.

He was about to give his standard greeting but was stopped cold. It wasn’t just Danny and Julian: a neatly formed trio of scouts was standing at attention, saluting. The boy named Randall was at their side holding a white box.

“Good evening, Sir,” Tony said cheerfully. “Reporting early, with dessert.”

Randall elevated the box. “My mom sent a chocolate cake.”

Mark recovered quickly and laughed. “Come on in guys. I wasn’t expecting you this early. I just got out of the shower.” He stood aside and ushered them in. Tony is a surprise; I forgot that I invited Randall.

All four were delighted to have caught Mark in his briefs. They didn’t stare, but they got a good look—a very good look—as they came in.

“Let’s go right into the kitchen with that.” He led the way—I need to get rid of this blasted ice cube.

The boys were equally pleased with the view from behind. Randall glanced at Julian, who pretended he didn't notice anything special. Tony stuck his tongue out of the corner of his mouth and grinned at Danny, wowing his eyes. As usual, his antic nature sprung into action: he reached forward, vigorously flexing the fingers of his left hand like a claw; just inches away Mark's left cheek worked away—under fresh cotton briefs, it was such a temptation. Danny rolled his eyes and jabbed him in the ribs. Luckily, Mark didn't see anything.

Julian was conflicted: this yummy peek was a welcome surprise, and went into his image bank automatically. But sharing it with three others guys wasn't so hot—what if they figure out how I feel about Mark? Mark's kind of puffy down there… ordinarily, Little J would react quick… I hafta keep him limp somehow. Why would Mark be puffy? Oh! He said he was in the shower… Sometimes Little J does that when I'm in the shower… maybe Mark does the same thing. The problem right now is Little J—watching those buns in motion is an automatic wake up call.

"There's pop in the fridge, guys." Mark gestured for them to help themselves while he deposited the ice cube in the sink—it wasn't needed now. He stepped over to the cupboard to fetch some plates and forks.

Roger, unaware that he had just been given a reprieve, enjoyed being jostled across the room so vigorously. He didn't grow any larger, but he wasn't in a hurry to shrivel up, either—freshly laundered cotton felt good and provided a comfy nest.

Randall took the box over to the table and carefully lifted out the cake. From a bakery of course, it rested on a disc of reinforced corrugated cardboard. He'd never seen his mother bake a cake. She always bought them, and she *always* found good ones.

"Wow, pretty fancy!" Julian took the chair next to Randall. Must have four layers.

"You guys want root beer… or root beer?" Tony asked cheerfully.

"I have some coke and orange on the back porch, but it isn't very cold."

"We can split one." Julian gestured to Tony; he didn't like root beer especially—it fizzes up. I'll let Randall have most of it.

Mark put the plates and forks next to the cake. He extended the cake knife handle first.

Randall looked at the knife wide eyed. He didn't have any experience cutting a cake. He shook his head. "Umm, maybe you can do that better."

Mark nodded. If he was one of my scouts, I'd use this as a teaching moment. Since we're a little short on time, it makes sense to cut it myself. He stood in place, cut it down the center, turned it 45 degrees to the right and focused on the horizontal line. He cut the half circle into five parts—a generous portion coming from a cake this size. To the naked eye, the slices looked perfectly equal.

"Whoa… how can you do that?" Impressive as it was, Randall's peripheral view was even more impressive: Mark's midsection was to his *immediate* left. If he turned his head, he'd be looking straight at what he shouldn't. Reluctantly, he kept it aimed forward—but his *eyes*… Wow. A newly showered man in freshly laundered briefs *inches* from your face is bound to cause a reaction. He covered his lap automatically, fearing his probable response would be seen. The wakeup signal had already been received… darn these pants: they're unable to make allowances down there. How am I going to prevent The Problem?

During this demonstration of excellence in practical geometry, Tony and Danny had seated themselves across the table and were ostensibly opening bottles and having a chug. The view couldn't have been better—and a more appreciative audience couldn't have been found. Tony in particular was adept at studying a view like this while appearing to be doing something else entirely. He recalled at once the conversation he had at camp that day across from the archery range. Geoff was studying Mark through a pair of binoculars. Now he understood why.

Danny's attempts to not look failed; he masked it somewhat by taking a few too many gulps of root beer; as a result, a persistent need to belch threatened to develop into a case of hiccups.

Julian's problem was like Randall's, but from the other side. Mark was standing between them. Little J had come awake the second Mark had accidentally rubbed against Julian's right forearm with his bare thigh; combined with the same aromas that had invaded Randall's nostrils, nothing could have stopped Little J from saluting enthusiastically. The smell of a freshly showered man is like nothing else in the world—briefs, no matter how recently laundered, do not eliminate the underlying essence; if anything, they provide an excruciating temptation to nuzzle. Julian had a nose, recently trained, that wanted to do just that.

These were the boys who had just spent a weekend in a hexagon tent becoming expert at you-know-what you-know-where. Before the first bite of cake was consumed, four erections stood ready for action. It did not make things easier when Mark proceeded to place the slices of cake onto the small plates and deliver them one at a time around the table. He did this still standing there, every reach providing an opportunity for Roger to nudge the cotton barrier and demonstrate how ineffective it was at hiding his presence; Roger enjoyed being rocked back and forth; he liked how the cotton felt when he stretched against it. In his present state, it clung to his contours in a most satisfying manner. He was disappointed when Mark stepped around to sit at the end of the table between Julian and Tony.

Oblivious to all this, Mark attacked his piece of chocolate cake with enthusiasm. He had stopped paying attention to Roger; this puffy state had lasted stubbornly off and on ever since that group grope in Tiberius three days ago—presumably it will take care of itself eventually. Most of the time he didn't feel it; as long as it was stable, it was easy to ignore.

"This is great cake, Randall." Five layers! Thick icing, *sinfully* thick. After Mark had eaten about half of his piece, he stood and reached across for the box. This provided a rapid but even better view of the cotton briefs' front and how thoroughly—how handsomely—its occupant filled the available space.

"Where did she get this?" I don't see any identification… the top and sides are blank.

"Gosh… I don't know. She gets these all the time for her bridge games." He gulped, glad to change what his mind was doing. "Probably somewhere near the campus." I've never been along when she bought one.

"Well, be sure to give her my thanks and my compliments." He stood again and returned the box to the other end of the table, secretly hoping that Randall intended to leave the leftover half. He sat and took another bite. "If you think of it, ask her, will you? It would be good to know where to get a quality cake. You can't tell when knowing something like that might come in handy."

Julian, seated directly at Mark's right, had no choice but to observe… how could he close his eyes? Why would he? When a man's mid section appears in profile inches from your face, you check it out—every detail. That it was Mark's mid section made it doubly special. When it appeared the second time, Little J strained to escape.

Mark enjoyed another bite of cake—this impromptu snack was a nice surprise and most welcome; that drive-in hamburger wasn't a full meal. The opportunity to sit informally with the boys for a minute was most welcome. He gave Danny a small congratulatory wink for working out the root beer problem. He took a deep swig from his own bottle and produced a small > *erp.* < He glanced over his shoulder to check the clock and did a double take: "Wow! Look at the *time*!" He stood abruptly. "You guys carry on. I gotta get dressed!" He ran out of the kitchen.

The four boys watched the exit in awe—then looked at each other. At last they could relax a minute and *say* something.

But no one did… their minds were too busy. One of the unexpected benefits of the Initiation turned out to be the no talk rule: they had learned the value of meditating about strong images such as the one now crowding their thoughts, *without* words. They continued to look at each other, amazed. They all had the same insight. They didn't need to do the usual, the predictable adolescent hardy-har-har. They *valued* what they had seen. It went onto a memory shelf, ready to be recalled—the sooner the better. Mark's quick exit was thrilling—the factor of rapid motion, front and rear, enhanced the spectacle considerably.

Julian had an idea. He grabbed the root beer bottle and scooted his chair back. He pressed the bottle against the bulge Little J had caused. He looked across to Danny. "This should work." The instant cold did just that. He passed the bottle to Randall. Danny and Tony scooted their chairs back and did the same thing.

"You deserve ten points for this," Danny was *delighted.* "It works!"

It was amazing. They grinned at each other and sat forward to finish their cake; Randall was still puffy, but that was because of the tight pants as much as anything. They would have started KP, but just then Mark raced across the front room, roaring.

"C'mon, men! We gotta get outa here!"

They hurried to catch up.

"Randall gets to sit in the front seat," Mark added as he locked the front door behind him: he's a guest tonight. "That happens when you bring a cake," he winked.

17 Naming the Country Squire 2

Randall was glad it was dark out. It provided more latitude when it came to focusing on forbidden areas—crotches, to be specific; the cover of darkness was most helpful. I shouldn't even be thinking about this. Putting Little R to sleep with a half empty bottle of root beer a few minutes ago was a first. Why take a risk? Well, for one thing, an opportunity like this doesn't come along every day: a crotch on display on *both* sides? For another, it's customary, if not automatic, to check things like that out—especially when it's safe, when no one will be the wiser. On the right, sitting by the door, is Julian—my all-time favorite. It's possible to sit by him now without getting all hot and bothered by the sexy smell, but only just. On the left is the scoutmaster, just added to the list. After that episode in the kitchen, how could he not be?

Julian was flipping through his steno pad, checking on something for the meeting; Mark was driving, intent on getting there on time. Thus, Randall was at liberty to review their status. Julian had receded; enough bulge remained to reassure anyone that it was a boy's lap; the root beer bottle had worked fine for him too. The scoutmaster's valise rested against his shins.

Mark was more interesting... at first glance, his slacks seemed perfectly ordinary. Same color as the shirt... part of the uniform. But... something was different. Due to the highlights created by the dashboard, the thigh muscles and his right knee were emphasized. The fabric clung to his leg as if molded there. The crotch area, similarly, appeared to have been formed especially to accommodate what was between the legs. After watching the cake being served,

Randall had a fairly good idea of what that looked like in a standing position; the dashboard lights did such a good job it was hard to look away. He knew better, but this could be the only opportunity to get this close a look. The short Eisenhower jacket barely covered the belt—the entire lap is there for the eye to behold.

Until recently, anyone older had not been of any interest. The Hayden Park experience had changed that; four of those guys were older—two of them were *seniors*. At first glance, Mark didn't look much older than them. A door had been opened; that's why his eyes were focused: his imagination was at work. What's in that intriguing loaf shaped area just inches away? Not defined like it had been in the kitchen, the bulk suggested it was similar to Beta—without the curve. From personal experience, Randall knew what could be done with it.

I'd better look straight ahead... I don't need The Problem now, of all times. He couldn't see his own lap—the scoutmaster's hat covered it. Mark had entrusted it to him when they climbed in. "It's your job to hold this while we're in transit; it's too wide to wear in the car, and you're sitting on the hat rack." It is wide—a big flat disc for a rim... if you were to sail it like a Frisbee it would look like a flying saucer. State troopers wear these.

I am worried a little about developing The Problem again. Wearing these pants will make it worse if it happens. His mother had made him change into these at the last minute. She can be stubborn about how I look. "You're an invited guest!" she scolded. School clothes would not do. Mothers get their way on things like that. I couldn't exactly explain the problem—my waist size is the same as when she bought me these, but everything below the belt line is bigger or taller or longer. The folds of cloth that provide room for "unexpected growth" were almost non-existent.

Anyway, I need to keep my eyes on the road and my mind on something else; I don't want to ruin things before I even get there! Julian's comment about not wanting to be a sex fiend came to mind... maybe I've turned into one. The odd thing is, maybe I don't care. Lately, sex has been pretty much all fun.

"Hey, Mark," Tony chirped merrily from the back seat. "We went on a campout last weekend!"

"Good for you!"

"It was a two nighter!"

"Better yet." Mark was impressed. "Who is we?" The Tiger patrol's campout isn't until spring. Tony is the life of the party in that patrol.

"Us four and a couple of other guys from school."

Mark gave Randall a friendly nudge with his right leg: "You went, too! Great." He felt a nostalgic twinge; I used to do that… take off Friday after school on a campout: one of my favorite things. "I remember you telling about your mountain trips."

Randall nodded, flattered that Mark remembered. The sensation from that nudge was nice… good thing this seat is plenty wide. If my left leg was pressed against Mark's the way my right leg is against Julian, I wouldn't be able to stop The Problem; wouldn't take much… even so, he risked a quick glance: no change… it's probably just air.

"Must have been a Hayden Park trip." Two nighters this time of year were unusual unless there was no school on Friday.

"Yeah. Still counts though, doesn't it?"

"You bet! Make sure Danny puts those points down." Tony will need them eventually. "I sure wish I had been along. I haven't been on a campout since last summer." The remark was automatic—truth is, I couldn't have gone anyway—I was busy in Raleigh.

The four campers smiled to themselves. They too wished Mark had been along; they had a good idea of what he would have brought to the party.

Something inside Mark was at work; the Raleigh trip was not the disaster he had expected. He had mixed feelings—it had a positive side, sort of. He wasn't sure what that was yet, exactly… at any rate, thoughts about that are forbidden tonight. His attention turned back to the meeting.

As they pulled into the church parking lot, Mark gave the dashboard an affectionate pat. "Good boy." The dashboard clock showed that they were in time—two minutes to spare, technically. Seeing the crowd of scouts waiting at the Parish Hall door always gave him a boost. "We made it, men!" he announced, proudly. He gave Randall a wink as he reached across to retrieve his valise. "Thanks for playing hat rack."

In the back seat Tony and Danny unclasped hands. They were fond of holding hands nowadays. Young romances thrive on constant physical contact—hard to get away with if you're boy with boy. It's more fun when a little danger is involved—it would have been okay if Julian or Randall had turned around—Mark, on the other hand… awful risky; but it's dark in the back seat. They got out on opposite sides; they had developed a how-to-appear-in-public strategy, and shifted into it automatically. Even in the troop, no one knew they were steadies.

"Stick with me, Randall," Julian opened the door eagerly; scout meetings were one of his favorite things. He was itching to show off his special guest. Concentrating on that helped neutralize the lingering aftereffect of what happened in the kitchen. "It's a little confusing at first, 'cause everyone's scrambling to get things ready." He tucked the Troop Nine Scrapbook and steno pad under his left arm and led the way.

Randall watched in awe as Mark strode toward a large building: what long legs! When he's in a hurry, you almost have to run to keep up; with that hat he looks foreboding.

Adjacent to the church a signboard in the patch of lawn read "Parish Hall." His family wasn't involved with a church, so this was a little foreign. From what I've seen so far, religion isn't a major part of these guys' lives; maybe you don't have to be a member of the church. In any case, I'd better be careful what I say.

The crowd opened as Mark approached, then closed right behind, swallowing him like quicksand—there must be forty or fifty guys! Randall had no idea there would be so *many*. They're a happy bunch, all excited about something. I never tried anything close to this in Pullman; I avoided crowds like the plague. Going into an unfamiliar group this size would have been too scary—but things are different now… I have a new bunch of friends; I don't need to worry. I can tell that I'm going to have an interesting time. He grinned… if nothing else, I can let my eyes play tourist. Boys are boys, after all. Scout uniforms can't be much worse than regular clothes.

Mark unlocked and opened the door; like water behind a bursting dam, the scouts poured in. Randall was glad they were at the back. When they entered at last, what he saw was confusing—the scouts had taken off their coats and fanned out in every direction. This doesn't look like a meeting; everyone is doing something—sitting down and coming to order isn't the way they do things around here. It reminded him of an ant colony, all these identical kerchiefs hustling about. He followed Julian to the coat racks—half a dozen units on wheels stood at one side; plenty of hooks. Through the cross traffic they went—he kept up as well as he could. He drew a few curious glances—no surprise. His light blue shirt and cream colored dress pants stood out: I'm the only one not in a scout uniform. So many *younger* kids; half of them are shorter than me. Some must be *seventh* graders! Others were a lot older—at least taller; they must be juniors and seniors.

The big barn of a room must be 40 or 50 feet long. At the far end, Mark stood by a table at one end of the stage or platform that stretched the full width. Julian and Danny headed there—soon they were joined by three others. It's the guys from the car buying trip! *amazing* how different they look in a uniform. One of them had a small instrument case… must be a musician.

"Julian, grab a chair for Randall, will you?" Mark pointed to a folding chair dolly. "You can sit up here with the Flaming Arrows."

"Here ya go," Julian opened the folding chair. "For now, just stay here and watch, I guess; everyone has a bunch of stuff to do before we start the meeting. Eventually, Mark or me or someone will keep you company… okay?"

Randall nodded; it felt a little conspicuous, sitting on the platform like an exhibit; but no one seemed to pay him any attention. Busy as a beehive out there… he watched the scoutmaster brief his leaders. The tall one is Tom—he's the one that drove us around to look at cars—Nick's boyfriend. He's as tall as the scoutmaster; looks part Indian in a way, with that straight hair. Danny, of course… he lives across the fence from Julian. The other guy is the musician; I don't know him. Well; better not stare. He turned to watch the seemingly random activity out in the room; it wasn't particularly noisy, just busy. He had never wondered about what went on at a scout meeting… but now that I'm here, might as well see what they're like.

One group was setting up a table at the side—looked like a serving table. Probably for refreshments. Another cleared the central area of stray tables and chairs. A few groups huddled at random locations talking about something. A couple of boys brought something onto the platform and put it on the table behind him, next to Julian's scrapbook… an exhibit or project of some kind. Another crew retrieved some flags from a storage closet; they positioned them toward the front of the platform, two on each side. The stars and stripes identified one. Don't know the others—probably the state flag and… who knows, a troop flag, maybe… do churches have flags? Everyone has something to do… no one just sat around. It seemed to be the middle of something rather than the start. Eventually I suppose this will make sense…

> ***ta-ta-ta… ta-ta-ta… ta-ta-ta!*** <

Randall almost jumped; the bugler had just given some kind of a signal. That's what was in that case. Sure is loud inside—lucky I'm behind the guy.

Everyone finished up what they were doing and headed to the center of the room. They went through some sort of process automatically, and in a couple of minutes stood in a rough formation. These were pre ordered positions. Flaming Arrow guys stayed on the platform but lined up on the right—except for Tom, who had stepped to the front edge. The scoutmaster stood a few feet behind him, slightly to the left.

"Fall in!" Tom commanded in a strong voice that filled the room. A couple of stragglers scurried into place. "Attention!" He paused a couple of seconds. "Dress right, dress!"

Impressive transformation—in a few seconds the rows were in perfect alignment. If it weren't for the variation in height, they would have looked identical. Randall sat forward and hesitated for a moment, wondering if he should do anything besides sit. He looked over to Julian to see… he mimed something, but it was hard to figure out… the gesture seemed to say stay put, so that's what he did.

Tom turned to the scoutmaster and saluted. "The troop is assembled, sir."

Mark returned the salute. "You may proceed."

Tom turned and gestured to a scout in the front row. The scout stepped forward a few feet and saluted; Tom returned the salute. "Life Scout Kruger will lead the Pledge of Allegiance." He nodded, signaling him to begin, and turned toward the flag. All the scouts saluted as they recited the pledge.

Randall stood at once and faced the flag, hand over his heart. He had been trained to do this in grade school and had it memorized. He always skipped the two added words, agreeing with his father who used to rant about it: "It's against the Constitution to say 'under God.'"

The Scout Oath and Scout Law were next, also led by a scout called forward from the group—all obviously arranged in advance. Those guys must have done something to earn the privilege. Randall sat quietly and listened. The words were admirable enough, but the regimentation and uniformity did not appeal. Impressive in its way, but… too tidy. If I had my druthers, I'd never tuck my shirt in—or polish my shoes. He had what he thought was a healthy disdain for uniformity. Like his father, he was secretly an intellectual snob, and proud of it.

Next, roll call; they didn't go through the list: each patrol reported in, and two were absent. Randall relaxed during all this procedural stuff; his attention wandered momentarily… his eyes accidentally landed on the scoutmaster's backside—it was standing in place about six feet away as if on exhibit for his benefit. The slacks were doing a superb job of showcasing Mark's right bun—the cloth clung like it had in the car… to the same leg. The contour was revealed—displayed—almost as if he were wearing ballet tights. What would it be like to touch, to *feel* the shape: When he moves, a line shows: the bottom edge of his briefs. I saw those briefs a few minutes ago—I didn't notice the line at all, but it must have been there.

Buns were not usually what attracted Randall's eye, but this was special—it was a continuation of what he had found so impressive, so sexy, around front. His attention to the meeting faded rapidly—indulging himself, he focused on the beige slacks. The left bun was less interesting: Mark's wallet was the main feature. It filled the depression featured so impressively on the other side—it was so appealing he wanted to approach and run his hand, his fingers into and across the concave area… and continue around the smooth bulbous rear with his palm… to the center where the slacks, instead of being flat like most trousers, revealed the valley between the muscular cheeks. Oh-oh… he stopped himself. A warning sensation from below: without thinking, he had begun to imagine he was employing the special routine—the one he had learned in the hexagon tent—a sure way to develop The Problem.

Just as he had resolved to think about something else, the scoutmaster, who had been rattling off a series of instructions that made no sense to an outsider, mentioned Julian's name. He looked up: Julian was headed his way.

"Don't look so worried," he smiled. "Come along a for minute—I get to introduce you." He giggled, "this way, I don't have to do it over and over again!"

Julian's manner set him at ease, but still… standing in front of forty or fifty guys staring right at you isn't the easiest thing to do. He listened patiently, trying to ignore yet another danger message being sent from below—thinking about it made things worse. Standing up and walking a few feet had loosened the area around Little R—the *wrong* thing to do right now; please, Little R: go back to sleep.

"Everyone, I'd like you to meet Randall Hallstrom. He moved here last summer from *Washington*, the *state*—you know, north of California, on the Pacific Ocean. He's a mountain climber! *Real* mountains, ones with *glaciers* and everything. They have scads of those out there. He knows how to rope up, how to use an ice ax—you name it, he's either done it or knows about it—I've seen some of the pictures he took—man, you wouldn't believe some of the stuff he's done. It's just like in National Geographic! So when you get a chance, be sure to introduce yourself and ask what it's like to climb a mountain thousands of feet high way out west."

Randall was in total shock: he'd never been presented in public, never been praised like that—never felt his face turn as red as fast as it must have; it was all he could do to not wet his pants or worse. At least I wasn't asked to say anything… I've climbed to the top of only *three* mountains, been on *one* glacier… somehow he mustered a weak smile and gave a tiny wave. They all waved back! Several faces looked at him as if he was a movie star or something. A couple of real young ones in the front caught his eye… evidently awestruck, their mouths were hanging wide open. He turned to Julian for help: what am I supposed to do?!

Julian gave him the usual big grin and conducted him back to the chair; it was still in the same place: in plain view. That didn't bother him quite as much now—but his head was still swimming. I'm used to going unnoticed. Wow…

He lost focus on what was going on temporarily, but looked up when it was clear that something new was happening. He hadn't heard the order, but the formation was falling apart and scouts were headed every which way again. Julian pulled a chair over and sat down with that big grin.

"Hey, you did great. I know you're kind of shy, so… anyway, that's why I didn't warn you. I figured you would worry about it too much."

He had no defense against Julian's smile. All was forgiven. "What's going on now?"

"Oh. This is small group time." He pointed to a circle that had formed close to the platform. "That group is Tenderfoot scouts; they're working on their Second Class rank. Every group out there is working on some kind of advancement—either a rank or a merit badge. We have 20 minutes, then we'll assemble again—tonight we're doing drill. Sometimes we have a special class or merit badge thing; otherwise, we practice marching. After drill we break up again into patrol meetings. Then we have a refreshment break. After the break is the official meeting. Tonight is big because it's nominations to name the car. Each patrol has to make a nomination; they have until the next meeting to campaign; then we'll have speeches and vote.

"Name the car?" What fun! "Like pilots name their planes?"

"Yeah! Mark wants it to belong to the troop—in spirit, at least. So… are you okay for a while? I hafta go join the Star group."

"Sure, don't let me get in the way. Should I just stay up here?"

"Yeah, probably be best. Nobody's doing anything secret. I haven't talked to anyone, or I'd let you tag along with me."

"It's okay; I'll be fine." He wanted to make a comment on the speech, but he could do that later. He watched Julian scurry over and sit with one of the groups. They were all sitting cross-legged on the floor in small circles. Too bad I can't roam around and do some serious crotch evaluations—on the other hand… he rethought that… might be a quick way to attract a Nels type. So far I have avoided that fate… best not to rock the boat. All these scouts aren't into boys. I know of five that are, and *that* is pretty amazing.

The scoutmaster is crouched down on one knee talking with one of the groups. He has no idea that his entire executive patrol—with the possible exception of the bugler, is into boys. Speaks well for those guys—they do a good job of playing it straight. Not one is a femme, which helps. None of these guys are. I haven't seen or heard one this whole year, come to think about it. I always feel sorry for them… the Nels type loves to harass them most of all.

Oh-oh… darn it… a new message from below: Little R wants to

be adjusted—he's been complaining for a while, now… I sat down too fast. He's twisted sideways—the tip is jammed against my right leg and he doesn't like it. These tight pants don't help, either. How do I adjust without being seen? All alone up here, nothing to hide behind… it's not possible. I'll just have to suffer. Actually, adjusting might free him *too* much… then what? If he were to go all the way up?! Perched up here, that would be a disaster. As a compromise, he crossed his legs; sometimes that worked.

For the next fifteen minutes he tried to focus on other things—while his eyes appeared to be gazing around at this group or that, his mind was at work searching for innocuous subjects—he needed to distract Little R. He reviewed academic assignments, ran through every music score he could think of… anything to keep from developing The Problem. He was successful for the most part—it didn't get any worse—but it didn't get any better, either.

> ta-ta-ta… ta-ta-ta… ta-ta-ta! <

The bugler startled him out of his torpor once again. He checked the wall clock—sure enough, twenty minutes had passed. Amazing how fast that had gone!

"Fall in!" Tom commanded.

The scoutmaster is standing to the side again—interesting. He never gives the orders—Tom always does that.

The next fifteen minutes went by rapidly—some kind of marching practice. Everyone except Mark and Tom was out on the open floor performing this or that command. As far as Randall could tell, they had it down from the start, but Tom was a perfectionist.

He'd have various moves done over and over again—sometimes he pulled out a few guys to demonstrate a point. During all this Mark wandered around observing, taking notes. The demonstration of strides was interesting—Tom had three guys, each a different height, come forward and take their natural step. They were supposed to find an average that they could all do—this made it possible for them to move together perfectly. The short guys had to stretch, the tall ones had to take shorter steps.

Every patrol worked on that for a while, until the bugler played his signal again. Tom ordered the troop to fall in; he complimented them and said a few words about what they would work on next and reminded them about the Veteran's Day Parade. Then he ordered them to fall out for the patrol meetings. Everyone grabbed a chair from the dolly; The Flaming Arrows didn't have their own circle—each one sat with a different patrol. Mark did that for a while too, then circulated, paying attention to each group. There was no way to make out what anyone said; too many were talking at the same time. Randall tried to see how many of these guys he could recognize from school. Hmm—the uniforms take over and hide them like a mask of some kind. Even the ones I know are hard to pick out at first glance.

After a while, Mark came up onto the platform and sat in the empty chair. "How are you doing? Completely bored yet?" He gave Randall a friendly tap on the shoulder.

"No!" He was thrilled to be asked. "It's fascinating. I never understood about marching before. I see how you compensate for the big difference in strides. It's obvious once you see that; I never realized how complicated marching is."

"We're fortunate there—my predecessor was a West Point man; he left behind his instruction manual—one of a kind. I try to keep the tradition as well as I can—I used to be a member of this troop myself, and I remember how much that meant to me. We show off in public whenever we can—Fourth of July, Veterans Day, Memorial Day. It's fun to do and the crowds love it. It feels good to have people applaud a job well done."

At once Randall could see why Julian was so drawn to this man—practically worships him. A big brother substitute I suppose… he isn't old enough to be his father. Randall was too polite to ask his age—must be under thirty though…

"So, any questions?" the boy's speech impressed Mark. His intelligence is obvious. I should meet his parents.

"I did wonder about one thing," Randall hesitated, but it sort of nagged at him. "How come you don't do the commanding? All I see is Tom. Shouldn't the scoutmaster be in charge?"

"Aha! I'm glad you asked that." I was right—this boy sees what is important. "It's my job to teach leadership. I can't do that very well if I do all the leading, can I? What I do is set an example and give the boys every opportunity possible to learn by doing—there is no better teacher than experience."

What a brilliant approach. No wonder the guys think he's the best. He's not on an ego trip—I could make a list of about a dozen teachers that could benefit from taking Mark's approach.

"It's almost time for the refreshment break. I wanted to ask something: how do you plan to get home—you don't have a car, do you?"

"I have a bicycle. It's at Julian's house."

Mark nodded. That raised a question. "Did you ride all the way with that cake on the handle bars?"

"No," he laughed. "My mom dropped it off."

"Tell you what: how about I take you home afterwards. We can pop your bike into the back. I want to meet your parents."

Why does he want to meet them? Randall didn't know how to react.

Mark could see the concern.

"Here's a confidential tip: parents generally care who their boys spend an evening with and what they do. I need to allay any concerns—besides, I want to find out the name of that bakery!" Mark always wanted to be in touch with the parents.

Again, Randall was impressed. Obviously Mark will impress them—reassuring them won't hurt me any. "Wow, sure! If you don't mind going out of your way."

"It's not out of my way. Besides, there's nothing on TV tonight anyway. Maybe you can show me some of those mountain climbing photos." He winked.

> *ta-ta-ta... ta-ta-ta... ta-ta-ta!* <

"At last! Time for punch and cookies!" Mark stood. "I'll turn you back over to Julian now." He gave a friendly tap on the shoulder. "See you later."

Naturally, Randall watched him walk over to the table. The backside in motion was almost as thrilling as the conversation had been. The buns are even sexier… the tan fabric faithfully displayed every nuance of the gluteus muscles at work. He looked away quickly, lest it contribute to his ongoing problem. His view of this regimented society was under serious review; he could tell when he had made a hasty judgment—this was a clear case.

"Hey, guest of honor!" Julian chimed as he hurried over. "Let's go get a cookie!" They look homemade—my favorite thing.

Randall stood—the honorific was mildly annoying, but Julian was just trying to lighten things. He's always bubbly happy about everything. You couldn't be grumpy or worried with Julian on your case. He followed along, trying to ignore the faint buzz below… I shouldn't have watched Mark walk away. The problem that had plagued him all during the meeting was as bad as ever.

"Make way, make way," Julian commanded. "Special guest gets to go to the front!" He made a point with his arms as if he were about to do the breaststroke.

Another blush spread across Randall's face—that's the second time tonight he's done that to me… does my face look as red as it feels? Randall had never learned what to do about blushes because he rarely had the problem. Again, he thought Julian was talking about someone else at first. His eyes flicked back and forth nervously, expecting to see someone frown at being pushed aside. To the contrary: nothing but supportive interested expressions. You can't have *dreams* this good!

"Take two," Julian ordered, moving from the cookie tray to the fruit punch. Three pitchers, full to the brim, sat next to a stack of paper cups.

After that cake, Randall wasn't especially hungry, but they did look tasty. His mother never baked cookies. She usually gets Oreos.

He took two and folded them into a napkin. He followed along, both hands full—Julian sat in one of the empty patrol circles. Randall parked on his far side. Thanks to the fanfare, the whole world had watched him go all the way to the refreshment table: fixing The Problem was impossible—a little worse now because of that short talk with Mark. I can't do a thing about it now, either: my hands are full. He shrugged, hoping it would take care of itself… nothing else I can do. > *sip…* < …mmm—one of those tropical fruit drinks. The chair to his right was a good temporary resting place for the cup; he wrapped one cookie in the napkin and tucked it into his shirt pocket for later. The napkin is a good idea: these are a little oily.

"So, are you glad you came tonight?" Julian winked. "You're supposed to say yes, by the way." He took a bite of cookie. "Yum!" he wowed his eyes. Maybe there will be extras…

"Hi," said an eager voice. "My name is Alex… Alex Trent." He gestured to the scout at his right. "This is Clint—Clint Walker." He stuck out his hand. "I'm really glad to meet you."

Randall fumbled awkwardly and shifted the cup to his left hand temporarily; he shook hands with both guys. What a contrast—Alex is a muscular athletic type; Clint was more like Randall himself. Indeed, he felt an instant kinship with Clint, as if they were cousins. His face looks vaguely familiar.

Clint's reaction was similar, but he already knew who Randall was—they were in the same English class. I doubt if he recognizes me—we haven't ever spoken to each other… don't know why. He returned Randall's smile; when the guest's attention had returned to Alex, it was safe to re-check: Clint always had an eye out these days, and a seven o'clock bulge below the belt made him curious. Ever since Julian's introduction, he'd been keeping his eye on the crotch: is he growing one or just big down there? Clint had a secret hobby of spotting guys that had boners going—or growing. He rarely found out for sure if they were hard, but it was a fun pastime. English class will be more interesting now, no doubt about that.

"My father used to take me on climbing trips," Alex said enthusiastically. "I don't think any were as dangerous as yours, though."

"Oh? That's interesting. Where do you go climbing around here, anyway?" Dad would like to know where he could find a good climb.

Alex blushed. "The biggest one I went to was one called Bald Mountain… or was it Bald Peak? I dunno for sure… I was only nine years old at the time." He changed the subject. "What's it like on a glacier?"

While Randall conversed with Alex, Julian watched proudly. I knew he could do it. Maybe now he won't be so shy all the time. Several had gathered to listen. "Hey you guys, grab a chair; feel free to join in."

The circle filled at once, and other chairs were appropriated—eventually eighteen boys were attending, greatly interested. None of them had ever met a person from Washington, the state. A few, if the truth were told, were interested in the same thing that still preoccupied Clint. Two Tenderfoot scouts in particular: they sat cross-legged on the floor in the very front, eager to hear every word. Eyes open wide, they were positioned perfectly to see every detail, head on.

Randall hadn't forgotten that his crotch had an unresolved conflict, but he had put it aside for the moment, unaware that it was visible. The light cream color of the slacks reflected the light such that every detail possible was visible or enhanced. In these pants it didn't matter whether he was swelling or not.

It wasn't that he was endowed too generously down there; but it did become an honest six and a half inches when he allowed it to grow—or when it grew on its own. It so happened these pants were small for him now—he had grown more than an inch and a half since his mother had proudly purchased these; they were his junior high graduation slacks—the pale cream color was symbolic—only top ten graduates were dressed in these special trousers. Along with a special blazer and bow tie, he looked very classy at that ceremony.

No one here could know about or appreciate the former significance of these pants, no matter how expensive they looked. What mattered now was how they fit: the cuffs were an inch above his shoes. More critical, his growth over the summer was sufficient to take up the slack usually built into the panels on either side of the fly. He lacked several cubic centimeters of space where it was needed most of all: the crotch. This was the one pair of pants in his closet that tended to show off what he had—especially if Little R had lodged himself just right. Lack of room contributed to The Problem: resistance was the same as adding pressure. Little R enjoyed being pressed: it was encouragement, always welcome—and Little R was ready to respond.

The longer Randall sat there expounding on his mountain exploits, the more secure and confident he felt—and the more intently a few in the audience stared—hoping to see it grow. Fortunately, he was not aware of this—had he been, it would have been impossible to prevent Little R from satisfying their curiosity. As it was, he had been able to hold his own. Answering lots of questions about what it was like out west kept him occupied—the usual ones about how many Indians there were, what mountains he had climbed and so forth… it was all very exciting and ego building. He had never been given this kind of respect; it was intoxicating—*enabling*.

Julian needed to confer with Nick—his Assistant Scribe duties called. He tapped Randall on the shoulder. “See you later. I gotta go talk with Nick before the meeting.”

“Oh… sure.”

He didn’t have time to react—Julian’s chair was occupied at once by Tony—who, not coincidentally, happened to be standing behind him.

“Let me tell you guys about the *campout* we had last weekend!” Tony boasted, putting an arm around Randall’s shoulder. “This is the guy who rescued us all from being attacked in the night by wild beasts of all sizes!”

Tony’s style was well known, so it was taken for what it was worth with laughter and a few applauding hands. His comic relief was always fun. The fact that he had been on a campout with the visitor was to his favor. For all his clowning around, Tony was regarded as a competent scout.

Randall was startled; he knew Tony well—very well in a special way—not as the troop did, but as the experience in Hayden Park had taught. He didn't think for a minute that Tony would talk about that. The problem was the arm around the shoulder and the small hug. It sent a signal downward—an *instant* signal. And Randall felt an instant response. Unless an inspiration came along to prevent it, he feared that Little R would find a way to spring out of his blind alley—and soon. Oh-oh… Randall could feel him getting underway.

What can I do with all these guys staring right at me? A yet to be tasted cookie was in his left hand and half a cup of punch in his right; both were directed to hide what they could before it was too late. With any luck, that bugle will sound—maybe before Little R is all the way up: he could tell that was probably going to happen now, no matter what—Tony's arm was still around his shoulder.

The paper cup is worthless… I need that cold root beer bottle! I don't dare rest my hand down there; touching will make it worse… the cup is suspended just above. There's no place to put the cookie—he held it in place… maybe it will help cover things.

Little R would have enjoyed being pressed down from the outside by Randall's hand, but he didn't need assistance now—Tony's hug had done the trick. He had been dislodged at last. Relishing his newly acquired space, Little R pressed his tip forcefully against the right thigh, seeking full freedom… ever so slowly he gained distance in regular increments: seven o'clock… seven fifteen… seven thirty… the endeavor showed through the fabric… eight o'clock… eight fifteen… The left side of his shaft, upward curve clearly visible, seemed to be boastfully inviting anyone close by to pull out a ruler and take a measurement. Nine o'clock… nine fifteen…

Randall, meanwhile, couldn't look down to see if he had covered himself adequately—a dozen or more pair of eyes would follow his at once; nonetheless, he could feel Little R on the move. There was nothing he could do. To make it worse, he could feel nervous sweat beginning to form on his temples.

Those sitting opposite were unaware of Randall's situation. Most, not given to looking down there, were none the wiser. Clint, however, was positioned perfectly to see the drama unfold from start to finish. He stared, thrilled… felt himself doing the same thing… luckily, he was not the object of anyone's attention. His suspicions had been correct… he hadn't predicted this, but he had wished for it awfully hard—maybe I helped by using my will power.

On the other side of the circle, Andy noticed the spectacle as well—the view wasn't perfect, but he could tell the kid was growing one. The power of suggestion is a force few can resist: Andy felt himself start… a favorite sensation. He glanced around… nobody was looking his way. All clear. Slowly he moved his hands to cover… and assist. The meeting is minutes away—no one will pay any attention then.

Those who had been annoyed by having an obstructed view were soon given a nice surprise—inadvertently, Tony came to their aid.

"Hey, you guys, give the guy a break—he hasn't been able to drink his punch or eat his cookie!" He nudged Randall's leg with his own and patted him on the back. "Go ahead—drink up before it gets too warm… your ice has melted."

Oh boy… what can I do? Randall raised his cup and took a drink, knowing that half of his lap was now exposed, including most of Little R; when he took a bite from the cookie, he felt the last stage being achieved, thanks to the assist provided by Tony's nudge. Little R completed his move upward—the last opposition had been overcome. There was no doubt about what occupied the hospitable valley at the ten o'clock position in his lap: the underside of a full-fledged erection was visible to all. Little R had arrived at the top of the right leg at last; he gave a victory pulse, gratis; he'd earned a good brag.

The scene was thrilling for any who were paying attention—and several were. The total number was not known, of course, but Andy got his eyes full, as did Clint. Others took note as well—Robin and Doug certainly, and Shawn, newly awakened to these things, was unable to prevent his jaw from dropping. He knew Randall slightly, being in Concert Band; unfortunately, as a drummer, all he ever saw was his back; he planned to keep an eye out anyway. Paul, about to make arrangements with Doug for an after the meeting dare, did a double take. Instantaneously, each of these had a sympathetic event of their own begin. Had Randall looked down at the two Tenderfoot scouts sitting cross-legged, he would have seen the stiffies that had been pulsing away for several minutes already—one, considerably larger than the other, was destined one day to be among the larger ones in troop history.

Tony was the last to notice. He felt responsible and guilty—this was a fellow Initiate. Before he could think of anything, the bugle sounded. While everyone scurried into action, Tony spoke low. "Hey, don't sweat it; hardly anyone can tell," he lied.

Randall looked at him accusingly. He didn't know what to say, so he handed Tony the empty cup. He walked back to the platform, sat in his chair and crossed his legs. He had no idea who had seen his problem and what they must think. Maybe Julian can help me figure out what to do. The problem was not helped any by the fact that he had seen a few bulges appear. Normally that would have been a nifty bonus. Now it was proof that he had been seen. Be philosophic about it, Randall… all I can do is hope they forget about it. Fat chance—*I'd* never forget seeing something like that. So the best hope is that they won't *talk* about it.

Unable to focus on the official goings on for a while, he nibbled at the cookie until it was gone. Tom was conducting a standard business meeting, for all practical purposes. Nick read the minutes of the previous meeting and praised the Zebras for bringing the punch and cookies; Danny gave an official report about a number of subjects including a list of points being awarded for various things—as well as twenty five points to himself, Julian and Tony for the campout. Randall tried to look interested—and he was. But it took a while to recover from his awful embarrassment. Hopefully, no one would tell Mark.

Nominations were the last item of business. Each Patrol Leader stood and placed in nomination their choice for the official name of the new car: Panther Patrol: **General Patton**. Tiger Patrol:

Scoutmobile. Lynx Patrol: **Troop Nine Transport**. Wolf Patrol: **Mark's Mean Machine**. Badger Patrol: **George Washington**. Zebra Patrol: **Lady Luck**. After the nominations, Tom turned the meeting over to the scoutmaster.

Mark stepped forward: "Excellent nominations, men. Next month we will decide by secret ballot. Let's see which Patrol can win over the most votes. Remember though: vote for what you think is best for the *Troop*." He checked his clipboard. "I have a couple of special notices. First, a reminder that we'll be taking the annual Troop picture just before the parade on Monday; be here 15 minutes early. Next, congratulations to Norman and Casey for their excellent Life project model. If you haven't checked it out, it's on the table up here with the Scrapbook. I recommend you try to steal an idea or two. I'm awarding them each a 25 point bonus." He pointed at the Wolf Patrol: Norman and Casey stood and took a bow. After the applause, he continued; "It's Wolf night, I guess. If you haven't checked out the Scrapbook lately, you should. It's the outstanding work of Julian, a former Wolf. The camp scenes have all been added now. Everyone who is pictured gets five points."

Cheers erupted.

"That's five points *per picture*." He grinned. "A big hand for the best troop artist of all time, Julian." He gestured for him to take a bow. "Now, here's Tom."

Tom stepped to the front. "Anything for the good of the order?" He scanned the Troop. Tony stood; it was the standard ploy he always tried to get a bonus point. "Tony?"

"I suggest a big round of applause for our special guest from the State of Washington!"

The idea pleased Tom. "Objections?" Hearing none and not allowing time for anyone to do so, he declared, "By unanimous consent, a hurrah and bravo to our guest !" He motioned everyone to stand and join him: "Hurrah! Bravo!" He was unaware that Randall had any problem.

Embarrassed once again, Randall stood. At least Little R was back where he belonged. He took a mini bow and sat back down, moved. The look on Tony's face when he made the suggestion made up for everything. Emotionally, he was in unfamiliar territory. The humiliating incident during the refreshment break seems to have been dismissed by everyone… but being cheered and applauded? Dazed, he stared straight ahead unable to think.

Tom proceeded with the meeting. He nodded at a scout poised at Julian's side—the one with a guitar.

"Life Scout Webster will lead us in the closing song." Tom joined the scoutmaster. The troop stood.

Max strummed his guitar and played the first bars of *O Christmas Tree*.

Randall recognized the tune at once… he couldn't think of the words right now… I *know* this music!

Max led the Troop in the Vesper song:

Softly falls the light of day,
As our campfire fades away.
Silently each Scout should ask,
"Have I done my daily task?
Have I kept my honor bright?
Can I guiltless sleep tonight?
Have I done and have I dared,
Everything to Be Prepared?"

He finished with a flourish of improvised strumming.

Tom stepped forward. "Troop dismissed!" The meeting was over.

That answered Randall's question. In spite of the fact that they were meeting in a church building, it did not begin and end with some sort of homage to God. Another barrier to his favorable opinion had been removed. As he stood up, a crowd stormed up to look at the Scrapbook. A couple of them stepped out of the throng and approached.

"Hiya," Sid said, all smiles. "We couldn't get close to you during the break. Do you always attract a large crowd?"

Randall was taken aback. How do I answer a question like that? He had never met Sid, and did not know his style.

Julian overheard and raced over—"Hey, Sid." He turned to Randall. This is Sid. We've been best friends since grade school." He punched Sid in the arm. "You have to be careful around him, though… he loves to pull jokes on you."

"Gotta keep you on your toes," Sid nodded. "If it wasn't for me," he aimed his left thumb at Julian; "he'd never have made it to high school." He stuck out his right hand. "Sid Thomas is the name. This guy is Kurt—Kurt Davis. He can row a canoe faster than you can run—not to mention that he could pick you up and toss you across the room if he had a mind to."

Kurt shook his head but held his tongue; he reached out. "Hi." He was curious about the glacier, but…

"How'd you guys meet, anyway?" Sid asked mischievously.

Julian gave him a wry grin. "We just bumped into each other in the hall one day."

"Aww, isn't that nice… and it was love at first sight!" He looked at Kurt. "Don't you just love it when that happens?"

Julian put his arm around Sid and gave him a sorrowful look. "It was fate. What's a guy gonna do?" They put their hands on each other's shoulders and bumped heads; they did a pretend cry.

Randall and Kurt looked at each other awkwardly and blushed.

Kurt cleared his throat. "So, how tall a mountain have you climbed?"

"Hard to say, exactly… I've been on a couple that were over nine thousand feet; the highest I've been on the very top of was 8760."

"Whoa… what's it like?"

"The air is thinner… you tire out real quick. The fun part is signing the book."

"Book?!"

"Yeah… most named peaks have a metal box chained to the rock. Inside is a visitor's book. It's interesting to flip through and see who's been there, what year, y'know, stuff like that."

"Must be kinda windy up there…"

"Depends. If it's nasty weather below, you better believe it's worse on top. It wasn't bad the day I went up."

"Time to hit the road, guys," Mark announced from across the platform. Valise packed and ready, hat planted atop his head, he was ready to head out.

"See ya around," Sid gave Randall a mini tap on the shoulder. Kurt nodded, and they headed for the coat racks.

Julian hurried to get his scrapbook. Danny and Tony were standing by, ready to go.

Randall just noticed: the flags were put away and the room was all cleared, ready for whatever was scheduled next. Everyone was gone! *Amazing* how efficient these guys are!

Julian returned and gave him a prod. "When I was talking to Danny I snagged us an extra cookie!" He plopped one into Randall's hand, "Let's split, as they say." He skipped off the platform.

Randall hurried along behind. I'll save the cookie for later. A secret inside pocket in his coat served as a regular nook for stashing Oreos and other treats. Oil spots won't matter there; in fact, he planned to transfer the one in his shirt pocket to the same location.

Outside, the parking area was almost empty. "Where'd they all go?" I've never seen that many kids vanish so fast… we aren't that far behind.

"Home, where else? It's a school night." Julian noticed Randall's puzzled expression. "Some have their own cars. The rest are picked up by parents. The meeting always ends on time, so they know when to be here. Until Mark got the station wagon, my mom always brought and took us home; she never had to wait once."

So it wasn't because they were in a hurry to leave. He glanced at Mark. He knows what he's doing all right.

One pair hadn't reached their car: that big husky kid has the skinny blond in a headlock giving him a knuckle rub. Sid was his name; he's laughing, so it's in good fun… he must have made one wisecrack too many. What's the other one's name? Sid and… it will come to me. I'm pretty good at remembering names.

That "love at first sight" quip had hit home… the truth is, I was *already* in love. What about Julian? It's looking pretty good.

As they approached the Country Squire, Tony gave Danny a quick goose and scooted around the other side before he could strike back. Randall admired Tony for his daring—he does all those things I'd be too chicken to try. Seeing that gave him a small buzz—memories from the park popped into his head. He glanced at Julian's backside. The bottom half showed under his jacket. One day, maybe I can give him a surprise goose. He chuckled. What would his reaction be, anyway? What does that feel like? He'd seen guys doing that it a few times after PE class… but no one had ever done it to him. Oop… hello Little R… he reached down and made a small adjustment while he could.

In a few minutes, he would be home where he could take these pants off—*forever*.

18 The Hallstroms at home

Randall never imagined his bike could fit into the back of the station wagon; no problem at all with that third seat folded down. The four mile drive from Julian's house, about twice the distance from the church, wouldn't take long… the problem now was thinking of something to say. It's stupid to just sit here. What can I say that isn't corny? The scoutmaster's hat, on the seat between them, gave him an idea: "How long have you been the scoutmaster?" Maybe he just moved up from the ranks.

"Seven years, counting this one. It was supposed to be temporary, but…" he shrugged. "During my last year in college, the scoutmaster had a fatal heart attack and they were stuck. Somebody thought of me—who or why I don't know." That was the roughest six months of my life—it was right after Erik died; the scoutmaster duty is what kept me going. "Anyway, at the end of the year they asked me to stay on. So I did. For a while I assumed it was for just another year. So far they've asked me to stay on every year. I guess we're stuck together, for better or worse."

"I always thought scoutmasters were older."

"They generally are. My case was special. They were in a jam; no one else would take it on. I was twenty-one, so I was qualified, legally. My background helped; I was an Eagle Scout and had served as Senior Patrol Leader—so I knew what to do. I'd only been gone from the troop for three years, so half the guys knew me. I've kept things pretty much the same. Once in a while we try something new, but I see no reason to fix what isn't broken."

Mark's scoutmaster still stood as his idol and example. We called him the General. I'll never fill *his* shoes. That's why I insist that the boys call me by my first name. Pat says I don't want to be a grownup yet—she has a point.

"Turn left here… it's the third house on the right."

"Okay if I pull into the driveway, or should I park on the street?"

"Either one is okay… the driveway is best; the house is set back quite a ways."

Randall rarely brought anyone home—certainly not this late, and certainly not an adult. This was the first time he'd brought anyone to this house. He wasn't worried, but maybe he should have thought to call ahead somehow. Mom might have her hair all put up—she always fusses with it if she has something coming up the next day…

Mark waited in the anteroom while Randall went to fetch his parents. Chamber music, not loud, came from a room nearby. He wasn't especially fond of it, but it was better than the top ten this time of night. An enlarged photograph of a mountain scene caught his eye. He studied it closely—very alpine; makes me want to pack my kit and hike up there first thing in the morning, wherever it is.

His nose twitched: pipe tobacco. Not as bad as cigarettes, but still, takes getting used to. It figures, in a way; pipes were commonplace among professors when I was in college; almost a status symbol. An image appeared in his mind: a balding grey haired man with metal frame glasses halfway down his nose… unbuttoned vest, of course. I wonder if Randall's father fits the stereotype. Probably not, if he's done much mountain climbing.

"Good evening," said a charming voice, just emerging from a room down the hall to the right.

"Mom, this is Mr. Schaefer. He was kind enough to give me a ride home."

"Good evening, Mrs. Hallstrom; Mark Schaefer." He extended his hand; her appearance took him by surprise—she looked ready to sit for a portrait. Presumably she had attended a formal event earlier in the evening. Her demeanor was friendly and welcoming; the family resemblance was clear in spite of the fancy hairdo.

Randall had ducked into the room at the left; he and his father emerged in a few seconds. Mark was pleasantly surprised. The man was not professorial at all—hale, hearty and fit; he had left the pipe behind.

"Helgar Hallstrom," extended his hand, delighted; this is a nice surprise. Expecting to see a middle aged insurance broker or some such, his eyes did an instant scan up and down. Yes, *indeed.* He patted his son on the back. "Randall has given you good marks, sir, and I can see why. Can you stop a while and chat?"

"I'd like that, if you have the time. I'd hate to think I'd be keeping you from finishing a stack of term papers."

Hallstrom gave a hearty laugh. "I'm on top of that just now, thanks." He glanced at his wife to see if she had something to say.

"That would be very nice; I wasn't expecting company, but there's always something on hand. Would you like a glass of wine perhaps, or…"

"Please, I don't want to upset your routine. Don't make a fuss. We can just sit around the kitchen table and talk a bit, as far as I'm concerned. Formalities are not my thing." The pleased look on the father's face confirmed his hunch. The wife is the fussy one… the tea and crumpets type.

"Excellent!" Hallstrom extended his arm toward the kitchen-dinette. "Eloise is always ready for the impromptu occasion." The man's arrival is perfect: this will get my mind off the news. All they can talk about is the President's speech last night. I don't like the way international affairs look these days—too much sabre rattling. First Berlin, now Cuba.

Eloise led the way.

Mark left his hat on the small table by the door.

"May I take your coat?" Helgar extended his hand.

"No need; I'll just put it on the back of the chair." It made departing easier; many parental visits taught the same basic lesson: when I give up my coat it's harder to make a graceful exit. Asking for your coat can make you seem somewhat abrupt or rude—why leave people with a bad impression?

Randall detoured to the mudroom to shuck his jacket.

Eloise gestured to a chair, indicating where Mark was to sit. She had gone to some trouble to find this table—it was custom made locally, perfect for four people. "Now, what about that wine… or are you a teetotaler?"

"Not guilty. Whatever you have open would be fine. On scout nights I always wait until after the meeting to have my after supper glass." He draped his jacket over the back of the chair.

"Red or white?" Eloise maintained a respectable range of wines. She knew what any occasion required. A man who had a glass of wine after supper was a man who met with her approval.

"I prefer red, not very dry. But please, don't open anything just for me." He surveyed the kitchen and its furnishings. Quality, but not ostentatious. This is where they have breakfast. It felt homey. "I understand that Randall has a sister."

"Yes, indeed," Helgar replied. "Asleep already. In bed by eight, asleep by 8:30. You'll have to find a reason to drop by earlier in the day."

This wasn't the first time Randall had observed adults performing social niceties—it had never made a difference to him before. He was generally happy with how it was going… parents are okay if you give them some slack. Dad's reaction so far is excellent. The kitchen table meant they could just be plain people—his father disliked all that lace-and-doily stuff his mom thrived on. She's a lot more fun when she's in the kitchen; even though she says she doesn't like to cook, she's good at it.

"What I really wanted to do was thank you for sending that cake," Mark said as she opened a pantry door. "I want to know the bakery that came from."

Eloise turned and beamed with gratitude and pride. "Yes, they do make the best, don't they?" She reached for a bottle of Cabernet Sauvignon—a good room temperature wine. "It's from Nancy's over on eighteenth. I'm so pleased you enjoyed it. They have an excellent variety. They do all of Amanda and June's desserts, you know.

"Well." Mark nodded as if impressed. He knew Amanda's by reputation, for the most part; too out of the way to be a regular destination. He turned to Randall's father… the professor who didn't look like a professor. "Randall has told us some about your mountain climbing. I have to say, I am impressed. That's one area where I haven't done much." His face is intriguing… Mark was inclined to study it, but thought better; I see where Randall got his nose.

Helgar beamed. "That's the biggest regret I have about taking a position here. Nothing is nearby. Certainly nothing alpine." He gestured to Randall. "Bring some of your photography."

Randall hopped up at once and ran to his room. Thanks to Mom, I know right where the box is. His room hadn't had time to slip back to normal.

"Nothing tells the story like Randall's photos. He does his own processing, you know." Hallstrom was quite proud of his son's skill. He continued to marvel at the man seated at his table… so fit… handsome, too. His eye risked another glance downward. Fit *indeed.*

Eloise brought a tray with three generous glasses of Cabernet and placed them carefully. Odd, but she liked this man in spite of his being in a uniform. The wedding ring isn't a surprise… he reminds me of Helgar ten years ago. She sat and put her hand on the stem of her glass, expecting her husband to take the hint. He did.

"Let's drink to a long life," Helgar lifted his glass.

"With lots of adventure," Mark added, lifting his glass.

"To adventure," Helgar echoed, and took a sip. I like that idea.

Eloise lifted hers without adding a toast; adventure was the perfect word; this man seemed to create an urge, a need.

Randall brought in an open top box filled with photographs. "One day I'm gonna put these in an album."

"You should recruit Julian. He's a pro at scrapbooks." Mark helped himself to the top snapshot. "Where was this taken?"

"Ooo, that was in the Sawtooths! Remember, Dad?" He looked back at Mark. "Those are in Idaho, right across the border." He pointed to the tallest one in the long jumble of craggy peaks. "That's Thompson Peak… it's 10,751 feet high! Too much for us, of course. We camped by Redfish Lake though… that's the best access. The lake is over 6,500 feet. Too cold for swimming."

Eloise and Helgar exchanged glances. This was a new, wonderful experience. They had never seen their son in this sort of setting. He made them feel proud. They also couldn't get their eyes off the scoutmaster. Eloise was surprised to discover that her response to the uniform was… was what? She wanted to say erotic, but that's absurd. Why would I think that? It must be because he reminds me of someone… before Helgar.

Helgar was pleased—he was lucky to have seated himself such that he could see the entire man. Those slacks, especially, had awakened his alter ego, as he called it. I haven't found anyone in this town yet… perhaps my secret appetite is asserting itself. He had not looked for a replacement for Walter. Getting settled in had taken all his time and energy. He missed his bi weekly romps—pun intended. Maybe I have made a discovery. Well timed, Randall!

Eloise stood and went to the refrigerator. Some cheddar and sliced apple was required… maybe a Rye Krisp? or Wheat Thins… yes. While the men talk mountains, I'll make up a plate… we should do more entertaining. For bringing this man here, Randall's stock just went way up.

Mark selected another photo. This one he flashed to Helgar. "This camp looks very high. The trees, the plants are unlike anything you'll find around here." He watched the man's face closely. What is so interesting about this guy? The nose, maybe—and the straight blond hair. Must be purebred Viking. Bright blue eyes... all he needs is a horned helmet and a big sword...

"Ah, yes. Between six and seven thousand feet, I'd say. That's in the North Cascades, west of Lake Chelan. We spent over a week there; my grad assistant was along." One of our better trips, in *every* way. "Fortress Mountain. A serious piece of climbing." Late July, if memory serves; plenty of snow left.

"North Cascades?" Mark had not heard of that range. "Are they in Canada?"

"Partly, yes. Northwest Washington is a vast sea of rugged mountains. In part, they're the upper end of what is known as the Cascades. North and east of Mount Rainier, if you know where that is—above Seattle. Mount Baker and Glacier Peak are the best known in that group. The name tells what's there, for sure. They're the tallest because they're volcanic. Most of the others are upthrust bedrock, tilted and gnawed away during the ice age, like the Rockies.

Randall took the opportunity to study Mark's body. He could see all of him from here. The slacks were doing their thing again. I can't see the crotch as well as I'd like... I got an incredible view of the front standing in the hallway... I didn't see that at the scout meeting. The fabric is consistent—it follows the contours of Mark's lower abdomen and the tops of his thighs almost as well as it did the back. What he saw while the cake was being served was revealed—not as well, but well enough: the full length—it wasn't hiding behind the fly, but resting along the right side. Intriguing, if not inviting... the thigh and knee looked even hotter than they had in the car.

I never thought of a leg as being sexy... There's a first time for everything, they say; the proof is sitting less than two feet away. He sat up close to the table... maybe I can get a better look at what's hiding between those legs. Ooo, yes. Not a loaf now... look at that. The cling factor is *very* evident. It's in the same condition as before:

not hard, not growing… but not a limp noodle, either. Too bad I'm not sitting where Dad is.

Mark sat back and held the snapshot close. So this is a Cascade meadow. Very different—only conifers; shows what a couple thousand more feet is like. "I've never been much above five thousand feet."

Helgar used the moment to take another sip—and a good look at what had happened when Mark sat back in his chair—in that special place. *Very* fit; no paunch, and *look* at that thigh. The sensation in his own lap was very nice. It *has* been too long, hasn't it? He would allow it to develop freely, as it wished. If nothing else, Eloise and I are due for a bit of the old in and out.

Meanwhile, Randall settled in; he put his elbows on the table and rested his chin—this formed a tripod that made it possible to glance between Mark's lap and the box of photos without giving away what had attracted his eye. The same warning signal Little R sent at the meeting arrived, loud and clear. One problem with Little R: every time he goes hard he expects to get a hand job before very long; he stays super ready to fill up again—never goes completely asleep.

Randall wasn't worried about that—I can hide The Problem easily enough sitting at the table. I've done that before. So he fanned his legs occasionally; that always felt good, and it helped Little R slide up into his happy position unnoticed. Of course, I'd better not do that too much… sometimes that takes me to the edge. I want to save that for later. Besides, I don't need to attract any attention. His parents were unaware of his sex life, now that he had one; he planned to keep it that way.

Soon photographs covered most of the table; father and son had a great time sharing memories of various hikes and climbs and telling Mark all about the Pacific Northwest. Eloise was thrilled; she learned more about those trips here than she had heard after the trips themselves. She felt a part of that experience for the first time. The apple slices, cheese and crackers were perfect with the wine—so much so, a second glass was accepted with enthusiasm.

Randall considered asking if he could try a small glass, but thought better of it. Things are going well as is...no point in triggering parental instincts. Intriguing, though, to see how the wine mellowed everyone. He fetched a small glass of water and shared the nibbles. This is the most fun I've had with my parents since I was a little kid. When he crossed the room, no one noticed the stiffy—I centered it behind the fly; it's less visible when I do that.

This visit was not what Mark expected; I'm enjoying myself immensely. It's educational as well as hospitable. The second glass of wine wasn't the best idea, but I can handle it. When Eloise opened another bottle he didn't object... it's only a three or four mile drive home. The crackers and cheese should offset the alcohol. The subject of Randall joining the troop didn't come up, fortunately. There isn't a vacancy right now—and he's a little old to start. In scouts, you have to start at the bottom.

Mark was unaware that he was the object of intense interest—all the way around. All three Hallstroms would have hopped into bed with him, given the chance. Helgar intended to do just that. Something inside said 'go for it.' But I have to plan it; there's homework to do on this. Good timing indeed, Randall!

Mark glanced at his watch. "I have overstayed my welcome, I'm afraid. There's someone at this table who has school tomorrow." He winked at Randall, and stood.

"My!" Eloise glanced at the wall clock. "I lost all track."

Helgar checked his watch. "Yes, as did I." He hated to see Mark leave, but they had reached a comfortable stopping point. He stood and extended his hand. "You are good company, sir."

"Mark, please." He grinned at Eloise. "People called Sir have to starch their shirts. I hate to iron shirts—I'm sure you agree."

Randall froze briefly, amazed: he had just noticed his father's hard-on—something he had never seen in his *life!* What caused that?!

His own erection had started to recede—it went back up at once; it's still behind the fly, so I doubt they'll notice… fortunately, they're paying attention to Mark. Dad must be eight or nine inches! Wow. Pretending to be sorting photographs, he checked on Mark… no stiffy, but *plenty* of dangle. I *love* those slacks. His eyes played back and forth… he couldn't pick one over the other. I want my camera! I *need* my camera!

"You're wonderful hosts. I've enjoyed my visit very much." Mark turned to Randall. "I am impressed by your photography!" If it weren't so expensive, it would make a good merit badge. Randall would be an ideal instructor. He picked up his coat and headed toward the hallway.

"You are welcome to drop in any time," Eloise smiled. She meant it too, which surprised her. It's an odd sensation to sincerely mean a pro forma remark.

Randall followed them to the door like a good boy. He enjoyed watching Mark's backside—the tight waist length jacket emphasized the shape and contour; next to his father's, it was the winner. Although, if Dad had a pair of those slacks…

19 Right up to midnight

a: Julian b: Mark

a: Julian confers with Inside guy

What a *day!* Julian ruminated while scrubbing his teeth over the bathroom sink. It wasn't surprising that Mark decided to take Randall home. It's the sort of thing he would do for any scout—why not Randall? > *giggle* < He was so *funny!* He got a stiffy and couldn't hide it.

What's so funny about that? How would you feel? Inside guy just showed up.

You're right… I'd hate it. But it wasn't *that* bad, really. Only a few guys saw it, and they won't tell. They probably liked it. That's what I told him, too.

Easy to say. Someday it will happen to you. You won't think it's funny then.

We'll see. Anyway, overall it was a great night for him. He made some new friends, and impressed everyone. He won't be so afraid any more, be so shy.

And maybe he'll start looking at someone besides you.

Exactly. I think he's gotten the picture about that anyway. He's a smart kid. He can figure things out without being told.

Is that enough? Are you sure you're not being a chicken not to tell him you can't be his boyfriend?

I don't think so. Why hurt his feelings? I *like* him; I want to stay his friend. Besides, after doing the Initiation, there's no suspense, no curiosity about what's there, you know, that kind of thing. We've done a little here too, remember. We're kind of like blood brothers.

Aren't you afraid he'll get a crush on Mark?

Julian rinsed his mouth and put away the toothbrush. He looked in the mirror, right in the eye: "No, I'm not."

He sure got horny enough after watching Mark serve that cake.

"Well, duh! Who wouldn't?!"

Oop. I said that too loud. Mom will think I've gone crazy. He frowned at the dummy in the mirror and mouthed the words: keep your yap shut, stupid.

You said it, I didn't. Don't change the subject; we were talking about Randall. You saw how he watched Mark all during the meeting.

So?

How do you know that isn't why he got a stiffy?

It probably was. None of us could go all the way down after seeing him in those skivvies. His new pants were almost as bad—I mean, as good. I had to force myself to look away. Little J was just waiting for an excuse. Mark's buns are *Choice*. I learned that at camp. I look at them every chance I get.

"One of these days," speaking low, staring at his reflection, "I'll get to draw him nude, like Randall."

Yeah, right.

"Just wait. You'll see..."

The cake serving episode popped into his mind… on purpose he'd pushed that to the back during the meeting. Now Little J was awakening. He stood back to see what the mirror showed lower down… how visible am I with this combination on… hmm… these pants aren't as good as Mark's. Maybe I should get a pair of those. They're a lot sexier than scout pants or Levi's. He watched the mirror… that's fun to do once in a while. Little J grew slowly. Hmm… these don't show that much; they're still a little big. Mom always gets them a size too large so I can grow into them. Just as well… I get one or two stiffies most days; I always get one in typing class—being able to get one without panicking is kind of nice, actually.

That's what pants are for, y'know.

Yeah, yeah… and keeping me warm. Anyway, I don't need to go around trying to look sexy all the time; I have other things to think about. Besides, Geraldine takes care of that; she's the one who decides what I should wear. He patted the bulge lovingly; "one of these times, I'm going to clock you." He turned to leave. Mom is still up reading… she won't look. He opened the door and turned off the light.

"'Night, Mom." He headed for his room: I have an appointment with a certain drawing stashed in my closet. It has a good view of Mark's buns in skivvies—not the same pair, but skivvies all the same.

"Good night, dear… sleep tight; see you in the morning." She put her book down and reflected… how complicated his life will be in a couple of years. The President's speech last night had her worried. He's bound to get bombarded with war talk at school. She recalled how school was for her during the war; I hope it doesn't come to that. They still draft boys, even though Korea was over long ago.

He still talks to himself… he's done that since early childhood. It's one of his dearest idiosyncrasies. It helped keep him her little boy. She'd never tried to eavesdrop, but it was hard not to be a little curious.

Julian closed his door and started to undress. "Take it *easy*," he whispered. Little J was impatient—a wet spot had appeared in the bikinis. I was showing them to Randall just before I put on my scout uniform. Just for fun, he put on the other pair…

> ***hee-hee-hee!*** <

Oop… he covered his mouth quickly. I don't want Mom to ask what I'm laughing about. But it was *funny*: for once, Randall thought he looked sexy. He thinks he's boring looking… looks fine to me. He was too chicken to leave them on… afraid his mom would find them by mistake.

I wanted to see what they would be like at a troop meeting, so I left them on. A good thing, too—even though they felt kind of sexy, they helped keep Little J in line. That's why he didn't show much a minute ago in the bathroom, either. Otherwise, maybe they aren't such a good idea; too itchy around the balls—it's more comfy when things hang loose.

He straightened his scout uniform and hung it in the closet. Little J can wait; I like to feel him push and nudge. In a second I'll set him free—first things first: get the Kleenex handy and stash some skivvies under the pillow in case a trip to the bathroom is needed—or worse, if Mom comes in: I have to Be Prepared.

She doesn't know I started to sleep in the nude a couple of months ago… some things you do without asking permission. Running to the bathroom bare naked with a stiffy wasn't something he wanted her to see, either. She doesn't know how much I've grown down there—especially since last summer. She's the one who made me put on undies in the first place… when I was little, I ran around naked. She got me skivvy-trained in the first grade.

The idea of sleeping nude was another idea I got at camp—Danny and Tom slept nude in the crew tent: I saw them. It felt strange and wonderful at first; now it feels weird *not* to. Sometimes, after I turn off the light, I pretend a certain someone is sneaking under the covers; that too is Being Prepared: in case a miracle ever happens, I'm ready.

There—almost set. He turned on the headboard lamp and crossed the room to turn off the overhead. The chair had to be located exactly—that way the drawing would be positioned just right when it was propped up against the back… perfect. He returned to the closet and pulled out one of the drawings of Mark he had made in the cabin—the second one, the one with his back turned. It was on one of the large sheets of paper that Uncle Max had given him: two feet tall and a foot and a half wide. With that kind of space, you can draw *lots* of detail.

While I was drawing this, Mark started to grow—I saw the very front come into view… it was pretty hot, peeking from behind his leg like that. I knew it was puffing up because he hadn't moved, and I didn't see it when I started drawing. I didn't add it in… didn't want him to know I saw anything. It was just before lights out; I got a better look a minute later when he went into the bathroom… was *that* ever hot. He was half way up by then—pointed straight ahead. I never did figure out why that happened… he was looking toward the door the whole time. Little J does that on his own lots of times—it must be something they all do.

Mmm… that's what I remembered when Mark was serving the cake: him growing puffy in the cabin. Tonight that was *so* hot! It wasn't hard, but wagged like it would be pretty soon.

Julian had seen what the other guys hadn't. They didn't know he'd seen Mark in skivvies a lot: every night and most mornings before breakfast for two weeks, last summer… I'm an expert on the subject. He was a little puffy tonight, no doubt about that. But, even limp, he fills a pair of skivvies. I figure he's four inches limp and eight completely hard. I got a glimpse of that by accident when I had to wake him up that time he slept in: he tossed back the covers without thinking, and swung around to sit on the edge of the bed—he wasn't wearing anything at *all*. He folded his arms over his lap real quick; I pretended I didn't see anything—

He giggled aloud again… "I got to pretend I didn't see anything *lots* of times." It was *special* because I knew that he had gone to bed with his skivvies on. Other than that one peek, Mark was always in his skivvies.

During the two week camp Julian devised a ten point scale: zero was limp, ten was hard. I saw it at eight once… a six and a couple of fours… Tonight was a three… anything that stays in place without bending when you walk is a three or better. Tonight it stayed in place no matter how he moved; it was sort of stuck there. Little J does that sometimes. When they’re limp, the tip sort of flops back and forth when you walk; you don’t see the pole effect the way you do with a three and up.

Okay: off with the bikinis. “Happy now?” Little J bounced back and forth eagerly. “In a minute, in a minute…” he pulled back the covers. Tonight I want to be in the open air—it’s fun to watch Little J sometimes. He stopped a second to glance across the bed… the curtains are *mostly* closed; good enough. Mom wants them closed *tight*. She’s like that… always worried about burglars and peeping Toms… honestly. No one is out there; too cold, for one thing. For another, they’d need a ladder.

He hopped up and scooted back against the pillows; some nights I like to sit and study the picture for a while and pretend I’m listening to Mark talk. I don’t always get a stiffy—sometimes I think about other things, like when Mark showed how to do things, or when he talked about serious stuff at the conferences. Most of the time I use the other drawing for that. Tonight, no talk; I’m using the other one, the sexy one that shows his buns.

Mark offered to pose for this at the last minute, just before taking his shower. It was a huge favor, unexpected. Of course, Mark didn’t know it was a dream come true—or that I had a pose already planned. All I had to do was tell him where to stand and relocate myself. I sat cross legged at the foot of his bed, holding the drawing board with my left hand. I was only eight feet away! The drawing board made a perfect shield—it hid Little J completely. Mark didn’t know that Little J went up full just after I started to draw.

Tonight is perfect for this drawing: after all the yummy views at the kitchen table, and after watching his buns walk around the meeting room… not to mention the view when he stood behind Tom—from the Flaming Arrow table, that was *something*: a perfect profile—the front and the rear: *man!* Since I’m Assistant Scribe,

I got to sit over there with Nick and take notes. Tonight Little J and I are *both* horny. Saving up makes fantasy nights special… *stronger*—more real.

Sitting up made it possible to look at the image without straining… the portrait could do its magic unassisted… the low light allowed the drawing to transform into the real man; Julian had studied him very carefully when he drew this. Little J in hand at last, he began. Mmmm… as always, the drawing blurred the image being depicted emerged.

…he was in the cabin at Camp Walker looking at his secret love. Mark was standing at the table, his back turned. For reasons of prudence and decorum, he was wearing his briefs. The stance was relaxed; left leg bent at the knee, the weight shifted onto the right leg. The torso was twisted a quarter turn to the left—looking at the door across the room as if to see who was about to enter. This put the face in profile, partially framed by the window above the table. Both hands rested on the hips, obscuring the elastic waistband; a relaxed, but dynamic position—suggesting he was in motion. The left bun was slack—the right firm and tight.

The fantasy began by focusing on the area under the left hand. Resting on the hip, it defined the lower midsection, and drew attention to the left bun, relaxed, yet firm. The cloth, having been in use all day, was tired and damp with perspiration; it rested on the skin with indifference… no argument, no enthusiasm… it was exhausted, ready to be tossed into the laundry drawer—its duty performed faithfully again for the umpteenth time, retirement to the rag box not far off. It was hot and muggy that night—once in a while I could see sweat running down the side of his face.

At this point, the familiar scenario underwent a modification: the camp memory was three months old; tonight's image of the left cheek was from a much closer vantage point—instead of eight feet, it was *inches* from his face… and it was less than three *hours* old. It supplanted what he had preserved last summer… a favorite scenario had become refreshed, refueled, recharged.

The fantasy always began by portraying what the cotton briefs would look like while being stretched across Mark's left cheek… they were being pushed from within: around front, he was enlarging. The new image replaced saggy and tired cloth with freshly laundered cotton—he could still smell the fabric softener and what was being covered: the midsection of a freshly showered man. The bare thigh had just brushed against his forearm, leaving a glow of its own.

Another modification to the routine: he had new tools to employ. The techniques he had learned last Friday in Hayden Park added depth, subtlety and intensity. He was enabled—and impelled—to employ them with the new information.

The fantasy continued in slow motion… the first event was always a change in the underlying form: the passive, convex gluteus muscle compressed… it became concave, betraying its active participation in the expansion that had begun up front… from 3 on the scale, the shaft grew… a bulge appeared, just visible to the right of the wrist… it grew to a 4…

Another squeeze… now it pointed straight out… 5; an upward arc begins… 6. Now the hands push the hips forward, pressing the tip even more tightly against the cotton… 7. The cheek muscles relax… the hips pull back like a slingshot: the cotton stretches across the back until the two orbs become as one… they hold momentarily… then spring forward: the rounded contour vanishes… the muscles compress: the shaft reaches 8. Clenching tighter, the muscles grab the cloth behind and push again… around front the fabric is stretched over a 9. The tip is at the waistband, unable to advance farther. The shaft distorts… two thumbs abandon their position on the hips and pry the elastic—it pulls outward: Mark's eight inch masterpiece springs free, at a flaring 10, ready for action.

Eyes closed, the show continued with unseen images—the *felt* images from the hexagon tent took over, seamlessly. The body turned and approached slowly, stopping less than a foot away. Julian raised his right hand and grasped gently, his fingers explored the girth, the length… his left hand joined to pull down the foreskin. The right finger polished the tip with the drop of fluid that had just issued…

continuing down and around until the entire shaft glistened. His nose followed the same course…

Julian slid down and continued on his back… he took his time. He was practiced at this… his hand caressed and worked the dream man with skill—it was so clear in his mind it might as well have been real… so real, Little J believed it was the dream man giving him pleasure in return…

The scenario continued, employing skills learned at summer camp—Danny had been his teacher for the most part… the Geoff method was the best of all his lessons… his tongue served as a substitute for this last stage—the one where he takes the shaft into his mouth… he takes his secret love to a glorious finish.

The session was one of the more extended and enjoyable he'd ever had… he was exhausted. He drifted into a glowing afterzone that soon turned to a light sleep. Uncovered, his headboard light still on, the picture still on the chair—for the present, attending to these did not concern him.

Fortunately, his mother no longer stopped to do a last minute tuck in. He had pleaded with her to discontinue that—*I'm in high school now*. So she didn't stop by on her way to bed; she didn't see the light under the door or hear anything. All was well.

He awoke with a start—*brrr!* Pull up the covers! He turned off the lamp and curled into a ball… soon he was back to dreamland…

From that point, however, sleep was a mix: happy times present and past struggled with worries about what was coming up. For several days he had put out of his mind what was going to take place in a few weeks… and what was going to ruin his life every Wednesday until then: tomorrow was his first dancing lesson with Geraldine. Time and excuses had run out; all the ways to avoid facing it were used up. No scrapbook, no scouts, no drawing Randall tomorrow—only Geraldine and Mom.

And… messy sheets when he woke up in the morning.

b: Mark's post meeting self-debrief

Mark closed the door and locked up. It's one of those nights: too late to do anything, and too early for bed. No point in turning on the TV—the late news is nearly over… besides, that might disturb Pat. She's either reading in bed or asleep. I showered before the meeting, so no need for that… > *yawn* < Truth is, I drank too much wine. Eloise uses a large wine glass—ten ounces at least; we're used to a six or eight around here. That second bottle didn't have much left. I must have downed almost half a bottle, all told… *way* too much. I know better, but I was so intrigued by them. I planned to stay five minutes and I was there over an hour.

I'll get a book and read in bed; I haven't done that in a while. He headed for the stairs… a slow, deliberate step was required… he was much steadier sitting down. I'm not drunk, but I feel prit-tee mellow. Wow… it sure snuck up on me. I'll put these in the closet tomorrow… he hung his windbreaker and hat on the bannister post and headed up the stairs.

They're an interesting pair—an egghead scientist who climbs mountains and a grand dame that plays bridge. They say opposites attract—there's the proof. They're a happy couple and good parents, that's clear enough… and fun to be with. Randall looks more like Eloise but his nose is direct from his father. I suppose the little girl has blond hair and blue eyes. It's too bad he can't join the troop. The boys liked him at once. A mid-year vacancy rarely comes along, but you never know.

Mark wasn't so far gone that he couldn't do his usual after-scouts routine—he disrobed as usual… hung his shirt on the hanger with the new slacks. How easy these made the evening go… I was right about that… a happy discovery. The kerchief draped over the shoulder, he tucked the outfit in the closet. It won't be needed until the troop marches on Veteran's Day.

After doing his teeth he stopped by the small bookcase and pulled out a paperback. I haven't read any of these…he grabbed without looking at the title; one is as good as another. He tossed it onto the pillow and finished undressing. Underwear and socks were placed on the floor within reach—an old habit. He turned on the reading light and paused: forgot to flip off the overhead.

Covers pulled back, pillows propped up… ready at last. He slid in and got set to doze off with a book in hand. Half an hour will do the trick… just so I don't go to sleep too soon. What do we have here? *The Curious Case of Meriwether Upshaw*—a Geoffrey Hannibal Mystery by Adelaide Smythe-Winter. A detective novel… why not. I used to like these well enough. Erik practically swallowed them whole. He skipped all the intro pages and began the first paragraph: a dark rainy night. Of course it is. Most of them are; probably a murder or a kidnapping…

Mark's eyes were aimed at the page…they moved across horizontally, following the words in the right sequence, but the formulaic phrasing didn't grab his attention; his thoughts began to shift to other images and ideas. His eyes had seen many things during the day and his memory was still busily arranging its long term filing cabinet. The aftereffect of the wine was still apparent: he was only semi-conscious in the usual sense.

On the page he read, *A tall awkward figure struggled against the wind on the soggy heath...* but his mind drifted, allowing various images to replace words… the statue of the youth at Pompeii appeared… subtly, a fresh set of impressions from tonight's troop meeting superimposed, then began to replace what was there… the bronze hair turned golden blond… Julian's head was there now. The torso wasn't Julian's, but the legs could be… Julian's buns are much more shapely… he watched them appear… soon it was Julian reclining atop the perch in the center of the pool, surrounded by campers. The sterile lifeless bronze figure had vanished.

He shook his head slightly to clear out the intrusion; the image of the printed page returned briefly*: ...a light was now visible in the distance: Henry Isaacs knew at last that he would make it in time to give warning...* words blurred and faded into another pair of buns… they look familiar… it's the statue of David… no, it's Tom. Tom stands like that. Mark had seen him standing just that way dozens of times at the lake, dripping wet, smiling at the water polo team—some trying to avoid looking at what was hanging between his legs; one or two openly studied it in awe. At times it was a struggle to look the other way—or pretend it wasn't unusual… The statue rotated magically, and there it was… not the limp white marble mini-dick of the David, but a half filled real flesh masterpiece, foreskin beginning to pull back… the awed expressions transferred onto other faces… the swimmers on the dock were replaced by fresher images—a study circle at tonight's meeting—

Mark shook his head again, more forcefully. His eyes had unfocused and allowed his mind to wander all over the place. I've read three pages… the new paragraph makes no sense at all. I don't remember a thing! He flipped back to the beginning and started over. *A tall awkward figure struggled...*

This time his attention was diverted by a familiar sensation: he looked to the right of the book and was not surprised to see the tent. Roger was about three quarters up. If it weren't for the weight of the blankets, he would be all the way up.

"So, you're back." Roger pulsed a couple of times. Mark had made a promise after taking the shower; that was hours ago—Roger was tired of waiting. "So be it." He closed the book and reached behind to turn off the reading lamp. I don't want to read Adelaide Smythe-whatever, anyway.

He fluffed the pillow and slid down until he was prone. "You were a good boy at the meeting tonight, Roger." Didn't demand attention *once*; must be the slacks. Just like at work, I'm not aware they're there… extremely comfortable. Of course it's impossible to hide Roger if he gets out of line… but that's true with any of my pants.

He closed his eyes and began a slow, gentle routine, one he used from time to time when he wasn't in a hurry. Prolonging the experience was enjoyable; subtle variations were possible… his mind was released to wander freely—specific scenarios from the past were no longer needed. For months relying on physical sensations alone had sufficed. Tonight, still glowing from a bit too much Cabernet, he watched various images pop in and out like they had when he was trying to read… the spa statue was there from time to time, as was the room without any light—the sensation of many hands exploring his body, his own hands exploring someone… maybe Erik, maybe another memory from his scouting days. Swimmers at the lake… several images from years ago that he hadn't expected to remember… Julian's laugh and smile popped in suddenly, replaced by Tony's… faces in the Life Scout circle tonight… those faces melted and became the faces above naked boys on the dock at Camp Walker… now Julian is bending over, searching for an extension cord in the bottom drawer… resistance to recalling that collapsed tonight; the urge that always popped into his head, the sensation of stroking those orbs… exquisite. It was replaced in turn by Geoff standing in nature's own in the moonlight at two in the morning—a picture that intruded frequently in spite of all his efforts to suppress it; tonight he let it join the parade, along with Peter's backside waltzing down the corridor between the cubicles…

Scanning though these memories was like flipping through a magazine in a waiting room… unsatisfying, almost distracting; his mind tired of this eventually and stopped at one that he hadn't expected to pop up… it was one of his stronger *forbidden* fantasies… fantasies that he didn't want to pursue… thrilling because it frightened… off limits, buried so deep he thought himself safe… it was supposed to have been long forgotten…

He was standing in the cabin, posing… being drawn in pencil by the blond genius… sweat ran down his chest and his right armpit, and he couldn't do anything about it—it was still humid and warm; even the open window and door were no help; he wanted to hop in the shower this minute. But he had promised he would pose one more time—this time, standing. Julian had positioned him carefully. It was a comfortable stance.

The problem with standing in a fixed position is that the mind has to find something to do besides notice minor physical discomforts like beads of sweat turning into rivulets… or the blasted itch on the right side of his groin. He couldn't stand that another second. He reached down with his right hand and gave himself a good scratch. The left side was okay. He put his hand back on his hip, confident that his pose was unchanged. That felt so much better.

A side effect, unintended as side effects usually are, took a while for Mark to notice. Roger had been rousted from a contented sound sleep by the vigorous scratching and had been readjusted from his position on the right side; as a result, he now hung to the left. It was different over here… the cloth was in contact all along the top, and the perspiration under his shaft made the perch atop the left testicle slippery. As usual, when Roger was rousted by of any kind of movement, change in position, or contact, he was inclined to respond as if an inquiry had been made: do we want to stretch a bit, or maybe, who knows, have a good toss?

Of course Roger was interested: it was overdue, and the hot humid weather was bothersome. Rising up would allow some air in, if nothing else. He opened the startup valves and began a slow fill. This was routine… no authorization was required. In a while he’d send an affirmative pulse, indicating that he was ready.

Mark had been about to review a water polo play when he became aware that something was different below. He couldn’t look without breaking the pose. It felt puffy down there—Roger is touching the front of the briefs. Am I about to have a problem? Not good. At least my back is turned.

Being unable to move or get a visual reading of what was underway caused a level of concern and tension that increased the problem. Trying to avoid thinking about it was impossible—the more you try, the worse it gets. Your fear becomes a prediction—a forecast. The pulse below became noticeable… and entirely pleasurable. I must have grown half an inch. The early stages of an erection always felt so good. With hands off, the pleasure seems heightened… the next inch forms more rapidly. Soon, unless there is a miracle, it will begin to lift free… Feeling the surface of his cock expand was exciting… he’d never paid it this kind of close attention. What can I do? My back is turned, but if this continues, and it will, I need a way to hide it. Mercy… he could feel the blood rush to his temples; as the blush appeared, a tingle zoomed down his spine and jabbed his scrotum from behind… the telltale sensation of an early drop preparing the channel…

Mark stopped suddenly: he interrupted the fantasy before it could go where he feared it was headed… Julian is off limits. The finish is approaching… I can't allow it to happen there.

Change focus: a recent memory came to mind: a special sensation felt only once, just days ago. Let it take over… emptying Roger into an unknown, unseen mouth while each of his hands felt a separate shaft pump out massive payloads… *unh!* home at last… Roger required several pumps to complete his mission… a bit more than usual.

"Whoo! That was a *wild* one, Roger." He relaxed, hand in place while his heart rate returned to normal. Recalling that moment at the Pompeii had worked.

Mark never debriefed after satisfying Roger—he saw no point in analysis of that kind. Introspection was usually uncomfortable and unproductive. As far as he was concerned, fantasies were of no importance in and of themselves—they were merely Roger's companions, his rally squad. Tonight's were unusual, but the wine had taken an active role; this made them easy to dismiss. That anything in his subconscious might need attention never occurred to him.

Oh boy… I didn't bring along a towel—this was unplanned. What a mess… at least I kicked the blankets off. When did I do that? Helps a lot. Roger in hand, he swiveled to the edge of the bed. Maybe I can get to the john without spilling or leaving a trail—with his left hand cupped underneath to catch the excess, he crouched awkwardly and made his way to the bathroom.

His elbow located the wall switch and turned on the light. A hand towel will do… he stepped to the sink… Roger's reflection in the mirror wagged proudly: still up full.

"Yes, you did fine; no need to brag." Roger wanted a second go, but Mark was ready for bed. "No seconds tonight." Mark washed his hands and wiped away the remainder with the hand towel. He yawned and turned to leave. "Time for lights out, men." I'm done for the day.

Roger was used to being put off like that. He would do what he often did in this situation: inspire some nice erotic dreams. A lot of images were on file, waiting—many that Mark hadn't seen in a while.

Indeed, Roger and the crew in the development center deep in Mark's subconscious had fun playing fifty-two pickup the rest of the night; most of the memories they selected were from scouts when he was a member of the troop ten years ago. Everything was pre Erik—until he was surprised and delighted by a few present-day boys appearing alongside. The fantasy crew cleverly interchanged players. Forbidden pleasures now mingled with his own boyhood… fantasies that he had never consciously entertained had a field day. They awakened him a few times, but only just—not enough to remember what had disturbed him. Geoff in particular, and Julian… they had replaced Li'l Joe and Sam, his best buddies at camp… we tried a little of everything my third year.

This satisfied Roger temporarily, but it was not progress: it was a holding action. Mark was still unable to do what was needed: he didn't know how. He had never learned to hunt. His adolescence was focused on hiding his identity, not exploring and developing it. When he and Erik discovered each other, the need vanished. The predatory instinct had never been strong in the first place. That's why his fantasies were now much the same as they were before he met Erik. They were the fantasies of a boy still in the closet, still discovering who he was. The man having them needed more.

The memory that triggered the atypical nocturnal spill was from the present. In the morning he had no idea what had caused him to do that—especially after that epic load last night. He hadn't had a wet dream in *years!*

Perhaps Peter's valiant attempt at the Pompeii wasn't a failure after all. Maybe Mark didn't require an Erik to sweep him off his feet and carry him into the future. Erik was not in any of his dreams this night. Developing the skills that had been left abandoned and undeveloped ten years ago would be work—awkward and uncomfortable work. Fortunately, Mark was the kind of person who thrived when taking on a big challenge.

20 The Sadie Hawkins Day Dance

Julian's eyes were frozen in an unfocused stare. It was a good thing that the parking lot was smooth and level, because walking like a zombie was all he could manage right now. That was easy enough in this rubber coat.

The full weight of what he was about to do had taken him over. He was escorting Rita Mitchell—that's *Dance Team* Rita Mitchell—to the Girls' Gym; that's where the event was being held. He was dressed in a special costume—custom made by Geraldine. He was supposed to look exactly like the Li'l Abner character in the comics. She had cut out a panel from the Sunday funnies and tacked it on the bulletin board in his room so he could study it. They even made him wear his hiking boots so he would look more authentic.

That part was okay; but then she pulls out this huge yellow rain slicker—*rubberized*—heavy as the dickens, and wraps me up and snaps me in tight as if I might blow away in the wind or something—man. I have to admit it keeps me warm; still, I feel like something that wandered off the Gumby show. I can't even see my feet.

It was fun to watch Geraldine and Mom fuss and cluck over the costume; surprisingly, it was even fun to take dancing lessons from Geraldine. It wasn't as hard as I expected—I'm pretty good at it, from what she says. But now it's the *real thing*. Mom and Geraldine aren't here. I get to do this all by myself.

He looked over at Sammy, Barbara's date. Lucky guy; he has on a regular school jacket. I don't know him, but he seems okay—sort of tall and skinny. But it's good to have some company. Since we're in Barbara's car, Sammy rides up front. Fine by me… this big yellow coat would really stand out up there.

Julian wasn't a shy person and he usually didn't care one way or another about how he looked. But even a dummy like me knows when he looks really silly. It's a safe bet I'm the only one wearing a yellow raincoat, so rubberized it could practically stand by itself; if need be, you could stand it in the corner along with the umbrellas—or better yet, park it on the back porch. At least I have Li'l Abner's hat on instead of whatever goes with this yellow thing. I feel like a big traffic cone—one that wears a straw hat and bobs across the parking lot on hiking boots. I'm tempted to stick out my arms and waddle across making goofy noises. If it wasn't for Mom and Geraldine, I prob'ly would.

Julian hadn't done a whole lot of dancing in his life; he expected to be pretty clumsy no matter what, so wearing boots might not make that big a difference. I didn't wear them for the lessons because they always squeal and squeak on the hardwood floors. They do that on any kind of floor. I bet they'll be super bad tonight: the dance is in the girl's gym.

Why do I hear Rice Krispies all of a sudden? He glanced up at the brim of his straw hat. Is it gonna rain? He held up his arm… sure enough, teeny droplets had appeared everywhere on the bright yellow sleeve. It wasn't supposed to rain, but you never know. At least I'm dressed for it.

In spite of all the coaching and rehearsing, he was still worried; I don't want to mess this up. The real thing is never the same as practice. Geraldine's over an inch taller than me, so the lessons were kind of awkward. At least I'm a little taller than Rita; I wonder if that will make a big difference on the dance floor. Her waist will be lower… that might help.

This isn't like the sock hop I went to last year at Wallace. That wasn't a real date, for one thing—I went with Sid; we had a lot of fun goofing around. We didn't do any *actual* dancing with a girl. But I saw what it was like; that's why I didn't ever go to another dance… until this came along. Boy, oh boy, did it ever make Geraldine happy.

And Mom was too—although she isn't as fanatical about it. At least it took care of that movie date problem—for a while, anyway.

He wasn't attracted to Rita, especially. When it came to being attracted, girls were not all that interesting. His sights were fixed on one person, and no one was likely to get in the way of that. Certainly not a girl.

But he felt an obligation to her for inviting him—and getting him out of that movie date. It was a huge compliment, evidently—at least that's what Geraldine said, and she knows all about this stuff. I plan to have fun—might as well; and I want Rita to have fun too. Just so I don't foul up… do they let you take your boots off if they squeal?

He braced himself. Pretty soon, we'll be right under that big light over the fake barn door—it looks like the decorations committee has gone all out on this. Put on your smile and try to look like you know what you're doing. He looked over at Sammy… he looks just as worried as I am… comforting, in a way.

—w—

Rita was in her element. Mischief was on her mind most of all, and she was very pleased at how things were going. She had just made certain that Barbara's Wolf Gal earmuffs fit perfectly; her prospects tonight with Sammy are excellent. Now it's time to show off. My taste in men is going to make me look very good tonight—wait until Sherri gets a look at what *I* have in tow. This blond masterpiece is quite a catch. She lifted his left arm and tucked hers underneath; he's such a sweetie! Why he doesn't have a flock of girls following him everywhere is amazing. He hasn't been broken in yet. Well I'm just the one to do that! She promised herself that she'd behave—at least for a while. Who knows what might happen? There isn't much I won't be able to get away with. She had learned long ago that all she needed to do was be alert; when to nudge, when to back off—these were practiced skills.

First thing is to put him at ease, make him feel safe and in control. He'll follow the clues, no problem there; boys are so easy to play; this one will be a breeze. Those deep puppy dog eyes are special.

What is Big Man On Campus Tracy doing tonight, do you suppose? Besides not coming to the Sadie Hawkins Dance with me, that is. The true benefit of tonight's dance will be the new Tracy. Taking her for granted was not going to remain a problem after tonight; those so-called "alum nights" will be over, or else. His facial expression when I told him I had invited someone else to the dance was *delicious*. Having his complete attention was more thrilling than I expected… I could get used to that… in fact, I plan on getting used to that. This is the first time I've strayed from Tracy—there will be a *lot* of talk about that! I might as well enjoy myself while I'm at it. She smiled with satisfaction: yes… this blond cutie will give them *lots* to talk about.

She was eager to get inside—the air is a little cooler than expected; Daisy Mae's costume is a summer outfit. The raincoat covers everything well enough; at least there's no wind. She looked eastward—the moon was blurred by a surprise mist that had come up. Hmm… the forecast said clear skies tonight. I'm counting on that later at Fowler's Point. This costume will simplify things there… that's where to go after a dance if you want to do any *serious* necking. With this outfit, even a complete amateur could figure out what to do.

She glanced over at her date… it's odd, really—he looks kind of like Li'l Abner; a little shorter. Funny about the hair—he has Daisy Mae's blonde, and I've got Li'l Abner's brunette! Otherwise, we look perfect.

She sent a silent request to the moon to shoo away the clouds while she was busy dancing.

—∞—

These pants feel weird. Julian was used to his pants being more on the tight side, held on with a belt. Geraldine got these overalls from Jake, one of the guys on her landscape crew… said he needed a new pair anyway. They're a couple of sizes too big, so she rolled the pant legs up high and pinned them so they wouldn't roll back down—the socks are supposed to show above the boots. She made them look just like the comic strip by sewing brightly colored patches over the torn places and on the knees; she unhooked the right bib strap and pinned the loose corner inside. Just as well: it was almost ready to fall off on its own.

The strap in the back is folded inside too—which means that only one shoulder strap is keeping the thing on. I don't want to think about what would happen if it fell off my shoulder—in a flash I'd be standing there in my skivvies; the red polo shirt doesn't go much below my belly button. I've never had a polo shirt before. Basically, it's just a T-shirt with a collar and pocket. Fire engine red—urg. Not my favorite color. But it was nice of Geraldine to buy it. She could have gotten a larger size… "Oh, no… this will do just fine," she says and squeezes my shoulder. I caught her giving Mom a wink—which means it looks sexier if the shirt is a little tight. Honestly.

When this is over, I'm gonna box these overalls up and bury them in my closet. I'll give them to Uncle Max next summer; he wears these things all the time. After tonight I won't need them.

He turned around to see who was behind—the cars are pouring in. Will anyone from the troop be here? None of the Arrows are coming… neither is Sid… Jeremy either. It would be nice if I knew at least one person… oh well. Randall, the lucky guy, avoided detection by the girl squads—once in a while you could see them out there surrounding some poor unsuspecting guy like they did me. Some guys *want* to go, and are glad to be caught; I saw that a few times too… come to think of it, lots of guys appreciate it because they're too chicken to ask a girl to go out. I know how that feels.

We're in the front of the pack… I wouldn't have minded being late. But here we are anyway, standing under the huge floodlight. The outside entrance was decorated with huge doors opened wide as if a giant red barn had been reserved for the event. Bales of straw were stacked on both sides.

"Hi!" Rita chimed with an exaggerated wink, flashing her dance program at the girl taking tickets. Dotty was one of her *inside* circle. She leaned close—Dotty had some special, secret information. "Perfect!" Rita was delighted. She turned to Julian enthusiastically.

"We have the best spot!"

"Great!" He smiled back as if he knew what she was talking about. *Nyugh!* the sudden urge to rub his nose was hard to ignore; a big whiff of her perfume just now almost bowled him over. He grinned at Rita's friend. "Hi." One syllable words are easy enough. I'm impressed a little though; the girl is a junior, and treats Rita as an equal. Her stare made him want to zip inside as quick as he could. Oh… maybe it's the yellow coat.

He pulled the gymnasium door open like a gentleman and ushered Rita in just the way Geraldine taught him. They walked into the "barn."

> *Squip-squipp—squip-p-p--* <

Oh, no! The tire tread boot soles were just as bad as he had feared; the freshly polished floor made the sound extra crisp. What am I gonna do?

"Ahem!"

Before he could take another step, Miss Audrey Fredericks, the head girl's PE teacher, barred the way. With a frown on her face she pointed at their feet and swung her arm to the left, forefinger aimed at a stiff bristle doormat. "Shoes," she commanded. She looks different. The costume did not diminish her foreboding demeanor… at least two inches taller and ten pounds heavier than Julian, she looked like Lucille Sweeny in the comics, only with a frown.

The command to wipe off shoes wasn't a surprise: one of the first rules spelled out in P.E. class was how to treat the gymnasium floors. It was required to clean your soles of any sand or dirt before walking on the gym floor. In the Boys' Gym, you had to take your shoes clear off and *leave* them off. He stepped onto the doormat and drew his feet backwards… boy, is it ever stiff! He chuckled… this is what dogs do in the park; they piddle on a tree then do this… I never figured out why they do that.

Miss Fredericks nodded at last and allowed them to pass. When he stepped on the floor his boot soles didn't squeal… he took another step… whoa. He glanced back at the coarse floor mat. What do you know… I need to get one of those. Do they make smaller sized ones?

The light was subdued, so it took a minute to see the setup. In place of tables and chairs, bales of straw were scattered around the perimeter, creating a home base for each couple. Reservation numbers matching the dance program were pinned on one of the bales in each group. Rita grabbed Julian's hand and pulled him forward.

"We're over there—it's one of the best locations!" She led the way across the dance floor to a cluster of three bales; the number 32 was pinned atop the bale that stood on end. She removed her raincoat and reached back to grab a hanger from a portable clothes rack conveniently located behind their straw bales. As a member of the decorations committee, she knew what was where. She indicated with a nod where to hang the slicker.

"Oh—yeah." Julian hopped over to grab a hanger. Boy, am I glad to be rid of this! I feel about ten pounds lighter. He put the hat on top of the upright bale of straw and looked around—I lost track of Sammy and Barbara. They must have their own bales; too bad. He was curious about their costumes; I couldn't see what was under their coats. About the only thing I noticed was her oddball earmuffs and Sammy's shoes—they're the exact opposite of hiking boots: classy—the kind that have a second layer on the toes with small holes punched in a fancy pattern—shoes for going to church in, basically; they look brand new.

> plop! <

An odd rubbery sound came from behind. Oh, no: the slicker fell off the hanger! He stepped around to look… there it is, resting on the floor. Might as well leave it be; at least the stupid thing didn't roll away.

Julian surveyed the layout. Wow… this is really something… so well organized. I had no idea it would be such a big deal; Geraldine was right about that. A big Sadie Hawkins sign stretched across a platform in one corner. A disc jockey was sorting through a stack of LPs. Behind him a rack displayed covers of the record albums he would be playing. Huge speakers were spread around the gym, aimed at the wall—this diffused the sound and allowed the volume to be turned way up. To set the mood before the dance started, Moon Mullican's *Shine on, Harvest Moon* was playing at a low volume. Strings of small lights had been strung from special wooden stands—the effect suggested a barnyard. Alternating white and yellow bulbs led to a small stage. Split rail fence units bordered the sides and back; the disc jockey stand had the same kind of fence. Rita's right about the location—he had an urge to grab his sketchbook and make a couple of drawings. Silly… I don't have it with me.

"Turn around a jif." Rita had a 3 x 5 card with a big number 32. She pinned it on the back of his overall strap. "This way they can tell who we are when they do the judging."

"Judging?" If they're judging how good I dance, there's no point. He didn't say that aloud.

"They have *lots* of awards at this dance—you'll see." She turned him around to get a good look at his outfit. "You look perfect! Oh—remember to put on your hat later. That will cinch us for best costume." She leaned over and gave him a sisterly peck on the cheek. She winked, noting the lip print. *Now* it's perfect. "How do *I* look?"

She glanced down at her Daisy Mae blouse. She'd never been able to wear anything like this before—the special order strapless demi-cup felt sexy; it was certainly doing its job tonight. I'll pretend everyone is admiring the big polka dots. She did a slow rotation so that he could see the full effect of her outfit. She loved the way the sleeves felt; she wasn't worried about them slipping—the elastic held them in place halfway down her shoulders. Too bad Tracy can't see me…

Julian gulped. He hadn't really looked at her until this minute. Am I glad the lights are dim. The comic strip page Geraldine had put on his bulletin board came to mind—Daisy Mae was depicted as well as Li'l Abner. Maybe it *didn't* exaggerate the girl's top and bottom curves: half of Rita's boobs are pushing out the top! And her skirt is so short! She better not bend over or sit down wrong. He had not noticed before that she had such a large rear end. She isn't fat or anything—but she's… really *big*. Her buns have to be twice as big as mine.

"Wow," he managed. He looked her in the face. Obviously she wanted something more. "You look exactly like the cartoon!" Is it okay to wear such skimpy clothing? She's practically naked. Personally, I'm happy with my blue denim tent.

Rita was slightly disappointed… Tracy would have started to drool the second I took off my coat. Later on he'll be a little more enthusiastic—a few minutes on the dance floor will do the trick. She sat on the bale of straw and patted the space next to her. A few things needed to be covered before making the rounds. That's why we had to arrive early—obviously he doesn't know what's expected—but he's smart enough, I can tell that much. Rita rarely left anything to chance.

Julian sat down where he was told, right next to her. It took a minute to get used to that: not only did it bring him closer to that uggy perfume smell, it forced him to see down the front of her bulging blouse: he tried not to notice—but it was hard. It looked like they would pop out completely if they got the chance; they were half way out already. Those are *weird*… made him glad he wasn't a girl. Having to deal with them all the time must be a real pain. Finally, she held the program so that it blocked the view. She wanted to explain how the dances were planned in advance—I'm gonna be exchanged to dance with another girl about halfway. That's pretty scary…

After Rita completed the briefing, she led Julian on a mini tour to meet some of her friends and compare costumes. It felt good to move around. Some of the other guys looked a lot more comfortable; lots of cutoff jeans with ragged bottoms… those would be a lot better than these bib overalls. It's too cold, or I could have worn my work cutoffs—no, on second thought, those are way too short. He laughed to himself… they'd sure go with Rita's skirt! At least I don't have to wear a flannel shirt. Lots of kids had corncob pipes and raggedy straw hats. Some couples wore matching shirts and blouses. Not everyone has a costume… a few of the kids have regular school clothes.

He wasn't the only Li'l Abner. Must be six or seven guys in overalls. One had both bib straps; some had the right side unhooked, some the left. His overalls looked more used and worn than the others—and bigger. I'm the only one with big heavy boots. There are other Daisy Maes too. Rita is more like the cartoon than the others as far as boobs are concerned. They all have big butts.

Rita did all the talking. All he had to do was smile and look interested. No problem. He tried to figure out some of the costumes while she chattered away. It was hard if they didn't have the name written down somewhere. When they were talking to a guy named Teddy—he had a big gold sheriff star pinned on his shirt—a loud fanfare erupted from the speakers. The evening was about to begin.

"Oo, quick," Rita grabbed Julian's hand and hurried back to their straw bales.

The first thing they had to do was walk in a big circle before the judges. They were giving points for the costumes; Rita grabbed the hat and put it on him just the way she wanted. Where are the judges, anyway? I don't see them anywhere. Just as well. It helps me act natural. Walking a full circle around the dance floor helped put him at ease; he didn't have to talk or say anything.

Just as they got back to their bale, the music came on: Ricky Nelson singing *Hello Mary Lou*—that meant the first dance had begun. A couple came out onto the floor and started to dance—Julian didn't know who they were. Right after that, other couples joined in.

He took a deep breath and held out his hand—thank you, Geraldine—he followed her lesson to the letter. From the beginning it went just fine… no squeaks at all. Soon, they were well into the song… hey, this is easy! The beat was clear… it took no time to get the hang of how to do this. His self-confidence was building steadily. This is fun! Then—

"Ouch!" Rita stumbled awkwardly; they had to stop.

"Oh, man—I'm sorry—are you all right?" The second it happened he knew: his right boot had trod on her left foot. He felt awful. He looked down and felt even worse: she's *barefoot*!

Rita winced. She had taken off her street shoes for the costume parade and not bothered to put them on again—Daisy Mae was always barefoot in the cartoon; it felt better to dance barefoot, anyway. Something had to be done differently: her foot really hurt. She looked around quickly—luckily, no one was paying attention. "I think it's all right…" she didn't want to scare him, but she had to know how bad it was. "Let's sit down a minute." She led him back to their bale.

Julian was devastated. I am such a *clod*. The whole night is ruined. And, it's my fault… How am I going to face Geraldine? And Mom? The *first* dance! Cripes. What do I do now? He watched her walk… she's limping!

Rita sat and swung her left leg up onto the bale. If only it wasn't so *dark*. She looked up at Julian—he looks so sorry. Her heart went out to him. "It's not *that* bad. Come here and look at it, will you?" She smiled reassuringly. It never hurt to play the maiden in distress.

He jumped forward at once and got down on his knees. The foot isn't bleeding, at least… what should I do? he looked up—oh. Droplets of sweat broke out on his forehead… I'm lucky it's this dark. Otherwise I'd probably be able to see what I'm not supposed to see.

"Go ahead, look real close—is the skin broken?" She could tell that he was afraid. Getting him to handle her foot was an unexpected bonus. That will come in handy later… give him some confidence.

He bent close and looked around both sides. "It looks okay!" He grinned wide.

"Feel it, try to tell if it is sprained…" She wiggled her toes. They felt much better now. She looked out to see if they were being watched. Not yet.

He took her foot into his hands and… what should I do? He gave it a small twist to the right and looked up. She nodded that it was okay. He twisted it the other way a little and checked again.

"Look at the toes." His hands holding her foot felt very nice; now if he'll explore a little…

He touched the big toe and looked up. Ok; then the next one… okay. Hmm. He lifted each of them up and down, very gently; nothing seemed to hurt. Maybe I bruised the top or something. He tried pushing lightly above the toes.

"Ooo!" Rita cooed. "That helps. Do that some more."

Julian did a few tentative pushes with his fingertip. He looked up and saw her smiling and nodding. He rubbed a little, then made a circular movement. Danny's massage at summer camp gave him an idea of what to try.

"Mmm, yes, that's wonderful," Rita purred. This had taken a turn for the better. She watched him concentrate… perfect. But we mustn't get carried away. When he included the ankle, she wiggled the foot to indicate that he could stop. "That was very nice. You have fixed it; I'm all better now. We can go back to the dance. But—maybe you could take off those boots?"

"Oo, yeah!" Julian attacked the laces on his right boot then and there. What a relief. I'm so glad she's okay. The night isn't ruined after all.

Rita watched him remove the boots. This is going nicely. *Very* nicely. As Patsy Cline sang, *I Fall to Pieces,* she extended her arm to be escorted back onto the dance floor. The string of lights set off his profile and highlighted his wavy blond hair. He might be new and awkward, but he is *very* handsome.

Taking the boots off made a huge difference. Considering his inexperience, he was surprised at how well he was able to do; dancing is fun. Rita is definitely easier to dance with than Geraldine.

The bop and the two step were the most common, which was good; those were the ones he had practiced. By the fifth dance he had adjusted well to the way she moved. Sometimes she varied things by putting her hands on his shoulders—he was supposed to put his hands on her waist. This made them dance face to face instead of side by side. That was better in a way; it was easier to avoid stepping on her toes. Sometimes she reversed that because her arms got too tired and she put her hands on his waist behind his back.

These different positions made it more interesting. When he checked around it looked like everyone was doing pretty much the same thing, 'cept for this one guy—he took up a lot of floor space doing some special fancy stuff. People had to steer clear of the area by the DJ. It looked interesting, but he couldn't watch them and pay attention to his feet at the same time. Besides, doing those things with Rita wouldn't be a very good idea. The boobs would probably pop out—that overhead toss thing would show off *everything* down below, for sure.

He didn't keep track of how many dances there were; sometimes they played a set and went on to a second and third song without stopping. When it came time for the exchange, the DJ announced that a five minute break would happen while everyone got squared away. Rita led us over to straw bale number 58. That's where the guy named Teddy was. His girl is named Theresa. I didn't know her at all, but I've seen her in the hallway a few times. "Moonbeam" was her character; she wore a super wide belt.

She was fun. First they did a special dance called the mashed potato. It was weird. He didn't see the point. You held both arms out in front while you took turns grinding one foot and then the other; you were supposed to flutter your arms one at a time too. The concept was that you appeared to be mashing potatoes with your feet. It took a while to get the hang of it. They never said why it was called that, either. Where do they mash potatoes with their feet?

It's a good thing that dance was with Theresa; watching Rita jiggle and flutter might have been scary. He really thought she was going to pop out of that blouse any minute. I like dancing with Theresa… she's very friendly. We talked a little during the next song—it was a regular dance, not a potato.

"Why don't I ever see you around?" Now that she had seen him up close, her interest deepened. He dances very well. Where did Rita discover this one?

Julian shrugged. "Don't know." I'm not hiding or anything.

"What do you do for lunch?" Theresa had an idea that after tonight he'd be free. Rita's not about to dump Tracy. Terrible Teddy wouldn't mind if I had some fun on the side.

"I have second lunch. I usually sit in the atrium." Now that it's so cold out, I'm back inside during lunch. He didn't mention that he always had lunch with Randall.

"You never eat in the cafeteria?" No wonder I never see him. Who eats in the atrium?

"Sometimes. My mom makes me a lunch every day. Once in a while I get a carton of milk or a cup of juice."

"Well, someday why not join us?" She smiled coyly. "We always have a good time." She twirled again. "Bring along your lunch."

"Okay…" Julian was flattered; Mom and Geraldine always nag at me about making more girl friends. All I ever do is scouts and hang out with Randall. Well, that's all I want to do. I could rack up some points with them by having lunch in the cafeteria a few times! I can bring Randall along! "Yeah! I'd like that." He nodded. This might help with the movie problem, too.

He liked Theresa most of all because she didn't smell as strong—that perfume of Rita's is pretty potent.

Julian's smile took Theresa by surprise. His face seemed to transform when he smiles… it made her heartbeat increase. She didn't remember that happening before. "We sit over near the windows on the south side." She looked closely every chance the dance allowed… the combination of dark pupils and bright blond hair was exotic and magical… his dark eyebrows made the eyes stand out even more… and *perfect* eyelashes. Boys don't have eyelashes like that! *perfect* white teeth and full lips… he's like a poster come to life.

Second lunch is perfect. Now then… do I tell anyone? Wait a second… no. Let him be an "unexpected" surprise. No point in giving Brenda a heads up. She might just pounce before I've had a chance to get acquainted. Besides, Teddy will be there too. Life gets complicated at times. Rita will be back with Tracy, that's practically guaranteed—he'll be right at her side starting Monday morning. She sure knows how to keep him in line. They'll be having lunch somewhere else—by themselves.

Teen Angel finished playing and the DJ announced a twenty minute refreshment break. Teddy and Rita rushed over to join them in the center of the dance floor.

"Isn't this fun?" Rita gushed, lunging at Julian; she ruffled his hair and gave him a hug. She stood back and grinned wide, pleased with herself; Terrible Teddy had held her close during *Teen Angel*, and precisely what she intended had occurred. Out of the corner of her eye she could see him failing to hide what had arisen below his belt.

"Yeah!" Julian grinned. The hug was unexpected, but it was okay this time… the perfume was a lot fainter now. Maybe it wears off or something. I hope she doesn't have a stash of it in her handbag.

Rita realized too late—I shouldn't have winked at Theresa… she's looking downward—Teddy's receding erection had stalled at the nine o'clock position.

"What do we do now?" Julian asked eagerly.

"Isn't he cute?" Rita grinned. "Now is when you and Teddy go to the refreshment table and get us punch and cookies!" She reached her left arm over to her friend. "Us hens will wait for you back at the nest!" She looked at Theresa—"yours or mine?"

Theresa wasn't ready to react. "Yours, I guess." She wasn't jealous or angry, really, but still… She gave Rita's polka dot blouse a baleful glance. I hadn't occurred to her to try anything like that with Julian. Well now. If Teddy can play a little…

"C'mon." Teddy nodded toward the refreshment table. He was a junior, so he knew the routine. Besides, he needed to make an adjustment; standing in the crowd at the table is a good place for that—no one will notice.

Julian was eager to do this. He was thirsty and ready for a break. Teddy seems like a good guy—kind of muscular. Reminds me of Kurt. "You a wrestler?" Might as well be friendly.

Teddy looked at him sharply. "What makes you think that?"

"Because you're so muscular, and everything." Julian held up his arm and flexed, to show how small his bicep was. Maybe he plays football.

Teddy was flattered. "Naw, I'm just in good shape. I work out and such with my pa." He looked at Julian a second time, curious… "How'd you get hooked up with Rita, anyway?" Is Tracy history? Serve him right if he was.

The question threw him. "Hook up?"

"Well, yeah—I mean, in case you haven't noticed, she has the biggest jugs in the room. There's lotsa guys here that wouldn't mind being in your shoes tonight," he nodded forcefully as his left hand worked to solve his problem; it was hard to do via his pocket, but reaching under his belt wouldn't be very cool. This was one time a hole in this pocket would have come in handy.

Julian blushed. Unknown to Teddy, he'd be glad to turn the assignment over to any or all. No way could he say that, though. He noticed Teddy's problem… ooo-ee…. bad place to get a stiffy! How did *that* happen? Oh, I get it: Rita's boobs! He calls them jugs! He wanted to laugh but was able to hold it in. Good thing it's kinda dark. I'd like to fix it for him, but I can't do that either. He looks about Chuck's size down there; I wonder if it curves to the left.

*Don't think about that **now**,* warned the Inside guy.

Yow… an image of Beta had begun to form… that will cause Little J to wake up real quick. He shook his head and focused on Teddy's question.

"Dunno. I don't really know her at all. One day she stopped me in the hall and handed me that flower. I didn't even know what it meant." He shrugged. "Beats me why I got picked." He leaned close—"I didn't even know how to dance—I had to take *lessons!*"

Just a minute—is this guy for real? "You never been to a dance before?!"

"Sock hops at Wallace."

Teddy pondered the import of this... so he's from Wallace. Maybe that explains it. "You come in your car or hers?"

Julian laughed. "I don't have a car! I can't even drive yet. I get Driver's Ed next semester. We came in Barbara's car. They picked up Sammy then came after me."

Wow. Teddy had a small envy attack; after the dance this kid will be in the back seat with those jugs. Wow.

It was their turn at the table. A sign on the post read: "Kickapoo Joy Juice Here." Two punchbowls were being administered by girls clad in gingham. The puffy shoulders looked like some of Lucy's grade school dresses; they had those ribbons too.

"Lemonade or Fruit Punch?" asked one holding up an empty cup.

What would Rita like? He looked at Teddy for advice.

"Take one of each; she can pick the one she wants."

Good idea. "One of each, thanks." His eye fell on the plate of cookies. Urg... the store bought kind, little round factory things. Taste awful. He took two for each cup anyway and slipped them onto the saucers. He stood to the side and waited for Teddy.

"Hey, Wolf!" Norman gave Julian a nudge in the ribs.

"Hey, wow!" His hands were full or he would have elbowed Norman back. Norman was now Patrol Leader of the Wolves, his old patrol. I miss being in that patrol... but being in the Flaming Arrow is good too.

"Looks like you're doin' pretty good," Norman gave Julian the double Groucho eyebrow lift.

He smiled and shrugged. Norman was referring to his "date." I'm not about to brag or anything. "Who brought you?"

"Ann Jeffries." They'd been steadies for almost a year, so it figured, really. The punchbowls drew his eye. "What's the red one?"

"Some kind of fruit—I haven't tasted it yet." Probably too sweet. I got lemonade because it doesn't fizz up. I hate carbonated drinks; make me feel too full.

Teddy appeared with his punch cups, ready to go back to bale number 32.

"Hey, do you know Teddy?"

Norman looked over—he knew of Teddy; he's all right, for a football player. He nodded. "Hey."

"Hi," Teddy nodded, impressed. Norman Miller was just made the captain of the basketball team. This kid isn't as out of it as I thought.

"Catch you later," Norman moved up to the punchbowl table.

Julian concentrated on the task of carrying two cups of punch across the dance hall—it wouldn't do to splash punch all over the place. I'm pretty good at this; I learned how to run a cup of coffee back to the cabin last summer. Mark always wanted a cup first thing.

Rita and Theresa were sitting together talking excitedly about something—so excited that they merely paused to take a cup, wink thank you, and carry on as if they had been served by anonymous waiters.

Teddy gestured toward the other bale; they sat beside each other like obedient servants, and sipped their punch.

Julian's eye landed the lettering on the big sheriff star. "What's 'F F' mean?"

"Fearless Fosdick," Teddy grinned. He reckoned his costume was about the easiest to make in the entire dance: a yellow paper star, pinned on his black shirt. All I had to do was buy a cheap hat.

Julian did not recognize the name; Teddy's about the only guy that doesn't look like a hillbilly. He doesn't look like a sheriff either… prob'ly best not to ask.

Teddy had been thinking about the comment at the refreshment table. "First dance? Really?" Kinda hard to believe.

Julian figured the sock hop didn't count, especially since he'd goofed off, fake dancing with Sid more than anything. He didn't offer an explanation. Inside guy had alerted him: on this matter, explanations could cause problems. He looked around the room… are any other boys here like me? Maybe I'm not the only one that got snagged by mistake.

Could be, Inside guy observed… *you know, this date might come in handy at school, just like at home with Geraldine and Mom.*

Julian nodded. It never hurts to look normal. People usually think you're just like they are because that's what they want; no reason to disappoint and cause trouble. Just smile and keep your mouth shut.

Teddy nodded back, knowingly. He remembered his first dance. Boy was I ever clueless. The girls were always a step ahead. I never could figure them out. Not worth the trouble to try. I always had a good time; sometimes they left me horny as hell, but sometimes I got my rocks off pretty good. Theresa usually put out when it counted.

"Don't sweat it," Teddy advised sagely. "You're doin' fine." No point in alerting him to the after-the-dance part. Nobody's *that* stupid. Besides, Rita has it all planned. I just wish I was gonna be the one in that back seat. He shook his head in envy. Man.

Another fanfare burst from the DJ stand. An intense beam of light from the Disc Jockey's platform appeared suddenly—the Drama Department's brand new Altman follow spot illuminated the small stage at the opposite corner of the dance floor. "Can I have everyone's attention?" A dazzling eighteen foot wide pool of white light surrounded the Girls' League President; a microphone had replaced the refreshment table. The awards were about to be presented.

It seemed to take *forever*. Julian had never heard of so many silly awards. It looked like they tried invent one for everybody! Dogpatch stuff… lots of laughs, though; people were having a great time. He joined in by applauding and laughing along with everyone. He didn't get what most of them meant; the costumes gave a hint, but not being a fan of the comic strip didn't help matters. The funniest one was Pantless Perkins; the kid came out barefoot in a nightshirt. Hard to tell if anything was on underneath. Julian focused on the mid section… yeah… no wag; that means he's wearing skivvies; too bad.

Then, at last, one he did understand: the best Li'l Abner costume. Incredibly, the possibility that he might win had never occurred to him. But the girl on the platform had just said his name. It took a minute to sink in. He looked at Rita in shock.

Rita was not surprised, of course—this was part of her plan. And, he *was* the best Li'l Abner. While the boys were getting refreshments, she'd made the last minute preparation: the rawhide boot strings were now tied together, creating a handle. At the applause, she grabbed his left hand and forced him to take the boots. Then she plopped the straw hat back on his head and pushed him onto the floor.

Julian had never been the center of attention like this; he didn't know what to do or not do. But he'd had such a good time it was only right to show his appreciation. Besides, this is for Geraldine, not me; that delighted him most of all. Happily, he skipped across the room swinging the boots with his left hand and holding down his straw hat with his right. He bowed low to the presenter, and gave her a big smile. The expression on her face sort of gave him goose bumps… weird. He accepted his award—the certificate read, "Best Li'l Abner." He waved it at the audience and ran back to bale number 32. I can hardly wait to give this to Geraldine.

The fun wasn't over: as soon as he got back, the announcer asked, "And who is the best Daisy Mae?" She looked around as if she was searching the room. She paused and held up her clipboard. "Rita! Rita Mitchell!"

Julian's jaw dropped. I don't believe it! But it's probably the right call—when it came to the boobs, Rita had them all beat.

Next, completely unexpected, she grabbed his right hand and pulled him alongside. She wanted him there when she got her award. He barely had time to drop the boots and certificate. They were there in a flash—it went so fast his head spun. This is *terrific*—it meant Rita had a great night! Bringing a clumsy guy like me didn't matter. Mom and Geraldine will be proud. Maybe they'll lighten up some about girlfriends—if Geraldine had her way, I'd have a new one every day.

"Ladies and gentlemen,"said the President of the Girls' League Association, "I present this year's official Queen of the Sadie Hawkins Day Dance, Rita Mitchell!" The crowd erupted in applause, whistles and cheers.

Proudly, he watched the other girl on the platform put a brightly colored wreath around Rita's neck—it's made out of those Sadie Daisies!

As the certificate was awarded, Rita smiled graciously. She curtsied and quietly asked the presenter to keep the certificate until later—she needed her hands free. In a swoop, she jumped on Julian and gave him a huge kiss on the lips. She took her time and, lest he try to escape, held the back of his head firmly—a full five seconds.

Julian was not prepared for anything like that—but something clicked in his head, and he pretended to be pleased. When she stood back, he gave her a big grin and a perfect Geraldine bow—unaware of the garish imprint covering his lips.

The crowd cheered and laughed; one guy slapped his knee and pointed gleefully. Julian bounced on his toes… this is really *fun!*

He did not notice the sudden attention many girls were giving him. Rita had showcased him perfectly—Julian's life at Jackson High School had been relatively quiet and anonymous up to now; the Sadie Hawkins Dance kiss changed that instantly. Every girl in the school now knew who he was, or soon would. And several, beginning tonight, would have their eyes on Rita's prize blond discovery.

Delighted with herself, Rita gave Julian a big hug before putting her hands around his neck—her signal that it was time to dance.

The DJ took that as his cue and started the next set with Neil Sedaka's *Stairway to Heaven.* The floor filled with couples. As the song progressed, the spotlight—centered all the while on the prizewinning pair—narrowed slowly to black.

Rita needed to frame her next words with care, so she waited a few minutes into the dance. After the spotlight had closed and they were surrounded by couples, she purred, "That was some kiss, Julian." Actually, it was rather wooden: she had pounced without warning, usually a bad idea. But her instincts were pretty good about these things. Now the barrier was down for later on. Before the night is over, I'll have him trained and asking for more.

How can she say that? Julian puzzled. I didn't think the kiss was good at all. Danny's kisses back at Camp Walker came to mind—the only real kisses I ever had. There's no comparison.

What if she really thinks that? What did Geraldine say again? 'Don't expect to get a kiss right away, Julian… these things take time. Maybe by the end, just before you take her home you can try something…' Sheesh! As if I wanted to do that anyway. I'm not worried. If Geraldine only knew. It must have been a lot harder when she and Mom were my age. Besides, Rita's taking *me* home.

Nah… it isn't a big deal… it was just a big thanks, a sudden burst of energy; it didn't mean anything, really. How could it? She's just naturally affectionate is all. And grateful. He looked around… people had stopped paying attention to him and Rita; everything was back to normal. One good thing was that daisy necklace. It sat right across the middle of Rita's chest. It wasn't big enough to cover things completely, but as far as Julian was concerned, it improved the view. Is she supposed to wear that for the rest of the dance? I wonder if it itches.

Just then Rita answered his unspoken question. She pulled her arms away and took it off. "Can you wear this for me? The stems are too scratchy." Without waiting for an answer, she put it around his neck. "You can give it back when we go back to our little nest." She wasn't about to give it away… she planned to wear it all day Monday. She could hardly wait to see Tracy's face.

Julian couldn't do anything but smile and silently agree; his chest was well protected. As they resumed dancing, he noticed that off near the door some guys were standing around talking about something. Their dates were a few feet away, dancing with each other. That's okay; at the sock hop lots of girls danced with each other. I bet none of the boys were doing that though. Too bad. Now that I think about it, what would it be like to dance with a boy? Huh. He couldn't quite imagine it, but still, he had to ask himself: 'why not?' Dancing is *fun*. Why does it have to be with a girl all the time?

I'm gonna ask Nick about that. I bet he knows. What would it be like to dance with Randall… hmm. Doesn't fit, somehow. Of course, there's only one person he wanted to dance with. Fantasizing about it now wouldn't help any, either. Maybe later… what an idea! I never thought of that before… he smiled his secret smile.

Without a pause, the second song in the set began: *Itsy Bitsy Teenie Weenie Yellow Polka Dot Bikini.* It was perfect. They did the bop step and had a great laugh. The crowd joined in and chanted the refrain at the end of each verse. By the last stanza, practically everyone sang *"…an itsy, bitsy, teenie, weenie, yellow polka-dot bikini!"* in unison. That's funny: I'm dancing opposite the *least* teenie weenie polka dots in the room. He had stopped worrying about the blouse emptying its contents—afraid he'd have to catch them or something. How far would they fall, anyway? That blouse must have some kind of special built in grabber or something.

A short pause after the last chord of *Bikini* … the DJ put on the third song in the set: *Moon River*.

"Oh, that's my *very* favorite song," Rita sighed. She put her hands around Julian's back and started a slow two-step. She pressed her cheek to his and closed her eyes. Soon her mind wandered… dreamt about other times, other places; before long, she was revisiting one particular dance—the one that had made Tracy hers. She forgot, for a while, that she was dancing with Julian.

He was startled a little when she pressed so close—the cheek-to-cheek thing was new… without breaking his contact, he glanced around at the other dancers—most were doing the same thing. Well… okay. Maybe that's what you're supposed to do during the slow songs. It was easy to do, actually—no worry about getting your feet in the wrong place. I haven't stepped on her toes at all. Lucky the perfume has worn off… otherwise this wouldn't be much fun. I hope the flowers hold up…

Rita's hands had slipped downward gradually and were now resting on his buns. He didn't pay much attention to that at first, since the overalls were so loose and rough; earlier in the evening she had slipped her hands into the back pockets for a minute, which he thought was kind of fun. But when she slipped her hands into the open sides between the front bib and the panel in back, he paid attention real quick… what is she *doing?!*

"...you dream maker, you heartbreaker..." Andy Williams' smooth voice was in contrast to the words he was singing.

Rita was extremely fond of this texture… caressing cotton that's stretched tight over a boy's buns is one of the best teases she knew… Tracy *loves* it when I do this. These little buns are firm, and *so* sexy… after a while, if she wanted, she could slip her fingers under the elastic in the back—a gap was waiting there by the spine, a small gap, sometimes a half inch, sometimes more if the back is arched, perfect for one fingertip, then another. What would these cheeks feel like… they're so warm. The muscles now under her palms were a reminder—one *fabulous* time with Tracy, she'd explored that gap and moments later cupped his amazing glutes in her hands; under the tight cotton, she had massaged and squeezed in time to the music, thrilled by his inviting, pleading, begging, *demanding* thrusts…

Julian's shock soon gave way to an unexpected sensation—pleasure. It was so strong that it held him in check—he had to see what this was about… the music was hypnotic… she was caressing his buns now—it was like last summer. Instantly he was in the supply tent at Camp Walker and Danny was massaging his buns, slowly and gently. He could feel every finger pressing, pushing, stroking, pulsing… he would be turned over soon and…

Little J awoke, dissolving Julian's reverie in an instant. He broke into a sweat. The skivvies were resistant to Little J at first, which intensified the pleasurable tingle in the early stages of arousal. That hastened the enlargement, which, thanks to the gentle swaying back and forth with the music, provided even greater pleasure—each pulse in the upward arc was a special treat. A side benefit of the dance was eliminating the need for any manual adjustment to relieve discomfort—the two-step movement provided what was required. In six steps Little J was roaring ready, in full salute.

The gentle rubbing back and forth caused by the dance steps was oh so nice—but oh so scary. Flashes of the recent Initiation activity burst into his consciousness… enhanced by the rhythm of the music, reinforced by her skilled massage strokes. He saw Delta, then Gamma… He wanted the song to end right now! Little J, on the other hand, didn't. His balls were humming, too—

"…We're after the same rainbow's end…"

Julian was scared but he was thrilled… Little J was taking over; gradually, he transposed the sensations Rita was producing on his backside: now they were his own hands at work caressing the buns of the six foot two man of his dreams—the man named Mark who was standing in front of the table in the Camp Walker cabin. This was the imaginary world he dissolved into every time he saw that image. Somehow, at this moment, in the center of the dance floor, it seemed more real than ever. The friction Little J was enjoying in front was a direct reminder of Zeta—somehow he had joined in. Julian's conscious mind had been moved aside; now he was in the tent at Hayden Park and Zeta's nose was at work, this time in sync with Andy Williams' mellow voice…

Rita caught herself at last—she didn’t allow her fingertips to invade that secret entrance after all. Her good sense had returned. Instead, as the song reached the last refrain, she grasped the gluteus muscles with both hands and pulled Julian tight, pressing him in a last embrace. She did not place a kiss, though she considered it; the sensation of her breasts and torso pressing against him was very nice… the hardness she had caused below was larger than she had expected. She was careful to withdraw her arms without making a direct contact… that was saved for later. *Mmm*... that’s *two* of those tonight!

“Last dance special!” exclaimed the DJ. No need to announce the title for this one.

> **Boom-boom-boom!** < *“Come on baby, let’s do the Twist!”*

Chubby Checker had come to the rescue.

21 Fowler's Point

Everything moved so fast that Julian was unable to think—all around him people were doing this Twist thing. It was kind of like the mashed potato, only they were wagging their butts as well as squishing their feet… so that's what he did too. It was a good thing, because it took his mind off what had just happened.

Once he had figured out how to do the dance, his mind started to process the last few minutes. When Rita pressed herself like that she must have been able to tell I had a stiffy. Even the overalls couldn't hide that, not when she was pulling me so close. I thought she was going to leave *dents* back there, she pulled so tight! Little J went limp at once; the dance did a great job shrinking him down the rest of the way.

The boobs weren't a factor… ever since he was little, his mom or Geraldine would hug him like that; no big deal—sort of like a pillow or something under their shirt. But no girl, even his mom, had ever felt Little J when he was hard. And, Little J had grown during the summer, just like the rest of him had. Now when he's up, there's no hiding the fact… *except* if I'm wearing tent-sized overalls. Why did she have to pull so tight like that? She would never have known if she hadn't done that!

What am I gonna do? What must she think? Did I wreck the evening after all? Cripes. I couldn't help it if Little J woke up like that. Technically, it was her fault. Why did she have to do that with my buns?

He had forgotten about his summer camp study of buns and his discovery that it felt really great when they were stroked and rubbed like that.

I can't blame her, come to think about it. How could she know? You can't very well go around warning people not to massage your buns, can you? Maybe she won't say anything about it. Maybe she'll pretend it didn't happen. The dance had been such a great time—much better than I ever expected. I might like to go to another one.

The Twist was replaced by some background music, sort of like what they play in the elevator.

"That's all, folks!" said the DJ. "Drive safely!" The overhead lights flooded the room, turning it into a gymnasium that needed to be put back into shape for school on Monday.

Julian looked to see if Rita was mad—but she was grinning from ear to ear. Boy did that make him feel great. She isn't mad after all.

"You were terrific!" she clapped her hands together. "Let's get our things," she took his arm. "Barb and Sammy will come over to meet us."

Wow. He couldn't believe his luck. She must not have felt Little J after all. What a *huge* relief! The overalls just went up a notch in his opinion. That was a *very* close call.

Rita had reached the same opinion of the overalls for the opposite reason. She already had a plan that would take advantage of their extraordinary design properties—she'd never met their equal when it came to simplifying things. When the gym lights came on, she took a good close look at her prize for the first time—the decorations she had put on his face made him look even more delicious. It was hard not to stare.

Sammy and Barbara's bales, it turned out, were two places away; as they passed by, Rita signaled her to bring Sammy along.

Sporting a giant grin, Julian stopped to slap Sammy on the back. He was giddy because of how things had turned out—no worries after all… "Wow! Did you know how to do that last one?"

Sammy had not tried, in fact. "No way," he shook his head. He still hadn't recovered from *Moon River*. He grabbed his coat.

Rita gave Barbara a meaningful grin as they arrived at her bales. She put her hand on Julian's arm: "We're going to the powder room for a jif." She had to have a short talk. "Do you want to wait for us here?"

"Sure." It wasn't a question. Sammy returned a what-else-can-we-do shrug. Julian sat on one of the bales; that was what he wanted to do more than anything. It felt so good to sit down. He didn't pay any attention to the girls—they were chatting up a storm, headed for the girl's locker room. He wiggled his toes.

"You need to go?" Sammy was under pressure.

"I can hold out for a while."

"I need to pretty bad," he crossed his legs. "Do they have a boy's room around here?"

"Gosh. This is the *girls'* gym…" there must be a way. He looked around… "I know! We can ask that guy!" He pointed to the DJ.

"Yeah!"

They raced across the floor; the DJ was coiling some power cords.

The directions weren't complex; they negotiated a couple of turns and found their way to the regular boys john in the south hall. They knew this one—used it all the time, since it was close to P.E. They rushed in and headed for the urinals… the tall kind, standing along in a row—eight of them.

"Just in time!" Sammy unzipped as he scurried over to the closest unit.

The smell of disinfectant cakes almost overwhelmed; each urinal had one sitting atop its drain, awaiting the next golden shower. That—and the power of suggestion—was all it took: Julian felt the urge too. He stepped up, skipping the one right next to Sammy—just good manners. Oh-oh. How do I do this? He had not faced this problem until now—the zipper in these overalls was about four inches below and almost a foot away from his skivvies' front door—stupid to use either one, really. I know! He slipped the shoulder strap off and held the side so the overalls wouldn't fall to the floor. Like always, he pulled the top of his skivvies down, lodged the elastic band under his balls, and gave Little J a shake. Problem solved; no big deal.

Ordinarily that would be true—not this time. Below, the shake was interpreted differently. Little J had been shut down so suddenly a few minutes ago that a call to duty was unexpected. No problem; it just took a little longer to get underway. There isn't much difference between a shake to urinate and a shake to wake up; as far as Little J was concerned, an order is an order.

"Man!" Sammy beamed; he was *so* relieved. "The pause that refreshes." He glanced at Julian's equipment.

"For sure…" he looked over at Sammy's full-bodied stream, unaware that Little J was slowly waking up.

Being held steady by a couple of warm fingers always felt nice… Little J could tell that Big J wasn't in a hurry—he never is when he's emptying the tank. Little J could take his time.

"Whoa, you weren't kidding!" Julian laughed."You could put out a fire with that!" He thought of the fat guy in the faculty restroom; his sounded like this looked.

Sammy blushed. He was secretly proud of his endowment; Mr. Nine was still about a third hard because of that slow dance—it had helped stop him from wetting his pants though.

Julian took a second look: his eyes wowed. Big guys like Sammy hafta use their whole hand to aim. He must be about halfway hard. It's almost as big as *Tom's!*

Without warning, his vision blurred… now he was looking inside his head… it's *Alpha*… he could remember his hand holding Alpha's shaft like that while Alpha was at work on Little J…

Sammy was used to this reaction. "Nine and a quarter," he grinned. "I call him Mr. Nine."

"Wow!" Julian shook his head… he hadn't expected his brain to do that kind of image swap automatically. I have to pay better attention. The brief memory of Alpha was an alert: Little J is waking up. I can feel the change between my fingers… it's getting harder to piss… I have to head him off.

Just keep talking as if nothing is happening. Inside guy to the rescue.

What to say? Ah: the size. "Where do you put it?" I always wondered about that.

Stop staring at it, stupid!

Sammy laughed. "It's easy most of the time, since I'm so skinny; loose pants hide things pretty good. It's still up partway because of that slow dance." He looked at himself proudly. "That's why I had to untuck my shirt." I was up all the way because of that.

"You too?!" Amazing. "What did she do?"

The echo in the room amplified the sound of their voices; the ceramic tile and the glossy enamel on the smooth plaster walls reflected rather than absorbed. Afraid that anyone walking by in the hallway could hear what they were saying, Sammy looked around—had to make sure no one else had come in. Watching his stream dwindle, he aimed into center of the disinfectant disc… he spoke low: "I was okay until she started feeling me up." He grinned, "I never had a girl do that before." His eyes wowed. I'm hoping she'll do that again, later tonight. His attention returned downward… he focused on the sudsy overflow… his stream was boring a hole in the pink cake.

"Wow!" So they *all* do that! "Mine did that *too*." He shook his head—Geraldine didn't expect that part, obviously.

Sammy flipped and wagged Mr. Nine a few times to shake off the last drops, and pulled his foreskin forward with a tight squeeze and wagged again.

Out of habit, Julian took careful notice of his ritual; as always, it was being filed away for possible reference. After all, it wasn't every day you could watch someone like this without getting a wisecrack or two; Sammy wasn't one of those idiots. He's nice. He likes girls, but that's no big deal.

"I hate it when I have leftover drops," Sammy explained. "They always leave a stain in my shorts." He tucked himself away. "I hate stains in my shorts." He was still swollen down there… takes time to shrink down—one of the burdens of being blessed with nine inches.

"Mm," Julian nodded; not a big problem for me. With the help of Inside guy, a stalemate had been achieved with what was his problem; almost finished, he aimed his last bit at the cake like Sammy had… at a small crater in the center… how long does it take to dissolve all the way through?

"So, what are you gonna do tonight?" Sammy was fishing for a tip or two. He had never been on a necking date before. Presumably, Julian had. All you had to do was look at him—anybody with looks like his could get whatever he wanted. Look at who he's with! Not to mention the lip prints on his face!

"Do?"

"Yeah, y'know, after we leave here." It's only ten thirty and I don't have to be home until midnight.

There… finished. Without thinking, Julian performed Sammy's flip, wag, and squeeze sequence; he pulled his skivvy waistband out so that his equipment could fall back into place.

Better not do that in public after this, warned Inside guy.

Right… Little J appreciated that squeeze a little too much… I hafta be careful, especially considering what happened out on the dance floor. I've never grown a stiffy in the boy's room—not a good idea, *ever*. The one thing I never expected tonight was having a Little J problem. He pushed down the flush lever.

Sammy wanted to know what it was like to press up against those huge tits, but he was too chicken to ask.

Julian ignored the glow trying to establish control below and returned his attention to Sammy's question. "Gosh, I don't know. Whatever Rita says, I suppose. It's her show." He pulled the overall strap back onto his shoulder.

"Yeah, that makes sense, doesn't it?" He grinned wide. I don't have to make a plan—I can just leave it up to Barbara! Brilliant! Especially after what she did on the dance floor… she knows what she wants to do—and, come to think about it, that's pretty much what I have in mind myself. He hesitated to ask anything else… didn't want to look like a total dumbass.

Julian had not given any thought to this… plenty of time left before I'm supposed to be home… Mom said eleven, but Geraldine scolded her and insisted that I be able to stay out until midnight. I don't know why it's such a big deal. But girls know about this stuff; might as well let them do the figuring. So far, they have been pretty much right. 'Cept for Little J, of course. That was accidental… they don't need to know about that.

That won't happen again. Why would it? Anyhow, my buns will be out of reach. I'll be sitting most of the time. I doubt if she'll want to do that anyway… I don't need to put a do-not-touch sign back there or anything. We'll probably go get pizza. I could use a bite to eat after all that dancing.

"C'mon—I gotta put my boots back on." The nice feeling below will fade soon enough once I start walking; Little J will go back to sleep in a minute. They hustled back down the hallway.

"Isn't this *fabulous!*" Rita exclaimed, gesturing to the moon. It was almost full—tomorrow it would be. The sky had cleared, and there was no wind. She made a silent kiss at the moon. She and

Barbara had firmed up the game plan for the rest of the evening—she was *very* ready.

This yellow slicker felt silly, but it kept the cold out. Rita's mood was catching; when she held her hand out Julian took it gladly. They skipped all the way to the car.

Barbara's parking spot was a ways out—she had been late signing up for a slot; first come, first served. Rita rubbed her arms. "Hurry, hurry!" she called out. "If she doesn't get here quick, I might have to get in there with you!" She planned to do just that, later on. It wasn't exactly a blanket, but it was the next best thing… maybe even better—she reached out and fiddled with one of the snaps.

"Are these hard to open and close?" she asked sweetly.

He looked down. "Kinda, yeah. They hafta use these things out in the wind and rain, y'know. It wouldn't be much of a raincoat if it was blowing open all the time."

"Oh. That makes sense." She smiled to herself. The idea of being snapped in was *very* hot. The possibilities for the evening kept multiplying. Her original plan was hands only—maybe I should reconsider. Barbara planned to go farther, but then she needs to; she doesn't have any notches on her belt yet; it was high time she did.

Well—as long as I have the night free… why not? I don't have to worry about Tracy tonight. Plenty of time for him tomorrow; what I do or don't do tonight doesn't matter, *really*, since Tracy won't know, either way. He's afraid of the worst happening anyway—that's why he'll shape up.

Rita had just given herself permission to do whatever she felt like when the time came.

Barbara unlocked the passenger door for Sammy and headed around the front of the car.

"Turn on the heater!" Rita was exaggerating, of course; all a part of her strategy; if I'm held nice and close, I won't get a chill, will I? She gave the daisy necklace a small tug. "Put this under the back window, will you?" It needs to be in good shape tomorrow; keeping it out of harms way is important.

"Good idea." Julian was glad to take it off, actually; she worked hard for it. This way, I won't wreck it. When Sammy unlocked the rear door, he held it open so she could slip in first. After she scooted over he climbed in partway… reaching the shelf under the rear window is kinda tricky with this blasted coat on. Carefully, he laid the flower necklace out flat; as an afterthought, he took off the straw hat and put it in the center. Boy, do I hate this coat—now I hafta turn around and sit down. That won't be very easy either.

Julian was mistaken about going for pizza. Instead, they were on the way to Amanda and June's Pie and Pastry Shoppe.

"We don't want a big meal this late at night," Rita explained. "You'll *love* this place. They have more kinds of pie than you *ever* heard of."

She was quite right about that. It turned out to be a popular place on Saturday night. Julian looked around—some of these couples had been at the dance. Another Li'l Abner was over by the window in one of those circle booths; three couples were crowded together. Several waved as they walked by. Most were eating ice cream and drinking hot cocoa. Looked real good. He waved back, grinning wide. He wasn't used to kids he didn't know paying attention to him. At first he didn't understand what was going on… but then he figured it out. It's because I'm with Rita.

He leaned close to Sammy. "Are we supposed to pay for the refreshments or are they?" He wasn't sure if the Sadie Hawkins rules were still in force.

Sammy's eyes went wide in terror. "I don't know," he whispered. "I didn't bring any money!"

Julian put his hand over his mouth. I can lend him some, but I don't know if I can pay for all four. Oo-ee. "Better order a *small* size." He checked to make sure his billfold was still in the left front pocket of the overalls; it always had a five-dollar bill in case an emergency came up; Mom always makes sure of that.

Sammy nodded thanks.

The waitress showed them to a booth—one of the last three that were open. Julian gave Sammy a wink; Rita had whispered something in her ear. Maybe she reserved this. It felt nice to be with someone who had that kind of smarts. He tilted his head slightly: she's kind of like *Geraldine!* Yeah… no wonder this is going so well. I just figured that out. Julian was pleased with himself. Most of the time I don't figure stuff like that out until way later.

It was very warm, so they took off their coats at once. Rita took charge and stuffed the slicker on the window side of the bench and tossed her raincoat on top. She then slid in, leaving just enough room. Barbara did the same on the other side. The escorts wordlessly followed the unspoken instructions to sit down and snuggle up.

They were given fancy menus and a glass of water; any quality restaurant did that… Julian knew that because his mom and Geraldine took him to a restaurant sometimes. Maybe even this one—it seems kind of familiar.

When Rita scooted close, Julian realized that they had been given one menu per couple. It didn't matter; we can share, no problem. She leaned close and ran her right finger down the list of pie flavors. Her left hand reached over and took his right hand off his leg and held it. After holding hands all night on the dance floor, it wasn't a big deal. Besides, it's just like I figured: sitting down like this puts my buns out of range.

"Isn't this nice?" she cooed, scooting a little closer. She wanted their legs to touch, but the overalls sort of neutralized the effect she was after.

Across the table, Barbara had achieved the same thing, but her leg and Sammy's felt each other's body heat; he was responding as predicted. Barbara glanced up with what seemed like a straight face. The brief pursed lip pulse told Rita that she was behind. She wasn't concerned. Obviously Sammy was not a tough assignment.

Rita had a more subtle task—that's one reason she picked it. It isn't as much fun when it's too easy.

Julian liked the homemade look of the cookies under a covered round display on the counter when they entered. He didn't order one though… Maybe one day I'll come back. The prices were more important than the flavors; I'm not a huge pie fan, although Miss Carter from across the street makes good ones—she always brings one over at Thanksgiving. I like the pumpkin better than the mincemeat, unless there's ice cream. His eyes scanned up and down the right column: hot chocolate is fifty cents. I have enough to get four of those.

"How about some cocoa?" He gave Rita a grin. "It will warm us up!"

"Great idea!" Sammy echoed.

Rita and Barbara gave each other a look of satisfaction. Perfect. They would be out of here in no time and on the way to Fowler's Point.

"You are so smart!" Rita kissed her forefinger and touched his cheek. She squeezed his hand by mistake—it had been slipping into Julian's lap according to plan… she was hoping to find out whether anything was going on down there yet. Now it rested on his thigh again. That's okay… best not to hurry. The open side of the overalls was tempting, but…too risky. If this were Tracy her hand would be in there right now. Being in a public place like this would turn him on. The time will come soon enough… it has to be done when there is no escape route.

Hot chocolate is filling. They all felt that without talking about it; no one wanted a second cup. Rita was ready.

"Have you ever been to Fowler's Point?" She looked eagerly at Julian as if she had a special surprise or a birthday present to whip in front of his face.

He didn't have time to answer because Barbara bounced up and down on her bench.

"Oh, that's *perfect!"* She turned to Sammy— "Especially tonight! That full moon—it will be right over the town!" She included Julian. "You can see the whole town from up there. At night it's *spectacular!"*

As planned, the boys were eager to go up to Fowler's Point. Julian had never been there, and he had a thing about views, this could be perfect to draw. Sammy wanted to go because he had heard about what goes on up there, and even now Mr. Nine was getting ready. This hot restaurant made him perspire; he wanted to leave before he got a case of the pits—and before his problem was too big to hide. When Barbara insisted on paying for everyone, his worries were over.

Amanda and June's Pie and Pastry Shoppe was located on the edge of an upper middle class neighborhood. The restaurant parking lot was also upscale, landscaped with islands of lawn and closely trimmed shrubs. It matched the well-groomed city park across the street; that's one reason it was popular. As another draw, the establishment had two areas set aside specifically for dog owners. After walking their dogs in the park, patrons could tether their pets in a safe, sheltered area while they went inside. Water and chew toys were provided.

The staff policed the area regularly in case an owner had not picked up after his or her animal. There were occasional infractions, but they were always caught the first thing in the morning before they opened for the day. In ten years there had only been one complaint.

On the night of November 10, 1962 at 10:41 p.m., one of the light posts in the parking lot went dark—its bulb had burned out. It so happened that five minutes earlier, the passenger side of Barbara's 1956 ultramarine and ivory Plymouth Savoy had parked beside that very light post. Barbara was a skilled driver: purposely, she parked close to the curb so that her passengers could step onto the soft, well-trimmed strip of lawn. The illumination provided by the light post had helped her be precise—her white sidewall tires were never in trouble.

After half an hour of hot chocolate and polite conversation, the eager couples left the restaurant with nice warm tummies and great enthusiasm. Behaving like true gentlemen, the escorts assisted their dates to the driver's side doors and guided them into their seats. Sammy gave Julian a thumbs up sign and scurried around the front of the car as fast as he could. Julian gave Sammy his signature Cheshire cat grin and headed around the rear to his door.

How could they have known that shortly after the light post went dark, a very impatient Grace Connally looked the other way while her properly leashed dachshund left a small deposit—in a dark area that no one would notice, of course. She was tired and anxious to pop "Weenie Girl" into the car so she could get home in time to watch the late news.

How could the in-a-hurry-to-be-on-their-way foursome have known that "Weenie Girl" had blessed the exact spot that Sammy's right foot would need to use when, fifteen minutes later, it was about to re-enter the car?

"Ooo," Rita complained as Barbara started the engine. "How could it get this cold in here? We weren't inside that long!" It was, in fact, warmer than the outside; she was merely reinforcing her cuddle strategy.

Julian would have wrapped his arm around her, but this blasted slicker wasn't that easy to work with. Instead, he gave a token nod of agreement, and tried to scoot toward the center.

> *wb-wbbpl-wbbl-wpp* < The yellow rubber protested, unable to accommodate the simple task of moving across a seat while being sat upon; outdoors please, preferably in a cold rain.

"How far away is it?"

"Six miles, I think." Six point three miles, in fact. Barbara had checked that last week and had timed how long it took to get there. She cranked the heater fan knob over to high. "Sammy, can you find something on the radio?" She reached her left arm forward to push the reverse button. She loved the way her pushbutton transmission simplified driving.

Sammy bent forward. His sister had talked some about what radio stations played the best songs at night. Let's see… 1340 on the dial, wasn't it? or was it 1360?

>….*fwipytlrstbp*…< He turned the dial hurriedly. There! Ricky Nelson! I like Ricky Nelson. He sat back; the TV show is okay, but Ricky's singing is really good.

Three cars were at Fowler's Point already. Rita made a quick judgment and sat forward. "Park all the way to the left," she spoke low so only Barbara could hear. At least one side needs to remain clear; with any luck, no one would park very close on the right side either. She didn't want any "neighbors" to spook her tender unsuspecting blond. She swung around fast and looked at him eagerly. "See?" she pointed.

"Whoa…" The view, even from the car window, was impressive. "Look at that!" He sat forward and put his right arm on the back of the front seat. Rita leaned in and sat as close as possible. They surveyed the sea of lights while Barbara carefully slowed the car into place.

Julian's artistic eye kicked in at once. I want to get a better look. "Can we go outside and see? For just a minute?" Obviously this was a candidate for being drawn up. I need a better view so I can figure what to do.

"Sure!!" Exactly what Rita wanted. They could stroll and gaze for a while, while Barbara got started. That way, when we come back, we can join in. Much easier that way—removed the need to talk a lot. She nodded, "I'd like that."

He opened the door and removed his left arm from around her; getting out of the car was kind of awkward with this slicker on—it doesn't like to scoot. Once the coat was re-snapped, he held his hand out like a gentleman to help her alight from the car. Geraldine had made a point about doing that: I'm always supposed to help the girl get in and out of places.

The second the rear door closed, Barbara made her move. "Hi," she said, moving her face close to Sammy. She batted her eyes.

Rita had told her in the powder room, 'Don't let him start talking. Pounce before he has a chance to say a word.' Barbara's left hand pressed on Sammy's thigh and slowly crept upward… on a direct path to the discovery she had made when *Moon River* was playing at the dance.

Sammy was transported in an instant—to the same place he was an hour ago—this time, she's kissing—kissing hard. Automatic. He was on automatic. Mr. Nine was already erect—what had started in the restaurant had continued without pause; he was almost two thirds up by the time they got back to the car. He hadn't worried about it showing, since it was so dark. Now, it was clear that he didn't need to worry anyway: she had checked on Mr. Nine first thing.

It's getting warm in here… he took off his coat.

Barbara stopped kissing long enough to remove her coat. Bunched up on her left side, it made an excellent support. She swung her left leg across the center and faced him—proof positive that push button controls mounted on the dashboard were superior—no gearshift column stood in her way. The column in Sammy's lap was was what drew her interest.

"We shouldn't walk in front of them," Rita indicated the other cars. She narrowed her eyes to see if she knew anyone… no… I don't know any of these cars. Just as well.

"Oh… yeah." That's right. We don't want to wreck their view; it's no trouble to cross behind.

This was considerate, typical for Julian; in fact, he wasn't even likely to look their way—if he had, he would have seen that their view was, in reality, a steamed up pane of glass. As far as the view was concerned, walking in front of them wouldn't have mattered at all.

"But I want to go all the way to the other side." Otherwise, I can't pick the best vantage point. This *has* to be drawn up. He glanced up at the sky, then at the horizon. He focused on the tiny lights below; with a slow wide horizontal stroke, he defined a particular area that had caught his attention.

"It's kind of like a *mirror.*" Enthusiastically, he looked for patterns… do any of the lights cluster like the stars? That's an idea… might have to fudge some, but…

Rita cocked her head and gave Julian a second look. He's serious. Hmm. I have an *artist* on my hands. Her imagination kicked in… she was posing naked on a crimson velvet drape, her left knee elevated, her right hand covering her front to give the illusion of modesty…

Julian continued forward, studying the horizon. That will be an important part—might help decide where to frame the view; the Moon will be in the upper left…

Rita had grown a little chilly. She wanted to get back into that cozy car… no way to tell how far along they are… better stick it out a little longer. She scurried up close to Julian's side. Ten minutes. I'll give her ten minutes.

—ᴡ—

Sometimes, when you're necking on a cold autumn night, it helps to have the radio going—especially if the song on the radio is a good one. It covers the deep bass drone of the engine and the tenor roar of the heater fan pretty well—and it will hide lots of other sounds, personal sounds, from the couple in the back seat when they return; they won't know how far you've gotten. That's what Barbara was thinking when something rare happened, something special—and she didn't hear it at all. She and Sammy had moved ahead in their mutual pursuit of *what-it-would-be-like-if* much faster than either had anticipated. The sound of the sixteen year-old boy's jism striking the headliner of her 1956 Plymouth Savoy four door sedan went unheard.

The sound, somewhat akin to a squirt from a Windex bottle into an empty Styrofoam cup, should have drawn some kind of attention; it was a first time ever event. The headliner fabric, driven suddenly against the steel roof was cushioned slightly by a thin foam backing—perhaps that's why Sammy didn't hear it, either. Possibly he was too occupied losing control to notice the finer details of his exquisite explosion.

Since it was a first time event for Barbara, she did not understand what had taken place. Her playmate had been taken to the point of no return for the third time that night, and he let fly with an uncontrolled jet that had velocity sufficient to go five feet in the air had he been outdoors. But he was spread legged on her car seat kissing her madly while she stroked his pulsing nine and a quarter inch staff of life. Both her hands working around it, she was thrilled when it suddenly tensed; she did not know that the pulsing she felt was a series of emissions. She thought he was merely pulsing with heightened pleasure due to her masterful massage routine. She was fascinated from the start by the properties of the foreskin sliding up and down his incredible pole.

She had not known about that; she thought that when a boy was hard, everything was fixed and rigid—like a huge finger, say, or a "third leg." She had not worked up the courage to kiss it yet, but it was on her list. At first, the overflow from the smaller pulses went unnoticed as well—but when her new toy became slippery, it was obvious that something different was going on. She sat back and looked down at the masterpiece poking upward between her hands. The light from the radio dial illuminated the exotic sight.

Her jaw dropped in shocked surprise when she realized what had happened—what was still happening. A giant drop oozed out the top… stunned, she watched it flow downward until it reached her left thumb; she squeezed as if to allow it to spill over—it did, after being joined by another drop summoned by the squeeze.

"Sorry," Sammy said, short of breath. "I couldn't hold it any longer." This was one of the best hand jobs ever; he grinned wide. He did not know this was Barbara's first time—especially because of how good a job she did. A girl had never done this for him before… Man… she must really be experienced. I really lucked out.

"Oh." Barbara didn't know what to do next. Rita had not explained this very well after all. Do I keep stroking? How much more is there? How do I clean this up? What about me? Is that all? Is the night over already? She had plans for his hands that she had not even started… She was uncertain what to do, how to react.

Sammy couldn't see her face well because the radio light was behind her head now. He needed to say something, since Mr. Nine had stopped the involuntary pulsing. As luck would have it, a handkerchief was in his right front pocket. He reached for it.

"You really know how to please a guy!" he gushed, looking down to see where to mop up the joy juice. She was still holding him. He smiled with unearned self-assurance. "Let me clean this up. He needs to rest for a minute. Then you can do it again, if you want." I sure hope she will.

Fortunately, the large drip that threatened to fall from the headliner had stabilized and spread horizontally, absorbed by and large by the soft fabric. It would go unnoticed for weeks and ever afterward remain a mystery.

Barbara gulped. She watched him tidy up, fascinated; she had recovered somewhat from the shock. "Um… how many times can you go?"

"Twice, most of the time. Some days I can go three, but it takes a while. I usually have to sleep a little, you know… then it's no problem." He tipped his head and considered. "I don't think I can do that many before curfew. Second one? No sweat!"

Barbara was thrilled. This is so much *better* than Rita said. Maybe Tracy isn't as potent. Her eyes blazed, eager to get back to work. The thought that she had surpassed Rita in this art was enormously satisfying. She reached out and took the handkerchief. Gracefully, she wiped her hands and placed it on the dashboard. With a suggestive grin, she took Sammy's empty hand and placed it on her breast; she slid her arm behind his back. It's his turn to do the massaging; soon I'll be all the way on my back. I have a different plan for Sammy's second time.

Sammy was ready—had been a long time; a stack of fantasies was ready and waiting. He drew the first one that surfaced. Mr. Nine is beginning to pulse already, this is the best night of my life!

Rita tugged at Julian's sleeve, then turned him away from the vista. She attacked the top snap of the slicker. It wasn't hard to undo after all. "I'm freezing." She unsnapped the second one. "You have to let me share this for a while."

"You want to go back to the car?" He had seen what he needed to for now.

"No, not yet." She unsnapped the remaining clasps. And pulled herself inside.

Gosh. He didn't expect this, but there was plenty of room, so it was okay… Except for the bottom and top two, he refastened the snaps securely—that way her head could poke out the top.

"We need to give Barbara and Sammy a minute or two alone, don't you think?"

"Oh… yeah." Julian just remembered what Sammy said back in the john. He was hoping to get somewhere with Barbara. "Good idea." Think of that: Rita is willing to wait in the cold a little to help her friend out. That's very thoughtful of her. He closed another snap to keep the cold air out.

Rita threaded her right arm around his back. "You're so sweet," she hugged. "Tell me some more about what you see out there." She was a little curious about that; a few clues to work with would help. In ten minutes, or sooner, they would be in that nice cozy car with these coats off. A frontal assault would be a bad idea; she wasn't dealing with a jock like Tracy; another approach would be wise. The mini massage of his backside on the dance floor was proof enough that he'll get there…

Julian wasn't sure how to describe what he saw that was different from what she could see for herself. He tried to put himself in Mr. van Horn's shoes. After a short pause he pointed to a cluster of trees that stood out along the horizon. "See those trees?"

Rita moved her hand up to his shoulder and put her fingers around the strap in back—as though using it for a place to hold on. That's what she was doing, for now. He didn't flinch, so…

"That's what they call a focal point." He looked down at her face to see if she understood. Her smile assured him that she did, so he continued. "The first thing you do is locate your focal point."

Focal Point? She suppressed an urge to grin… I identified that on the dance floor; she could still feel the impression she had forced it to make. Discovering unintended *double entendres* was a special pleasure—especially if they were naughty. She moved her left hand across the front. Again she grasped, this time where the strap hooked onto the bib; she explored the steel button and the buckle mechanism. Familiarizing herself with how it detached might pay off later. She listened to what he was saying for a while; nothing gave her a hint about what would turn him on. Something would, she was certain of that. There was no mistake about what happened during *Moon River*—focal point, indeed; she had a plan that involved providing him with a special one—in just a little while.

Julian held out his right hand and stretched it in front of his eye. He squinted and formed a frame corner with his thumb and forefinger. "See, if you decide your focal point, then you can locate the corners of your drawing…"

Rita leaned forward to see—

Wow… she's taking an interest in this. "Move your head around until you see the focal point where you want it to be. That's how to decide if the drawing will be vertical or horizontal." He watched her weave her head around randomly, trying to see what he was talking about. He waited eagerly, watching her facial expressions.

Rita tried, but she couldn't quite see how this worked. What she did see was that as long as he was interested in creating a drawing, his mind would not drift her way—she had a different idea about how to decide the question of vertical or horizontal: time to get back into the car. "Ooh, I think I see what you mean!" she lied. She pulled on his overall strap, forcing an awkward hug. She nuzzled behind his ear and whispered. "I think we can go back to the car, now."

"Oh, yeah. Sorry about that—I sorta got carried away. I do that sometimes, 'specially when I see something new." He turned toward the car. "Say—you want to go back like this—together?" he grinned. Being wrapped up like this made him think of the sack races they used to do in Cubs. Those were fun.

"Why not?! Let's!" She stepped forward.

Julian giggled as he tried to get into sync with her. I don't want to step on her foot again. He leaned left as far as he could and paid careful attention… oop… I almost tripped on my own foot! This is a little tricky…

The bright Moon enabled Rita to see his face clearly; he pokes the tongue out of the corner of his mouth when he concentrates. How cute is that?! The full mouth kiss-print on his lips looked newly planted. Ah, yes: a kissing lesson. I remember now! She had her start clearly in mind. They had reached the car: she poked her left hand through a gap and unsnapped the slicker. With her right hand she opened the car door and zipped inside. "Quick, don't let all the heat out!"

Still laughing, Julian jumped in after and slammed the door. The change in temperature was unexpected. "Wow, is it ever hot in here!" The windows are all steamed up. He struggled to take off the slicker. Don't need this in here! Freeing himself was awkward—I should have taken it off before getting in. At least the snaps are already open.

Activity in the front seat continued without pause.

This blasted thing! Folding it is next to impossible. As well as he could, he tucked it to his right, by the door. It tried to unfold itself. He turned it over and pushed hard… there. The springy rubber material did not like being compressed and folded; he gave a test push. It stayed put. Good; there isn't any other place to put the thing.

While Julian struggled with the slicker, Rita sat forward and removed her raincoat—it was lightweight and cooperative. A quick peek over the seat: the moonlight shining through the windshield was more than sufficient—Barbara had scored—Sammy had begun to explore the delights of his focal point in the horizontal position. No need to look carefully—his bare backside was visible halfway down to the knees. Rita wasn't expecting them to be so far along. The movement, somewhat in pace with the music on the radio, told her that she need not worry—her own program would not be interrupted. The sight of Sammy's flexing gluteus was a goad, certainly—a sight she had seen last summer, one that banished hesitation and whetted the appetite. Nothing I do will be noticed by those two, vertical or horizontal. She stuffed her coat away on the left and zoomed into place. Time to begin! It's a good thing the windows are fogged over.

"That's better… isn't it?"

"Boy oh boy." Amazing, how warm it had gotten in here. As she snuggled close it dawned on him: better? she wasn't talking about the temperature. Gosh. His eyes looked forward; there's supposed to be two heads up there… gosh. All he could see was a handkerchief on the dashboard—it looked like a small white tent. Because of the music and the fan, he couldn't hear anything—it looked like the seat moved a little. What is Sammy doing? It had not occurred to him to consider what Sammy had in mind when he asked about that in the boys' room… What to do or not do in a car wasn't on Julian's radar even. The fact is, Julian didn't even have a radar. Indeed, he made it a policy to ignore that sort of thing whenever the guys talked about it. Maybe I should have paid some attention… Unconsciously he wiped a bead of sweat off his left temple.

Swiping away perspiration was taken as a positive sign—he's ready. So am I. First though, the setup: "Did you have a good time at the dance?"

Julian gave a sigh of relief: a question he could answer. "Oh, yeah!" Geraldine popped into his head. "I sure want to thank you for inviting me. I would never be able to go otherwise." He nodded sincerely.

"I'm so glad." She ran her right forefinger up his left arm to the sleeve of his polo shirt. "I had a good time too." Idly she played with the cuff as she spoke. Her left hand took a complementary route and meandered over to the small pocket on his left pectoral. She gave a playful tug. "You look very good in red."

"You think so?" That's interesting. I've never liked red very much… maybe I should take a second look at that.

Rita ran her left palm over to his right shoulder and rested her hand on his neck. The skin was slightly moist—he's beginning to perspire. She toyed with the area behind his ear. "It's getting awfully warm, isn't it?"

Julian wasn't panicking yet, but it had become a possibility. This sort of situation was new. Geraldine didn't talk about this, and I haven't thought about it at all. A faint sensation at the base of his neck teased his pleasure center in a new way—it was a cousin of what he felt when Mark pinched that special spot between his neck and shoulder.

"I don't want to disturb them, but…" she pulled her left forefinger down the back of his neck as if it was a squeegee. "Should we ask them to turn the heater down?" She had collected a few drops of perspiration.

Gulp. She's right about the temperature in here for sure. Maybe I should roll down the window… no… can't do that without asking Sammy… At this point he didn't want to know what Sammy was doing, actually. He searched for another idea… nothing came to mind… he had trouble focusing on the question. The radio is kinda loud…

Being caught by surprise was the problem—he had never thought about being in this kind of situation. He had heard some things during the last year or so, but tuned out because it didn't interest him. Broken fragments of conversations bounced around in his head—remarks, comments, anecdotes overheard in the locker room or on the job last summer… conversations about what might be happening right this minute. Nothing was clear enough or complete enough to be of any use. This is like that saying of Geraldine's about being in high school; you're supposed to know these things automatically or something. He didn't feel at home here… he wasn't afraid, exactly, but he was a little worried about Little J… that tickle she caused behind my neck… I felt an echo down there… Little J hasn't gone back to sleep completely.

Oh—what did she say again? Was that a question? He looked her in the eye briefly—very briefly. "Gosh…" a bead of sweat ran down his temple.

Rita took courage in what she saw—*and,* in what she *didn't* see: no flashing red light—not even a caution light. "Would you feel better if you took this off?" She tugged at the pocket.

"Man, would I ever!" What a brilliant suggestion—it's the obvious answer. This shirt is hot, these overalls are hot… and, he didn't have another solution handy. He didn't stop to think.

Julian did not connect the dots. Subconsciously he was still behaving under Geraldine's rules and commands. All relations with Rita came through that filter. His own ego was not in play; he had no goal for the evening, other than to please Geraldine, his mother, and Rita. So far, that had worked out; so far he had been having a fun time. He knew nothing of the hidden agenda that had maneuvered him into this unfamiliar place. He looked at Rita again to see if he should, really, take off his shirt.

Rita nodded reassuringly and sat back.

The shoulder strap fell off at the same time; it had to in order for the shirt to come off. Julian did not notice—the relief he felt was so pronounced, nothing else registered in his mind.

"Thanks!" Boy, did that help. The temperature quickly readjusted to a tolerable level. It was still warm, but not sweat box warm. Maybe now I won't get a case of B.O. He wiped his forehead off with the polo shirt and placed it atop the rain slicker… I can slip it back on easy enough after it cools off a little.

Rita adjusted rapidly to the surprise of having reached this stage so early on, so *effortlessly*. Usually, her top was the first item to go—Tracy always began there. How long will it take Julian to think of doing that? She was a patient huntress… after a few minutes, with the right prompting, it will happen automatically. She stroked his shoulders gently, first one, then the other. "You have a well shaped body, Julian." She tried to affect an objective tone.

The sensation was familiar: it was like the one that woke up Little J at the dance—Danny's massage last summer had paid attention to the same contours… that morning episode in the supply tent was a sensual event and memory that remained central in his pleasure center; it was one of his strongest erotic switches. Just as he feared, Little J had taken the call—he's coming to life again, in a hurry. How can I stop him?!

Rita was good at this; she knew how to massage a male torso. Tracy was the primary recipient of her skill, but he was not the only one who had met that good fortune. Indeed, she was a proud practitioner, one who believed that perfection is reached by practice—and by variety: the summer up north this year was especially good there. Julian was now in for the latest super treatment. She stroked his pectoral muscles in a special tender choreography all her own. His perspiration was like fine body oil. Her ministrations were slow and deliberate—gradually, as she felt him respond, she would apply her skills in those areas that she knew would remove any resistance; he was putty in her hands. Oh, how she enjoyed doing this…

Trying to keep up with this was difficult and awkward—it was new and unprepared for… analyzing and rationalizing wasn't doing any good. Julian had failed to cancel the orders dispatched to Little J—a fierce competition for his attention took over: Little J is pointed sideways, unable to lift. I don't dare reach down to make an adjustment—that would only encourage him. Besides, Rita's hands are in the way.

True to character, Little J was eager to play; he'd been shut down twice tonight—making up for that was top priority. He was about to run out of room down here already… the pressure that caused felt good too. Eventually help will come along to fix the problem—it always does.

Julian did not realize what Rita was up to; he was unaware that he had become so completely vulnerable. That bib strap falling to the side had allowed space to open in front. Not only that: his conscious mind had lost contact with current events—weaponless, it sought desperately for a place to hide. Several alternatives were immediately available. Unaware that Little J had taken charge, his imagination flashed between Danny in the cabin last summer, and the five Greek names in the tent… both jockeyed for dominance. Which would prevail? Which would be the inspiration to carry Little J to his goal?

Meanwhile, Rita had discovered that without tension from above, the denim bib had no strength, no protective capability—it could not constrain anything. With undetected deftness, she worked the loose fabric outward in gradual increments. The base of the strap aided in the enterprise—it enabled her to widen the bib's spill, maximizing the open space. A gulf had opened in front of Julian: revealed in full was the one and only item of cloth remaining on his body—other than two oversized overall legs and a pair of socks. The white cotton fabric seemed to glow in the dark.

Because the air temperature was so high, Julian did not feel exposed. He had not looked down. His mind was elsewhere—under the hypnotic effect of Rita's massage, enhanced by the music and the background hum of the fan, his brain had replaced reality with fantasy: images of Danny and the Initiates soon gave way to his extensive store of Mark scenarios. In his imagination, he had sculpted Mark's torso in much the same way that Rita lovingly stroked every inch of his abdomen—her skill, in concert with those he had learned during the Initiation, amplified and enhanced his fantasy in thrilling new ways.

Dealing with Little J directly was not possible—Julian was fully occupied by the forces inside his head: Little J was on his own. Impatient by nature, Little J was not content to wait for help from above. Goaded by the underlying hum and constant sympathetic vibration of the car's 270 cubic inch V-8 engine, he raged and pulsed, desperate to find an escape. Little J wanted nothing further to do with cotton underwear.

The moon shining through the foggy window spotlighted the white briefs. Rita could see the entire package, still under wraps. That was about to change thanks to a combination of factors: an opening had begun to appear in the center. The sitting position provided enough slack to allow the built in entrance to open of its own accord. Dark because the moonlight could not reach in, something—and she knew what it was—was about to appear: her "focal point" was on the way. Gradually she had expanded the massage coverage… she would soon be within a few inches of the elastic waistband. His deep breathing intensified, betraying an accelerating heartbeat. A glance at his face told her all she needed to know: his glazed unfocused eyes revealed that he was spellbound—he had surrendered completely. She continued her ministrations with gentle subtlety… haste was not necessary, and not wise.

Julian's manhood, after pressing desperately, had worked into the built-in access and was about to explore the route outward that, ordinarily, was never used. The sitting position allowed direct entrance to the passageway—it opened a little wider each time he exhaled; and each time Little J pulsed his demand to be free, he inched a little farther into the escape opening. He would have sprung free by now, but the scrotum was caught under the lining along the base of the right thigh.

Rita had become fully engaged—after the surreptitious release of her support clasps, she had focused her eyes on the dynamic event taking place less than six inches below her skilled hands and fingers. Her lips puckering, she *willed* it to appear… she watched each undulation, each expansion of the valve like opening of the underwear… any second *it* would appear, and her fingers would be there, ready to surround it gently, to reward its valiant escape into the open air. This was a new variation of a favorite part of the ritual—one she had not performed with Tracy.

The form was visible, pressing tight against the cotton, stretching it taut. Pushed to its maximum tolerance, only the stubborn trim along the edge of the garment's front opening was able to stop the escape of its desperate prisoner—the edge of its tip had begun to appear… the deep color flushed as it pressed yet again… to no avail; it forced the supporting shaft to bow outward into partial view, as if in preview: it was about to spring free at last.

If only he would pump! She could see it beginning to peek out… the dark hole was beginning to fill in… *Pump, will you,* ***pump!*** It looked like he might do that at any moment… she repeated her silent command: soon she would have it in hand; her prediction was six and a half inches… maybe seven. She had not determined yet whether he was circumcised—a little more needed to show before she could be certain.

Her next step was planned already—in one move, her left hand would reach down and pull the panties aside just before she swung around to sit on what she would have in her right hand. This Daisy Mae skirt is *made* to perform a straddle…

A muffled vocal sound in the front seat was followed by a springy bounce. Some kind of adjustment was being made, a graceless awkward shifting of position. Rita grinned. Barbara will have lots to talk about tomorrow. She returned her eyes to her enterprise, grateful that she did not have to contend with a steering wheel.

Julian was vaguely aware of a rustling noise up front, but it didn't jar the picture in his mind—his hands were approaching Mark's pelvis. He had studied that part of Mark's anatomy carefully—he had actually seen it briefly, which made a huge difference. His eyes were closed now… he was transported to that world where these emotions, these feelings were allowed…

Rita pictured herself riding now, impaled—thighs open wide, straddling, ready to power her program; she knew when and how to employ her pelvis…

Sammy was in the wrong position, that's all there was to it. Even with nine inches I can't do what she wants without making a big shift. That isn't going to be easy, especially since I can't get these blasted pants below my knees. "I have to move some," he whispered.

Barbara knew this. She was ready now—freeing up her undergarments while doing all this kissing and caressing was a huge accomplishment. She knew he'd have to get on top completely to go any farther. "I know… go ahead, but try not to let the others know what you're doing," she spoke as softly as she could. She didn't want Rita to know how far along they were.

"Right." Slowly he twisted his torso… and with a big push, got out from under her thigh, allowing her to shift over. The seat creaked, but it held. Next, with great effort, he freed his right shoe from the pant leg—victory is at hand! now I can get the leverage I need to get my left knee in position… he swung his foot forward—

> *Crack!* <

His shoe connected sharply with the heater vent. *Darn!* The trouble is my long legs… did I break it? From the sound he could tell it was a plastic frame, not made to be kicked in the night by a size eleven brogue. No way to reach down there and see… he tapped around with his toe… nothing is loose… seems all right.

"It's *okay,*" Barbara whispered urgently. "We can look at it *later…*"

Sammy completed his move at last; he was exactly where he needed to be. Barbara was ready, and took him in hand again… she had never done this, but she had sure studied all about it.

There is a wonderful gloss spread over the real world when ecstasies of sex and romance are in process. Various states of undress, awkward positions, disheveled hair and clothing—random disorder, the result of hurried urgent needs being met by the most expedient route available—these do not interfere because the participants are not worried about how they might appear—their current sensory receptors define the world, and it is beautiful.

Until something shatters the gloss, that is. Sammy's unfortunate kick to the wall of the passenger well popped the bubble. That was the shoe that had picked up an uninvited passenger. The heel of a wingtip brogue has a sharp front edge—and when new, a crisply sculpted logo stamped into the smooth surfaced sole; both areas are made-to-order depositories for things stepped upon—whether it be grass clippings, mud, or soft, highly malleable tokens left by Grace Connelly's five year old dachshund named "Weenie Girl."

When even a small quantity of that material becomes lodged in a car heater's air vent, the effect is almost instantaneous—especially if the temperature setting and fan are on the high position.

Just as Rita's right hand was on the way to grasp Julian's pulsing six inches the second it sprang free, a rich rancid stench struck her nostrils full force.

Just as Barbara was directing the tip of Sammy's enormous instrument toward her most sacred place, she too received a blast of sour rank air.

Both boys got the aromatic punch in the nose at the same time.

"Eeew!" four voices screamed in unison.

The gloss was gone, utterly—it had been replaced by the instinct to escape.

It wasn't pretty. Sammy's pants dangled on his left foot as he burst out the passenger door, and he landed on his backside in the gravel; at least his shirt was still on. Barbara's blouse was wide open and her bra hung by one strap; her panties were down to her knees. But her skirt was in the right place, so when she leapt out of the driver's side it fell into place. She was the lucky one.

In the back seat, Rita had secretly loosed her bra and blouse from behind, and she was exposed from the waist up; she had not yet made her adjustment below—her Daisy Mae skirt needed none; it was already wide open. The sole obstacle to beginning her lap dance could be pulled to the side in an instant—Julian wouldn't know how to do what Tracy always did, but she could take care of it with ease. She didn't get the chance.

Julian, who had not even noticed Rita's spectacular topside, was worse off than the others: his overalls fell to the ground as he jumped out, causing him to trip and fall flat on his face. The laws of physics enabled Little J to make his long sought escape, too late for anyone to see. Fortunately, when the door swung open, the yellow rubber slicker sprang out and unfolded precisely where it would be needed a split second later. The polo shirt made the least dramatic exit; it had slipped off the end of the seat earlier and was resting on the doorsill when the exodus began. It was the last item to depart, landing on the gravel without making a sound.

The radio and the fan played on, oblivious, and loud: four doors opened wide had unleashed a sudden torrent of sound—not particularly welcome by the occupants of the other cars—nor to the wildlife. At least one steamed up window lowered an inch—presumably someone was free enough to check out what was going on over there. Whoever it was chose not to intervene.

Could it get worse? Only if a car were to come into the parking area before the escapees had time to cover themselves. Alas… only Julian was spared; he had the good fortune to pull up his shoulder strap in the nick of time… caught standing in the center of a curious bright yellow semi-circle, he was the only one to escape having private areas of his anatomy bathed in a brilliant splash of white light. It took three or four seconds for the beams to swing away and head to the other side of the promontory—but it seemed like an hour.

All four were frozen like a deer in the middle of the highway staring at a blinding light—unaware that it was about to be punted into eternity by a speeding car whose driver hadn't seen it in time. Two topless girls on the left side of the car, one in the world's skimpiest mini-skirt; and on the right side, a tall gangly kid with his pants around his ankles—wagging an incredible erection that looked like it was a foot long if it was an inch. Who even noticed that the blond hick in overalls wasn't wearing a shirt?

In their haste to dress and sort out what had fouled the atmosphere inside the car, no one checked to see if that late arrival was anyone who attended Jackson… in other words, anyone who might have recognized them.

22 The day after

"Good morning, this is Geraldine." She glanced at her watch… it's a little early, but you never know. She always answered her telephone as if a prospective buyer was at the other end. Sundays are always popular for working people who want to see a property or two.

"You might want to come over here," Francine whispered.

Geraldine went cold. "Why—what's happened?" Whatever it is, it had to be something to do with Julian—last night was the big dance.

A pause… Francine didn't know how to answer.

"Is he all right?"

"I think so—he's still asleep…"

"Franc*eeene…*" Geraldine *hated* being kept in suspense.

"I'm going to let him sleep in. He didn't get in until midnight." Julian's usually asleep by eleven.

"MMmm!" Geraldine approved. "What did he have to say?"

"I don't know… nothing—I dozed off and he snuck by me. When I woke up he was in bed, sound asleep. From what I can see this morning though, I think everything must have gone fine…"

"What do you mean, 'see'?"

"He still has lipstick on his face—he didn't wash up."

Geraldine squealed in delight. "I'm coming right over! Don't let him wake up!" She dashed across the room to fetch her purse and keys.

—𝔪—

Julian was having the *strangest* dream…

he was trying to get to the boys room, but this heavy rubber coat slowed him down. everyone's standing around… no one will help. there's Norman and Teddy, but they're too busy talking about the punch. Sammy's there already, blasting away with that fire hose; the spotlight makes it look even bigger. what's it like to have one that big? after playing with Alpha and Beta he almost knew. man, what if I can't get this blamed thing open when I get there? the pressure is getting kind of bad—Little J wants to go this minute!

> *Klink-le lingkling-ing!* <

Julian awoke with a flinch, eyes wide open—teaspoon… clattering on the kitchen table! What's going on? Am I late? It's *Sunday*—what about church? His head wasn't fully awake.

I have to take a whiz, *now!* He tossed the blankets aside and leapt out of bed. In three steps he was past the drawing table and poised to race out of the room—*skivvies!* He stopped just in time… I don't dare run to the bathroom nude—especially not with a stiffy! He doubled back and slipped them on… thank goodness they're right by the bed. He zipped back to the bedroom doorway, grabbed the frame as an anchor and catapulted himself around the corner toward the bathroom without stopping to think about anything. I have to get there *fast!* The fact that his bedroom door wasn't closed didn't register.

> **Wham!** <

"Ow!" His elbow clipped the bathroom door—it bounced back and slammed shut behind him. He lifted the toilet seat and pulled the waistband down just in time.

Startled, Geraldine and Francine stopped talking and looked at each other. Francine raised a finger to her lips in a silent shush. She cupped her ear. "I think it's the under-pressure-in-the-morning problem." She tilted her head, expecting to hear the telltale sound. "He doesn't always think to piddle before going to bed." Men. His father was the same way.

"Ahh," Geraldine nodded, reassured.

—⁂—

Man alive! I don't think I've *ever* been this hard. He had to bend over and *force* Little J to point into the bowl. "So, *start* already!"

Little J was being stubborn. He enjoyed being up full in the morning. Why should he always have to go down just because Big J wanted to take a pee? He was going to stay up for as long as he could.

Geraldine listened intently for her cue: the second Julian opened the bathroom door, she intended to summon him: she wanted a report before he could do anything else. Her peek into his room a few minutes ago was a disappointment—he had turned in his sleep, making it impossible to see the lipstick smears. She had to see for herself what he looked like. She'd persuaded Francine to let him stay out late for a reason. She knew from experience that a boy needed some time to get around to doing anything, especially on a first date. That extra hour is *crucial*; she was *dying* to know the details.

Little J was forced to relent. But he didn't give up completely—unfinished business needed attention; he'd been forced to stop suddenly last night, *three times*, and they never got going again before Big J went to sleep. Little J wanted to take care of that first thing, now that he was awake. Sometimes Big J forgot that there was no going back after a certain point. It could be painful if the job didn't get finished—last night's delivery needs to be made, that's all. If Big J doesn't take care of this pretty soon, Little J would find a way to make him pay attention.

Darn it… there's more left in the tank… > *ungk!* < He tried to force it out, but Little J refused to go limp enough. The flip, wag and squeeze thing Sammy did last night might work… *oo*-oo: that wasn't such a hot idea… don't want another stiffy… I hafta get dressed for church. He tucked himself away, pointing Little J down. I'll just have to finish later. He pushed the handle.

The second she heard the flush, Geraldine leaned toward the doorway; when the bathroom door swung open, she sang out: "We're in here, Julian!"

Oh boy. I should have known she'd be here. Ordinarily it wouldn't matter; all my life I've run around in my shorts when Geraldine and Mom are around—no big deal. But Little J is trying to go back up… I shouldn't have done the Sammy thing. "I'm in my skivvies!"

Geraldine grinned at Francine. "So what else is new?" She winked mischievously. "We promise not to look. We're at the kitchen table." She grinned. Silly boy… he didn't mind last week during the costume session; I've seen him in his undies his entire life.

Francine was amused by her boy's sudden attack of modesty—rarely one of his traits.

Julian grimaced. It's a good thing I stopped to put these on! They could have been sitting in the living room and seen everything! He held his hands in front and scurried into the kitchen. His regular chair was pulled out, waiting. Thank goodness for that. Maybe Little J will go back to sleep before I have to stand up again.

Francine watched her boy scoot into his chair. My… it's hard to believe he's grown so tall. His uncombed hair warmed her heart—in the morning he still looks like my little boy. Except for the lip prints…

Geraldine was able, just barely, to keep a straight face. Rita's bright red lipstick marks were still clear—they could have been planted there five minutes ago. She waited as long as she could, which was about two seconds. "Well?"

Julian looked at Geraldine with a big grin—he had not spent a minute thinking about this, but that's okay. This dance is important to her… she was there to see me off when Rita came to pick me up—she gave me a special hug and told me to have a good time. She even put the hat on my head.

"Boy, were you ever right!" he started eagerly; the expression on her face made him feel good. "It was so cool, they way they had it set up." He described the farmyard and all the layout details, and then all about the costume parade. "I never did see where the judges were, either." He paused to think…

Francine was on the way to the refrigerator. "Maybe they were teachers." She poured his glass of orange juice. I wonder… should I make breakfast? She glanced at the clock—we'll never make it to church anyway…

Julian considered that… come to think about it, how many teachers were there? Other than Miss Fredericks, I didn't see any around. "Dunno," he shrugged. "Anyway," he looked back at Geraldine. "I wasn't the only Li'l Abner!" He told all about the variations in the costume… he wanted to go through the evening in the order it happened—telling about the award has to be last. "But I was the only one with boots."

"What's the matter with that?" Li'l Abner always wears boots.

He told about how he had stepped on Rita's foot. "I thought I'd wrecked everything." His look of fear turned into a grin. "But she was okay. She asked me to take them off…. was I ever glad. It was *way* easier to dance."

Geraldine recalled the dance lessons. Fortunately, he had not worn his boots for those.

Soon, Geraldine and Francine were swept up into the event. His infectious enthusiasm was so detailed it almost came to life—at times they felt like they had been there. He talked a mile a minute. Francine was so happy: his first dance went well after all; she had been worried a little… the one thing he never talked about was girls. There's nothing to worry about… he had a *terrific* time.

"Next we did the exchange dance." He paused a second to finish off his juice. "I got to dance with Theresa for that one."

Geraldine and Francine exchanged a surprised look.

"She was fun to dance with. She even knew how to do the Mashed Potato."

"The what?" Francine had never heard of a *dance* called that…

Julian checked Geraldine… she shook her head no too. He scratched his head. "It's kinda hard to describe…" he thought a sec. "I know!" A demonstration… he scooted his chair back and stepped out into the center of the kitchen. Plenty of space. "You hold your arms out in front, and one at a time you shake them up and down like this." He shook his left arm. "Then you take the opposite foot, and you pretend you're squishing a potato under it." He bent and squished an imaginary potato with his right foot. "Then you switch and do it with the other foot."

He demonstrated the entire sequence several times. "'Course, you do it in time with the song." He returned to his chair. "They never said why it was called that."

The ladies were at a loss for words; he certainly learns to dance fast. The bizarre dance step had just demonstrated something besides a new dance: Julian was growing up: defined muscles had begun to show on his chest and legs. The smooth undeveloped boy they were used to seeing run around the house was a creature of the past. Luckily, he was fully clothed last night. Both ladies formed an image in their mind of the very attractive girl that had picked him up at the door. Unfortunately, they had not gotten acquainted when she stopped by… the other couple was waiting in the car, so a proper interview wasn't possible.

"Anyway, it was lucky that Theresa knew how to do that. I was sure glad it wasn't Rita!" When he saw the expression on their faces he realized his goof. On purpose, he had not mentioned anything about Rita's boobs. How am I going to get out of this?

They're staring so intently… where are you, Inside guy? Oh well… he shrugged. "See, when Theresa did the arm thing, she also shook her top back and forth real good." He demonstrated by moving his shoulders back and forth.

They're still staring… he took a deep breath. "Y'see, Rita wore this Daisy Mae blouse… it was just like the one in the funnies, y'know? Half her chest poked out the top." He hesitated, unsure how to say this. "I was afraid… I mean… what if they popped all the way out?"

The ladies exploded in hysterics.

Julian was nonplused. It wasn't funny *at all.* He'd worried about that most of the dance. Their reaction amazed him. Maybe it's because I said chest. Well, I couldn't very well say *boobs*, could I? What are you *supposed* to call them, anyway? Who do I ask?

They had a breakfast break. They had to; the ladies couldn't stop breaking up. The image painted by his words took a while to manage.

Just as well… gave him time to think a little. Little J had gone to sleep, mostly; a little puffy because of demonstrating the potato—that started to wake him up again. I could feel him swinging back and forth, up and down—he likes that. It's a good thing I didn't do that any longer. He's real touchy today… not so good, considering what I haven't told yet. Some of it has to do with Little J—I don't dare talk about *that*. I have to figure a way around it. They don't *know* about him, for one thing… doesn't disappear like he used to. I've looked in the mirror: even limp you can see him, easy—'cept in the boxers.

After breakfast he went to fetch the certificate. This will be fun. Geraldine was adding sugar to her coffee when he came back. He held it behind his back and waited. When he had their attention, he asked. "Guess what?"

Francine and Geraldine looked at each other and shrugged.

Julian whipped the certificate from behind and held it toward Geraldine. "We won. I was made best Li'l Abner!" He placed the certificate on the table beside her coffee.

Geraldine's mouth dropped—she turned red, enormously pleased. She picked up the award and stared at it. Francine leaned close to see… and gave her a sisterly hug.

"They had this big spotlight on, and I had to go clear across the room all by myself. But I didn't care; I ran all the way, swinging my boots—Rita made me take them along, 'cuz it was part of the costume. I pretended you were there… you're the reason I won. All I did was wear the clothes." Seeing how happy they are is great… you don't get to see that every day.

Tears filled Geraldine's eyes. She tried to blink them away, but it was no good. She looked up at Julian, but was unable to form words.

He bent over and gave her a hug. "Thanks, Aunt Geraldine." He hugged his mom too and sat back down.

The ladies took a minute to calm themselves. After patting the stray teardrops dry and refilling their cups, they were ready for Julian to continue.

"Guess what happened next!" he bounced up and down in his chair. Their eager expressions were terrific. "Rita won best Daisy Mae!" He clapped his hands together. "She grabbed my hand and pulled me along." He paused. "I don't know why. I didn't deserve any credit—maybe she didn't want to go over into the spotlight all alone…it was super blinding." Julian remembered her taking a bow… by then it was clear that her boobs weren't going fall out, so he wasn't worried. Best not to mention that—don't want to cause another laughing jag.

"They called her the Queen of the Dance, and she took a bow to everyone. Then she swings around and gives me this giant hug, and smacks me one, right on the mouth!" He looked down at the table.

He did not see the wide-open eyes across the table—he was too busy recalling the details and keeping them in the right order.

Geraldine had grabbed Francine's hand under the table and gripped tight. He had just described the first kiss! Is that the one he's still wearing?

"Well, she was so happy, I couldn't really blame her, y'know. She was so grateful and all. So I bowed a thank-you to her afterwards."

"Then they had a slow dance—the *Moon River* song—she really liked that one. She pulled me super close and pressed her cheek right next to mine when we danced." He saw his mom's eyes go big. "It was okay… no big deal—practically everybody I could see was dancing that way. After a while, they made the spotlight squeeze down until it was gone."

Geraldine wondered if the press was there. The lead photo and headline were easy to picture. She reconsidered her first reaction; Rita had turned into her ally after all… Julian can't escape notice now; they'll be fighting over him before Thanksgiving.

"The last dance was just the opposite! The *Twist*! Do you know that one?"

The ladies shook their heads.

"It's kind of like that Mashed Potato. Instead of waving your arms you pump them like you're running up the stairs or something. And you wag your rear all the time you're mashing your feet." Julian shook his head. "I don't get what they see in those dances, to be honest. People were all over the place—sometimes you couldn't tell where your partner was."

He didn't tell why he was glad it was the next dance—skipping over Rita's surprise massage during *Moon River* and what it had caused was important—telling about *that* would be a very bad idea.

"Then they turned on the gym lights, and it was all over!"

The ladies sat back and relaxed. Time for a break—the next part could be the big news part. Geraldine took charge. "What a *wonderful* time, Julian…you describe it so well. But before you tell about the rest of your date, I need to visit the powder room." She stood and looked at him affectionately. "Don't you *dare* go away!" She turned to Francine. "Too many cups of coffee. Start another pot, will you?"

"Thank you, Julian," Francine looked her son in the eye. "I can't tell you how happy I am for you. I'm so glad you had such a good time. I wish my first dance had been that nice."

His concern was automatic.

"No, no, don't mistake me. I didn't have a *bad* time. Not a bad time at all. It wasn't as special as yours, I guess. I didn't win any prizes." She had to ask this. "What did you think about the big kiss?"

"**Don't you *dare* talk about that until I get back!**" Geraldine shouted from the bathroom. "**Make that coffee**!" She had left the door open a smidge just in case. Very wise.

Julian and his mom looked at each other sheepishly and giggled. Automatically they got up and went across to the sink. Julian assisted by emptying the old grounds while his mom rinsed out the percolator.

"There. That's better," Geraldine announced, re-entering the kitchen. She gave Francine a do-you-need-a-potty-break-too? look.

Francine nodded. It wasn't pressing, but it would be a good idea. "Be right back," and she stepped gingerly out. "Same rules, Geraldine!" she added, halfway to the bathroom.

Julian thought the ladies in his life were funny. Geraldine was his mom's boss, but they were more friends than anything. Sometimes they were rivals, sometimes scrappy, but mostly they were pals. He liked that.

“So, what *did* you think?” Geraldine whispered. Maybe I can coax something out before she gets back.

Julian crossed his arms and shook his head. “Hafta wait,” he smirked. He didn’t get a chance to say no to Geraldine, ever—that was fun too.

Geraldine gave a mock pout.

He loved it. Then he felt the pressure himself. The cold water from cleaning the coffee insides made him want to go. “I get to go next.”

“Well hurry, then,” Francine reentered the room. “We’re waiting.” She went to check the coffee.

Zoom! He raced to the potty.

—ᵒᵒᵒ—

Emptying the tank was easy this time; Little J was asleep—or was until Julian wagged him good afterwards. On purpose he had not done the Sammy squeeze again—but Sammy’s comment about leaving stains had made an impression; might as well add a few extra shakes.

If Little J had been able to stretch and yawn like a person, he would have; he did the best imitation he could, tucked back into his skivvy nest. It always felt good to nuzzle against the cotton when Big J was standing up. He didn’t need a squeeze; he’d been on standby all morning.

Julian felt the tingle. “Don’t you dare do that,” he whispered. “I still hafta tell about the car.”

It felt a little silly, talking to Little J like that. But really, I have to tell why I came home late and tell about what the guy at the gas station found out. I have to be real careful because of what almost happened. It *didn’t* happen, so why even tell anything? Besides, I haven’t had time to think about that whole massage thing yet. I still don’t understand how a girl was able to give me a stiffy! *Twice!* The *same* night. Something weird is going on, that’s all.

Little J didn't get any bigger… but he didn't go back down all the way, either. He liked being slightly puffy. That was how he'd stay for a while. He was on standby, ready to do another stretch or two, first chance.

—~—

When he returned to the kitchen, Julian could tell he had it figured right—from the way they sat it was easy to see that this was the part they had been waiting to hear about all morning. He had a plan. I'll tell about everything *except* the Little J part. That's what I did before and it worked just fine. No reason to think I can't do that again. He scootched to get comfy—kitchen chairs are kinda hard after a while: I'm not used to sitting here for hours like they are.

"I thought we were gonna go for pizza," he began. "I heard some kids talking about that. But Barbara took us to this fancy pie place over by that park. I don't remember the name…"

"You mean Amanda and June's?" Geraldine took clients there frequently; I've closed a lot of sales there over the years. I always take Francine there… she has an uncanny ability to choose the perfect dessert.

"Yeah!" The name was on the menu. "Real fancy place. We had cocoa. It was good and hot—perfect because it was so cold outside."

Geraldine was curious about where they sat, but chose not to interrupt.

"Then Barbara suggested that we go up to a place called Fowler's Point. It sounded neat—she said you could see the whole town from up there." He looked at his mom eagerly. "She was *right*, too! It's super up there. I wish I had my sketchbook along, but I didn't. So I studied it good."

I'm getting ahead of myself… "See, I asked Rita if we could get out of the car to look at it for a minute. The back seat wasn't any good for getting a good look."

“What did Rita say?” Geraldine asked evenly, carefully masking her suspicions.

“Oo, she thought that was a brilliant idea. So we got out and went over to the edge.” He explained all about what he had seen, the fascinating interplay of the stars shining down on the sea of lights below, and how he located several possible compositions. “There were a couple or three other cars up there—no problem; we just walked around behind so we wouldn’t block their view.”

“Were they from the dance too?” Geraldine was surprised there weren’t more.

“Dunno—I didn’t look in.” That would be kind of rude. One arrived later, but I can’t talk about *that*. “I want to go up there in the daytime. I bet I could get lots more ideas if I saw it under the sun instead of the moon.”

“Didn’t you get cold?” Francine was worried that he might have gotten a chill.

“Nah, that big rubber coat was plenty warm. But Rita got cold real fast. So she asked if she could get in there too, since there was lots of room.”

Geraldine perked up at that bit of news.

“It wasn’t that bad, actually… her perfume was mostly worn off before the dance was over.” He looked at Geraldine and twisted his nose. “It was pretty potent when we first got there.” Unconsciously, he rubbed his nose. “She was very considerate, I thought. She said that we should let Barbara and Sammy have a few minutes alone. Huddling with me for a little wasn’t that big a deal. That’s when I explained to her how I was going to draw up the picture.

Francine stirred her cup absentmindedly, picturing a girl cuddled up in that yellow rain slicker with her boy. She exchanged a glance with Geraldine.

“But she got cold after a while anyway, so we went back to the car.” He broke into a big grin. “That was fun! We pretended it was like a sack race. Kinda awkward at first—I was afraid I might step on her foot again… but we made it okay.” He shrugged, “kinda surprising, since we never practiced." He paused to think a second… the tricky part is coming up. "Boy, were we surprised!" Julian wiped his brow, remembering the heat. "The heater was going full blast all the time we were outside, and it was like a *furnace* in there! So we had to take off our coats." He gave Geraldine a news flash: "Y'know, those slickers aren't all that easy to take off when you're in the back seat of a car." He paused again… do I tell about what was on the radio?

You didn't pay any attention to the radio, silly. Inside guy had shown up at last.

Geraldine had to concede that the slicker was overkill; I didn't have a good choice there—it was about the only thing the crew was able to come up with. She stirred her cup again. Buying something for a single occasion didn't make sense.

The sound caught his attention. I better get back to telling the story. "See, the motor was running, the fan was going full blast, and the radio was on, pretty loud. Rita says, 'should we ask them to turn it down?' She was talking about the heater, I think. I thought maybe we could just roll down the window or something. The thing is, they were…" how do I say this? "I mean Barbara and Sammy… I don't know what they were doing; I couldn't see them because it was too dark."

That was a fib… the white handkerchief on the dashboard was all I could see up front… it wasn't dark at all because of the moon outside.

"Rita said she didn't want to disturb them." Another fib! Yikes… telling this is harder than I thought. Julian had never faced a task like this… he didn't have a script, and he hadn't prepared. '*Go slow'* was all Inside guy could suggest.

Geraldine rolled her eyes. She'd been in the back seat herself eons ago—front seat, too; filling the gap required little or no imagination.

Francine took a careful sip—she felt Julian's discomfort… there was no way she could help.

Julian continued, a little awkwardly… "It was hard to hear on account of the radio and the fan and the motor still running. So she had to sit pretty close anyway." He gulped and rocked his head back and forth trying to find the right way to word things. "Rita asked about things, you know, if I had a good time, what I thought was best, about the dance and stuff… she noticed that I was starting to sweat pretty good. I was afraid I'd get a case of B.O. or something, you know?"

I wish I had a glass of water right now, actually. This is getting tricky. How much should I tell?

Hang in there... you're doing okay, but try no to tell any more fibs. Inside guy was usually straight laced about things like that.

"Rita was very considerate. She wasn't trying to cuddle up close because she was cold—the radio was so loud I had trouble hearing her talk. 'What?' I said. I was feeling kinda funny, actually—sort of woozy. So she says, 'why not take your shirt off?'"

Julian looked up, the desperation he had felt clearly visible. "Well, that's exactly what I wanted to do, so I did."

He didn't hear the faint chirp that came from Geraldine; his eyes had blurred… he was focused on sorting out what parts he could tell and what parts he didn't dare mention… his memory wasn't *entirely* clear…

Francine's knuckles had turned white; her hands were in her lap, clenched tight as she watched her boy laboring to talk. She wasn't surprised at Julian's eagerness to take off the shirt—that's been true his entire life. But in this case, it might not have been the best thing to do.

Just like the old days… Geraldine couldn't count the times he had shed his shirt at the office when he was little; he didn't wear a shirt all summer. But this is different… it feels suspicious somehow. It *was* Rita's suggestion, after all. What if it was planned?

Julian took a deep breath and exhaled, as if he had just stepped out of that furnace; in his memory, he had. "Boy oh boy was I glad she thought of that!" He sat back, relieved. "I felt so good all of a sudden. I could breathe again."

The ladies relaxed with him—they had begun to share his tension, his discomfort as if they too were baking.

"She was very complimentary—she started to say nice things about me, you know, my shoulders and stuff. I guess she could see me well enough, even though the windows were all steamed up, 'cause the moon was up high." He paused to collect his thoughts, and to fight Little J down again.

Little J had been lying in wait all this time; the part about the hands feeling across the shoulders and neck was the go signal… and he was good to go.

The detail about the widows being steamed up caught the ladies' attention at once: now they were on the edge of their chairs…

… Of course they were steamed up! An image flashed into Geraldine's mind… Julian's uncovered torso, glistening with perspiration in the moonlight… she had just seen that torso demonstrate the Mashed Potato. For a second she pretended to be in Rita's Daisy Mae blouse… If I had been sharing that cozy back seat, what would I do?

… A claustrophobic urge made Francine want to open the car door so her boy could escape—the steamed up windows, the stifling heat, the radio… the bursting Daisy Mae blouse…

The ladies held their breath awaiting Julian's next words.

"All of a sudden, Sammy had some kind of problem up front. He was moving or trying to do something, and he kicked the heater by mistake. It made a loud crack sound. That's when it happened." Julian had just leapt over the key part. He sensed victory.

"IT?" asked Geraldine and his mom in unison.

"All of a sudden there was a terrible *smell* everywhere. It was awful, and strong—*thick* or something. We couldn't *breathe,* it was so bad. So everybody had to jump out of the car as fast as they could."

He did not describe the various stages of undress; he hadn't seen them all. Sammy's pants were down around his ankles, but I better not tell about *that*. I never did figure out why my overalls fell off. I couldn't see the other side of the car; by the time I had put myself back together, so had everyone else. I don't need to tell about that car shining its headlights on us.

"At first, we couldn't find what it was. It was too dark. Finally, Barbara says 'turn off that radio!' So Sammy plugged his nose and reached in. It helped, a little. Then he checks his shoe and sees—he stepped on some dog do-do somewhere."

Geraldine and Francine covered their mouths to hold in their shock and laughter—they had to hear the sorry end.

"The problem was, nobody had a flashlight. Barbara was about to go *crazy*, and Rita says, 'Let's go for help.' So I asked if I should try to borrow a flashlight—there was another car about twenty feet away. It made sense to me, but she didn't want bother the other people up there; she's always so considerate."

Geraldine glanced at Francine… odds are, she knew they didn't want to be interrupted... Geraldine had been here before: no one in their right mind taps on a steamed up window at the town's favorite necking spot.

"So, we climbed back in and she drove as fast as she could. We left all the windows down so we could keep fresh air. I could still smell it, so I plugged my nose and poked my head out of the window the whole way. It was cold, but that didn't matter. That gas station on Banner Street was open, and we pulled in. The guy helped us as much as he could—he had an extra big flashlight—but he said that we'd have to get to a shop. Some of the do-do was squished through the safety grille: it had to be taken apart to be cleaned. I took his word for it. Barbara tried to get him to fix it then and there, but he didn't want to do it—all he did was turn the thing off." Julian wrinkled his nose. "Who could blame him? He had to be free to wait on other people when they came in. He stuffed a paper towel in the vent opening; that helped some, actually."

"Well, there wasn't anything we could do. Besides, it was almost midnight already, and I was supposed to be home—I think everyone was. Rita and Barbara were in kind of a bad mood anyway. So they brought me home first.

"I felt so sorry for Sammy. It wasn't his fault, really, but it sort of was." He had watched Sammy use the gas station hose to clean off the shoe. "Man… what if *I* had stepped on it, with my boots?!" I checked just to be sure.

"When I got home I came in as quiet as I could… I didn't want to wake you up or anything, so I just tiptoed into my room. I was really tired, so I fell asleep quick. He paused. "It seems kinda funny now, but it wasn't last night. Poor Sammy."

"Poor Barbara," said Geraldine. She assumed that Sammy's kick was a simple accidental reflex… it wasn't too hard to imagine what might have caused something like that.

"Poor Rita," said Francine, suppressing a smile. She had a hunch that her boy had been rescued in the nick of time; she wasn't sure if Rita was up to something, but if she was, her son was defenseless. There had been no talk about back seat rules—or dangers.

What a relief… I got through it. I only told two fibs, and I didn't have to tell about Little J—that's the important thing. He took a deep breath. "Mom?"

"Yes, dear?"

"Can we go up there today? You know, to that Fowler's Point?" I want to make that sketch.

Francine paused. That was the last thing she had thought about doing. One look at Julian's face was all it took. "Why, yes. I've not been up there myself." She issued Geraldine a silent invitation.

Absolutely, Geraldine nodded back.

"First, though, I think you should wash your face."

Julian tilted his head.

"How long since you looked in a mirror?"

Huh. "Dunno… not since I finished putting on the Li'l Abner clothes, I guess." Didn't even cross my mind.

Francine kept a straight face and pointed to the bathroom.

Geraldine had a grin that he didn't like. What is she talking about? He hurried to look.

He saw the lipstick marks on his face for the first time.

"Oh, *NO!*" He stared at himself in disbelief. I remember the big smack in the spotlight. A zillion people saw that! He swung his head back and forth and saw the small but vividly clear imprint on his left cheek. How did I get *that*? She didn't do that in the car…

He walked back to the kitchen like a zombie and looked at his mom then at Geraldine, his mouth hanging open. He wanted to shout out 'why didn't somebody tell me,' but couldn't say a word. He stood there for a minute, mute; then turned slowly and returned to the bathroom. The one on my cheek… when did she do that? I don't remember her kissing me besides that one time… was it during that Moon River dance when she pulled me tight? No… he shook his head. She was cheek to cheek the whole time, even when she pulled me tight. This is weird. No wonder that gas station guy looked at me that way. I thought it was the yellow coat.

Does this stuff come off if it's been there all night? He turned on the hot water tap. No, wait. Take a shower: better do a full scrub-down. He felt uggy, soiled, marked. It was like losing his… what's the word? Not honor… but it was a matter of pride to never have kissed a girl. Worse yet, the whole world knows about it.

Little J was happy; the skivvies coming off meant that his chance had come. The shower is a great place to take care of things; we'll get caught up at last. No need for a go signal… before the water was up to temperature, Little J was roaring ready.

In the kitchen, the ladies had a new task. While relishing the comedic narrative Julian had delivered, they had to adjust to the mixed picture they had just seen. The shocked horrified look on his face was priceless—however… the bulge in his shorts was totally unexpected. Their little boy was no longer a *little* boy!

Francine had an unwelcome flash of memory—she had seen Adrian more than a few times in a very similar state. In ten years, except for his eyes, Julian will look just like him.

A ripple of secret pleasure accompanied Geraldine's memory. She could see Adrian as clearly in her mind's eye as if it was yesterday. What a wild time that was! His boy will be just as magnificent—of that she had no doubt. She looked at Francine—the stone cold look on her face revealed that she had seen the same thing. Geraldine helped by breaking the silence.

"Do you think he likes her?"

Francine hadn't considered that. "I have no idea…" she pondered. "He thinks she's considerate. He said that more than once."

"Mmm…" that word certainly applied to Julian; shrewd would be a better word to describe Rita. Geraldine feared that her plan might have gone too well… I'm not ready for Julian to *settle down*.

They stared at each other briefly. The sound of the shower and ceiling fan in the background filled the void while they sorted out their thoughts. Silently, they were in agreement about one thing: their boy had survived a close call.

"If he asks her out in return, I guess we'll know." He never talks about girls. Francine knew better than to press him.

Geraldine hated to be in suspense about anything—especially this. But she was smart enough to sit back and watch… for a while. It was obvious that Julian had left out a few details. It's too bad he's not still on the crew… that would have been a good secondary source.

Julian dried his hair with vigor—the last step after taking a nice long shower. He tucked the towel into the rack and stepped over to the mirror… no trace of Rita's imprint remained. Good; he was done with Rita as well. He was grateful to her in a way, but having that dance over and done with was a big relief. He still hadn't completely worked out what had happened—how did I end up with Little J poking out like that? I was so wrapped up thinking about Mark I lost track of everything else.

He stepped back and took a fresh look at himself. Boy, it's great to do this without that stool. Hmm. There's Little J, looking satisfied, still half puffy. Julian wasn't satisfied though. Quick ones in the shower never really satisfied.

The dark hairs around the base were easy to see now. They had shown up finally, last summer. After searching for them every week—ever since the *seventh* grade—wouldn't you know, it was Sid who saw them first. Hard to believe that was only five months ago.

He and Sid had "compared notes" about their relative progress one day in the cabin; Sid was well ahead in the race to grow pubic hair. Randall has a full crop already. What causes that, anyway? Maybe you have to have to be Swedish or something. That can't be it, Swedes are blond too… it must have something to do with having dark hair, though… Tony and Danny have super jungles down there.

He wagged Little J back and forth a couple of times. It always felt nice when it was puffy. Little J responded, as expected.

"Man, it doesn't take much to get you going, does it? I just gave you a good one!" I sure wish you could talk. What's going on down there, anyway?

One thing Julian *had* figured out: he wasn't in charge of Little J all the time. That was troubling—especially after what happened at the dance and afterward, in the car! It didn't do one bit of good to say no. I tried that a hundred times, but once Little J got started, he went right up anyway, no matter what or where. Now I appreciate Randall's problem at the troop meeting—the same thing happened to me last night.

"The thing is, I don't wear baggy overalls around all the time." The dummy in the mirror nodded in agreement.

I was lucky to have those on. What if it hadn't been at night? What if that awful smell hadn't happened? It was a miracle in a way—if that hadn't happened, Rita would have seen you for sure. *Look* at you!

Little J rose up again, unassisted. Julian watched, fascinated. He had always liked the feeling down there when that happened. I'm gonna time that one of these days. Sometimes it's real fast, like now—it was super fast when she rubbed my buns, too—like somebody flipped a switch. !!! Whoa! I just remembered something… Mark warned me! Julian turned around and looked at his bare buns in the mirror. Last summer, at camp—all that fuss about Choice Buns. One night in the cabin I asked Mark what Choice Buns meant. He asked if I had ever wanted to pet a puppy or a kitten, and why. I told him I did; I liked to because I liked how they felt. He told me that I'd have to be on my guard—that some people liked to pet buns for the same reason.

He looked at the reflection for a minute… they didn't look particularly special. About the only buns that looked special were Mark's. I wouldn't mind petting those. He turned back around; there's Little J again, wagging away as usual.

"I'm not giving you another one now!" Cripes. Mom and Geraldine are still yacking away in the kitchen. I hafta go into my room and put on some clothes so we can go up that hill.

Just in case, he wrapped the bath towel around himself and checked the mirror again—this is the same wrap style Mark used in the cabin. It's okay, 'cept Mom's towels aren't anywhere as big. Is anything revealed the way Mark was… hmm. He didn't have a stiffy like I do… I'll walk fast.

23 Lunch with Theresa

Amazing how fast the school year is zooming ahead… Julian was on his way to meet Randall at the bicycle rack. Ever since the campout, they had met there and gone into the building together—it simplified things. He didn't think of Randall as a boyfriend, but as a buddy, like in scouts.

Speaking of scouts, Mark sure looked impressive marching in the Veteran's Day parade yesterday—the TV station had two different cameras; they showed us marching in front of City Hall! It's weird to see yourself on TV. Mark and the Flaming Arrow Patrol were the front line, just like on the Fourth of July. Getting to march down Main Street right next to him—boy, was that ever great. Little J was good the whole time—at least during the actual parade. Afterward—well, it wasn't Little J's fault Mark gave me that special squeeze on my shoulder. Nobody noticed; it was after we were done marching.

How do I put that parade in the scrapbook? Do they keep those movies? I should check on that. The best thing about yesterday was having lots of time to get caught up on homework.

Two things were on Julian's mind this morning: first, asking Mr. van Horn how to draw a night picture—the view from that Fowler's Point was a lot more interesting at night. The trip up there on Sunday didn't help much. The autumn trees would look better in a watercolor—too late this year, since over half the leaves are gone. I hafta wait until sixth period for that. The other thing, the most important one, is telling Randall about the dance. I need to tell him about what Little J did; maybe he'll have an idea about what caused that. At least no one else knew; if it weren't for Sammy, Rita *would* have. Talk about a close call. Telling about Sammy and his shoe will be fun.

Too bad I can't do that before lunch—he doesn't know it, but we're going to eat in the cafeteria today. I made the mistake of mentioning Theresa's invitation to Mom and Geraldine when we went up to Fowler's Point. Now it's *required*; me and my big mouth. But with him to keep me company, what can go wrong? I've been meaning to look around in there anyway—that's one place I haven't done any drawing. I can tell him about the dance after school.

Julian checked out the half dozen bikes parked in the racks—Randall's isn't here. Good… that gives me a minute to check out the area… drawing this up will be fun. Where would I draw this from? He put his books down by the base of the light pole and did a slow walk-around in search of a good perch—where you draw from is what defines what you draw. Other students were arriving, so he had to stay out of the way and keep an eye out for Randall—he'll be here any minute. Hmm… too bad I can't climb up the light pole; I bet it looks cool from up there…

A puff of wind peeled back the left side of his jacket, revealing his sky blue shirt. Normally, Monday is blue shirt day, but since there was no school yesterday, I put on blue today. Might as well—the yellow one is still in the laundry. He buttoned it up securely and returned to the light pole to wait.

The shirt wasn't visible now because his jacket was buttoned up completely. That was just as well: he didn't know yet *why* keeping his shirt covered would be a good thing to do this morning—nor why he might have been better off if he hadn't worn it. He didn't realize that the blue shirt made him look *extremely* attractive, almost *irresistible*; that's why Geraldine had selected it. Wearing it was like standing in a spotlight. That was the *last* thing he needed, but he didn't know that either. He didn't know lots of things, but he figured that was no big deal—everyone in the world was in the same boat there, if you thought about it.

Today, assuming what he didn't know was "no big deal" was not going to be at all helpful—for example, not knowing what other people, girls most of all, had been talking about for the last two days. On the phone, after church, and about everywhere in town: in over a hundred separate conversations, Julian had been referred to as one of the major highlights of the Sadie Hawkins dance. Interest in him had skyrocketed; a mythology had begun to form—partly because no one knew his name. The memory of him accepting the award, and the dance with Rita in the spotlight was on its way into Girls' League Association Legend, along with a superb series of photographs—some of which would appear later in the yearbook. His mysterious, exotic appearance was reported far and wide all weekend; he was now famous: he was a celebrity. Dozens of girls had put him at the top of their find-out-all-about-him list. Had he overheard any of these conversations, his face would have turned the same color of red as that polo shirt that he planned never to wear again.

At least one head turned to watch him walk over to the bicycle rack after his mom dropped him off. Had he noticed, it might have served as a warning that something was afoot. He had no idea he was about to walk into a changed world.

Julian never paid attention to whether or not he was an object of interest. He had learned at an early age to discount all that nonsense; the more the moms gushed over him at home or at Geraldine's office, the more immune, the more insensitive to it he became. They had fawned over him mercilessly, fluffing his hair and talking silly. He just smiled and thought about something else until they got tired and quit; it had become a basic part of his survival toolkit long ago. That stuff simply didn't matter. That's why it was fine for his mom and Geraldine pick his wardrobe—saved a lot of work, letting them figure that out. That excess adulation, for as long as he could remember, had served to numb any concern about his looks. He felt no need to challenge or disagree with them, but it would be stupid to think it made any difference. He was born this way; taking any credit for it would be pretty stupid.

The only time he could remember worrying about how he looked was last summer at camp; when Nick said he had "Choice Buns," it threw him into a flurry of concerned study and activity. At the end of the week he realized that worrying about it was stupid.

He couldn't help what they looked like, and he couldn't help what anyone thought about them. They were just his butt, and all he did was sit on it; study finished, end of research. As long as they didn't massage him back there: that's new. I don't need to worry about it happening again; I can always sit down or walk away.

So Julian didn't pay any notice to whether anyone was looking at him or not. His mind was always occupied with something—scouts, a drawing, a class assignment. Unless he was looking for someone, who was out there or what they were doing didn't matter. Of course, if it was another boy sitting close by staring at him, like Randall used to… but that's different. He understood what it was like to have a crush on someone; Randall's will wear off, eventually.

As far as he knew, people ignored a person being dropped off curbside; few students arrived that way because it was socially unacceptable. It suited him just fine. It so happened that today, from the moment his mom dropped him off, heads had begun to turn his way. His jacket did not hide the wavy light gold hair. It also so happened that no one else in the school had hair like his—boy or girl. He was noticed at once; the news of his arrival was passed along in eager whispers.

—ꟿ—

Randall spotted the light blond head in the distance… excellent. The boy leaning against the bicycle rack was waiting for him to arrive. Either he's a tad early today or I'm a tad late… a glance at his watch verified that Julian was early. Looks like he's spotted something to draw. He hasn't done one from there yet. Julian has a way of tilting his head when he plans a drawing. Watching him draw was one of Randall's favorite activities. I hope he can wait until spring for this one.

"Happy November 13," he dismounted cheerfully.

"What's November 13?" Yesterday was the holiday.

"Today's date." Randall's dad pulled that one on his mom once in a while. Her reaction was always fun—she always thought she had forgotten something. It was especially funny because his father was the one who always forgot things.

It took Julian a second to get it; with a wry grin, he aimed one of Mark's pantomime pistol shots to the face with his right thumb and forefinger.

Randall enjoyed the look on Julian's face. He secured the bicycle and collected his books from the pannier baskets. As he transferred the clarinet case to his right hand, he glanced up. "So what did you do yesterday?" The offhand tone of voice was intended to mask his eagerness to hear about the dance. Every detail of what happened was essential—he wasn't worried that Julian would be swept away into a reformed life by that girl, but he did wonder what went on: two days had gone by: no word, no phone call. Why? It wasn't just any old event. I wanted to call him all day but chickened out.

"Look good on T.V." It was Julian's turn to have fun.

Randall frowned.

"Don't you watch the news? Troop Nine was in the parade; you watched us practice for it."

Randall blushed. How could I forget?! I was out in the photo lab and lost track of the time. "Sorry…" embarrassed didn't cover how he felt. He had wanted very much to see that. I knew about it, too: Marching Band practiced for weeks. Concert Band never parades, so I didn't pay attention.

Julian was surprised that Randall didn't watch the news. Oh well; no big deal.

"So you're all recovered from Saturday night, then," he quipped. Concern about that was the real reason the parade had slipped his mind.

"Just barely," he laughed. He stopped in mid thought. Being around Randall had caused him to think about things differently… especially what words to use. Randall was big on making puns; Julian had just done that by accident.

Randall caught on fast. "*Really*?" Bare, as in taking off clothes? He looked at Julian in disbelief.

"Almost. Saved at the last minute. But you have to wait. There won't be time to tell you until after school."

"What's the matter with lunchtime?"

"That's the bad news. We have to eat in the cafeteria today."

"*What?!* Why?"

"'Cause I had to promise my mom." Julian shrugged.

Oh. Randall knew about that. When you have to promise your mom, there's no point in arguing; obviously he had to agree. It would really be nice to know why, though. As they approached the giant staircase something out of the ordinary wiped the frown off his face… a group of girls had stopped talking to watch them pass by. Why would they do that? He was about to ask, but Julian had picked up his pace. He hurried to catch up. He turned back to check, and sure enough: they were talking about Julian and him. One of them was pointing; another beckoned to a fourth to come over and join them; what are they talking about?

Since the traffic was primarily one way before school, they didn't encounter anyone head on until they reached the top floor. Julian's locker was to the left, and Randall's to the right. This is where they always parted.

"See ya second period." World History was the one class they had together. Julian walked briskly—I want to get to English class a little early. For a change, I'm super ready.

"Yeah…" Randall had a funny feeling. He wasn't one to take premonitions seriously, nor omens, but something was going on. As Julian hurried down the hallway a couple more girls stopped to look at him. Why? That is, other than the obvious reason; he had grown used to being the one who did that. Sharing was not a welcome thought.

True to character, Julian didn't notice a thing. In fact, even when he took off his jacket and hung it in his locker, he failed to notice an audible gasp from six feet away as he shut his locker and made sure the lock was engaged.

His locker and most of his classes were on the top floor, along the Sophomore Hall. Sophomore girls were a minority at the dance, so he went unnoticed as usual—for the *most* part.

Classes had been fairly routine this morning, if a little disappointing. Why do they always call on you when you *aren't* prepared? In spite of the dance on Saturday and the parade yesterday, I got all my homework done. Too bad you can't put a sign on your desk saying 'pick me today.'

Maybe you deserve to be ignored when you want to show off; that's the lesson: you're supposed to be ready every day anyway, so you don't have a brag coming when you are. Hmm. Figuring out that doesn't make me feel much better… I'm starting to sound like Inside guy.

His third class was P.E.; it always interrupts things. Today we had to do laps around the gym… boring, but it provided time to rest his brain—and come up with boring observations. Now I get to go back up to the third floor. Next year I'm gonna try to get P.E. fourth period. That way I won't have to be going up and down the stairway all the time.

"Hey! Julie!" Tracy yelled.

Unaware that he was being addressed, Julian didn't react. He had a World History assignment due Friday… I'm in trouble. I still have a lot of reading to do before I can write the report; spent too much time on the illustrations. He pulled on his left sock.

Tracy frowned. "I say, **Julie!** What's the matter, pretty boy? You hard of hearing?"

That penetrated. Julian looked around as he pulled on the other sock.

"Better watch out," Jason warned. "That guy's out to get you." Never mind the fact that Tracy was a year older, had a fullback's build, and was forty pounds heavier. Since they were both in Troop

Nine, Jason buddied with Julian in P.E. He had figured out what was going on.

The shout had come from the bench on the far side—that's where the upper classmen dressed, off limits to mere sophomores. Julian recognized the guy, but didn't know his name.

"I hear you couldn't get it up after the dance. Why would *that* be, Julie?" Tracy had not heard that at all, but getting the truth was not his concern—getting his girl back in line was. She took this goldilocks to the dance instead of me!

Julian turned red. How could this guy know about the dance? In fact, I didn't try to get it up, but it happened anyway. After that, the date turned into a complete fiasco. Does this guy know about that? The image of Barbara's car speeding back to town with a head poking out of all four windows flashed into his mind.

"That's Rita's steady." Jason spoke softly. "She asked you out instead of him. *Bad* news. He's really pissed."

Julian's jaw dropped. I didn't know that. Why didn't someone *say* something?

Tracy took the blush and the dropped jaw as proof positive that Julian was guilty of something. In three strides he was across the room, over the bench and in Julian's face. He pinned him against the locker with his left arm; his right hand grabbed Julian's crotch.

Julian turned white with terror—he didn't know what to say or do. Over this guy's shoulder he could see the big guys laughing it up. Where did Jason go?

Tracy stared hard at his captive. He hadn't thought this through, so didn't know what to say, exactly. The goal was to scare the shit out of him so he wouldn't go near Rita ever again. "Well?!" He tightened his grip on Julian's basket. He could feel it resisting… good.

Julian did not know what the question was—nor was he able to say a word. He'd never been in this kind of situation. In the fourth grade I had an argument with Gene over a game of marbles, but…

"Ai—!" Suddenly, Tracy was pulled back; someone had collared him around the neck and the hand that had grabbed Julian's balls was now being forced behind Tracy's back.

It's Tom!

"What's your problem, Trace?" Tom asked, keeping his tone of voice conversational.

Tracy struggled to get free but to no avail. Tom was stronger, taller, and experienced at this—three big brothers had seen to that years ago.

"None of your business. Get off me!" He tried to free himself by kicking at Tom's leg in a clumsy wrestler's move. Tom was too fast and too smart. *"Aiee!"* Tracy's right arm was about to dislocate.

Tom spoke firmly, but politely. "Any time a buddy of mine is in trouble, it's my business." He gave the arm another pull upward between the shoulder blades. "I don't know what your beef is, but I know Julian. You are now going to apologize to him; then we can see about your complaint." He waited for a reply.

Beads of sweat broke out across Tracy's forehead. He'd never been bested like this. He was smart enough to know that he was powerless—trapped between the bench and the lockers.

"Did I hear anything?" Tom asked, tilting his head politely. "I didn't think so." He gave another upward push.

"**Aaah!** *Sonofabitch* that hurts!" Tracy was in agony, but he wasn't yelling for help—yet.

"What was that again? You need to speak up."

There was a considerable group watching by now. Tom was worried that a coach would show up and ruin things.

"All right, *all right!"* Tracy pleaded. "I'm sorry!"

"Hmm," Tom loosened the hold slightly. "I like what you said. I like it a lot. Trouble is, I don't believe you. Say it again, only nicer."

Tracy fumed with rage; the reduced pressure on his arm was carefully calculated. He had to agree, or his right arm would take weeks to recover. Somehow, someday, I'll pay Tom back, in spades. "Right." He took a couple of deep breaths and looked Julian in the face. "I'm really sorry." What he was truly sorry about was not knowing the kid had Tom for a protector.

"Gosh, Trace, that was much better," Tom said pleasantly. "I like the way you said that. Now let's sit down a minute and wrap this up, shall we?" Tom pulled him back sharply, forcing the back of his knees against the bench. Tracy sat with a hard thump. Tom released the headlock and sat next to him pressing his left hand firmly on Tracy's thigh; he kept a tight grip on the right arm, still held prisoner in a hammerlock between the shoulder blades.

Tracy knew that trying to escape wasn't worth the risk: Tom could dislocate his arm with ease; he was smart enough to behave. His eyes darted back and forth, desperate to find a way out. All he could see was the row of lockers and the blond kid. He had seen the ring of a dozen or so guys standing behind with their arms crossed, looking at him in disbelief; none of them were about to help. Tom was a senior and one of the conference's best wide receivers—untouchable.

"What am I supposed to do now?" Man, if only he'd let up a little.

Tom winked at Julian to put him at ease; after this, he wouldn't get any more trouble from Tracy. "Well, why not tell us about your problem with Julian, for openers?"

"He took my girl to the dance on Saturday, that's what!"

"Oh, is *that* all!" Tom laughed. "So it's a simple misunderstanding."

Tracy looked Tom in the face, outraged. Misunderstanding, hell!

"Actually, *she* took Julian to the dance."

Tracy fumed some more… then stopped to think. He couldn't argue the point. "He didn't have to go…"

Tom lifted his left hand and patted Tracy's leg. "Oh, but he *did* have to."

Tracy looked back in disbelief.

"Think back to your sophomore year. Did a girl invite you to the Sadie Hawkins dance?"

"Well, sure." Everyone knows they have to go...

"Was she very popular, and super hot to boot?"

Tracy shrugged and shook his head. It was before he hooked up with Rita. Gwen was good enough to look at, but a prude at heart. Besides, looks didn't count for this dance—there wasn't anything you could do about *what* they looked like. They invited, you went.

"What do you suppose would have happened if Julian had said no to your Ree-ta?"

Tracy pondered that question a minute. She would have made him suffer big time, somehow. Probably call him a fairy and generally make his life hell. I get it now... I was out of line... the kid standing there in his skivvies isn't to blame. He stopped resisting.

"I'm sorry. It wasn't your fault." What do I do now? There's no point in picking on this kid. Although... it's easy to see what Rita was after. He looked Julian up and down... if he was a girl, I'd be pretty interested myself. He shook his head to clear that idea out; he could still feel the kid's tool in his hand. If I didn't know different, I would have sworn it was starting to grow. He gave it another glance... no way to tell for sure.

Tom released Tracy's arm and patted him on the back. He whispered in his ear. "I think you should shake his hand, don't you?"

Tracy nodded. It was agony to lift his arm, but he made the attempt. "No hard feelings, okay?" All the same... what went on after the dance? Did she go all the way with this kid? He glanced down again to see if there was reason to worry... he knew what Rita liked. Not all that big… he looked back up at Julian's face… maybe nothing happened after all.

Julian smiled wide and took Tracy's hand with a nod. He didn't want to hold it for long, though: a new problem was about to make things worse… a stiffy was on the way. It would take over any second if he didn't get out of here. Ever since the guy had released his grip, Little J had been celebrating… I don't need to be wagging a stiffy all the way to Mr. Frankel's class.

Little J didn't know who had grabbed him and squeezed. He didn't care about a detail like that. He was always glad to wake up and join in whatever was happening. Day or night, Big J could depend on his Little J. He'd been re-charged and ready to go since yesterday afternoon. He enjoyed waking up… one of his favorite sensations. Sometimes, when he gave a small pulse, he got a squeeze in return; he liked those squeezes. He sent Big J another pulse… the cotton covering his shaft tightened… another favorite sensation, especially when Big J was standing—it was easier to grow from a hanging position. Maybe this will be one of those new marathons where he got to go three times in a row. He wanted to get better at that; practice makes perfect…

Julian made it to Biology without too much trouble; running up the stairway to the third floor helped, but Little J wanted to play because Tracy's grab had felt strangely good. His balls tingled for a long time afterward. Is that another after-effect of the campout? I owe Jason big for getting Tom to rescue me.

Anyway, spending an hour with Beth put Little J to sleep. She was nifty today… he had given her the surprise cuttings from the campout, and today she showed him the full written report she had prepared to go with them. They planned to turn it in as a joint project for extra credit. For the first time he looked at her directly. She is sure different from Rita. I always figured that girls, being girls, were all the same. I should know better… Mom and Geraldine are way different. Sometimes I'm amazed at how stupid I can be.

No argument about that. Inside guy made wisecracks like that sometimes.

Inside guy was good at seeing lots of things, but he was limited to what was going on inside Julian's head. He wasn't any better at noticing the outside than Julian was. He didn't notice that some of the girls in his classes watched him a lot today; he didn't see the notes being passed, didn't hear the whispers.

Beth didn't notice those girls' behavior either. Nor did she expect to be landed on after class by a flock that wanted to know all about Julian. She was now important because she knew him personally. What's it like to sit by him every day?!

Beth didn't know about the dance—didn't know anyone who did, either. She had no idea what was going on. She was a loyal member of the Girls' League, but her interest was in the annual Mother-Daughter Tea, and in winning the scholarship. It felt good to be noticed for a change, but she was wary… her first instinct was to protect Julian, to defend him if needed. It came as no surprise that other girls were interested in him. How could they *not* be?

—·—

Randall had been able to leave Geometry class first today, and was at his locker when Mr. Frankel's door opened a few feet away. Julian was the third person to emerge. "Hey, Julian!" he hollered. Good—I'll be able to talk more about my suspicions on the way to lunch.

Julian skipped over happily. "You should see Beth's report!" Randall's is sure to be good too, but—

"Hey, glad I got you in time. We need to talk."

"What's up?" I was going to do that on the way to lunch anyway.

Randall chucked his books into the locker and grabbed his clarinet case. He paused… "Do we take our sack lunches or go through the line?" Normally, they had lunch elsewhere—wherever Julian was drawing.

"Sacks. I brought mine too. We can buy a milk or OJ though." He led the way to his locker at the other end of the Sophomore Hall.

Lest he be overheard, Randall talked low. "Have you noticed anything odd going on?" He glanced around to see if they were being watched. No one so far…

"Odd?"

"Yeah… with the girls."

"I never pay them any attention… 'cept Beth, naturally." Why is Randall? What's the point? He likes boys, like I do. "What do you mean, odd?"

"I can't tell, exactly… I don't want to sound crazy, but something is up... they seem to be looking at us… or at you or me, I'm not exactly sure." A couple in Geometry just now made him uncomfortable… I half expected one of them to come over and say something, but neither one did. I pretended to not notice. Maybe I should have asked them. But going up to a girl and asking what was on her mind was just about the last thing he was likely to do.

Julian looked around, all the girls he could see were looking at something besides Randall and himself. What's the big deal? "Tell ya what. When you see one doing that, let me know." He gestured to the one standing close to his locker as proof. "They look the same as always." He entered his combination and traded his books for the sack lunch.

He couldn't tell that the girl was, in fact, just *pretending* to consult her student guide. She was disappointed because he had a friend with him. She had planned to… well, say *hello*, at least. She'd had a locker three places down from his *all year*. How lucky is *that?!*

Randall didn't see through her pretense either; all the instances he'd seen so far were too blatant to miss.

Unconsciously, Julian adjusted himself as he turned; a slight tingle below persisted. Little J hadn't forgotten about Rita's boyfriend, I'll save telling about that for after school. Little J is almost asleep… I don't need any problems during lunch.

On the way down the grand staircase, he started to tell about the dance decorations and the costumes… might as well get that out of the way. Without thinking about it, he smiled back a couple of times at a girl passing by; he didn't know who they were, but they had given him a small wave and a friendly look. He continued his narrative about the bales of hay as they rounded the corner to go down the last flight of stairs.

Randall was concentrating on Julian's narrative and did not notice that some of the girls going up the stairs were delighted to see the blond beauty pass by… it would have reinforced his opinion that something was up.

—∾—

Julian was not a familiar face in the cafeteria, so his appearance was a total surprise. He and Randall headed for the station that sold milk and juice as if it was a daily routine. The blue shirt/blond head combination was noticed immediately, and caused an instant dropped jaw and moment of silent awe. It snowballed...by the time they reached the beverage counter, at least fifty girls and several boys had stopped to stare.

"Smells good today," Randall was tempted to go through the line, now that they were here.

"Mmm, sure does." Smells like they made Sid's favorite today: lasagna.

Randall debated with himself: OJ or grape juice? neither one is great with peanut butter...milk is worse...*oh:* they have *apple* now. Perfect.

When they finished paying for their beverages, Julian turned to look for the set of windows that Theresa talked about. He knew roughly where they had to be.

Randall noticed at once that they were being looked at or watched or *something,* by a *lot* of kids—whatever it was, the looks weren't threatening or hostile… but they were *weird.* "Umm, Julian…"

Julian spotted Theresa and her friends; now I know where to go. The expression on Randall's face stopped him cold. What's wrong? What is he looking at? He turned to see—Ohmygosh! All these… are they looking at *me*? Is my zipper down or something? These suntan pants did that sometimes… he glanced down at his fly… that isn't it. He looked back to the beverage window, nothing out of the ordinary. He glanced at Randall again… he's frozen. What should I do?

Smile, you idiot, and get over to Theresa's table.

Julian smiled wide, raised his milk carton high in a wave. "C'mon. Everyone's waiting." He had no idea what was going on, but Inside guy's on duty. Somehow, I'll make it through whatever this is.

They had the strange experience of seeing a crowd of happy faces waving back—a couple of girls by the coke machine were almost squirming with joy; another pair were hugging one another in delight. Julian's smile had always been magical, though he did not know that. Over the years he had learned to smile a lot because it always made people smile back—no big deal.

Again, Julian was mistaken: his smile was one of the salient features at the dance; his smile and bow to the crowd when he stood in the spotlight was a major point in the report circulating about Saturday night. He had just authenticated what everyone had heard and what many had seen *in person.* Julian's smile included his eyes: his incredible rich brown eyes and jet black eyelashes—eyelashes that always looked like they were professionally applied ten minutes ago. Combined with his wavy blond hair and flawless fair skin, his entire face radiated joy; it was genuine and automatic, always affecting anyone who encountered it.

Like the wake following a speedboat, his path to the set of tables by the window was followed by a widening swath of staring people.

The sound level went back up gradually as questions were answered and stories about Saturday were retold with added embellishment.

"Do you see who I see?!" Brenda nearly choked on the bite of lasagna she had just put in her mouth.

Lynne looked up—oh, wow. "I do… I *do*." She looked around rapidly—Rita isn't here yet. She looked at her friend. "What's going *on*?!"

"You tell me! Is she planning to join him for lunch?" What about Tracy?

"I don't believe this! Did she and Tracy break up?" Talk about scandal! Tracy and Rita always eat at the next table: they practically have reservations… no one is sitting there.

"Stay tuned, folks. We may be in store for a show—Tracy is a *lot* bigger."

"For sure." Nowhere as good looking, though… he looks even better close up—she remembered well what he looked like in the hallway when Rita gave him the Sadie Daisy. She grabbed Brenda's arm: "he's coming over *here!*"

They watched spellbound as the stunning blond in the wonderful sky blue shirt approached. He stopped to talk to Theresa! Why would he do *that*?! What *is* going on?!

"Hi!" Julian chirped as he stepped up to Theresa's table. He caught her by surprise. "I brought along a friend." He gestured to his left. "This is Randall." He grinned, waiting to be told where to sit.

Theresa gulped. She wasn't expecting this at all… but remembered in an instant that she had asked him to join her Lunch Bunch. Julian's big smile was even *hotter* in the bright lights of the cafeteria than it had been during the dance.

“Ooo, so you’re *here*.” She stood and gestured to the girls opposite to scoot over to make room. “Everyone, this is *Julian*! We had a dance together Saturday—I invited him to join us!” She glanced over to see if Rita and Tracy were there… best to be sure. She was confident that they were headed off in his car for a very special lunch. Rita wasn’t about to dump Tracy for this blond cutie… even though he is very pretty. She was pleased to see there wasn’t room for Brenda and Lynn to squeeze in anywhere.

Julian and Randall took their designated place on the bench. Their backs were to the bulk of the cafeteria, which was just as well. It relieved them from the awkward task of wondering what was being said by dozens of kids who were staring at them and talking in hushed tones between bites of lasagna and gulps of milk.

Theresa could see it though, and knew at once what the buzz was about. She had answered a couple of phone calls yesterday from girls that had heard that she knew him. I didn’t realize it was *quite* this important. But I can handle it; best of all, Rita isn’t here: he’s mine today!

Julian waved at Theresa’s boyfriend. “Hi Teddy; this is Randall.”

Randall poked up a hand and gave a small wave; shaking hands across a cafeteria table felt a little bold… he did not feel bold at all; quite the contrary. Most of these kids are *Juniors;* they’re also the social somebodies—the sort that mother would approve of highly—she’s keen on social status. She’s probably playing bridge somewhere with their mothers… small comfort.

Julian pushed his sketchbook to the side and pulled the contents from his paper bag. “Don’t let me interrupt anything; you don’t want your lunch to get cold!” He flattened the paper bag neatly and placed his sandwiches, apple, and carrot sticks atop it, as usual. Normally, this would be outside or in the atrium—the empty bag served as a placemat to keep the food safe and clean. Arranging them neatly in order was a habit formed on the work crew. Ordinarily he opened his sketchbook right away to look over his drawing; no point in doing that today.

He removed half a sandwich from the neatly folded wax paper and glanced at it—excellent: ham and Swiss cheese. He took a bite… *yum.* After a couple of chews, he noticed that no one was eating… everyone was watching him instead. "What? Is something wrong?" Randall was the only other person eating—a bite had been taken from his peanut butter and jelly sandwich, so…

"No, no, everything is fine!" Theresa jabbed Teddy with her elbow and took a forkful of lasagna. "Come on, dig in, everyone." I could kick myself for not having a plan. At least Brenda is at the next table.

Teddy regarded Julian more critically. At the dance I got the impression that the kid was a complete greenhorn. But he's a hit with the girls. Why did Theresa invite him to lunch? She didn't tell me… am I in trouble with her? Look at the *other* kid: nerd city! Who has *peanut butter and jam* sandwiches?! I just remembered: he's a friend of *Norman's*. He actually introduced me at the punch bowl. Norman is a *Senior*. He's about as big as they come around here. This is *deep.*

For Teddy, deep meant complicated and probably suspicious.

This is the kid that got to sit in the back seat with Rita and those *jugs*! Teddy had a good idea of what Rita had in mind, after that dance set with her… wow; I'm not about to forget *that*. It makes my balls itch to even *think* about it. He studied the kid's face. In the daylight he looks even more handsome; easy to understand why Rita grabbed him… heck of a lot better looking than Tracy. Huh… he *said* it was his first dance… but he did just fine out there… huh. Things don't add up here. This is *Deep*-deep… *triple* deep.

"Hi—I'm Julian!" he said brightly to the girl on his right. "What's your name?" She isn't a Wallace girl, I don't think. None of these kids are.

"Oh! Uhm, M-Marcie…" she stammered. She had never expected to meet him, let alone sit right *next* to him. How can he be so *friendly*?! The color returned to her face too rapidly… she had been in danger of fainting; now she couldn't stop a blush from making her look as stupid as she felt. Lucky, maybe, but *stupid.*

"Marcie!" He looked her in the face. "That's a nice name; I like that name." I've never met anyone named Marcie. What's her last name? It wouldn't be polite to ask. He returned his attention to the sandwich. I need to open up the milk…

Randall was inexperienced at socializing; I should follow Julian's example and introduce myself. He was able to look at the girl to his left briefly with half a smile; he managed a "Hi." Oh… I said it too softly.

Alice smiled back, delighted that he had broken the ice. He's the shy type, which helps. Maybe I can ask a few things about his friend without attracting attention. I was just as blown away as everyone else at the dance. I always knew that being connected to Theresa was a good idea.

"I'm Alice."

Julian heard and leaned forward. "Hi, Alice." He gave Randall a small nudge in the ribs. "Randall here is a little shy, but he's really kind of impressive. He's from Washington, the *state*!" He nodded eagerly. "He knows how to climb *mountains*! They have *scads* of them out there." I've seen some photos of his trips. "You know, *real* mountains… like they have in *National Geographic*." Kind of scary.

Aside from the scout meeting, Randall had never been praised in public. The feeling was unexpected and *incredible*. He blushed and did an aw-shucks shrug, but felt a foot taller. The impressed look on Alice's face was also unexpected. It was uncomfortable but it was wonderful, all the same. He gave Julian a grateful smile… what *went on* at that dance?! His world was turning upside down here and he couldn't find a way to get a grip on what was happening around him. He was not accustomed to feeling like this… how do you hold steady when the earth is shaking under your feet? This was a brief insight into what that must feel like.

Julian noticed that Teddy was looking at him; oh yeah—Teddy was all hung up about Rita's oversized boobs. Kinda funny—he got a stiffy at the dance because of those.

You're one to talk, Inside guy observed.

Not because of her *boobs*! But you're right. He took a sip of milk, then another bite of ham and Swiss. I'm okay as long as I'm sitting down. He gave Teddy a friendly grin. I hafta remember to tell Randall about him… Teddy has a good sized one.

The blond celebrity's attitude and demeanor was so disarming and genuine, that soon everyone was chatting and enjoying their meal like old friends. Everyone kept an eye on Julian, all the same. He was so exotic and so *new*. They didn't want to miss a word he said.

> ***ding! ding! ding!*** <

The Noon Announcements chime interrupted everyone's conversation. The PA volume was adjusted so that you had to shout to be heard over it. That was by design; the Principal had decreed that students must shut up and listen when announcements were made.

"Your attention, please," the school secretary's voice sliced through the air like a buzz saw with worn out bearings: *"This is to remind you that all this week, the Army, Navy, and Air Force recruiters will be set up in the main hall. Senior boys in particular are encouraged to visit one or all of them. The Marines will be here next week. That is all."*

That put a damper on things for a while. The senior boys in particular were sobered. The threat of war was still being felt, even though the Russians were starting to remove their missiles from Cuba. Once in a while the school world was forced to pay attention to what was going on in the "outside" world, like it or not. Lunches were finished without a lot of gaiety.

As people finished eating, Julian was introduced to everyone at the table—most of them were girls. That wasn't a problem—all his life he had sat around talking to girls—Mom and Geraldine and various other women. This was the same thing, pretty much. I like these kids just fine. Just goes to show you, doesn't it? You don't have to be from Wallace to be nice. Inside guy doesn't have anything to say… he must be off having his own lunch. He'll pop up if he's needed.

Inside guy had a good idea suddenly: *I'm still here; you should take down some of these names for your movie list.*

What a stupid idea. While I'm eating lunch? While everyone is looking at me? I'll try to remember some and put them down next period. I'm supposed to be having a good time, remember? These kids are *nice*! Taking down names? Julian had forgotten all about the sea of staring faces that had met him and Randall at the start of lunch.

Randall had gotten acquainted with Alice. He didn't remember *ever* talking to a girl for more than a couple of minutes. It wasn't as hard to do as he expected… or as unpleasant. That didn't mean that his eye had failed to check out all the boys. A couple of them in particular would be worth a close look when they got up from behind the table. Stan in particular tweaked his curiosity… maybe he could use a special tutor to help him in Math or Biology or something.

Meanwhile, Marcie's curiosity about the spiral pad had reached the tipping point.

"What does the number 3 mean?" It was super fancy, drawn by hand.

"That means it's the third one," he smiled. "I like to draw things."

Her eyes opened wide. She thought it was a notebook for whatever he had third period.

"Go ahead and look if you want." I brought it along out of habit. I always run across something to draw when I don't have it along, so I make a point of having it handy.

Marcie couldn't believe he had given permission—and so easily. Maybe it's just doodles… she pulled the sketchbook in front of her and opened it.

Theresa had been studying Julian's eyes and face, generally—the longer she looked, the more intrigued she became. Where has this kid been all my life? It's time to get back in charge of the conversation; he's my guest. "Where did you go before Jackson?"

"Wallace." These kids sure didn't; Julian could tell that at once. Maybe now I can see what kids from the other Junior Highs are like, for real. At Wallace the school spirit fanatics always ran these kids down. Sometimes those school reputations are a bunch of baloney. These kids seem just fine to me.

"Oh, that's nice. We went to Sheldon…" She was about to gesture that everyone at the table had gone to Sheldon when Marcie caught her eye—she's examining that notebook as if something was wrong. "What's the matter, Marcie?"

Marcie looked up and stared back; her vocabulary had gone missing. She handed the sketchbook across the table.

Theresa took it and gave it a look. She was impressed, but had not heard the conversation earlier and did not know it was Julian's work.

"Yes, what's the matter?" Julian was puzzled. Maybe I shouldn't have let her look at those…

Theresa looked at Marcie, waiting for an answer.

Marcie usually blushed when put on the spot, but not this time. "Nothing's the *matter*; it's just that it's so *good*. How can you draw like that?!" She hadn't finished looking at them either.

Theresa looked at the page, then at Julian. "You drew this?"

Randall grinned wide. He was enjoying this.

"Well, yeah." He shrugged, apologetically. "It's not that good, I admit. The ones toward the middle are a little better." He turned to Marcie. "I try to get better all the time… sometimes it doesn't show."

Theresa's jaw dropped. She turned to the next page. The front of the school appeared. "Julian!" she said softly.

He felt himself start to blush. I should have left that in the locker. He grimaced at Randall… maybe he knows what to do… wait a minute: what's he so happy about?!

"I've been trying to tell you," he whispered. Theresa's reaction wasn't a surprise, of course. Even so, it was nice to have his opinion confirmed. He gave her an approving nod: "They're *all* like that."

"Thanks a lot," Julian frowned.

"No problem," he smirked. Then he realized: now everyone will know. I don't want to share Julian. Too late.

Randall was smart and ethical enough to realize that he had no right to an exclusive. Maybe I can do my part by helping him get some credit for a change. That's the least a friend could do.

"Look at this!" She showed Teddy a sketch farther along. "That's… what's her name? Linda! Linda *Beech*! I sat next to her in the seventh grade!"

Teddy gave it a look. Sure enough. "That's her, all right."

"He drew that in the atrium a couple of weeks ago." Randall affected a ho-hum attitude.

"I like to draw people, too," he apologized. He had not asked permission, but she was so interesting… whatever she was reading must have been super good. She didn't budge for over ten minutes, other than to turn a page.

Several at the table got up and looked over Theresa's shoulder; they knew she wasn't about to pass the sketchbook around.

"How long does it take to draw one of these?" Murray, who had stepped over from the far end of the bench, was keen to know; he fancied himself a bit of an artist. I couldn't do anything like this.

"Depends. Just a head like that, maybe ten minutes. Longer if I do lots of shading and stuff… a whole person takes longer. But these small sized sheets aren't the best if you want to do a good job." As Theresa turned the page he added, "trees and buildings take longer—lotsa detail in those."

There was a brief silence while Theresa turned the pages—she did this with care so everyone behind could see.

Julian gave Randall an I'll-get-even-with-you-later look. Say! An idea just popped into his head: he checked the clock—twenty minutes until the bell. He turned to Marcie. "You want me to draw one of you?"

"Me?" she felt herself turning white again…

"Sure!" He turned to Randall. "See a good place?"

Randall knew exactly what Julian meant. He glanced over to the area where he'd had lunch the first day—looked good. It was off to the side where people rarely sat because of the overhead slant in the ceiling. He pointed to it.

"Perfect." Julian stood and reached his hand to Marcie the way Geraldine and his mom had taught him. "C'mon." He gestured to Theresa. "Bring the sketchbook. I sorta need that to draw on."

Attention to Julian from the general public had largely faded; but when he stood up, the few that had been watching and waiting noticed at once. Intent on following his every move, they sat up straight, ready to tag along. They watched eagerly as he strode confidently across to the tables under the north staircase. He held onto Marcie's hand the entire way, unwittingly granting her a status that she never dreamed would be hers. Eight or nine others followed. What is going on? They joined the parade.

When they got there, Randall took Marcie's other hand. "I'll show you where to sit."

Julian held out his hand with a smile, and took possession of the sketchbook. "It's okay to watch. I don't mind." For the next fifteen minutes, Julian entertained about seventy students; many were disappointed because they couldn't see very well. Half were not attendees at the Sadie Hawkins Dance—they were just curious to see what the fuss was all about.

Randall sat to the side this time so that others could see. He enjoyed watching Julian at work, but it was *fascinating* to watch a crowd watch him. A side benefit was being able to do his other kind of favorite watching. There were at least three that he could study for a long time, given the right opportunity.

One of the side benefits of his weekend in Hayden Park was being able to extrapolate certain moves learned there and apply them—in his imagination only, sad to say—to selected individuals. A long and a short version of this had evolved. The longer one was reserved for home use, of course. In public it has be the short version lest he lose control down below.

Randall, it turned out, was not the only boy there with that talent. Unaware that he had fallen under another's eye, he did not take care to sit as modestly as usual. By the time the period was over, he had attracted a fan of his own. Like Julian, he was blissfully ignorant.

"All done," Julian plopped the pencil into his shirt pocket. Can't do much more anyway—no pencil sharpeners around here.

Marcie ran up to see. Her expression said it all. Those in the back of the crowd knew at once that they would be in line, given a chance.

Julian was delighted by her reaction. "You want to keep it?" I *love* to give people drawings I do—one of my favorite things. Obviously she wants it; he signed the lower right corner before tearing it out of the tablet.

> ***Baaaaaaaaaz!*** <

The buzzer was harsher and louder in the cafeteria—it was designed to cut through all the conversation. Second lunch period had ended.

Julian was glad it had sounded; typing will be a relief after this… nice and quiet. But drawing Marcie was kind of fun. Her reaction made it double fun.

Theresa and six others rushed to his side before he had taken three steps. They all spoke at the same time with hurried entreaties for him to come again tomorrow. He already assumed he would—Mom and Geraldine will have a fit if I don't. After a week or two, I can sort of taper off or whatever. He checked to see what Randall thought.

Randall gave a nod. Delighted with Julian and with himself, he smiled. Now that the blasted dance is out of the way, after schools are back—that's what counts.

As the throng headed for the stairway for an afternoon of academic pursuit, Marcie stood staring at the drawing in disbelief. She had never had this kind of luck—and it was absolute luck: she had done nothing to deserve it. It was too early too fresh and too intense to analyze her feelings right now…

"Can I see, please, *pretty please*?" Joan touched the corner of the sheet.

Marcie gave her a stern look—the kind you give your best friend when they are on the brink of doing the unforgivable. "Be careful… *very* careful."

Her tone alerted all present to respect her wishes: they would feel the same way if it were theirs. One by one, all nine girls got a chance to hold it and look at it up close—each had begun to think of a way to have themselves portrayed like this. All ten girls were late to their fifth period class. It was worth it. One quality stood out above all: the drawing made Marcie look prettier than she is—yet it looked exactly right at the same time.

Neither Julian nor Randall paid attention to who had watched the portrait being drawn. Not that paying attention was of any importance—but the Dean of Boys had cafeteria duty that day, and he took great interest in what was going on. Not just because he was in charge of seeing that orderly behavior prevailed, but he had a built in interest in all the boys in the school—that was his job description. Julian had not come to his attention until today. He stepped close to the cluster of girls examining the drawing. From behind one he got a good look.

Holy Moly! If I hadn't personally witnessed that being drawn I wouldn't believe it. I have to find out who this kid is! How has he escaped my attention? A few staff members need to be consulted concerning this boy. The art teacher certainly, but also the principal—Roy, my boy, he addressed himself: I have a hunch about this kid; it may be a long shot, but this lad might be just who we're looking for. First off, I need to find out his name. He has to be a sophomore… but he was sitting with the juniors. *Very* interesting. Who is the other boy?

He hurried after them, intent on catching up. Oh-oh: the friend just headed to the left… *aha:* a music case in his other hand… he's headed for the band room. That simplifies things—he'll be easy to I.D. Skipping several steps to close the gap, Barnes started up the stairway. The blond head stood out; he followed at a distance. The plan was to see what room he entered; that would lead to a class list.

Secretly, Roy Barnes enjoyed playing private detective. In the past he had been able to identify students without asking a single question of anyone. Silly, but it was fun. And it had come in handy more than once.

24 Randall's photolab

Randall's house was farther from school than Julian's—another mile and a half. The extra distance provided plenty of time to tell the rest of the story about the dance and what happened afterward—when the passing cars weren't interrupting to toot a greeting, that is. It so happened that most of Theresa's Lunch Bunch lived in this part of town. When they saw the blond head, they squealed in delight, waved like he was an old friend and forced their boyfriend drivers to give a friendly beep.

"How many is that?" Julian waved with a smile.

"Seven." Randall joined in a cheerful wave as well; very odd, being noticed. "They're heading for that fancy pie place you went to after the dance." That bunch is too important to be seen at Sparky's. Admittedly, he had enjoyed talking to Alice… she wasn't stuck up at all.

"Oh? Where is that, anyway?" I was so busy fussing with that coat I didn't pay attention. Besides, it was dark.

"Over by the park," he pointed to the left. "It's about six or seven blocks from here. My mom goes there sometimes."

Julian nodded; Geraldine does too. He looked over his shoulder to see if any more cars were coming. I don't want to spend any more time on Theresa's lunchroom pals. Randall's opinion was important; so far he hasn't offered one. "So, what do you think?"

"Think?" Thanks to the latest interruption by Julian's new fan club, Randall had stopped laughing. Too bad I missed seeing Julian standing on that yellow slicker in the moonlight with his overalls down around his ankles—not to mention Sammy and his massive pole wagging in the breeze. "Watch where you step, I guess." Seems obvious. Hardly any thought required; dog piles aren't all that rare. He stopped and did an exaggerated inspection of his right sole.

"Not that! I mean what about Little J?"

Randall tilted his head; he didn't understand the question.

"How come he *did* that? I mean, Rita is a *girl*!" This had been bothering him more and more.

"Capital G," Randall nodded. He had gone to some trouble finding out who she was—without telling Julian, of course. He had to see if she was a threat of any kind. In his opinion, going to the dance was an act of heroic bravery—especially considering her behavior in the car. I'm not at all surprised; what surprised was how unsuspecting Julian could be.

"I mean, would *you* have that problem? What if a girl rubbed you on the buns? Would you get a stiffy?"

"Gaaa!" he laughed. "No way!" He had no intention of allowing himself to get in harm's way.

"Now I've got a whole flock of them wanting me to draw their picture." Usually that wouldn't be a problem; my whole life I've been surrounded by females telling me what to do—no big deal. They finally stopped fluffing my hair all the time… but they never tried to massage my buns before.

"Little J didn't cause a problem in the cafeteria, did he?"

"No, thank goodness." That would have been awful. "He's been good all day…" except for fifth period, of course… I think the chair in there causes that. "I didn't let any of them get close to my buns."

Randall broke up laughing, then stopped to think: that's right! We were *surrounded* by girls during lunch… for Randall, that was amazing in itself—a first time event. Julian isn't bothered by that at all—also amazing. He looked sideways at Julian... hmm... Julian hasn't actually talked about girls all that much. I've been assuming we're pretty much agreed about them... maybe it's more complicated. "So... do you ever think about girls?"

"*Eew*, are you crazy? *Never*." It wasn't an article of faith—it didn't need to be. What a dumb question.

Reassured, Randall gave a sage nod. "Maybe your buns don't know that."

"So I have stupid buns?"

"I sure hope so!" The idea that part of the anatomy could have reasoning power was a little far out. On the other hand... he couldn't deny that the occupant around front had a mind of his own—Little R was more independent by the day, or so it seemed.

"Besides, it wasn't *only* my buns; she didn't touch them in the car."

"That's *right*..." that complicated things. "What did she do again?" He had been so revolted by what Julian described that he didn't pay close attention to the details.

"She massaged my chest... everything from my neck down. With *both* hands! Real slow, like she was trying to *memorize* everything. I was sweating so much she used it as *grease*."

"*Gross!*"

"Yeah, looking back now, I agree... I must have a stupid chest and tummy too." Julian hated to admit this: "but at the time, it felt *good*... y'know?"

Randall looked at him, aghast. "No, I *don't* know... I've never had a girl paw me all over in the back seat of a car." Or anywhere else. The fact that Julian had allowed it to happen was a little troubling. "Did you tell her to stop?"

"No, but..."

"Think about it, Julian. There you are, practically naked, nobody is watching: the windows are fogged over and the two in the front seat are… well, they're *busy*. What was she supposed to do? Blush and cover her eyes?" If it had been me, I wouldn't have wasted time playing rub-a-dub dub; no sir: treasure hunt is what pops into my head—no map required.

"I see your point… she must have thought I *wanted* her to do that." That thought had not occurred to him before… huh.

"So, what did you think about?"

"Gosh, a little bit of everything—my mind was doing all kinds of stuff trying to not pay attention to what she was doing. I thought about school, scouts, all kinds of stuff—I tried to block out what she was doing… I was kind of paralyzed…" I don't *dare* mention that I was thinking about Mark; I pretended it was his chest being massaged, and that I was the one doing the massaging.

"Aha! I know: did you think about the Initiation? That was all touch and feel…"

"Of course!" I *did* think about that a little. A perfect excuse. "That must be it!"

"I get a stiffy every time I think about that." Randall nodded. It's a big annoyance sometimes.

"So… it's what I'm *thinking* that causes Little J to wake up?" Julian wasn't sure it was that simple… I didn't think about that when she rubbed my buns. I was thinking about Danny, back at Camp Walker. He's the only one who has ever massaged my buns… until Rita, that is.

"Has to be. If you had been thinking of Rita would Little J have come to life?"

"No way! At least I don't think so… I've never actually *thought* about Rita… I've never thought about any girl, as far as I can remember." In fact, Julian wasn't sure what that required. What do you think about if you think about girls? Boobs? That's what Teddy thinks about. Weird. As far as Julian was concerned, they were a handicap; one of the side benefits of being a boy was not having to deal with the things.

"Problem solved: next time you're stupid enough to allow a girl to rub your butt, just think of Rita," he laughed heartily; what an idea!

Julian laughed along with him. That was probably half right; but I'm not eager to do a test... The fact is I *let* her do whatever she wanted—I didn't want to know. I was like the ostrich hiding his head in the sand while the lion pounces.

Exactly: you have been warned. Inside guy had been tuned in to all this. *Next time you won't have dog do-do on Sammy's shoe coming to the rescue.*

So the moral of the story is to pay attention to what's going on... and run away while I can.

Paying attention is only half the job.

What's the other half? Julian wasn't expecting Inside guy to show up, but he always helps...

Thinking ahead, of course. Have a clue about what could be coming down the road; steer clear beforehand.

Oh. What a dummy... I should have figured something like that could happen.

Next time you have to have a plan.

What do you mean, next time?!

If Mom and Geraldine have their way, there will be. Remember, you're supposed to go to a movie one of these days. You have to plan it in advance.

Yow... I forgot about that. At least in a movie you get to sit the whole time. Compared to a dance, it's a safe place to be. All of a sudden going to a movie looked a lot better.

Better jot down some of those names before you forget.

Randall could see that Julian was still sorting this out, but the silence had gone on long enough: I have a plan for this afternoon. "You want to ride the rest of the way?"

"How could I do that?"

"Easy. Just sit on the handlebars."

Not exactly a seat... a chrome plated pipe, basically, with a bump in the middle—not very inviting. Handles at the ends for the operator, nothing for a rider to hold onto. But I've seen kids doing that... "Where do you put your feet?"

"Nowhere; they just hang down on either side of the wheel."

"Oh." It looked precarious. "What if we fall over or something..."

"Nah... I used to do this all the time. No problem." Randall wanted to get there as fast as possible... there might not be enough time to do everything. I've been planning this for a week—but after school is risky... never enough time... sooner or later, Mom shows up and takes control of your life. Mine is worse about that than Julian's: when supper is ready, you stop everything and go to the table, *regardless*. He turned around and moved his clarinet. "Put your books in the basket and hop up." The double basket in back often simplified things.

Julian was ready to dismount the minute they arrived. Riding up there is okay in an emergency maybe... but until they invent a seat pad for handlebars, I'll take a pass. The bump at the driveway lip was not fun at all: my tailbone took a direct hit. Vigorously rubbing himself to smooth out the dent that must have formed across his backside, he surveyed the grounds as he followed around back—man, this is a long driveway. The bicycle had a special parking place at one side of a wide breezeway—kind of a big hutch next to the gardener's potting shed. I worked on a couple of classy yards like this last summer. I wasn't ever in one of the houses though. You don't see a lot of these brick houses—kinda fancy.

"Mom and Dad have bikes too—so does Marietta," he tucked it into the empty slot. They retrieved their schoolbooks from the carrier basket. "When the weather is nice we get to go on 'outings.' My dad is kind of a health nut."

Wow… Julian looked at him in awe: a *Dad*! The one thing in the world I always wished I had. He had been in other kids' houses with dads, so he *sort* of knew what it was like. Look at the *set* of bicycles… he was walking into a different world: Randall's folks are *rich*. He never let on that he was rich or anything—seems like an ordinary guy. Julian thought back… I saw his mom in the nurses' room. She was sort of fancy looking, at that.

"I hope you don't mind going in through the mudroom. It's a long way around to the front door."

"Fine with me…" What's a mud room?

Randall took off his jacket and hung it on his peg. "You can hang yours there," he pointed to the visitor's strip—half a dozen empty pegs waited to be of service. "We'll leave our books on the bench for now." He didn't want to go right to his room.

Julian glanced around—not one bit of mud anywhere: the room is spotless. Small, but spotless. He had pictured a room that looked used… mud caked along the baseboards where it was hard to reach, a few smears on the wall, hip boots piled in a corner… nothing. This looks brand new… not even any dust. This room has never seen any mud. The inside door opened into the kitchen.

"Oh, Randall…" Eloise was pleased he had come in early today. She needed his opinion. "Why, hello." He's brought home a friend…

"Good afternoon, Mrs. Hallstrom," he bowed. She looked the same except she was wearing an apron.

"I recall now… you're the boy that collided with Randall!" She remembered the hair at once. That's the hair that insists you fluff it every five minutes just for the fun of it—even if you don't need to. I *covet* hair like that.

"I'm gonna show Julian the photo lab."

"Oh, that's nice. First though, I have a small job for you—one that your friend can help with." She pointed to the kitchen table.

The table was bare—four chairs pushed in neatly as if the maid had just put them in place.

"You'll like this job, I'm sure. Boys your age always need a bite after school. I need a taste test." She gestured to the table again. "Sit, sit. I won't be a minute." This is perfect: I don't need the extra calories. She never served anything that was untested, even if it was from Nancy's.

They looked at each other and shrugged. Moms are in charge. When you wander into their domain, they can draft you into service at once, no questions asked, no explanations required. The assignment was welcome, especially after that long walk.

Eloise went to the stove and opened the oven. She did a careful test with her forefinger: perfect! She grabbed a pair of hot pads and pulled out a twelve inch pie. The boys couldn't have arrived at a better time.

A terrific aroma permeated the air. Julian's eyes wowed. He remembered the cake: Randall's mom was an expert on where to buy good cakes. She must be an expert on pies, too.

At first Randall was a little embarrassed by his mother's imperious behavior; it's the very first time Julian has been here. But Julian didn't seem to be annoyed at all. Her request wasn't a surprise; he was used to being the official taster of new things for the bridge club. A glance at the clock told him that it might be a problem if it took long—it's 4:00. That left about 90 minutes before supper… hmm. That's calling it pretty close; might not be long enough.

For Julian, watching a mother serve up a slice of freshly warmed pie with care and finesse was an appetite enhancer—especially when she went to the refrigerator and extracted a half gallon of ice cream. A healthy scoop on the side… yum. Watching her bring the plates to the table added a dash of suspense.

Are you supposed to try the pie first, or the ice cream? Let's try the pie… *mmm!* What *is* this? I've never tasted anything like this before.

Eloise watched with care: first reactions tell all, really…

"Wow, Mom!" Randall took another bite. Being warm must make a difference. "They'll *love* this one!" He peeked under the crust… what's in here?

"This is a new flavor… they're letting me have an advance trial. If it's accepted it will be the first new flavor in *two* years! It's rhubarb-apricot! So… you like it then?"

Julian nodded enthusiastically. I'm glad I tasted it before she said what it is. He sliced off a small bite of ice cream… *ooo!*

"That's new too: pineapple-coconut sherbet." It's supposed to be the ideal companion.

"You'll get another prize with this, for sure." Randall took another healthy bite.

"It's supposed to give you a taste of summer when it's cold and dark out."

It wasn't like any summer Julian knew, but he wouldn't mind if it had been. My summers are simpler. This is a fancy taste, a rich people's taste. Nice place to visit. What's roobarb, anyway? I've had apricot jam before, but roobarb is new. I'll ask Mom when I get home. That reminds me… "Mrs. Hallstrom, can I use your phone? I need to call my mom. She doesn't know I'm here instead of at home."

"Why, certainly." Eloise was pleased and impressed. If her boy had a shortcoming it was not always calling in. "You can use the wall phone in here—or do you need to use the phone in the den?"

Julian did a double take: they have *two* phones? "This one is fine."

He had just finished telling his mom where he was when Randall's mom tapped his shoulder and gestured for him to give her the handset.

"Mrs. Forrest, this is Eloise Hallstrom, Randall's mother; I believe we have met."

What is she doing?

Randall's shoulders raised in a search-me shrug.

"Francine, then… Thank you so much… And you are to call me Eloise… I couldn't agree more. Please, if you will permit, I'd like Julian to stay for supper. That way he can meet Randall's father and have a little more time. I will be happy to bring him home, of course."

Julian and Randall stared at each other. Mothers love to pull surprises sometimes.

"Thank you for that. You are as charming as your boy, which is not a surprise. Do you have a be-home-by time?"

Randall's gears were whirling… this is *perfect*!

"Delighted. Do you need to speak with him? Of course. I look forward to it." Eloise handed the phone back.

"Hi." He smiled at Randall's mom gratefully. "Okay… yep. Thanks Mom… yep, I know… See ya." He put the handset on its hook. This phone looks just like ours… *two* phones: think of that.

He sat back down to clean his plate. So I'm staying for supper… wow. I had dinner at Larry's a few times, and at Sid's and Jeremy's, but that was back when I was a Cub. This is going to be way different.

Eloise watched Julian, her appreciation growing by leaps. He is the reason Randall has become so motivated and positive; he's never been this happy. I owe this boy. Whatever she could do to encourage and support their friendship was a priority. What remarkable eyes… I've never seen a boy with eyes like that. It made her look more closely at his hair… no, it's *not* bleached. Remarkable.

She stepped forward to collect the plates… I have a winner for sure! The plates are almost licked clean. All I need now is some flowers. Tomorrow it was her turn to be hostess.

"Thanks for the pie," Julian didn't wait for a reply—she was busy; he followed Randall back through the mud room. He scratched his head. Why mud room? Mud is the last thing you're gonna find around here; you'd have to go out into the back yard and dig a hole and make some. Words like that are annoying: not knowing them shows how stupid and uninformed you are. I *hate* that. Maybe all these fancy houses have a mud room… heck with it: I'm gonna ask. "Hey, Randall."

"Yeah?" he had reached the garage.

"Why do they call that a mud room?"

"No idea. That's what the lady who sold us this place called it," he shrugged. "It isn't a porch, exactly. Maybe this used to be a farmhouse or something. You know, take off your clodhoppers so you don't track mud into the house?"

"Oh." That made sense. One of these days, Julian, you need to practice using your brain. That was a perfect example just now… even a simple thing like that. Of *course* that's what a mud room is for: stopping mud. And you had to ask Randall to figure that out. He shook his head, disgusted with himself. Boy… if I'd asked Sid, he'd have had a field day. That's one thing I like about Randall: he isn't always looking for a way to poke fun.

He looked back: that wasn't ever a farmhouse… I guess if you have enough space you get to have a mud room whether you need one or not. If was mine, I'd rename it a coat room. They don't have back porch, so maybe that's what it is.

Randall unlocked the side door and walked into the expansive three-car garage. He flipped on the overhead lights. Two cars were parked inside: a Lincoln Continental and a Land Rover. A walled off section replaced most of what had been a third bay—or space for a boat.

Julian scooted to catch up. "Man!" He looked around. "This is *huge*!" It doesn't look this big from outside. Look at the *cars*… the very *fancy* cars.

"That's Mom's, mostly." He pointed at the Lincoln. Dad doesn't usually drive in town. He walks to work. Like I said, he's a health nut."

"What's that, then?

"That's the Rover. We use that to go on mountain trips." Dad hasn't come up with a trip around here yet.

Yow… I've seen those in National Geographic—kind of a super jeep. They drive these out to photograph lions in Africa and stuff like that. Look at that! They still have Washington license plates. This place is too amazing for words! A stairway to the left invited his eye.

"That goes to a caretaker's apartment. We don't use it except to store stuff. The people we bought this from had a live in gardener and handyman. We don't need that. Dad hires a yard service to take care of things." He pointed to the walled off area. "That's the photo lab. Dad had it built when we moved in last summer. It used to be a shop area for fixing cars and building cabinets and things. We didn't need that either. What we did need was a darkroom!" With a grin, he gestured to the door.

Julian had no words to express what was going on in his head. He had never encountered a place like this. Last summer the crew worked on some yards around here, but this was a cut above those… I was never inside one of the houses. The cost of something like this… no idea how to figure that. I bet our whole house could fit in here! The main house didn't seem that big… but who has a garage that can hold two cars, have six feet extra on all sides for walking around, and even more room in front? And build in a photo lab too?

"Come on!" Randall grinned. Julian's expression was unexpected fun. He flipped a switch next to the door. The blue light bulb above the door turned on. "That light tells whoever comes in here that the darkroom is being used… it's a warning light, basically." A square box was mounted on the wall. "This is an intercom. You can talk to whoever is inside. Just push the call button, and when they answer, you can talk. That way whoever is inside doesn't have to come to the door."

"I don't get it."

"If you're busy developing a print, you can't go answer the door just because someone knocks. You can't stop in the middle of most things without ruining them. It can be very touchy." Julian still doesn't understand. "When we get inside I'll show you what I mean, okay?"

Julian nodded.

"You need to know how this is set up. The first room you enter has no light at all. You can't go into the main darkroom until this door is closed. That way, no one can let in unwanted light—you can wreck your film and prints in a second if this kind of light gets in." He unlocked the door and opened it wide. "That's why this door stays locked when I'm working in there. Take a look first so you get an idea."

The darkness was absolute: the walls were painted black. A horizontal rail or guide was affixed to the wall at the left.

"When you close the door, you put your hand on that rail. It guides you around the blind into the main room where a safety light lets you see what you're doing. All the light in there is controlled *from* in there." He gave a gentle nudge. "Grab the rail."

Julian stepped into the void; Randall followed, closing the door. He flipped the switch that activated the safety light in the next room.

"Reminds me of a certain tent…"

Randall laughed. "Maybe this is why I figured out what to do so easily. I'm used to groping around in the dark."

A corner… "I just follow this around?"

"Yep."

"Aren't we supposed to hear eerie music about now?" The rail went six inches or so and another corner—aha! This is the end of a wall! This is *fun*… a few feet further in, a dim yellowish light began to fill the area… he kept going and looked to his right. "Whoa!" A whole room, full of strange things—counters, sinks, cabinets, unusual instruments…

"Well, here we are." Randall put his hands on his hips. "I take it you've never been in a darkroom before."

"No, not ever. This is *cool!*" I remember seeing something like this in a movie once. "How come you never mentioned any of this before?"

"Dunno," he grinned. "Same reason you don't go around babbling about your drawing tablets."

"Oh… I get it. You're right." But this is so… I don't even have a word for it. "How did you *get* all this stuff?!"

"My granddad. He was a professional photographer. He had his own studio. I used to go there after school and help. Vacations too. He taught me everything. His eyes went bad and he had to retire. He set me up with a full lab before he sold off his big studio equipment. Some of this he got for me brand new. If I'd been older, he would have turned over the business to me lock stock and barrel. I was his only grandson." Randall paused a second. I get a little sad if I think too long about Granddad Fletcher. "I miss him a lot."

"I had a granddad once… but he died when I was five years old. I don't remember too much, except I used to like to sit on his lap and listen to stories." I was their only grandson too. He looked around again… once your eyes adjust you can see everything real easy.

Randall pointed to the light in the ceiling. "That's called a safelight. It's specially made so you can see to work when you make prints. Photo paper isn't affected by it unless you leave it out for a long time. Film, on the other hand, has to be handled in complete darkness. A tiny bit of light will ruin it." He stepped over to a tall narrow door. "This is the drying closet. I hang film in here to dry after it's developed. It's important to keep it away from dust until it has dried good and hard—otherwise, dust can land on it and be stuck there for good. No way to undo that if it happens." He reached in and unclipped a long strip of negatives.

"This is something you'll recognize." He took the film over to one of the enlargers and glanced at the first few frames. He slipped it into a carrier, slid the carrier into place and flipped the enlarger switch. A large image projected onto the table below. He elevated the housing a couple of feet and turned the focus knob.

"Whoa!" It's that blasted hexagon tent. It gave Julian goose bumps. I can't tell who the guys are… the faces are black… the tent is white. It's a negative!

Randall was delighted by his reaction. This is just the beginning! While Julian studied the projection, he stepped over to a cupboard and opened a drawer inside. He selected a piece of 4 by 5 print paper and held it by the edge to avoid leaving fingerprints. He closed the drawer and the cupboard door to keep it light tight, and carried the paper back to the counter where he fit it into a print easel.

Julian stood back and watched, wide eyed… a genius is at work.

Randall lowered the image to the appropriate height, refocused, and turned off the light. He put the easel in place, set the timer, and pushed the button.

"Wow…" the image was smaller and brighter; it was on white paper. After a second the light shut off automatically.

Randall left it in place and stepped over to the long counter in the center of the room. Four large trays were lined up a few inches apart. "Here," he lifted the end tray—it was sitting on top of another one just like it. "Hold this a second… don't let it drip on your clothes." He removed the next tray and handed that over. "Take these over to the sink." He removed the next two and took them over. "These are really handy: you can leave the chemicals in their trays because they've been sealed by these—no air can get in. Otherwise, I'd have to put the solutions back into the jugs every time I stopped making prints. Saves a lot of time and trouble.

The list of questions was building up; but Julian didn't want to interrupt.

After taking the film back to the drying closet, he returned to the enlarger and opened the easel. "Come watch the magic." He carried the exposed 4 by 5 over to the first tray. When Julian was in position to see, he slipped it into the liquid face up. "This tray is the developer."

The image began to appear—this time it was a regular picture—the tent was darker rather than lighter. "Whoa… that's Chuck! And Tony!" he laughed. "Man, that is so *neat!*"

At the right moment Randall slipped a pair of tongs into the solution and grabbed the print; he pulled it out of the developer quickly. "This is the tricky part. You have to take this out and put it into the next solution real fast." He slipped it into the second tray. "If you don't, it will turn all black; you don't have any time to waste. This is called the stop bath—it stops the developer instantly." He counted to ten and moved the print to the next solution. "The next tray is called the fixer. It stabilizes the image and makes it permanent on the surface of the paper. It also breaks down the unexposed emulsion so that it can be rinsed away in the bath." He pointed to the fourth tray: "this one is called Hypo. Its job is to speed up the rinsing process so that all the unexposed silver grains get washed away. Otherwise, you'd have to wash the prints ten times longer. If you don't wash those away," he tapped the edge of a round contraption full of water—"the photo will get foggy eventually." He stepped over to the sink and turned on the rinse valve; the water began to circulate. It overflowed into a trough that emptied in the sink. "The tongs move along with the print; you never go upstream with them. After they're rinsed in water, you can reuse them in the developer."

Randall gestured to the third tray. "The print needs to be in the fixer for a couple of minutes at least; I like to leave them in for five, just to be safe."

"Safe from what?"

"Sometimes the fixer gets old; it gets diluted eventually by being used and exposed to the air. I cheat a little by using it as long as I can. Mixing it isn't my favorite thing.

"You make that yourself?!"

"Well, sure. It's not hard: add water and stir, basically." He gave the print a nudge. "While the fixer is fixing, let me show you around."

The full tour followed; from the supply cupboard to the drying rack, every piece of equipment and what it did was explained. Randall was a good tour guide, but there was a lot of information. Julian stopped trying to remember the details… too much data. But what it was for and how it was used was easy enough to understand. It was enormously interesting. In mid tour Randall moved the print from the fixer to the hypo without breaking stride.

By the end of the tour, the print had been in the rinse for several minutes. It was sitting atop the water trying to find a way to slip into the trough that emptied into the sink. Randall rescued it and handed it to Julian. "Bring it over here." He grabbed a paper towel and put it on the enlarger base. He flipped on the enlarger light. "Take a look in full light."

"Whoa…" It was magical. There they are, there's that blasted tent… the campout memories started to emerge.

"Now that you get to be here for supper, I thought you might like to help make a set of prints. We can make you a set too, if you want." He snapped off the enlarger.

"Wow." Julian was wide eyed. "I'd really like that!"

In the hour that followed, he helped make contact sheets, cut up 8 by 10 photo paper into a supply of 4 by 5 and 2 1/2 by 2 print sizes, load a paper carrier, and make two sets of prints. Time zoomed by; Julian proved to be an excellent lab assistant—he had a ball doing this. Randall showed him how to use the enlarger, the timer, and the proper way to use the chemicals and the tongs. They became an efficient production line.

While the prints swirled in the circular rinse tub, they had fun poking tongs into the water to keep them separated. Julian was intrigued by the interaction of the water current and the photos—it looked like they were trying to escape, but the water was doing all the work. The properties of the paper was a surprise… any other kind of paper would have turned into mush.

The intercom broke the silence. "Randall?"

"Hi, Mom."

"Supper in ten minutes."

"We'll be there in five. Thanks, Mom." He lifted a couple of prints out of the tub and carried them over to the drying rack. When they had them all on the rack, he turned off the rinse valve.

"Do we put these back?" Julian tapped one of the trays that they had put in the sink.

"Not yet. We may want to make another print after supper." He grinned. If his plan succeeded, he would have a special print to make—one that he'd been fantasizing about for a long time. "Time to head back through the cave," he pointed to the rail on the wall.

"So, you are the renowned Julian!" Randall's father exclaimed with hearty enthusiasm. Helgar Hallstrom stood and reached for a handshake.

Julian responded as well as he could, considering. "Hello, sir… thank you…" The man was over six feet tall, had long blond hair, a well-trimmed mustache, bright blue eyes, a deep voice and an iron grip. Other than the nose, Julian would never have associated him with Randall.

"Sit, everyone, sit," Eloise commanded as she entered bearing a large tray. She proceeded to put a small bowl of tossed salad on each pre-set plate. "I hope you're not French," she said in passing. "We start with salad in this house."

"Umm, fine." He had no idea what she meant. At home Mom just puts everything on the table at the same time. We don't have a separate dining room like this. Julian had sat at a dining room table before, at Jeremy's. But it wasn't quite as fancy as this—or as big. He and Randall were seated on one side of the table, facing his little sister. She's eight years old—she has blond hair like her dad; she's nice enough… stares a lot, of course. Not much else she can do, come to think about it. He smiled at her anyway. She looked all alone over there… she smiled back, so we're okay.

Randall's mother returned, each hand supporting a platter—one had sliced ham, the other, pieces of chicken—whether roasted or fried, Julian couldn't tell. They looked different from anything he had seen before.

"We have chicken parmigiana and honey baked ham. You may have either one or both, as you wish." She returned to the kitchen without breaking stride.

The food smelled fabulous. How could she cook all this so fast?

This time she returned gripping a casserole with one hand and a serving dish with the other. She placed the scalloped potatoes in front of her husband, the mixed vegetables in front of her place at the other end, and took her seat.

Helgar responded to her nod, and lifted a small glass of wine. "Here's to our special guest, Julian." Randall and his sister lifted their small glass of water and joined their parents. "To your good health and fortune." They nodded at him and took a sip.

Julian had not encountered this sort of thing before. He wasn't sure what to do, but didn't think he should toast himself. So he lifted his glass: "thank you for your nice welcome… I'm glad to be here." Kind of lame, but…

Helgar dug into his salad with gusto.

"He doesn't use dressing, but you are welcome to." Eloise pointed to a cluster of small bottles. "We have the usual kinds there. Please help yourself."

At home Mom puts it on the salad ahead of time. He reached out for one as if he knew what he wanted… stands to reason they'll all be good. He sprinkled a little across his bowl of tossed greens and handed it to Randall.

"Thanks, but I like the bleu." He grabbed another bottle and passed it to his mother. It was her favorite; letting her use it first was a smooth move he learned on advice from his father.

Out of the corner of his eye, Julian watched… blue dressing was a new thing… oh. It's white. Figures; like the mud room without mud, they have blue dressing without blue.

Helgar had begun his assessment the second Julian appeared. Not as tall as I expected. Randall's descriptions were colored by a degree of hero worship, certainly. But what a face! In a few years… well. He certainly has influenced Randall in a positive way. What Helgar was curious about, of course was the boy's orientation… So far I don't see a problem. He didn't expect one, of course. Randall is an intelligent boy, but still young enough, inexperienced enough to be hasty—particularly when he's up against a stunner like this. He finished his salad and spooned out a healthy portion of scalloped potatoes.

"One way traffic, to the right." He passed the potatoes to Julian. He didn't expect to see anything overt, but by the end of the meal he expected to glean a few hints that pointed one direction or the other.

For a kid who was used to sitting at the kitchen table with his mom, this was something else. Once before, a long time ago, Julian and his mom were guests at a fancy dinner like this—all he could remember was being told to keep the napkin in his lap—oh, and they had two forks. This was sort of like that, 'cept everyone is in regular clothes. This is like a movie—everyone sitting around a table, father at one end, mother at the other… feels nice. A few minutes into the meal, he noticed that soft music was playing somewhere. It covered all the chewing and munching… no one was talking… It seemed okay to not talk… maybe that's better manners than trying to eat and talk at the same time. On the other hand, maybe they're just being super polite. Maybe they expect me to say something… show that

I'm not just a bump on the log. He looked for an opening—I know: when he takes a sip of wine.

It didn't take long. "Mr. Hallstrom, may I ask a question?"

"Why, certainly." He was pleased by the boy's deference and tone. Ten points.

"It's that music. I've never heard that before."

"Oh, let's see..." he listened to a couple of bars. "Schubert. That's Franz Schubert... one of his quartets." Ten more points. "Do you like that kind of music?"

Julian paused to find the correct way to phrase his answer. "I think so, but I don't get to hear it very often. The one they're playing now, yes. It's interesting."

Ten more points: this boy pleases me. "What do you like about it?"

You and your big mouth. Inside guy just joined him at the table.

"Umm... I'm not sure exactly. It makes me sit back and think, maybe. No, that's not it... it's like... I don't know how to describe it. It's relaxing, but it's not putting me to sleep... it's the opposite of pop music—you know, the stuff on the radio that you always want to turn down because your brains get scrambled and you can't think until it's turned off—it's not full of stupid words that don't mean anything and they repeat over and over a hundred times." He shrugged. "I don't know anything about music, to be honest. I like some songs, but I like most of all for it to be quiet. Like on campouts and hikes—the natural sounds are what I like." Wind, water, birds...

Helgar was a Groucho Marx fan. He pictured Groucho in his mind, doing his eyebrow routine: the contestant just said the secret word: sounds of nature. Julian had just won an extra hundred points. He glanced at his wife—she sees it too. This boy is every bit as good as Randall says.

He was doubly impressed—the boy's sentiment, and the honest attempt to articulate something new and complex on the fly demonstrated a high level of self-confidence. Also impressive was the way Randall watched and attended his words: there was no doubt about his son's attachment. I see why, now—it's not just because the boy is so pretty.

"Randall has told us that you are an excellent artist. I'd like to see some of your work."

Julian blushed. The compliment was unexpected; I never know what to say when that happens.

"His latest sketchbook is in the mudroom." Randall remarked with a grin. Julian had passed the test: Dad likes him. I knew he would, but still it's good to know for sure.

"Well; after supper, perhaps I could prevail on you to give me a peek." Helgar raised his glass.

"Umm… yeah, sure." Now I know why Randall uses fancy words so much: his dad. Julian gave him a closer look. He had never met a man like this. Imposing, impressive, distinguished… and there was another quality that he couldn't find a word for. But to look at him, you'd never guess he was a professor… looks more like a football coach. Randall is one lucky kid, that's all.

Julian offered to help with the dishes—that's what he always did at home; but Mrs. Hallstrom shooed them all into the den. She wanted her daughter to do that. Julian understood at once. Doing the dishes with his mom was a big part of the day. That was the one thing he missed when he was at camp last summer. Just doing something with her at the end of the day made him feel good. This was Randall's sister's time to be with her mom.

For some reason, his dad was keen to see my sketchbook. I expected him to keep me there while he leafed through it, but after he opened it to the first page he said thanks and sat down. He said he'd look through it while we worked in the photolab. A relief, really…

it's uncomfortable to sit and wait for someone to look though your notebook—and boring.

So, here we are, going through the mud room again. "What did you say your dad's name is?" He's so different from Randall.

"Helgar—but I think it was Mom that said it."

"Oh… yeah… I expect that's a Swedish name." Randall said he was Swedish.

Instead of heading for the photo lab, Randall turned left as they entered the garage. "It means a flat rock that's spritely enough to skip across rapidly moving water." He always found that amusing; he pictured his father as a boulder that could wade through the water to cross the river if he had a mind to; the water would be a mere nuisance.

Julian didn't pay attention to where they were headed; he was still preoccupied by Randall's dad. The image of the man back there didn't match that meaning very well. Sprite didn't fit. Probably named after a relative. "So what's Randall mean then?"

They started up the stairway. "That's not a Swedish name; I'm named after my grandfather, Randall Fletcher. He was Scottish. The name means a guy that makes arrows that fly like a raven and bite like a wolf. But for me, it means a Scottish arrow flying like a raven and biting like a wolf on rapidly moving Swedish water." He opened the door to the upstairs apartment. "What I'm supposed to be biting isn't mentioned anywhere." He turned on the light.

"How do you know this stuff?"

"Looked it up; I did a report on it in the sixth grade." Miss Watkins was big on genealogy. He walked across the room and opened a large box.

"Huh. I don't know what my name means. My dad gave me my name and I don't know anything more about it." Mom is dead set against talking about that stuff.

"It's not hard to figure out." He handed Julian a large reflector panel. "You could find out in a minute in the library. Common sense says that your last name is what it says: Your ancestors lived in the forest. Your first name probably means you're connected to Julius Caesar somehow." He handed Julian the telescoping stand.

"How do you figure that?"

"That's the easy part: you should know that. Everything that starts with J-U-L is connected to Julius Caesar."

"Why would I know that?!"

"Because Mr. Quimby said so. You know, our history teacher? He said that in class."

"Oh." I don't always pay attention to Mr. Quimby like I should. My mind wanders off in that class sometimes.

"It was around the time he talked about Cleopatra and how she bore his son and named him Caesarion instead of Julius Junior."

I remember that: "He's the kid they killed in the desert, right?"

"Yep."

We haven't had that on a test yet. "What are these for?" More to the point, what are they?

"Bring them over here." Randall had crossed the room and was affixing a flood lamp to a stand. He took the second stand from Julian and opened it up. "We're setting up a temporary staging area."

A temporary what?

When Julian didn't ask, Randall looked at him. "You know what that is?"

"Not exactly."

It's where you will be standing in a few minutes when you pose for me and my camera."

Julian's jaw dropped.

"Fair is fair," he grinned, and took the reflector panel.

A complete surprise… the last thing he would have expected. He didn't disagree—not at all. But it had never been discussed—or mentioned even.

"I was going to ask you about it, but I could never figure out a way to bring it up. So I sort of hoped that once we were here, and you saw what I can do, you'd like the idea." He gave Julian a warm smile.

Julian tilted his head and regarded Randall anew: a dimension that he had not expected was there—his respect had just gone up a notch; no: two notches. The boy setting up equipment was no longer a shy kid from out west who needed a pal to show him around. He's a force to be reckoned with—a friendly force. This is Zeta, my blood brother who I can always trust. A wide smile replaced the surprised look.

—ꟽ—

"Well. It seems that Randall the First has proven to be absolutely correct about his grandson." Helgar lifted his glass in salute. He had been very fond of his wife's father.

"Daddy was always right about people; that's why he was such a good photographer. He had an inner eye… he always knew what would make his subjects look better than they were."

"Do you think Randall has found whom he needs?" Helgar was of mixed opinion about this… he didn't want his boy to hurry into any commitments.

Eloise pondered that… "He could do a lot worse, Helgar."

"True; too true." I know a few who paid dearly for jumping before they looked both ways.

"At least he hasn't attracted any bullies here. I credit Julian with that too; Randall has found acceptance among those boy scouts thanks to him. He's not isolated here the way he was back… in Pullman." she stopped herself from saying "home" just in time.

They would not be returning there for the foreseeable future. This is home now.

They were silent for a time, troubling over the next step, which they knew was closer than not: the talk. It's timing was critical. They believed it essential that Randall grow and develop on his own as much as possible. Their role was to be a support—guiding *indirectly,* as needed. They preferred to be silent in their omniscience, not controlling… the danger of that approach is to appear neglectful, or to assume things are on course when they're not. That's why the family outings and events… why every opportunity for Randall to ask or confide is available without hesitation or reservation. Their children came first and foremost; part of that, a very real part, was preventing the children from being aware of it.

"Thanks for tonight, Eloise; you have every bit as good a sense about people as your father. I shall have to find a way to reward you for your quick thinking this afternoon. The instant supper invitation was perfect." Prearranged meetings are never to be trusted; Helgar set great store in the spontaneous—as a man as well as a scientist. He picked up the sketchbook. "I want to look at these again. I wouldn't mind if Randall could arrange for us to see his other tablets." Randall says he's done these on his own—no training, no special art lessons. I don't know anything about art or how a boy like Julian can make it into a career. I'll have to ask about that.

"Mmm," Eloise nodded in agreement; I'll see to that. Yes… that might serve as an entrée to get acquainted with Francine. She wanted to meet the woman who had produced the marvel who had captured her son's fancy. More than just meet.

She smiled internally; she looked forward to Helgar's "reward."

25 Above Randall's photolab

After Randall set up a folding screen background with a basic set of lights, reflectors and diffusing panels, he had Julian try a set of potential stances. He'd learned from his grandfather the basics of shadow and contrast. This project had been brewing in his head for weeks, so it fell into place rapidly—once he had adjusted to the fact that Julian was doing all this in nature's own. That was a complete surprise—Randall hadn't even asked him to undress; Julian just did it automatically. It helped greatly: at once it clarified how the lights needed to be aimed and filtered. The short ladder permitted a couple of high angle shots. Julian assisted by suggesting angles and composition elements.

The first set was taken in Verichrome Pan, a 12 exposure medium format roll, using his Yashica A. It included all the essential views, angles and poses he had in mind; the raw material in that short roll was enough to do many things. Medium format negatives allowed enlarging beyond anything he would need.

Then he loaded his Nikon F with a 36 exposure cartridge of Tri-X. This was the fantasy roll—Julian would get to take half of the snapshots.

"Why don't you put that camera on the tripod?"

"Don't need to. The film in this is a lot faster—four times, almost. The other film is better for detail and enlarging, but you have to have all these floodlights or a flashbulb unless you're outside; and you have to make sure the camera is held steady—otherwise, you get a blurry image. With Tri-X you can use available light and a fast shutter speed."

Julian's head couldn't hold any more technical information—Randall knew what was up and that was enough.

"With this you can move around and get all kinds of interesting angles and you don't have to set things up in advance." He handed Julian the camera. "Look through the viewfinder at something…"

He pointed the camera at Randall's face. "You're all blurry."

"Use one hand to adjust the lens—with this camera you're looking at the subject from the same lens as the film; turn until it's focused. What you see will be what's in the picture."

"Ooo…" Randall's face filled the frame. "'What a big nose, you have,' said Little Red Riding Hood."

Randall laughed. "All the better to smell you with." Standing close like this made that easy enough.

He panned down. "'What a lot of clothes you have on,' said the camera man."

"Oh!" he giggled. "I forgot." He undressed rapidly. The deal was that he had to pose for some nude pictures too. It felt very strange at first. He was never comfortable without something on—but somehow, Julian was able to make him feel at ease, like it was natural or something. Amazing.

Randall had no way of knowing that Julian had always preferred to have as little on as possible. The social function and purpose of clothing was something he learned to put up with gradually and reluctantly. Once he was out of diapers, it had taken his mother over three years to keep underwear on him, indoors or out. In warm weather he wore a bathing suit or cutoffs and went shirtless. As far as Julian was concerned, clothing had only one purpose: to keep you warm. He dressed accordingly when he could get away with it—or when it was allowed. It wasn't a matter of philosophy—it all depended on how it felt. He wasn't an exhibitionist; modesty was never a factor in his thinking—Once in a while his mother still had to remind him it was time to put on his pants.

While Randall undressed, Julian took a closer look at the camera. Look at all the dials… it must take a while to learn how to use this. Grandpa had a real old one that folded out into a bellows, but mom says it's too delicate to use. She promised one day to get a new one. I'm not worried about it. The cost of the film and prints sort of put the whole idea on the bottom of the wish list. Besides, if something is worth remembering, I just draw it up.

Randall was ready. "How about this… one of us stands in a pose and the other one takes the picture—then we trade places. That way we'll have two sets with the same pose."

"Neato!"

"So all we have to do is decide who poses first." He hadn't planned the next step; having gotten this far was a miracle. Standing naked in the upstairs apartment with Julian had never even been a fantasy. He was running as fast as he could just to catch up with reality.

Julian had the camera, but he didn't know how to use it. "I think I should pose first. That way, you can get the camera all ready. When we trade places all I have to do is push the button. That way my pictures won't foul up."

"Good thinking." Julian doesn't know anything about shutter speed or aperture. This way we won't have to spend time going over all that. He took the camera.

Julian had several ideas about the anatomical and artistic elements of a pose; thanks to Leonard and Mark, he had considered several possibilities when they posed at camp. He had a few in mind. He stepped over to the sofa and lifted his left foot. With his hands linked behind his head, he twisted to look back over his left shoulder. "How's this?"

"Great." Randall got down on one knee and focused—a low angle shot felt right—Julian's balls were visible in profile from down here—yum. The twist in his back created diagonal folds in his skin that swooped upward, suggesting movement. He set the shutter speed and f-stop. The floodlights were still on, so this was easy to figure without a light meter: f/8 at 125th of a second. I'll do the entire roll with the 50mm lens. This setting will be good for everything as long as I leave these floods going. He snapped a picture. "Before you come over here, take a look at how I'm positioned."

Seeing Randall on his knees made Julian realize something: I can't do that when I'm drawing… huh. All of a sudden the potential of a camera was clear. If I'm drawing what I'm actually looking at, it has to be from eye level… wow.

"Notice that I have turned the camera sideways—that way the picture will be vertical. It will look just like what you see in the viewfinder." He advanced the film to the next frame while Julian skipped over and got down on his right knee.

Randall checked to make sure the camera was set right before taking his pose. No problem. He zipped over to the sofa and tried to mimic Julian's pose—it felt very odd… untypical as can be… I never stand like this. He wasn't sure he wanted to see what it looked like… still, it feels sort of good… sort of free.

Julian checked the focus… oo… interesting view. You don't get to look at balls from this angle every day… a drawing started to appear in his minds eye.

> *click!* <

Julian had just taken his first photograph. Wow, this is *so* cool!

After six poses, Julian realized that a camera could take several different angles of the same pose. He imagined his drawings of Mark as they would look from different angles—that might help me understand what I'm looking at better… I like to feel inside my head what the real figure is like—as if I was molding it with my hands. That's what I want the drawing to look like, as if I could almost "feel" it, as if I know what the other side looks like. The best thing about the Initiation was I got to "see" in 3-D with my hands. Yeah… maybe Randall will teach me how to use his camera; I can't go around feeling everything with my hands as if I was blind or something.

After another six sets of exposures, Julian was confident enough to think ahead about the remaining images… an idea occurred to him. "When I take this one, stay put. I want to try something, okay?" He pressed the button, put the camera down and stepped behind Randall quietly. "Close your eyes." He checked to make sure he wasn't cheating. He put his hands on Randall's buns and massaged slowly. "Keep them closed, now…" he looked around to see if his hunch was right. It was: Little R was swelling.

Randall felt an electric jolt as strong as any he could remember—the blood rushed to his face and scalp—at the same time it pumped full speed into Little R's wide open intake valves. He felt the tips of his ears turn red… he was back in the tent, but this was *better*.

"So…' Julian said softly as he reached around and cupped Randall's balls in his right hand: "I'll bet you're not thinking about Rita."

"*What?!*" He turned around, appalled. "You just ruined the best hard on grow I ever had!" He looked down at his raging Little R. Little J was bouncing a few inches away, just as hard.

"They had a race," Julian chuckled."I think it was a tie." It seems that rubbing buns has the same effect has having buns rubbed.

"We still have film to shoot!"

"I know. I figured we ought to get a few stiffies." He had a special reason. It had occurred to him that he'd need to draw one in detail at some point. You can't just order up a live model whenever you want; a good reference set will come in handy.

Randall was not about to argue—I have to come up with a triple secure hiding place, that's for sure! I was so proud of myself for not getting a stiffy up to now… not that I'm disappointed…

They had 12 more frames: six different positions to plan and document. It was fun; each frame made them even more horny. Horizontal poses, close-ups and special angles were an unexpected delight. The strong shadows made their bodies seem like living sculptures. By the end of the roll, both Little J and Little R were dripping with impatience—even that got into the last picture. This fit perfectly with what Julian had in mind.

"You're sure no one is going to come up here?"

Randall checked his watch. "We're okay for another hour."

"Perfect. I thought it might be fun to give you lesson number three."

"You mean…" Randall's eyes opened wide.

"Yeah." Julian had decided to jump ahead to the Geoff technique. Technically, that's lesson four. He wanted to combine all his oral knowhow into one lesson—one *last* lesson. "I was gonna do this in my bedroom, but I don't exactly want to wait until later…"

"Me either!" Randall glanced at the sofa. His mom kept that ready in case they had an overnight guest. "That's a hide-a-bed. Would that be okay?" I assume doing it on the carpet is sort of second best.

"Yeah!" Julian stepped over. "How does it work?"

In a few minutes they had the hide-a-bed set up. The floodlights were turned off, the sheets pulled down, pillows fluffed, and towels from the bathroom, as well as a supply of tissue, were at hand. To achieve a little atmosphere, Randall turned off the overhead and let the light from the bathroom spill into the main room. Just to be safe, he locked the door. "Everything's ready."

"Remember, this is secret."

Randall frowned. As if there was anyone I could tell!

"I just want you to remember the rule I set before: if I tell you about someone, you know, use their name, you won't ever pass it on."

"Oh yeah, sure." Randall thought a little. "I could always say I don't know," he shrugged.

"No. Don't do that. Be honest: Say that you won't tell any *whos*; you will only tell *whats*—make them understand how important it is to respect people. If you talk about anyone without their permission, you are hurting them whether you mean to or not. If you do that, you deserve the same thing." In grade school Julian had first hand experience—he had to console a girl who had been the victim of this. It wasn't easy. What had started out as a fun rumor had turned into a very bad experience. He swore that he would never be guilty of harming anyone just because he wanted to tell a fun story.

The deep conviction in Julian's eyes was compelling. Randall was smart enough to see the logic and the wisdom: if I were to mention a name, it would get passed on along with my own. That he would *ever* be in a position to talk about this was unimaginable, but he nodded anyway. "If, and it's a *big* if—I ever have the need, I'll say what you just said—and I won't tell it was you that taught me, either." He looked Julian straight in the eye: "Ever."

Julian felt a rush. Randall meant this with all his heart. Good. Better than good. He hopped onto the bed and patted the space next to him.

Randall was next to him in a flash, his heart pounding so hard he was afraid Julian would hear it.

"Say, this isn't bad." Julian scootched back and forth…"I've never been on one of these before." Not as good as a real bed, but better than a canvas cot. He propped his head up with the pillow as if he was about to read a book.

The hide-a-bed was *dreadful,* but Randall wasn't going to argue the point. He wanted the ceremony to begin, yet he was torn: Julian's beautiful face was in silhouette—I want to appreciate it for a minute. What I'm looking at would have been the best snapshot of all. The eyes are so *mysterious*…in the semi-dark room they became inscrutable; the brown pupils look almost black, like his eyelashes.

The light from the bathroom created highlights and shadows that emphasized Julian's smooth lush skin and his rich lips, ripe, swollen with sensual appeal—adolescent lips in their prime have such a powerful attraction—they seem to *need* kissing, to *require* it. Randall couldn't have articulated that, but he felt it to his core. He lacked the courage to follow his urge—he would curse himself later for being a chicken. Or, be thankful he hadn't totally screwed up the evening.

Julian wanted to set the stage first, sort of explain things a little. I'm hot to trot, but this is a *lesson*, all the same.

"This was back at Camp Walker, remember," he began. "Danny and I had to do Inspection every morning after KP. It was after everyone was gone from camp to a class or activity. Most days we had fifteen or twenty minutes extra. On some days Danny was so horny he couldn't stand it, so he'd come up with these tricks or excuses to "play around." He looked at Randall directly. "I didn't mind a bit, to be honest. I was so green and stupid… I wanted to know what it was all about. I *needed* to know; he wasn't taking advantage of me at all." Julian was using Danny's real name because Randall already knew him—he's a fellow Initiate; Randall had already sworn that he would never pass it on.

Unconsciously, Randall had satisfied a small itch along Little R's right side… his hand remained in place—inactive; his eyes continued to survey the prone beauty at his side… the sight of Little J in silhouette a couple of feet away was wonderful. He was listening, of course—but he couldn't resist feasting his eyes at the same time. Little J is just as ready as Little R: the light caught a small bead at the very tip, giving the illusion that a liquid diamond was being born. Again, Randall had to exercise his self-control… I've never seen Little J drip before, but I did feel it in the blackness of the Initiation tent… if only I had a way to take a picture.

…"One day after Inspection, he wanted to show me something he had learned the day before. We went to the cabin again, since no one was around. This time though—and this is *Super Top Secret*—I spread my blanket out on Mark's big bed instead of the floor."

"Mark's *bed?!"*

"Yeah—well, I figured it would be okay as long as my blanket covered everything up. My cot was worthless, and the floor was so darn hard… so why not?" Besides, I wanted to see what it was like on that bed anyway. Randall doesn't need to know *that*, of course…

Wow… this was one example of bravery that Randall really admired—I would never have dared that, no matter how safe it was.

"So anyway… Danny was all hot to show me something he had learned on his supply route. He and another guy had a delivery route after lunch—they took fresh stuff to some of the camps." Julian turned on his side and faced Randall. "This guy: boy, was *he* something. Part Cambodian, part English—super hot to look at. He grew up in California. They must get a head start on this stuff out there."

"Mmm." That didn't surprise. "Is he a surfer?" I've heard about those guys.

"Could be. I never found out that much about him. Anyway he taught Danny this special way to suck off somebody."

Randall could hardly believe his ears: his all-time top priority! At last!

"I s'pose you've been wondering about that some…"

"Umm… a little, yeah." His heart rate had doubled.

"Me too. Back then I had only thought about it." He was conveniently omitting an event here…telling about Sid was pointless. Besides, what he and Sid had done was nothing compared to what Danny did. It might as well have been my first time.

Out of sheer luck Randall caught a drip on his left arm—it would have fallen onto the sheet—he hadn't touched himself. Little R is *so* ready…

Julian sat up. "Roll onto your back." He got onto his knees and faced Randall from the side. "Now spread your legs open…" he pulled the right leg toward himself while Randall shifted the left leg. Julian climbed over and repositioned himself; now he was sitting on his heels between Randall's legs.

"I'm going to show you what he did, but first I need to tell you about one change I want to try."

Randall nodded.

"Y'see, after what we learned at Hayden Park, it makes sense. When he showed me what to do, it was from start to finish. When I shot, it was my turn to do him, start to finish." He put his hands on his hips. "If it's okay with you, I think we ought to do what we learned in the tent: when you're about to shoot you tell me to stop. Then you hold off and do me until I'm close. I stop then, and we trade again. I finish you—and then you finish me. What do you think?"

Randall was hardly in a position to make a reasoned judgment about this sort of refinement in something he had only dreamed about. He swallowed and garbled, "Your way, for sure." His mouth had become so filled with saliva he almost choked.

"Great!" I've wanted to try this ever since that campout. "Okay. Here's what you do—the way you start is *very* important. With your left hand you pull down so the skin is real tight. With Danny that was super important—he's not circumcised like we are." He pressed the sides of Randall's shaft and pulled downward until it was tight. A sizeable drop of pre-cum appeared.

"Oo, look who's ready!" Julian cooed. With his right forefinger he spread it around uniformly. "I love the taste of this stuff; it makes everything so much better, so *slippery*!" he grinned. Too bad I won't be able to see his face when I do this. "Oop! Little R wants a second coat!" He spread the new drop around. "There." He licked his finger and gave Randall a wink.

Randall was too numb to react; that would come later. Julian licking his finger as if it had been dunked in chocolate syrup was… unforgettable. The correct word to describe it, if there was one, would also have to come later.

"The most important thing is how you start: you keep the skin pulled down and, you suck real *tight*… *super* tight; you go real slow all the way down… you have to keep the suction and your lips real tight. You loosen up gradually, but not until things get going. You keep hold of the base so it won't slip out and flip away by mistake. With your right hand you massage the area gently—do some of the stuff we learned in the tent." He paused a second—this is where my plan starts.

"That is the first half: you stay still the whole time—no pumping. When you know you're close, you push on my shoulder—that way I can pull off in time. Okay?"

Randall nodded.

"I'll do a bunch of things with my tongue and lips—y'know, just to make it more interesting and feel better… I'll experiment a little. The idea is for me to go slow so every little nerve ending can be appreciated. Then, during the *second* half, you pump; my job is to hold tight and steady; you control where it goes, how far in, how far you pull out, you know, that kind of thing. It's best not to go too fast, or you'll shoot too soon—it doesn't feel as good as when you go slow.

"One other thing: don't be tempted to hold yourself or do any jacking while you suck—it will make you want to shoot too soon. The whole idea is to shoot into my mouth—every last drop. Then when you pull out, I'll swallow it."

"You'll *swallow* it?!"

"Sure. I like the taste." He saw the doubt… "You don't have to—it's not a requirement; I just like it, that's all."

Randall was fascinated; I had fantasies about doing that but figured I'd probably chicken out. Now I'm going all the way, for sure.

Julian was ready to do this—he wanted to do it really well because Randall deserved the best—but this is to be a one and only time. I like Randall more than ever now—but I don't want to get attached. If I hadn't promised, I probably wouldn't be doing this. Julian was afraid that if he played with Randall too much or too often, he'd lose Mark. He couldn't say why he believed that—but he did, and there wasn't a single person he could talk to about it. When it came to Mark, Julian took no risks.

He gave a friendly wink and bent down, his mouth open.

Oh... oh! Randall's arms shot out to the side automatically. The sensation of Julian's warm wet mouth moving slowly down his shaft was unlike anything he had ever imagined. The suction multiplied the intensity twofold, *threefold…* his fingers twisted randomly in the air in a vain attempt to diffuse the intensity to a more tolerable, more comprehendible level.

Like a hi-fi turned up too loud, the pleasure bordered on the uncomfortable… it leveled off, becoming a complex combination of pleasure sensations; awareness of an orchestration evolved gradually as he became more accustomed to what Julian was doing… the value of going slowly was absolutely clear. Being a passive recipient was as difficult as it had been in the Initiation—but that event enabled him to pay attention to this new technique as well as to experience it.

After the sixth cycle, the telltale signal at the base of his shaft and at the tip upstaged everything… his balls had elevated. He pushed Julian's shoulder hurriedly.

Julian released him at once and sat up. This could go wrong if Randall had waited too long. He watched closely; Little R throbbed in protest at this sudden cessation—so close to home…

Randall closed his eyes and concentrated on catching his breath—it was like watching a glass of water tipping precariously, nearing the balance point: will it spill or level off? His heart was going a hundred miles an hour… he inhaled deeply, trying not to feel Little R or what Little R was doing. Please, please… what if I waited too long…

Julian glanced down at himself. Oh-oh… I need to pay attention—Little J is in a hurry… a big hurry. Keeping him under control won't be easy; he returned to his side of the bed and laid back, legs spread. Randall can begin his turn when he's ready. Making Little J wait a little is a good idea.

The Initiation training had taught how to stop in midstream; it was a bit of an art, but most of all, it was an application of self-control and timing. When he was safely on hold, Randall sat up. There's Julian, waiting with his eyes closed—he looks like a Prince that's been put into a trance by an evil witch. My assignment is to bring him back to life. First though, it was essential to etch what he was looking at into his core memory. This is a once-only kind of shot—there are lots of sunrise pictures but in all my mountain trips, only one is burned permanently into my memory. What he was looking at this minute was another such—no camera could capture this.

He moved between Julian's legs. Now, what I've been waiting for so long: tasting one of these had been his dream fantasy forever. To think that his precious Julian would be first was good fortune beyond understanding. He bent down close… oh, wow… the *aroma*. He inhaled deeply and held Little J at the base just as Julian had instructed… he licked his lips and lowered his head.

It was the Initiation all over again—his mouth knew this object of beauty—the sensory knowledge he had learned with his hands and fingers and nose were applied in an instant. His tongue knew where to press, to sweep… he knew when to squeeze his lips tighter and when to rotate his head… he had done this before: writ larger with the addition of taste, the tongue enabled a new, more complex connection.

Julian was able to experience Randall's performance on two levels: as friend and as a teacher. Twice before he'd had one of these—first Danny, then Nick. Those were fantastic at the time, but this is the best so far… mmm… it was the effect of the Hayden Park experience. I felt that when I was sucking Randall—it was like I was back home, back where I was supposed to be… that crazy weekend keeps improving my life.

On purpose he refrained from thinking about Mark… that would make this go so fast it would be over in a second. Randall is doing a good job… *ooo*, an *excellent* job…

No metaphor could do justice to the experience Randall was in the midst of—the sheer joy of knowing exactly what Julian is feeling when I do something—because I still feel what he did a few minutes ago… I'm in a magic mirror, experiencing it as I perform it.

Time was suspended… the slow pace encouraged each level of pleasure to build… each upward pass was a new layer, each return downward pressed it tightly onto the previous layer, turning the shaft into a throbbing tower of ecstasy.

The crucial moment arrived—Julian didn't know for sure if it was too soon or too late, but he pushed Randall's shoulders gently. He had been doing so well it was very difficult to ask him to stop.

Randall sat back at once—he had been so absorbed that he had lost track of time. He might have been doing this for five minutes or twenty five… he didn't want to stop.

"Mmm." Julian cooed. Giving some sign to Randall that he was doing well seemed appropriate, but cluttering the air with words wasn't.

That sound made Randall's scalp tingle… Julian liked what I did… I feel so strong, so good, now—like I passed some kind of test.

Julian was in position for part two: he reached over and appropriated Randall's pillow and stuffed it under his own. The surprise on Randall's face reminded him that he hadn't mentioned this little detail. He touched Randall's knees "Put your knees up here…" he put his hands on his waist. "Then scoot up close."

As Randall moved into position, Julian drew his own legs together. The two dripping pleasure batons brushing each other as they passed by was a nice surprise; he looked at Julian directly for confirmation that he was in the right place.

Julian answered the question by grabbing Randall's buns and drawing him forward. He formed his lips into an open pucker and pulled Little R in.

Ohhhh, the *sensation*… he moaned softly… he felt Julian's tongue press upward as he pushed in, forcing the point to ride across the roof of Julian's mouth… 'Remember,' he warned himself… *go slow*… That will be the most difficult part…

Randall soon became aware of new sources of pleasure—the rocking back and forth employed several muscle groups in their most ancient role—creating an internal rhythm that made his prostate glow; his balls swung freely and hummed a silent song when they touched Julian's chin. Instinctively he ran his fingers through Julian's hair—gently, tenderly, choreographed unconsciously to match the movement below.

Julian caressed and massaged Randall's backside, and squeezed the muscles together—Randall understood at once and clenched them tight as he thrust inward. Julian held Randall's thighs—thrilled by the flexing muscle and sinew... the power, the strength—wonderful! He continued around, sending a forefinger to rest briefly on each side of the crotch... then to slowly trace along each side of the scrotum—Inside, the prostate sent its clarion call, announcing the impending discharge—the most intense pleasure yet radiated upward. Julian had pushed the launch button.

There was no stopping—Randall caressed and massaged Julian's golden fronds, flexing his fingers in ecstasy. Exhaling a guttural groan, he fired. He backed out, then fired a second time: his unique whimper betrayed the incredible intensity of the release. Three more enormous shots, and he was spent. He held still, perched forward—Little R continued to pulse in place. After a moment he relaxed and tried to recede—but Julian held him fast.

They remained in that position for several seconds... then Julian maximized the suction and pulled his head back slowly, lips squeegee tight.

The spasm was sudden and sharp—it would have made Randall collapse if Julian hadn't been holding on to him.

Julian looked up at Randall's face and waited... when he opened his eyes, he swallowed what remained; a telltale rivulet had run down his chin. "Tasty." He released Randall's buns.

The offhand tone was so out of sync with where Randall's mind had gone, it forced him to give a single laugh. He couldn't think of a thing to say. It served to snap him back to reality: it was his turn to be a receptacle.

Inadvertently, Julian had made it possible—and imperative—to proceed; otherwise, Randall might have sunk into a swoon, cradled himself in Julian's arms and fallen asleep. Instead, he returned to his side of the bed and grabbed the pillows. He was determined to prove he could do this.

Julian got into position and began his part two run. He had been planning to try this for a long time—though not with Randall. But he was delighted so far—it was a big improvement over what Danny and Nick had done. When it was time, he would do this with Mark. That's what his mind began to do. They say practice makes perfect, and this was about the only practice he was likely to get.

He was able to hold out for three thrusts just as Randall had, which was a nice surprise.

Randall was a quick learner; the fact that it was Julian meant his effort was absolute. When it was time, he accepted the emissions without hesitation. He tried to replicate what Julian had done… there was no way it could be improved. The one difference: he kept his eyes wide open—he wanted to be able to put himself back here in his mind whenever he felt the urge. He performed the final squeegee and waited for Julian to open his eyes.

Julian relaxed at last, but resisted the urge to lie down. He opened his eyes and was surprised by the expression on Randall's face. The strong shadows gave him a mysterious enigmatic quality.

Randall swallowed at last, certain that Julian would see.

Julian felt a rush of gratitude. "See what I mean?"

"Kinda sweet, isn't it?"

Julian nodded. A wave of emotion flooded him—Randall had been so selfless, and so good. An impulse grabbed hold—an expression of his friendship was required. He leaned down and pulled Randall into a sitting position and hugged as hard as he could—he didn't want to kiss him; that wouldn't be honest. But after tonight, their friendship had reached a new level. Julian felt enriched as a human being. He didn't have the vocabulary to express what he felt—the hug was a good substitute.

Randall was thrilled—surprised—and honored. Tears filled his eyes. He was wise enough to realize that Julian didn't love him…

but they had something special. He wasn't about to give up all hope… but he sensed that there was someone or something else that came first. No way to fight that, no point in trying. Preserve what there is… it may grow one day. He returned the hug but remained motionless, savoring the silence, the presence of his Prince.

The real world had returned. Julian leaned back and tapped Randall on the shoulder: "How are we doing for time?"

He checked his watch. "We have about twenty minutes."

"Can we clean up and show up five minutes early?"

"Yep. Let's take a few prints from the drying rack—that will show that we've been good boys."

"Good thinking." Julian rolled to the side and scooted off the bed. What?! He looked down… Little J's not going limp.

Randall had rolled off the other side and noticed a similar sensation. Wide eyed, he looked at Julian for an explanation.

"Whoa…" he saw Randall's… both were still *very* puffy.

"Does it take them longer to go down after doing that?"

"Dunno for sure." This didn't happen at Camp Walker… "Let's hope we'll be okay in ten minutes. Should we get dressed first?" Normally, Julian preferred to do that last.

"Maybe so… we can't go down there looking like *this*." My parents have never seen me with a boner. Tonight is *not* a good time to bring them up to date on that.

They dressed, and checked each other out. Neither could disguise the bulge. Julian remembered Mark's puffy state when he served that cake.

"We need a cold bottle of root beer!" Randall quipped. The small refrigerator up here is empty—unplugged.

"Maybe they'll go down enough… we can always put our hands in front, y'know, hold some pictures…"

They set to work. Randall decided to leave the staging area as is. "All we need to do is fold up the hide-a-bed." This evening's inspiration had made one thing obvious: I can set up a regular studio in this space. Who knows, it might come in handy.

They worked well as a team. In no time the sofa was back in its original position. Randall grabbed the cameras and led the way to the door.

Julian's brain, as usual, began to analyze what had transpired in this room; it stopped at the first imponderable. The subject heading was a major gripe: I don't like the word I'm being forced to use. Maybe Randall has an idea: "I have a question for your advanced scientific mind."

"That means I probably don't know the answer either; but I'll give it a shot." He turned off the overhead light and headed down the stairway.

"Why do they call it a blow job?"

"What?!" He stopped in mid step and looked back, nonplussed. It was very strange to hear Julian say that word. It was certainly not the question he expected.

"I mean, it's just the opposite. You don't blow at all."

Randall laughed. "I have to admit that I have never looked it up…" He shook his head; good old Julian.

"It really bugs me though. Why don't they have a word that tells what it is?! What we just did was wonderful, beautiful, *excellent.* The word they have is uggy and crude… almost disgusting."

"Y' know, you're right." He flipped on the blue light and opened the photo lab door.

"Who makes words like that up, anyway?"

"Dunno."

"Whoever it is, I bet they never had one or did one." He groped for the railing and led the way into the dark room. "Maybe they just watched."

"Good point..." he had never given this sort of thing any thought. "When you think about it, all the words about sex are like that." He didn't need to say them aloud. "Maybe it's just that way in English. Maybe the French or the Italians have better words."

"Hmm. Could be... how would you find out?" He stood aside.

Randall headed to the "dry" counter and set down the cameras. He proceeded to remove the exposed film. "Go to the library?"

"At Jackson?" Julian laughed. "I doubt if the school library would have very much. Say, I bet the college library would have something."

"If you think I'm going to ask Dad to look up blow job in the university library, think again!" He took the two rolls of film and tucked them into the back of a drawer. "If I get hit by lightning tomorrow, you'll have to rescue these."

"Oo, that's right. When are we going to develop them?"

"Good question." I could do it tonight, but that wouldn't be fair—Julian should be here. "I need to have something else to develop—that way no one will suspect anything. Any ideas?"

"Bring the camera to school tomorrow—you can take pictures in the cafeteria."

"Brilliant!" Randall began to see the possibilities... I'll photograph the girl that he draws, and the drawing too... But I won't tell him. The idea of documenting Julian's artistry appealed to him. Come to think about it, I'll take the close-up lens—I can photograph all his sketchbooks! He headed for the sink. "Let's cover up—we don't have time to make any more prints tonight."

As a matter of fact... I'll take the complete camera outfit tomorrow. That way I can slip on the telephoto real easy... a few crotches from today's lunch came to mind. I can play candid camera. In the morning I'll load a few cartridges.

"Just be sure the funnel corners line up." He handed Julian a tray he'd just rinsed off in the sink. After sealing the processing trays, they sorted the prints on the drying rack.

Julian's attention returned to his pet peeve. "What I'm gonna do is make a list of words that need to be replaced. Then I'll hold a contest. Somebody ought to be able to come up with a better idea."

"You're going to hold a contest to find a replacement word for blow job?!" I can hardly wait to see the campaign poster. He handed Julian his set of prints and headed for the blind. "Suck job wouldn't be much better."

"Mmm… that's another thing: why do they call it a *job*?" The whole thing's fouled up. "Are there any perfect words?"

"How do you mean?"

"You know, words that actually look and sound like what they mean."

Randall closed the photo lab door and pointed at the knob. "There's one."

Julian didn't follow his line of thought.

"Click. You know, when the door shuts, it goes "click."

"Yeah!" There must be hundreds like that. "*Sounds*! You just imitate the sound!" He thought a second. What other sound? "squeak!"

Randall nodded eagerly; they had discovered a new game. "Squirt."

As they left the garage, Julian came up with another: "Woof."

They were on a roll: "Plop."

"Burp!"

"Fart!" Randall opened the mudroom door.

Julian broke into a laugh… the word was funny, but funnier was hearing Randall say it. "Fizz!"

"Bump!" He opened the door to the kitchen.

"That rhymes with *rump*!"

Laughing, Randall led the way to the den; Mom and Dad will be watching TV.

Helgar looked up from his magazine; Eloise turned her head away from the television set. This was new: their son coming down the hall laughing and joking with a friend. That had never happened before. At first it seemed out of place, jarring. But when they saw Randall's face and demeanor, they were thrilled—he had never looked this radiant and jolly.

"Oop… sorry," Randall realized that he had interrupted the program.

"Not to worry, son." Helgar sized up the boys as they stood there. The sound of their laughter was quite wonderful. "Lucy is just now over." Not my cup of tea: they don't have Fred on any more. But Eloise watches it faithfully, week after week.

He could tell at a glance that the boys probably had a special time after supper—the way they held their hands in front told all. When he was their age, that was the only way he ever found to obscure the telltale receding bulge. Ah, those were the days… the memory prompted a sympathetic response in his lap. Yes… after Eloise returns home…

"What's so entertaining?" Eloise crossed the room and pushed the off button. The program was over—I don't need to see another cigarette commercial. She was pleased that Randall had been careful about the time.

Julian blushed. He didn't have an answer ready.

"Julian has a crazy idea that he can reform the English Language. He wants to replace words that don't fit or match what they represent."

"Oh?"

Use Milky Way. Inside guy to the rescue.

"It's just me being silly," he shrugged. "You know, things that are opposite of what they name—like the Milky Way. It isn't milky at all… it's crystal clear, unless its foggy out."

"Good point." Helgar would have pursued the idea, but Randall had thrust a set of prints into his hands.

Julian was quick to step over to show his set to Randall's mom… he didn't want to explain what was so funny. He was still enjoying the way Randall said fart.

26 A ride in the Continental

Julian had never paid much attention to cars. Unlike a lot of guys, he wasn't all revved up about having one, himself. It's a bad idea to spend time thinking about something you could never afford. Mom always says it's best to be grateful for what you have instead of feeling grumpy about what you don't. Makes good sense. Anyway, I like to walk—there's always interesting things to see along the way; when I'm walking, I can stop and look; in a car, I have to go on by. If I have to hurry, Mom takes me—or someone gives me a ride.

But this car was unlike any he had ridden in; he had to take notice. It's so fancy and plush! I've seen cars like this around—some of Geraldine's customers had one like this. Riding in it seems magical, like being in a spaceship—lots of instruments all lit up across the dashboard... super quiet... you don't feel any street bumps... seems bigger inside, too.

"This is a nice car."

"Why, thank you." It interested Eloise that he would have that observation—and that he felt moved to express it. It's an indicator of what I like about him. Randall might have a similar sentiment, but he rarely expresses his thoughts aloud.

Julian wanted to run his hand along the dashboard and see what it felt like—but that would be rude... besides, my hand is still recovering from that handshake Randall's dad gave me. It didn't hurt exactly, but almost.

"I'm so pleased that you were able to join us tonight. I know it meant a lot to Randall."

Julian kept a straight face, but enjoyed the moment: it's a good thing she doesn't know the details!

"I hope it didn't spoil any plans you might have had… I know you have lots of activities, what with boy scouts, and of course, your girlfriend."

Girlfriend?! What is she *talking* about?

"As you know, Randall wasn't invited to the dance; I'm afraid he isn't as far along as you are, socially."

What do I say to that?

Just smile and say something nice. Inside guy wasn't sure what to do here either.

"He's okay; he's just a little shy is all." Do I tell her that Rita isn't my girlfriend? No answer…"Actually, I'm not *that* far ahead… Rita's not my *girlfriend*, really. She just asked me to go to the dance."

"Oh, I see." Eloise hadn't meant to put him on the spot, but since the subject has come up…

"He gets along real well with Alice and Marcie at school."

That announcement jolted her like a thunderclap: she had never had a report of Randall so much as looking at a girl, let alone getting along with one—or *two?!* It had not occurred to her until this second that she could acquire intelligence from one of his friends—wait until I tell Helgar! "Alice and Marcie, you say?"

"Yeah. We have lunch with them."

"How nice." Her mind was going a mile a minute. "Randall hasn't mentioned either of them." This did not fit: a lunch hour romance? *Randall*?! My goodness… are they the reason he started putting up a sack lunch? I was never able to get an explanation for that.

"Yeah; well we just met a few days ago. Randall and Marcy figure out who I'm gonna draw next. That way, there aren't any arguments."

"Arguments? I don't understand."

"It's sort of complicated. Lately a lot of girls have wanted me to draw their face. I don't know why it's such a big deal. Anyway, Randall and Marcie set up a way to decide which one gets done next. Works out pretty good."

"Oh, I understand..." Eloise recalled seeing a portrait in the sketchbook. "You draw well, Julian. I can see why they'd like that. Maybe one day you can find time to do a sketch of Marietta." Her daughter was quite impressed by Julian at supper.

"Sure. I'd like to." I'd like to draw Randall's dad too, come to think about it.

"I have to warn you in advance that she'll want to keep it."

"'Course. I always give those away."

"That's very generous of you." Well. The list of questions that need answers is growing—none of them can be dealt with here or now. I didn't expect this turn of events. What to do? Asking a lot questions will make him uncomfortable... make him raise questions of his own. No, it's wise to go slowly... It had just become doubly important to get acquainted with Julian's mother. Comparing notes with her is a priority. It's just as well we're approaching their house.

Generous? Julian shrugged; not much he could say. Compliments were always nice, but he could never figure out what to say afterwards. Besides, the last thing I need is a stack of those portraits. I'm glad they want them.

She turned off the ignition and set the parking brake. "I need to talk with your mother about something—you don't mind, do you?"

"Gosh, no. I'm used to that," he chuckled. "Mom's always like to compare notes." That was true—when he was in Cubs they were always huddling about this or that. Hmm... tonight isn't a great time to have company... Julian was anxious to wrap things up so that he could deal with personal stuff... I need to think about what happened tonight, and talk to Mark... my "pretend Mark."

"Hi Mom," Julian sang out as he opened the door. It was only fair to give her a hint that he wasn't alone.

Francine looked up; Julian doesn't usually announce himself…

Eloise stepped in behind. "Here we are at last, safe and sound. I wanted to thank you in person, Francine, for allowing your son to dine with us this evening." She touched Julian on the shoulder, as if to release him back into his mother's care.

"Easily granted—thank you for extending the hospitality." Francine set aside her Good Housekeeping magazine and went to greet the visitor. "I hope you had enough to go around—his appetite has taken off lately." She put her arm around her boy's shoulder affectionately.

"I know what you mean," she laughed. "Rest assured, I've learned to have extra of everything: Randall's father has an extraordinary appetite—Randall has just begun to compete. I always have leftovers, just in case." Her real secret was placing the order with Sharple's properly. Eloise generally made only one or two dishes—the rest was prepared by one of the best delicatessens around: delivered ready to serve at whatever time she required.

"Please, won't you come in for a minute? It's a little chilly out."

"Why, thank you, I will," Eloise stepped forward and did a quick glance around. "The last time we met, there wasn't time to get acquainted. I should have paid a call sooner. I thought this would be a good chance to make a start."

Julian stepped over to close the door and waited… he wasn't sure what to do, exactly—it seemed rude to just go to his room, even though that's what he wanted to do.

"May I take your coat?" Francine was a little surprised that she would want to visit at this hour.

"Well, it *is* a little late to pay a call—why don't I just rest it on a chair." The television set is off; Francine may be an early to bed person.

Julian removed his coat while Randall's mom took off hers. He wasn't sure if he should hang around or what.

"We can sit here, if you like, or at the kitchen table..."

"The kitchen, by all means... let's don't make a fuss, please. I promise not to stay long."

Francine was glad about that, but glad also to have a sit down, however brief. She believed in being in touch with other boys parents for a number of reasons. Julian had never been a problem, of course, but it's wise to see from as many angles as possible—she couldn't expect Julian to know or remember to tell her everything.

Julian wanted to be excused—visiting with Mrs. Hallstrom wasn't exactly what he wanted to do right now... finally it occurred to him to yawn. That usually worked.

"You can go on to bed if you need to, Julian—" she looked at Eloise: "unless you need him—"

"Oh mercy, no; do feel free to retire, Julian." She smiled at him thankfully, and followed behind Francine. "Is your boy always such a perfect gentleman?"

Julian rolled his eyes. Randall's mom dressed fancy, but she was just like all the others. Perfect gentleman, blah blah blah... he could tell what they were going to say before they even started. They'll spend an hour trading compliments about Randall and me before getting to the point. He shook his head and hung his coat up in the hall closet.

"Can I get you anything?"

"No, please. Maybe a glass of water, if it's no trouble." Eloise looked at her closely—she looks more familiar than I remembered. I recall meeting her at school, but...

Julian headed for the bathroom. Time to do the teeth. With any luck, they won't talk for two hours.

Francine sensed something different—this wasn't the same woman at all—she felt a simpler, more genuine person than the rather imperious lady that had been in the office so often last summer. "I trust you and your husband have been happy with the house on Alton Circle."

That's it! Eloise smiled wide. "Please forgive me. I didn't make the connection until this minute. You're with Worthington Realty!"

"Yes. Geraldine enjoyed working with you. I do locating and research on most of the properties."

"Well, you have my admiration again—the house is wonderful in every respect. Both Helgar and Randall are able to do what they want, and my daughter and I are free to do our things too…

Julian closed the bathroom door. He didn't need to listen in; it's a good thing they're in the kitchen—when they sit in the living room, it's hard to block out the sound of their yakity-yak. He had permission to call it a day, and that was what he intended to do. First things first: he headed for the toilet.

Wow… he was surprised at how full his tank was… he giggled, remembering Sammy hurrying across the boy's john—'*the pause that refreshes!*' He looked down. "Say, why are you still so puffy?" I thought he was back to normal. Little J doesn't feel as puffy as he looks.

Nothing to worry about, Inside guy observed.

I s'pose your right. Little J has his own rules. It would be nice to know what they are, sometimes. I still don't know why he went crazy at the dance.

Inside guy still had nothing to offer about that, either.

He finished up and went over to the sink. He squeezed some toothpaste onto the toothbrush and got started; no point in asking the blond dodo in the mirror.

While he brushed, his mind wandered, landing on images at random—on purpose, he was putting off what he needed to think about until later... after he was closed up safely in his room.

The automatic garage door opener thing popped into his head—that and the intercom to the darkroom. An upstairs apartment... and don't forget the mud room. It must be nice to be rich. Oh well. I hafta give Randall credit there—I didn't know he was a rich kid at all until we got to his house. He acts like a normal guy. Just goes to show how stupid it is to judge people because of things like what they wear. At school, you'd think he was a regular kid, not poor, but maybe on the less-well-off side. My clothes look a lot fancier. O'course that's because of Geraldine, right?

The dummy in the mirror nodded.

Julian rinsed out his mouth and wiped off his face. There: all ready. What to do: shall I go into the kitchen and say good night like a perfect gentleman? He opened the bathroom door and hesitated. They're laughing about something.

Hollering won out: "G'night Mom... g'night Mrs. Hallstrom." There—less than perfect is best sometimes. As he stepped into his bedroom, they stopped laughing and returned his good night. Excellent.

Julian was in his usual position, sitting cross-legged on the bed, facing Mark's portrait. This is the one he used when a pretend talk was needed—the drawing that showed Mark's whole face. Julian and his Inside guy did all the talking of course... it was the only thing he *could* do for now. In real life I'm not allowed to talk to him about the things I want to. Last summer, Mark made it clear that for as long as he was a scout a wall stood between us. He didn't say that exact thing, but that's what he meant. He said that as long as he wore a scout uniform, he had to follow the rules, no exceptions.

That's why Julian planned to cease being a scout when he graduated from high school. A few weeks after that, I turn 18—that's when I have to be ready.

I'm ready *now*. It's so hard to wait, to live a secret… His main worry was not being accepted when the time came. Replacing Mark's first love, the one who died, was a tall order—if it's even possible; I have to prove that I am *worthy*. Julian refused to consider the possibility that Mark might find someone else.

A tear ran down his cheek: he felt guilty. I went too far tonight; I came too close to the line with Randall. It was sure lucky he didn't push any… especially since I was so close to kissing him afterwards. If he had turned his head even, I don't think I would have been able to resist. A big chunk of me wanted to roll around and kiss like mad…

How do you apologize to a drawing?

Stop beating yourself up. You didn't cross the line. Inside guy stepped in.

I was awful close…

No you weren't. You were making love to Mark, not Randall—and you know it.

Julian sniffed and reached for a Kleenex.

You're just tired of waiting, of being alone.

He nodded in agreement. I have two and a half years to go! What if…

Cut that out. We've already figured that; don't slip backward. As long as you are in his sight, doing good things with him and the patrol, he isn't going to wander off.

I hope that's true. Mark still treats me special—even though it doesn't look really obvious, I know he cares. As long as I don't foul up and force him to think about the rules… as long as I don't remind him how young and unqualified I am. When we were going through the scrapbook I could see how much smaller my legs and feet were—it's better than last summer, but I still have a ways to go.

You have to be strong... that's what Mark will respect. Besides, you need to grow a couple inches taller and sprout some whiskers.

Yeah, you're right. Mark would look kinda odd with me now… I'm practically a midget. He looked down at his lap. "A midget with a puffy dick."

That struck him as funny. He laughed at how silly that sounded. That snapped him out of it; he swung around off the bed. Returning Mark to the hiding place in the closet was next… no further discussion was needed. Little J isn't making any demands tonight anyway—he had his exercise already… boy, did he ever: how long will he be puffy?

The sensation of walking around with Little J so puffy was kinda fun. "Do I have to find a new name for you too?" Usually, he wasn't aware of Little J at all when he was just walking. "How about Mr. Puffy?" he giggled. "Puffy J? PJ for short."

Coming up with new names isn't as easy as I thought.

G'night, Mark. He fluffed up the clothes—that way no one could see the large drawings behind. He had turned his drawing board around so Randall's drawing didn't show—he always kept the drawing board in front of Mark's portraits, just in case.

He climbed into bed and curled into a ball. He enjoyed doing that—soon, the sheets would be nice and warm… systematically expanding the warm area with his body heat was a good way to drift off—he didn't remember ever getting the entire bed warm, he always fell asleep somewhere along the way.

> *yawn* < Boy, I'm tired. Now that his brain had sorted out the day, dropping off would be easy. Once again, Inside guy had helped take care of his worries. Tomorrow is planned—Randall will be taking pictures during lunch. After school he's going to show me how to develop film… that will be fun…

Julian did not hear any sound from the kitchen; he did not hear the fancy Lincoln drive away, then return again a while later. He slept soundly in spite of the fact that it was an active dream night—Mark dominating them as usual. They weren't all wish fulfillment dreams though…

He didn't hear the bedroom door open quietly… he didn't know that his mom had looked in—not to check on him, but to look at him lovingly for a moment before retiring. She hadn't done that in a long time. After talking with Eloise, she couldn't resist the urge. The news about Marcie and Alice was enormously interesting—news that she didn't plan to share with Geraldine just yet.

A few houses down the street, Mark had dozed off in front of the television set again. His dreams were troubled; it had been a long day at the store. An obnoxious flirtation from a couple of buxom lady shoppers—something he was never sure how to handle—had ruined his day. How do you make them satisfied customers when all they can do is make suggestive and leading remarks? When they work as a team like that, it's difficult. He never could tell if they were merely teasing and having a bit of fun, or if they were serious. Teasing, hopefully.

His dreams were nightmarish—he found himself trapped in a spa with only a towel for protection—a squad of women was stalking him. It was only a matter of time before they would discover which cubicle he was hiding in. He expected them to haul him bodily into the dark room and have their way.

His rescue came at last: by force of will, he transported himself back to Camp Walker. Surrounded by his boys, he was safe. He spent some quality time there with Julian—going over his scrapbook drawings, admiring his innocence and his beauty. Ah, his beauty… in his sleep, he didn't have to avert his eyes or his imagination.

> *Whack!* <

A sharp sound startled him awake… oh. The clipboard had slipped off the arm of his chair. The roar of white noise on the T.V. set told him that he had drifted off again. He shook his head… Go to bed, Mark. He shut things down and made his way upstairs, still half asleep. What was I dreaming about? Don't remember… made me feel good. Maybe it will start up again… he pulled up the covers… was it something to do with Julian? He shook his head and yawned. How long has it been since I looked at the scrapbook? I need to go over there one of these evenings.

27 Thursday, November 15

Roy Barnes was serving as the organizer and guide; he had assembled five staff members in the faculty lunchroom—five *hungry* staff members. Their regular lunch period was nearly over. The group had been asked to postpone lunch today to do a special assignment during the second lunch hour. The task was to observe what he had discovered on Tuesday and Wednesday. Included were Dr. Stanley J. Middleton, Principal, Ralph van Horn, Art teacher, Alistair Quimby, World History teacher, Lillian St. John, English teacher, and Ernest Ladendorff, Journalism advisor. Roy had begun by telling them the names of the two students that had brought them together.

"I thought of you, Ernie, because of what I saw yesterday: I may have found you a photographer."

"If that's true, I'll pay for *your* lunch!" Ernie "Mr. L." Ladendorff *always* needed photographers. The lunch today was courtesy of the boss, always a nice surprise. The extra prep period was *very* nice.

"Al has them in his second period class, so I think his input will be useful. The same for Lillian; though they are not in the same class, she knows both boys. Ralph is here because he knows the artistic one very well."

"Best talent I've ever seen," Ralph nodded. Now he understood why Julian had asked for a few sheets of drawing paper on Tuesday. One was about to turn into a portrait.

"*I'm* here," the Principal interjected, "because Roy thinks he has discovered the perfect ambassador for what we face next year." He paused for emphasis. "His timing couldn't be better: the timetable has been moved up. It will happen at the semester break."

That news commanded their attention. That was just a few weeks from now. There had been no announcement about this.

Roy continued: "I'm assuming that today will be the same as yesterday; if it isn't, I may need to make an adjustment. Don't worry about that. The plan is to eat among the students. You'll sit separately—where you'll have a good view of the west side, toward the stairwell; that's where they've been for the last two days. You all know Julian, so look for him and you'll be able to go from there. As you leave the line with your tray, I'll point each of you to a good spot. If you can, be sociable with the students—see if you can get any feedback from them about either of these boys. Try to be cool about it. After lunch we'll meet in Stan's office. I have arranged for a substitute to take your fourth and fifth period classes."

Four frowns. Teachers are always the *last* to know.

The Principal took over. "I know this is awkward and inconvenient—but it is very important. You four will be called on to report first; after you have your say, you can return to your students. It shouldn't take long." On the other hand, he didn't make that a promise.

Three shrugs; losing class time was always a hazard. Lillian was non-committal: she wanted more information.

"Do we stay put, or move around?" Alistair had never played secret agent before.

Roy laughed. "No, no… nothing like that. Just have lunch and be yourself; be interested and curious… don't be obvious about why you are there—that is to be a coincidence."

"Who is going to take my classes?" Alistair didn't want some unqualified yokel to mess with his curriculum.

"A secretary or aide will supervise while they study or read.

Four nods. That was harmless, at least.

The Journalism advisor was delighted at the prospect of gaining a photographer, so he had no objections whatever to the sudden change in his lesson plans for today—especially if it solved his problem tomorrow night. I might not have to hire someone to cover the game after all.

"I assume it's best that we not be seen by either of them?" Lillian didn't want to affect their behavior."

"Best, but not essential. Make it appear natural that you are there—your turn to do lunch duty; make a friendly gesture, you know—just so they don't suspect they are under any kind of scrutiny." Roy was experienced at this sort of thing.

"What *exactly* are we looking for?" Lillian was unclear about what was expected.

"I don't want to prejudice your observations by defining that in advance. Don't worry—you will see at once what has drawn my attention. It is entirely unique. Suffice it to say that we have a high level of confidence in your judgment." Roy sat forward and spoke to her directly. "An honest unbiased observation will tell us what we need to know. Combined with your knowledge of their academic work, this should round out your perceptions. That's why you were chosen: you already know these boys as well or better than anyone."

"So you don't want us to take notes, then?"

"Absolutely not, Alistair. That would attract the wrong kind of attention. The idea is to fade into the background as much as possible. We don't want any student to think twice about your being there today.

Ralph raised his hand. "Have you talked to Mark yet?"

Everyone looked his way with a blank expression.

"Mark is Julian's scoutmaster. I don't know his last name. But I do know that he could tell you a great deal more than any of us." Julian had made it clear more than once that Mark is a key figure in his life. "Julian keeps the troop scrapbook." He brought it to class one day; remarkable.

Roy and the principal looked at each other: Roy had a new assignment. "Any idea what troop?" There are half a dozen scout troops in town.

"Sorry."

Roy nodded. I'll chase it down. "Mark, you say? You're sure of the name?"

"Quite. He's like a big brother—hero figure; he can do no wrong. For Julian, the sun rises and sets with Mark."

Wow… Roy was glad to know that. The boy's performance as a scout will tell us a lot. The scoutmaster will know something about the home situation too, if he's worth his salt. "Thanks, Ralph."

> ***Bzzzzzzzz!*** <

The passing bell sounded in the cafeteria—so loud, it wasn't necessary to mount one in the faculty room.

"I take it we're ready, then?" The Principal stood. "Oh… before I forget: don't pass on what I said about next semester. The faculty meeting on Monday will include the official announcement. It would help if we don't have a bunch of rumors and buzz about it ahead of time."

Five nods. "Good." He led the group out of the faculty lounge and headed directly for the special faculty cafeteria line. I'll get a cup of coffee and call it lunch… he planned to move around. Food can wait until later.

One of Stanley Middleton's innovations was providing a fast lane in the cafeteria for his staff. Previously, teachers were expected to go directly to the front, effectively crowding into line. Displacing a student in line was almost entirely negative. Yet there was a legitimate reason for the teachers to be served first: many of them had a duty of some kind during the lunch period; the faster they could be served, the sooner they could be at their assignment. Middleton prevailed on the kitchen supervisor to allow for a special staff line on the kitchen side of the serving counter. After a few weeks it seemed so natural everyone wondered why it hadn't always been done that way. Today he went straight to the cashier and prepaid for the committee.

—∾—

Randall and Julian had planned to return to the cafeteria for the remainder of the week, at least—Julian to chat and do a sketch or two to please his mother and Geraldine, and Randall to assist and take more snapshots. They assumed it would be like before… with a little less fuss, maybe. Yesterday was a lot better. Randall had come up with the idea of drawing the next name—that avoided the hassle of picking one and offending everyone else.

Julian appointed Marcie to take care of that, since she had been the first to have her portrait drawn. To the great amazement of Theresa and her boyfriend Teddy, she rose to the occasion; they, along with most in the class, had regarded Marcie as an also-present-but-non-essential harmless type. That changed when Julian asked her to be his *aide de camp*. While Marcie set up the name drawing procedure yesterday, he had drawn Theresa's portrait out of courtesy.

Today was about the same, except that there *wasn't* less fuss at all—the news had spread. Julian and Randall were not yet accustomed to "being noticed," let alone be the center of attention. Still, when the eager and interested swarm—girls mostly, greeted them with hopeful grins and settled in around them, they took it in stride. Their regular place at the table had been kept open—Theresa had seen to that. The rest of the table was packed tight, as were a few others close by—several girls had shown up early to claim a good seat. All this kept Julian and Randall fully occupied; neither caught on to the fact that they were being observed by the adults in the room. They didn't notice, for example, that their English teacher was sitting only a table away, chatting quietly with one of the girls as she enjoyed her lunch. Had they looked around, they could have spotted others as well.

To the adults' credit, they didn't draw attention to the fact that they were keenly interested in these two boys. Their assignment to be observers had been a last minute surprise, veiled in mystery. From the anonymous stew otherwise known as the Sophomore Class, these two boys had emerged in the heart of the Junior Class dining area—and were *welcome* there. That had not happened before—it violated tradition in a major way. Something was afoot.

Lillian St. John was surprised by the spectacle. To begin with, she would never have guessed that Julian and Randall were even acquainted. But to see them in this context was nothing short of amazing: a crowd of upper class girls was fawning over them as if they were celebrities. What is going on here?

"Hi, Miss St. John." Melanie was surprised but pleased to see her in the cafeteria.

"Melanie! Good to see you." Perfect. This was one of her better students last year. She'll be able to tell me what's going on.

If anything was inconvenient today, it was the pressure to finish eating—the girls were impatient to see who would be picked next. Julian was annoyed a little; his mother had made a new kind of sandwich, and he wanted to enjoy it. He glanced at Randall's... looks similar. He leaned closer.

"Mom made my lunch today. Don't know why." He looked at Julian's sandwich. Oho... Randall did not believe in coincidence: his mother had connected with Julian's: the sandwiches were identical. This roast beef looked like it came from Sharple's Deli, his mom's favorite.

They nodded at each other: our mothers have joined forces. No problem, as long as it meant an improved lunch menu.They shrugged and enjoyed the fancy sandwiches. Julian took another peek into the sack to see if there was a slice of Mrs. Hallstrom's cake or pie. Not today.

It's a good thing that Julian didn't plan to keep his empty lunch sack; the minute he wadded up his wax paper and deposited his apple core, it was whisked out of sight; he hadn't even seen the hand that took it away. He looked at Randall. "I guess we're ready."

Randall nodded. His trash had been cleared as well. He leaned forward and gestured to Marcie.

She nodded and shook up the small Whitman Sampler box that sat on the table in front of her. Her mother had supplied that this morning. Inside she had placed little slips of folded paper: all the names that had been turned in yesterday were there along with ten new ones—thirty-seven in all. She opened the lid and reached in. "Jill," she called out. "Jill McNeal."

A squeal from the next table over revealed Jill's whereabouts. Congratulations from those nearby were genuine, though envious. Randall went over to serve as escort, as usual.

It was only the third day of this activity, but the pattern set on the first day worked so well that it was repeated yesterday; now it was expected—an audience was already in place near the stairwell. That's where the artist placed his subject.

Julian gave Marcie a grateful grin and crossed over to the location Randall had selected. The lighting was perfect—it would be nice to have a good drawing board. Oh well... I'm used to drawing on a cafeteria table… no big deal. I drew the big picture of Uncle Max on the table at camp. This is great: Mr. van Horn gave me this nice 9 x 12 drawing paper—a lot better for drawing than the sketchbook. Today I brought two pencils—freshly sharpened. I'm ready to go. Ooo… Jill is wearing glasses! That will be fun. I haven't drawn glasses since summer camp. You can do interesting things with glasses. First things first: he walked over and sat down by her.

"Hi… Jill?" She looks familiar…

She nodded eagerly.

"Say, aren't you in Mr. van Horn's class?"

Jill blushed and nodded. She already knew how well Julian drew.

"Neato. That's my favorite class! He gave me this nice paper." This is perfect; she knows what to do, how to sit still. "Sometimes I do better if I know a few things. Maybe you could say something about what you like, your favorite color, maybe a song or a hobby… whatever you want."

Jill was almost tongue-tied. Sitting this close was so *intense*, so… it was hard to look at him for very long for some reason—way too intense. "Color?" That's easy. "I like lavender most of all," she pointed to the bracelet on her left wrist.

Julian noted that the barrette in her hair matched… it was a set. "I like that color," he nodded. He had studied her face long enough to decide a basic pose. "If it's okay with you, I'd like you to look up there, in that general direction." He pointed to an intake vent over the foot of the stairs. "Think about something happy or nice, okay?"

Julian's bright grin forced a smile on her face. She remembered to breathe finally, and nodded. How can he be so nice?! Mesmerized, she watched him go to the other end of the table and sit. He picked up his pencil and… Oh! I almost forgot! She looked where he had pointed… nothing to look at… that's all right… her eyes blurred… savoring the last few minutes was all she wanted to do anyway.

The camera was a blessing: it gave Randall something to do and lessened the likelihood that he would have to visit with anyone in particular—in other words, a way to hide in plain sight. Talking with Alice was okay, but he had nothing else to say; it didn't make sense to just sit there. It was very nice of her to look after his clarinet—losing that would be a very bad thing.

Documenting Julian in the act of drawing was a privilege and a duty. Randall took pleasure and pride in his photographs; he put some of his grandfather's advice to use: what to look for, how to frame a shot, how to be ready in a moment for a surprise… but also how to not waste a lot of film taking the same shot several times. I loaded half a dozen cartridges yesterday, but there's no point in wasting film. The light conditions in the cafeteria presented no challenge to speak of. As long as I don't face the south windows, I can't take a bad picture in here. He moved around a little more today and tried some new angles. After taking a few close-ups of Julian and the girl being drawn, he stepped to the side and changed to the telephoto lens. He had several ideas of what he could capture with that.

They had developed yesterday's roll after school, along with the secret poses. Today we're planning to make a few prints—the negatives looked good, better than I expected. Indoor light isn't my long suit, so this is an excellent training ground.

About forty feet away, Ernest Ladendorff almost choked on his carrot stick: the boy had just opened a shoulder case and changed lenses. That alone told him what he needed to know. He looked at the clock. I'll leave in fifteen minutes: I want to see this kid right after school… I need to see him… I *have* to see him. Andy will know what to do—he's one of the best sports editors I've ever had on staff.

Several tables closer, Ralph van Horn had found a vantage point that would have been ideal if Julian were at an easel. Nonetheless, he was grateful for the chance to watch Julian work. During class several students need attention, so I'm seeing a few things for the first time. Phenomenal eye-hand coordination… he almost never has to erase a line. It's as if he had been trained professionally. Van Horn had always believed true talent was a gift you were born with; this is the first time he had seen absolute living proof. And he's working on a flat table! I need to scare up a small drawing board for him. I doubt if he'd want to fuss with a table easel.

The English teacher was enormously intrigued by what she had seen. They are so different as students… they see different things, respond differently to the same material. This strange assignment had opened her eyes a little. She had not spent any time thinking about that phenomenon, yet it was a central factor in both writing and understanding literature. Balancing the common experience and the individual variants is key to helping students master their language and culture. This is a learning experience for me as well. When I figure out a way, I need to thank Roy for this opportunity. I wonder if I'll be able to get a look at the drawing.

Quimby wasn't convinced this was a good use of his time. It isn't hard to see what's going on. The Forrest boy is the latest teen fad. Girls create those and toss them away next week. The surprise is that he's not a rock musician. Of course, I haven't been able to see the drawing yet, so there may be something to that... Ralph says he's good. The other boy is an excellent student—never misses class, solid test scores... listens well. An A student in every way. It's good that the other boy has him as a standard. He's a solid B student. I don't know what Roy wants me to see here... these boys are not a problem in any way that I can see.

—ᴧᴧᴧ—

Julian had found a solution for depicting the soft edge of the girl's sweater. All I need to do is press my thumb lightly along the line and give it a little twist. That softens it without making it look like a smudge... neato... discovering new tricks is part of the fun. He sat back and grinned at the girl to his left... she had seen it too. This has turned out to be a great way to use the lunch hour.

At first it reminded him of Geraldine and his mother and the gaggles of perfumed powdery ladies that always stood around talking about runs in their nylons and all that fingernail polish stuff. They used to play with my hair and pinch my cheeks as if I wasn't there... Most of the time I wasn't, in my mind. Giggling girls are just like giggling moms when you think about it. What can you say? It's the way they're born. At least they don't wear nylons at school... they do stink of perfume sometimes. That was another point that earned Marcie his approval: she doesn't smell at all.

As long as you don't turn your back—or if you do, be sure to sit on your butt—they can be fun. I haven't seen Rita since the dance, which is just fine with me, thanks. She must be paying attention to her boyfriend again. Good idea all the way around; she can play with his buns all she wants.

The girl now being drawn—Jill—had a couple of moles that gave her an exotic look. His artistic solution was to have her looking upward toward one of the ceiling fixtures—that made her chin line kind of special. With the light reflecting on those glasses, she looks sort of dreamy. He held it up briefly to compare the drawing side by side with the subject. Doing that helped make sure things were all straight; I need to work on the hair line on the right side…

At least today the kids aren't crowding so much. Being watched while I draw isn't so bad, really; it means that I'm doing something interesting at least—and besides, they're watching the drawing; they aren't so hung up on looking at me. I still don't get that. No one has said why these girls were all fussed over me to begin with. It has to be my hair. Geraldine always said they would freak out because of that… I guess she was right.

—∞—

Becoming anonymous or invisible was generally not possible for a building principal, so Stanley Middleton didn't try. What he did do was nod a lot and smile. Since he was known to do a casual drop in here and there, anywhere and everywhere, his presence was not in itself anything to take note of. He was careful to behave as he always did—a benign supervisor doing a routine visit. After a while he wasn't noticed. It was his goal to see the phenomenon from as many places as possible. One thing was apparent from the beginning: Roy's hunch appeared to be absolutely correct.

Not clear was what the other boys thought. Most of the "fan club" is female. Still, half the student body won is half the goal achieved: not a bad starting point. That's assuming, of course, that the lad is sympathetic and up to the challenge. The fact that he's a scout is encouraging. The meeting this afternoon will be very interesting.

He headed for the kitchen to refill his coffee mug. He planned to stay the entire period. Unusual, but some things one has to see for oneself. That includes getting a peek at that drawing.

28 Thursday afternoon

Randall was busily sanding the end of the dowel inserts—the final touch before assembling his custom drying rack. As usual, his mind was on other things—in this case, photographing the sketchbooks. Getting Julian to bring the others was no trouble. After we're through making our "special" prints, I'll do a proper job with the close-up lens; I can set it up in the apartment over the lab. Mom and Dad want to see Julian's other work—easy to understand that. This way they can see it whenever they want… and so can I.

There… rounding the ends of the dowels done! Now, I need find a finish for it… something dark—

"Hey," Andy gave a friendly tap on the shoulder. "What are you making, anyway?" He examined the assorted pieces of wood. An indirect approach to Mr. L's assignment seemed the way to go.

Randall was startled; a senior talking to me isn't exactly an everyday event. "It's going to be a drying rack. I'm almost ready to assemble it."

Andy was puzzled… doesn't look like a kit. "What do you dry on it?"

"Film reels and developing tanks." Randall expected more questions, but didn't mind. The guy is friendly enough. He looks sort of familiar.

"You do your *own* developing?!" Now I see why Mr. L is so worked up.

"Yeah." Wow… he picked that up fast; maybe he's a photographer too. "Do you have a camera?"

Andy cupped his hand in a mock attempt to tell a secret: "I have a Kodak Brownie from when I was a Cub Scout," he winked. "I keep it around, just in case." The puzzled look on Randall's face was sort of fun. "You don't know who I am: I'm Andy. I saw you at the Troop Nine meeting a while ago. I meant to talk to you sooner, but—"

"Wow, you're in Julian's scout troop?" He grinned wide. Randall tried to locate the face in his memory… Andy… Andy. Hmm.

"Yeah. I was hoping to see those mountain climbing photos sometime. We don't have any mountains like that around here."

"That's easy." A glance at the clock confirmed that there was plenty of time. "Come over to my locker a minute." He kept a small packet in his notebook just for this purpose.

Each student was assigned an in-class locker for storing small projects and personal items. Randall kept his books there during class. He opened his three ring binder and removed a small packet. "I started to carry these around after that meeting." He handed the prints to Andy. He raised his arm to get the teacher's attention. "I need to talk to Mr. Nelson a sec; be right back."

Andy browsed through the photos—about a dozen or so, taken from climbing trips out west. *Outstanding* pictures—make me wish I'd been along. Man, *look* at these… these were taken by that *kid*? He looked closely at the paper… this isn't from a film drop off—this is custom. Does he do his own *prints?!* I'll bet Mr. L doesn't know about *this*. Have I ever got news! Where does he do it? Maybe he has a job at some studio. As sports editor for the school paper and yearbook, Andy knew quite a lot about photography—but he was only a courier or assistant when it came to the pictures. Most of our photo work is hired out; we get a special rate at Camera World, but *nothing* is free. We don't have a darkroom at school. Hold on, hold on… he looked into the kid's locker… *whoa*. I didn't see that before: a carrying case… a *big* carrying case—that's what Mr. L was talking about! Camera World sells cases just like that.

Andy stepped over to listen… Randall was conferring with the shop teacher, explaining what his project needed. Wow! He's making that for a darkroom!!

Andy had positioned himself outside Mr. Frankel's room. He was under special orders: when Randall emerges from Biology, my assignment is to take him directly to Mr. L. I've never seen Mr. L so worked up. Not hard to see why. The prospect of having our own photographer is exciting—at fifty bucks a game, we can't afford to cover everything. It's hard to sell enough ads to pay for the ones we do. With this kid aboard we could double—maybe triple our coverage and save *beaucoup* dollars.

After discovering what Randall was making in shop class and examining the mountain prints, his brain had started to buzz about other things: at the troop meeting, Tony said he'd gone on a campout with this kid. A campout? with *Tony?* I don't need to know any more: I go *way* back with Tony. If Tony was there, then Danny was there: they're steadies these days.

I don't know much about Julian—but he's a friend of Danny's. It stands to reason this kid and Julian might have been "accidentally" put together. That's the kind of thing Tony would do, for sure. Maybe Randall and Julian are more than just good friends. I doubt if they're steadies like Tony and Danny; but if my hunch is right, Randall might be open to a certain amount of "specialized" sport—like we have at scout camp. Maybe there's more room in the tent… ever since Tony and Danny became steadies, I haven't had anyone to play with… we used to do lots of things together. Casey used to goof around, but now he's always *swimming*, trying to grow webbed feet or something.

Another reason this line of thought has potential: what I saw at the troop meeting—the kid got stiff while he was sitting in that chair next to Julian. I thought it was funny at the time, but it was pretty hot all the same. Possibilities…possibilities… maybe my "dry spell" is about to end. Plans were starting to form in his mind…Hold on, boy: he stopped himself. Walk carefully Andy, or you could screw it up.

> ***Bzzzzzzzz!*** <

Oh-oh… school's out… here we go! On your toes, Andy. Mr. Frankel's door opened.

Randall was the fourth student to leave the Biology class. It was a particularly good class today; he had been awarded fifty extra credit points for his paper on the Piedmont flora. The snapshots were a huge success. Whoops! All of a sudden, Andy appeared in front of him.

"Oh—hi!" he grinned. I like Andy for some reason.

"You look surprised."

"Oh! sorry. I forgot you would be here after class." The truth is, his mind was on what he and Julian were planning to do this afternoon: make some *very* special prints. Visiting the school paper office had slipped his mind completely.

"His room is on the first floor." He turned to lead the way.

"Hold on—I need to stop off at my locker." The camera case and books were there. He headed to the left. "I don't want to come back up here." After opening his locker, he slung the camera bag over his shoulder and paused to think… let's see…I'll need history and English tonight. He swapped the Biology book for World History and World Literature. After Julian goes home I need to put in a couple of hours—that's right: he doesn't know about this school paper thing. I have to swing by his locker on the way. He grabbed the clarinet case and shook his head... I sure wish I didn't have to carry this everywhere. Unfortunately, it was too valuable an item to leave here overnight.

Andy hadn't been to his locker yet; it isn't far from Mr. L's room. This errand came first.

As they approached the stairway, they met Julian.

"Hi, Andy!" What's he doing up here? He's a senior.

"Howdy." Just for fun, Andy extended his left arm to give the Troop Handshake; he didn't get a chance to do that very often. "I'm here to escort your buddy to a special meeting. You can come along—it's not secret."

"Oh." Julian grinned. "Okay!" sounds interesting. He glanced over to see if Randall could say what was going on. All he got was a "beats me" shrug. Julian shrugged back. I don't know Andy very well… he's a friend of Tom's, I think. "So, what's up, anyway?"

"Mr. L wants to see him—it seems that he saw Randall taking pictures in the cafeteria." He gestured to the shoulder bag. "Mr. L is *always* interested in photographers."

"Who's Mr. L?"

"He's the advisor for *The Cardinal*." He puffed up his chest: "It so happens that I am the Sports Editor. I'm sure you've read all my stories."

Blush… that's one kind of story I *never* read. "Um, sorry. I've never cared much for sports, to be honest."

"Well, to be *honest*, neither have I." As a participant, at least. "But when Mr. Barnes told me how I could use a portfolio of stories to help land a scholarship when I graduate, I jumped at the chance." It turned out to be fun and challenging—not to mention the visual treats. Locker room interviews had become a specialty—it's a regular slide show in there after a game. Andy had an unwritten list of the choicest jockstrap "prisoners" in the school—his great fantasy before going to bed every night was assisting one or more to escape. Celebrating their freedom was a joy to rehearse; one day, he would actually pull one off—the escape, that is—*and* the celebration.

"Hi, Julian," chirped a female voice as the trio rounded the corner on the Junior level.

"Hi," he waved back with his signature grin. No idea who she is… it's weird to have all these people know my name. He and Randall exchanged shrugs again. What's a guy gonna do?

Randall had worked out who Andy was… the one standing in the back—he started to get one and reached down to fix it—a big one, too… right after that the bugle went off. Is anything visible now?… hmm… could be, could be… pants aren't tight enough to be real sure.

—∾—

The Cardinal room was between the student body office and the school store. Not big enough to be a regular classroom, a staff of twelve or fifteen could fit in if they had to. Usually, six or so were on hand after school, but today Mr. L had cleared the room. He was sitting at his desk in the front.

Ernie Ladendorff wasn't going to wet his pants or anything, but if it had taken any longer for Andy to deliver the solution to his Friday problem, he would have gone in person to see what the blazes had gone wrong. When the door opened, he feigned being engrossed in proofreading recently submitted copy.

"Mr. L, allow me to introduce Randall—Randall Hallstrom." He smiled wide and bounced on his toes with a wink. He led the way to the desk, where the teacher had just stood, smiling politely.

Ladendorff extended his hand. "Glad to make your acquaintance."

Randall blushed; hurriedly, he tucked the clarinet under his left arm. Mr. L has a handshake like my Dad.

"And you are?"

"I'm Julian." The man in front of them looked different from other teachers; his sports coat had leather patches on the elbows… looks cool. The other cool thing was no necktie. That made him interesting, automatically. A potential portrait came to mind… standing… holding something… an open newspaper. Yeah…

Ladendorff knew who Julian was, of course. After the discussion in Stan's office, Mr. L was keenly interested in Julian: he's going to be a big newsmaker in a few weeks. Mum's the word on *that* for now. He was tempted to talk with him, but that had to wait: first things first. I need to start my trawl. He turned back to Randall.

"I happened to have cafeteria duty today, and I saw you taking photographs." The case over Randall's shoulder drew his eye. "What do you use?" He tried to appear knowledgeable.

Randall perked up at that; he was proud of his cameras, especially the one he had along today. He sat his books on a table and placed the case on the teacher's desk. He opened the safety clasp. "This is my Nikon F." He took it out of its slot and passed it to the teacher.

Mr. L had taken a mental snapshot of what the open case revealed: form fitting pockets lined in velvet held a sophisticated light meter, three lenses with snap on covers, several filters, and the camera. The lid had a supply pocket that rattled—filled with 35 mm film canisters more than likely. The other pocket must have lens cleaner and a packet of wipes. This case and its contents were worth well over a thousand dollars—closer to two. "Looks new." Like an AP photographer's outfit, in fact.

"Thanks; I take care of it. It's as good as they come for most applications. What I'm waiting for is one with a built in light meter. They say this will be obsolete in five years."

'Keep your cool,' Mr. L admonished himself. He knew enough about cameras to recognize that he was talking to an expert. "I'd be interested to see some of your work." Andy had told him about the mountain prints.

"Sure!" He turned around to the desk where he had put down his books, and opened the binder.

Andy gave Mr. L a smirk. What a cagey guy; you wouldn't know that an hour ago he was practically hopping up and down with excitement.

As the teacher looked through the set of prints, the room fell silent. Julian felt a need to contribute something. "You should see his photo lab. He does these prints all by himself!"

Ladendorff froze; did I hear that right? "That's interesting." He could see from Randall's reaction that it must be true. "I have to say that I'm impressed." He leaned back in his chair. "It so happens, I am always interested when I run across a good photographer. It *also* so happens that I have a small photo assignment that I could let you have if you're interested. If I like what you do there could be more... I might be persuaded to let you join *The Cardinal*. I know Andy and the others would enjoy having a photographer aboard."

Randall was taken by surprise. It was almost like he had won a contest. *Me*, on the *school paper*? Are you *kidding?!* He looked at Julian, amazed.

"Wow!" Randall deserves a break like this.

Andy was able, just barely, to keep a straight face. He glanced at Mr. L, who just gave him a conspiratorial wink. That made his day: he *felt* like an editor now. Wow is right.

"Do you have a flash?" He handed the prints back across the desk.

"Flash?" The question was a surprise. "Oh, yes. But I haven't used it much. I prefer using available light—I can always push process."

That was a level above Ladendorff's expertise. He awaited an explanation.

"If you double the developing time and cheat on the aperture, you can do lots—of course, it's a little grainy, but…" he noticed the blank reaction. Something his Grandfather said a couple of years ago came to mind… '*Don't look down on a flash, Randall. It's just another tool—sometimes it's exactly what you need. You need to learn what it can do...*' "I should learn more about using a flash. I can bring it along."

"Good. You might need it. We're talking about the football game tomorrow night. How fast a shutter speed does this have?" He pointed at the Nikon.

"That's no problem. Two thousandths of a second; I'm not sure what the flash default is—probably a hundredth." Randall had almost no experience shooting moving objects, but he didn't expect it would present any problems he couldn't solve; a 250th will be all

I'll need. What I don't know is if I can mix flash exposures with ones I push. They might get overdeveloped… I need to read up on that.

Mr. L smiled to himself; I have a photographer at last; the boy has already decided to take the assignment. Just to be certain: "So, you're interested?"

Randall looked at Julian quickly—he got a big grin and a nod. "Yes, I'd like to. I think I can do it, but I have to warn you: I've never photographed a sports event before. I'm not sure what you need."

"That's no problem: Andy here will be by your side the whole time. His job will be to tell you what and when. He's an old hand at this.

"Wow!" Randall and Julian exclaimed together. Julian planned to go along and learn about this. Someday I'll have a camera… besides, the idea of drawing an athlete in action was challenging… more interesting than doing faces in the cafeteria, for sure. A face in the gym is just as interesting—the rest of the body would be fun.

"Can Julian come too?"

"Certainly!" Mr. L was delighted by that question: he was already making plans to recruit Julian as a cartoonist. He had seen the drawing in the cafeteria well enough to know that Julian was a natural. One thing at a time. "Andy here can tell you the details about where and when to show up." He stood and extended his hand again. "I'm sure you will do fine. Thanks for taking this on. I look forward to seeing the results!" He reached out to Julian. "Nice to meet you too, Julian."

Randall's ego was bursting—a new and thrilling feeling. "Thanks for letting me do this. You won't be disappointed." He put away his camera. The best thing to do is make a graceful exit before the teacher has a change of heart. The fact that he would allow a complete beginner to do this is amazing. My first ever sporting event. Wait 'til I tell Dad.

Julian looked forward to this too—I should be going to the games anyway... Tom is on the team. Say... are any other members of Troop Nine on the team? He turned and gave Mr. L a farewell smile.

Ladendorff watched the boys leave. He gave his Sports Editor a wink and an okay, well done sign. With any luck, I'll have a staff photographer at last—and he's a sophomore! I'll have him for another *two years!* He suppressed the urge to shout a yahoo-hurray. I need a way to celebrate. Too bad I'm not a drinking man! I'd better scoot down and fill Roy in. I owe him a lunch. No time like the present. He headed toward the door.

One of these years they *have* to let me have a regular Journalism class. It was his pet peeve; this school is way behind the times. We should offer both Journalism and Photography. The only incentive I have to offer is some extra credit in their English class. For a photographer, it's all gratis.

"When do I get to see this photo lab?" Andy was hoping for an instant invite. He had stopped at his locker.

Julian and Randall glanced at each other... not *today*, of all days.

Randall was good at thinking fast. "Didn't you say you had a car?"

"Yep. A junker, but it gets me there." His 1948 Dodge four door was almost like driving a truck, but it was still going strong.

"Why don't you pick me up at my house tomorrow? You can come a little early and I'll show you around."

"Yeah!" Julian chimed. "After the game you can help develop the film!" He took it for granted that he would be there too.

"Sounds good." Second best; looks like I'm cutting in here... best be careful. These guys are sort of a team. I wonder if it's more than that. Andy was disappointed, but that's they way the ball bounces. "The JV game starts at seven, so I'll be there at six."

Whoa—supper is at 5:30. Cutting it close.

"Where do you live, anyway? You want me to take you guys home?"

"Thanks, but I have a bicycle. It's 4875 Alton Circle; third house on the right after you turn off 48th." They watched Andy jot it down in his handy pocket notepad.

So, it's near the University. Nice. Figures: that camera outfit says it all: that's not your average middle class camera kit. "Great. See you at six tomorrow. Actually, I'll see you fifth period first!" He reached out to Julian for another troop handshake. Obviously, I'm supposed to back off gracefully… these guys have a plan for this afternoon. What might that be? Andy didn't usually suspect the worst—or best, either—but when he did, he had fun with it.

I'm just as glad to be free this afternoon. Watching Mr. L recruit Randall was so *nifty*… Gives me an idea of what to do with Martin… or better yet, Aaron: two Tenderfoot scouts in my patrol need some *motivating*. He slammed his locker shut and headed down the hall; Julian and Randall were about to go out the bike rack exit. Hmm. Tony's fun with Randall at the last scout meeting came to mind. A *campout* of all things… that usually means a tent. With Tony and Danny? Andy smiled. Who knows? I think they're just buddies. I didn't pick up any serious vibes… they're not like Tony and Danny. Still, I'll bet they like to play…

28.1 What happened on Friday?

The answer to that question takes too many pages for this book. Explaining what happened on Friday takes more than eighteen pages. Julian gets called into the principal's office during seventh period—a major turn of events follows. Mark is there, so all goes well. Photographing the football game takes a chapter, and so does developing the film. Explaining why Julian was unable to attend the game will take another twenty pages. Rita and Tracy show up for lunch on Monday: interesting, to say the least. Then there's Andy's ingenuity, and Mark's adventures—or misadventures, depending on how you look at them.

This part of Julian's Sophomore Year has gone over the standard word limit by a fair amount: you don't need to be told that. Julian has met two sizable challenges and been able to prevail—Mark too has reached a new place in his ongoing internal tug of war, so this is a logical place to pause. Besides, you deserve a break—you need to be rested up before tackling the much dreaded movie date.

Several other characters minor and medium sized are slated to romp through Julian's world, some old and some new—he has another six months as a sophomore, and they are full of fun and surprise. Julian and Randall's paths lead in slightly different directions for a while—they don't diverge, but become parallel instead of congruent; anyone interested will be able to read all about the goings on, but not until *Julian's Sophomore Year, Part Two* is published. Hopefully it will be before too long; I'll do my best.

Thanks for riding along. I hope to see you again soon.

Eldot
June, 2015

a word from Eldot about the style…

When I was midway writing *Julian's Private Scrapbook*, I became annoyed by the cumbersome conventions of narrative fiction. Some experimentation evolved into a quest of sorts: to achieve the intimacy of the first person point of view from within a third person point of view perspective. It required mixing verb tenses in a new way and abandoning conventional rules of punctuation and paragraphing. I tinkered with those elements until I found an approach that worked.

By "worked," I mean it freed the reader from the burden of having to translate what they read as they read.

For example:

> The Sun was up already. If he were seen, it would mean failure. He ran as fast as he could, but it was too late. They'd seen him coming and shoved off. They were well downstream already.

This places present action in the past tense; it is awkward—and worse, it keeps the reader at a distance rather than inside the character.

What if I do this:

> The Sun is up already. If I'm seen, I'm out of luck… He ran as fast as he could, but he was too late. Rats, they saw me coming. They had shoved off and were well downstream.

Here the reader has to jump in and out of the character's point of view, and between present and past. It's unusual and maybe awkward at first, but it achieves something new. It lends a first person intimacy and involvement to material that is essentially passive when in the third person. It helps remove the dulling effect of using the narrative past tense "was" to a vivid alive "is," and it does so without the clutter of a lot of punctuation cues or paragraph breaks.

I have utilized this technique in varying degrees. In many places it is not used at all, in others it is extensive. My goal always is to get the reader into the character's perception to the maximum extent—unwashed grammar and all—while retaining the ability to see things from the outside.

So when you run across this phenomenon, that is what's going on—it's not a typo. I hope it makes the experience of following Julian more fun; a few of my old English teachers might be appalled, but others would grin.

Troop 9 1962-1963 Roster
Mark Schaefer, Scoutmaster

1 Panthers

1	Ryan Kruger	[17] L
2	Calvin Radcliffe	[16] L
3	Doug Tucker	[17] S
4	Ben Jasper	[15] 1st
5	Don Bennett	[14] 2nd
6	Edward Ashmore	[13] T
7	Arthur Branson	[13] T

2 Tigers

1	Andy Ashbaugh	[17] E
2	Tony Johnson	[16] S
3	Brad Fisher	[17] L
4	Chris Smith	[15] 1st
5	Shawn McGee	[14] 2nd
6	Martin Fetterman	[13] T
7	Aaron Breen	[13] T

3 Lynx

1	Gary West	[17] E
2	Max Webster	[16] L
3	Alex Trent	[16] L
4	Robin Simmons	[17] L
5	Paul Harris	[17] S
6	Jason Jones	[15] 1st
7	Sandy Smith	[14] 1st

4 Wolves

1	Norman Miller	[17] E
2	Casey Snyder	[16] L
3	Jeremy Baker	[15] S
4	Sid Thomas	[15] S
5	Barney Nichols	[15] 2nd
6	Billy Bradford	[14] 2nd
7	Kevin Ryan	[13] T

5 Badgers

1	Tommy Carlysle	[16] L
2	Don Felton	[16] S
3	Bruce Ruggles	[15] 1st
4	Freddy Scott	[14] 2nd
5	Josh Green	[14] 2nd
6	Chad Nelson	[13] T
7	David Bennett	[13] T

6 Zebras

1	Jim West	[17] E
2	Kurt Davis	[15] L
3	Cory Summers	[16] 1st
4	Justin Blake	[14] S
5	Tad Benson	[15] 1st
6	Clint Walker	[15] 1st
7	Dwayne Foster	[13] T

Flaming Arrow

1	Tom Dawson	[17] E
2	Nick Harrison	[17] E
3	Danny Laskey	[16] L
4	Frank Ferris, bugler	[17] L
5	Julian Forrest	[15] S

Ranks

E= Eagle	(6)
L= Life	(11)
S= Star	(8)
1st= First Class	(8)
2nd= Second Class	(6)
T= Tenderfoot	(8)

Ranking

chronological age in brackets [ ]

1-6 Patrol ranking in troop
1-7 Individual ranking in patrol

Appendix:

The Hayden Park Ceremonial Initiation

Oütis, pronounced oh-oo-tis: A secret society of men. Little is known about its origin; many claim it was created at Oxford University in England in the nineteenth century. Classical Greek culture was extremely popular, and part of the "revival" included exploring several ancient pagan religious rites. Only full members knew its true name, which was never written.

Claims that it originated in ancient Greece may have a basis, but to date no scholarly attempt has been made to verify that, since so little has survived. The only known credible source of information would have been housed in the Library at Alexandria, which burned in 30 B.C.

The name Oütis was borrowed from the Greek hero Odysseus. Translated into English, the word means "nobody," or "no one." In Homer's Odyssey, Odysseus used that as his name when he boastfully escaped Polyphemos the Cyclops. Odysseus and his crew had gotten him drunk and blinded him by piercing his one eye with a sharpened log; they had turned its point into a red hot ember in the fire. When help arrived in response to his loud calls, all the giant could say was that No One was responsible for his injury. The name has been borrowed often by persons wishing to remain anonymous. (Transliteration of Ancient Greek Οὖτις, in capitals ΟΥΤΙΣ, from οὔτις "nobody" or "no one").

A member of the society, nameless, has not given permission to use the written summary about the rite that he wrote in a letter to a colleague. The letter was discovered in a box of miscellaneous effects at an estate sale in the mid 1930s:

The “nameless” society practices a rite based largely on rituals attributed to pastoral cults that worshipped Dionysus, Hermes, and Pan, and to Spartan and Boeotian military traditions. A hexagon is sometimes used as a sign of recognition.

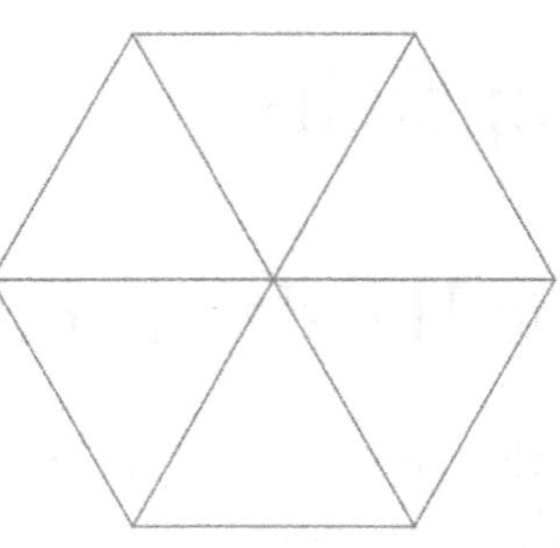

Six is regarded as a sacred number. The rites utilize six as an organizing element to guarantee maximum effect. Induction to full membership is done in groups of six. The Greek alphabet of 24 letters is divided into four groups of six letters. These represent the four levels of the initiation: manual [Anafluo], oral [Mousikos], between the legs [Diamerizein], and kissing [Kataphileo]

Greek Alphabet Names.

The first six letters in the Greek alphabet are used for Level 1 of the “Initiation:

Level 1: *Anafluo*—Greek for overflow, burst upward—in context, to masturbate. The activity was taught to Pan by Hermes; it was to release excess energy and tension in order to reduce his urge to ravish too many unsuspecting mortals. Pan is famous for his sexual powers, and is often depicted with an erect phallus. According to Diogenes of Sinope, Pan learned masturbation from his father, Hermes, and taught the habit to shepherds.

Level 2: *Mousikos*—In ancient Greece, oral sex was known as "playing the flute" (in latin, *fellatio*). Its praises were sung by Greek and Roman poets; its practice was fairly widespread. [letters: eta [H], theta [Θ], iota [I], kappa [K], lamda [Λ], mu [M]

Level 3: *Diamērizein*— The prefix *dia* means between, and *meria* are the thigh bones. Inter-femoral intercourse was a common outlet in ancient Greece because anal sex was considered demeaning to the receiving partner. The Ancient Greek term for this practice meant "to do it between the thighs." [letters: nu [N], xi [Ξ], omicron [O], pi [Π], rho [P], sigma [Σ].

Level 4: *kataphiléō*—passionate or fervent kissing, as opposed to a ceremonial or pro forma greeting. [letters: tau [T], upsilon [Y], phi [Φ], chi [X], psi [Ψ], omega [Ω]

A controversial fifth level has appeared in modern times, attempting to include anal sex. It is not regarded as a qualifying requirement for membership; the practice itself is not condemned or endorsed. The ancient practice of anal pederasty was never a part of the Oütis rite. Oütis was and is for post adolescent men.

ΟΥΤΙΣ Level One

A-Δ	B-Z	Γ-E	Δ-A	E-Γ	Z-B
A-Γ	B-E	Γ-A	Δ-Z	E-B	Z-Δ
A-B	B-A	Γ-Δ	Δ-Γ	E-Z	Z-E
A-Z	B-Γ	Γ-B	Δ-E	E-Δ	Z-A
A-E	B-Δ	Γ-Z	Δ-B	E-A	Z-Γ
[Louis]	[Chuck]	[Tony]	[Danny]	[Julian]	[Randall]

Of the six involved in the Hayden Park campout ceremony, only Louis was eligible—he was the only one who had started to grow a beard. A beard, or being able to grow one, was the first qualification for membership. His own initiation took place before he was of age. Whether this was due to his remarkably oversized endowment or not is probable, but not known. He was invited by an unknown person associated with an unnamed fraternity on an unidentified university campus.

Whether that invalidated his membership is also unknown. But he became an avid enthusiast at once and, unknown to his mentor, began his own chapter of the unknown society.

Glossary for You're in *high school* now

This section is provided for readers who are not familiar with the United States in the 1960s, and who have not read The Julian's Private Scrapbook series. Rather than bog down the story with explanations, the text assumes the reader knows what is being referred to. For those who don't, this should help. Many of these entries are still contemporary.

Baths: Bathhouses vary considerably in size and amenities—from small establishments with 10 or 20 rooms and a handful of lockers to multi story saunas with a variety of room styles or sizes and several steam baths, jacuzzi tubs, and sometimes swimming pools. Most have a steam room (or wet sauna), dry sauna, showers, lockers, and small private rooms. Many bathhouses are membership only. Customers pay only for the use of the facilities. Sexual activity, if it occurs, is not provided by staff of the establishment but is between customers, and no money is exchanged. (*see* **Pompeii,** *below*)

Betty Boop: an animated cartoon character created by Max Fleischer; she originally appeared in the Talkartoon and Betty Boop film series, which were produced by Fleischer Studios and released by Paramount Pictures. She has also been featured in comic strips and mass merchandising. She became one of the best-known and popular cartoon characters in the world. Betty Boop made her first appearance in 1930, in the cartoon Dizzy Dishes; she began as a caricature of singer Helen Kane.

Big Plan: When Julian discovered that his goal to win Mark as his life love partner could not be achieved during the two-week summer camp, he regrouped and did some serious planning. He realizes that he has to grow into the position—literally and figuratively. His new goal is to win Mark for his eighteenth birthday. All his dealings with Mark are calculated to achieve that goal. He will not confide that information to anyone.

Charlie Brown: Charles "Charlie" Brown is the main protagonist in the Peanuts comic strip by Charles M. Schulz. Charlie is a lovable loser, a child possessed of endless determination and hope, but who is ultimately dominated by his insecurities and a "permanent case of bad luck". He is often taken advantage of by his peers.

Cheshire Cat: A character in *Alice in Wonderland.* The animated film version featured a wide closed tooth open lipped smile.

Close order drill: The term comes from the tradition of close order formation combat, in which soldiers were held in very strict formations to maximize their combat effectiveness. An alternative to mêlée combat, it required strict discipline in the ranks and competent officers. As long as their formations could be maintained, regular troops could maintain a significant advantage over a less organized opponent. It is the basis for ceremonial performances by military units, marching bands, drill teams and scout units.

Coleman stove: Throughout its history, Coleman produced a wide variety of equipment primarily for camping and recreational markets.

Perhaps their most famous product is the Coleman Lantern, a series of lamps that were originally made to burn kerosene or gasoline. Current models use Coleman fuel (white gas) or propane and use one or two mantles to produce an intense white light.

Cuban Missile Crisis: a 13-day confrontation in October 1962 between the Soviet Union and Cuba and the United States, generally regarded as the event that took the Cold War closest to a nuclear conflict. The US had placed nuclear missiles in Turkey, aimed at Moscow; after the failed US attempt to overthrow the Cuban regime at the Bay of Pigs, Nikita Khrushchev proposed placing Soviet nuclear missiles on Cuba to deter any future invasion attempt. These preparations were noticed by the Defense Intelligence Agency, which secured clear photographic evidence of ballistic nuclear missiles on the ground. The United States considered attacking, but decided on a military blockade instead. The confrontation ended on October 28, 1962, when Kennedy and United Nations Secretary-General U Thant reached an agreement with Khrushchev. Publicly, the Soviets would dismantle their offensive weapons in Cuba and return them to the Soviet Union, subject to United Nations verification, in exchange for a US public declaration and agreement never to invade Cuba. Secretly, the US also agreed that it would dismantle all nuclear warheads deployed against the Soviet Union in Turkey and Italy.

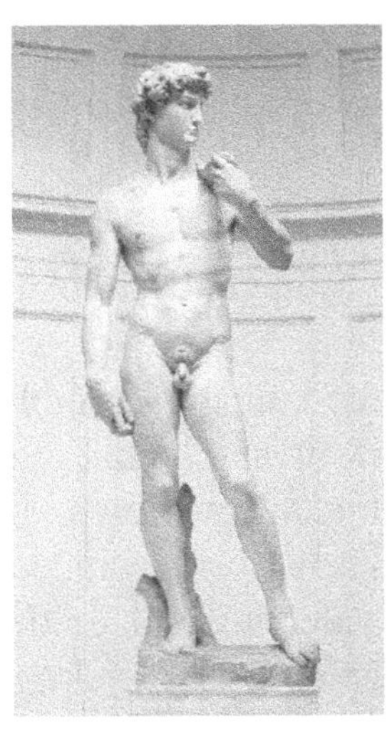

David: A statue by Michelangelo, an Italian sculptor, painter, architect, poet, and engineer of the High Renaissance who exerted an unparalleled influence on the development of Western art. He was considered the greatest living artist in his lifetime, and ever since then has been held to be one of the greatest artists of all time. A number of his works in painting, sculpture, and architecture rank among the most famous in existence. Two of his best-known works, the Pietà and David, were sculpted before he turned thirty. Despite his low opinion of painting, Michelangelo also created two of the most influential works in fresco in the history of Western art: the scenes from Genesis on the ceiling and The Last Judgment on the altar wall of the Sistine Chapel in Rome. At the age of 74 he succeeded Antonio da Sangallo the Younger as the architect of St. Peter's Basilica; Michelangelo transformed the plan. The western end was finished to Michelangelo's design; with some modification, the dome was completed after his death.

Farting Post: During summer camp, Tom accidentally farted at the breakfast table. Mark defused the situation by announcing that he would install an official farting post at a safe distance downwind. He selected a branch from the firewood stash.

Fifty two pick up: a children's card game using a standard deck of 52 playing cards; it is usually played as a practical joke. Any deck of cards will do, although the game works best with traditional playing cards. The game requires at least one unsuspecting player who wants to be initiated into the game. The first player, or "dealer", throws the entire deck into the air so the cards land haphazardly on the floor. The other player must then pick them up—all 52.

Ford Country Squire 9 passenger station wagon: a full-size station wagon built from 1950 until 1991, encompassing seven model generations. It was the premium station wagon model in Ford's full-size car range. The Country Squire was initially built as a full "woodie" (*right*).

After the mid-1950s the rear body used fiberglass covered by a vinyl appliqué printed to simulate wood. Fourth generation (1960–1964):
Prior to 1961, all Ford wagons used a two-piece tailgate assembly that required the operator to lift the rear window up and lock it into place via a mechanical support, and then drop the tailgate down. In 1961 the tailgate assembly was one piece with a self-storing window feature; it could either be rolled down into the gate via crank on the outside, or by an electrical motor actuated by an interior switch. A safety lockout measure required that the rear window had to be fully retracted before the tailgate could be lowered.

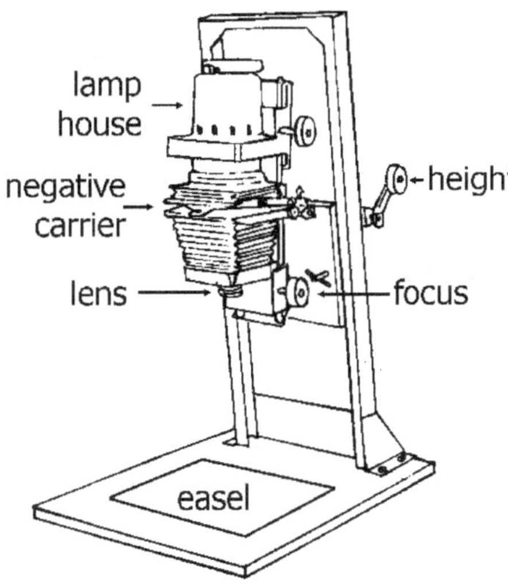

Enlarger: The Beseler 23C enlarger is one of the best enlargers made. Introduced in 1956, it is still in production today. Early models were light green color then changed to grey, then to black.

The maximum size print possible with a 23C depends upon the negative size and the focal length of the lens: 35mm negative with 50mm lens: 15 x 22 3/8 inches 6x6 negative with 80mm lens: 19 1/4 x 19 1/4 inches 2 1/4 x 3 1/4 inch negative with 100mm lens: 14 x 20 1/8 inches These are full frame sizes with no cropping. The 23C heads can be flipped to a horizontal position for wall projection; in that position, image size is only limited by the size of the darkroom.

Flaming Arrow: The leadership patrol of Troop Nine, an executive council. Includes the Junior Assistant Scoutmaster, Senior Patrol Leader, Scribe and Bugler.

Fortress Mountain: Located in the Glacier Peak Wilderness, Fortress is one of the highest peaks in Washington State, at 8760 feet. Two commonly used routes attain the summit. Three main faces, each with a radiating ridge: Pass No Pass is on the west; a large snowfield is at the base of the north face; the Chiwawa River

Basin lies below the southeast face. Multiple high points on the Fortress massif are above or slightly below 8000 feet. The view from the summit includes nearby Glacier Peak, Bonanza, Fernow, Seven Fingered Jack, Maude, and most of the volcanic summits. This area is also rich in wildlife: a combination of bear, deer, marmots, ptarmigan, and mountain goats. The climb itself is nothing more than a rock scramble in mid summer. Steep snow in the early season requires the use of an ice axe.

Four point GPA: A system of converting letter grades [A, B, C, D, F] to a numeric average. A=4, B=3, C=2, D=1, F=0. The grades are converted to the number, then added together. That number is divided by the number of grades being averaged, giving the Grade Point Average.

Geoff’s Poker Club: The boys from Atlanta formed a special club for playing strip poker. It provided a game master that decreed what sexual acts were to be performed at the end of the game and by whom.

Gerbera Daisy: Gerbera is a genus of ornamental plants from the sunflower family. It was named in honor of the German botanist and naturalist Traugott Gerber. It is also commonly known as the African Daisy. Gerbera is very popular and widely used as a decorative garden plant or as cut flowers. It is the fifth most used cut flower in the world (after rose, carnation, chrysanthemum, and tulip).

Greek Alphabet: See appendix, page 554.

Groucho Marx of the Marx Brothers hosted ***You Bet Your Life*** with announcer and assistant George Fenneman. The quiz show aired on both radio and television. The show debuted on ABC Radio in October 1947, then moved to CBS Radio in September 1949 before making the transition to NBC-TV in October 1950. In 1960, the

show was renamed ***The Groucho Show*** and ran a further year. Most episodes are in the public domain.

The play of the game was secondary to the interplay between Groucho, the contestants, and occasionally Fenneman. Each show was begun by confiding a secret word to the audience. If a contestant happened to say that word at any time in the interview, a stuffed cartoon bird dropped on a string with a fanfare; the contestants were awarded a bonus of 100 dollars. Groucho generally steered the interview in a manner that improved the chance they would use the word. It was the first game show to have its reruns syndicated.

Hayden Park: A nature reserve near the high school in Troop Nine's town. Hiking trails, campsites, park benches and picnic areas make the five acre park a favorite. (*see map on page 201)*

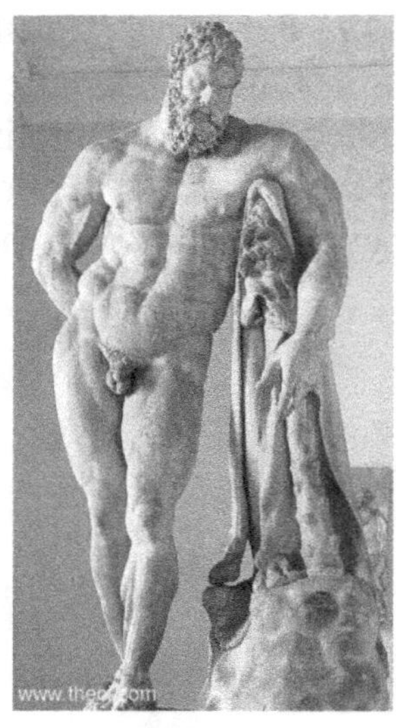

Hercules: the Roman name for the Greek divine hero Heracles, the son of Zeus (Roman equivalent: Jupiter) and the mortal Alcmene. In mythology Hercules is famous for his strength and for his numerous far-ranging adventures. The Romans adapted the Greek hero's iconography and myths for their literature and art under the name Hercules. In later Western art and literature and in popular culture, Hercules is more commonly used than Heracles as the name of the hero. Hercules was a multifaceted figure with contradictory characteristics, which enabled later artists and writers to pick and choose how to represent him.

I Love Lucy: a landmark American television sitcom starring Lucille Ball, Desi Arnaz, Vivian Vance, and William Frawley. The black-and-white series originally ran from October 15, 1951, to May 6, 1957, on CBS. After the series ended in 1957, a modified version continued for three more seasons with one hour specials, known first as The Lucille Ball-Desi Arnaz Show and later in reruns as The Lucy–Desi Comedy Hour. In 1962, Ball began a six-year run with **The Lucy Show**; Both Desi and Frawley ["Fred"] were dropped from the cast. In 1968 another sitcom, **Here's Lucy**, ran until 1974—ending her long run as a CBS sitcom star.

I Love Lucy was the most watched show in the U. S. in four of its six seasons, and the first to end its run at the top of the Nielsen ratings. The show is still syndicated in dozens of languages across the world.

Previously, T.V. shows were produced live in New York for eastern and Midwest audiences. West coast viewers saw live programs only through low-quality kinescopes, a 35 mm or 16 mm film of the live show as seen on a closed-circuit television monitor; videotape had not yet been developed.

I Love Lucy's pioneering use of three cameras became the standard technique for most sitcoms filmed in front of an audience. The process resulted in a much sharper picture quality compared to blurry kinescopes.

Ice axe: a multi-purpose ice and snow tool used by mountaineers both in the ascent and descent of routes which involve frozen conditions. It can be held and employed in a number of different ways, depending on the terrain. In its simplest role, the ice axe is used like a walking stick in the uphill hand, the mountaineer holding the head in the center, with the pick pointing to the rear. It can also be buried pick down, the rope tied around the shaft to form a secure anchor on which to bring up a second climber, or buried vertically to form a stomp belay. The adze is used to cut footsteps as well as scoop seats in the hillside and trenches to bury an ice axe belay. An ice axe is not only used as an aid to climbing, but also as a means of self-arrest in the event of a downhill slip.

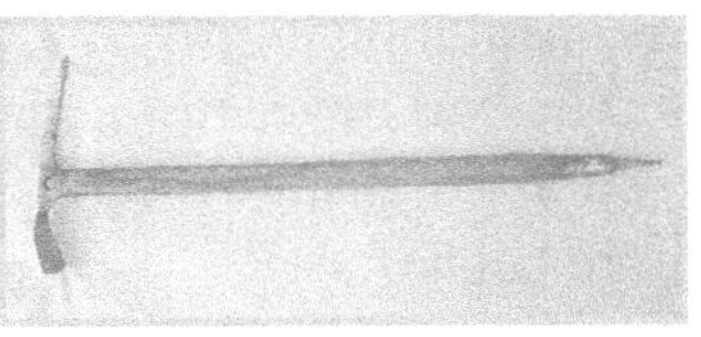

Julian's costume:

Costume elements for the Sadie Hawkins Dance: straw hat, overalls, slicker, hiking boots.

Julius Caesar: (July 100 BC – 15 March 44 BC) a Roman general, statesman, Consul, and notable author of Latin prose. He played a critical role in the events that led to the demise of the Roman Republic and the rise of the Roman Empire. Caesar's conquest of Gaul, completed by 51 BC, extended Rome's territory to the English Channel and the Rhine. After assuming control of government, he began a program of social and governmental reforms, including the creation of the Julian calendar. He centralized the bureaucracy and was eventually proclaimed "dictator in perpetuity." But the underlying political conflicts had not been resolved, and on the Ides of March (15 March) 44 BC, Caesar was assassinated by a group of senators led by Marcus Junius Brutus. A new series of civil wars broke out, and the constitutional government of the Republic was never restored. Caesar's adopted heir Octavian, later known as Augustus, rose to sole power, and the era of the Roman Empire began.

Junior Assistant Scoutmaster: Highest position for a scout in the troop.

Junior High School: Grades 7-9. Before the reforms of the 1970s, High School was a three year program, grades 10-12.

Kodak film: In the 1960s, digital photography did not exist. Amateurs and professionals had to use film of one kind or another. During most of the 20th century Kodak held a dominant position in photographic film. Photographic film is a strip or sheet of transparent plastic base coated on one side with a gelatin emulsion containing microscopically small light-sensitive silver halide crystals. The size and other characteristics of the crystals determine the sensitivity, contrast and resolution of the

film. During chemical development, the silver salts are converted to metallic silver, which blocks light and appears as the black part of the film negative. Color film uses at least three layers. Dyes, which adsorb to the surface of the silver salts, make the crystals sensitive to different colors. Typically the blue-sensitive layer is on top, followed by the green and red layers. During development, the exposed silver salts are converted to metallic silver, just as with black-and-white film.

Life: The scout rank between Star and Eagle, awarded when the Scout serves in a position of responsibility for six months, performs six hours of community service and earn an additional five merit badges (three of which are required for the rank of Eagle.

Li'l Abner and Daisy Mae: Li'l Abner is a satirical American comic strip featuring a fictional clan of hillbillies in the impoverished mountain village of Dogpatch, Arkansas. Written and drawn by Al Capp (1909–1979), the strip ran for 43 years, from August 13, 1934 through November 13, 1977. Comic strips typically dealt with northern urban experiences before Capp introduced the first strip based in the South—although Capp was from Connecticut.

Li'l Abner Yokum: was 6' 3" in his stocking feet (when he wore stockings), and perpetually 19 "y'ars" old. A naïve, simple-minded and sweet-natured hillbilly boy, he lived in a ramshackle log cabin with his pint-sized parents. He inherited his strength from his irascible Mammy, and his brains from his less-than-brainy Pappy. The family name is an intentional combination of yokel and hokum. Abner was a country bumpkin so gullible that he could be tricked by a small child. Typically he had no job, but sometimes worked as a "crescent cutter" for the Little Wonder privy company, later as a "mattress tester" for the Stunned Ox mattress company. Abner's main goal in life was evading the marital designs of Daisy Mae Scragg, the virtuous, voluptuous, barefoot Dogpatch damsel. For 18 years, Abner slipped out of Daisy Mae's crosshairs.

Daisy Mae Scragg: was hopelessly in love with Li'l Abner throughout the entire run of the comic strip. Abner exhibited little romantic interest in her voluptuous charms (much of it visible thanks to her famous polka-dot peasant blouse and cropped skirt). In 1952, Abner reluctantly proposed to Daisy to emulate the engagement of his comic strip "ideel," Fearless Fosdick. Abner and Daisy's ceremony, performed by Marryin' Sam, was permanent. When Capp finally gave in to reader pressure and allowed the couple to tie the knot, it was a major media event. It made the cover of Life magazine on March 31, 1952—illustrating an article by Capp entitled "It's Hideously True!! The Creator of Li'l Abner Tells Why His Hero Is (SOB!) Wed!!" Abner became relatively domesticated. Like Mammy Yokum and the other "wimmenfolk" in Dogpatch, Daisy Mae did all the work, domestic and otherwise—while the useless menfolk generally did nothing whatsoever.

Lucille Sweeney: sister of Roscoe Sweeney, Buz Sawyer's comic-relief sidekick, was the lead character of the Buz Sawyer Sunday strip, a comedy about rural and suburban life. Roscoe and his sister lived on a small farm. She became controversial as the first girl to play on a varsity football team. Buz Sawyer was a popular comic strip created by Roy Crane; it had a long run from 1943 to 1989. During World War II, the adventurous Buz Sawyer flew as an ace Navy fighter pilot in the Pacific Theater where he had numerous adventures with his sidekick Sweeney. Buz rejoined the Navy in the 1950s and flew carrier-based reconnaissance attack jets over Vietnam during the 1960s.

M-1950 (5-man arctic) tent, hexagonal (Army): Lightweight, pole supported tent to provide shelter for five men and their equipment in extremely cold, or cold-wet conditions.

Dimensions: 6'-7"L × 2'H to 8'-6"H (Eave to Peak) Floor Area: 113.2 sq. ft. Weight: 56 lbs. Cube: 3.8 cu. ft.
Erection: Five Soldiers - 15 Minute
Fabric: Cotton Color: Olive Drab

Mark Antony: Marcus Antonius, (January 14, 83 BC – August 1, 30 BC), was a Roman politician and general. As a military commander and administrator, he was an important supporter and loyal friend of his mother's cousin Julius Caesar. In 54 BC, Antony became a staff officer in Caesar's armies in Gaul and Germany. He proved to be a competent military leader in the Gallic Wars. Antony and Caesar were the best of friends, as well as being fairly close relatives. After Caesar's assassination, Antony formed an official political alliance with Octavian (the future Augustus) and Lepidus, known as the Second Triumvirate. It broke up in 33 BC; disagreement between Octavian and Antony erupted into civil war, the final war of the Roman Republic. In 31 BC, Antony was defeated by Octavian at the naval Battle of Actium, and in a brief land battle at Alexandria. He and his lover Cleopatra committed suicide shortly thereafter. His career and defeat are significant in Rome's transformation from Republic to Empire. Marlon Brando portrayed Antony in the 1953 film version of Shakespeare's play.

Nikon F: introduced in 1959, Nikon's first SLR camera. [SLR = single lens reflex: the viewfinder and the film use the same lens.]

One of the most advanced cameras of its day, it was replaced by the quite similar Nikon F2 in 1973. Aspects of its design remain in all of Nikon's subsequent SLR cameras, through the current D digital models (which still share its Nikon F-mount for lenses). The "F" in Nikon F was taken from the letter F in 'Reflex,' discontinued with introduction of the present day Nikon D digital cameras.

The Nikon F proved the superiority of the SLR design, and of the Japanese camera manufacturers. It was the first SLR system to be adopted and used seriously by the general population of professional photographers because of its combination of design elements, including interchangeable prisms and focusing screens. It had a depth-of-field preview button and the mirror had lock-up capability; it had a large bayonet mount and a large lens release button, a single-stroke ratcheted film advance lever, a titanium foil focal plane shutter, various types of flash synchronization, a rapid rewind lever and fully removable back. It was well-made and durable. Unlike most 35mm camera systems, the Nikon F had a wide range of lenses, covering 21 mm to 1000 mm focal length by 1962. Nikon was among the first to introduce 'mirror lenses' – lenses which allow the light path to be folded and thus more compact than the standard telephoto designs.

With the introduction and continued improvements being made in digital photography, the F6 was the last of the Nikon F film SLRs. The Nikon F revolutionized the photographic market, stealing the thunder of German manufacturers Leica and Zeiss. The F also had a reputation for being extremely resilient to damage or mechanical failure.

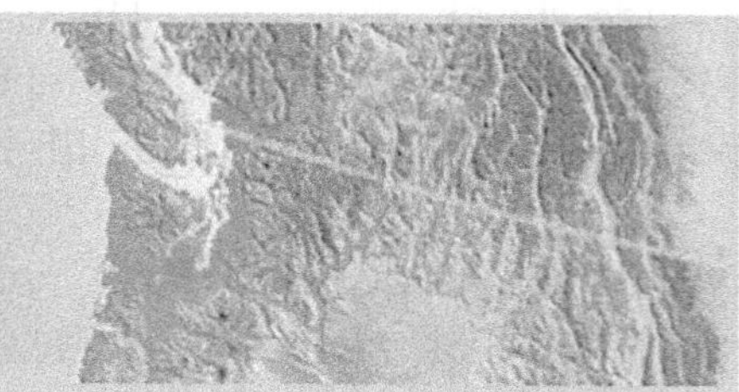

North Cascades: a section of the Cascade Range of western North America. They span the border between the Canadian province of British Columbia

and the U.S. state of Washington. The portion in Canada is known as the Canadian Cascades, including the mountains above the east bank of the Fraser Canyon as far north as Lytton, at the confluence of the Thompson and Fraser Rivers.
Predominantly non-volcanic, they include stratovolcanoes Mount Baker, Glacier Peak and Coquihalla Mountain, which are part of the Cascade Volcanic Arc.

The Pause that Refreshes: an advertising slogan of Coca Cola, first used in 1929. It soon became an everyday slogan for any number of applications.

The Piedmont: The Piedmont is a plateau region in the eastern United States between the Atlantic Coastal Plain and the main Appalachian Mountains, stretching from New Jersey in the north to central Alabama in the south. The fall line marks its eastern boundary with the Coastal Plain. To the west, the Piedmont is mostly bounded by the Blue Ridge Mountains, the easternmost range of the main Appalachians. The width varies, being quite narrow above the Delaware River but nearly 300 miles wide in North Carolina. The total area is approximately 80,000 square miles. The name "Piedmont" comes from the French term for the same physical region, literally meaning "foothill", ultimately from Latin "pes montium", meaning "the foot of the mountains." The region is named after the Italian region of Piedmont, the lowlands which abut the Alps.

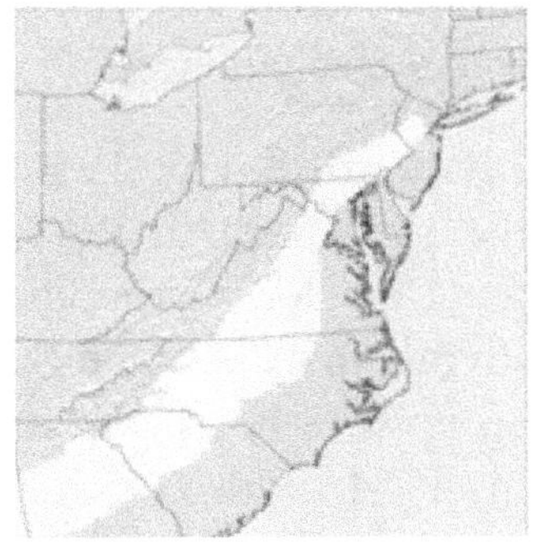

Pig-Pen: a character in the comic strip *Peanuts* by Charles M. Schulz. Known for his perpetually filthy overalls and the cloud of dirt and dust that follows wherever he goes, he is very good at playing the drums; he is also shown playing the double bass, and plays third base on the Peanuts baseball team. Charlie Brown is the one character who accepts Pig-Pen unconditionally for who he is.

Piñata: a container often made of papier-mâché, pottery, or cloth; it is decorated, and filled with small toys or candy, or both, and then broken as part of a ceremony or celebration. Piñatas are commonly associated with Mexico. The idea of breaking a container filled with treats came to Europe in the 14th century, where the name, from the Italian pignatta, was introduced. The Spanish brought the European tradition to Mexico, although there were similar traditions in Mesoamerica. The Aztecs had a similar tradition to honor the birthday of the god Huitzilopochtli in mid December. Today, the piñata is still part of Mexican culture, the cultures of other countries in Latin America, as well as the United States, but it has mostly lost its religious character.

Plymouth Savoy, 1956: The Plymouth Savoy was produced from the 1954 through 1964 model years by the Plymouth division of the Chrysler, Corporation of Highland Park, Michigan. As with Plymouth's Plaza and Belvedere models, the Savoy was named after an upscale hotel. When introduced in 1954 with 1955 model paint schemes, the Savoy was Plymouth's mid-level car—priced between the base Plaza sedans and the top-line Belvedere models. In 1955, the Savoy got new power steering. In 1956, the line added a hardtop coupe and the Custom Suburban station wagon, and the dashboard pushbutton transmission; seat belts were added for safety. The Highway Hi-Fi record player was also optional.

(*right:*) passenger well heater vent that caused the problem at Fowler's point.

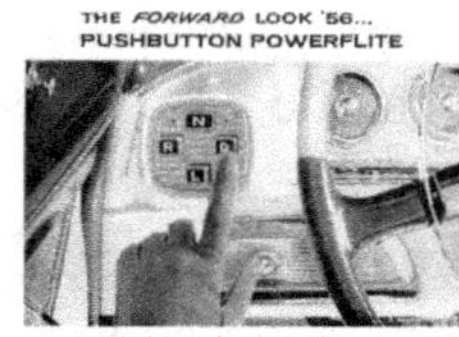

Pogo: the title and central character of a long-running daily American comic strip, created by cartoonist Walt Kelly (1913–1973) and distributed by the Post-Hall Syndicate. Set in the Okefenokee Swamp

of the southeastern United States, the strip often engaged in social and political satire through the adventures of its anthropomorphic funny animal characters. Pogo combined both sophisticated wit and slapstick physical comedy in a heady mix of allegory, Irish poetry, literary whimsy, puns and wordplay, lushly detailed artwork and broad burlesque humor.

Pompeii: an ancient Roman city near modern Naples; along with Herculaneum and many villas in the surrounding area, it was mostly destroyed and buried under 13 to 20 feet of ash and pumice in the eruption of Mount Vesuvius in 79 AD. With a complex water

system, an amphitheatre, gymnasium and a port, its population was approximately 20,000. Three public baths have been excavated, as well as several villas. Erotic sculptures and frescos are common. Many objects that lay beneath the ash have been well preserved because of the lack of air and moisture. These artifacts provide an extraordinarily detailed insight into the life of a city during the Pax Romana. During the excavation, plaster was used to fill in the voids between the ash layers that once held human bodies. This allowed one to see the exact position the person was in when he or she died.

Push processing: a film developing technique that increases the effective sensitivity of the film being processed. The film is developed for more time, possibly in combination with a higher temperature, than the manufacturer's recommendations. This results in overdevelopment of the film, compensating for underexposure in the camera. Push processing allows films to be used under lighting conditions that would ordinarily be too low. This technique alters the visual characteristics of the film, such as higher contrast, increased grain and lower resolution. **Pull processing** involves overexposure and underdevelopment, effectively decreasing the sensitivity of the processed film by developing the film for a shorter time, and possibly at a lower temperature. Pull processing displays the opposite change in visual characteristics. This may be deliberately exploited for artistic effect. Digital photography cannot use these techniques; some of the effects can be imitated by various computer programs such as Photoshop.

Quik: a chocolate powdered flavoring mix introduced in the United States in 1948, as Nestlé Quik. It enabled the user to create hot cocoa with water as opposed to powdered cocoa, which requires milk. In the 1950s, it was launched in Europe as Nesquik. In countries with the Quik term (including the USA, Canada, Mexico, and Australia, where it was originally marketed under the name Nestlé's Quik), the name was changed to the worldwide brand Nesquik in 1997.

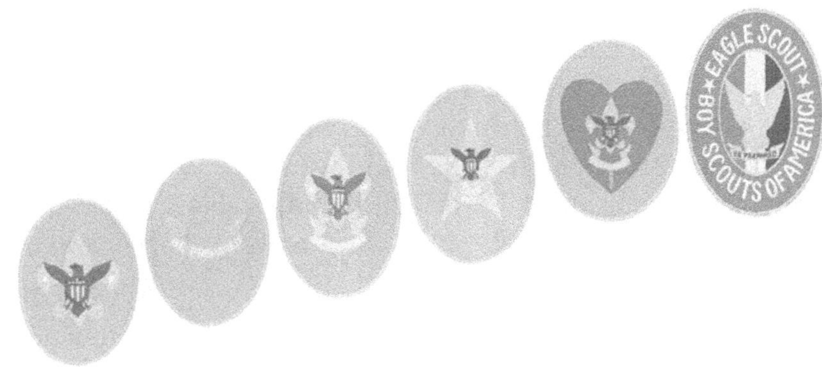

Ranks: in the 1960s the advancement program in the Boy Scouts of America was symbolized by earning six levels of achievement, identified as ranks. Tenderfoot, Second Class and First Class have progressively harder requirements in the areas of Scoutcraft, physical fitness, citizenship, personal growth and Scout Spirit. Star, Life and Eagle are designed to develop leadership skills and allow the Scout to explore potential vocations and avocations through the merit badge program. The Star and Life ranks require that the boy serve in a position of responsibility and perform community service. Originally, First Class was the all around Scout and the final and highest rank. Later ranks were originally recognitions of earning merit badges beyond First Class, and not properly ranks. Now these additional ranks form a second tier where Scouts can further develop leadership skills and explore potential vocations and avocations through the merit badge program.

Star: Star is the rank above First Class. Star is awarded when the Scout serves actively in the troop, team or crew in a position of responsibility for at least 4 months; performs at least six hours of community service; and earns six merit badges (four of which must be required for Eagle Scout rank).

Rip Kirby: was a popular comic strip featuring the adventures of the lead character, a private detective created by Alex Raymond in 1946. Displaying the talents of more than a dozen writers and illustrators, the strip had a long run, spanning five decades. After World War II, Raymond did not return to work on any of his previous successful comic strips (Flash Gordon, Jungle Jim, Secret Agent X-9) but began the new strip in which ex-Marine Rip Kirby returns from WWII and goes to work as a private detective, sometimes accompanied by his girlfriend, fashion model Judith Lynne "Honey" Dorian. The artistic merits were of special interest to Julian.

Royal Typewriter: The Royal Typewriter Company was founded in January 1904 in a machine shop in Brooklyn, New York by Edward B. Hess and Lewis C. Myers. In December 1957, Royal announced it had just produced its 10 millionth typewriter. Computers and word processors have replaced typewriters by and large. Now known as Royal Consumer Information Products Inc., Royal's product line has evolved to include cash registers, shredders, PDAs/electronic organizers, postal scales, weather stations, and a wide range of original and compatible/ remanufactured imaging supplies to support today's most popular printers, faxes, and copiers.

Sadie Hawkins Day: Sadie Hawkins Day is a pseudo-holiday that originated in Al Capp's classic hillbilly comic strip, Li'l Abner (1934–1978). This inspired real-world Sadie Hawkins dances, where girls ask boys out.

Original story: Sadie Hawkins was the daughter of one of Dogpatch's earliest settlers, Hekzebiah Hawkins. The "homeliest gal in all them hills, she grew frantic waiting for suitors to come acourtin'." When she reached 35 still a spinster, her father was even more frantic—about Sadie living at home for the rest of her life. In desperation, he called together all the unmarried men of Dogpatch and declared it “Sadie Hawkins Day.” A foot race was decreed, with Sadie in hot pursuit of the town’s eligible bachelors—and matrimony as the consequence. The concept is a variation of the myth of Atalanta, who, reluctant to marry, agreed to wed whoever could outrun her in a footrace. “When ah fires [my gun], all o’ yo’ kin start a-runnin! When ah fires agin—after givin’ yo’ a fair start—Sadie starts a runnin’. Th’ one she ketchesl’l be her husbin.” The town spinsters decided that this was such a good idea, they made Sadie Hawkins Day a mandatory yearly event, much to the chagrin of Dogpatch bachelors. In the satirical spirit that drove the strip, many sequences revolved around the dreaded Sadie Hawkins Day race. If a woman caught a bachelor and dragged him, kicking and screaming, across the finish line before sundown—by law he had to marry her.

In popular culture, Capp’s creation captured the imagination of young people, particularly in high schools and on college campuses. By the early 1940s the comic strip event had swept the nation and acquired a life of its own. By 1952, Sadie Hawkins Day was reportedly celebrated at 40,000 known venues. It became a day-long event observed in Canada and in the United States on the Saturday that follows November 9. Outside the comic strip, the practical basis of Sadie Hawkins Day is one of simple gender role reversal. Women and girls take the bold initiative by inviting the man or boy of their choice out on a date—almost unheard of before 1937—typically to a dance attended by other bachelors and their assertive dates. When Capp created the event, it wasn’t his intention to have it occur annually. However, due to its enormous popularity and the numerous fan letters he received, Capp obligingly made it a tradition in the strip every November for four decades. Sadie Hawkins Day has long been celebrated on the first Saturday of November.

Sawtooth Mountains: The Sawtooth Range is part of the Rocky

Mountains, located within a few miles of Stanley, Idaho, in the Western United States. Much of mountain range is within the Sawtooth Wilderness, part of the Sawtooth National Recreation Area. It encompasses an area of 678 square miles spanning parts of Custer, Boise, Blaine, and Elmore counties, and is bordered to the east by the Sawtooth Valley. Thompson Peak (10,751 feet) and Mount Cramer (10,716 feet) are the range's two highest peaks.

Stratolounger: a line of furniture for the home. It was originally made by the Stratford Company in the 1950s

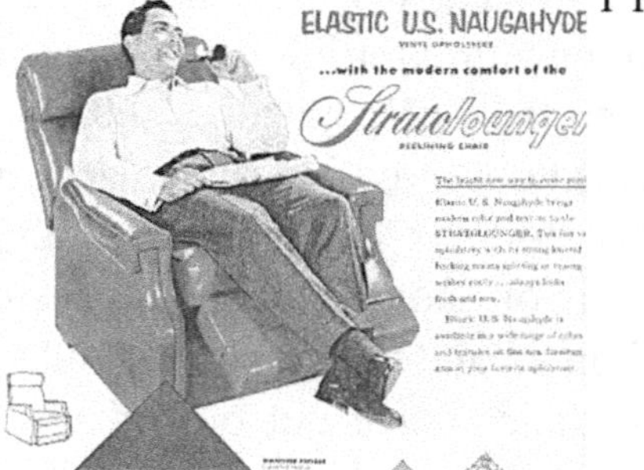

Sweetgum tree: Liquidambar styraci-flua, commonly called the American sweetgum, is a deciduous tree native to eastern North America. A popular ornamental tree, it is recognizable by the combination of its five-pointed star-shaped leaves and its hard, spiked fruits. A medium-sized to large tree, it grows anywhere from 33–50 feet in cultivation and up to 150 feet in the wild state with a trunk up to 2–3 feet in diameter. Trees may live to 400 years. The tree is symmetrical and crowns into an egg shape when the branches get too heavy, usually after its first two years of cultivation.

(Below left: sweetgum leaves in the fall. Right: sweetgum fruit pods.)

Suntans: A lightweight cotton twill trouser, originally the summer uniform for the US Army and Air Force following WW II and the Korean War. It became very popular as domestic apparel in the 1950s and 1960s. An alternative to the heavier blue denim jeans and gabardine dress slack, suntans held a crease and could be worn in formal or informal settings. Gradually, as the pale tan or khaki color was joined by other colors, the term suntan fell out of use.

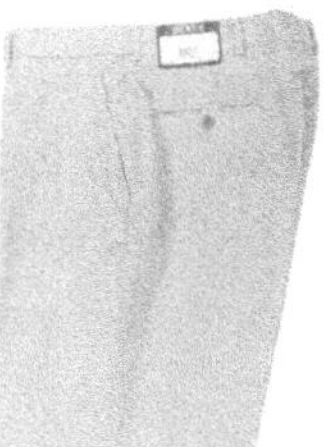

Tang: a fruit-flavored drink popular with hikers and climbers because of its low weight. Formulated by General Foods scientist William A. Mitchell in 1957; sales were poor until 1962, when NASA used it on John Glenn's Mercury flight and subsequent Gemini missions. Since then it was closely associated with the space program. Two tablespoons per 8 ounces of water provides 9 grams (0.32 oz) of sugar; 40 kilocalories (167 kJ); 100% RDA of vitamin C; 10% RDA of vitamin A, calcium, vitamin E, riboflavin, niacin, and vitamin B6, and no caffeine.

The Rifleman is a television program starring Chuck Connors as rancher Lucas McCain and Johnny Crawford as his son, Mark. It was set in the 1870s and 1880s in the town of North Fork, New Mexico Territory. The show was filmed in black-and-white, half-hour episodes and aired on ABC from September to April 1963 as a production of Four Star Television.

It was one of the first prime time series on American television to show a widowed parent raising a child. The Rifleman's gimmick was a modified Winchester Model 1892 rifle, with a large ring lever drilled and tapped for a set screw. The lever design allowed him to cock the rifle by spinning it around his hand. Connors demonstrated its rapid-fire action during the opening credits on North Fork's main street.

Tiberius: Tiberius was Roman Emperor from 14 AD to 37 AD. Born Tiberius Claudius Nero; a Claudian, Tiberius was the son of Tiberius Claudius Nero and Livia Drusilla. His mother divorced Nero and married Augustus in 39 BC, making him a step-son. Tiberius was one of Rome's greatest generals, conquering Pannonia, Dalmatia, Raetia, and temporarily Germania; laying the foundations for the northern frontier. But he came to be remembered as a dark, reclusive, and sombre ruler who never really desired to be emperor; Pliny the Elder called him tristissimus hominum, "the gloomiest of men." After the death of his son Drusus Julius Caesar in 23, he became more reclusive and aloof. In 26, Tiberius exiled himself from Rome and spent his final years at the Villa Jovis on the island of Capri.

According to some, it was a center of wild parties and orgies. He left administration largely in the hands of his unscrupulous Praetorian Prefects Lucius Aelius Sejanus and Quintus Naevius Sutorius Macro. Caligula, Tiberius' grand-nephew and adopted grandson, succeeded the emperor upon his death

Troop Nine Scrapbook: A project started by Julian when he joined. It was fashioned after the one he had done as a Cub Scout.

Under God: The Pledge of Allegiance of the United States is an expression of loyalty to the federal flag and the republic of the United States of America, originally composed by Francis Bellamy in 1892 and formally adopted by Congress as the pledge in 1942. The Pledge was supposed to be quick and to the point. Bellamy designed it to be recited in 15 seconds. Prior 1954, no endeavor to get the Pledge officially amended succeeded.
To celebrate Lincoln's birthday in 1954, President Eisenhower was sitting in Lincoln's pew at New York Avenue Presbyterian Church. The pastor delivered a sermon based on the Gettysburg Address. He cited Lincoln's words "under God" as defining words that set the United States apart from other nations. Eisenhower acted on the pastor's suggestion the next day; on February 8, Rep. Charles Oakman (R-Mich.), introduced the bill. Congress passed the necessary legislation and Eisenhower signed it into law on Flag Day, June 14, 1954. All states except five (Hawaii, Iowa, Oklahoma, Vermont and Wyoming) give time for the pledge to be recited as part of the school day.

Westminster chimes: The Westminster Quarters is the most common name for a melody used by a set of clock bells to chime on each quarter hour. The number of chime sets matches the number of quarter hours that have passed. It is also known as the Westminster Chimes, or the Cambridge Chimes from its place of origin, the church of St Mary the Great,

Cambridge. The chime melody is also used in some doorbells and school bells. Most of the schools in Japan and Taiwan play the chimes to signal the end and beginning of periods. The Elizabeth Tower at the north end of Westminster Palace *(above)* in London, strikes the chimes every day. Big Ben is the nickname for the great bell of the clock.

We're No Angels is a 1955 Christmas comedy starring Humphrey Bogart, one of the rare comedies that he made. The cast included Peter Ustinov, Aldo Ray, Joan Bennett, Basil Rathbone, and Leo G. Carroll.

Three convicts escape from prison on Devil's Island just before Christmas. One has a pet viper named Adolphe. At a nearby French colonial town they go to the only store that gives supplies on credit. The Ducotels - Felix and Amelie, and their daughter Isabelle - operate the store. The escapees notice that his roof is leaking, and offer to fix it. They plan to remain there until nightfall, steal clothes and supplies, and escape on the ship waiting in the harbor. As they stay in the store, they grow fond of the Ducotels and have a change of heart: they offer their services—including conning people and falsifying records to make the store appear prosperous in time for the hard hearted owner and his son when they arrive. With the help of creative accounting and Adolphe, the Ducotels' problems are solved.

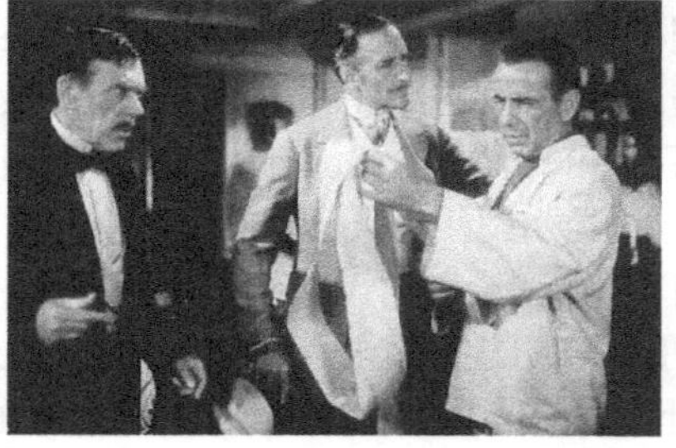

Wide Receiver: The wide receiver (WR) is a position in American and Canadian football that functions as the pass-catching specialist. Among the fastest and most agile players in the game, they are frequent highlight-reel favorites. The wide receiver's principal role is to catch passes from the quarterback. On passing plays, the receiver attempts to avoid, outmaneuver, or simply outrun defenders in the area of his pass route. Once a pass is thrown in his direction, the receiver's goal is to first catch the ball and then attempt to run downfield. Some receivers are perceived as a deep threat because of their flat-out speed. Tall height and light weight are advantages at the receiver position.

Yashica-A is a medium format 120 film TLR camera. Introduced in 1956, it was a basic model with a top shutter speed of 1/300. It was in production until 1969. Usually black, cameras produced between 1957 and 1959 had grey leatherette with either black or grey metalwork. Each roll of 120 film had 12 frames. The picture size is 6x6cm. Featuring twin 80mm f/3.5 lenses, the upper lens was for the viewfinder. The view was reflected onto a screen with grid lines, mounted on top of the camera; a cover shield unfolded to provide a light baffle. The lower lens exposed the film. A rim-set shutter featured speeds of 1/25, 1/50, 1/100, and 1/300. It has a connection for synchronizing flash bulb exposures; its leaf shutter is capable of flash sync at all shutter speeds.

Shutter speed is selected by rotating the shutter speed dial; aperture is set by adjusting a lever on the outside of the shutter speed dial. Film is advanced by manually turning the advance wheel until the next frame number appears in the red window on the back of the camera.

Song Credits

The songs referenced in the text are described briefly in the order they were cited. They were selected because they are representative of the time period and would have been likely choices.

Volare—Dean Martin. This was on the radio at Julian's house during the opening scene. Written by Franco Migliacci and Domenico Modugno, it was released as a single on 1 February 1958. It spent five non-consecutive weeks atop the Billboard Hot 100 in August and September 1958 and was Billboard's number-one single for the year. Modugno's recording subsequently became the first Grammy winner for Record of the Year and Song of the Year in 1958. The song was later translated in several languages and recorded by a wide range of performers, including Bobby Rydell, Dean Martin, Al Martino, David Bowie, Cliff Richard, Frank Sinatra, Louis Armstrong, Luciano Pavarotti, Dalida, Gipsy Kings and Barry White.

One Track Mind—Bobby Lewis issued this as a follow up to his first Beltone hit *Tossin' and Turnin,'* a Reggie Adams song. Lewis was raised in an orphanage, and ran away from his foster home at age 14. He worked carnivals, and eventually joined the Leo Hines Orchestra in Indianapolis as a singer. In late 1960, while appearing at the Apollo Theater in New York, Lewis stopped at the offices of Beltone Records, a small independent outfit in Manhattan, and was prevailed upon to cut *Tossin' and Turnin'*. The single was issued at the end of 1960, and lightning struck in 1961: the single rode the charts for 23 weeks, eventually hitting the number one spot on both the pop and R&B

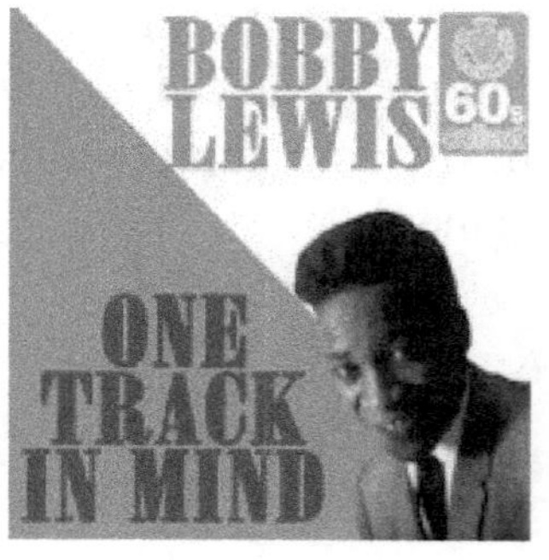

charts. Sales of the record were so strong that for the only time in its history, Beltone issued an accompanying album, *One Track Mind*, which also was on the top 100. The song came to be his signature. Lewis has been consigned to rock & roll history, somewhat unfairly, as a one-hit wonder.

Does Your Chewing Gum Lose Its Flavour (On the Bedpost Overnight?)— a novelty song by Lonnie Donegan. Released as a single in 1959, it peaked at number 3 in the UK Singles Chart; it was Donegan's greatest chart success in the U.S., reaching number five on the Billboard Hot 100 chart in 1961. The song is a cover version of *Does The Spearmint Lose Its Flavor on the Bedpost Overnight?* by Billy Rose, Ernest Breuer, and Marty Bloom and first released in 1924. The song is humorous in content; each verse describes a dramatic or urgent scenario leading up to the asking of the titular question.

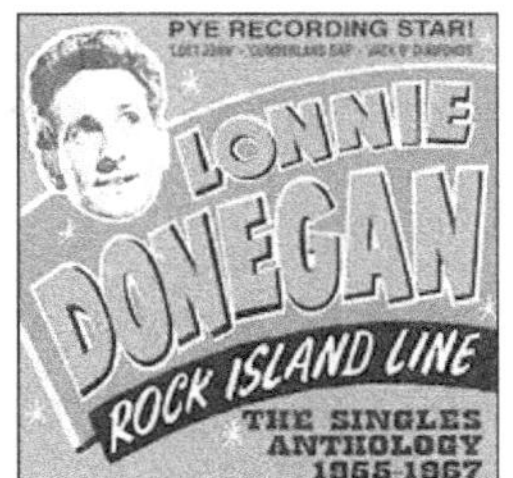

Shine on Harvest Moon—Moon Mullican. This was pre-dance background music. A popular early-1900s song credited to the married vaudeville team Nora Bayes and Jack Norworth. It was one of a series of Moon-related Tin Pan Alley songs of the era. It became a pop standard, and continues to be performed and recorded even in the 21st century. Aubrey Wilson Mullican (March 29, 1909 – January 1, 1967), known as Moon Mullican, was an American country and western singer, songwriter, and pianist. His performance of *Shine On* at the Grand Ole Opry on New Years Day 1955 was released on Artco Records C-685-L.

Hello Mary Lou—Ricky Nelson. First song played at the dance. Written by U.S. singer Gene Pitney and Father Cayet Mangiaracina, was first performed by Johnny Duncan in 1960, and later by Ricky Nelson in 1961. Nelson's version, issued as the B-side of his No. 1 hit "Travelin' Man," (Imperial 5741), reached No. 9 on the Billboard music charts on May 28, 1961. The song features an influential guitar solo by James Burton, often cited by later guitarists such as Brian May. Piano was by Ray Johnson, who had succeeded Gene Garf as Nelson's regular session pianist in November 1959.

I Fall to Pieces—Patsy Cline: a single released by Patsy Cline in 1961, was featured on her 1961 studio album, Patsy Cline Showcase. *I Fall to Pieces* was Cline's first #1 hit on the Country charts, and her second hit single to cross over onto the Pop charts. It was the first of a string of songs that would be written by Hank Cochran and Harlan Howard for Cline; it became one of Cline's most-recognizable hit singles. It has been classified as a country music standard.

Teen Angel—Mark Dinning. Written by Jean Dinning (1924–2011) and her husband, Red Surrey, and performed by both Jean's brother, Mark Dinning, and Alex Murray in 1959 on MGM records. The song was not an instant success, with radio stations in the U.S. banning the song. The song is about a girl who is out on a ride with her boyfriend. Their car is stalled on a railroad track when he pulls her to safety. But when she runs back, she gets run over by a train. Despite the reluctance of radio stations, the song

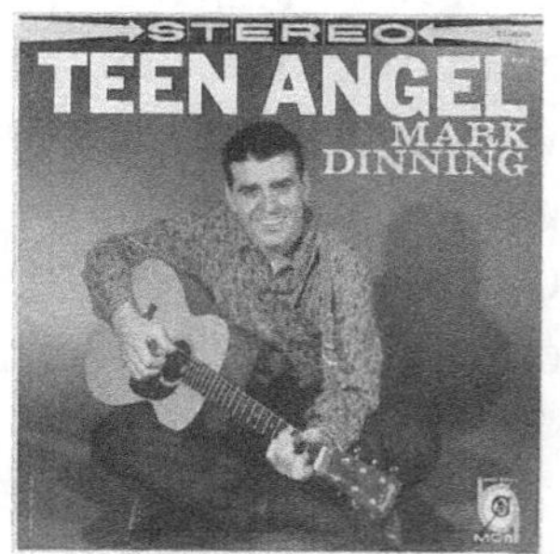

continued to climb the charts. In the last week of 1959, the single jumped from #100 to #50 on the Billboard Hot 100 chart. It went on to reach #1 on the U.S. Billboard Hot 100 (February 1960).

Stairway to Heaven—Neil Sedaka. Written by Neil Sedaka and Howard Greenfield. It was released as a 45 rpm single off of Sedaka's 1960 album Neil Sedaka Sings Little Devil and His Other Hits. In 1960, the song peaked at number nine on the US Billboard Hot 100 chart. The personnel on the song included King Curtis on saxophone, Don Arnone, Art Ryerson and Everett Barksdale on guitar, Milt Hinton on bass, and Dave "Panama" Francis on drums. This song is not to be confused with the Led Zeppelin song, *Stairway to Heaven* released a decade later.

Itsy Bitsy Teenie Weenie Yellow Polka Dot Bikini—Bryan Hyland. A novelty song telling the story of a shy girl wearing a revealing polka dot bikini at the beach, it was written by Paul Vance and Lee Pockriss and first released in June 1960 by Brian Hyland with orchestra conducted by John Dixon. Hyland's version hit #1 on the Billboard Hot 100 on August 8, 1960. The story told through the three verses of the song: (1) the young lady is too afraid to leave the locker where she has changed into her bikini; (2) she has made it to the beach but sits on the sand wrapped in a blanket; and (3) she has finally gone into the ocean, but is too afraid to come out, and stays immersed in the water—despite the fact that she's "turning blue"—to hide herself from view. Trudy Packer recited the phrases "One, two, three, four/Tell the people what she wore", heard at the end of each verse before the chorus; and "Stick around, we'll tell you more", heard after the first chorus and before the start of the second verse.

Moon River—Andy Williams. Composed by Henry Mancini with lyrics written by Johnny Mercer, it received an Academy Award for Best Original Song for its first performance by Audrey Hepburn in the 1961 movie Breakfast at Tiffany's. It also won Mancini the 1962 Grammy Award for Record of the Year and Mercer the Grammy Award for Song of the Year. Since its original performance, the song has been covered by many other artists. It became the theme song for Andy Williams, who first recorded it in 1961 and performed it at the Academy Awards ceremonies in 1962. He sang the first eight bars at the beginning of his television show and named his production company and venue in Branson, Missouri after it.

The Twist—Chubby Checker. The song that gave birth to the Twist dance craze; it was written and originally released in early 1959 by Hank Ballard and the Midnighters. The song, and the dance the Twist, was popularized in 1960 when the song was recorded by Chubby Checker. His single became a hit, reaching No. 1 on the Billboard Hot 100 on September 19, 1960 and then setting a record by being the only single to reach No. 1 in two different chart runs when it resurfaced and topped the chart again on January 13, 1962.

Chubby Checker and Dick Clark)

Exposure for Checker's performance on American Bandstand and on The Dick Clark Saturday Night Show helped propel the song to the top of the American charts.

American Bandstand was an American music performance show that aired in various versions from 1952 to 1989 on the ABC network. Hosted from 1956 until its final season by Dick Clark, the show featured teenagers dancing to Top 40 music, introduced by Clark. At least one popular musical act would appear in person to lipsync one of their latest singles, which often made sales skyrocket.

Julian's Class Schedule:

Per 1: English
Per 2: World History
Per 3: PE
Per 4: Biology
Lunch
Per 5: Typing
Per 6: Art
Per 7: Geometry

Randall's Class Schedule:

Per 1: PE
Per 2: World History
Per 3: English
Per 4: Geometry
Lunch
Per 5: Woodshop
Per 6: Concert Band
Per 7: Biology

Passing bell: In some schools the bell or buzzer that ended a class period is referred to as a passing bell, indicating that a specified time period is allowed to pass to the next class—usually four or five minutes, depending on the size of the school. Some schools had a special "tardy" or second bell that allowed students with a great distance a little more time to get to a class without a late penalty.

Index of names

(This index provides a quick assist to readers who would like to follow a particular character, or to see a character's relative importance at a glance in this book. Many were featured in previous books about Julian, and some will be in books that follow. An **S** *at the end of an entry refers to supplementary material at the back of the book. Numbers in Italics indicate the character is referred to by a pronoun or title e.g., Mom, Dad)*

Name **Brief description** **[chapter** || page]

Art Frankel: Biology teacher; astute and progressive. He gets Julian and Randall to the school nurse after their accident. [**6** 71 || **8** 107-10, 113-14, 119-20, 133 || **13** 229 || **15** 241 || **23** 446, 447 || **28** 537, 538]

Audrey Fredericks: Head Girls' P.E. Department, teacher, Girls' League advisor. Husky and butch, nicknamed Lucille because of her similarity in appearance to the comic strip character, Lucille Sweeney. [**7** 92 || **14** 234 || **20** 360 || **22** 417]

Barbara: Rita's friend and lieutenant at the Sadie Hawkins Dance—owns her own car. [**1** 10-12 || **14** 233 || **20** 355-7, 361, 371 || **21** 382, 3, 387, 388-398, 399, 401, 408-10 || **22** 424-6, 429-30 || **23** 442]

Ben: Employee at Oglivy's Emporium; mentioned only. [**4** 41]

Bernard Withers: Geometry Teacher. [**15** 241, 269]

Beth Johnson: Julian's lab partner in Biology. [**8** 108-9 || **11** 167, 171, 175 || **12** 197 || **23** 446-48]

Bruce Ruggles: First Class scout in the Badger patrol. Seriously overweight. Mentioned only. [**9** 138 || **S** 551]

Carl: Men's Clothing salesman at Oglivy's Emporium; mentioned only. [**3** 31]

Casey Snyder: Life scout in the Wolf patrol; mentioned only. [**17** 321 || **28** 537 || **S** 551]

Chuck *[Beta]*: Senior Master at the Initiation in Hayden Park. [**12** 194-6, 198, 200, 202, 204, 205-219 || **13** 221, 223, 4, *227,* 228-31 || **15** 249 || *17 302, 320* || **20** 370 || *21 414* || **24** 478 || **S** 555]

Clint Walker: Star scout in the Zebra patrol; he has a growing sexual attraction for Alex, his hero figure. [**17** 315-6, 318-319 || **S** 551]

Cousin Val: Lives in Newport RI; Rita's cousin is a year older—they spend summers at Greenwich Bay playing with the boys. [**1** 11-13 || **14** 233]

Danny Laskey: Life scout, Senior Patrol Leader of Troop Nine. He will become Junior Assistant Scoutmaster at the end of

4, 5, 6, 7, 8, 9, 10, 14 || **2** 17 || **3** *23, 24, 26, 27,* 29, 30, *31, 34, 39* || **5** *50,* 51, 2, 54-7, *58, 59,* 60-69 || ***6*** *71, 73, 77, 80* || **7** 84, 85-6, 92-7, 100-5 || **8** *116, 118, 119, 122, 123,* 131-3 || **9** *137,* 139, *141, 143, 145,* 147, *150* || ***10*** *151, 154, 5* || **11** 165-71,*174, 5* || ***12*** *197, 203* || ***13*** *226* || ***15*** *247, 249, 252, 255, 259, 262, 268, 269, 270* || ***17*** *325* || ***19*** *338, 9, 340, 342, 345* || ***20*** *355, 6, 7, 359, 365, 368, 373, 375, 6* || ***21*** *381, 386, 390* || **22** 413-32, *434* || ***23*** *436, 7, 438, 440, 446, 455, 459, 460* || **24** *467, 472,* 473, *482, 4, 5, 486, 487,* 488 || ***25*** *491* || **26** *511, 513,* 514-16, *517, 520* || ***27*** *528, 532*]

Frank Ferris: (Frankie) Troop Nine Bugler. He has been a sexual playmate of Danny's for fun, not romance. [**9** 139-146 || **10** 155 || **12** 195, 6 || **S** 551]

Fred: Henchman of Nels, Randall's childhood bully in Pullman, Washington. [**8** 128]

Geoff Staples: A scout from Atlanta that had a significant impact on several Troop Nine members and on Mark as well when they were at summer camp. He is mentioned only. [**2** 25 || **4** 43, 47 || **5** 54, 67 || **7** 90 || **8** 122, 133 || **9** 143 || **15** 256 || **16** 296 || **19** 345, 347, 349, 352 || **25** 494, 497 || **S** 562]

George Nelson: Woodshop teacher; mentioned only. [**28** 536]

Georgia: Waitress at Sparky's Drive-In. [**14** 244, 248, 252]

Geraldine Smathers: Real Estate Agent, friend and employer of Francine Forrest. She has adopted Francine and her son as family—she has no other. [**1** 3, 7-9 || **3** 23-29, 35, 37-8 || **5** 55, 58, 59, 60, 61, 62, 63, 66-8 || **6** 72, 73 || **7** 84, 85-6, 92-97, 100-106 || **8** 131-3 || **10** 157 || **11** 165, 6, 169, 170, 171, 173, 5 || **14** 237 || **15** 243, 247, 249 || **19** 339, 345 || **20** 355, 356, 7, 8, 9, 360, 1, 2, 364, 5, 6, 368, 373, 374, 5, 6 || **21** 381, 385, 387, 390, 394, 402, 3, 4 || **22** 413, 414, 415-32, 434 || **23** 436, 7, 446, 455, 459, 60 || **24** 463, 467 || **26** 511, 516, 517, 520 || **27** 527, 532, 3, 5]

Hazel: A neighbor that visits Francine and Julian from time to time, usually with homemade cookies or a freshly baked pie. She's the unofficial news bureau of the neighborhood. Mentioned only. [**8** 131]

goal was transformative. He retains his secret goal to win Mark. [**1** 3-15 || **2** 17-18 || **3** 23-40 || **4** 42, 47 || **5** 49-70 || **6** 71-4, 77, 79-81 || **7** 85, 86, 92-97, 100-106 || **8** 108-10, 111, 112-133 || **9** 135-9, 140, 141-150 || **10** 151-159 || **11** 166-75, 176, 7, 8, 9 || **12** 189-91, 192, 196-99, 202-4, 206, 208-19 || **13** 225-7, 229, 30 || **14** 234-39 || **15** 241-270 || **16** 287, 292, 294-99 || **17** 301, 2, 3, 305, 6, 7, 308-10, 312, 313, 314-17, 320, 21, 22, 323-25 || **18** 327, 332 || **19** 337-45, 347, 349, 351, 2 || **20** 355-7, 358-80 || **21** 381-396, 399-411 || **22** 413-434 || **23** 435-462 || **24** 463-488 || **25** 489-510 || **26** 511-521 || **27** 523, 4, 5, 7, 527-30, 531, 532-3 || **28** 535, 6, 7, 8, 539-545 || **28.1** 547 || **S** 551, 555, 7, 565, 580, 590]

Kurt Davis: Life scout in the Zebra Patrol. An encounter at camp with Sid was the beginning of a personal relationship. [**17** 323-5 || **20** 370 || **S** 551]

Lillian St. John: Julian's English teacher. [**6** 72 || **27** 523-5, 528]

Louis *[Alpha]:* Grand Master at the Initiation in Hayden Park. He provides the hexagon tent. [**12** 194-6, 198, 9, 202, 3, 4, 205-13, 215, 16, 17, 18, 19 || **13** 221, 223, 4, 226-27, 230 || ***14** 235* || **15** 241, 249, 252, 4 *255, 260* || ***21** 385* || ***22** 414* || **S** 555, 6]

Lucy Graham: Childhood acquaintance; Julian liked her cat. [**1** 8, 10, 11, 14 || **7** 97, 100-103 || **20** 371]

Lynne: Assists Rita in the Sadie Hawkins "draft." [**14** 233, 237 || **23** 451]

Marcie: Theresa's friend in the cafeteria; Julian draws her portrait. [**23** 453, 454-7 || **26** 512, 13, 520 || **27** 527, 29, 32, 534]

Marjorie Thomas: Sid Thomas' mother. [**1** 4]

Mark Schaefer: Scoutmaster of Troop Nine. Major protagonist. He is a retail purchasing agent and manager. When he was a senior in college, he was asked to replace his former scoutmaster who died from a heart attack. This and his marriage of convenience have helped him to cope with a devastating personal loss [see Erik, above]. He devotes all his personal time to scouting. He is unaware that

Pat Schaefer: Wife of Mark; a Registered Nurse, studying to become an M.D. Their marriage is one of mutual convenience, not romance. They have been friends since high school. [**4** 41, 2 || **5** 54 || **7** 83-5, 86-92, 97-99 || **11** 162, 163, 181, 187 || **16** 283, 292 || **18** 328 || **19** 346]

Paul Harris: Star scout, member of the Lynx patrol; mentioned only. [**17** 319 || **S** 551]

Peter Gustafson: RN, colleague of Pat Schaeffer. [**11** 162-5, 181-186 || **16** 271, 272-83, 284, 5, 7, 8, 289, 293 || **19** 349, 352]

Petey: Randall's childhood rival, henchman of Nels the bully in Pullman. [**8** 127, 8]

Phil Young: One of the Masters at Tony's Initiation; mentioned only. [**13** 224]

Phyllis Simpson: Sells cosmetics at Oglivy's Emporium. [**2** 20-21 || **4** 42 || **7** 91]

Ralph van Horn: Art Teacher at Jackson High School. [**10** 155 || **14** 235, 238-9 || **15** 246 || **21** 399 || **23** 435 || **27** 523, 529, 531]

Randall Hallstrom: Recently moved from Pullman Washington. Sophomore, in Julian's World History class. [**6** 74-6, 78-9, 81-2 || **8** 110-123, 126-131, 133 || **10** 151-59 || **11** 166, 170, 174, 5, 175-80 || **12** 189-93, 196-99, 202-19 || **13** 222, 226, 228-31 || **14** 235 || **15** 241-69, 270 || **16** 294-99 || **17** 301-25 || **18** 327-36 || **19** 337, 8, 9, 340, 345, 6 || **20** 359, 368, 377 || **22** 433 || **23** 435, 6, 438, 40, 447-61 || **24** 463-87, 88 || **25** 489-510 || **26** 511, 12, 13, 16, 17, 18, 19 || **27** 527-31 || **28** 535-45 || **28.1** 547 || **S** 555, 590]

Rita Mitchell: Buxom daughter of an attorney, very bright and sexually precocious. Member of the Girl's Dance Team, she has been one of the social elite all through school. [**1** 10-15 || **14** 233-4, 235-8 || **15** 245, 6 || **20** 355, 6, 357-67, 8, 369, 370, 1, 2, 3, 374-80 || **21** 381, 2, 3, 387-94, 395-6, 7, 8, 399-411 || **22** 416, 17, 18, 19, 20, 21, 424, 5, 6, 7, 8, 9, 430, 432, 4 || **23** 436, 437, 442, 445, 6, 7, 448, 451, 2, 3, 4, || **24** 464, 466, 7 || **25** 493 || **26** 512 || **27** 532 || **28.1** 547]

Robin Simmons: Life scout in the Lynx patrol. Mentioned only. [**17** 319 || **S** 551]

talented actor and clown. At the end of summer camp, he fell in love with Danny, causing a major change in his behavior. [**9** 143 || **12** 189-91, 194-99, 200, 202-220 || **13** 221-5, 226 || **15** 249, 50, 254, 6, 7, 265 || **16** 287, 294-99 || **17** 303-4, 317-321, 322, 324, 325 || **19** 349 || **22** 433 || **24** 478 || **27** 537 || **28** 545 || **S** 551, 555]

Tracy: Rita's boyfriend, football player, a Junior. [**1** 11, 13, 15 || **14** 233, 4 || **20** 358, 362, 363, 368, 9, 370 || **20** 377-8 || **21** 388, 391, 398, 399, 404, 405, 407, 410 || **23** 441-446, 451, 452, 3 || **28.1** 547]

Uncle Max: Julian's name for Sarge Oliver. [**3** 30 || **6** 80 || **19** 341 || **20** 359 || **27** 529]

Zack Peters: On Geraldine's yard crew; gives Julian an issue of Playboy Magazine on instructions from Geraldine. [**1** 7, 8 || **3** 36 || **5** 66 || **7** 96, 7 || **8** 125]

a word about the author

Eldot, a nom de plume, is a simple cipher: the author's first initial, followed by a period, spelled phonetically [L. = Eldot] Why? Two reasons: in 2011, when his first novel was published, the subject matter was more sensitive and controversial than it is today. The concern was that one or more "conservative" groups might choose to make a fuss about the content. Lest relatives, friends or former colleagues be inconvenienced or victimized, the nom de plume was adopted to serve as a shield. Secondly, the author didn't want opportunistic individuals in the media to distort what the book was seeking to achieve. In fact, media treatment of the subject was the major motivation to write Julian's side of story in the first place.

Four years have gone by; the Julian novels have been well received. All five print books have positive critical reviews. It makes sense to pull back the curtain and let the reader get a peek at the culprit. The potential for controversy still exists, but the extremist groups have lost their clout. It's harder to be a pioneer nowadays: social media and the cell phone have changed the landscape; the Julian novels are not weakened, but made more topical than ever.

Eldot has lived in the Pacific Northwest for most of his life. In order to dodge the draft and avoid the Viet Nam war, he took an occupational deferment to teach high school Drama and English. The interminable nature of the war and the draft lottery kept him in that occupation so long that he stayed there afterward, having been quite successful. Why change a good thing? The refuge had morphed into a career. He became a local and state leader in his profession. After thirty terrific years as an educator, he retired. Now he's taken up writing. The novels are not autobiographical.

You're in high school now is his twelfth book.

Leland Alan Hall

Publications:

1960: Emperor Commodus Prompt Book: Use of Masks in Drama
[*Honors Thesis, a translation from the Greek, housed at U of O Library*]
2011: *Little J and Roger* [eBook only]
2012: *Barr's Meadow*
The Poker Club
The Shooting Gallery
Thunder and Lightning
2013: *The Champions*
Inside Eldot's World: a literary gazetteer [eBook only]
2015: *You're in* high school *now*

about the Julian novels

Julian's Sophomore Year was to have been the title of this book. Alas, it grew too much—a side effect of the author's approach to composition: organic as opposed to pre-determined outline. Allowing internal narrative to develop as needed leads to this; so long as doing so serves the story goals—and the reader's endurance—they are allowed.

At about chapter 20, it became clear that it would be impossible to tell all that's important about Julian's sophomore year within a single volume. Finding a good place to pause was required—that proved to be an artistic challenge. It took another five chapters to find a suitable point in the action.

Inside Eldot's World

—a literary gazetteer for

Little J and Roger and/or *Julian's Private Scrapbook*

Thus, the original title has been reassigned to serve as a series title. This means that there will be at least one "sequel" to get through rest of the sophomore year.

That's what happened with the first Julian novel—in that instance, a two-week timespan at a summer camp became a series of five novels entitled **Julian's Private Scrapbook**. *You're in high school* covers a little over four months.

An extensive discussion of this phenomenon is discussed in *Inside Eldot's World,* available to download free at most eBook vendor locations. That book also goes into detail about the controversial

aspects of the content as well as a number of literary topics.
[a deluxe interactive PDF version is available at http://www.diphra.com/Gazetteer.html].
Julian's story is fictional; it is an attempt to address the failure of society and the media to deal honestly with the problems that young people face when it comes to sexual identity and development. It rises from years of observation and experience, and frustration. The vehicle chosen is unusual, if not unique: romantic comedy. The perspective is from within the characters: it is what they see, think, and feel—the view that is generally never allowed a voice. That, of course, is what can lead to controversy.

The "system" fails to recognize or remember that individual human beings under the age of 18 are conscious beings: learning, setting goals, and making life direction decisions at every turn. That is the world readers enter in these pages.

You're In High School Now is not dependent on the previous Julian novels; reading them is not a requirement. But many of the characters are the same; their memories include what has gone on before, and are factors in their behavior. Anything that the reader needs to know is explained within the new story, so referring to the earlier books is not necessary. However, for any who are not acquainted with the previous books, a listing is below:

The Julian's Private Scrapbook series

The two week summer camp of 1962 is the setting. The story is divided into five parts, roughly equal in length. Each part is written as if it were a stand alone, and has its own title. They are meant to be read in sequence, however, for a full and complete reading experience.

Barr's Meadow, Part 1: 261 pages, 105,000 words Published November, 2011

The Poker Club, Part 2: 294 pages, 106,800 words Published December, 2011

The Shooting Gallery, Part 3: 293 pages, 106,600 words Published February 2012

Thunder and Lightning, Part 4: 322 pages 114,500 words Published March, 2012

The Champions, Part 5: 360 pages 129,600 words Published April, 2012

All are available in hardcover, paperback, and eBook versions at any bookstore and online at Barnes & Noble and Amazon, as well as the publisher's website: http://www.julianssprivatescrapbook.com/

Independent BlueInk Reviews of all five books follow on the next pages

Barr's Meadow: (Julian's Private Scrapbook: Part One) Eldot

Xlibris, 248 pages, (paperback) $15.99, 978-1-4691-4512-9
(Reviewed: December 2013)

Pleasant, nostalgic and ingenuous, *Barr's Meadow* is set at a Boy Scout camp in the early '60s, the fictional story of a gay young man named Julian.

Julian, nearly 13, is handsome, enthusiastic and affable, as well as a skilled artist. Julian has a crush on Scoutmaster Mark. Mark — who, while married, has been open to same-gender sex in the past — has resolved to confront this with sensitivity and fraternal affection, realizing that Julian's trusting nature could make him the victim of more predatory scouts.

Author Eldot (who writes under one name) explores the daily activities of scout camp and the politics of sex between teenage boys. The author focuses mostly on the gay characters and Julian's sexual thoughts, but this is not really gay erotica (although the back cover warns: "Not for sale to persons under 18"). With the exception of two somewhat explicit (though not heightened) passages, it reflects on same-gender, male sexuality while generally avoiding the salacious.

Eldot gets inside the heads of the characters, including Julian and Mark, as in: "Mark stepped around to the other side of the bed and watched Julian hustle. He bounced on his toes unconsciously. He had faced the unknown here and it had gone very well. I was right about this."

Barr's Meadow is comparable to other teenage boy coming-of-age narratives, such as *The Last Picture Show*, minus the cynicism, sophistication or relative depth. This doesn't mean that it's poorly crafted; only that Eldot's prose is simple, direct and seeks to examine the lives and thoughts of guys who are only beginning to view the world with introspection. Eldot walks the precarious line between making the boys evolved and depicting them as saints. He allows them moments of tenderness and nurturing without suggesting their virility has been tainted.

Barr's Meadow, the first in a series, never breaks through to the transcendent realms of literary brilliance, but it is intelligent, moving, well-grounded and memorable.

The Poker Club: Julian's Private Scrapbook, Part Two
Eldot
Xlibris, 279 pages, (paperback) $15.99, 978-1-4771-1834-4
(Reviewed: March, 2014)

This unusual novel is sure to cause controversy for its subject matter. The second in a projected five-novel series, the book takes place at a scout camp during the summer of 1962, and follows several groups of boys as they form friendships, learn new skills, and fall in love. Much of the book concerns their various sexual explorations; indeed, the "Poker Club" of the title refers to one group's method of beginning such activities – and the author is careful to note on the back cover that the book "is meant for mature readers."

In between the sex, several plotlines start to form. Julian, who has a crush on his scoutmaster Mark, learns more about life matters while interacting with his fellow scouts. Tom, an older boy who has been with many other boys, finds himself falling for Nick, one of his earlier conquests and now a friend. Geoff, a co-founder of the Poker Club, recruits other scouts to join in the fun, including Tom and Nick.

While the extensive explicit sex scenes can feel somewhat exploitative, generally they are handled well, combining experience with innocence in an endearing way. Julian in particular, while certainly experienced in some sexual matters, still has much to learn. His sweet, innocent looks make Mark and the other scouts want to protect him from such things, so that, for instance, while a remark about "choice buns" makes Julian curious about what that means, he doesn't learn the answer until nearly the end of the book.

The developing relationship between Tom and Nick is also fascinating; in the previous book, Tom hoped to seduce Julian but now only wants to be with Nick and feels guilty for his earlier pursuits.

The author includes a summary of the first novel along with maps of all locations. If readers are open to the subject matter, they will find intriguing insights into the complex world of boys in this unique novel.

Also available in hardcover and ebook

The Shooting Gallery: Julian's Private Scrapbook Part Three
Eldot
Xlibris, 287 pages, (paperback) $15.99, 978-1-4771-4986-7
(Reviewed: April 2014)

The Shooting Gallery is the third in Eldot's five-part series: "Julian's Private Scrapbook." We find ourselves in a Boy Scout Camp, where our pubescent hero, Julian Forrest, comes of age in June 1962. Julian is a prodigy when it comes to drawing, a talent that garners many accolades. As we might expect, there are other skills to be mastered at camp: swimming, canoeing, archery, cooking — and, in this case, sex. In *Barr's Meadow* (Part 1) readers came to appreciate Julian's beauty, exuberance, affability and guilelessness. There, Eldot laid out the rituals and routines of scout camp: inspection and clean-up, naked swimming and campfire sing-alongs. In the midst of this cheery beehive, Julian had his first sexual experience with another scout; another encounter involved two older, more experienced boys.

In *The Shooting Gallery*, the author again presents the everyday activities we might expect, but now, sexual behavior is more frequent. While this kind of intimacy is often explored in fiction, it's much rarer to find it imbued with positive, canny eroticism, as it is here. In *The Shooting Gallery*, the tone is somewhat Utopian; the characters are not influenced by the usual shame or taboos society places on sex between males. Boy Scout Camp becomes a refuge where characters freely (though conscientiously) experiment with same-gender eroticism.

Eldot not only examines male-only sexual episodes, he anchors them in verisimilitude. Unlike more fantasy-driven erotica that sets up outlandish, compulsive scenarios, the sex here arises organically from the plot. The author goes inside the heads of the characters, so that we understand their bashfulness, their longing or curiosity. There is a nonchalant, playful tone that removes the stigma of queer intimacy that easily might have tormented teenaged American men in 1962.

All in all, *The Shooting Gallery* is a satisfying, intelligent story, notable for its warmth and credibility. It's perfect for those who appreciate homoerotic content without the usual overblown raunch so common to the genre.

Also available in hardcover and ebook.

Thunder and Lightning: Julian's Private Scrapbook, Part 4
Eldot
Xlibris, 327 pages, (paperback) $15.99, 978-1-4797-5684-1
(Reviewed: May 2014)

This unusual novel, the fourth in a five-part series, takes place at a scout camp during the summer of 1962 and follows several groups of boys as they form friendships, learn new skills, and fall in love. Much of the novel depicts their various sexual explorations, and the author clearly alerts readers to such content. "This series is meant for mature readers," he writes on the back cover. "…This book should be stored in a place not accessible by persons under 18."

In between the sex, several plotlines progress from the earlier books. Tom, an older boy who had been with many others before committing himself to Nick, makes amends for his past treatment of Kurt, an earlier partner. Nick advises Kurt on how to overcome his fear that his past with Tom will sabotage his relationship with his current partner Sid. Julian continues to improve his artistic skills, drawing beautiful portraits of the lifeguard Leonard and his scoutmaster Mark, while taking on further responsibilities in the campground. In a new development, Geoff, another older boy, becomes attracted to Mark and devises a plan for seducing the unwitting scoutmaster. Meanwhile, Mark begins to confront his past trauma.

While the extensive sex scenes may make some readers uncomfortable, they are handled well, showing the tenderness between the boys. Their relationships are fascinating to watch, as many are now committed couples, yet their emotional bonds are strong enough to allow them to learn new positions and techniques in sessions with more knowledgeable boys. Geoff's pursuit of Mark is handled humorously, leading to a situation where both attempt to conceal their erections. The author helpfully includes summaries of the previous novels, a glossary of terms and characters and more at book's end.

Thunder and Lightning is a charming read in spite of the controversial subject matter. As it shows further growth in the series' characters and their relationships, it sets the stage for the concluding tale.

Also available in hardcover and ebook.

The Champions: Julian’s Private Scrapbook, Part Five
Eldot
Xlibris, 375 pages (paperback) $15.99, 978-1-4797-8041-9
(Reviewed: June 2014)

The conclusion to a sexually infused five-novel series, The Champions takes place during the last day of a scout camp during the summer of 1962 and follows several groups of boys as they deepen their relationships, build on new skills, and ponder life after camp. Much of the novel depicts their various intimate explorations, from a final ejaculation contest known as “the Shooting Gallery” to the couples pleasuring each other on the bus ride home. In between, several plots building during the previous books reach their end.

Geoff, one of the oldest scouts, makes his move — even with his injured foot — to seduce the scoutmaster, Mark, in the middle of the night. Julian, while working on his remarkable drawings, befriends Sarge, the camp’s quartermaster, and draws out the gruff retired Army man’s soft side, even calling him “Uncle Max.” Tom, continuing his process of maturing, learns how to get out of uncomfortable situations without the help of his lover Nick, and even becomes a confidante to other scouts worried about their relationships.

Mark comes across as one of the strongest figures in this novel, encouraging all the scouts under his care to become the best that they can be. He makes plans for Julian to receive art lessons after camp, further developing his talent. He shows his tremendous strength, both physical and moral, during his late-night encounter with Geoff. It's no surprise that his troop wins all the prizes at the last day's competitions, or that Julian has a crush on the scoutmaster.

Charming and humorous, with sex scenes that are erotic without being over the top, the novel successfully ends the series, while leaving open the possibility of further adventures. The controversial subject matter may make some readers uncomfortable, but for those interested in a sexual adventure told from a gay perspective, this is a wonderful look at boys transitioning between childhood and adulthood.

Also available in hardcover and ebook.

www.ingramcontent.com/pod-product-compliance
Lightning Source LLC
Chambersburg PA
CBHW051537030726
47592CB00001B/9

* 9 7 8 1 8 9 3 0 7 5 7 7 1 *